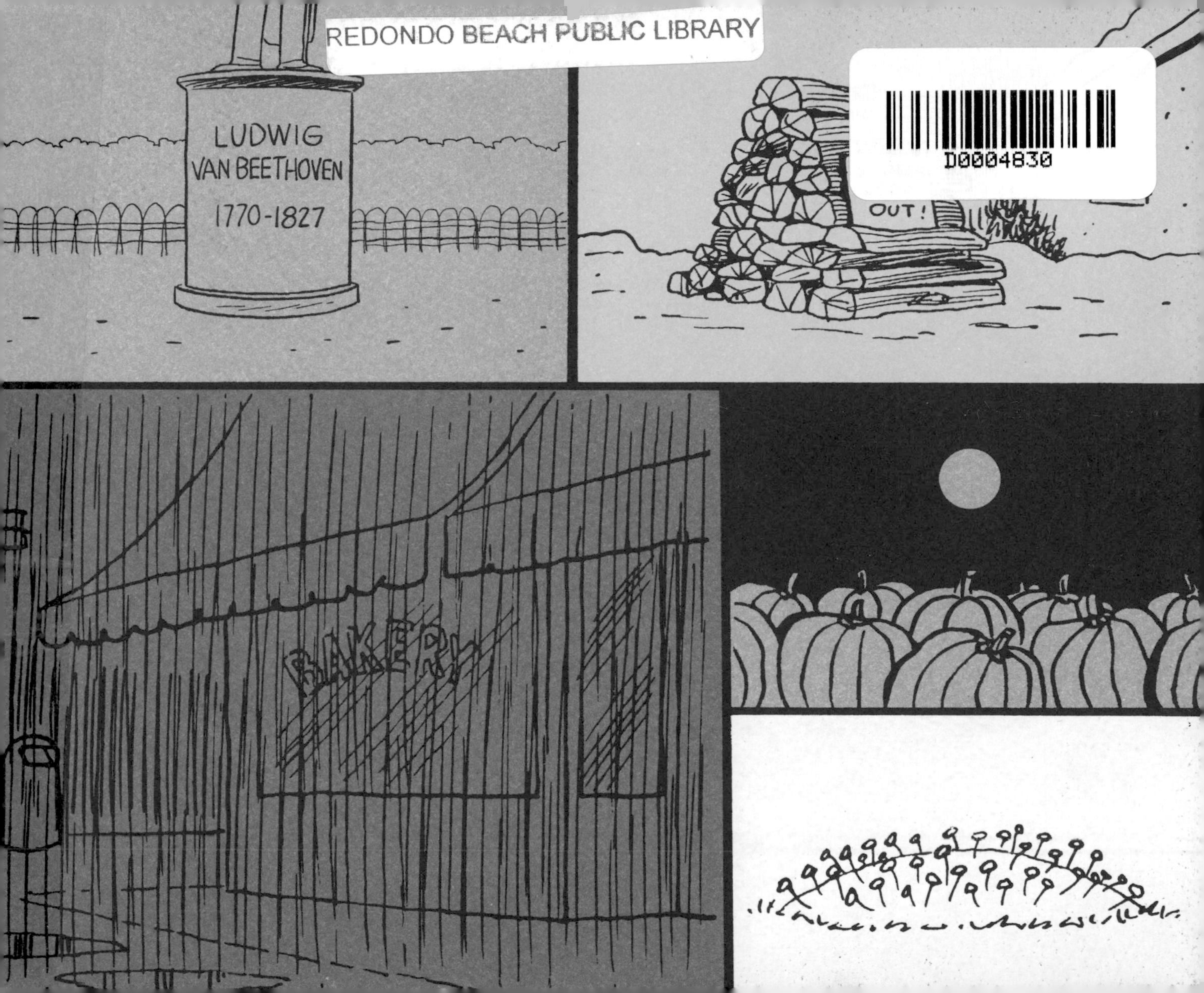
LUDWIG
VAN BEETHOVEN
1770-1827
OUT!
BAKERY

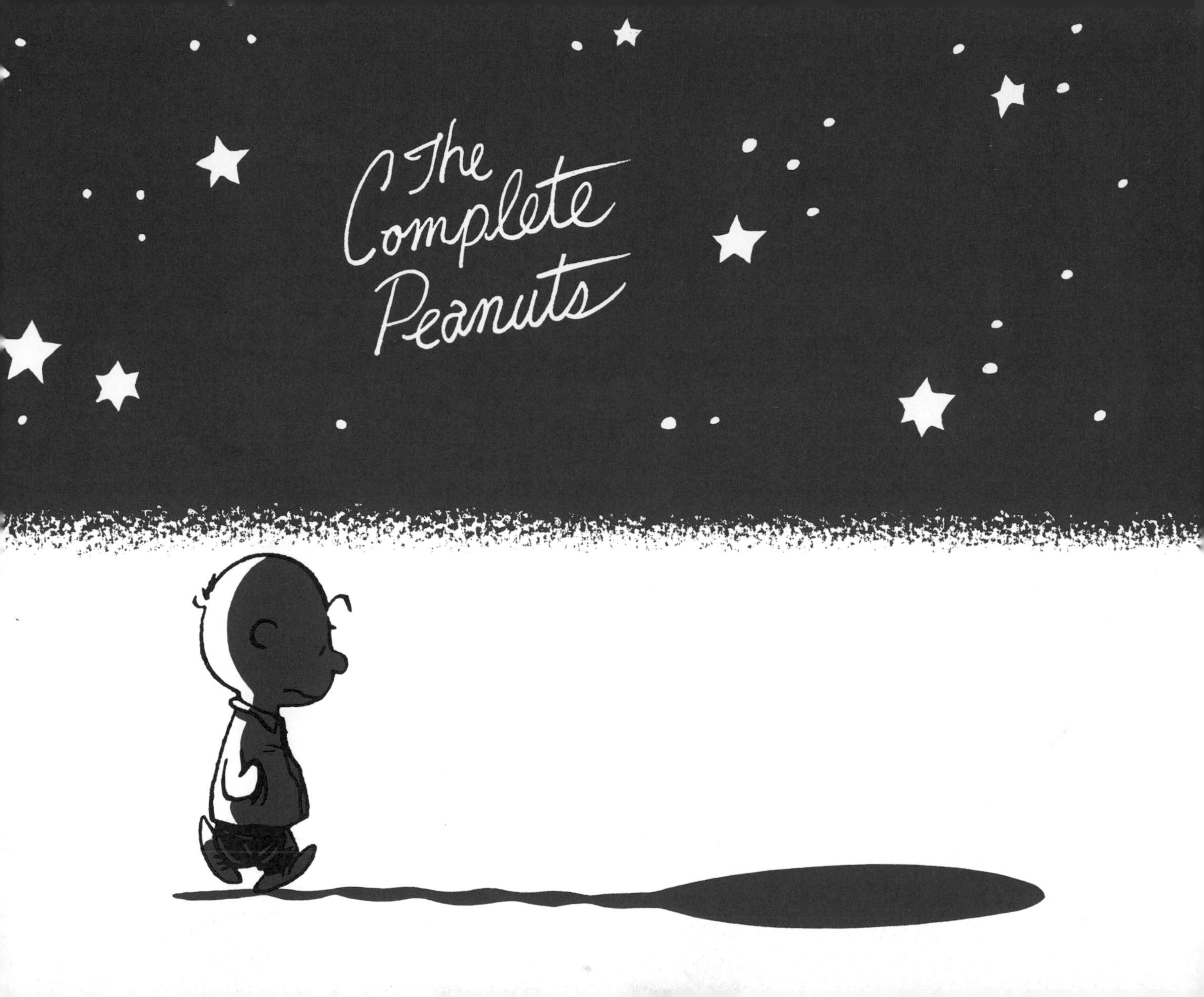
The Complete Peanuts

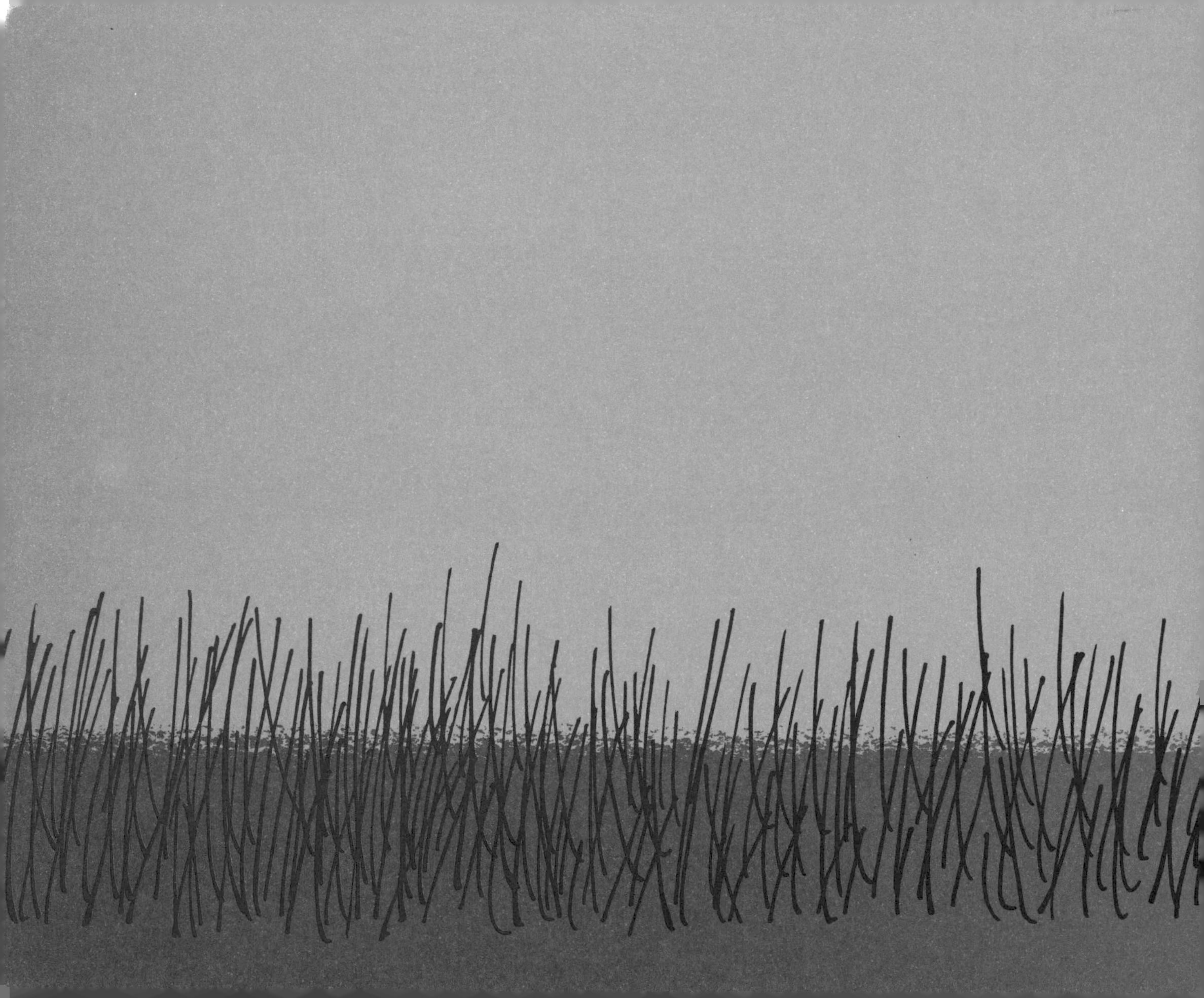

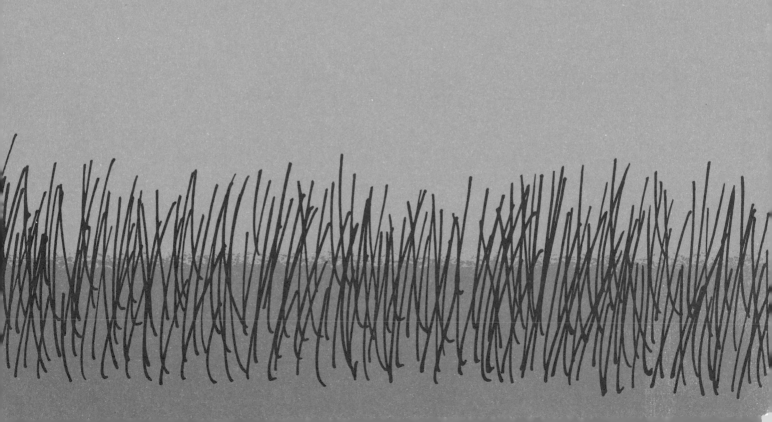

THE COMPLETE PEANUTS
by Charles M. Schulz
published by
Fantagraphics Books

Editor: Gary Groth
Designer: Seth
Production Manager: Kim Thompson
Production, assembly, and restoration: Paul Baresh and Adam Grano
Archival and production assistance: Timothy Chow & Marcie Lee
Index compiled by Amber Zeop
Associate Publisher: Eric Reynolds
Publishers: Gary Groth & Kim Thompson

Special thanks to Jeannie Schulz, without whom
this project would not have come to fruition.
Thanks also to the
Charles M. Schulz Creative Associates,
especially Paige Braddock and Kim Towner.

Fantagraphics Books, 7563 Lake City Way, Seattle, WA 98115, USA. For a free full-color catalogue of comics,
call 1-800-657-1100. Our books may be viewed on our website at www.fantagraphics.com.

ISBN: 978-1-56097-723-0
Fourth printing: August 2013   Printed in China

CHARLES M. SCHULZ

THE COMPLETE PEANUTS

1963 TO 1964

I WANT TO TALK TO YOU
THIS MORNING ABOUT THE
"GREAT PUMPKIN".....

◘ FANTAGRAPHICS BOOKS ◘

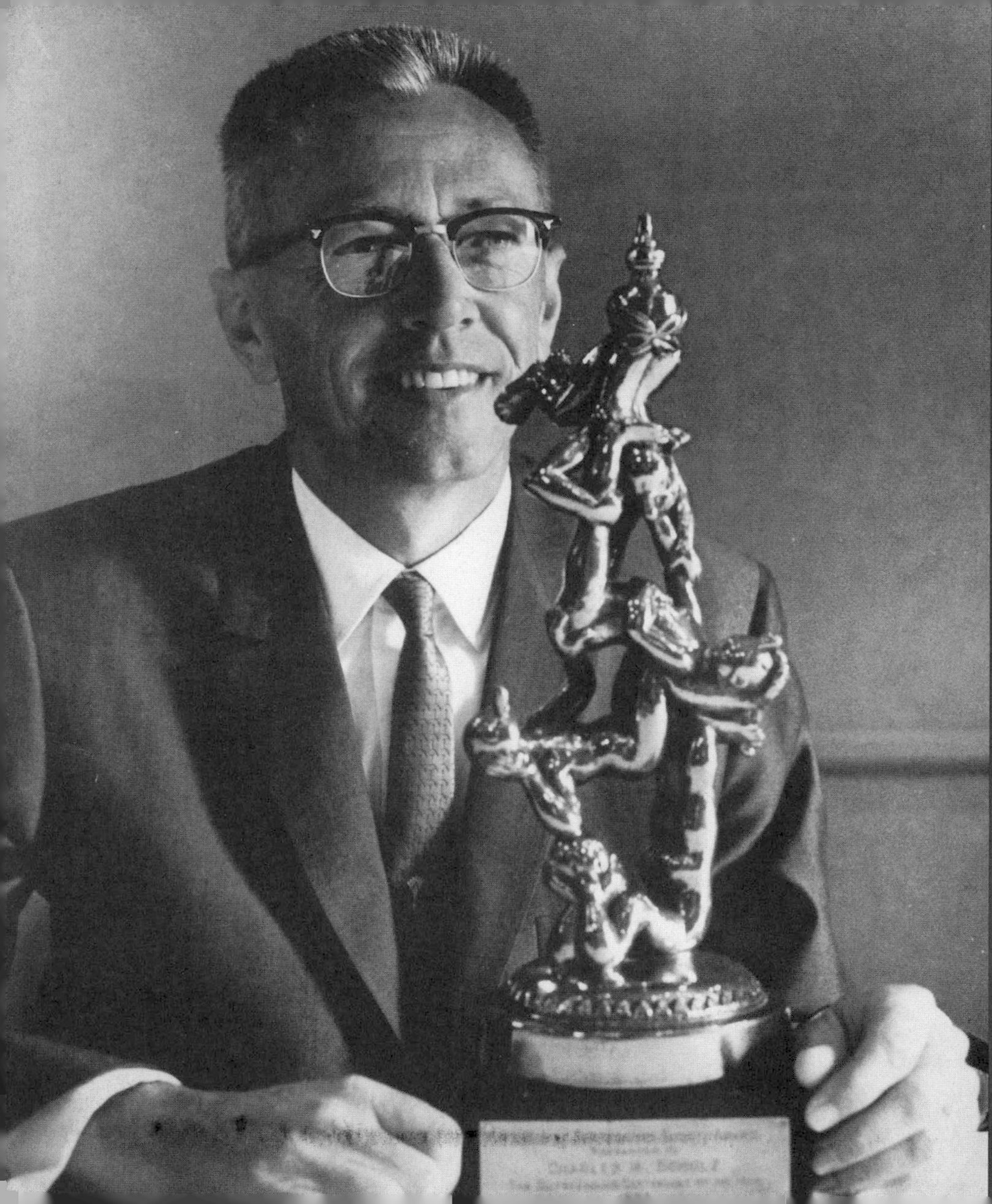

Charles Schulz with his second Reuben award, circa 1964.

FOREWORD by BILL MELENDEZ

In 1960 I was working for Playhouse Pictures, a small animation house in Hollywood that created television commercials. My boss called me into his office one day and told me that he wanted me to fly to Northern California to meet Charles Schulz, because we were going to do a commercial for the Ford Falcon using the *Peanuts* characters.

That's how I met "Sparky" in his studio in Sebastopol, California, about an hour's drive north from San Francisco. Little did he or I know we would eventually spend forty years together animating Charlie Brown.

Sparky's office was away from the main house. It was really very basic, nothing fancy, with his favorite books throughout the room. (His final studio in Santa Rosa, California was very similar, and his previous studio is now on display at the Charles M. Schulz Museum.) Of course, the one thing I remember more than the studio was that he had a three-hole golf course on the property. (He was a very

good golfer, usually averaging a seven handicap.) He had a single secretary at the time — Sue Broadwell, who was still working for the Schulz family in 2006 at the museum. So it was really a "one-man band" in every respect.

Sparky wrote *Peanuts* and drew every line of the strip, including the panel borders and the lettering! Now he would be turning his characters over to a new process, where animators would be involved with the art. Neither he nor I knew for sure how the characters would play in animation and how the characters would ultimately sound. This was a huge step for him and he told me of some of his concerns. He was very interested in the animation process itself, and I described the various steps. He seemed fascinated by it.

He was immediately warm and friendly, and after the first hour, it was almost like we had been friends for years. He was pleased to hear that I had worked on some of Disney's greatest features, including *Pinocchio* and *Dumbo*.

He discussed the philosophy underlining his characters, including the fact that he hated "bulliness" in any form and how Charlie Brown had to survive a lot of bulliness.

I went back to my animation studio, and we eventually worked out a storyboard involving the *Peanuts* characters talking about the Ford Falcon. We auditioned a bunch of kids. We then sent the storyboard and the audition of the kids' voices that we had selected to Sparky. After reviewing it, Sparky was very pleased, and he said simply: "Let's do it!" He was even more pleased with the first commercial when it was broadcast.

Then in 1963, Lee Mendelson produced a documentary on Sparky and wanted to include a minute or so of animation (that's all Lee could afford), and Sparky told Lee to get in touch with me at Playhouse. I met Lee and we ended up producing two minutes of animation of some of Sparky's favorite daily strips.

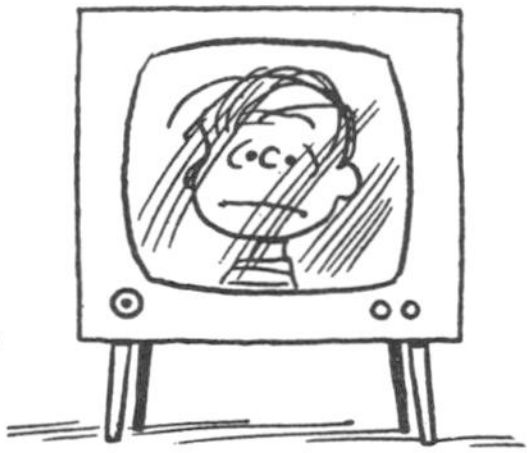

But Lee couldn't sell the documentary, so we were all in limbo for two years. Meanwhile, I had formed my own small animation company, Bill Melendez Productions. Then in 1965, the McCann Erickson Agency (who had seen the documentary) called Lee to see if Sparky and the animators had ever considered doing a Christmas show, as their client Coca-Cola was interested. Lee said "yes," indeed they had, and the agency replied that they needed an outline in their hands in five days in Atlanta. Lee hung up the phone in shock... called me and Sparky... said that he felt that he had just sold a *Peanuts* Christmas show ... and we both asked him what show was that!? He replied: "The one we all have to put together tomorrow!"

So I flew up from Hollywood... Lee picked me up at the San Francisco airport... and we drove up to Sebastopol to meet with Sparky.

Believe it or not, in just a matter of a few hours, we had put together an outline for a Christmas show to send to Coca-Cola. We started out with some of the Christmas strips Sparky had already done about school plays. Then Sparky said: "If we're going to do a Christmas show, then we ought to talk about the true meaning of Christmas... maybe have Linus read something from the Bible." This lead to us talking about doing something with a Christmas tree that could stand as a metaphor for Charlie Brown himself. Lee had used the jazz music of Vince Guaraldi in his documentary, and he suggested that we could blend the Guaraldi jazz with traditional Christmas music.

We sent the outline to the McCann Erickson Agency and Coca-Cola, and a week later we got a call that would change all of our lives. John Allen from McCann said simply: "OK, fellas, it's a go. Coke wants to do *A Charlie Brown Christmas*."

So we had the outline, we had the voices (the kids from the Ford commercials still sounded the same), we had the basic story based on strips about a Christmas play, we had the music, but the only other thing we "had" was six months — not a lot of time. But everything went so smoothly from start to finish that we really never had any problems. Sparky approved my storyboard... we recorded the voices in Hollywood and he approved the soundtrack... and we jumped right into the animation. We were very lucky to have done the Ford commercials and the few minutes for the documentary, so we didn't have to do any experimenting. And lo and behold, six months later, the show went on CBS on Dec. 9 1965 and almost half of the television viewers in the country tuned in. And thus a forty-year partnership proceeded to do fifty *Peanuts* specials. Who would have thunk it!

Our animators have always been praised for what has

been called a seamless transition from the comic page to animation. I think it's because Sparky and I had agreed from the start that we should keep the animation simple — just lift the characters off the comics page and move them, not try to embellish how they looked, and to keep the backgrounds simple as well.

The only real animation problem we ever had was turning around Charlie Brown's round head, of translating the two-dimensional image on the page into the illusion of three dimensions in animation. We eventually worked it out. Of course Snoopy was an animator's dream! One of my favorite scenes was when Snoopy flew his dog house in the *Pumpkin* show.

Sparky contributed many creatively unconventional springboards for some of the specials we produced. He had been a soldier in WWII and he decided that we should do a special tribute about the fallen Americans in WWI and WWII. So we took the animated characters to the landing beaches and cemeteries of Normandy and to Flanders Field, combining the animation with live-action footage. The show — entitled *What Have We Learned, Charlie Brown?* — won a coveted Peabody Award (our second, the first being for *A Charlie Brown Christmas*).

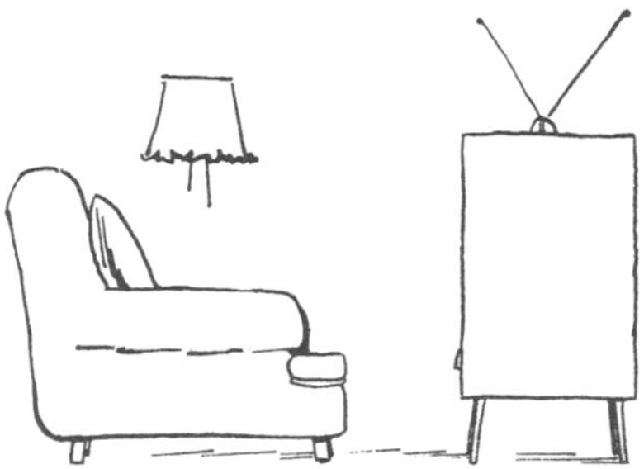

Then we did a special — *Why, Charlie Brown. Why?* — about a little girl, a friend of Charlie Brown's, who develops cancer. The research we did on that show was both heart-wrenching and very inspiring, and the show had quite an impact across the country.

We even did a show based on a dream Sparky had. He called me one day and said: "I had this funny dream about Snoopy becoming a sled dog at the North Pole, and I think we should do it as our next special." That became *What a Nightmare, Charlie Brown* and it became one of our favorites.

This is America, Charlie Brown was the first-ever, animated, network miniseries. Its premise was that the *Peanuts* characters participated in everything from the Mayflower Voyage to the writing of the Constitution to the creation of the Space Station.

One incident in one of those shows — "The Smithsonian and the Presidency" — sums it all up for me. As they tour the Space Museum, Charlie Brown and Lucy wonder why there are space modules named "Snoopy" and "Linus." Then they wonder, in the History Museum, why there is a *Peanuts* comic strip posted in the Entertainment section that shows their likenesses. Somehow combining the animated show with actual history is about as all-encompassing as you can get.

So that's a how a single commercial in 1961 lead to fifty network *Peanuts* specials and four *Peanuts* feature films.

It was all so serendipitous, a miracle of timing and creative convergence: The fact that Sparky and I came to know each other in 1961... that Lee met him in 1963... that we started the shows in 1965... that we found Vince Guaraldi... that we used real kids for the voices... that we eschewed a laugh track... Somehow it seems like it was all meant to happen. And what a wonderful experience to work with Sparky and Lee and all the wonderful animators to bring such joy to families around the world... and to spread the wonderful philosophy of Charles Schulz. All of these events came together and resulted in decades of friendship and fruitful creative work. How fortunate we all were to be part of this.

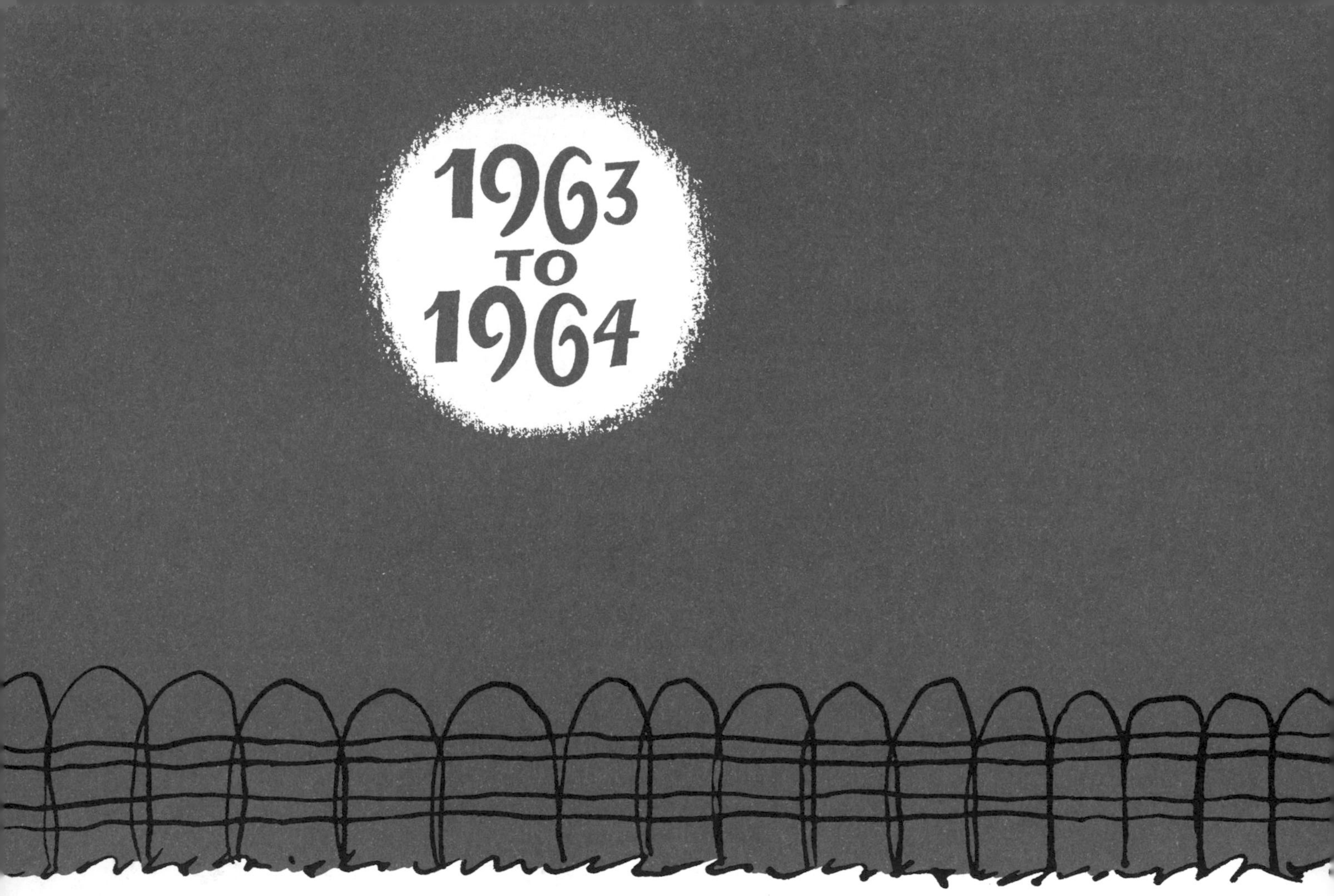
1963
TO
1964

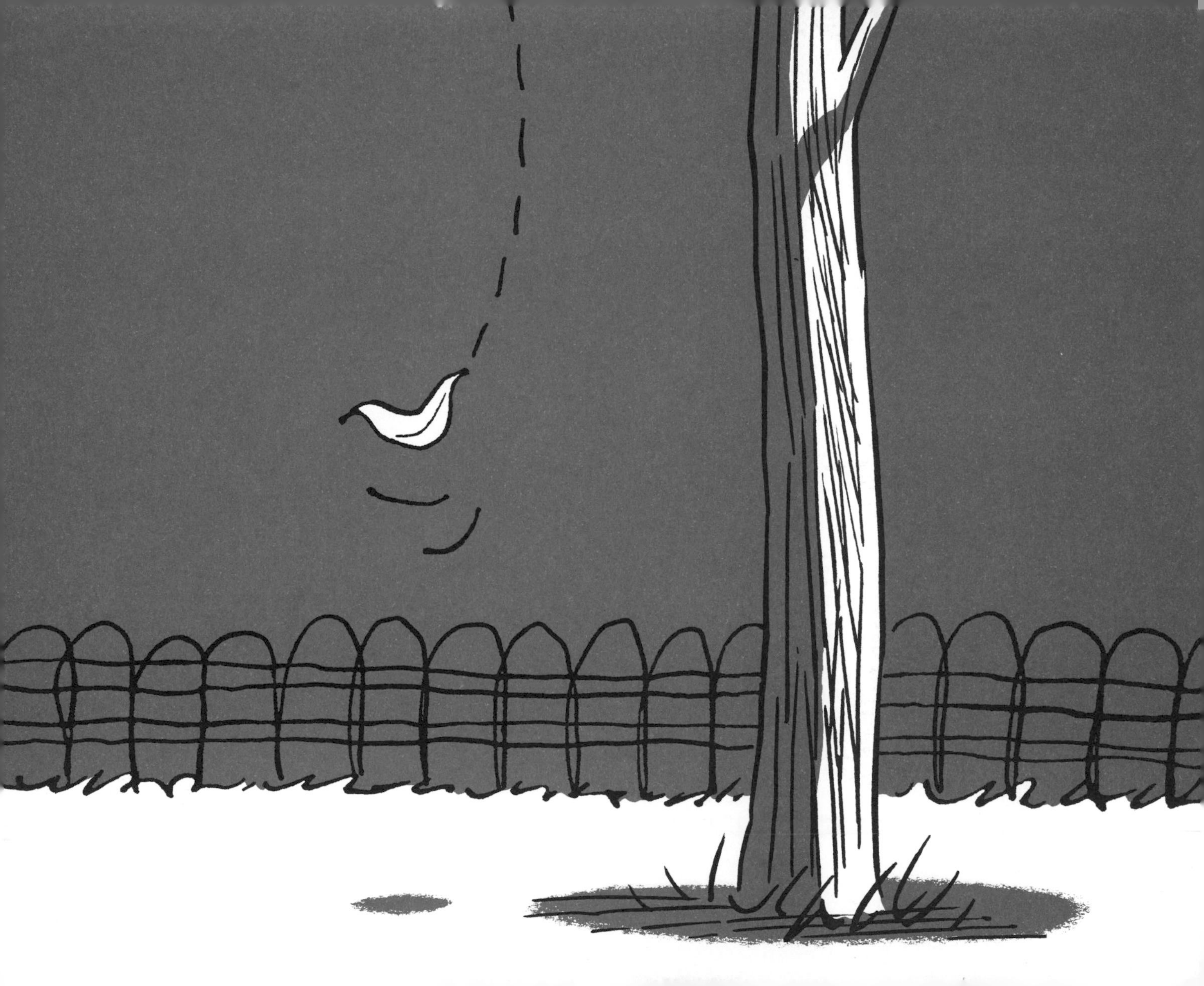

SEE? WHAT DID I TELL YOU?

WHAT?

1-1

THIS YEAR IS NO BETTER THAN THE LAST ONE!

DID YOU THROW THIS SNOWBALL AT ME?

GEE, I DON'T THINK SO...THAT DOESN'T LOOK LIKE THE KIND I MAKE..I USUALLY PAT THEM A LITTLE MORE FIRMLY TO INSURE ACCURATE FLIGHT...

1-2

I ALSO TRY TO MAKE THEM A SHADE SMALLER THAN THIS, AND TRY TO USE SNOW WITH A BETTER TEXTURE...THIS SNOW DOESN'T SEEM..

I THINK SHE SENSED I WAS PUTTING HER ON!

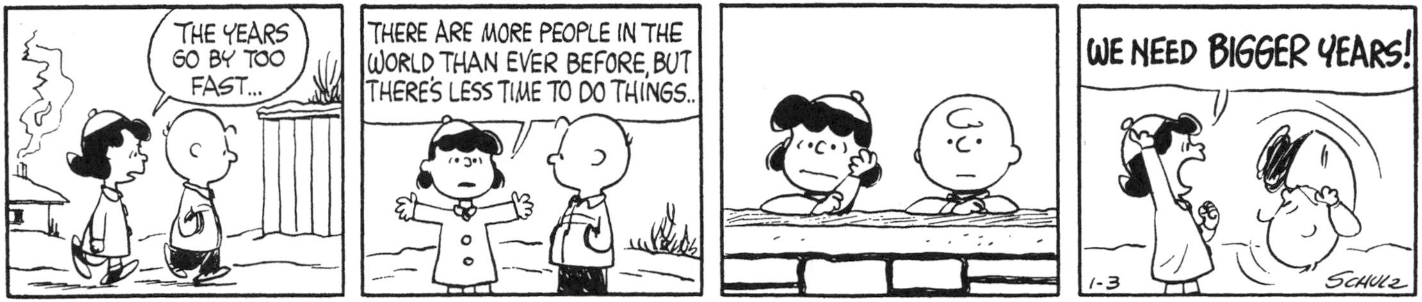
THE YEARS GO BY TOO FAST...
THERE ARE MORE PEOPLE IN THE WORLD THAN EVER BEFORE, BUT THERE'S LESS TIME TO DO THINGS..
WE NEED BIGGER YEARS!
1-3
SCHULZ

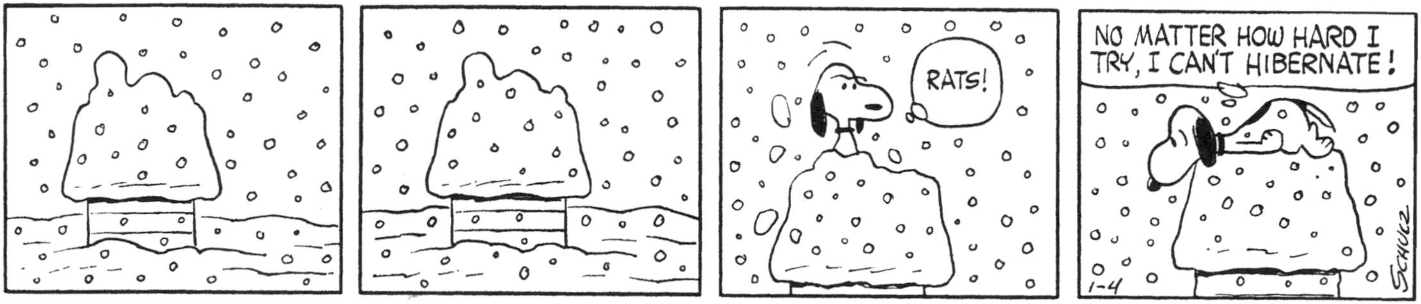
RATS!
NO MATTER HOW HARD I TRY, I CAN'T HIBERNATE!
1-4
SCHULZ

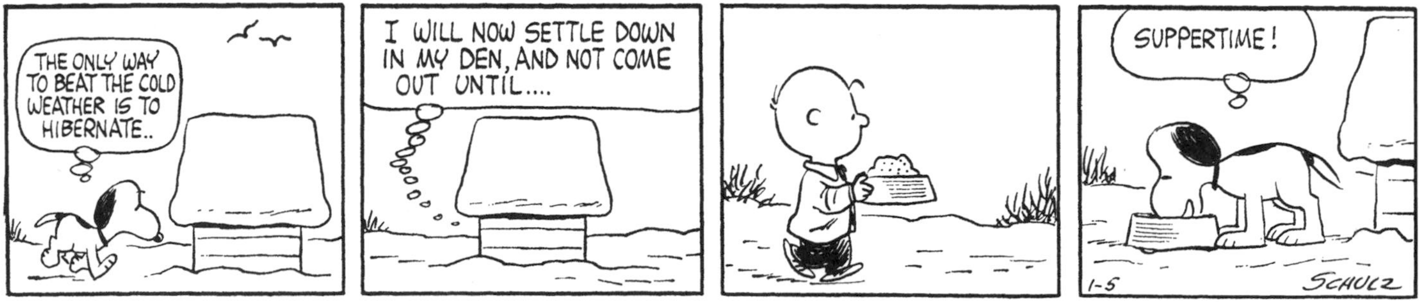
THE ONLY WAY TO BEAT THE COLD WEATHER IS TO HIBERNATE..
I WILL NOW SETTLE DOWN IN MY DEN, AND NOT COME OUT UNTIL....
SUPPERTIME!
1-5
SCHULZ

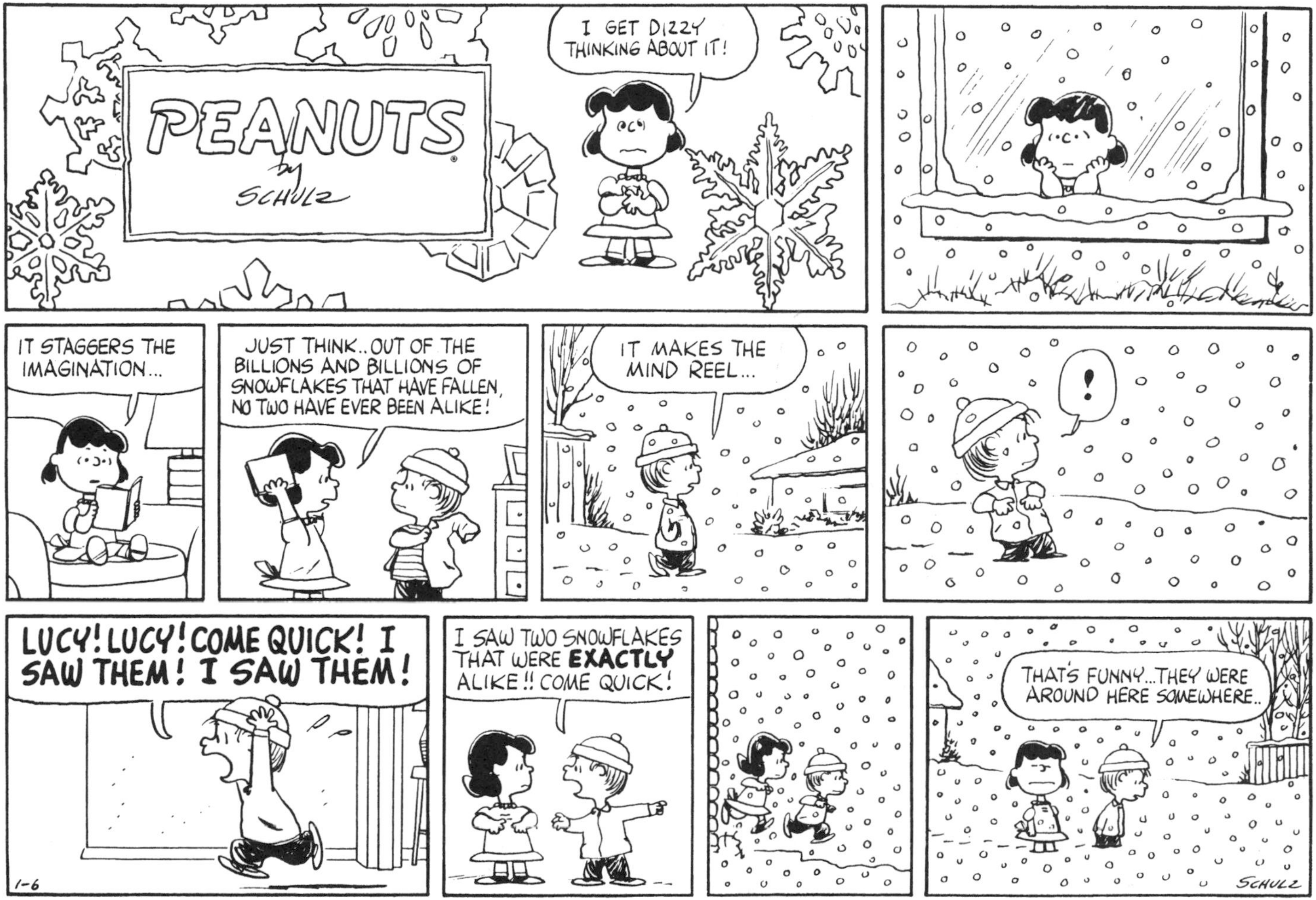
PEANUTS
by SCHULZ
I GET DIZZY THINKING ABOUT IT!
IT STAGGERS THE IMAGINATION...
JUST THINK..OUT OF THE BILLIONS AND BILLIONS OF SNOWFLAKES THAT HAVE FALLEN, NO TWO HAVE EVER BEEN ALIKE!
IT MAKES THE MIND REEL...
!
LUCY! LUCY! COME QUICK! I SAW THEM! I SAW THEM!
I SAW TWO SNOWFLAKES THAT WERE **EXACTLY** ALIKE!! COME QUICK!
THAT'S FUNNY...THEY WERE AROUND HERE SOMEWHERE..
1-6
SCHULZ

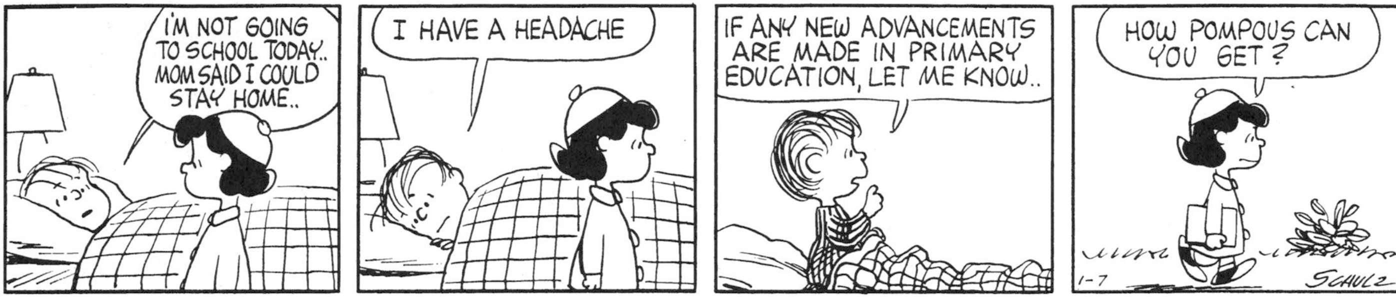
I'M NOT GOING TO SCHOOL TODAY.. MOM SAID I COULD STAY HOME..
I HAVE A HEADACHE
IF ANY NEW ADVANCEMENTS ARE MADE IN PRIMARY EDUCATION, LET ME KNOW..
HOW POMPOUS CAN YOU GET?
1-7
SCHULZ

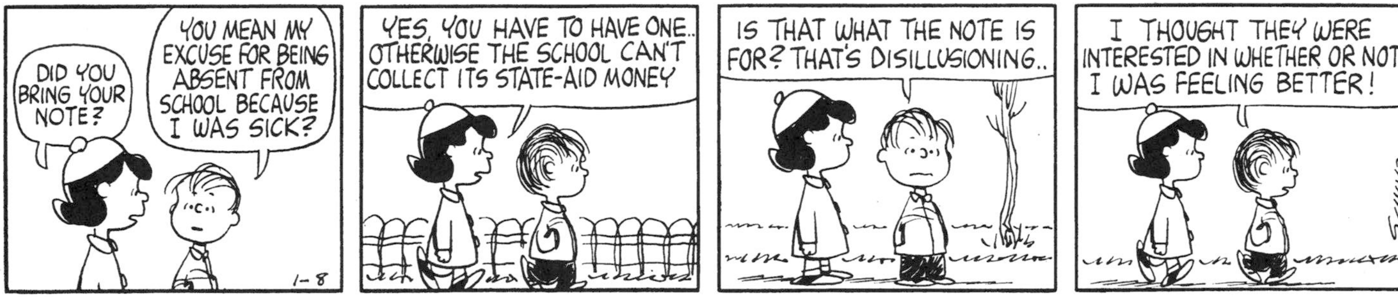
DID YOU BRING YOUR NOTE?
YOU MEAN MY EXCUSE FOR BEING ABSENT FROM SCHOOL BECAUSE I WAS SICK?
1-8
YES, YOU HAVE TO HAVE ONE.. OTHERWISE THE SCHOOL CAN'T COLLECT ITS STATE-AID MONEY
IS THAT WHAT THE NOTE IS FOR? THAT'S DISILLUSIONING..
I THOUGHT THEY WERE INTERESTED IN WHETHER OR NOT I WAS FEELING BETTER!
SCHULZ

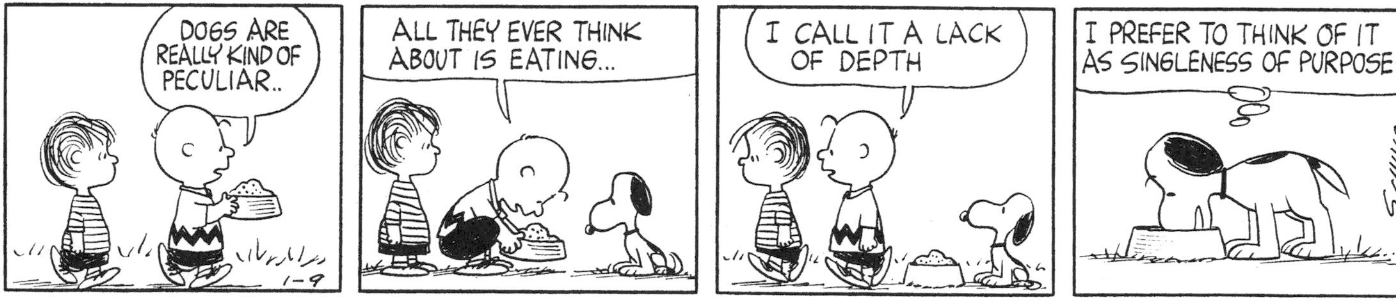
DOGS ARE REALLY KIND OF PECULIAR..
1-9
ALL THEY EVER THINK ABOUT IS EATING...
I CALL IT A LACK OF DEPTH
I PREFER TO THINK OF IT AS SINGLENESS OF PURPOSE!
SCHULZ

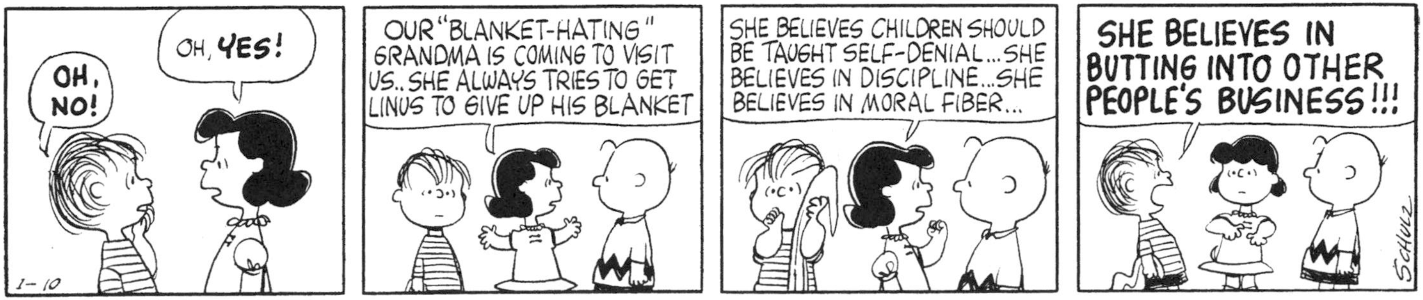
OH, NO!
OH, YES!
1-10
OUR "BLANKET-HATING" GRANDMA IS COMING TO VISIT US.. SHE ALWAYS TRIES TO GET LINUS TO GIVE UP HIS BLANKET
SHE BELIEVES CHILDREN SHOULD BE TAUGHT SELF-DENIAL...SHE BELIEVES IN DISCIPLINE...SHE BELIEVES IN MORAL FIBER...
SHE BELIEVES IN BUTTING INTO OTHER PEOPLE'S BUSINESS!!!
SCHULZ

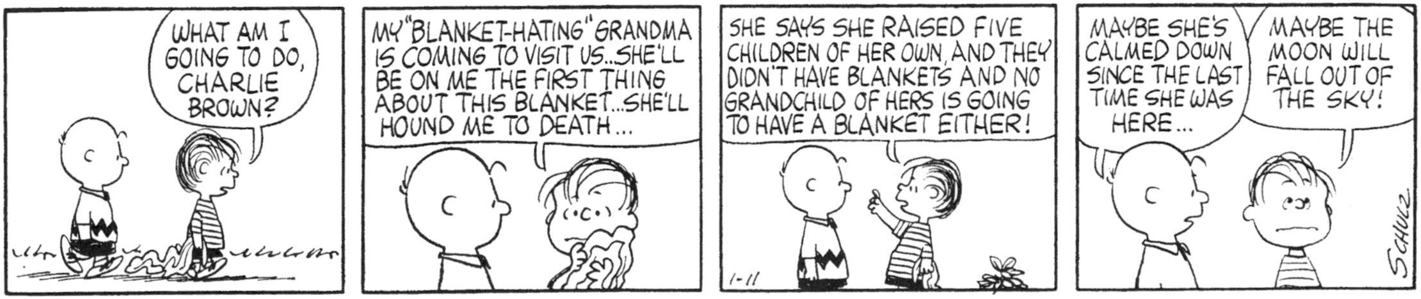
WHAT AM I GOING TO DO, CHARLIE BROWN?
MY "BLANKET-HATING" GRANDMA IS COMING TO VISIT US..SHE'LL BE ON ME THE FIRST THING ABOUT THIS BLANKET...SHE'LL HOUND ME TO DEATH...
SHE SAYS SHE RAISED FIVE CHILDREN OF HER OWN, AND THEY DIDN'T HAVE BLANKETS AND NO GRANDCHILD OF HERS IS GOING TO HAVE A BLANKET EITHER!
1-11
MAYBE SHE'S CALMED DOWN SINCE THE LAST TIME SHE WAS HERE...
MAYBE THE MOON WILL FALL OUT OF THE SKY!
SCHULZ

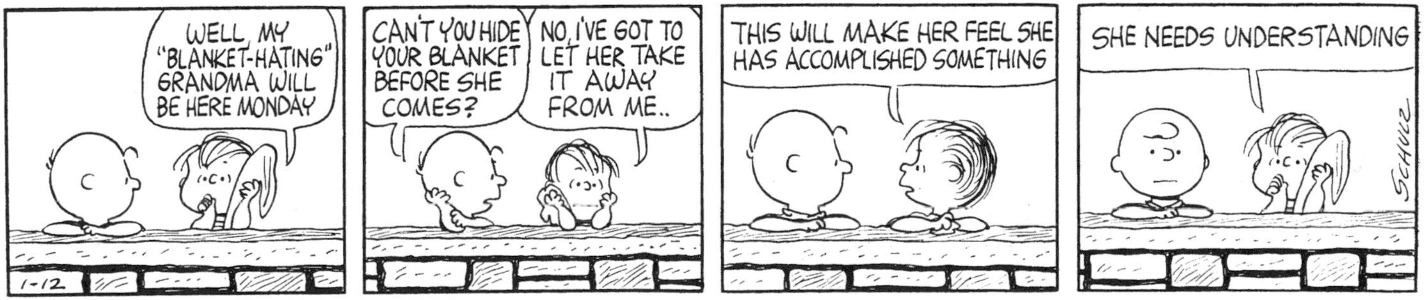
WELL, MY "BLANKET-HATING" GRANDMA WILL BE HERE MONDAY
1-12
CAN'T YOU HIDE YOUR BLANKET BEFORE SHE COMES?
NO, I'VE GOT TO LET HER TAKE IT AWAY FROM ME..
THIS WILL MAKE HER FEEL SHE HAS ACCOMPLISHED SOMETHING
SHE NEEDS UNDERSTANDING
SCHULZ

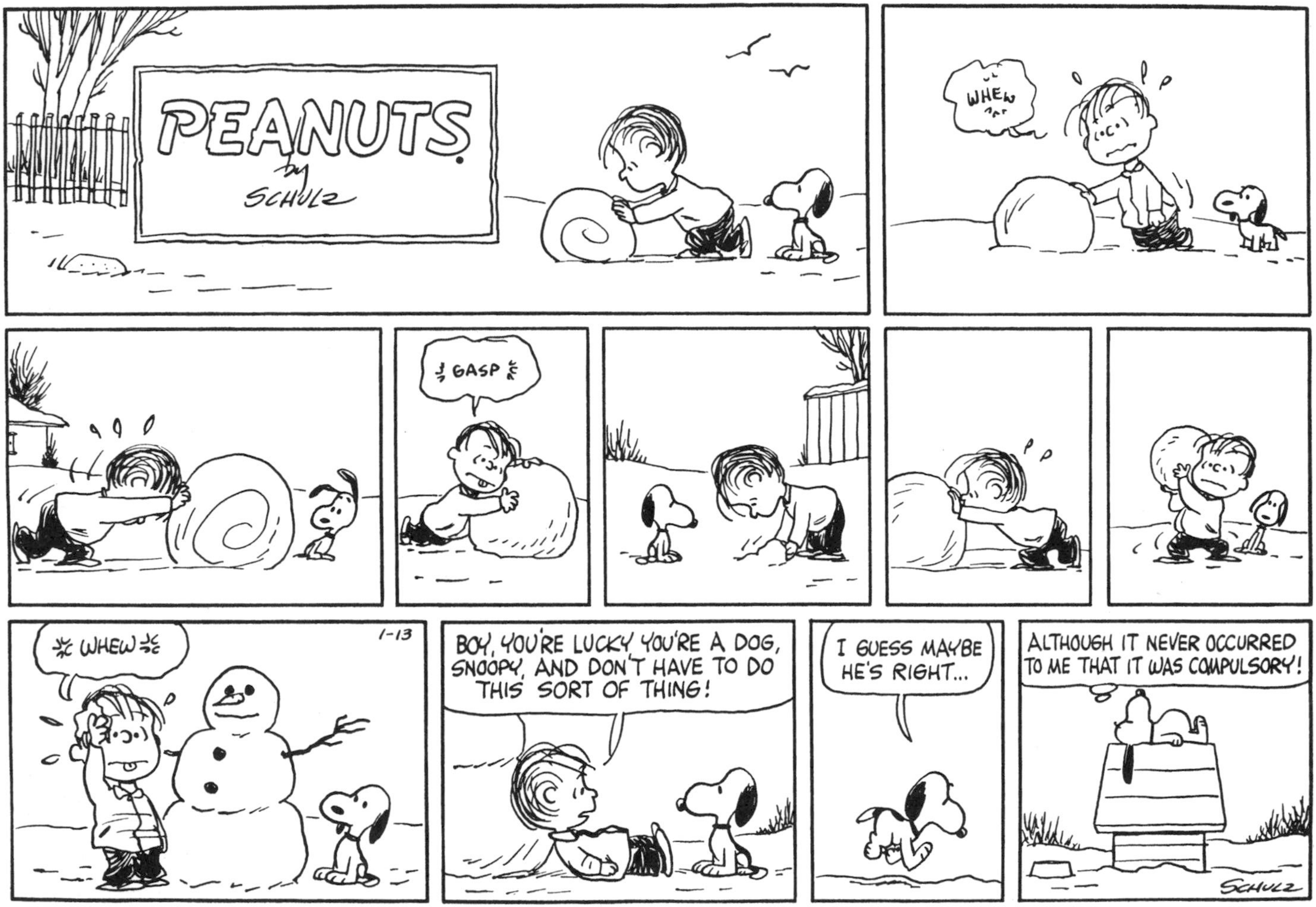
PEANUTS
by SCHULZ
WHEW
GASP
WHEW
1-13
BOY, YOU'RE LUCKY YOU'RE A DOG, SNOOPY, AND DON'T HAVE TO DO THIS SORT OF THING!
I GUESS MAYBE HE'S RIGHT...
ALTHOUGH IT NEVER OCCURRED TO ME THAT IT WAS COMPULSORY!
SCHULZ

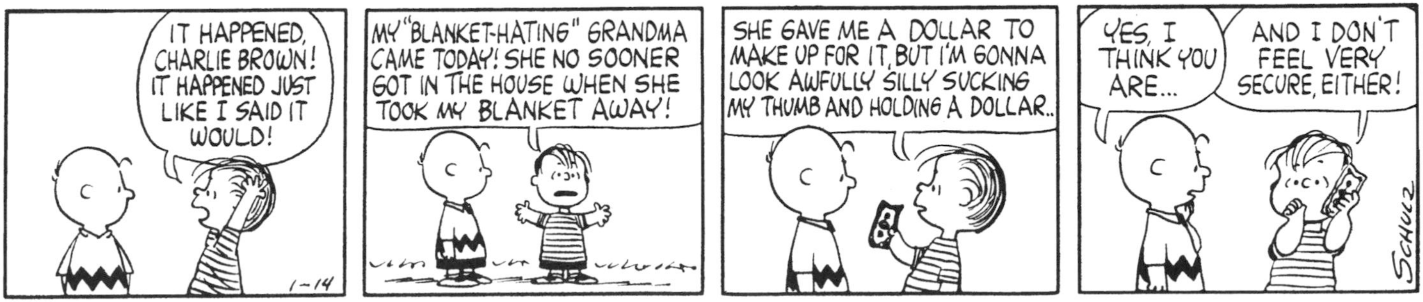
IT HAPPENED, CHARLIE BROWN! IT HAPPENED JUST LIKE I SAID IT WOULD!
1-14
MY "BLANKET-HATING" GRANDMA CAME TODAY! SHE NO SOONER GOT IN THE HOUSE WHEN SHE TOOK MY BLANKET AWAY!
SHE GAVE ME A DOLLAR TO MAKE UP FOR IT, BUT I'M GONNA LOOK AWFULLY SILLY SUCKING MY THUMB AND HOLDING A DOLLAR..
YES, I THINK YOU ARE...
AND I DON'T FEEL VERY SECURE, EITHER!
SCHULZ

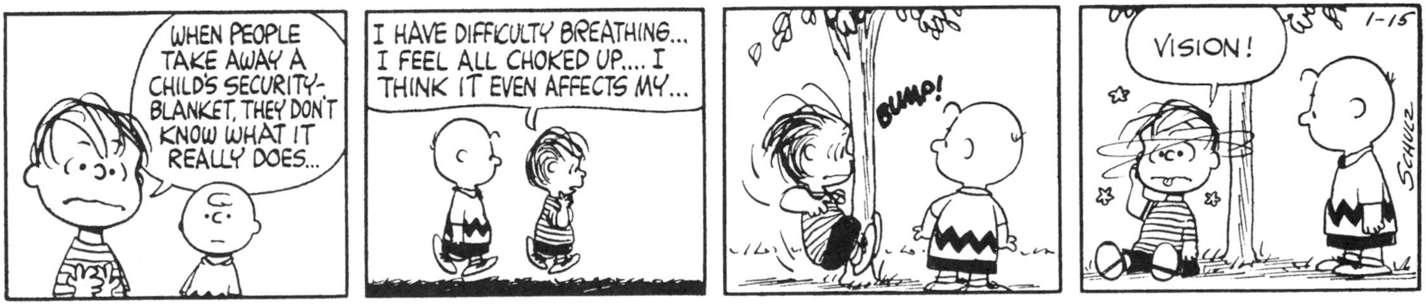
WHEN PEOPLE TAKE AWAY A CHILD'S SECURITY-BLANKET, THEY DON'T KNOW WHAT IT REALLY DOES...
I HAVE DIFFICULTY BREATHING... I FEEL ALL CHOKED UP.... I THINK IT EVEN AFFECTS MY...
BUMP!
1-15
VISION!
SCHULZ

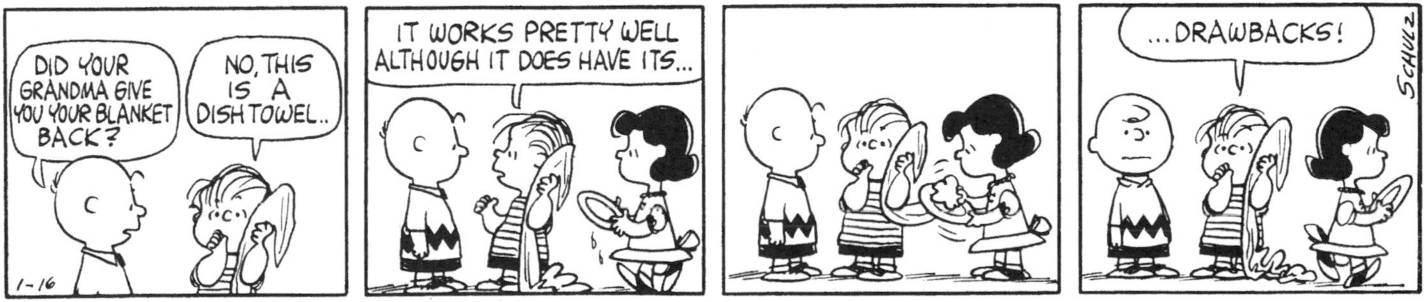
DID YOUR GRANDMA GIVE YOU YOUR BLANKET BACK?
NO, THIS IS A DISHTOWEL..
1-16
IT WORKS PRETTY WELL ALTHOUGH IT DOES HAVE ITS...
...DRAWBACKS!
SCHULZ

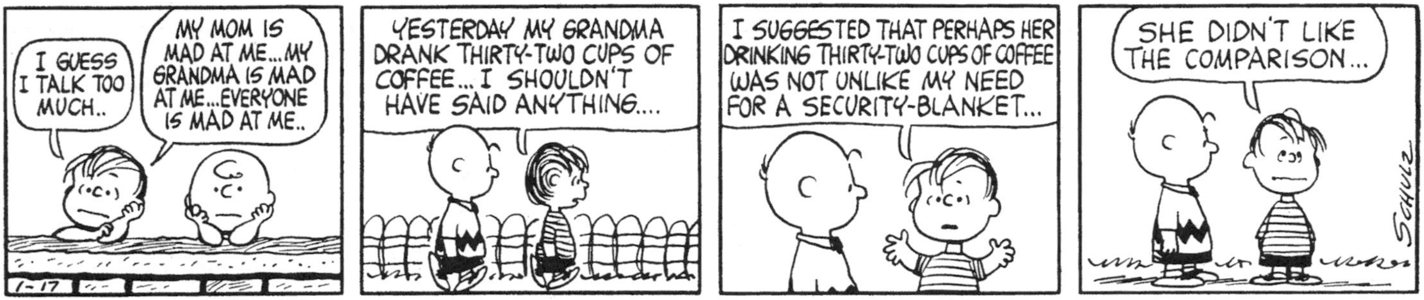
I GUESS I TALK TOO MUCH..
MY MOM IS MAD AT ME...MY GRANDMA IS MAD AT ME...EVERYONE IS MAD AT ME..
YESTERDAY MY GRANDMA DRANK THIRTY-TWO CUPS OF COFFEE... I SHOULDN'T HAVE SAID ANYTHING....
I SUGGESTED THAT PERHAPS HER DRINKING THIRTY-TWO CUPS OF COFFEE WAS NOT UNLIKE MY NEED FOR A SECURITY-BLANKET...
SHE DIDN'T LIKE THE COMPARISON...
1-17
SCHULZ

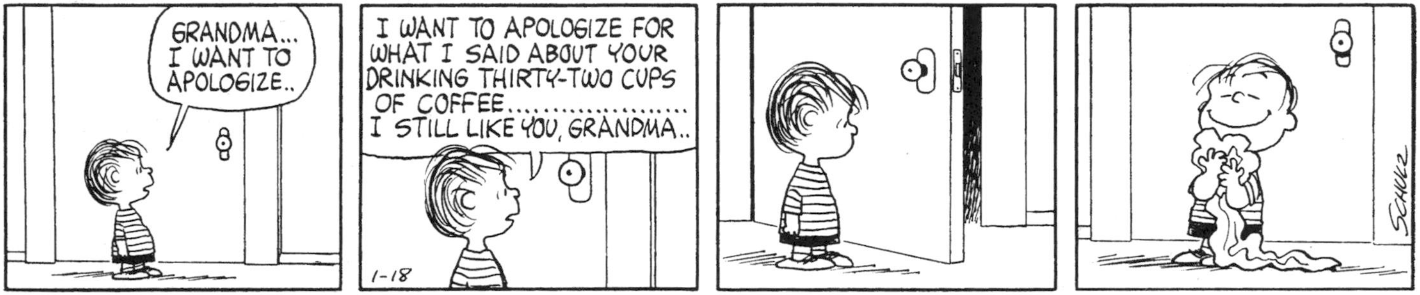
GRANDMA... I WANT TO APOLOGIZE..
I WANT TO APOLOGIZE FOR WHAT I SAID ABOUT YOUR DRINKING THIRTY-TWO CUPS OF COFFEE.................... I STILL LIKE YOU, GRANDMA..
1-18
SCHULZ

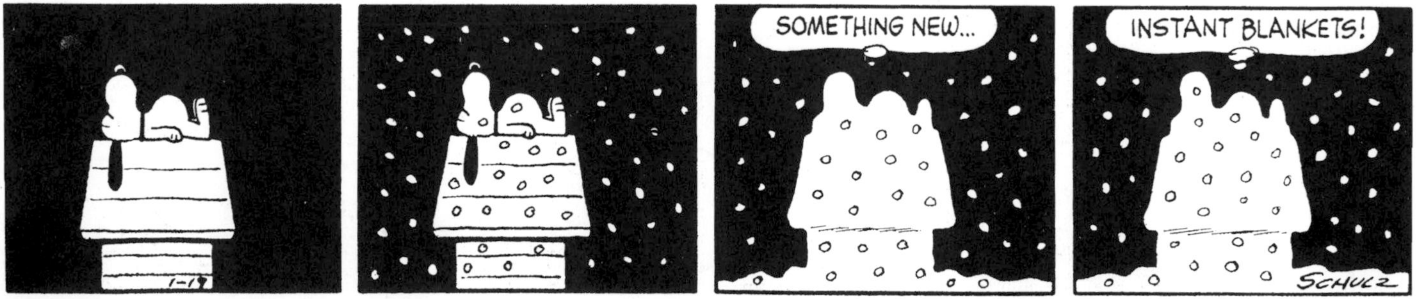
SOMETHING NEW...
INSTANT BLANKETS!
1-19
SCHULZ

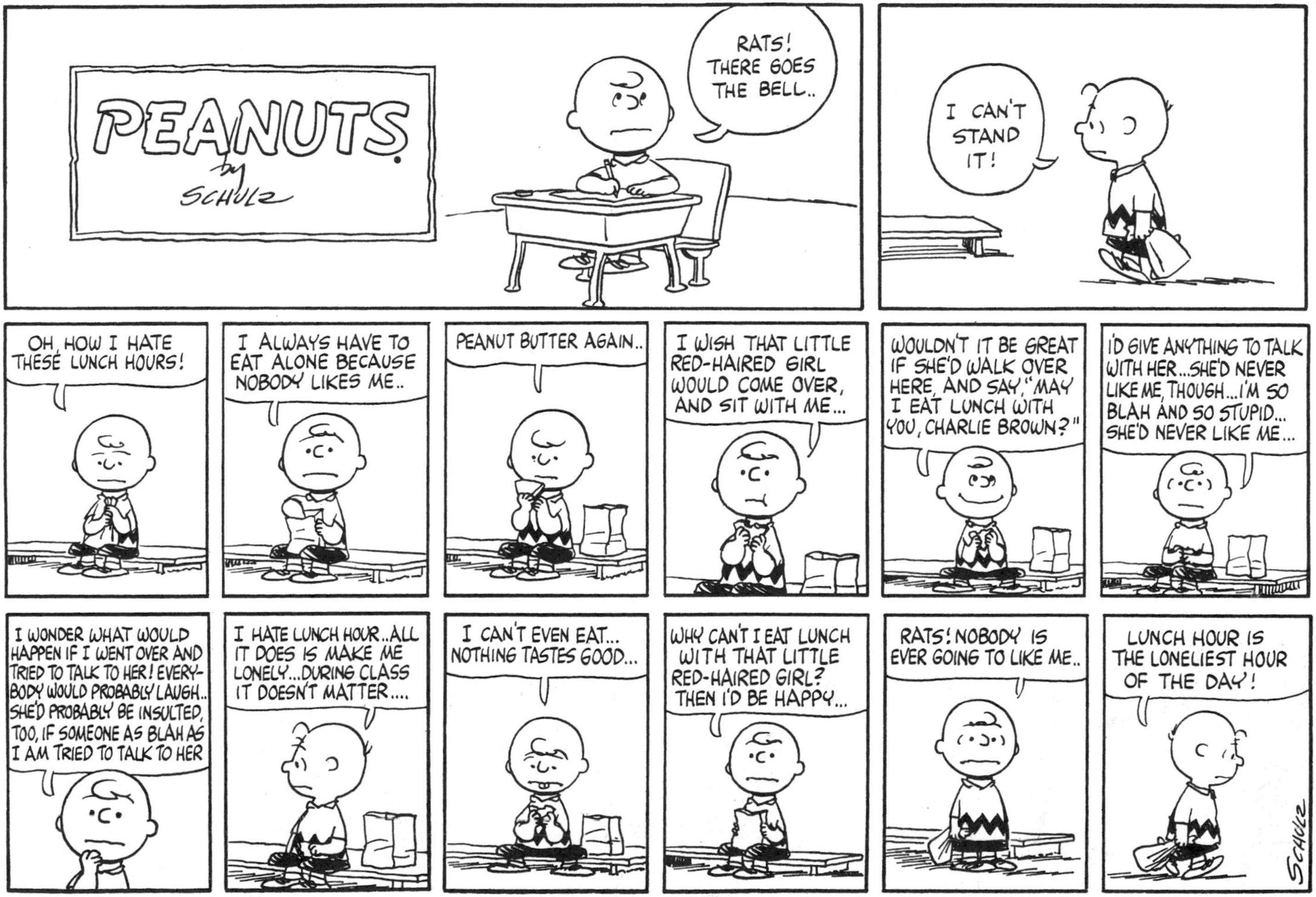
PEANUTS
by SCHULZ
RATS! THERE GOES THE BELL..
I CAN'T STAND IT!
OH, HOW I HATE THESE LUNCH HOURS!
I ALWAYS HAVE TO EAT ALONE BECAUSE NOBODY LIKES ME..
PEANUT BUTTER AGAIN..
I WISH THAT LITTLE RED-HAIRED GIRL WOULD COME OVER, AND SIT WITH ME...
WOULDN'T IT BE GREAT IF SHE'D WALK OVER HERE, AND SAY, "MAY I EAT LUNCH WITH YOU, CHARLIE BROWN?"
I'D GIVE ANYTHING TO TALK WITH HER...SHE'D NEVER LIKE ME, THOUGH...I'M SO BLAH AND SO STUPID... SHE'D NEVER LIKE ME...
I WONDER WHAT WOULD HAPPEN IF I WENT OVER AND TRIED TO TALK TO HER! EVERYBODY WOULD PROBABLY LAUGH.. SHE'D PROBABLY BE INSULTED, TOO, IF SOMEONE AS BLAH AS I AM TRIED TO TALK TO HER
I HATE LUNCH HOUR..ALL IT DOES IS MAKE ME LONELY...DURING CLASS IT DOESN'T MATTER....
I CAN'T EVEN EAT... NOTHING TASTES GOOD...
WHY CAN'T I EAT LUNCH WITH THAT LITTLE RED-HAIRED GIRL? THEN I'D BE HAPPY...
RATS! NOBODY IS EVER GOING TO LIKE ME..
LUNCH HOUR IS THE LONELIEST HOUR OF THE DAY!
SCHULZ

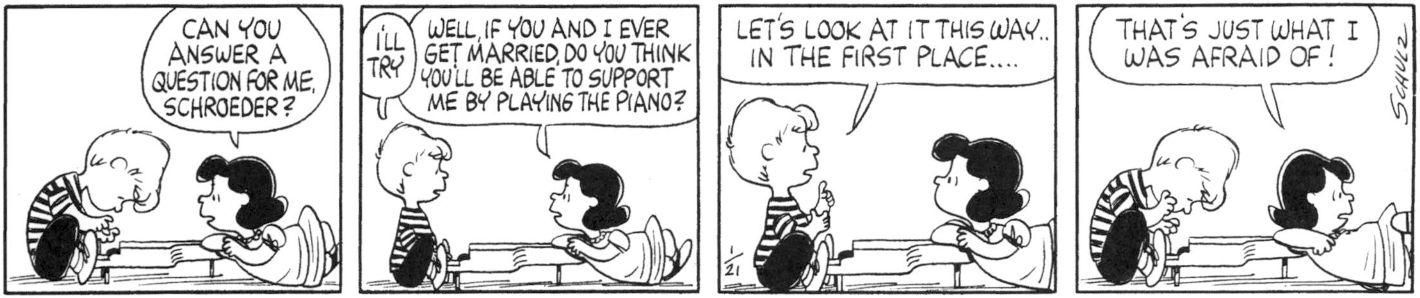
CAN YOU ANSWER A QUESTION FOR ME, SCHROEDER?
I'LL TRY
WELL, IF YOU AND I EVER GET MARRIED, DO YOU THINK YOU'LL BE ABLE TO SUPPORT ME BY PLAYING THE PIANO?
LET'S LOOK AT IT THIS WAY.. IN THE FIRST PLACE....
THAT'S JUST WHAT I WAS AFRAID OF!

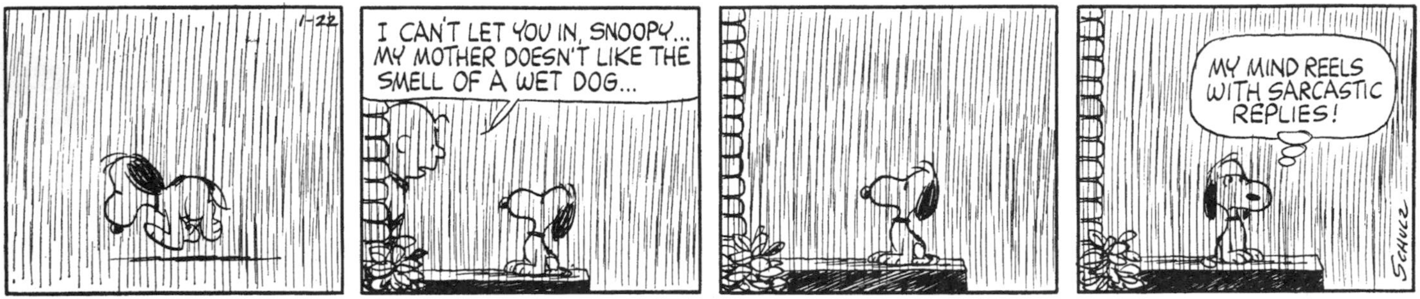
I CAN'T LET YOU IN, SNOOPY... MY MOTHER DOESN'T LIKE THE SMELL OF A WET DOG...
MY MIND REELS WITH SARCASTIC REPLIES!

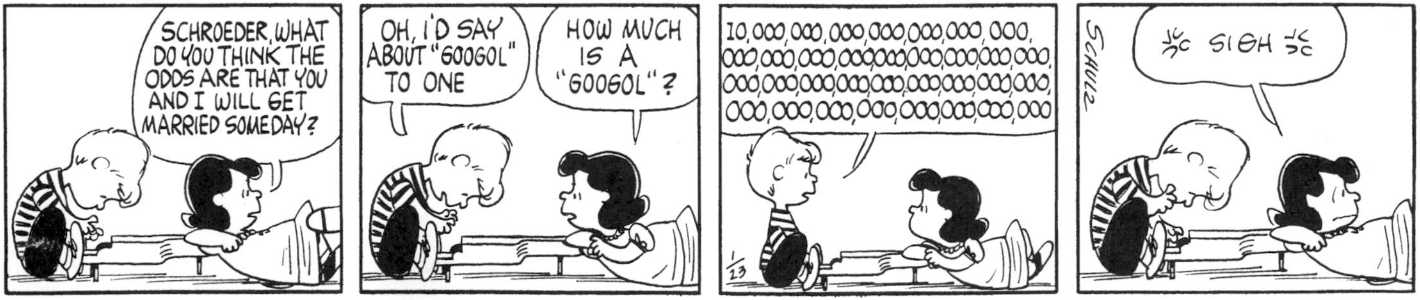
SCHROEDER, WHAT DO YOU THINK THE ODDS ARE THAT YOU AND I WILL GET MARRIED SOMEDAY?
OH, I'D SAY ABOUT "GOOGOL" TO ONE
HOW MUCH IS A "GOOGOL"?
10,000,000,000,000,000,000,000,
000,000,000,000,000,000,000,000,000,
000,000,000,000,000,000,000,000,000,
000,000,000,000,000,000,000,000
SIGH

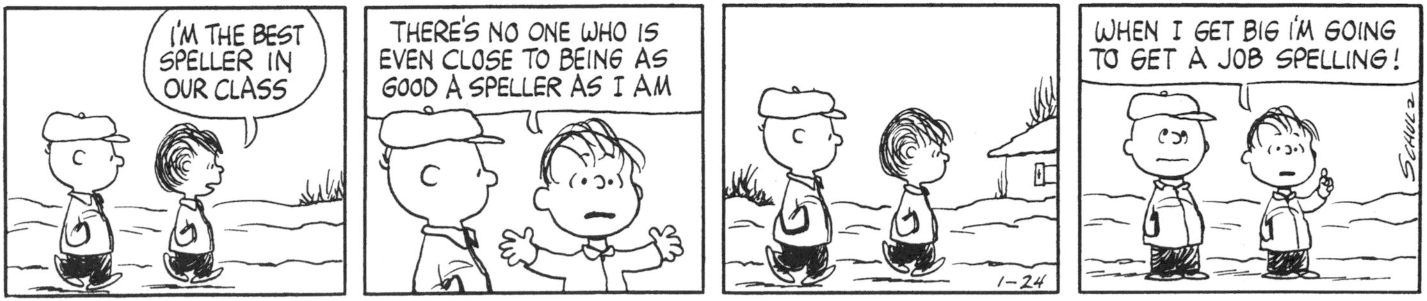
I'M THE BEST SPELLER IN OUR CLASS
THERE'S NO ONE WHO IS EVEN CLOSE TO BEING AS GOOD A SPELLER AS I AM
1-24
WHEN I GET BIG I'M GOING TO GET A JOB SPELLING!
SCHULZ

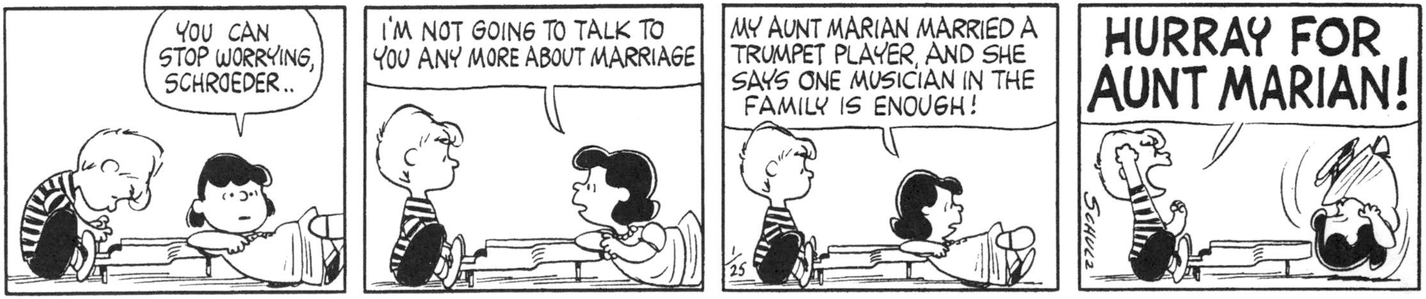
YOU CAN STOP WORRYING, SCHROEDER..
I'M NOT GOING TO TALK TO YOU ANY MORE ABOUT MARRIAGE
MY AUNT MARIAN MARRIED A TRUMPET PLAYER, AND SHE SAYS ONE MUSICIAN IN THE FAMILY IS ENOUGH!
1/25
HURRAY FOR AUNT MARIAN!
SCHULZ

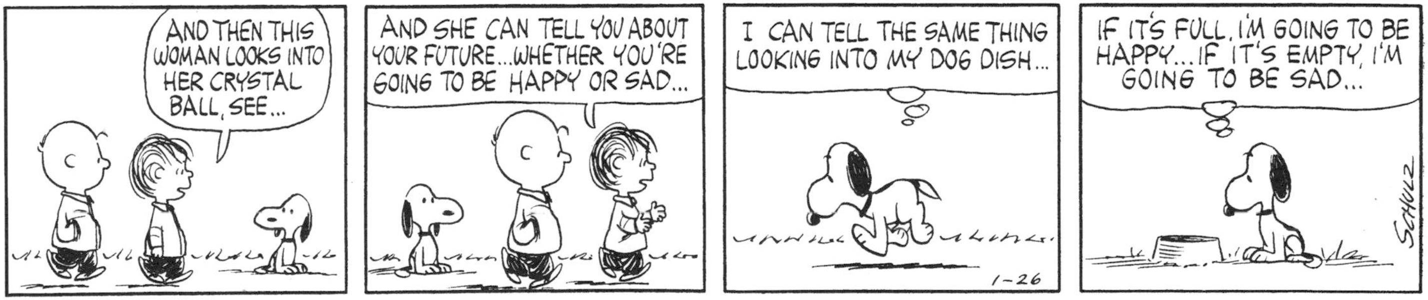
AND THEN THIS WOMAN LOOKS INTO HER CRYSTAL BALL, SEE...
AND SHE CAN TELL YOU ABOUT YOUR FUTURE...WHETHER YOU'RE GOING TO BE HAPPY OR SAD...
I CAN TELL THE SAME THING LOOKING INTO MY DOG DISH...
1-26
IF IT'S FULL, I'M GOING TO BE HAPPY... IF IT'S EMPTY, I'M GOING TO BE SAD...
SCHULZ

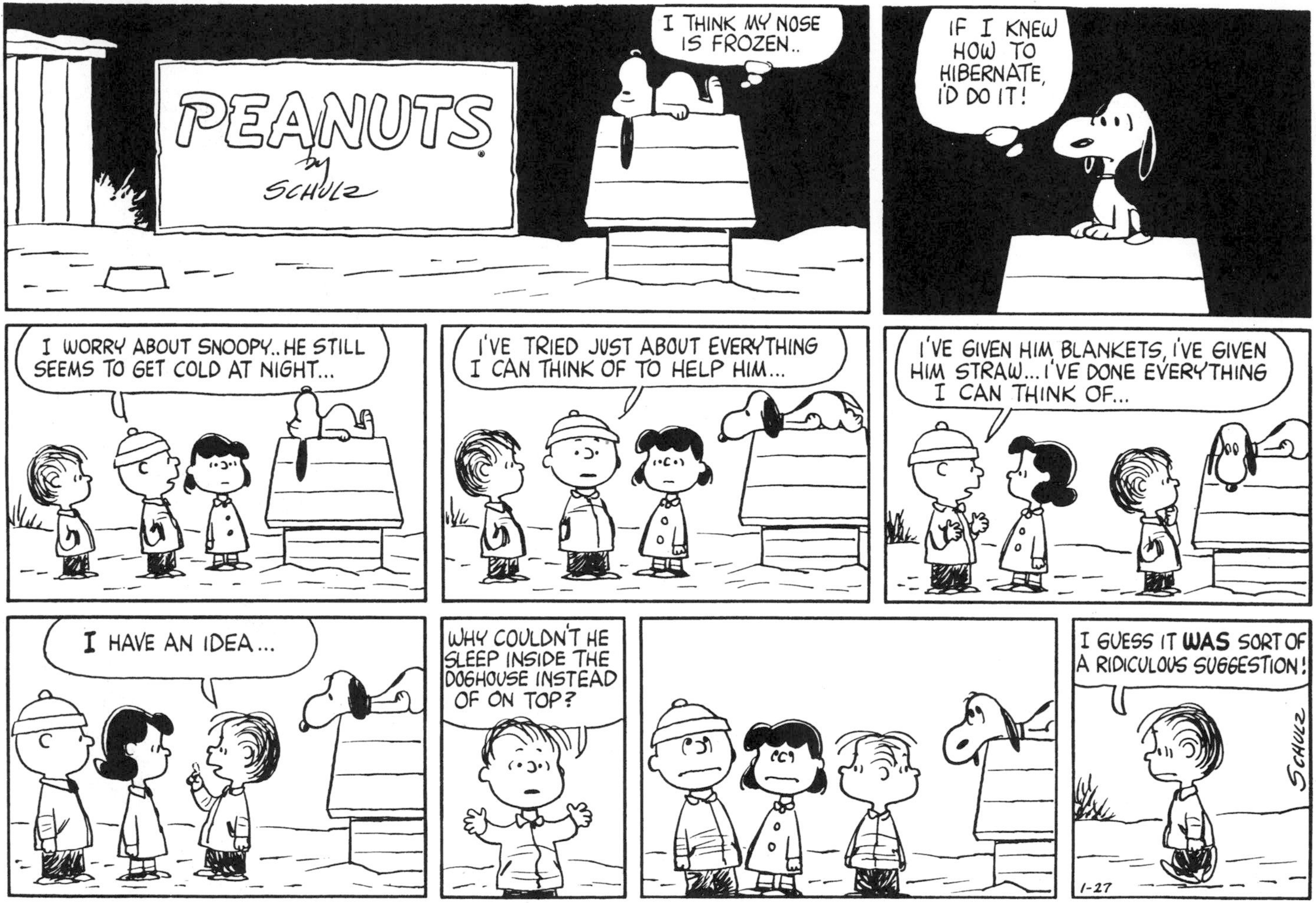
PEANUTS
by SCHULZ
I THINK MY NOSE IS FROZEN..
IF I KNEW HOW TO HIBERNATE, I'D DO IT!
I WORRY ABOUT SNOOPY.. HE STILL SEEMS TO GET COLD AT NIGHT...
I'VE TRIED JUST ABOUT EVERYTHING I CAN THINK OF TO HELP HIM...
I'VE GIVEN HIM BLANKETS, I'VE GIVEN HIM STRAW... I'VE DONE EVERYTHING I CAN THINK OF...
I HAVE AN IDEA...
WHY COULDN'T HE SLEEP INSIDE THE DOGHOUSE INSTEAD OF ON TOP?
I GUESS IT WAS SORT OF A RIDICULOUS SUGGESTION!
SCHULZ
1-27

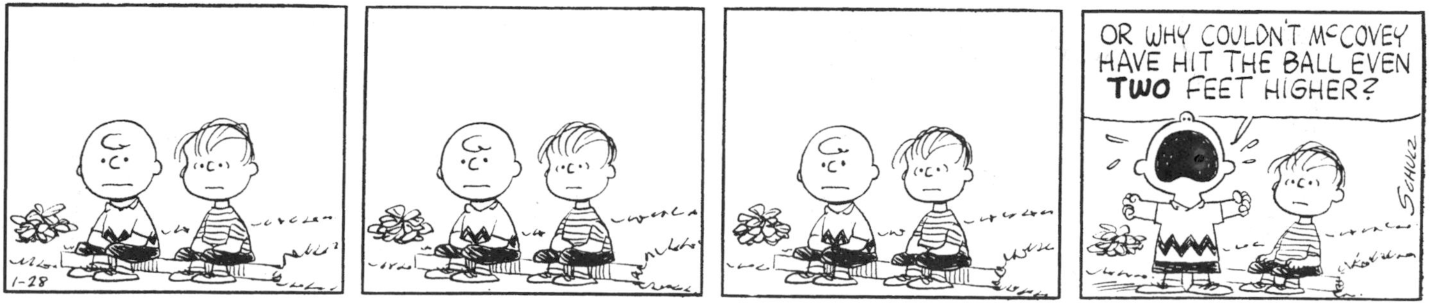
1-28
OR WHY COULDN'T M^c^COVEY HAVE HIT THE BALL EVEN **TWO** FEET HIGHER?
SCHULZ

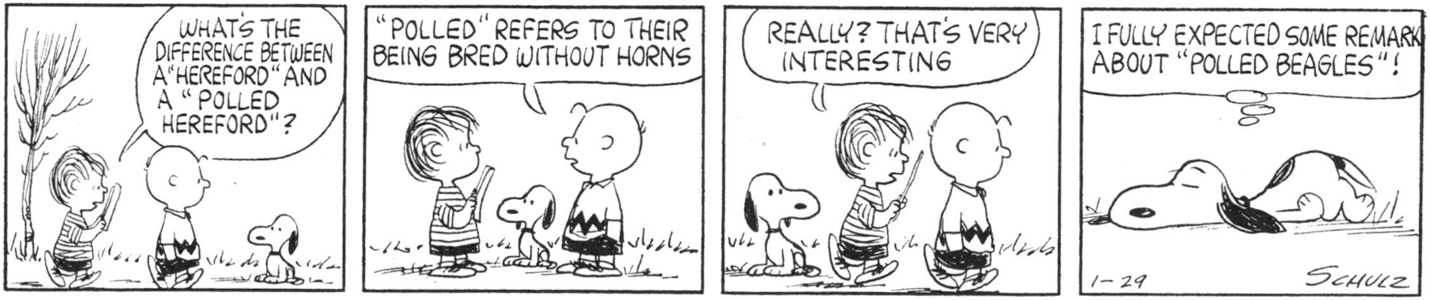
WHAT'S THE DIFFERENCE BETWEEN A "HEREFORD" AND A "POLLED HEREFORD"?
"POLLED" REFERS TO THEIR BEING BRED WITHOUT HORNS
REALLY? THAT'S VERY INTERESTING
I FULLY EXPECTED SOME REMARK ABOUT "POLLED BEAGLES"!
1-29
SCHULZ

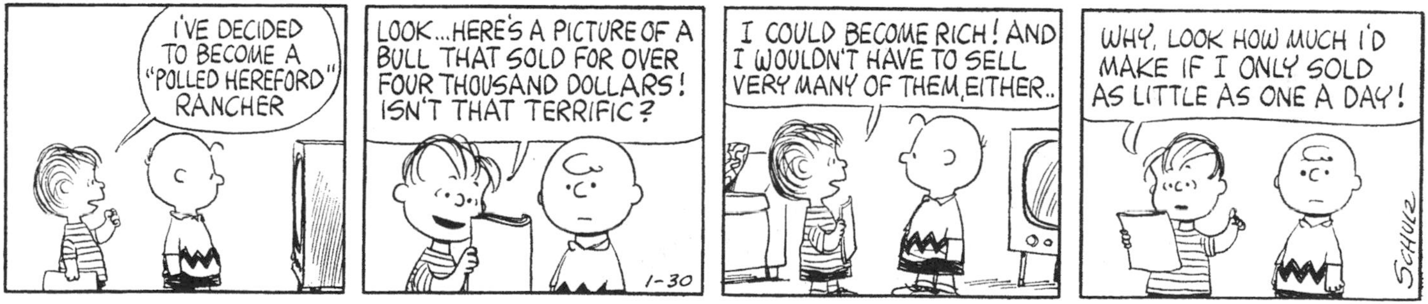
I'VE DECIDED TO BECOME A "POLLED HEREFORD" RANCHER
LOOK...HERE'S A PICTURE OF A BULL THAT SOLD FOR OVER FOUR THOUSAND DOLLARS! ISN'T THAT TERRIFIC?
1-30
I COULD BECOME RICH! AND I WOULDN'T HAVE TO SELL VERY MANY OF THEM, EITHER..
WHY, LOOK HOW MUCH I'D MAKE IF I ONLY SOLD AS LITTLE AS ONE A DAY!
SCHULZ

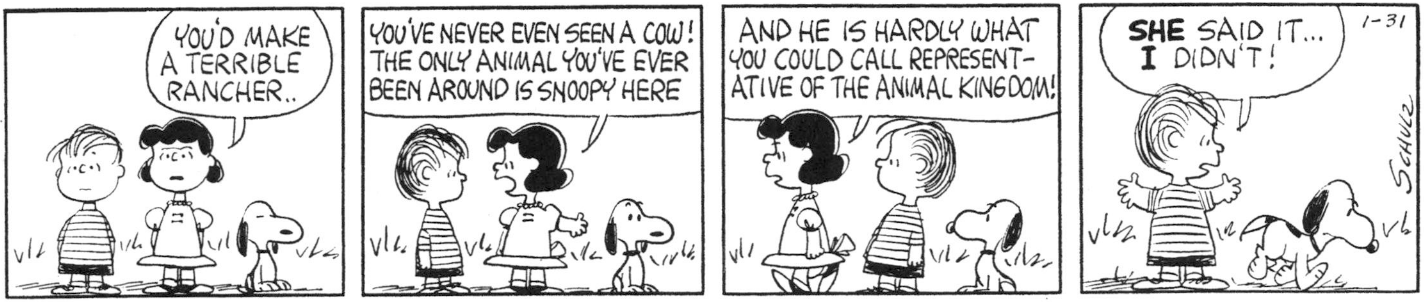
YOU'D MAKE A TERRIBLE RANCHER..
YOU'VE NEVER EVEN SEEN A COW! THE ONLY ANIMAL YOU'VE EVER BEEN AROUND IS SNOOPY HERE
AND HE IS HARDLY WHAT YOU COULD CALL REPRESENTATIVE OF THE ANIMAL KINGDOM!
1-31
SHE SAID IT... I DIDN'T!
SCHULZ

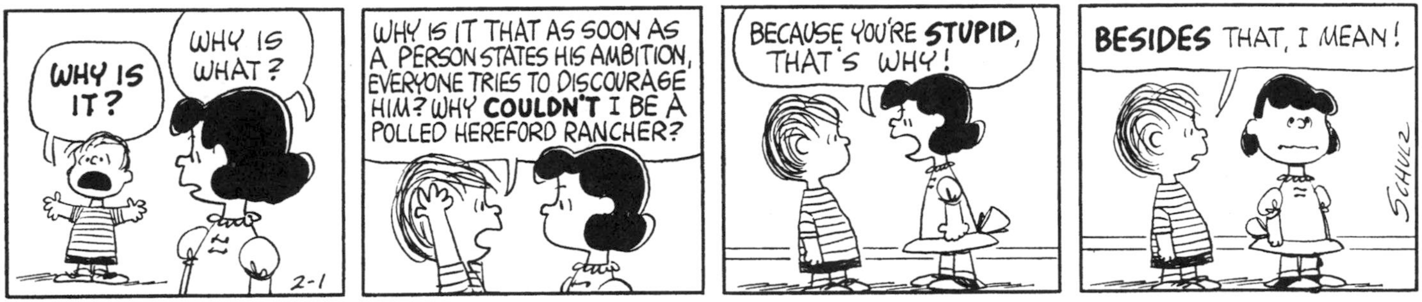
WHY IS IT?
WHY IS WHAT?
2-1
WHY IS IT THAT AS SOON AS A PERSON STATES HIS AMBITION, EVERYONE TRIES TO DISCOURAGE HIM? WHY COULDN'T I BE A POLLED HEREFORD RANCHER?
BECAUSE YOU'RE STUPID, THAT'S WHY!
BESIDES THAT, I MEAN!
SCHULZ

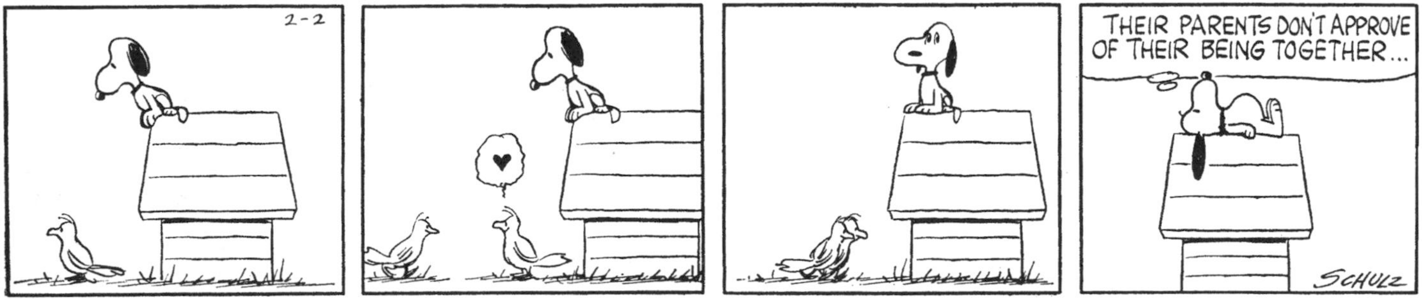
2-2
THEIR PARENTS DON'T APPROVE OF THEIR BEING TOGETHER...
SCHULZ

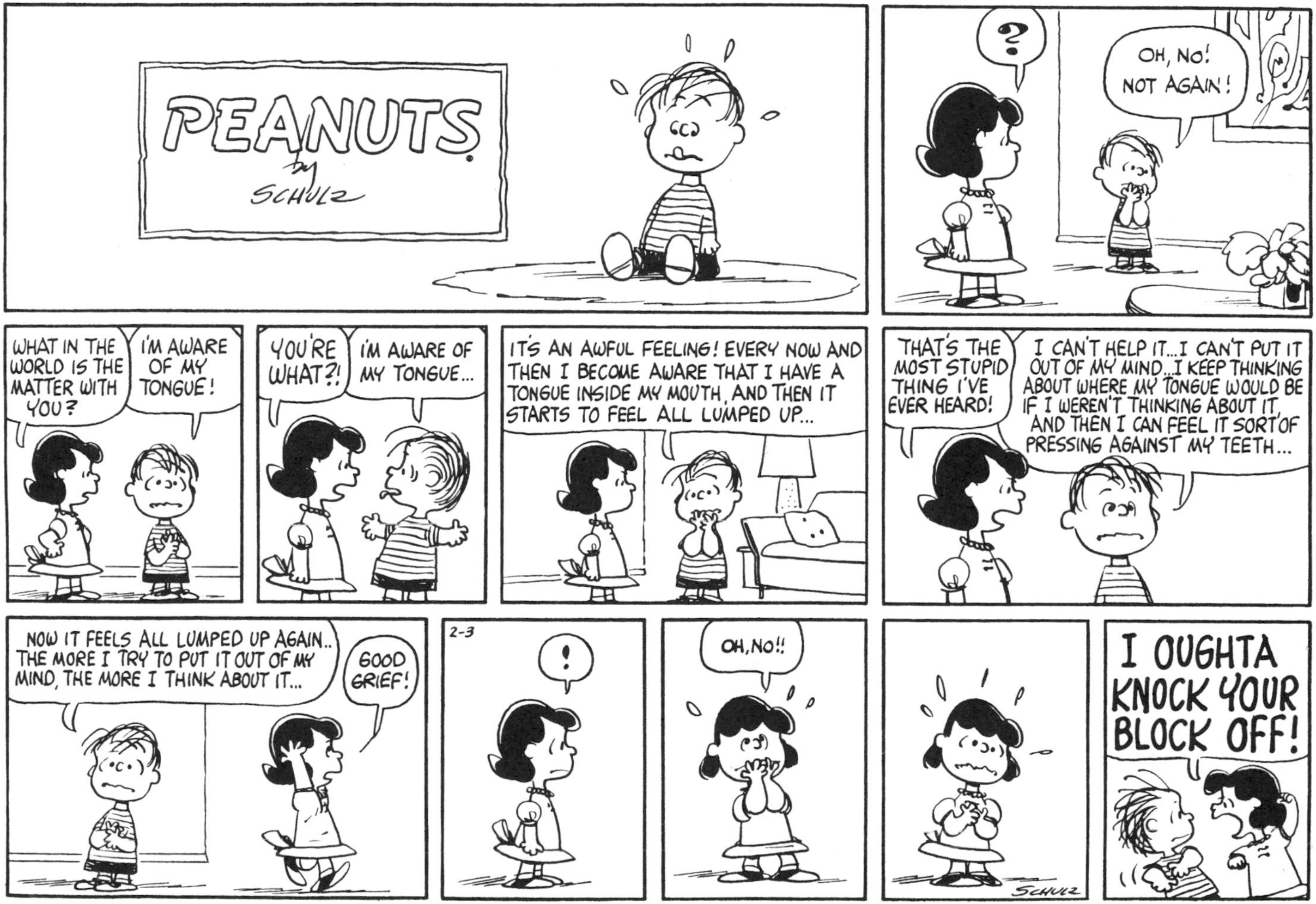
PEANUTS
by SCHULZ
?
OH, NO! NOT AGAIN!
WHAT IN THE WORLD IS THE MATTER WITH YOU?
I'M AWARE OF MY TONGUE!
YOU'RE WHAT?!
I'M AWARE OF MY TONGUE...
IT'S AN AWFUL FEELING! EVERY NOW AND THEN I BECOME AWARE THAT I HAVE A TONGUE INSIDE MY MOUTH, AND THEN IT STARTS TO FEEL ALL LUMPED UP...
THAT'S THE MOST STUPID THING I'VE EVER HEARD!
I CAN'T HELP IT...I CAN'T PUT IT OUT OF MY MIND...I KEEP THINKING ABOUT WHERE MY TONGUE WOULD BE IF I WEREN'T THINKING ABOUT IT, AND THEN I CAN FEEL IT SORT OF PRESSING AGAINST MY TEETH...
NOW IT FEELS ALL LUMPED UP AGAIN.. THE MORE I TRY TO PUT IT OUT OF MY MIND, THE MORE I THINK ABOUT IT...
GOOD GRIEF!
2-3
!
OH, NO!!
SCHULZ
I OUGHTA KNOCK YOUR BLOCK OFF!

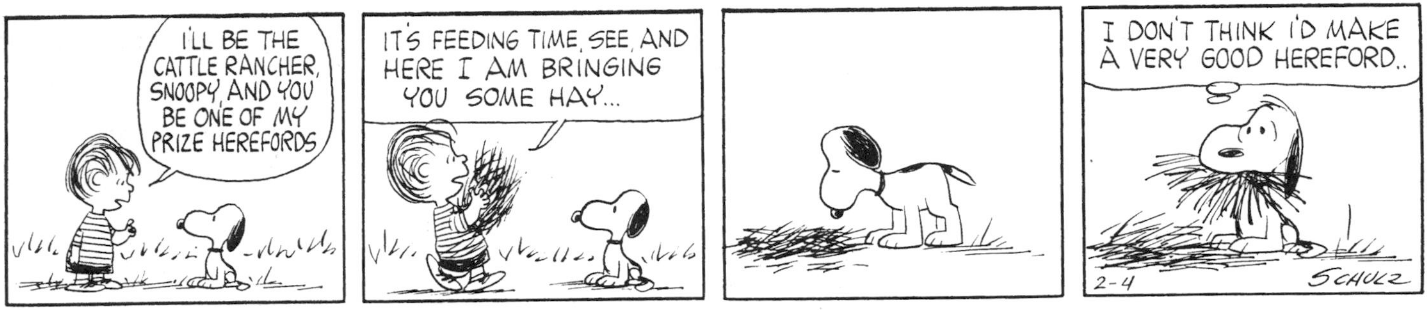
I'LL BE THE CATTLE RANCHER, SNOOPY, AND YOU BE ONE OF MY PRIZE HEREFORDS
IT'S FEEDING TIME, SEE, AND HERE I AM BRINGING YOU SOME HAY...
I DON'T THINK I'D MAKE A VERY GOOD HEREFORD..
2-4
SCHULZ

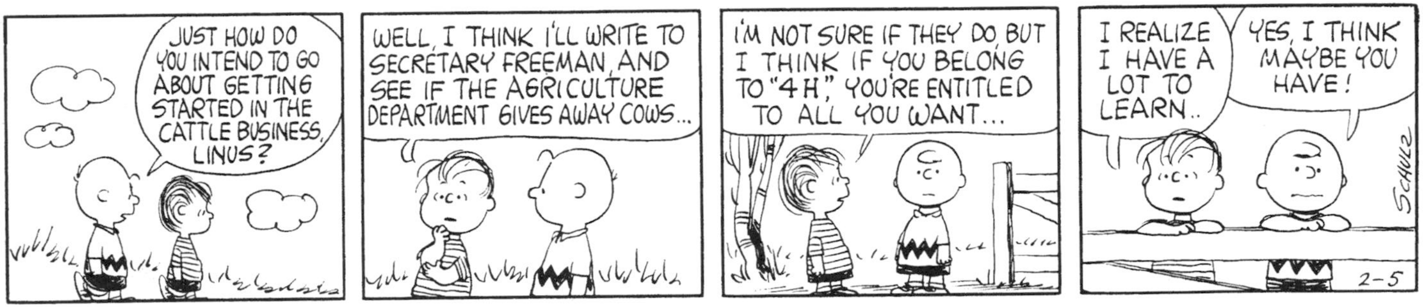
JUST HOW DO YOU INTEND TO GO ABOUT GETTING STARTED IN THE CATTLE BUSINESS, LINUS?
WELL, I THINK I'LL WRITE TO SECRETARY FREEMAN, AND SEE IF THE AGRICULTURE DEPARTMENT GIVES AWAY COWS...
I'M NOT SURE IF THEY DO, BUT I THINK IF YOU BELONG TO "4 H," YOU'RE ENTITLED TO ALL YOU WANT...
I REALIZE I HAVE A LOT TO LEARN..
YES, I THINK MAYBE YOU HAVE!
SCHULZ
2-5

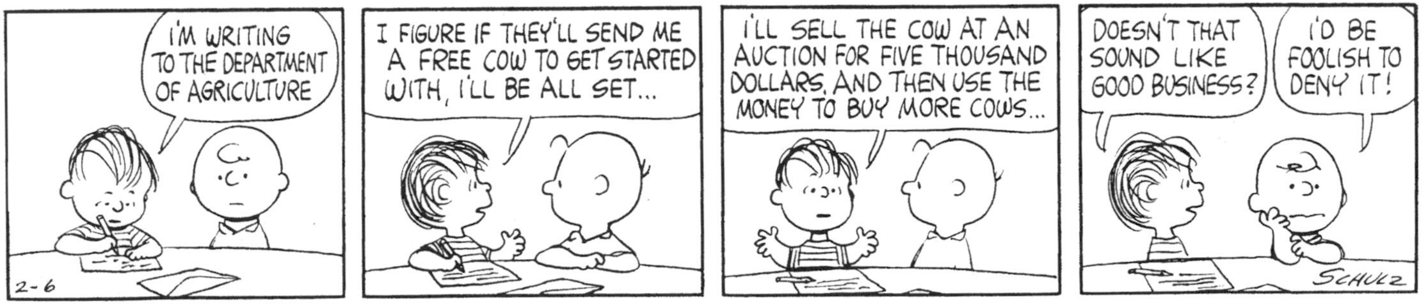
I'M WRITING TO THE DEPARTMENT OF AGRICULTURE
2-6
I FIGURE IF THEY'LL SEND ME A FREE COW TO GET STARTED WITH, I'LL BE ALL SET...
I'LL SELL THE COW AT AN AUCTION FOR FIVE THOUSAND DOLLARS, AND THEN USE THE MONEY TO BUY MORE COWS...
DOESN'T THAT SOUND LIKE GOOD BUSINESS?
I'D BE FOOLISH TO DENY IT!
SCHULZ

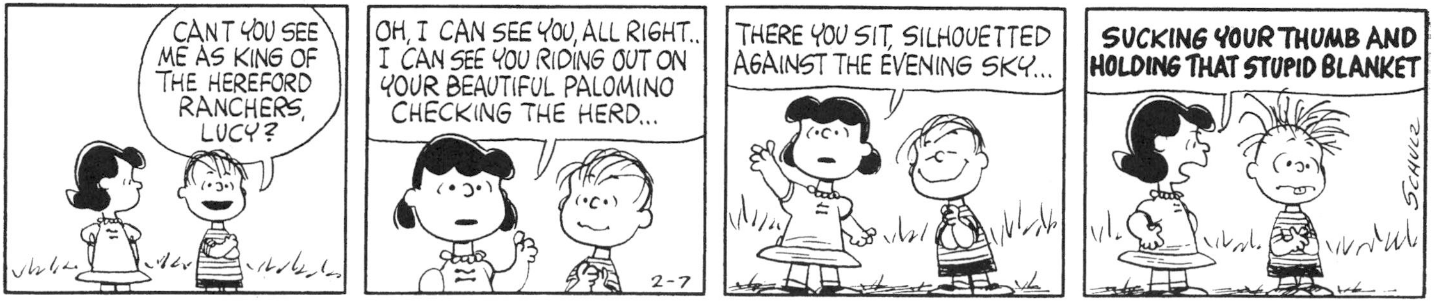
CAN'T YOU SEE ME AS KING OF THE HEREFORD RANCHERS, LUCY?
OH, I CAN SEE YOU, ALL RIGHT.. I CAN SEE YOU RIDING OUT ON YOUR BEAUTIFUL PALOMINO CHECKING THE HERD...
2-7
THERE YOU SIT, SILHOUETTED AGAINST THE EVENING SKY...
SUCKING YOUR THUMB AND HOLDING THAT STUPID BLANKET
SCHULZ

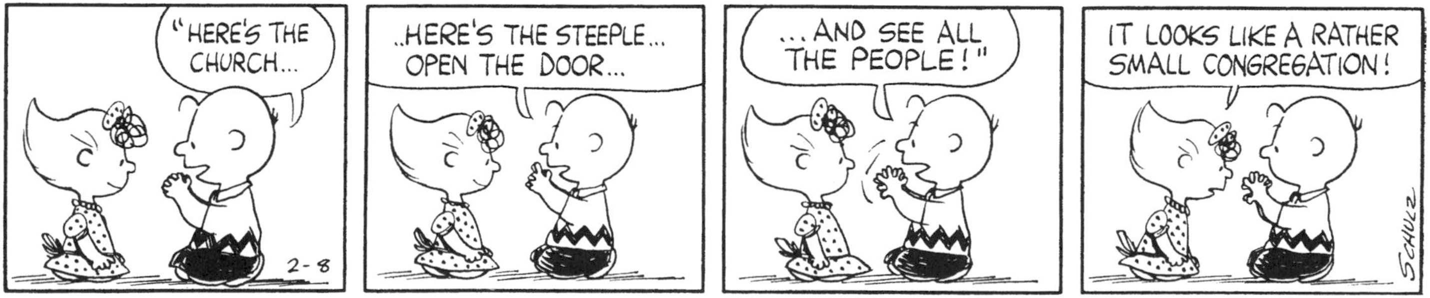
"HERE'S THE CHURCH...
2-8
..HERE'S THE STEEPLE... OPEN THE DOOR...
... AND SEE ALL THE PEOPLE!"
IT LOOKS LIKE A RATHER SMALL CONGREGATION!
SCHULZ

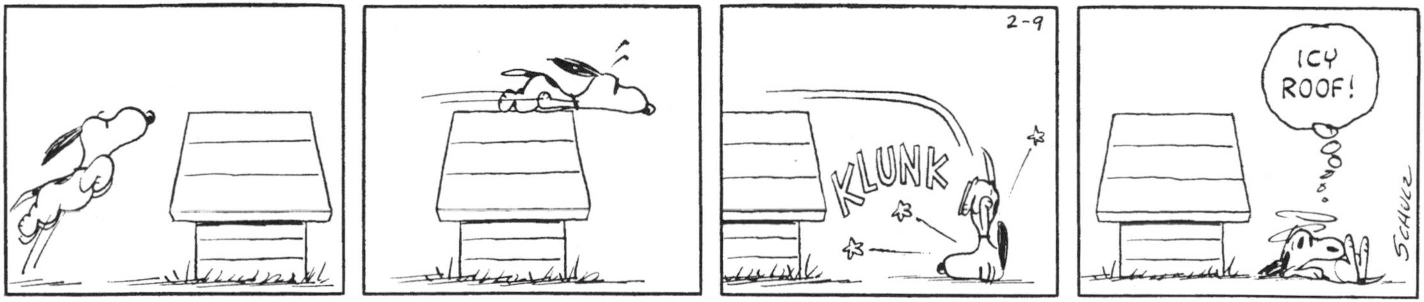
2-9
KLUNK
ICY ROOF!
SCHULZ

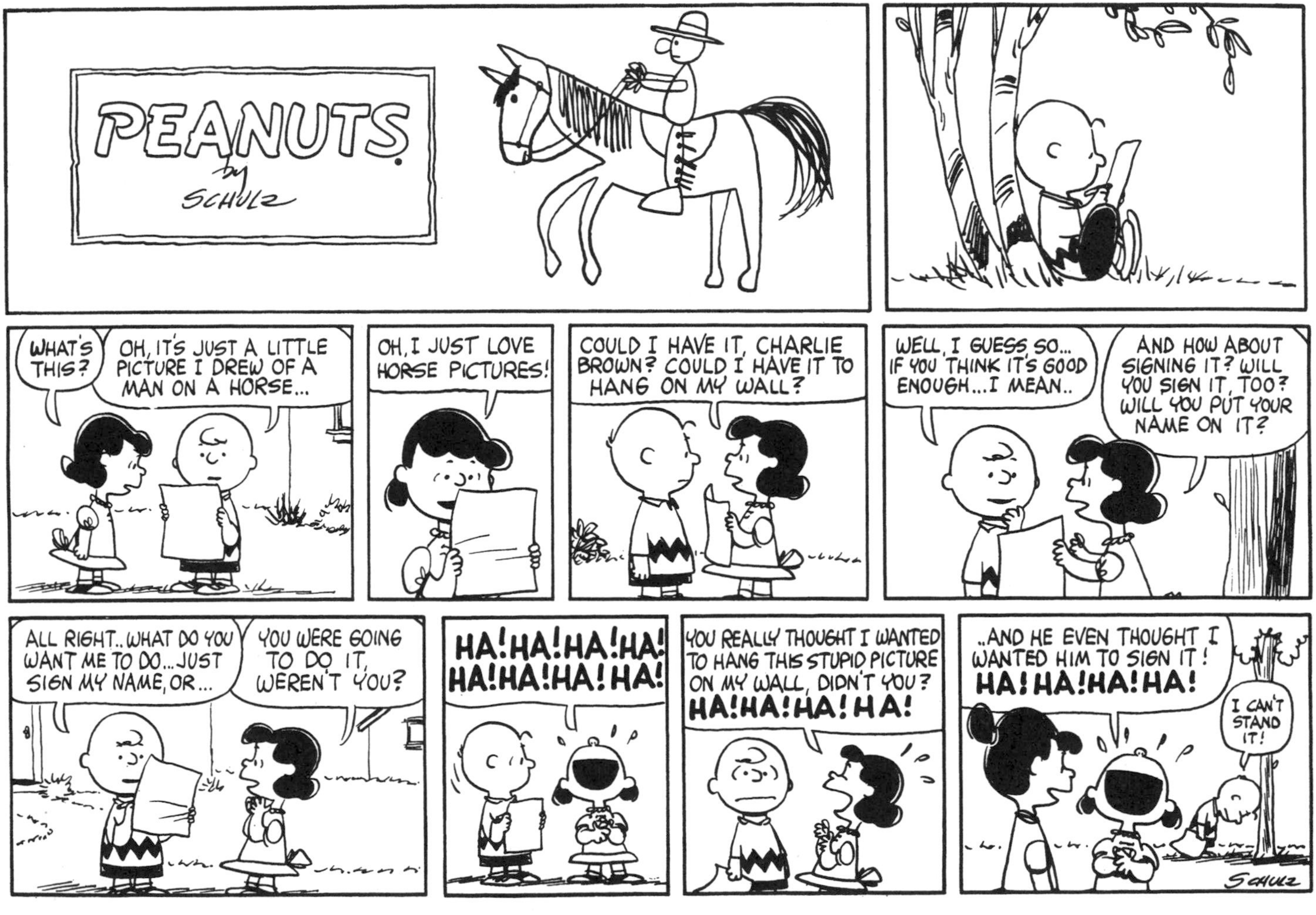
PEANUTS
by SCHULZ
WHAT'S THIS?
OH, IT'S JUST A LITTLE PICTURE I DREW OF A MAN ON A HORSE...
OH, I JUST LOVE HORSE PICTURES!
COULD I HAVE IT, CHARLIE BROWN? COULD I HAVE IT TO HANG ON MY WALL?
WELL, I GUESS SO... IF YOU THINK IT'S GOOD ENOUGH... I MEAN..
AND HOW ABOUT SIGNING IT? WILL YOU SIGN IT, TOO? WILL YOU PUT YOUR NAME ON IT?
ALL RIGHT.. WHAT DO YOU WANT ME TO DO... JUST SIGN MY NAME, OR...
YOU WERE GOING TO DO IT, WEREN'T YOU?
HA! HA! HA! HA! HA! HA! HA! HA!
YOU REALLY THOUGHT I WANTED TO HANG THIS STUPID PICTURE ON MY WALL, DIDN'T YOU? HA! HA! HA! HA!
..AND HE EVEN THOUGHT I WANTED HIM TO SIGN IT! HA! HA! HA! HA!
I CAN'T STAND IT!
SCHULZ

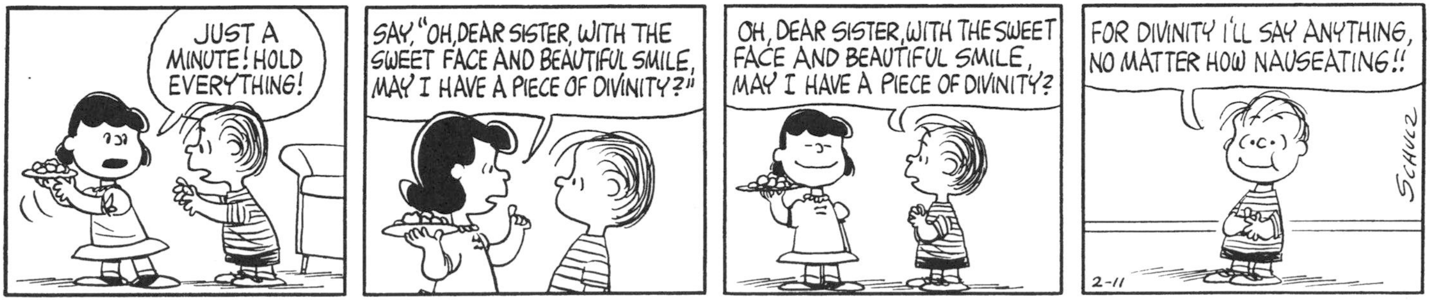
JUST A MINUTE! HOLD EVERYTHING!
SAY, "OH, DEAR SISTER, WITH THE SWEET FACE AND BEAUTIFUL SMILE, MAY I HAVE A PIECE OF DIVINITY?"
OH, DEAR SISTER, WITH THE SWEET FACE AND BEAUTIFUL SMILE, MAY I HAVE A PIECE OF DIVINITY?
FOR DIVINITY I'LL SAY ANYTHING, NO MATTER HOW NAUSEATING!!
SCHULZ
2-11

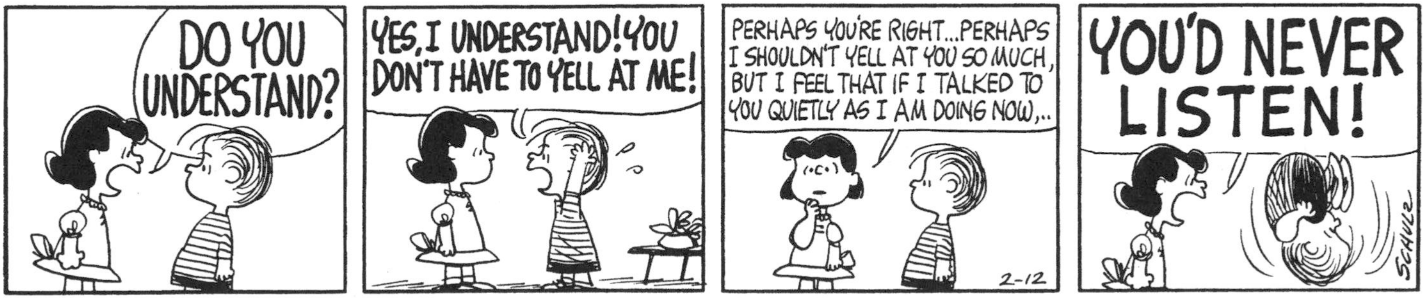
DO YOU UNDERSTAND?
YES, I UNDERSTAND! YOU DON'T HAVE TO YELL AT ME!
PERHAPS YOU'RE RIGHT...PERHAPS I SHOULDN'T YELL AT YOU SO MUCH, BUT I FEEL THAT IF I TALKED TO YOU QUIETLY AS I AM DOING NOW,...
2-12
YOU'D NEVER LISTEN!
SCHULZ

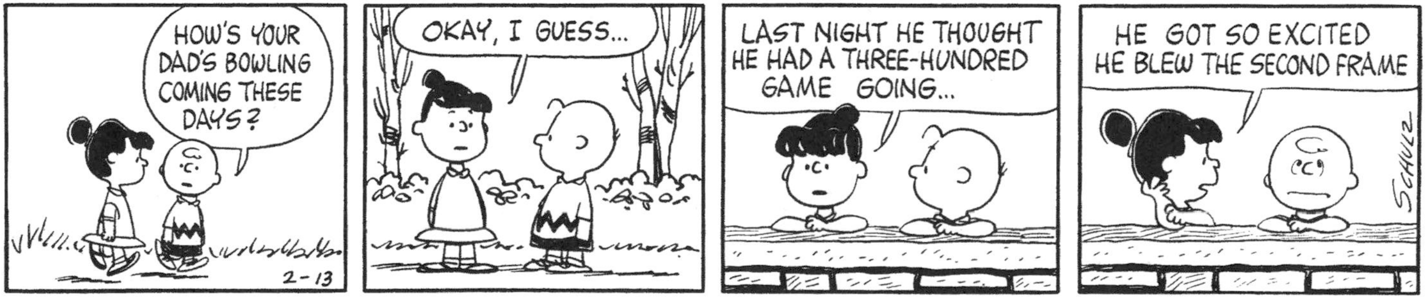
HOW'S YOUR DAD'S BOWLING COMING THESE DAYS?
2-13
OKAY, I GUESS...
LAST NIGHT HE THOUGHT HE HAD A THREE-HUNDRED GAME GOING...
HE GOT SO EXCITED HE BLEW THE SECOND FRAME
SCHULZ

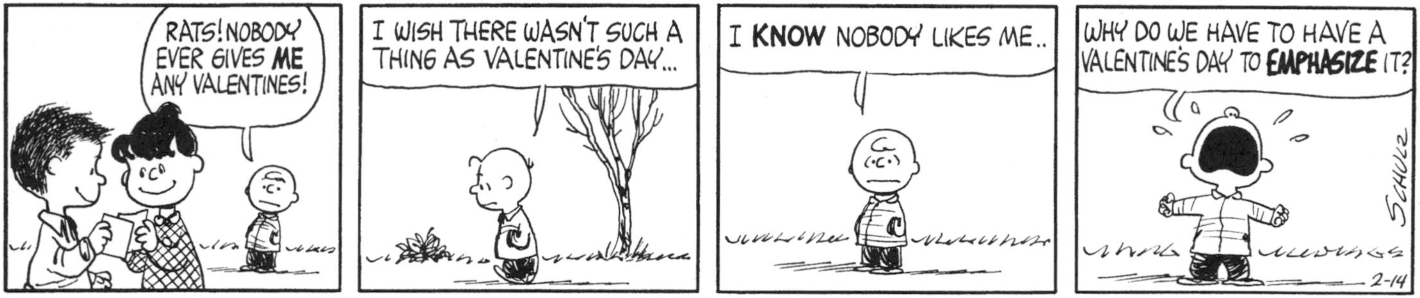
RATS! NOBODY EVER GIVES **ME** ANY VALENTINES!
I WISH THERE WASN'T SUCH A THING AS VALENTINE'S DAY...
I **KNOW** NOBODY LIKES ME..
WHY DO WE HAVE TO HAVE A VALENTINE'S DAY TO **EMPHASIZE** IT?
SCHULZ
2-14

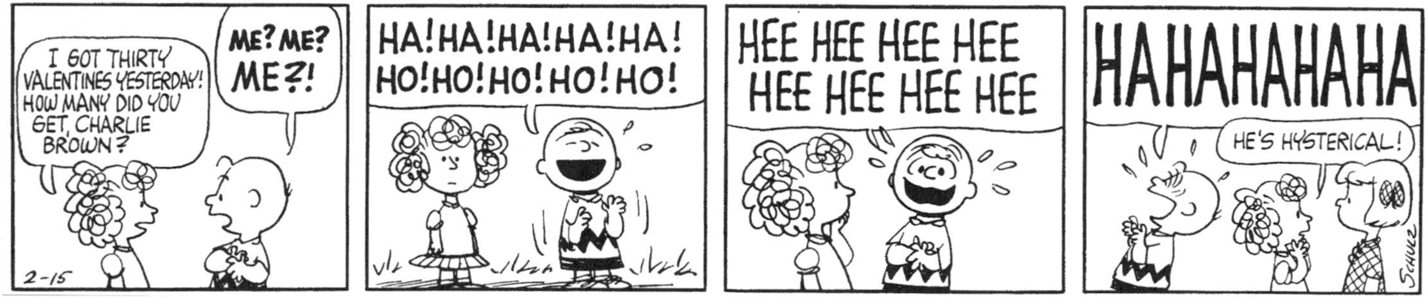
I GOT THIRTY VALENTINES YESTERDAY! HOW MANY DID YOU GET, CHARLIE BROWN?
ME? ME? ME?!
2-15
HA! HA! HA! HA! HA! HO! HO! HO! HO! HO!
HEE HEE HEE HEE HEE HEE HEE HEE
HAHAHAHAHA
HE'S HYSTERICAL!
SCHULZ

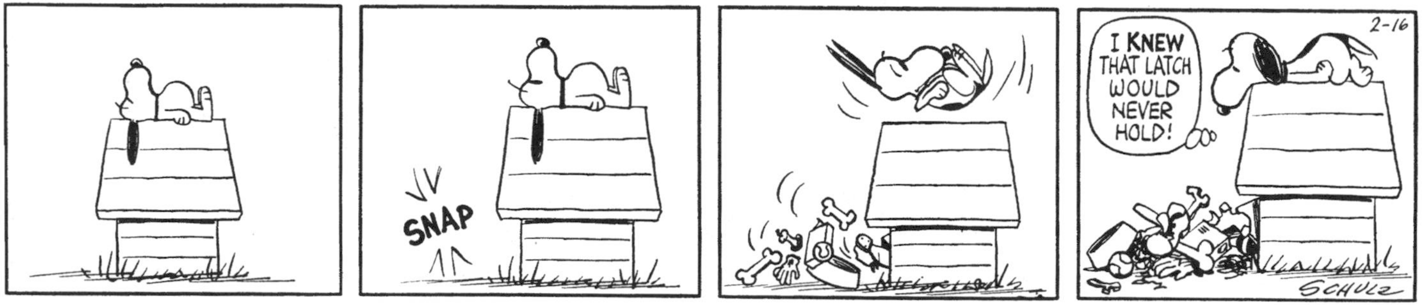
SNAP
2-16
I **KNEW** THAT LATCH WOULD NEVER HOLD!
SCHULZ

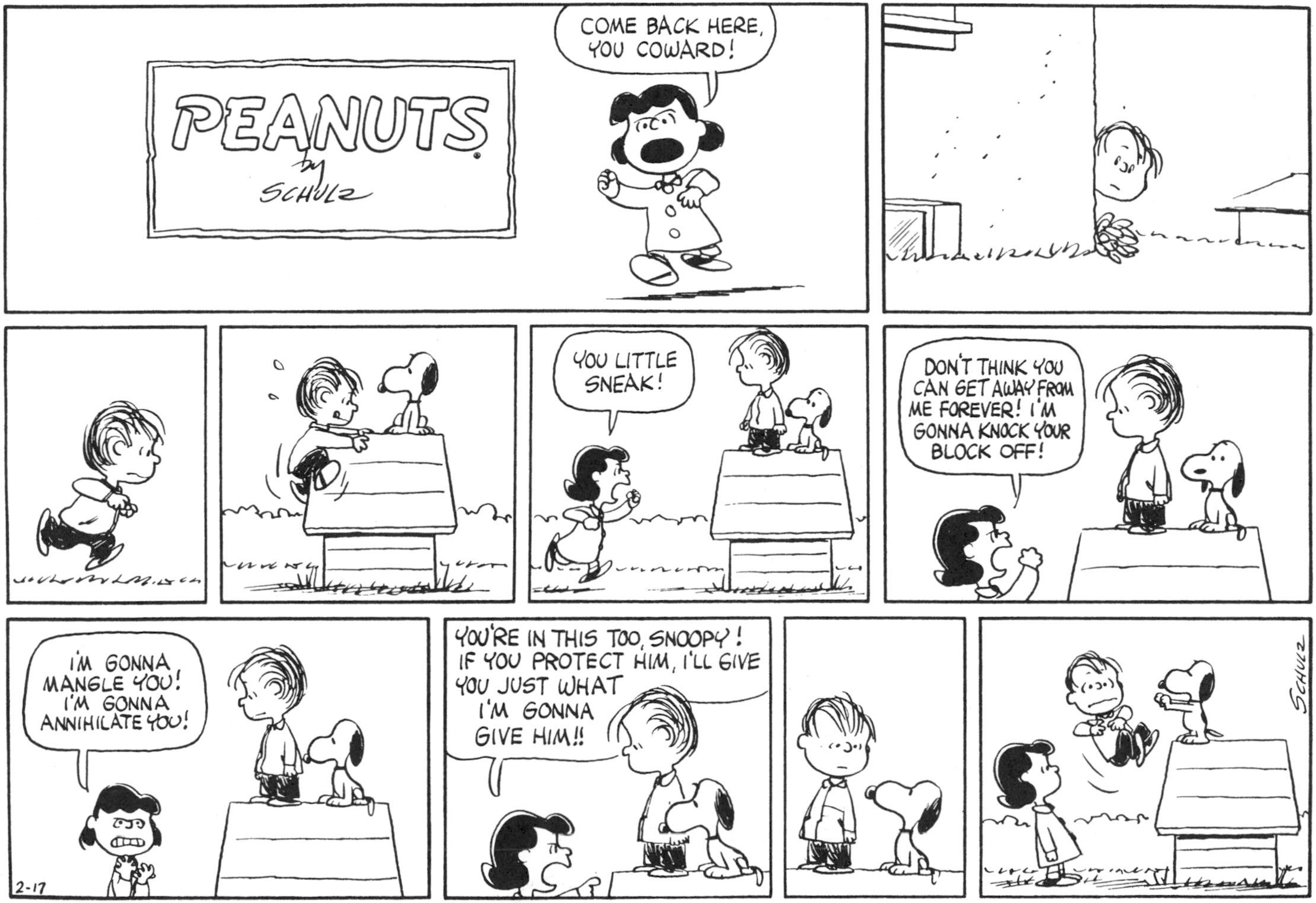
PEANUTS
by SCHULZ
COME BACK HERE, YOU COWARD!
YOU LITTLE SNEAK!
DON'T THINK YOU CAN GET AWAY FROM ME FOREVER! I'M GONNA KNOCK YOUR BLOCK OFF!
I'M GONNA MANGLE YOU! I'M GONNA ANNIHILATE YOU!
2-17
YOU'RE IN THIS TOO, SNOOPY! IF YOU PROTECT HIM, I'LL GIVE YOU JUST WHAT I'M GONNA GIVE HIM!!
SCHULZ

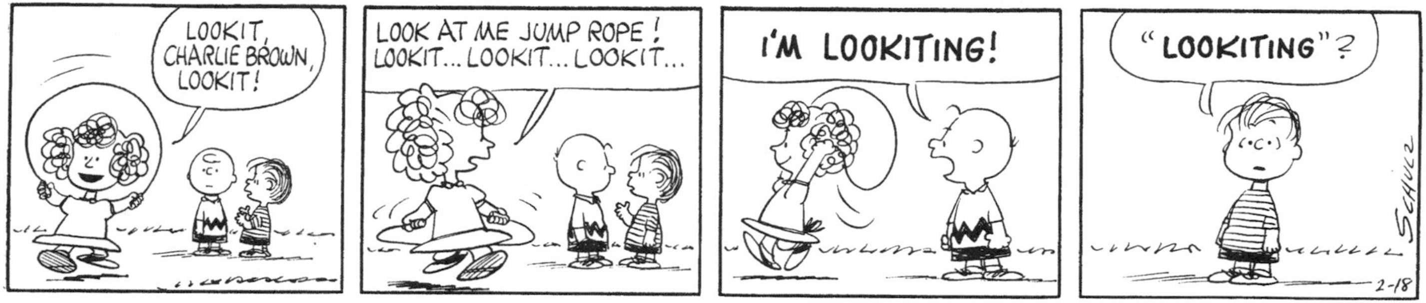
LOOKIT, CHARLIE BROWN, LOOKIT!
LOOK AT ME JUMP ROPE! LOOKIT... LOOKIT... LOOKIT...
I'M LOOKITING!
"LOOKITING"?
SCHULZ
2-18

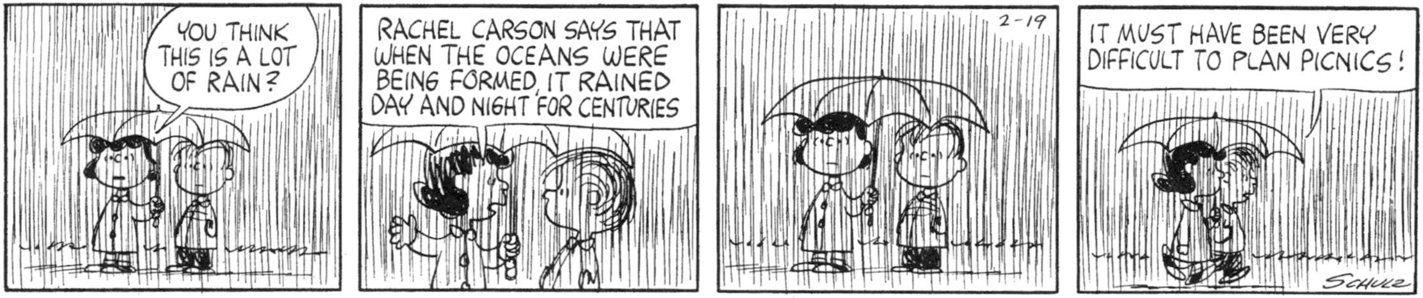
YOU THINK THIS IS A LOT OF RAIN?
RACHEL CARSON SAYS THAT WHEN THE OCEANS WERE BEING FORMED, IT RAINED DAY AND NIGHT FOR CENTURIES
2-19
IT MUST HAVE BEEN VERY DIFFICULT TO PLAN PICNICS!
SCHULZ

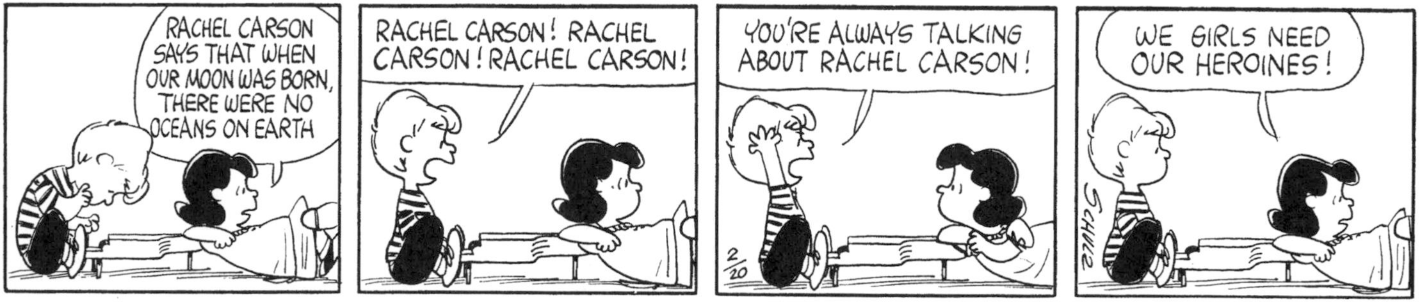
RACHEL CARSON SAYS THAT WHEN OUR MOON WAS BORN, THERE WERE NO OCEANS ON EARTH
RACHEL CARSON! RACHEL CARSON! RACHEL CARSON!
YOU'RE ALWAYS TALKING ABOUT RACHEL CARSON!
2/20
WE GIRLS NEED OUR HEROINES!
SCHULZ

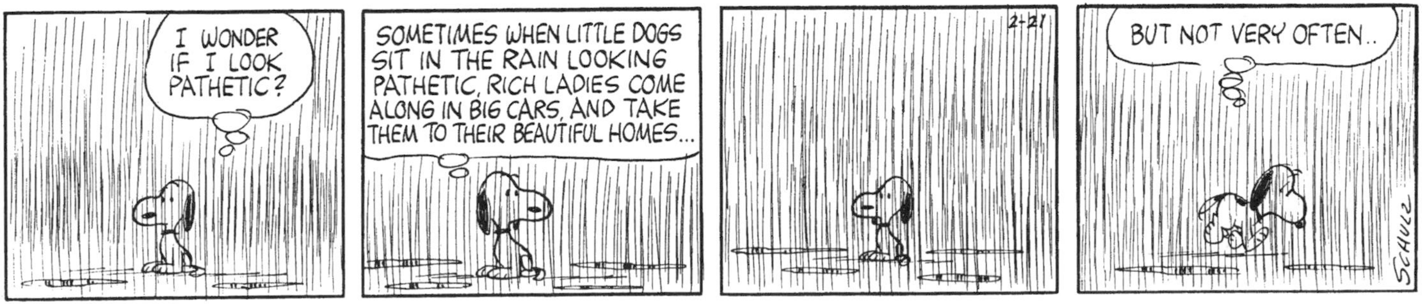
I WONDER IF I LOOK PATHETIC?
SOMETIMES WHEN LITTLE DOGS SIT IN THE RAIN LOOKING PATHETIC, RICH LADIES COME ALONG IN BIG CARS, AND TAKE THEM TO THEIR BEAUTIFUL HOMES...
2-21
BUT NOT VERY OFTEN..
SCHULZ

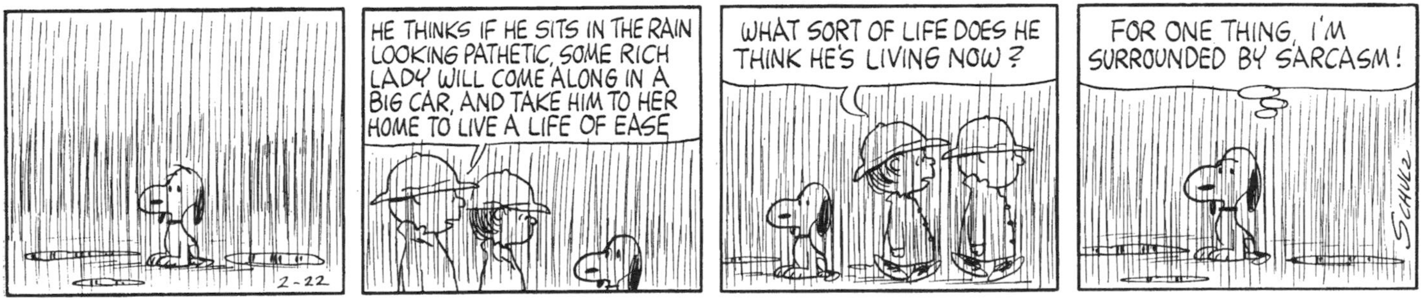
2-22
HE THINKS IF HE SITS IN THE RAIN LOOKING PATHETIC, SOME RICH LADY WILL COME ALONG IN A BIG CAR, AND TAKE HIM TO HER HOME TO LIVE A LIFE OF EASE
WHAT SORT OF LIFE DOES HE THINK HE'S LIVING NOW?
FOR ONE THING, I'M SURROUNDED BY SARCASM!
SCHULZ

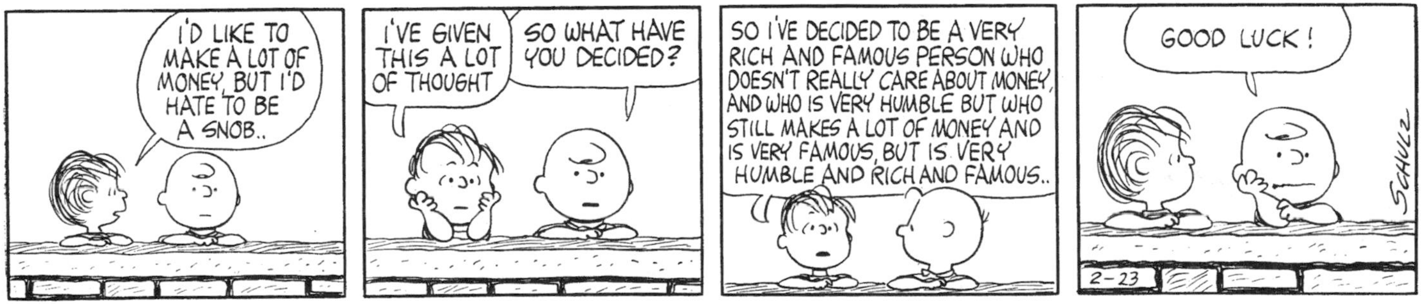
I'D LIKE TO MAKE A LOT OF MONEY, BUT I'D HATE TO BE A SNOB..
I'VE GIVEN THIS A LOT OF THOUGHT
SO WHAT HAVE YOU DECIDED?
SO I'VE DECIDED TO BE A VERY RICH AND FAMOUS PERSON WHO DOESN'T REALLY CARE ABOUT MONEY, AND WHO IS VERY HUMBLE BUT WHO STILL MAKES A LOT OF MONEY AND IS VERY FAMOUS, BUT IS VERY HUMBLE AND RICH AND FAMOUS..
GOOD LUCK!
SCHULZ
2-23

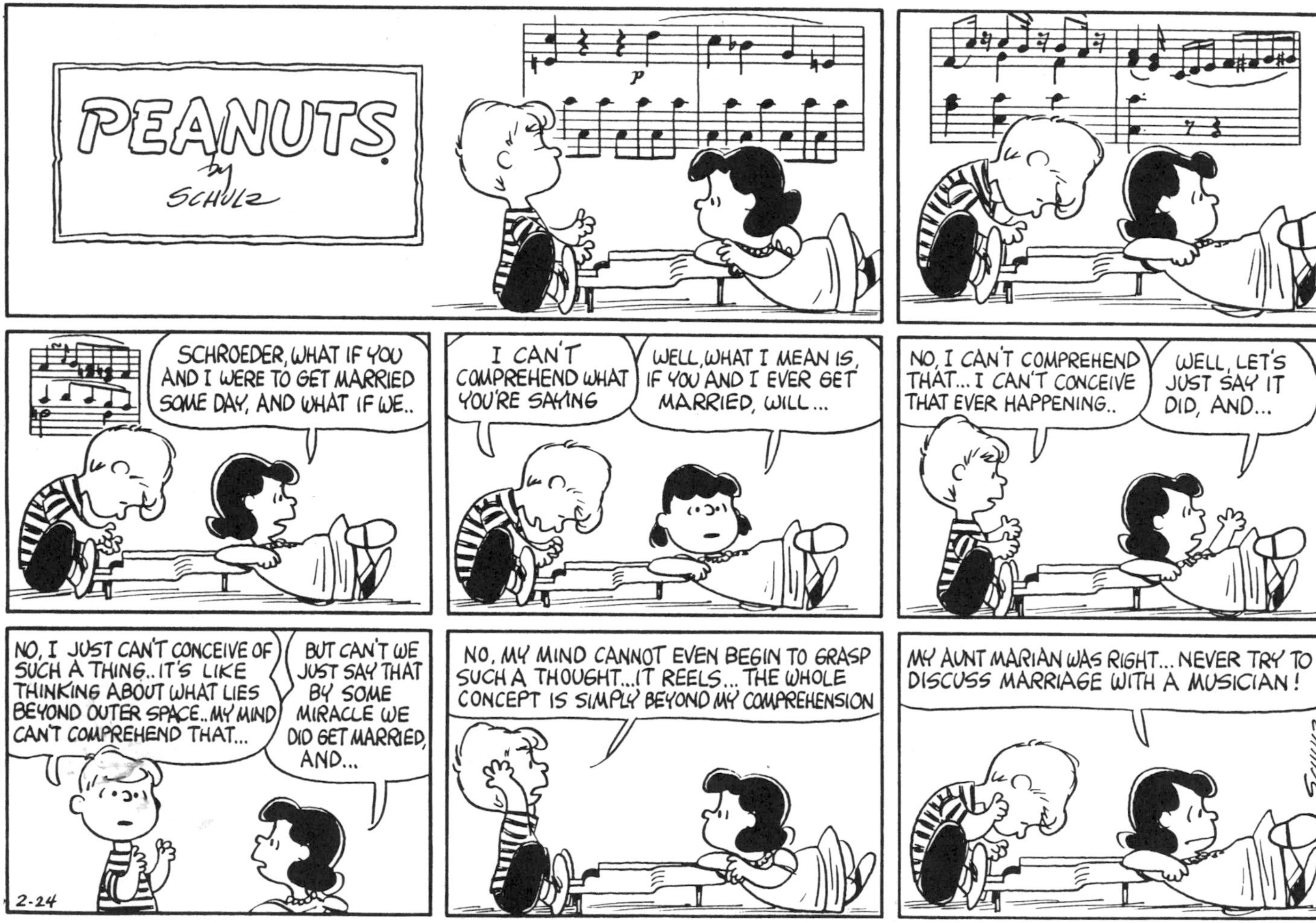
PEANUTS
by SCHULZ
SCHROEDER, WHAT IF YOU AND I WERE TO GET MARRIED SOME DAY, AND WHAT IF WE..
I CAN'T COMPREHEND WHAT YOU'RE SAYING
WELL, WHAT I MEAN IS, IF YOU AND I EVER GET MARRIED, WILL...
NO, I CAN'T COMPREHEND THAT... I CAN'T CONCEIVE THAT EVER HAPPENING..
WELL, LET'S JUST SAY IT DID, AND...
NO, I JUST CAN'T CONCEIVE OF SUCH A THING.. IT'S LIKE THINKING ABOUT WHAT LIES BEYOND OUTER SPACE.. MY MIND CAN'T COMPREHEND THAT...
BUT CAN'T WE JUST SAY THAT BY SOME MIRACLE WE DID GET MARRIED, AND...
2-24
NO, MY MIND CANNOT EVEN BEGIN TO GRASP SUCH A THOUGHT... IT REELS... THE WHOLE CONCEPT IS SIMPLY BEYOND MY COMPREHENSION
MY AUNT MARIAN WAS RIGHT... NEVER TRY TO DISCUSS MARRIAGE WITH A MUSICIAN!
SCHULZ

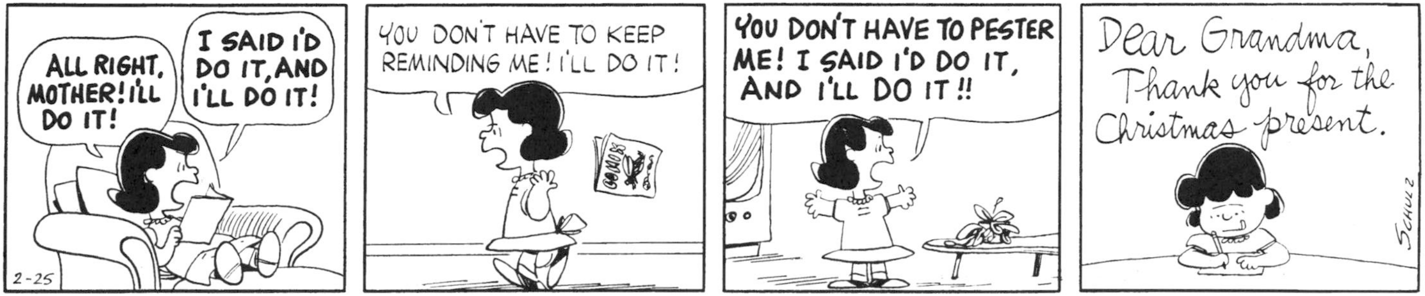
ALL RIGHT, MOTHER! I'LL DO IT!
I SAID I'D DO IT, AND I'LL DO IT!
2-25
YOU DON'T HAVE TO KEEP REMINDING ME! I'LL DO IT!
YOU DON'T HAVE TO PESTER ME! I SAID I'D DO IT, AND I'LL DO IT!!
Dear Grandma, Thank you for the Christmas present.
SCHULZ

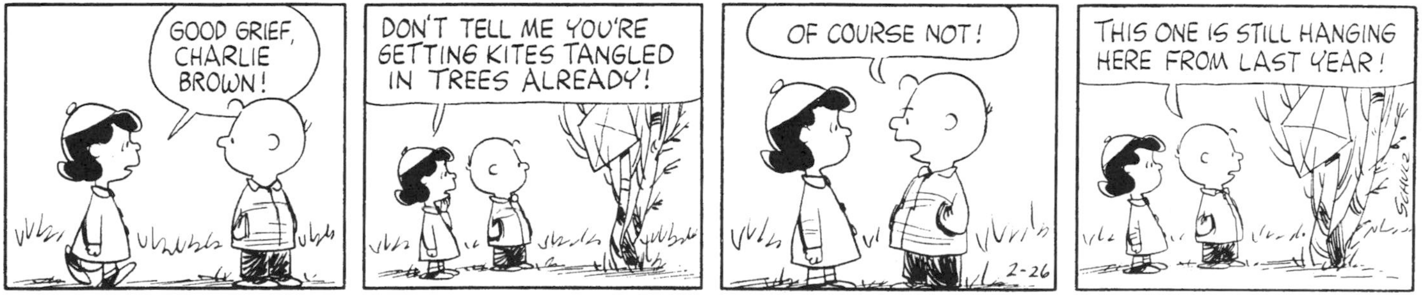
GOOD GRIEF, CHARLIE BROWN!
DON'T TELL ME YOU'RE GETTING KITES TANGLED IN TREES ALREADY!
OF COURSE NOT!
2-26
THIS ONE IS STILL HANGING HERE FROM LAST YEAR!
SCHULZ

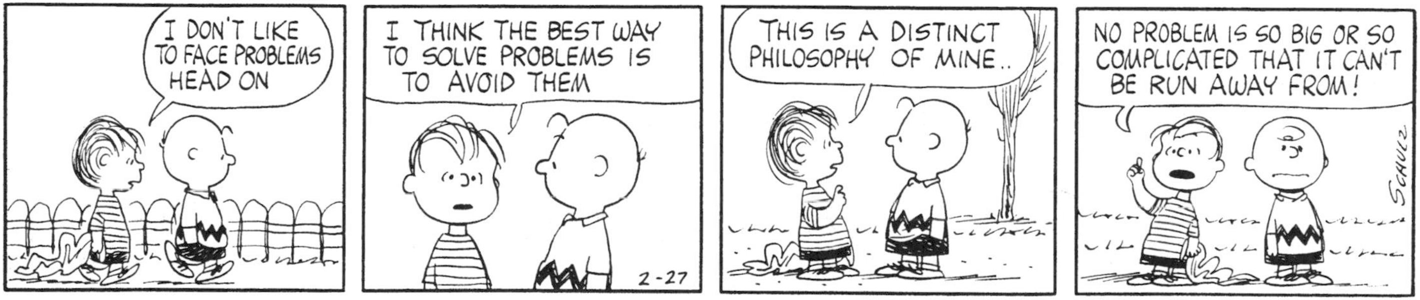
I DON'T LIKE TO FACE PROBLEMS HEAD ON
I THINK THE BEST WAY TO SOLVE PROBLEMS IS TO AVOID THEM
2-27
THIS IS A DISTINCT PHILOSOPHY OF MINE..
NO PROBLEM IS SO BIG OR SO COMPLICATED THAT IT CAN'T BE RUN AWAY FROM!
SCHULZ

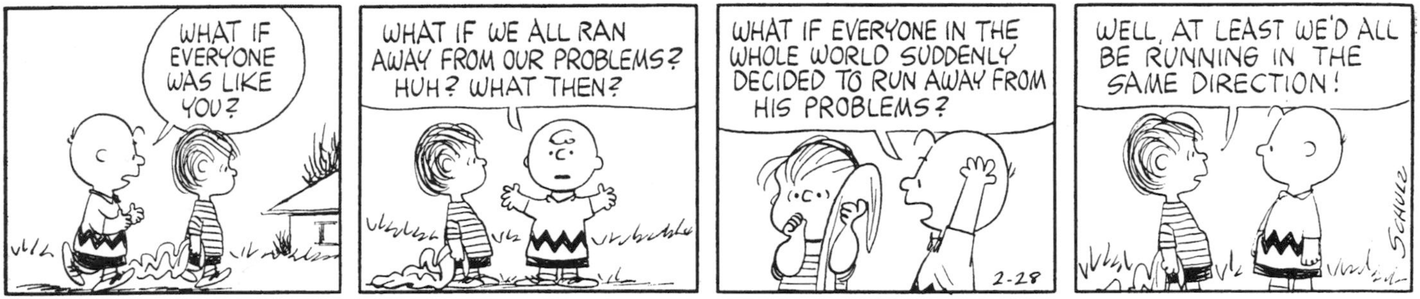
WHAT IF EVERYONE WAS LIKE YOU?
WHAT IF WE ALL RAN AWAY FROM OUR PROBLEMS? HUH? WHAT THEN?
WHAT IF EVERYONE IN THE WHOLE WORLD SUDDENLY DECIDED TO RUN AWAY FROM HIS PROBLEMS?
2-28
WELL, AT LEAST WE'D ALL BE RUNNING IN THE SAME DIRECTION!
SCHULZ

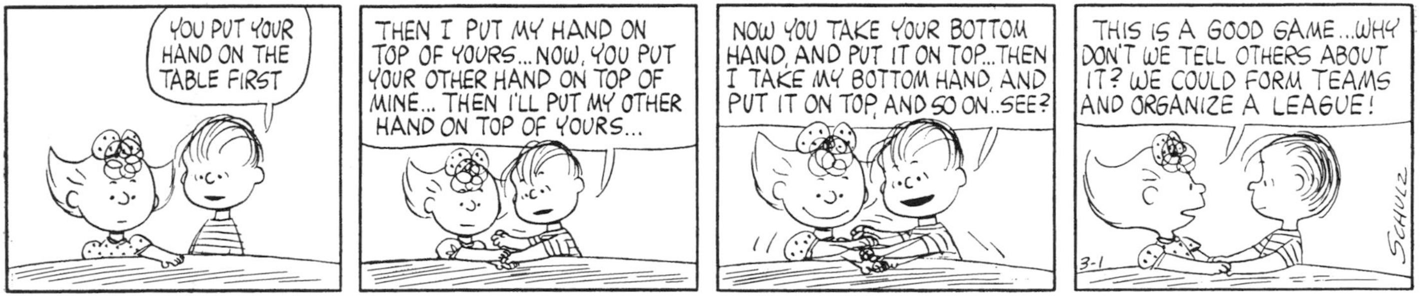
YOU PUT YOUR HAND ON THE TABLE FIRST
THEN I PUT MY HAND ON TOP OF YOURS...NOW, YOU PUT YOUR OTHER HAND ON TOP OF MINE... THEN I'LL PUT MY OTHER HAND ON TOP OF YOURS...
NOW YOU TAKE YOUR BOTTOM HAND, AND PUT IT ON TOP...THEN I TAKE MY BOTTOM HAND, AND PUT IT ON TOP, AND SO ON..SEE?
THIS IS A GOOD GAME...WHY DON'T WE TELL OTHERS ABOUT IT? WE COULD FORM TEAMS AND ORGANIZE A LEAGUE!
3-1
SCHULZ

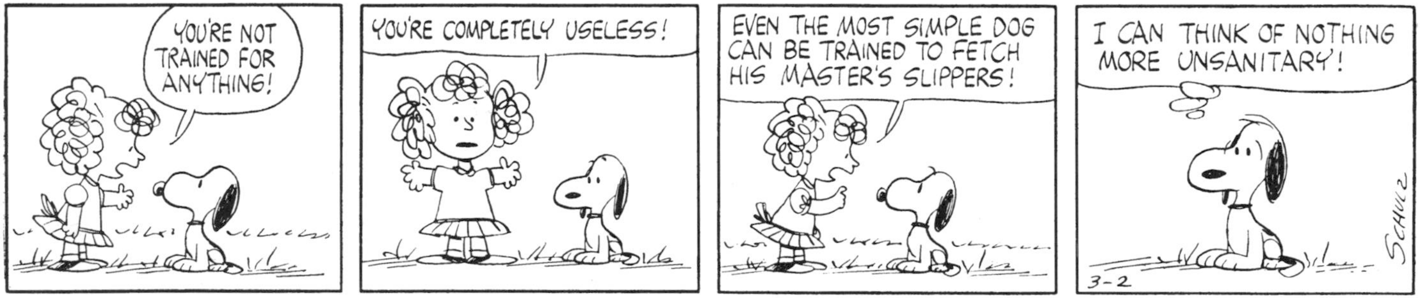
YOU'RE NOT TRAINED FOR ANYTHING!
YOU'RE COMPLETELY USELESS!
EVEN THE MOST SIMPLE DOG CAN BE TRAINED TO FETCH HIS MASTER'S SLIPPERS!
I CAN THINK OF NOTHING MORE UNSANITARY!
3-2
SCHULZ

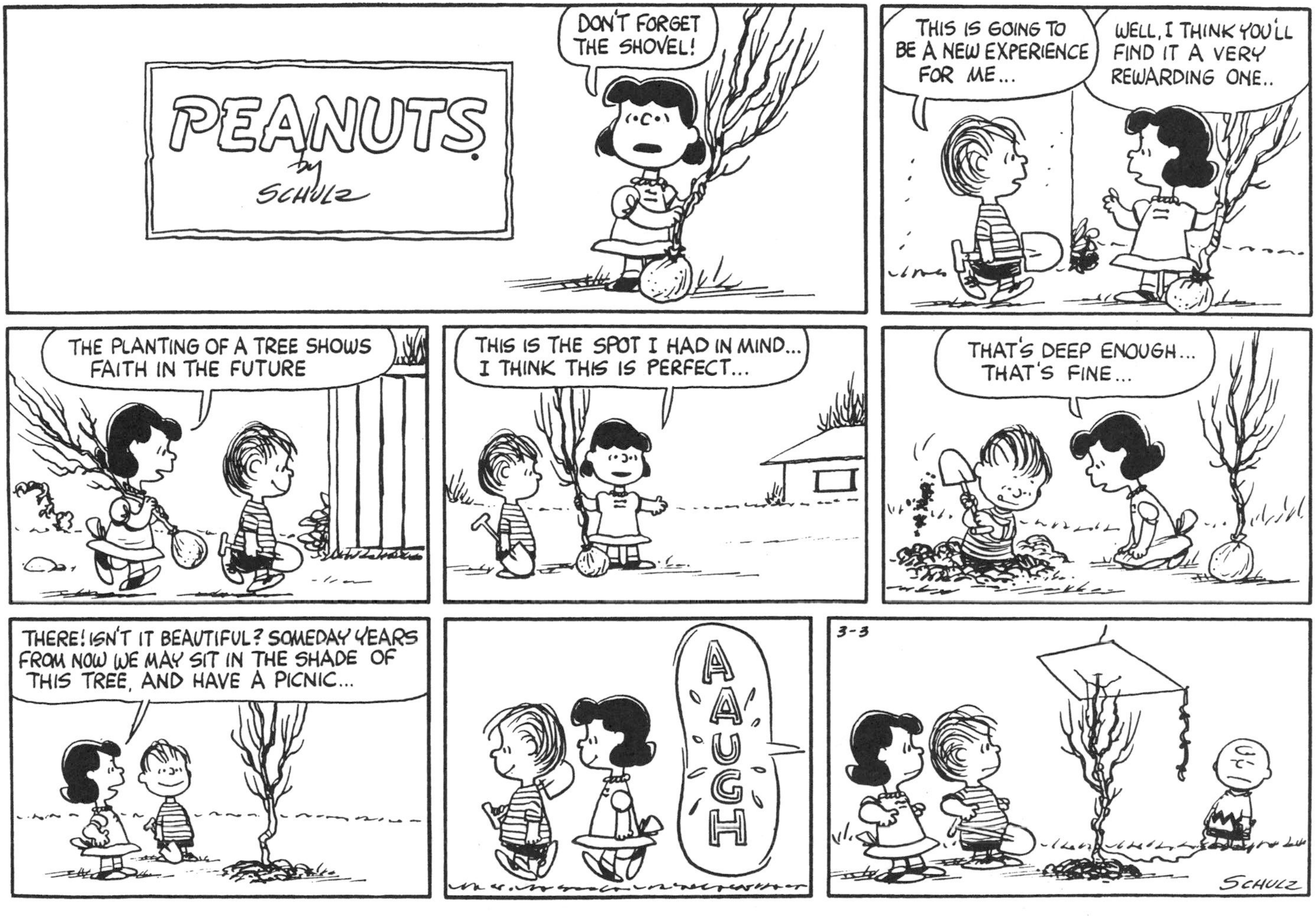
PEANUTS
by SCHULZ
DON'T FORGET THE SHOVEL!
THIS IS GOING TO BE A NEW EXPERIENCE FOR ME...
WELL, I THINK YOU'LL FIND IT A VERY REWARDING ONE..
THE PLANTING OF A TREE SHOWS FAITH IN THE FUTURE
THIS IS THE SPOT I HAD IN MIND... I THINK THIS IS PERFECT...
THAT'S DEEP ENOUGH... THAT'S FINE...
THERE! ISN'T IT BEAUTIFUL? SOMEDAY YEARS FROM NOW WE MAY SIT IN THE SHADE OF THIS TREE, AND HAVE A PICNIC...
AAUGH
3-3
SCHULZ

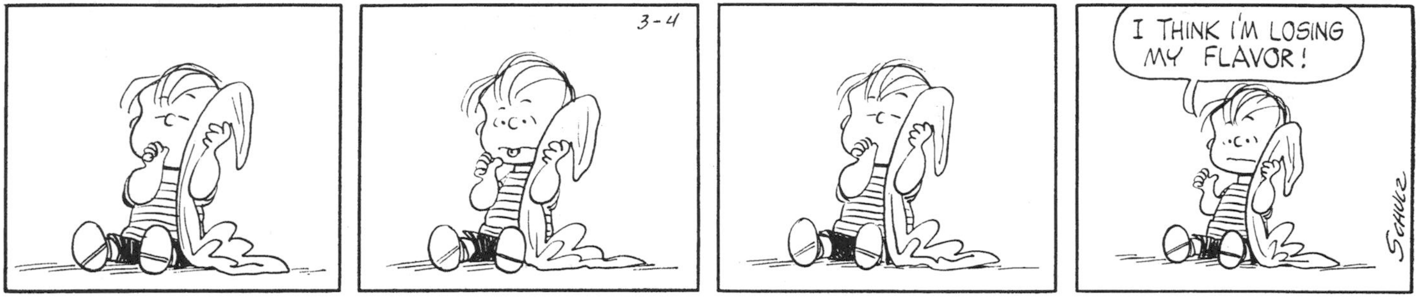
3-4
I THINK I'M LOSING MY FLAVOR!
SCHULZ

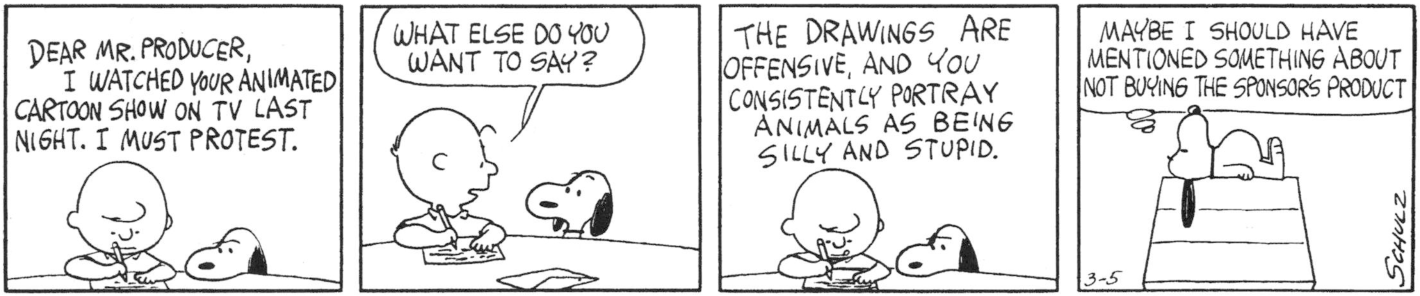
DEAR MR. PRODUCER, I WATCHED YOUR ANIMATED CARTOON SHOW ON TV LAST NIGHT. I MUST PROTEST.
WHAT ELSE DO YOU WANT TO SAY?
THE DRAWINGS ARE OFFENSIVE, AND YOU CONSISTENTLY PORTRAY ANIMALS AS BEING SILLY AND STUPID.
MAYBE I SHOULD HAVE MENTIONED SOMETHING ABOUT NOT BUYING THE SPONSOR'S PRODUCT
SCHULZ
3-5

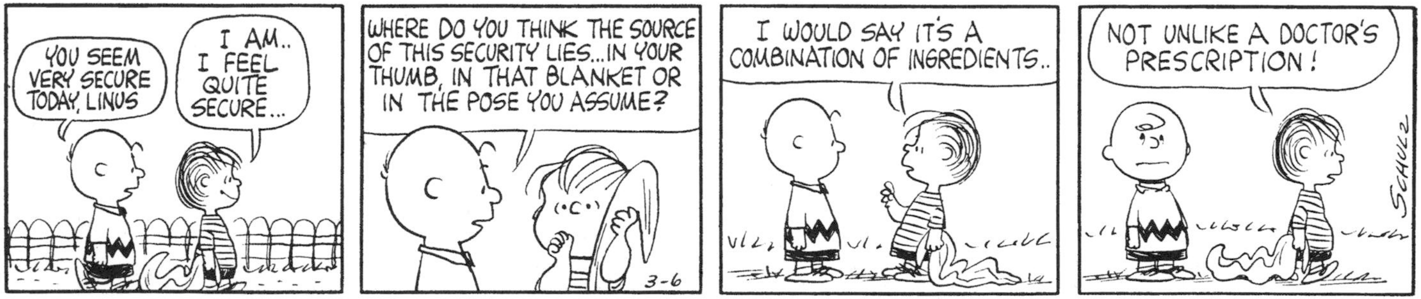
YOU SEEM VERY SECURE TODAY, LINUS
I AM.. I FEEL QUITE SECURE...
WHERE DO YOU THINK THE SOURCE OF THIS SECURITY LIES...IN YOUR THUMB, IN THAT BLANKET OR IN THE POSE YOU ASSUME?
3-6
I WOULD SAY IT'S A COMBINATION OF INGREDIENTS..
NOT UNLIKE A DOCTOR'S PRESCRIPTION!
SCHULZ

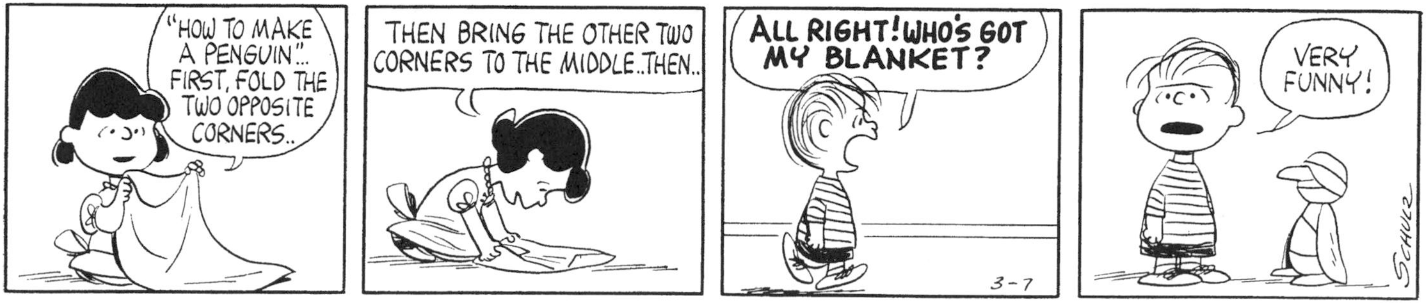
"HOW TO MAKE A PENGUIN"... FIRST, FOLD THE TWO OPPOSITE CORNERS..
THEN BRING THE OTHER TWO CORNERS TO THE MIDDLE..THEN..
ALL RIGHT! WHO'S GOT MY BLANKET?
3-7
VERY FUNNY!
SCHULZ

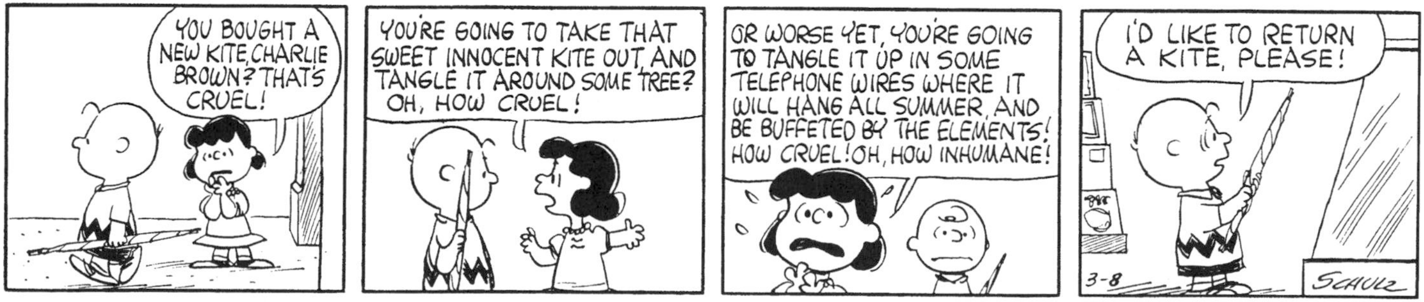
YOU BOUGHT A NEW KITE, CHARLIE BROWN? THAT'S CRUEL!
YOU'RE GOING TO TAKE THAT SWEET INNOCENT KITE OUT AND TANGLE IT AROUND SOME TREE? OH, HOW CRUEL!
OR WORSE YET, YOU'RE GOING TO TANGLE IT UP IN SOME TELEPHONE WIRES WHERE IT WILL HANG ALL SUMMER, AND BE BUFFETED BY THE ELEMENTS! HOW CRUEL! OH, HOW INHUMANE!
I'D LIKE TO RETURN A KITE, PLEASE!
3-8
SCHULZ

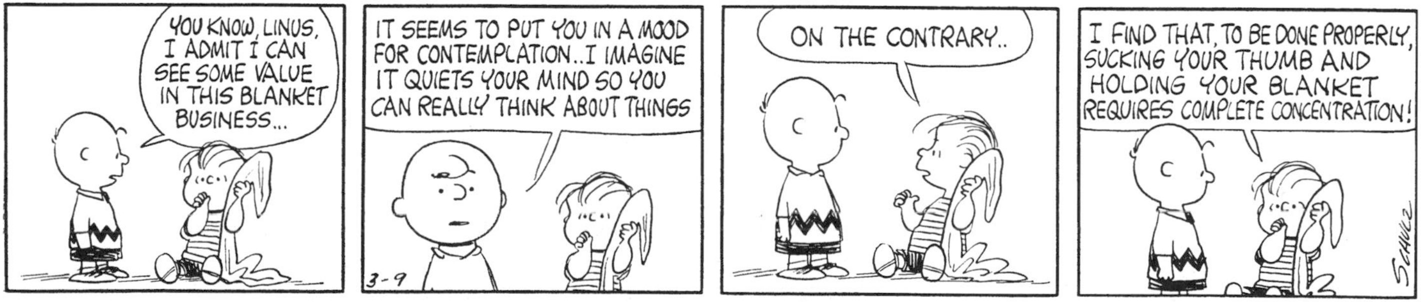
YOU KNOW, LINUS, I ADMIT I CAN SEE SOME VALUE IN THIS BLANKET BUSINESS...
IT SEEMS TO PUT YOU IN A MOOD FOR CONTEMPLATION..I IMAGINE IT QUIETS YOUR MIND SO YOU CAN REALLY THINK ABOUT THINGS
3-9
ON THE CONTRARY..
I FIND THAT, TO BE DONE PROPERLY, SUCKING YOUR THUMB AND HOLDING YOUR BLANKET REQUIRES COMPLETE CONCENTRATION!
SCHULZ

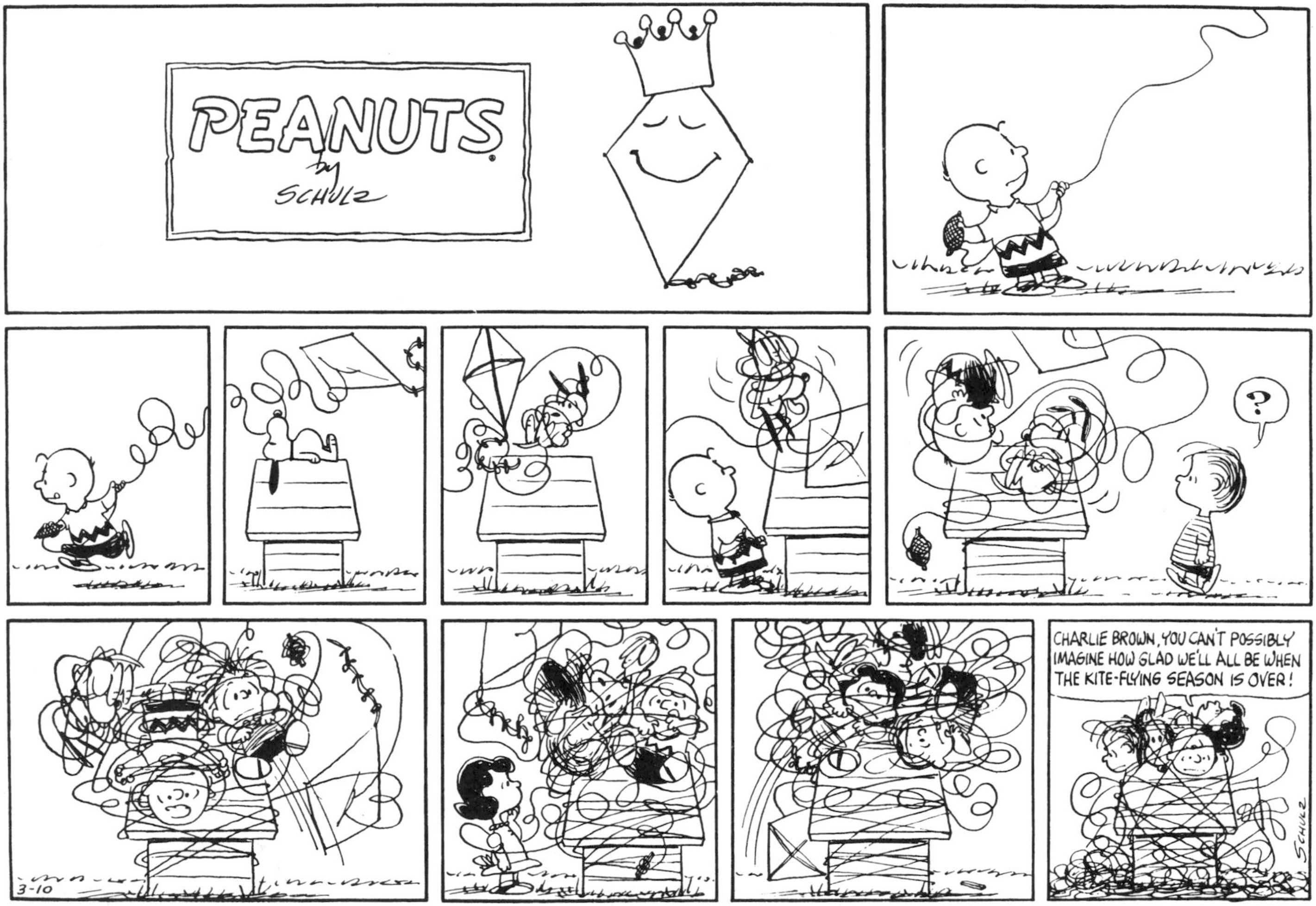
PEANUTS
by
SCHULZ
?
CHARLIE BROWN, YOU CAN'T POSSIBLY IMAGINE HOW GLAD WE'LL ALL BE WHEN THE KITE-FLYING SEASON IS OVER!
3-10
SCHULZ

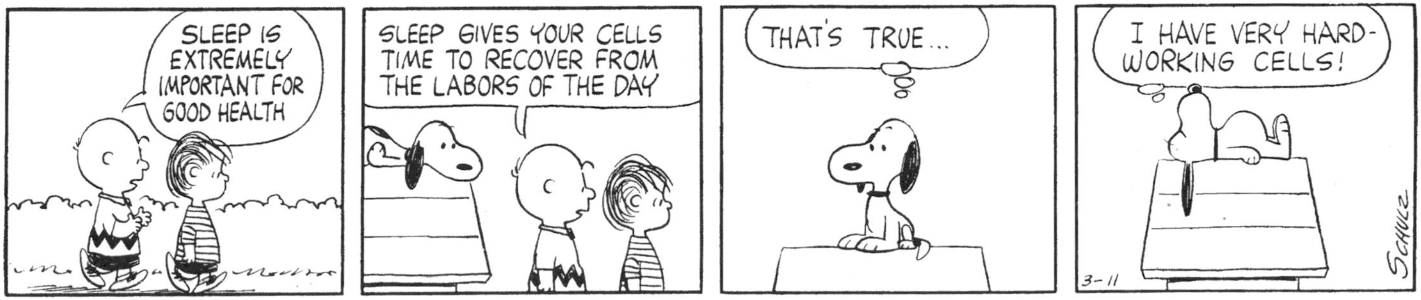
SLEEP IS EXTREMELY IMPORTANT FOR GOOD HEALTH
SLEEP GIVES YOUR CELLS TIME TO RECOVER FROM THE LABORS OF THE DAY
THAT'S TRUE...
I HAVE VERY HARD-WORKING CELLS!
3-11
SCHULZ

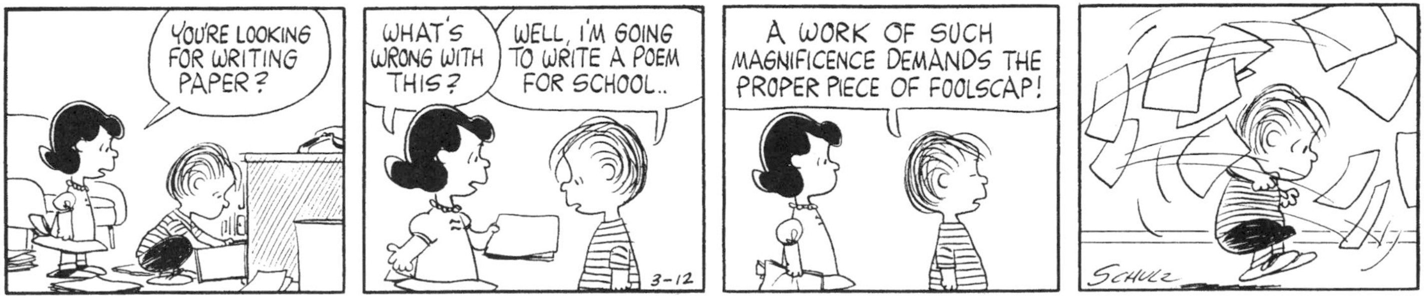
YOU'RE LOOKING FOR WRITING PAPER?
WHAT'S WRONG WITH THIS?
WELL, I'M GOING TO WRITE A POEM FOR SCHOOL..
3-12
A WORK OF SUCH MAGNIFICENCE DEMANDS THE PROPER PIECE OF FOOLSCAP!
SCHULZ

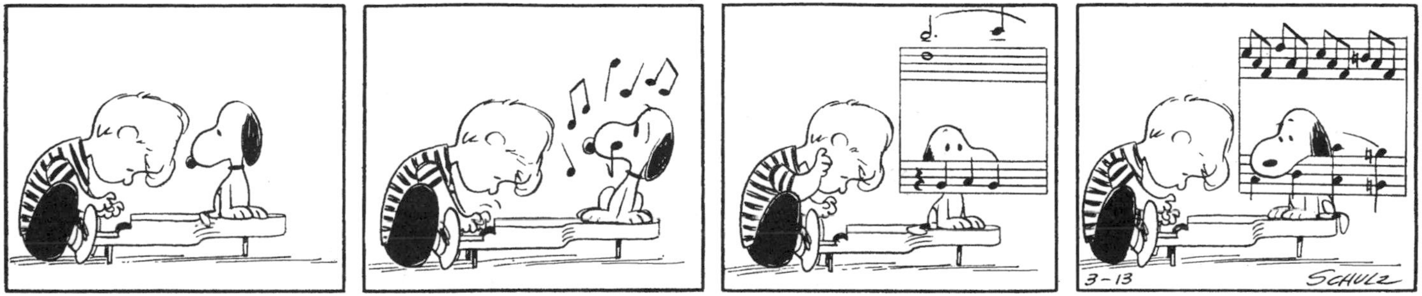
3-13
SCHULZ

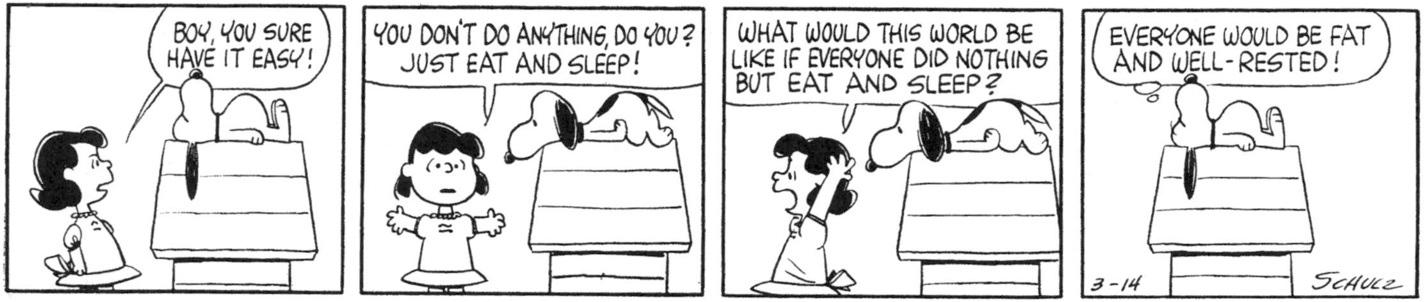
BOY, YOU SURE HAVE IT EASY!
YOU DON'T DO ANYTHING, DO YOU? JUST EAT AND SLEEP!
WHAT WOULD THIS WORLD BE LIKE IF EVERYONE DID NOTHING BUT EAT AND SLEEP?
EVERYONE WOULD BE FAT AND WELL-RESTED!
3-14
SCHULZ

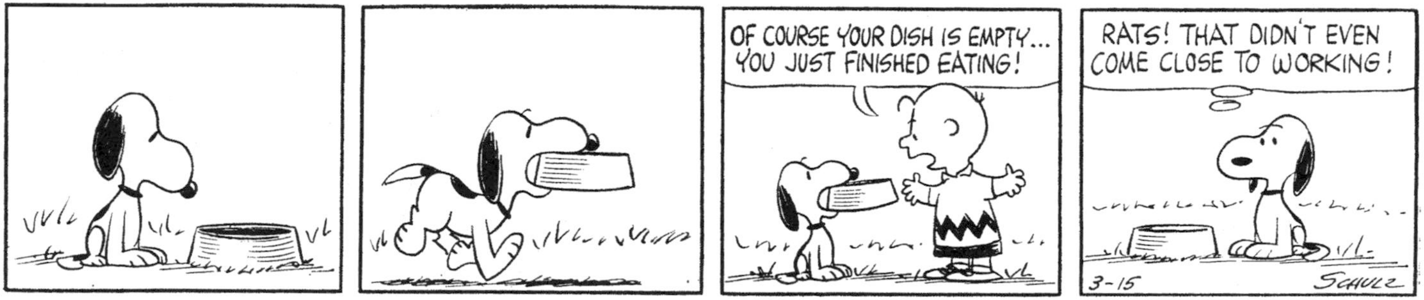
OF COURSE YOUR DISH IS EMPTY... YOU JUST FINISHED EATING!
RATS! THAT DIDN'T EVEN COME CLOSE TO WORKING!
3-15
SCHULZ

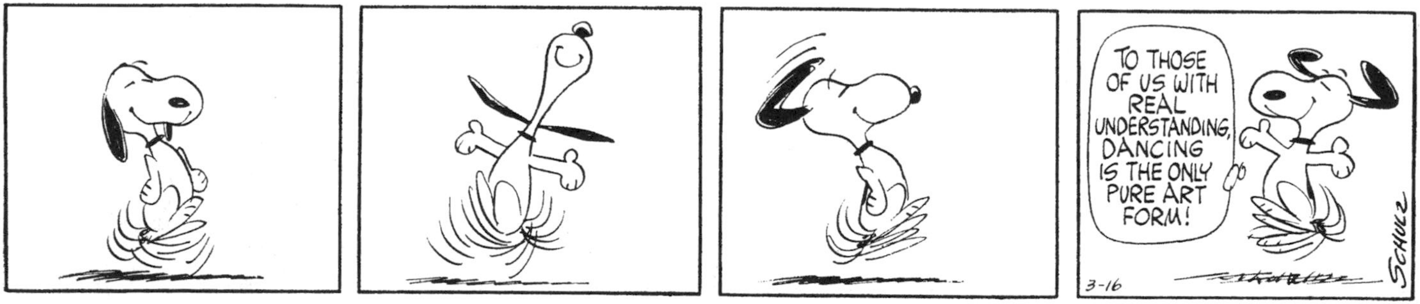
TO THOSE OF US WITH REAL UNDERSTANDING, DANCING IS THE ONLY PURE ART FORM!
3-16
SCHULZ

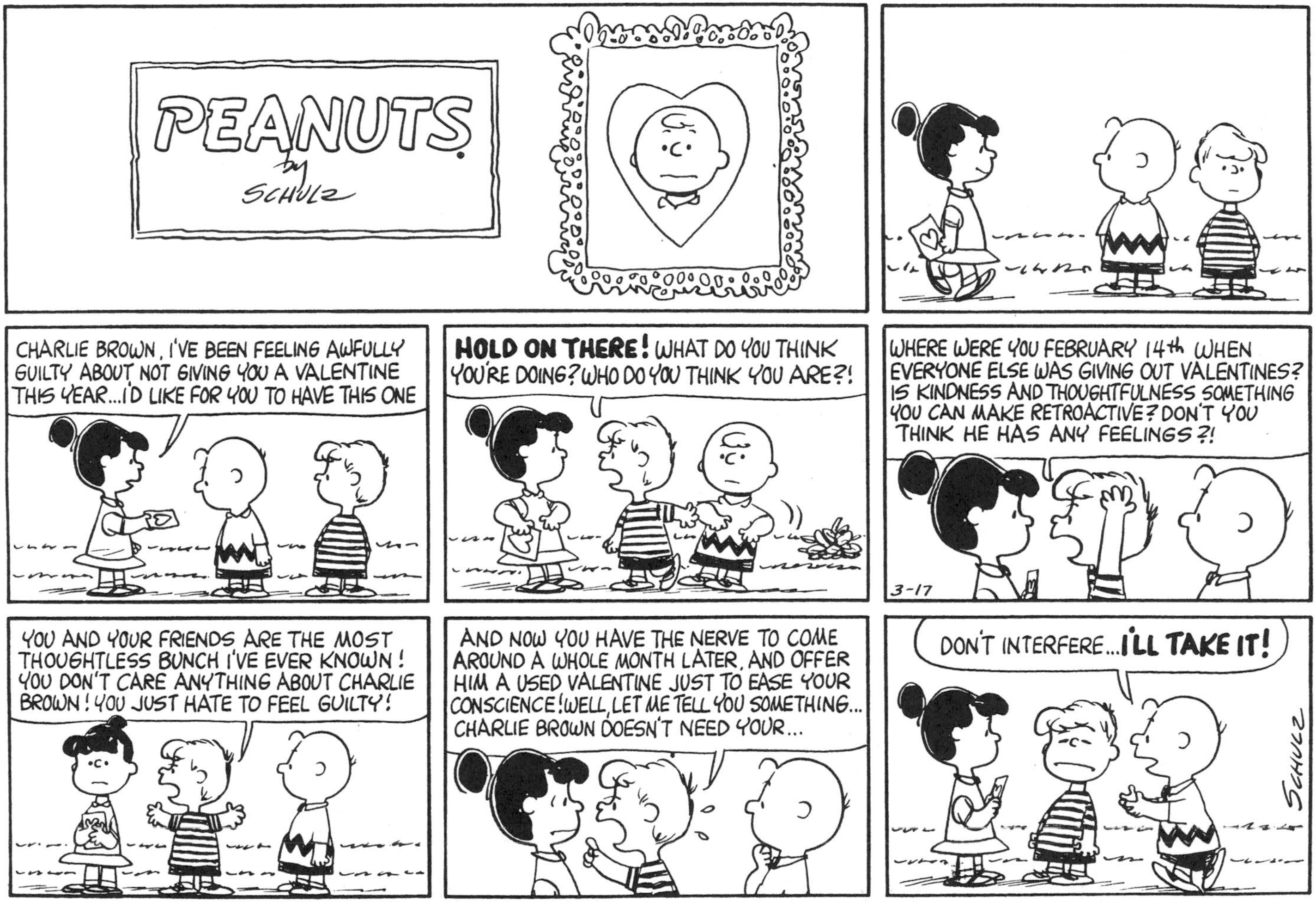
PEANUTS
by SCHULZ
CHARLIE BROWN, I'VE BEEN FEELING AWFULLY GUILTY ABOUT NOT GIVING YOU A VALENTINE THIS YEAR...I'D LIKE FOR YOU TO HAVE THIS ONE
HOLD ON THERE! WHAT DO YOU THINK YOU'RE DOING? WHO DO YOU THINK YOU ARE?!
WHERE WERE YOU FEBRUARY 14th WHEN EVERYONE ELSE WAS GIVING OUT VALENTINES? IS KINDNESS AND THOUGHTFULNESS SOMETHING YOU CAN MAKE RETROACTIVE? DON'T YOU THINK HE HAS ANY FEELINGS?!
3-17
YOU AND YOUR FRIENDS ARE THE MOST THOUGHTLESS BUNCH I'VE EVER KNOWN! YOU DON'T CARE ANYTHING ABOUT CHARLIE BROWN! YOU JUST HATE TO FEEL GUILTY!
AND NOW YOU HAVE THE NERVE TO COME AROUND A WHOLE MONTH LATER, AND OFFER HIM A USED VALENTINE JUST TO EASE YOUR CONSCIENCE! WELL, LET ME TELL YOU SOMETHING... CHARLIE BROWN DOESN'T NEED YOUR...
DON'T INTERFERE...I'LL TAKE IT!
SCHULZ

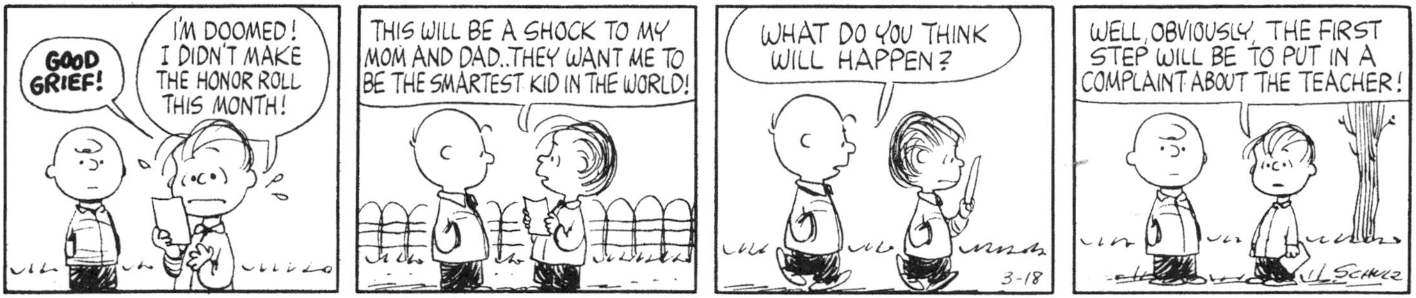
GOOD GRIEF!
I'M DOOMED! I DIDN'T MAKE THE HONOR ROLL THIS MONTH!
THIS WILL BE A SHOCK TO MY MOM AND DAD..THEY WANT ME TO BE THE SMARTEST KID IN THE WORLD!
WHAT DO YOU THINK WILL HAPPEN?
3-18
WELL, OBVIOUSLY, THE FIRST STEP WILL BE TO PUT IN A COMPLAINT ABOUT THE TEACHER!
SCHULZ

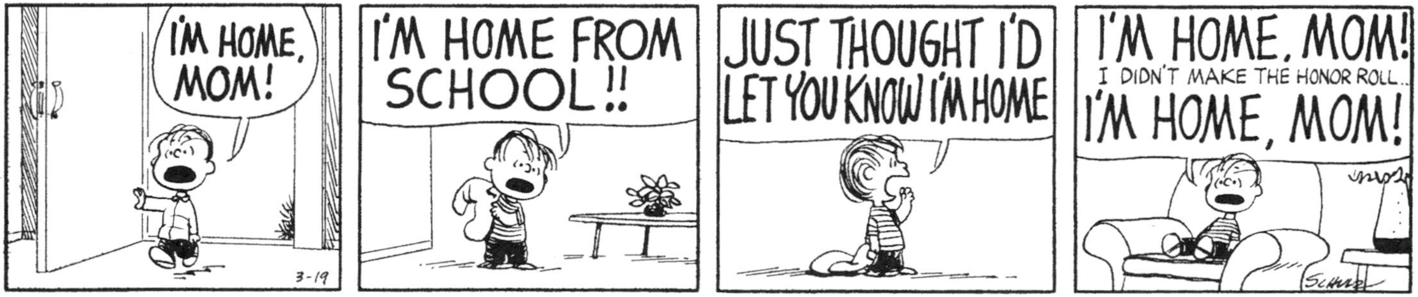
I'M HOME, MOM!
3-19
I'M HOME FROM SCHOOL!!
JUST THOUGHT I'D LET YOU KNOW I'M HOME
I'M HOME, MOM!
I DIDN'T MAKE THE HONOR ROLL..
I'M HOME, MOM!
SCHULZ

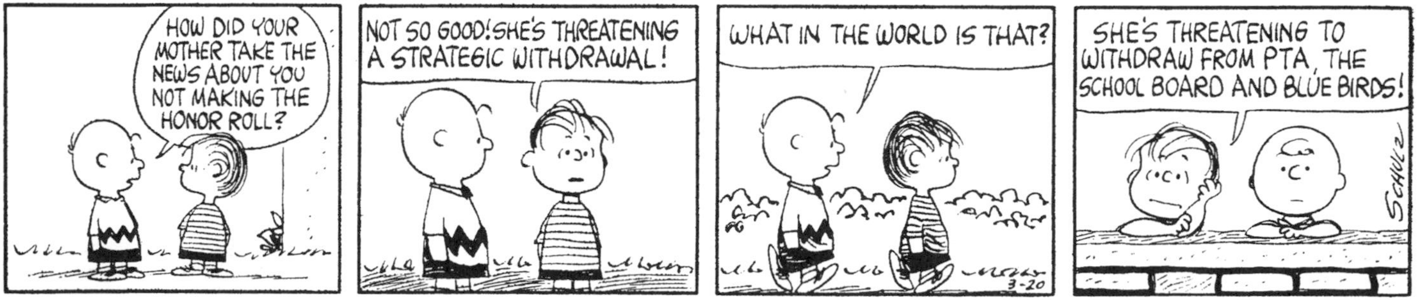
HOW DID YOUR MOTHER TAKE THE NEWS ABOUT YOU NOT MAKING THE HONOR ROLL?
NOT SO GOOD! SHE'S THREATENING A STRATEGIC WITHDRAWAL!
WHAT IN THE WORLD IS THAT?
3-20
SHE'S THREATENING TO WITHDRAW FROM PTA, THE SCHOOL BOARD AND BLUE BIRDS!
SCHULZ

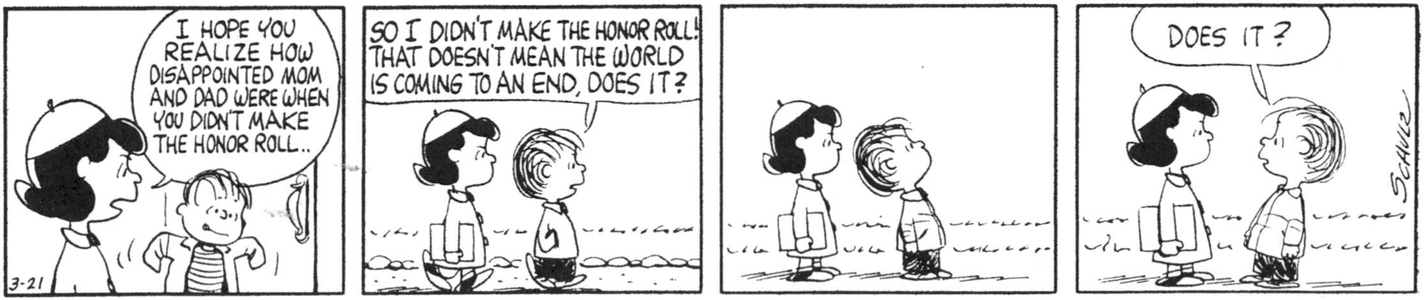
I HOPE YOU REALIZE HOW DISAPPOINTED MOM AND DAD WERE WHEN YOU DIDN'T MAKE THE HONOR ROLL..
3-21
SO I DIDN'T MAKE THE HONOR ROLL! THAT DOESN'T MEAN THE WORLD IS COMING TO AN END, DOES IT?
DOES IT?
SCHULZ

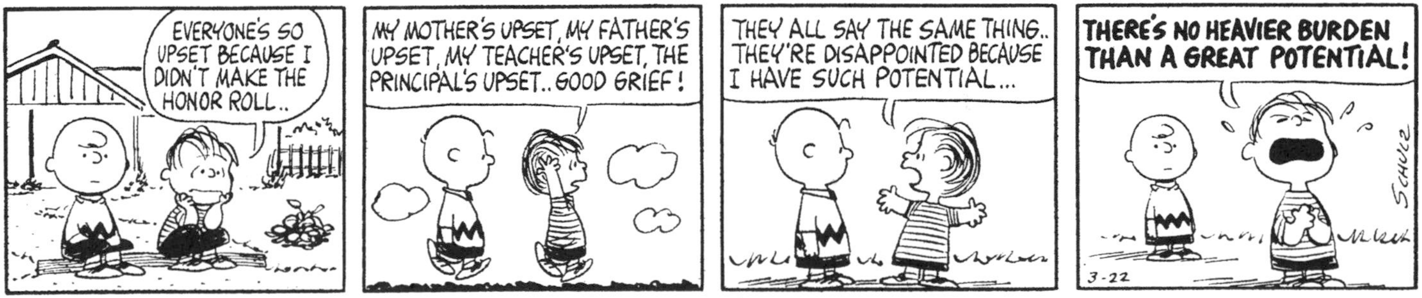
EVERYONE'S SO UPSET BECAUSE I DIDN'T MAKE THE HONOR ROLL..
MY MOTHER'S UPSET, MY FATHER'S UPSET, MY TEACHER'S UPSET, THE PRINCIPAL'S UPSET.. GOOD GRIEF!
THEY ALL SAY THE SAME THING.. THEY'RE DISAPPOINTED BECAUSE I HAVE SUCH POTENTIAL...
THERE'S NO HEAVIER BURDEN THAN A GREAT POTENTIAL!
SCHULZ
3-22

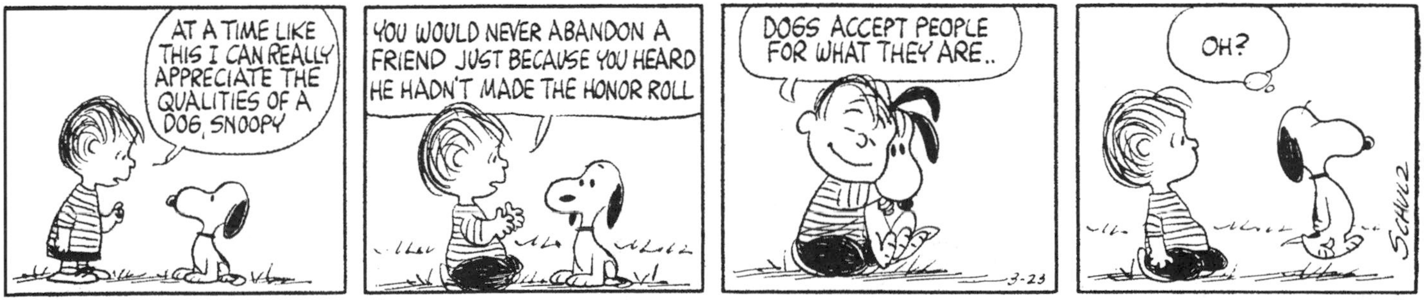
AT A TIME LIKE THIS I CAN REALLY APPRECIATE THE QUALITIES OF A DOG, SNOOPY
YOU WOULD NEVER ABANDON A FRIEND JUST BECAUSE YOU HEARD HE HADN'T MADE THE HONOR ROLL
DOGS ACCEPT PEOPLE FOR WHAT THEY ARE..
3-23
OH?
SCHULZ

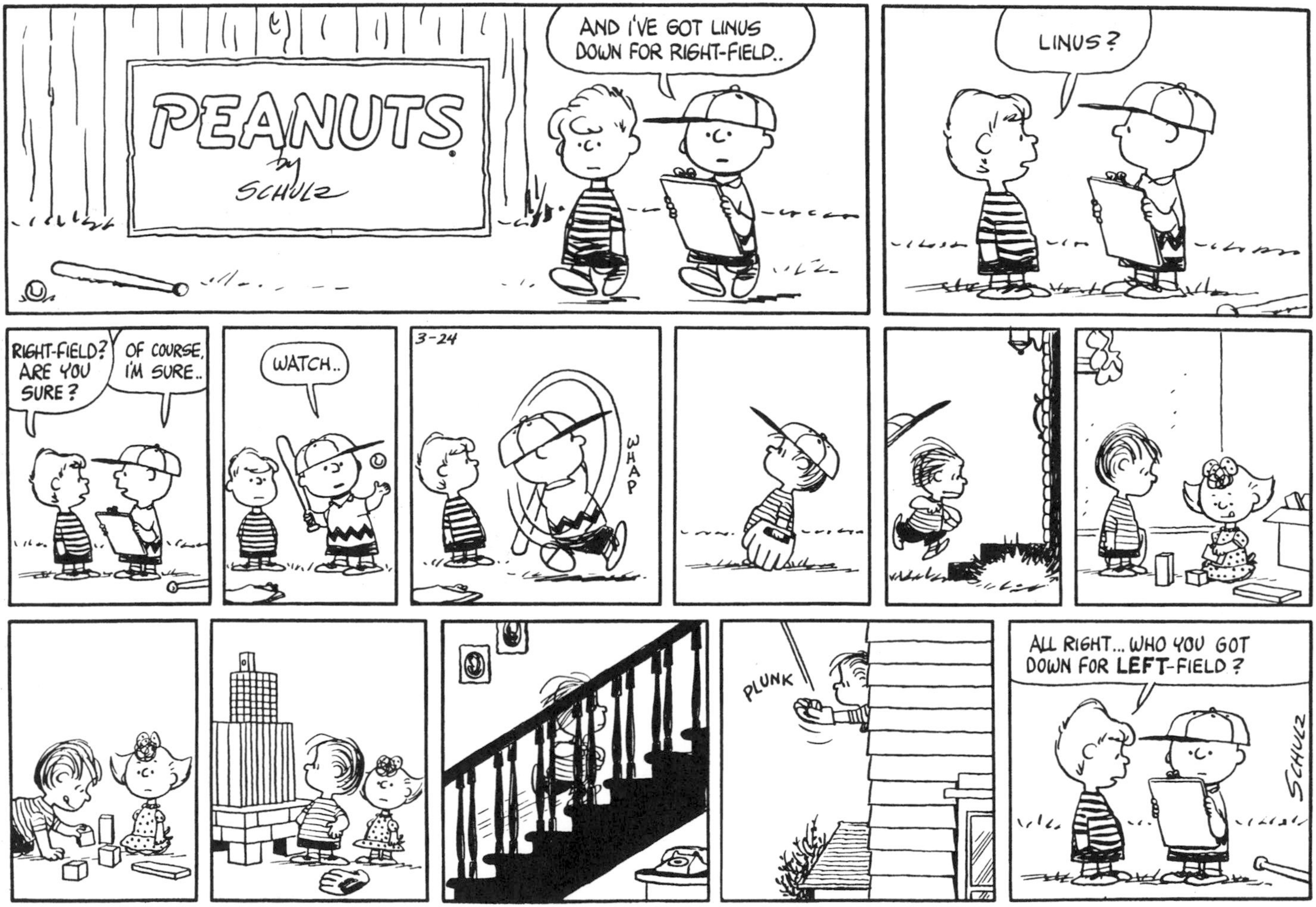
PEANUTS
by SCHULZ
AND I'VE GOT LINUS DOWN FOR RIGHT-FIELD..
LINUS?
RIGHT-FIELD? ARE YOU SURE?
OF COURSE, I'M SURE..
WATCH..
3-24
WHAP
PLUNK
ALL RIGHT... WHO YOU GOT DOWN FOR LEFT-FIELD?
SCHULZ

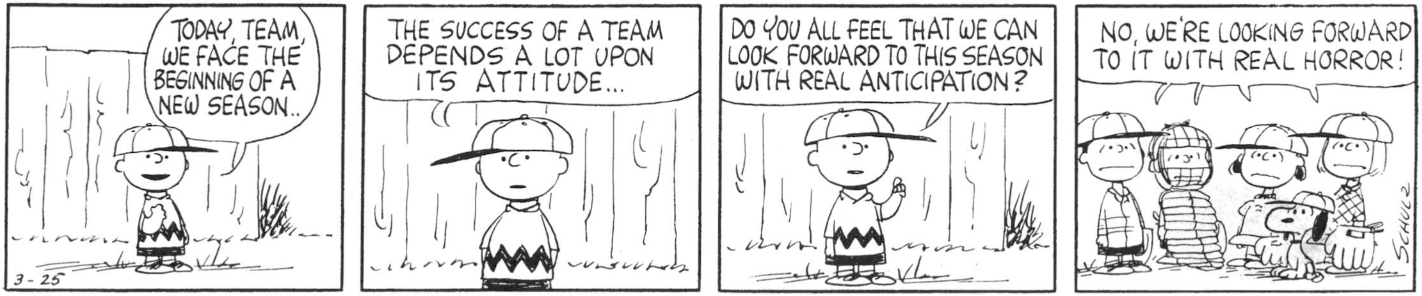
TODAY, TEAM, WE FACE THE BEGINNING OF A NEW SEASON..
THE SUCCESS OF A TEAM DEPENDS A LOT UPON ITS ATTITUDE...
DO YOU ALL FEEL THAT WE CAN LOOK FORWARD TO THIS SEASON WITH REAL ANTICIPATION?
NO, WE'RE LOOKING FORWARD TO IT WITH REAL HORROR!
3-25
SCHULZ

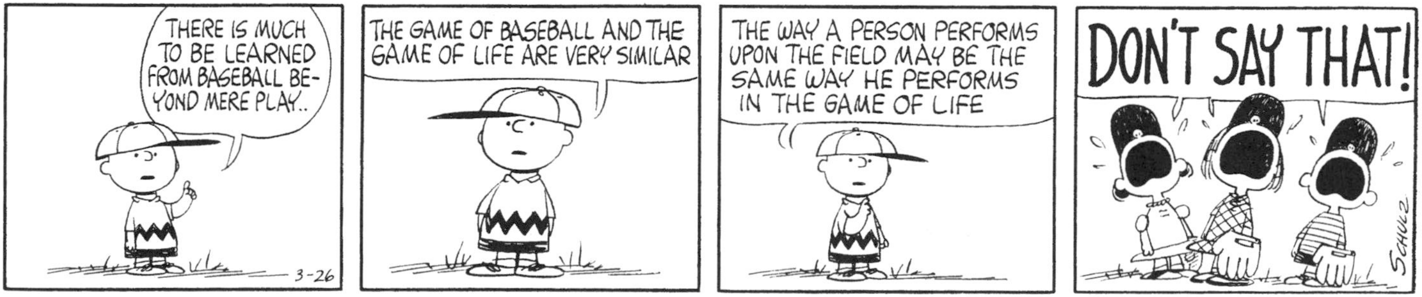
THERE IS MUCH TO BE LEARNED FROM BASEBALL BEYOND MERE PLAY..
3-26
THE GAME OF BASEBALL AND THE GAME OF LIFE ARE VERY SIMILAR
THE WAY A PERSON PERFORMS UPON THE FIELD MAY BE THE SAME WAY HE PERFORMS IN THE GAME OF LIFE
DON'T SAY THAT!
SCHULZ

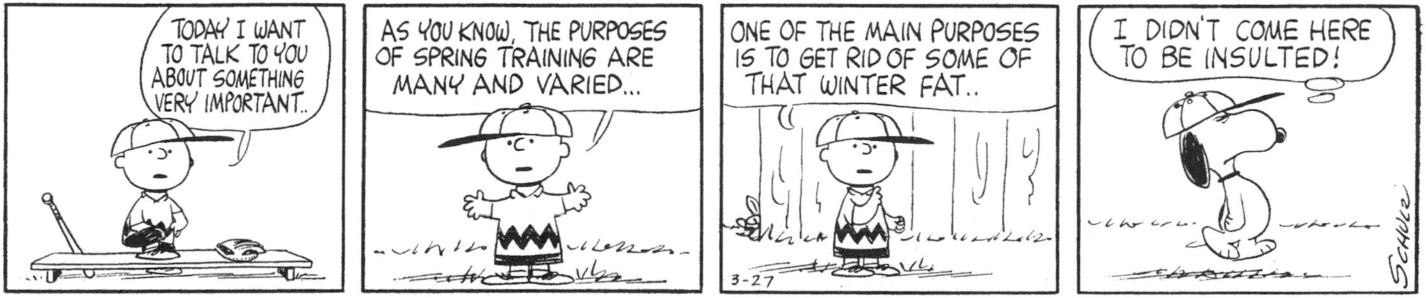
TODAY I WANT TO TALK TO YOU ABOUT SOMETHING VERY IMPORTANT..
AS YOU KNOW, THE PURPOSES OF SPRING TRAINING ARE MANY AND VARIED...
ONE OF THE MAIN PURPOSES IS TO GET RID OF SOME OF THAT WINTER FAT..
3-27
I DIDN'T COME HERE TO BE INSULTED!
SCHULZ

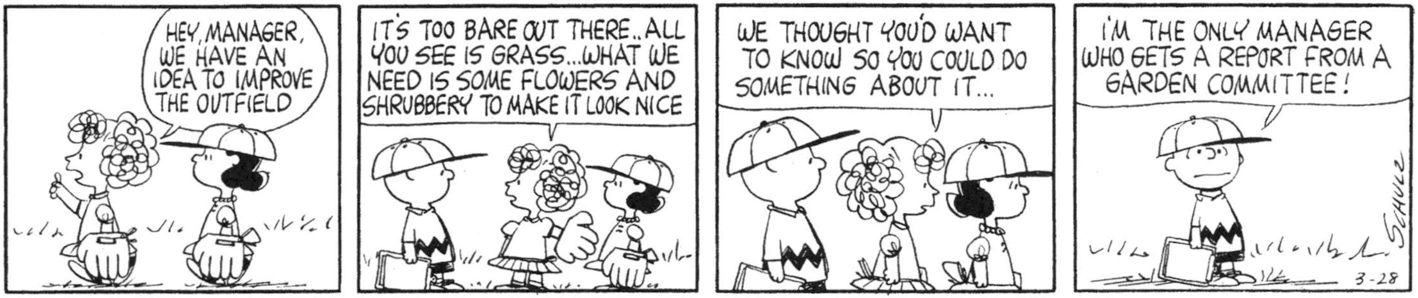
HEY, MANAGER, WE HAVE AN IDEA TO IMPROVE THE OUTFIELD
IT'S TOO BARE OUT THERE.. ALL YOU SEE IS GRASS... WHAT WE NEED IS SOME FLOWERS AND SHRUBBERY TO MAKE IT LOOK NICE
WE THOUGHT YOU'D WANT TO KNOW SO YOU COULD DO SOMETHING ABOUT IT...
I'M THE ONLY MANAGER WHO GETS A REPORT FROM A GARDEN COMMITTEE!
SCHULZ
3-28

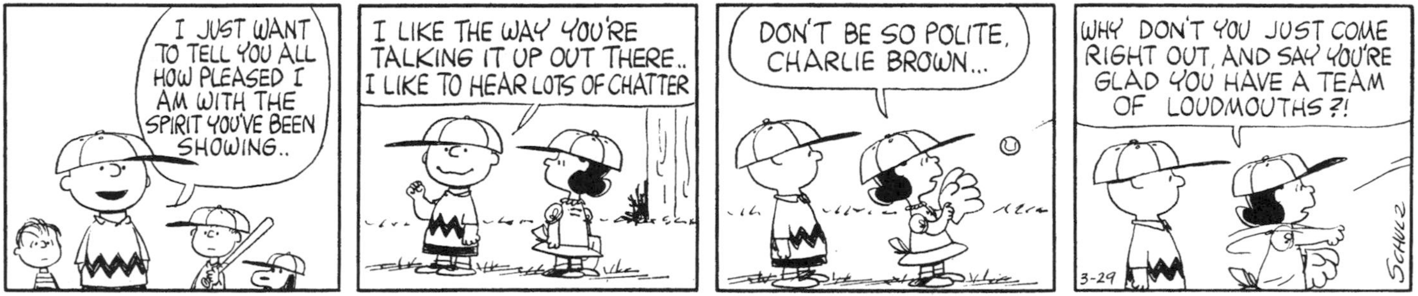
I JUST WANT TO TELL YOU ALL HOW PLEASED I AM WITH THE SPIRIT YOU'VE BEEN SHOWING..
I LIKE THE WAY YOU'RE TALKING IT UP OUT THERE.. I LIKE TO HEAR LOTS OF CHATTER
DON'T BE SO POLITE, CHARLIE BROWN...
WHY DON'T YOU JUST COME RIGHT OUT, AND SAY YOU'RE GLAD YOU HAVE A TEAM OF LOUDMOUTHS?!
3-29
SCHULZ

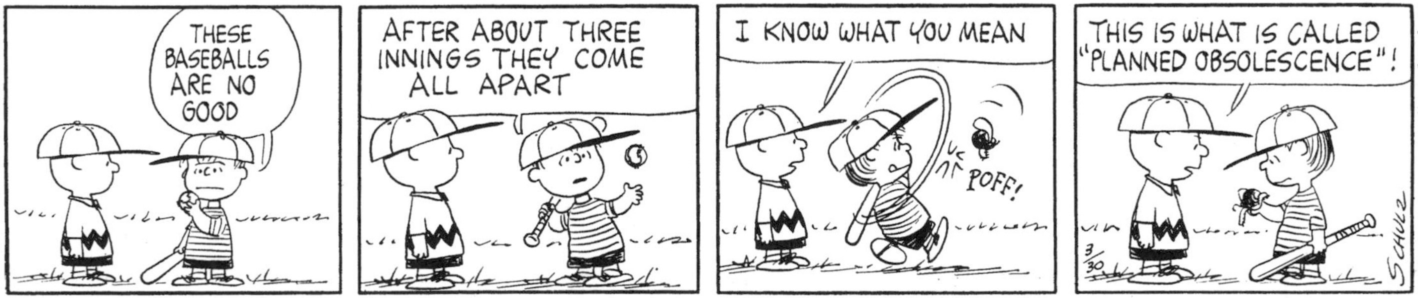
THESE BASEBALLS ARE NO GOOD
AFTER ABOUT THREE INNINGS THEY COME ALL APART
I KNOW WHAT YOU MEAN
POFF!
THIS IS WHAT IS CALLED "PLANNED OBSOLESCENCE"!
3/30
SCHULZ

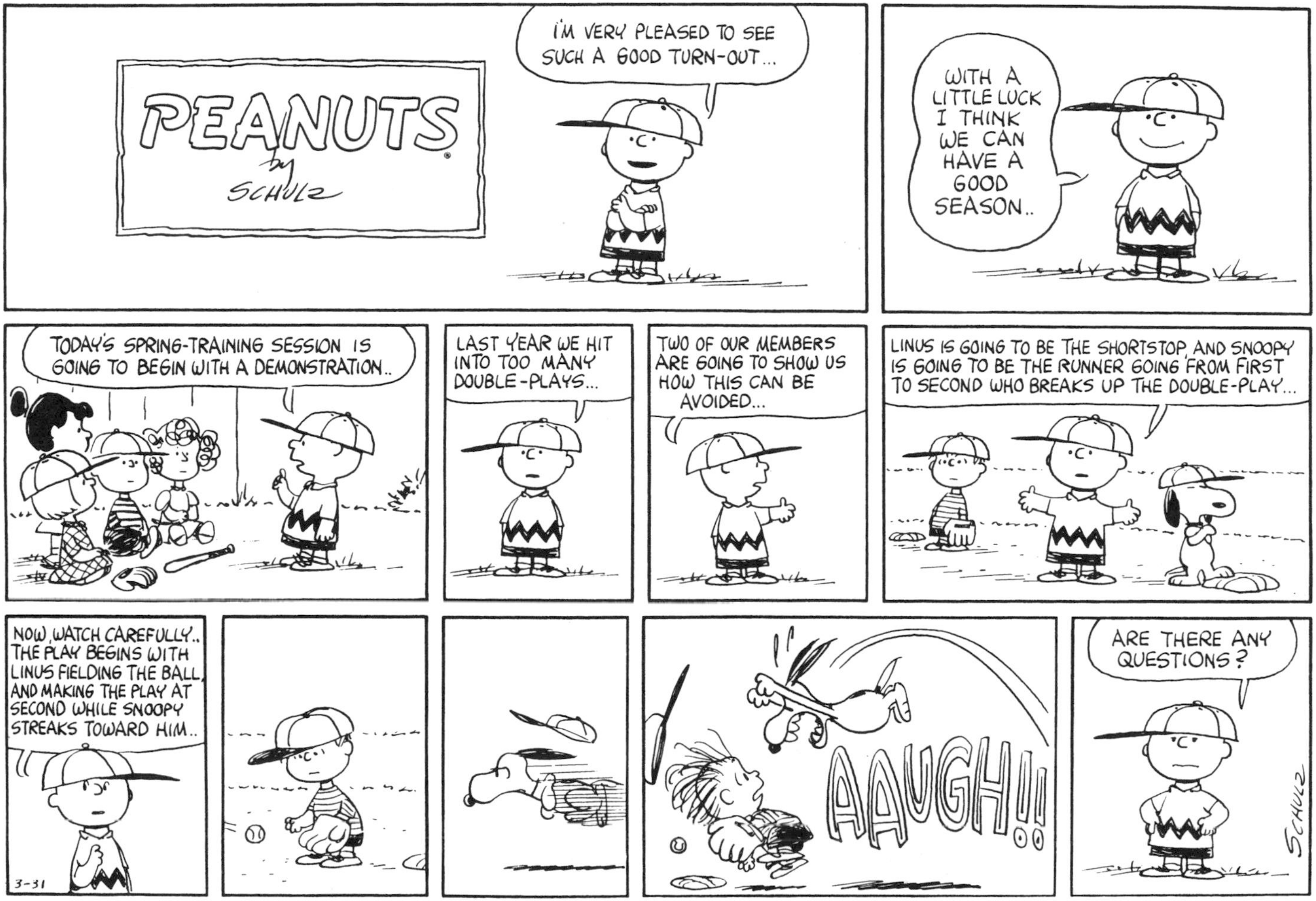
PEANUTS
by SCHULZ
I'M VERY PLEASED TO SEE SUCH A GOOD TURN-OUT...
WITH A LITTLE LUCK I THINK WE CAN HAVE A GOOD SEASON..
TODAY'S SPRING-TRAINING SESSION IS GOING TO BEGIN WITH A DEMONSTRATION..
LAST YEAR WE HIT INTO TOO MANY DOUBLE-PLAYS...
TWO OF OUR MEMBERS ARE GOING TO SHOW US HOW THIS CAN BE AVOIDED...
LINUS IS GOING TO BE THE SHORTSTOP, AND SNOOPY IS GOING TO BE THE RUNNER GOING FROM FIRST TO SECOND WHO BREAKS UP THE DOUBLE-PLAY...
NOW, WATCH CAREFULLY.. THE PLAY BEGINS WITH LINUS FIELDING THE BALL, AND MAKING THE PLAY AT SECOND WHILE SNOOPY STREAKS TOWARD HIM..
3-31
AAUGH!!
ARE THERE ANY QUESTIONS?
SCHULZ

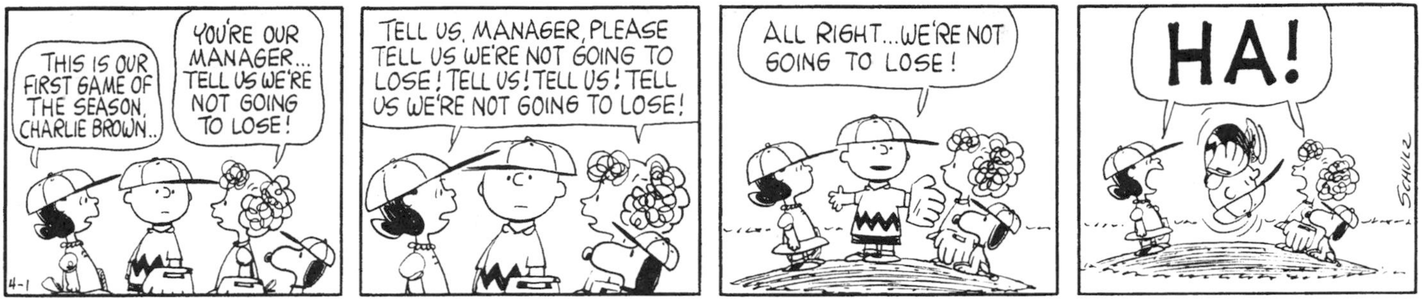
4-1
THIS IS OUR FIRST GAME OF THE SEASON, CHARLIE BROWN..
YOU'RE OUR MANAGER... TELL US WE'RE NOT GOING TO LOSE!
TELL US, MANAGER, PLEASE TELL US WE'RE NOT GOING TO LOSE! TELL US! TELL US! TELL US WE'RE NOT GOING TO LOSE!
ALL RIGHT...WE'RE NOT GOING TO LOSE!
HA!

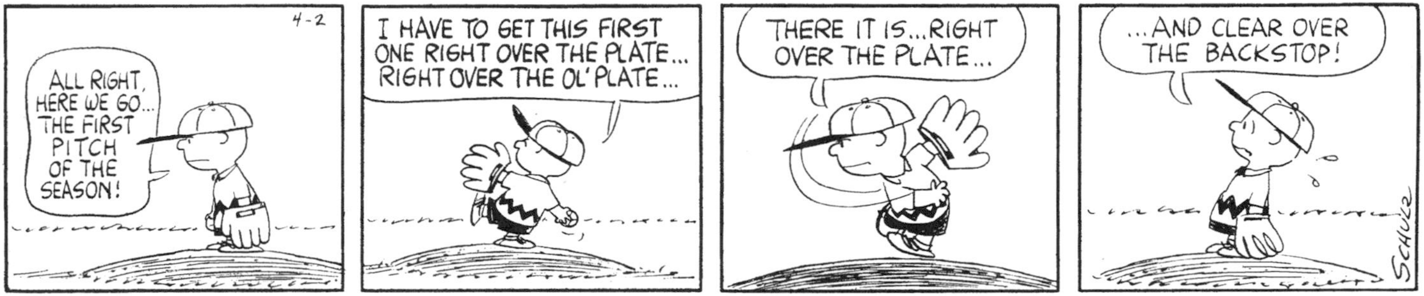
4-2
ALL RIGHT, HERE WE GO... THE FIRST PITCH OF THE SEASON!
I HAVE TO GET THIS FIRST ONE RIGHT OVER THE PLATE... RIGHT OVER THE OL' PLATE...
THERE IT IS...RIGHT OVER THE PLATE...
...AND CLEAR OVER THE BACKSTOP!

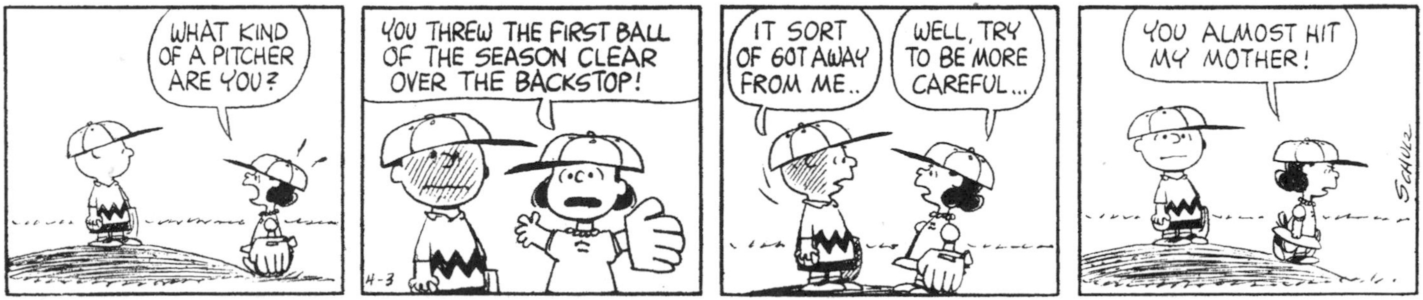
WHAT KIND OF A PITCHER ARE YOU?
YOU THREW THE FIRST BALL OF THE SEASON CLEAR OVER THE BACKSTOP!
4-3
IT SORT OF GOT AWAY FROM ME..
WELL, TRY TO BE MORE CAREFUL...
YOU ALMOST HIT MY MOTHER!

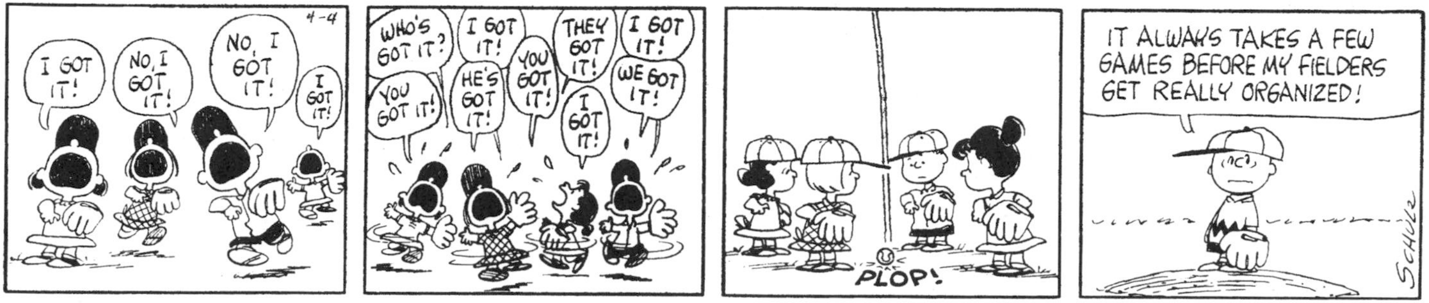
4-4
I GOT IT!
NO, I GOT IT!
NO, I GOT IT!
I GOT IT!
WHO'S GOT IT?
YOU GOT IT!
I GOT IT!
HE'S GOT IT!
YOU GOT IT!
THEY GOT IT!
I GOT IT!
I GOT IT!
WE GOT IT!
PLOP!
IT ALWAYS TAKES A FEW GAMES BEFORE MY FIELDERS GET REALLY ORGANIZED!
SCHULZ

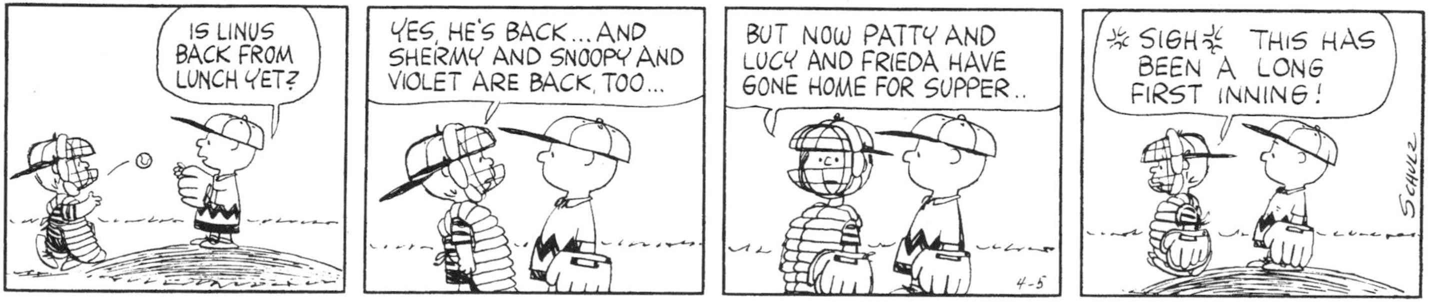
IS LINUS BACK FROM LUNCH YET?
YES, HE'S BACK... AND SHERMY AND SNOOPY AND VIOLET ARE BACK, TOO...
BUT NOW PATTY AND LUCY AND FRIEDA HAVE GONE HOME FOR SUPPER..
4-5
SIGH THIS HAS BEEN A LONG FIRST INNING!
SCHULZ

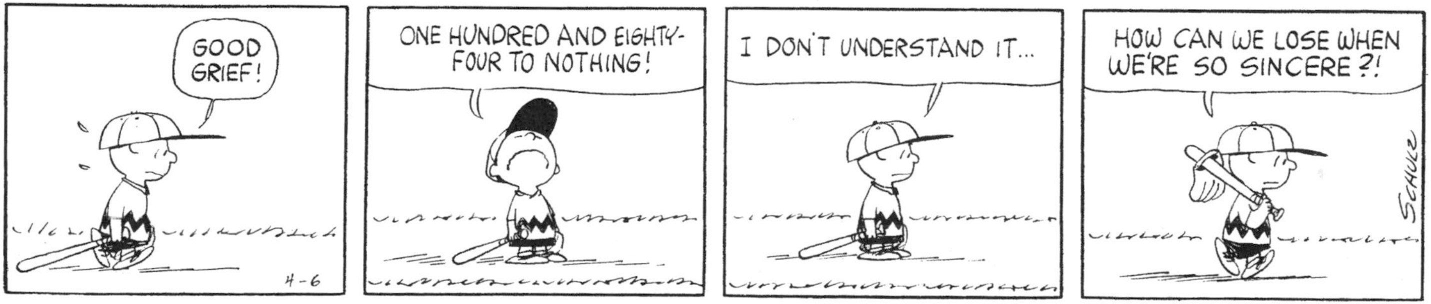
GOOD GRIEF!
4-6
ONE HUNDRED AND EIGHTY-FOUR TO NOTHING!
I DON'T UNDERSTAND IT...
HOW CAN WE LOSE WHEN WE'RE SO SINCERE?!
SCHULZ

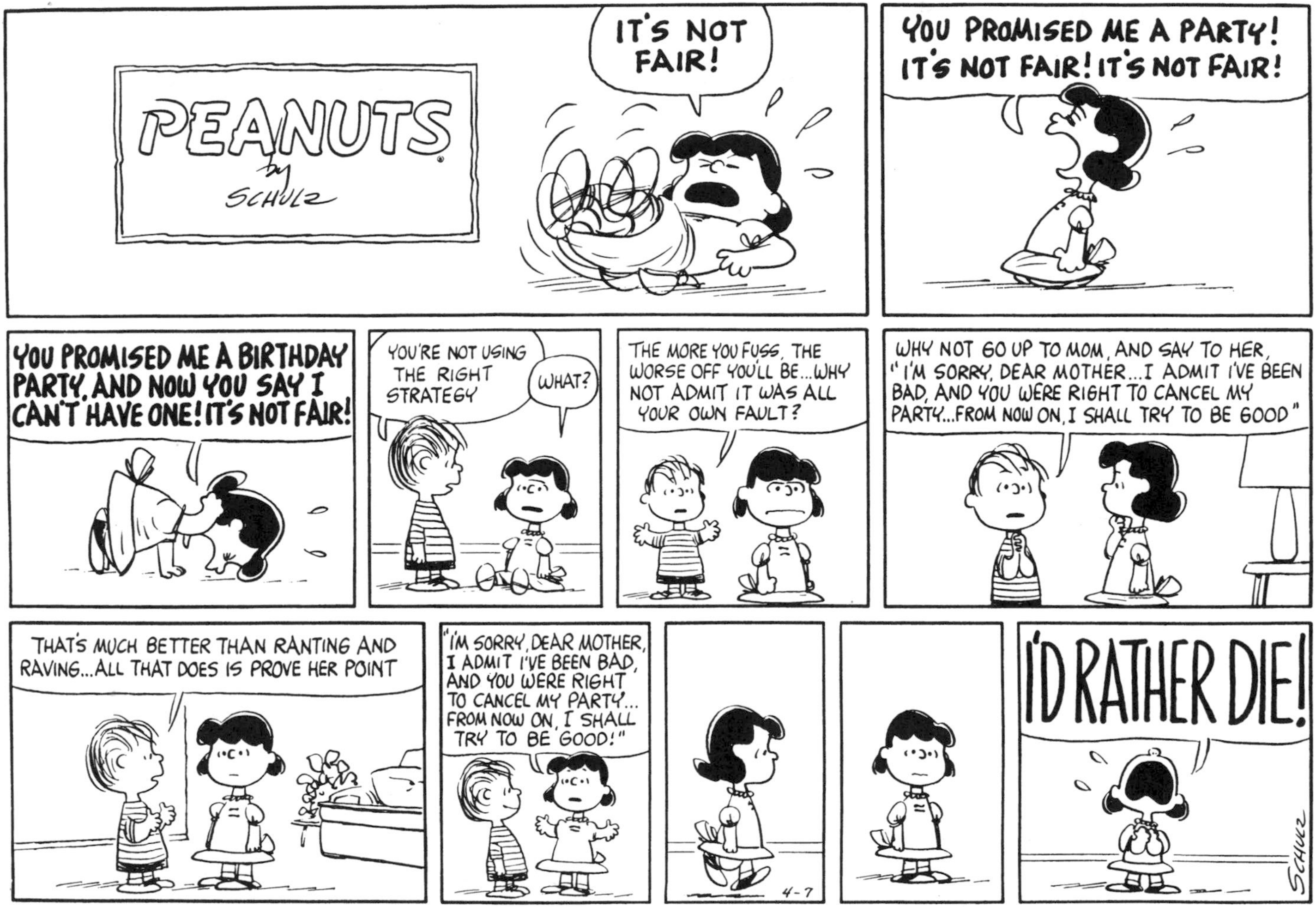
PEANUTS
by SCHULZ
IT'S NOT FAIR!
YOU PROMISED ME A PARTY! IT'S NOT FAIR! IT'S NOT FAIR!
YOU PROMISED ME A BIRTHDAY PARTY, AND NOW YOU SAY I CAN'T HAVE ONE! IT'S NOT FAIR!
YOU'RE NOT USING THE RIGHT STRATEGY
WHAT?
THE MORE YOU FUSS, THE WORSE OFF YOU'LL BE...WHY NOT ADMIT IT WAS ALL YOUR OWN FAULT?
WHY NOT GO UP TO MOM, AND SAY TO HER, "I'M SORRY, DEAR MOTHER...I ADMIT I'VE BEEN BAD, AND YOU WERE RIGHT TO CANCEL MY PARTY...FROM NOW ON, I SHALL TRY TO BE GOOD"
THAT'S MUCH BETTER THAN RANTING AND RAVING...ALL THAT DOES IS PROVE HER POINT
"I'M SORRY, DEAR MOTHER, I ADMIT I'VE BEEN BAD, AND YOU WERE RIGHT TO CANCEL MY PARTY...FROM NOW ON, I SHALL TRY TO BE GOOD!"
4-7
I'D RATHER DIE!
SCHULZ

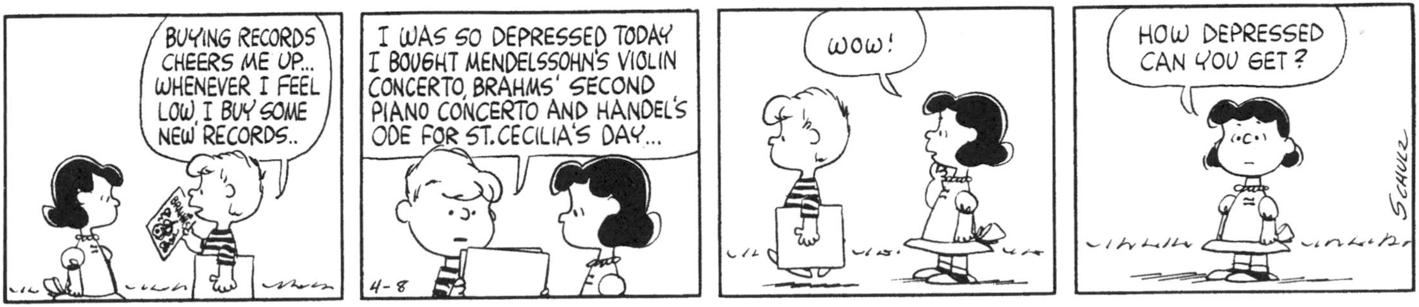
BUYING RECORDS CHEERS ME UP... WHENEVER I FEEL LOW I BUY SOME NEW RECORDS..
I WAS SO DEPRESSED TODAY I BOUGHT MENDELSSOHN'S VIOLIN CONCERTO, BRAHMS' SECOND PIANO CONCERTO AND HANDEL'S ODE FOR ST. CECILIA'S DAY...
WOW!
HOW DEPRESSED CAN YOU GET?

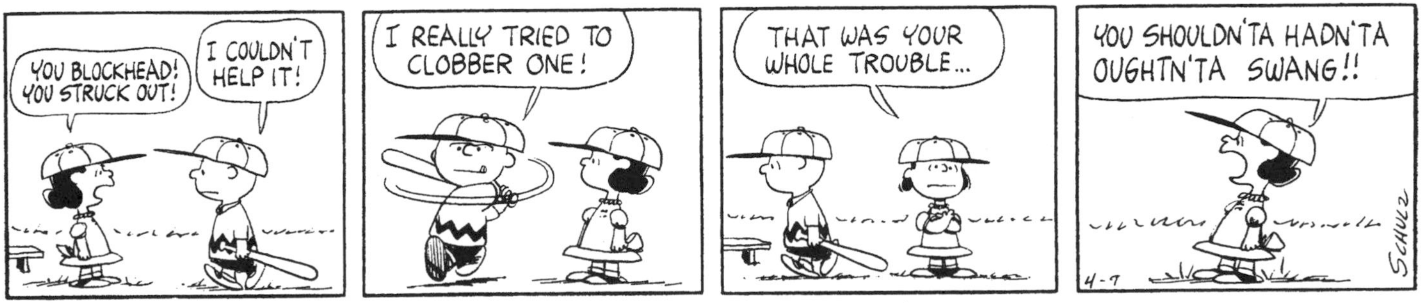
YOU BLOCKHEAD! YOU STRUCK OUT!
I COULDN'T HELP IT!
I REALLY TRIED TO CLOBBER ONE!
THAT WAS YOUR WHOLE TROUBLE...
YOU SHOULDN'TA HADN'TA OUGHTN'TA SWANG!!

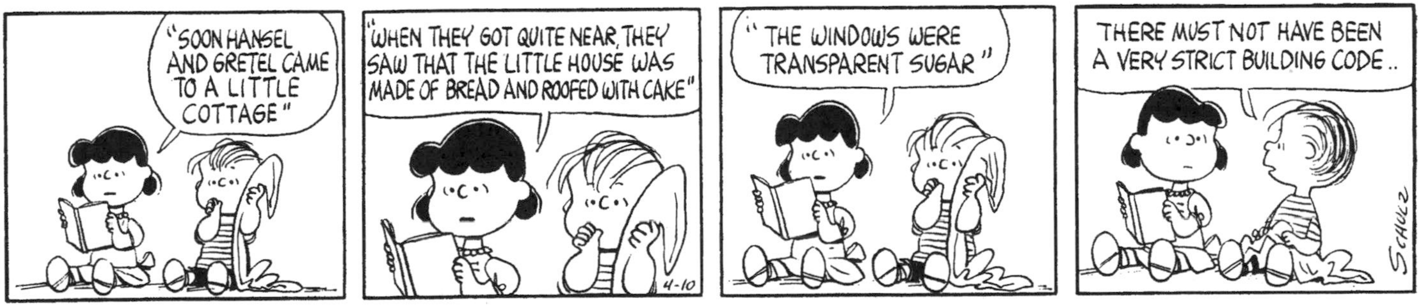
"SOON HANSEL AND GRETEL CAME TO A LITTLE COTTAGE"
"WHEN THEY GOT QUITE NEAR, THEY SAW THAT THE LITTLE HOUSE WAS MADE OF BREAD AND ROOFED WITH CAKE"
"THE WINDOWS WERE TRANSPARENT SUGAR"
THERE MUST NOT HAVE BEEN A VERY STRICT BUILDING CODE..

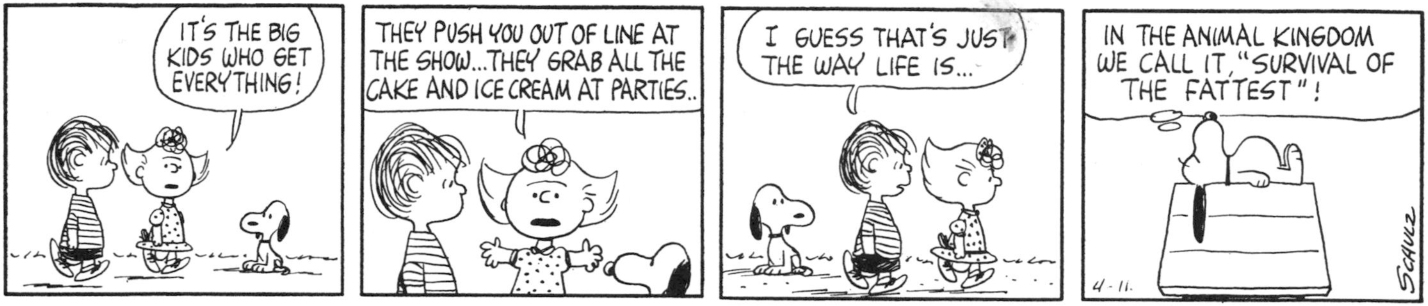
IT'S THE BIG KIDS WHO GET EVERYTHING!
THEY PUSH YOU OUT OF LINE AT THE SHOW...THEY GRAB ALL THE CAKE AND ICE CREAM AT PARTIES..
I GUESS THAT'S JUST THE WAY LIFE IS...
IN THE ANIMAL KINGDOM WE CALL IT, "SURVIVAL OF THE FATTEST"!
4-11.
SCHULZ

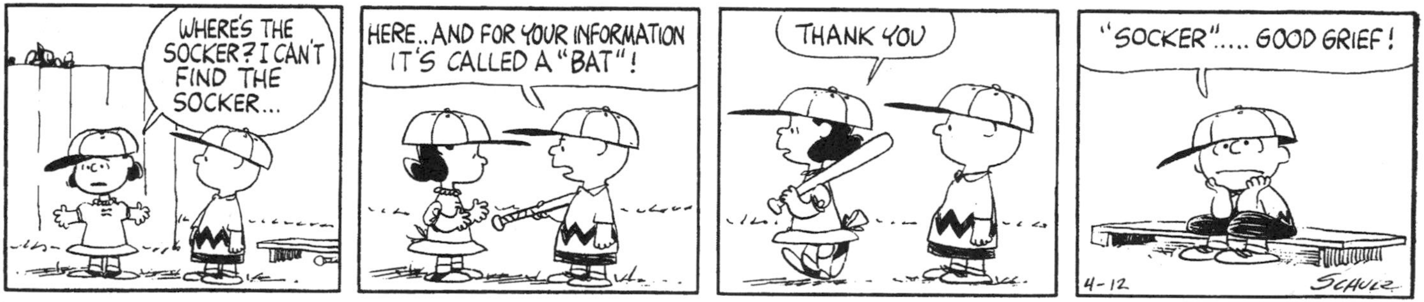
WHERE'S THE SOCKER? I CAN'T FIND THE SOCKER...
HERE..AND FOR YOUR INFORMATION IT'S CALLED A "BAT"!
THANK YOU
"SOCKER"..... GOOD GRIEF!
4-12
SCHULZ

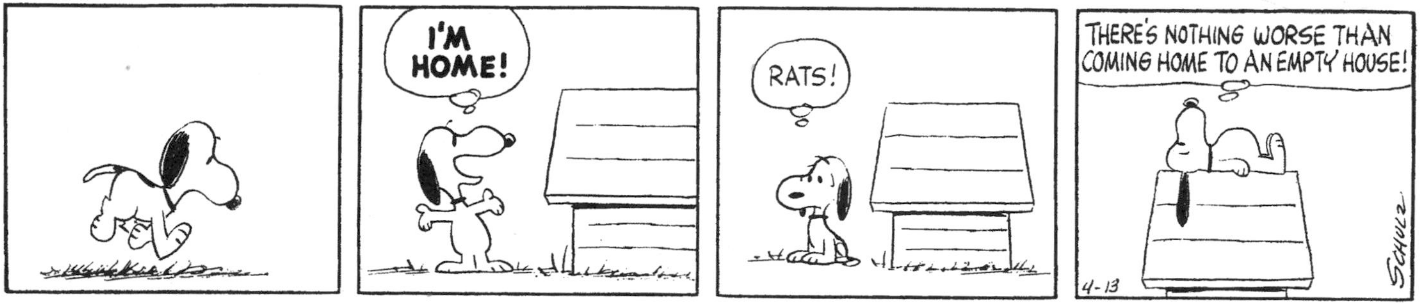
I'M HOME!
RATS!
THERE'S NOTHING WORSE THAN COMING HOME TO AN EMPTY HOUSE!
4-13
SCHULZ

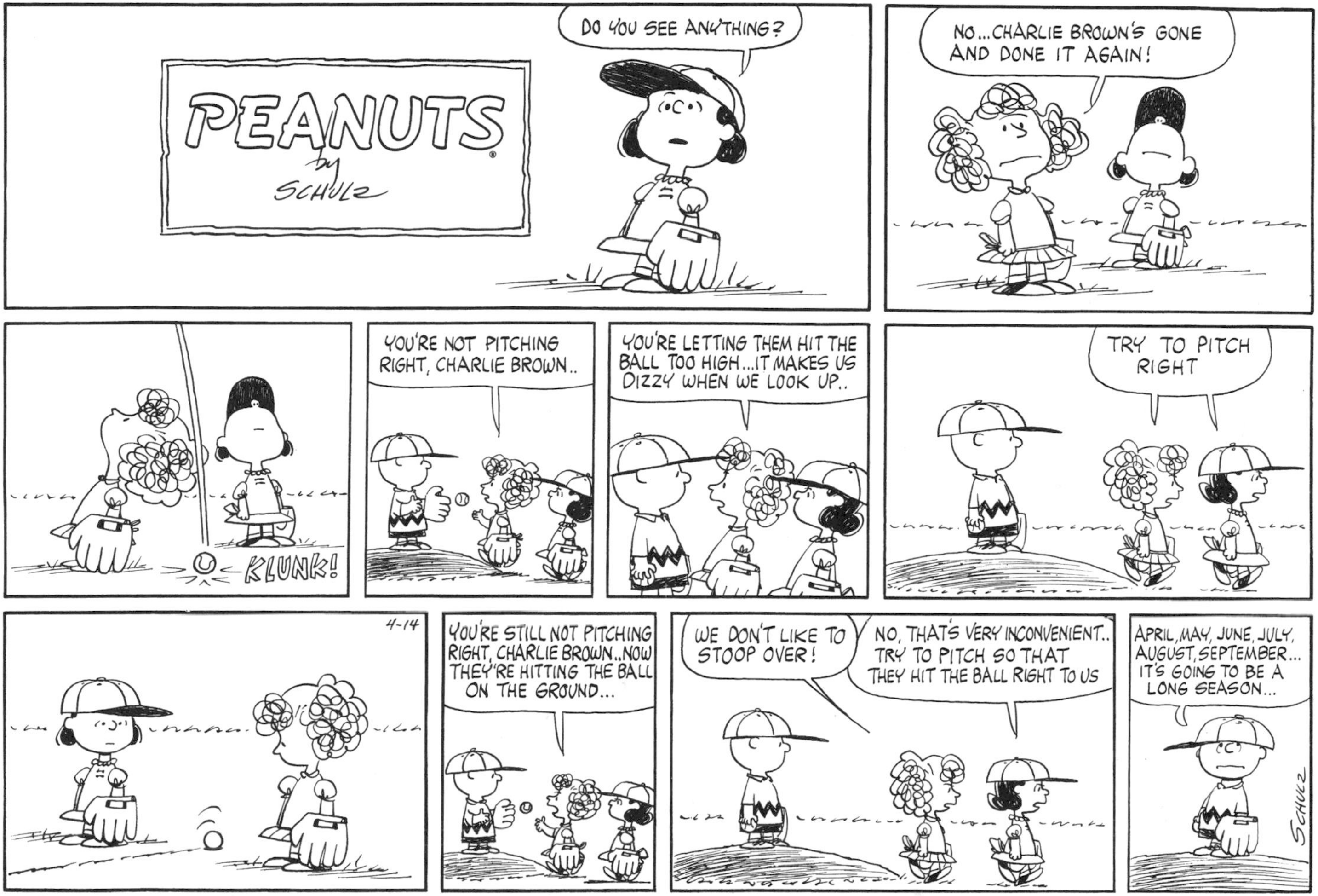
PEANUTS
by SCHULZ
DO YOU SEE ANYTHING?
NO...CHARLIE BROWN'S GONE AND DONE IT AGAIN!
KLUNK!
YOU'RE NOT PITCHING RIGHT, CHARLIE BROWN..
YOU'RE LETTING THEM HIT THE BALL TOO HIGH...IT MAKES US DIZZY WHEN WE LOOK UP..
TRY TO PITCH RIGHT
4-14
YOU'RE STILL NOT PITCHING RIGHT, CHARLIE BROWN..NOW THEY'RE HITTING THE BALL ON THE GROUND...
WE DON'T LIKE TO STOOP OVER!
NO, THAT'S VERY INCONVENIENT.. TRY TO PITCH SO THAT THEY HIT THE BALL RIGHT TO US
APRIL, MAY, JUNE, JULY, AUGUST, SEPTEMBER... IT'S GOING TO BE A LONG SEASON...
SCHULZ

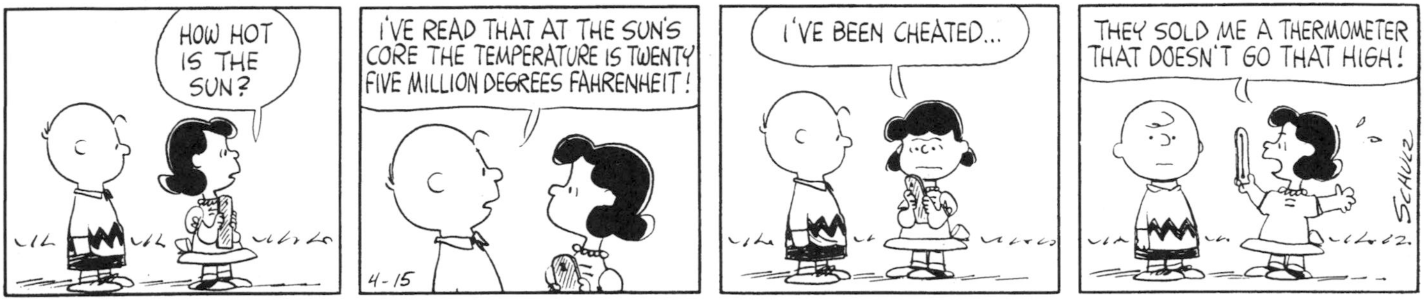
HOW HOT IS THE SUN?
I'VE READ THAT AT THE SUN'S CORE THE TEMPERATURE IS TWENTY FIVE MILLION DEGREES FAHRENHEIT!
4-15
I'VE BEEN CHEATED...
THEY SOLD ME A THERMOMETER THAT DOESN'T GO THAT HIGH!

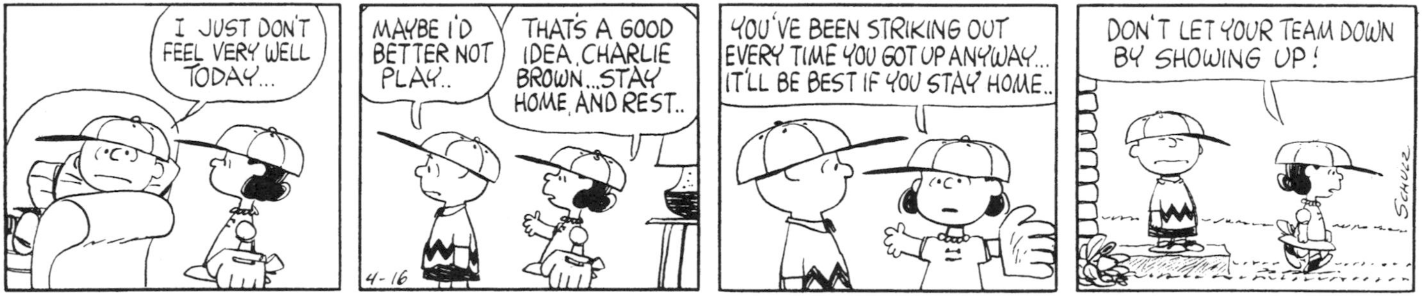
I JUST DON'T FEEL VERY WELL TODAY...
MAYBE I'D BETTER NOT PLAY..
THAT'S A GOOD IDEA, CHARLIE BROWN...STAY HOME, AND REST..
4-16
YOU'VE BEEN STRIKING OUT EVERY TIME YOU GOT UP ANYWAY... IT'LL BE BEST IF YOU STAY HOME..
DON'T LET YOUR TEAM DOWN BY SHOWING UP!

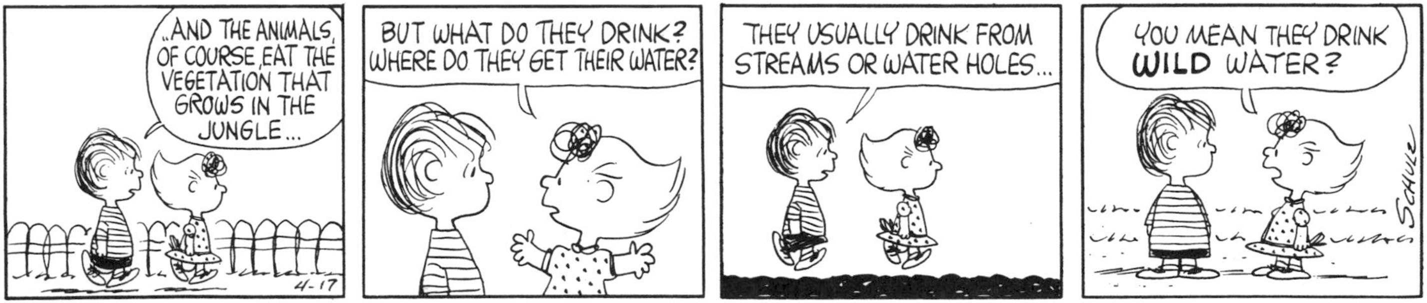
..AND THE ANIMALS, OF COURSE, EAT THE VEGETATION THAT GROWS IN THE JUNGLE...
4-17
BUT WHAT DO THEY DRINK? WHERE DO THEY GET THEIR WATER?
THEY USUALLY DRINK FROM STREAMS OR WATER HOLES...
YOU MEAN THEY DRINK WILD WATER?

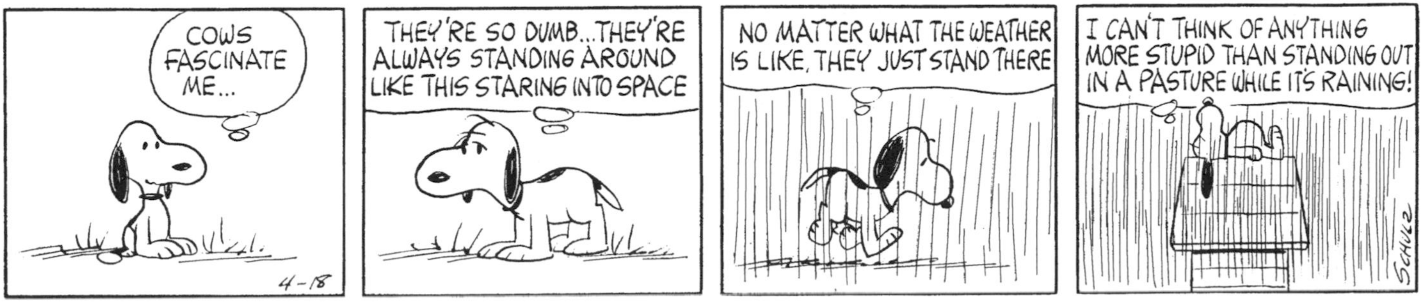
COWS FASCINATE ME...
4-18
THEY'RE SO DUMB...THEY'RE ALWAYS STANDING AROUND LIKE THIS STARING INTO SPACE
NO MATTER WHAT THE WEATHER IS LIKE, THEY JUST STAND THERE
I CAN'T THINK OF ANYTHING MORE STUPID THAN STANDING OUT IN A PASTURE WHILE IT'S RAINING!
SCHULZ

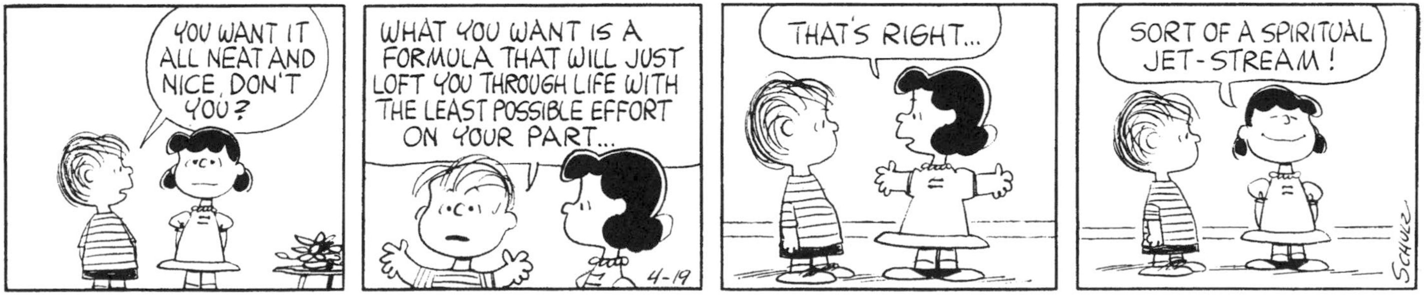
YOU WANT IT ALL NEAT AND NICE, DON'T YOU?
WHAT YOU WANT IS A FORMULA THAT WILL JUST LOFT YOU THROUGH LIFE WITH THE LEAST POSSIBLE EFFORT ON YOUR PART...
4-19
THAT'S RIGHT...
SORT OF A SPIRITUAL JET-STREAM!
SCHULZ

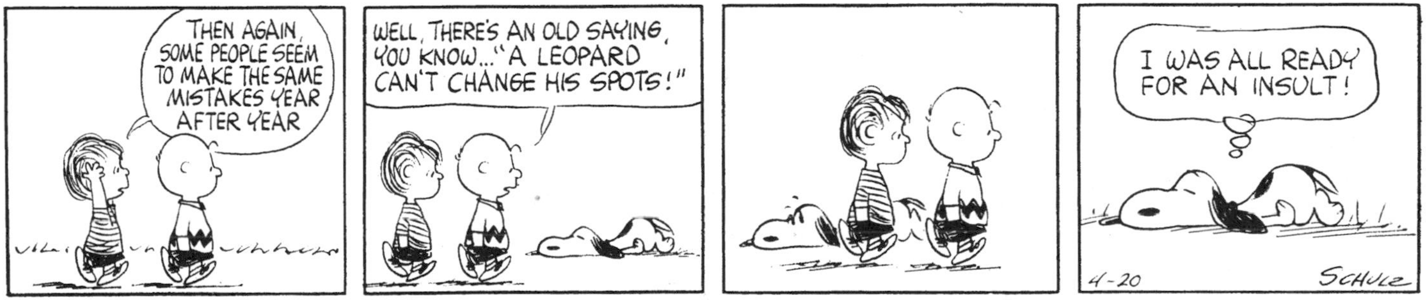
THEN AGAIN, SOME PEOPLE SEEM TO MAKE THE SAME MISTAKES YEAR AFTER YEAR
WELL, THERE'S AN OLD SAYING, YOU KNOW..."A LEOPARD CAN'T CHANGE HIS SPOTS!"
I WAS ALL READY FOR AN INSULT!
4-20
SCHULZ

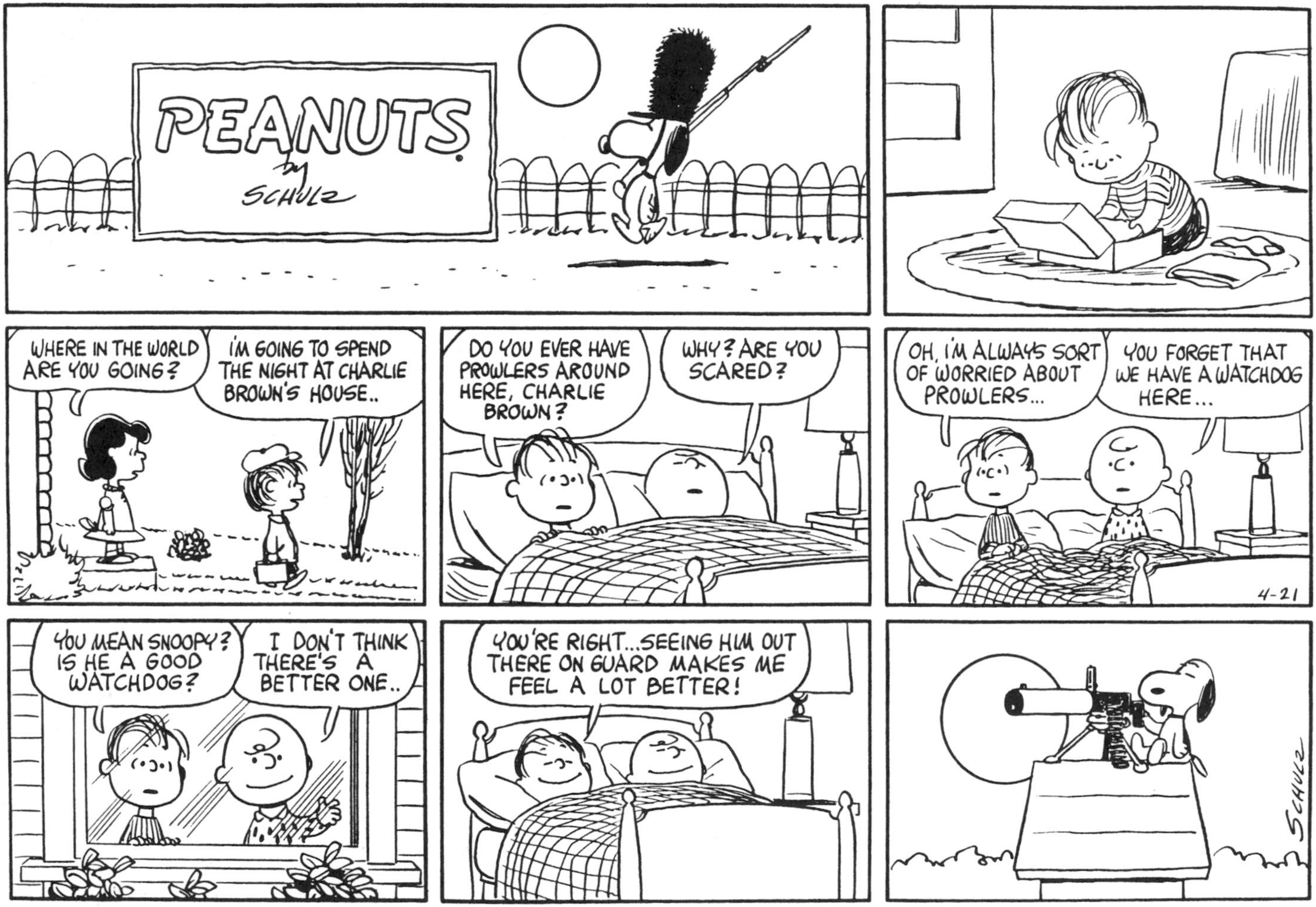
PEANUTS
by SCHULZ
WHERE IN THE WORLD ARE YOU GOING?
I'M GOING TO SPEND THE NIGHT AT CHARLIE BROWN'S HOUSE..
DO YOU EVER HAVE PROWLERS AROUND HERE, CHARLIE BROWN?
WHY? ARE YOU SCARED?
OH, I'M ALWAYS SORT OF WORRIED ABOUT PROWLERS...
YOU FORGET THAT WE HAVE A WATCHDOG HERE...
4-21
YOU MEAN SNOOPY? IS HE A GOOD WATCHDOG?
I DON'T THINK THERE'S A BETTER ONE..
YOU'RE RIGHT...SEEING HIM OUT THERE ON GUARD MAKES ME FEEL A LOT BETTER!
SCHULZ

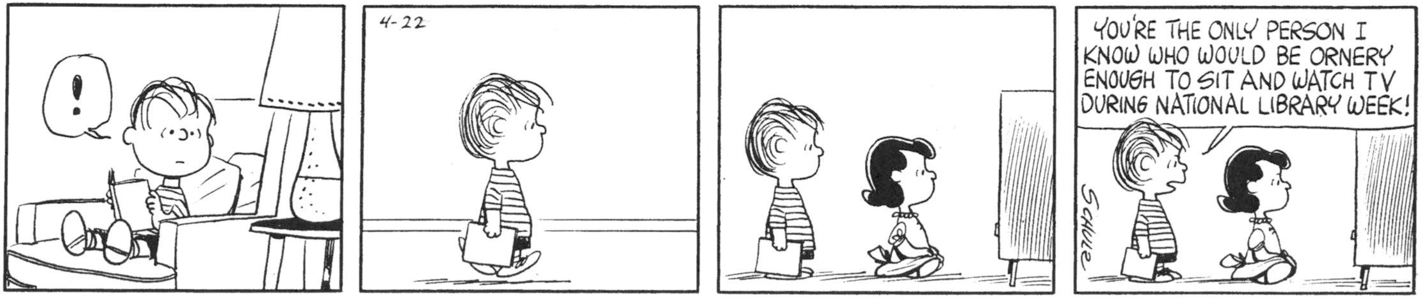
!
4-22
YOU'RE THE ONLY PERSON I KNOW WHO WOULD BE ORNERY ENOUGH TO SIT AND WATCH TV DURING NATIONAL LIBRARY WEEK!
SCHULZ

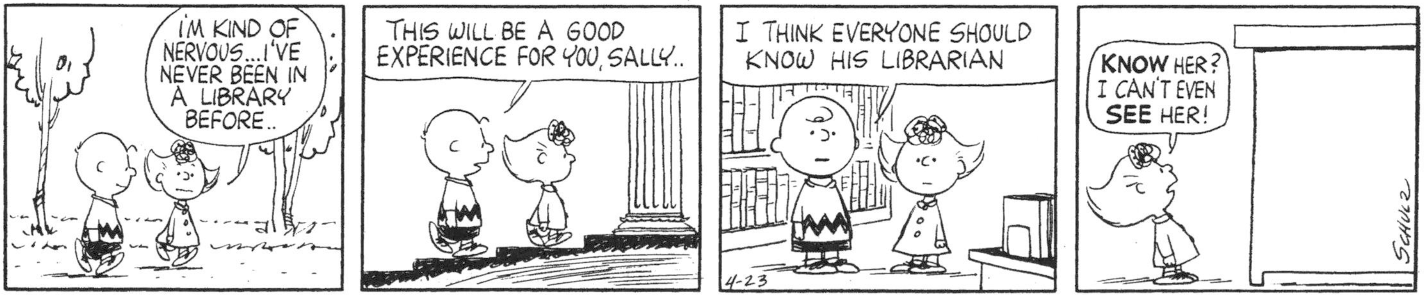
I'M KIND OF NERVOUS...I'VE NEVER BEEN IN A LIBRARY BEFORE..
THIS WILL BE A GOOD EXPERIENCE FOR YOU, SALLY..
I THINK EVERYONE SHOULD KNOW HIS LIBRARIAN
4-23
KNOW HER? I CAN'T EVEN SEE HER!
SCHULZ

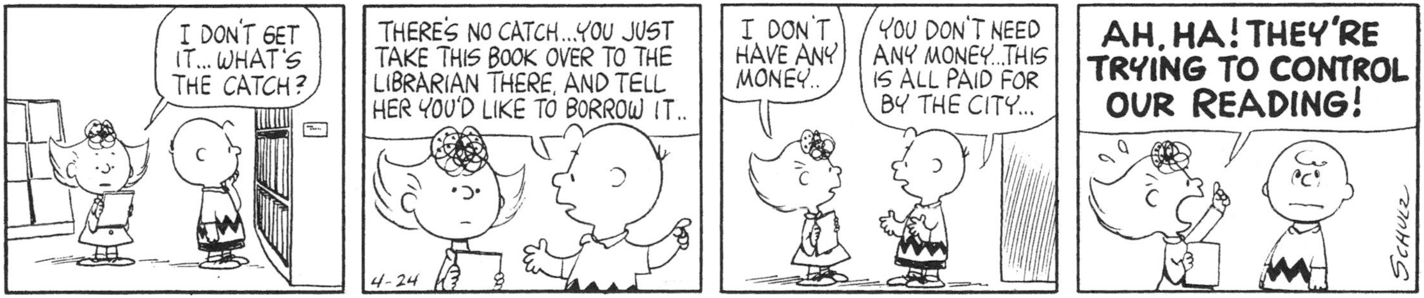
I DON'T GET IT... WHAT'S THE CATCH?
THERE'S NO CATCH...YOU JUST TAKE THIS BOOK OVER TO THE LIBRARIAN THERE, AND TELL HER YOU'D LIKE TO BORROW IT..
4-24
I DON'T HAVE ANY MONEY..
YOU DON'T NEED ANY MONEY...THIS IS ALL PAID FOR BY THE CITY...
AH, HA! THEY'RE TRYING TO CONTROL OUR READING!
SCHULZ

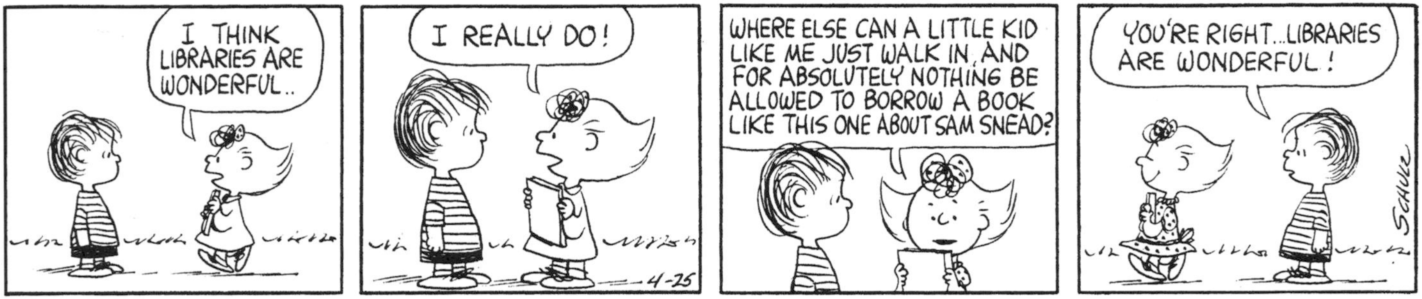
I THINK LIBRARIES ARE WONDERFUL..
I REALLY DO!
4-25
WHERE ELSE CAN A LITTLE KID LIKE ME JUST WALK IN, AND FOR ABSOLUTELY NOTHING BE ALLOWED TO BORROW A BOOK LIKE THIS ONE ABOUT SAM SNEAD?
YOU'RE RIGHT...LIBRARIES ARE WONDERFUL!
SCHULZ

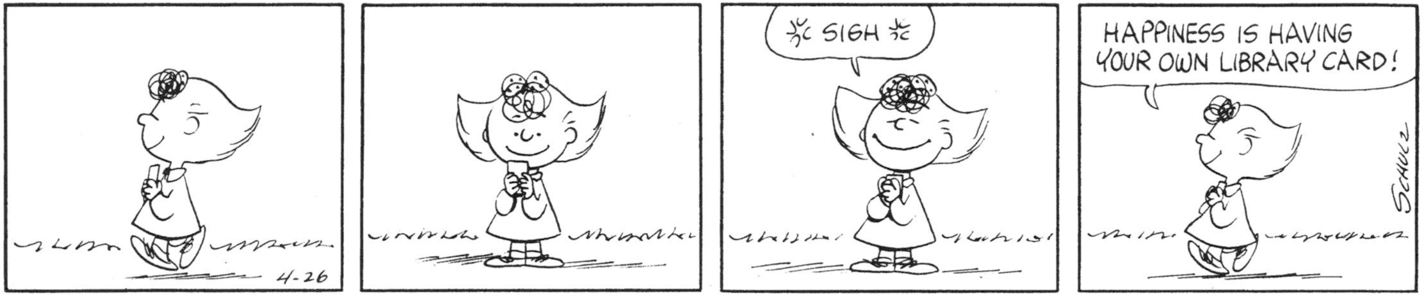
4-26
SIGH
HAPPINESS IS HAVING YOUR OWN LIBRARY CARD!
SCHULZ

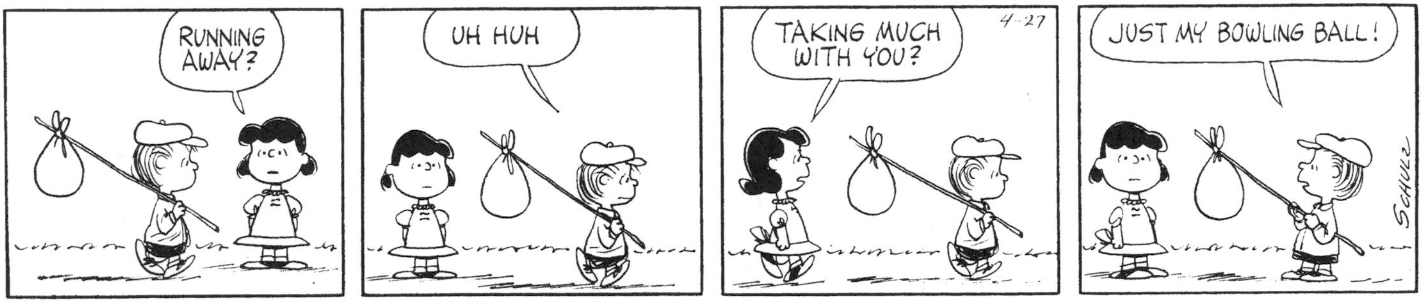
RUNNING AWAY?
UH HUH
4-27
TAKING MUCH WITH YOU?
JUST MY BOWLING BALL!
SCHULZ

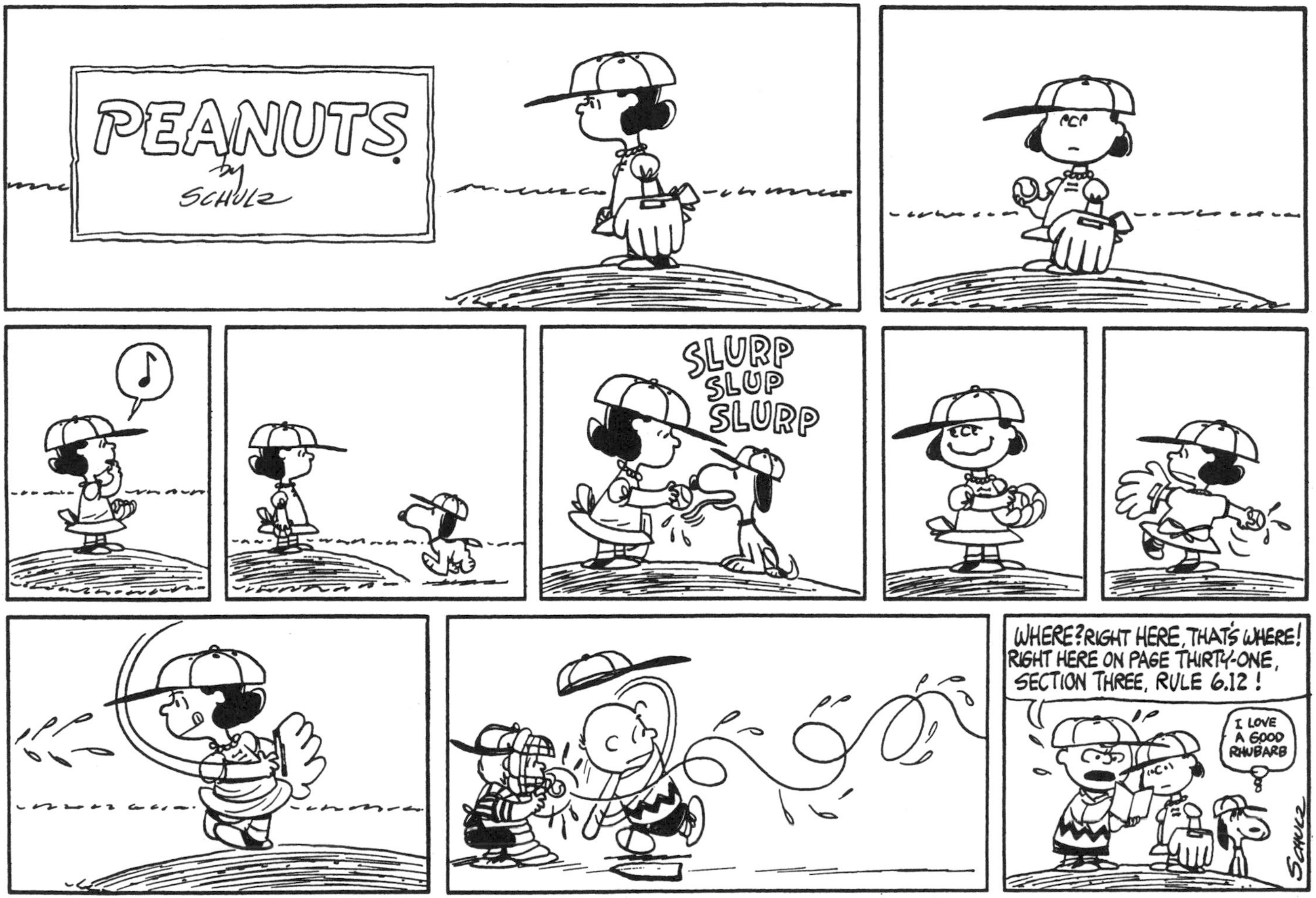
PEANUTS
by SCHULZ
SLURP
SLUP
SLURP
WHERE? RIGHT HERE, THAT'S WHERE! RIGHT HERE ON PAGE THIRTY-ONE, SECTION THREE, RULE 6.12!
I LOVE A GOOD RHUBARB
SCHULZ

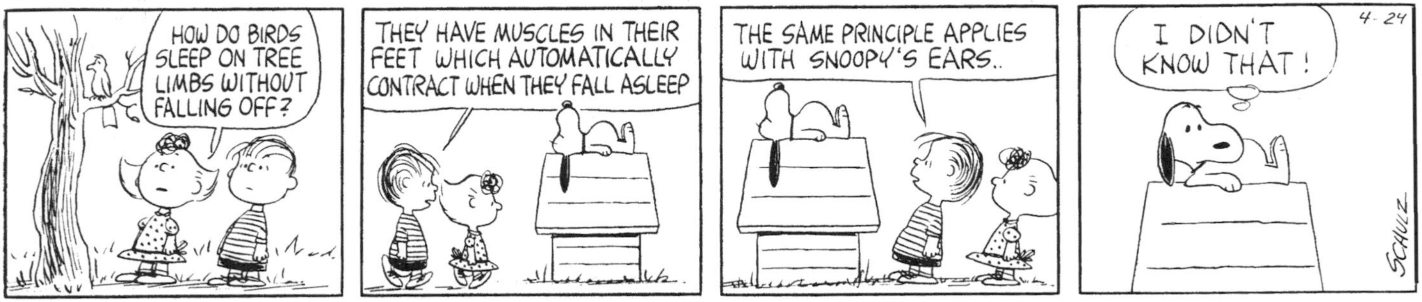
HOW DO BIRDS SLEEP ON TREE LIMBS WITHOUT FALLING OFF?
THEY HAVE MUSCLES IN THEIR FEET WHICH AUTOMATICALLY CONTRACT WHEN THEY FALL ASLEEP
THE SAME PRINCIPLE APPLIES WITH SNOOPY'S EARS..
4-24
I DIDN'T KNOW THAT!
SCHULZ

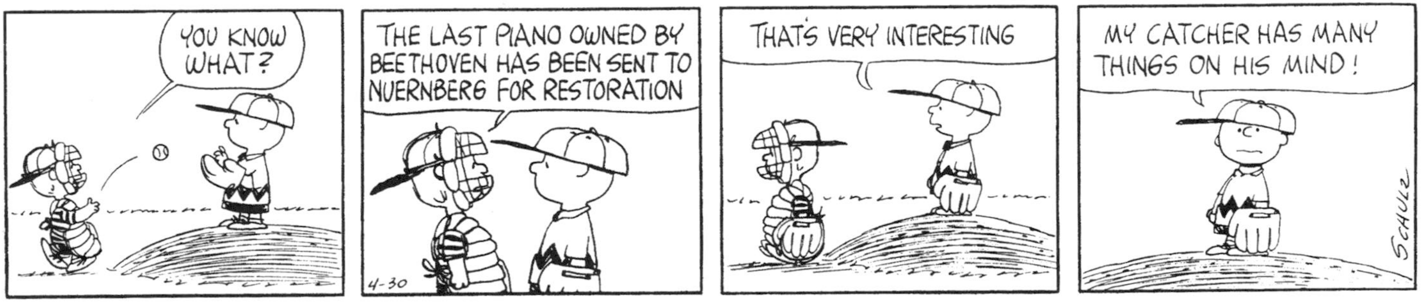
YOU KNOW WHAT?
THE LAST PIANO OWNED BY BEETHOVEN HAS BEEN SENT TO NUERNBERG FOR RESTORATION
4-30
THAT'S VERY INTERESTING
MY CATCHER HAS MANY THINGS ON HIS MIND!
SCHULZ

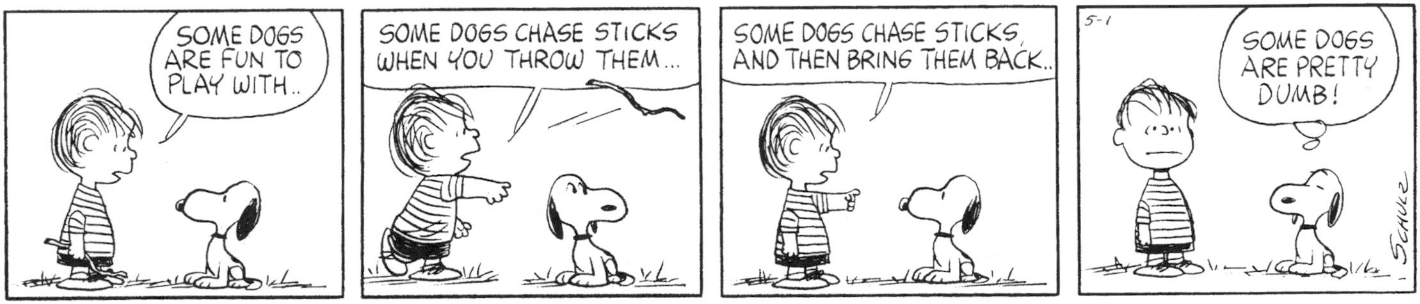
SOME DOGS ARE FUN TO PLAY WITH..
SOME DOGS CHASE STICKS WHEN YOU THROW THEM...
SOME DOGS CHASE STICKS, AND THEN BRING THEM BACK..
5-1
SOME DOGS ARE PRETTY DUMB!
SCHULZ

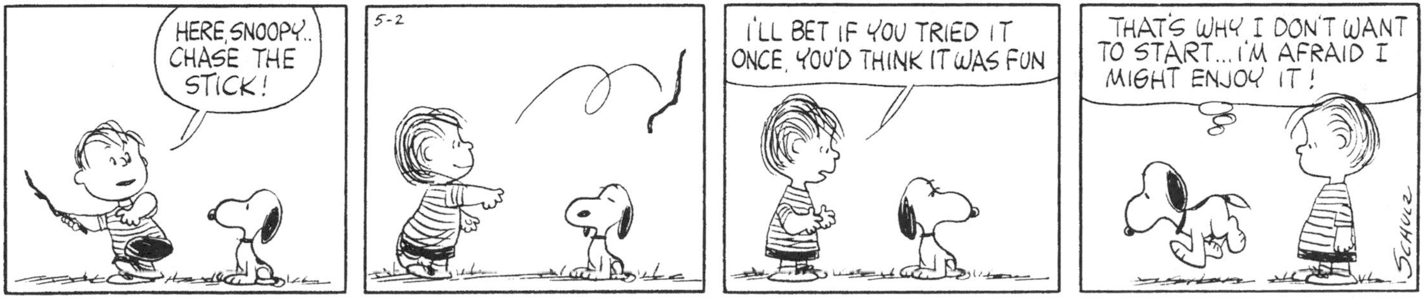
HERE, SNOOPY.. CHASE THE STICK!
5-2
I'LL BET IF YOU TRIED IT ONCE, YOU'D THINK IT WAS FUN
THAT'S WHY I DON'T WANT TO START... I'M AFRAID I MIGHT ENJOY IT!
SCHULZ

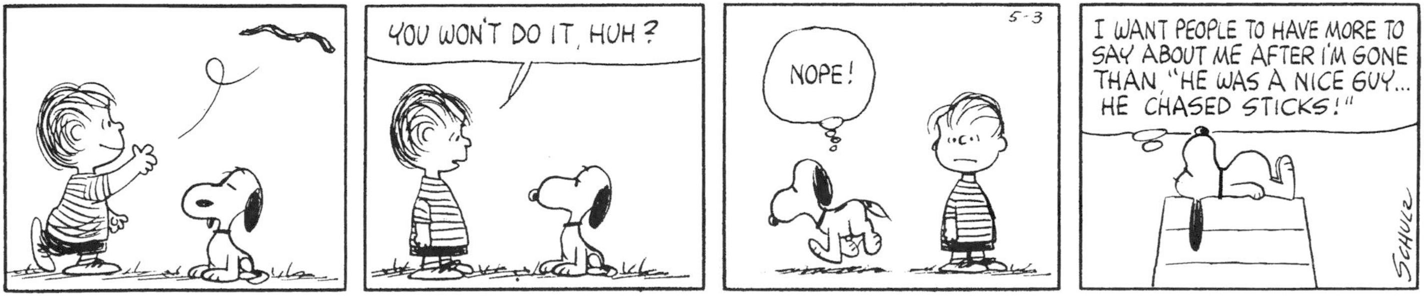
YOU WON'T DO IT, HUH?
5-3
NOPE!
I WANT PEOPLE TO HAVE MORE TO SAY ABOUT ME AFTER I'M GONE THAN, "HE WAS A NICE GUY... HE CHASED STICKS!"
SCHULZ

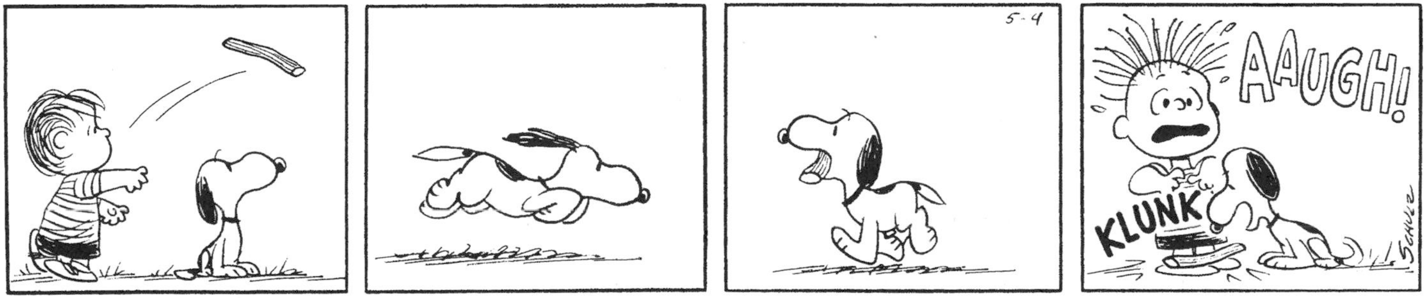
5-4
AAUGH!
KLUNK
SCHULZ

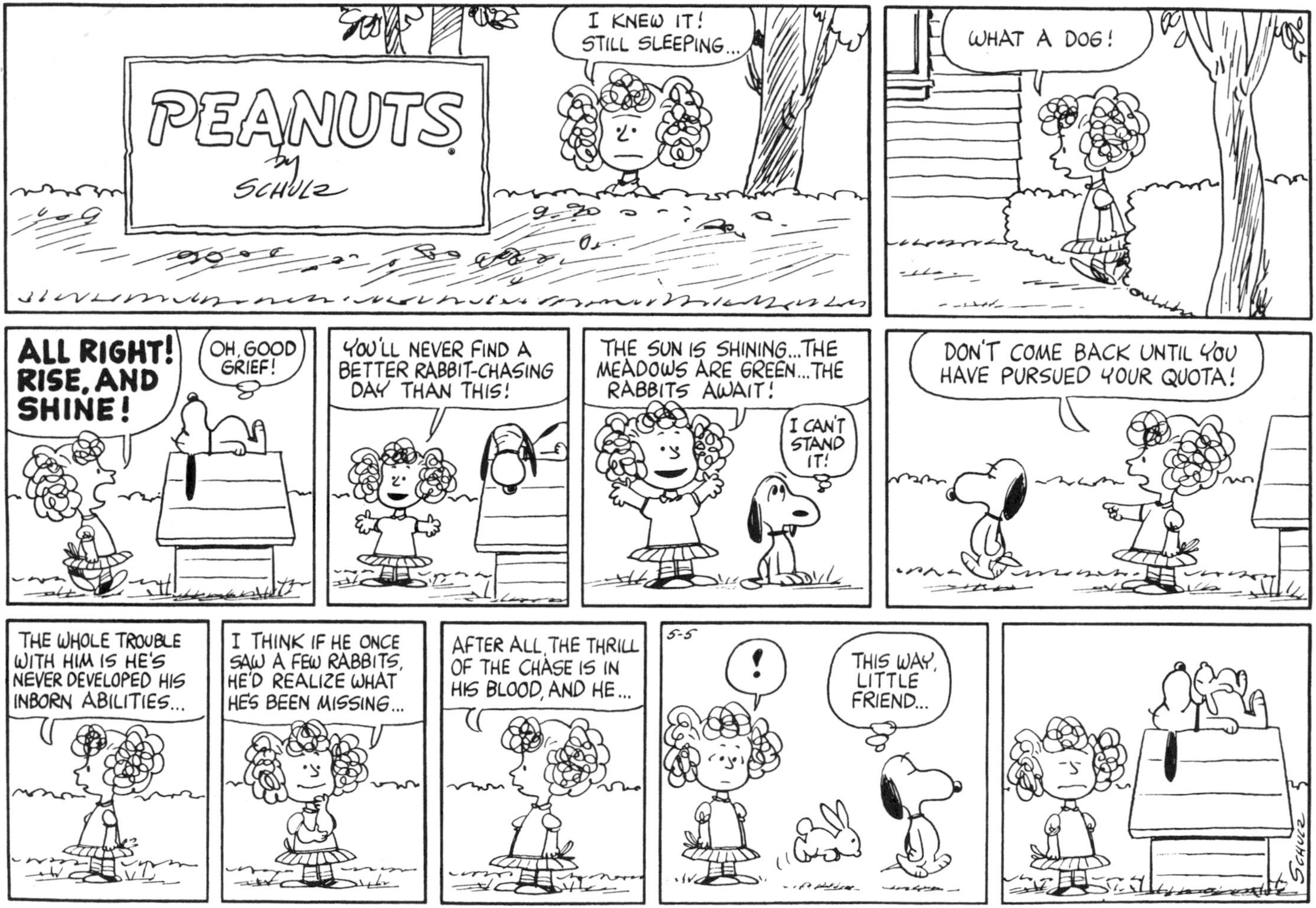
PEANUTS
by SCHULZ
I KNEW IT! STILL SLEEPING...
WHAT A DOG!
ALL RIGHT! RISE, AND SHINE!
OH, GOOD GRIEF!
YOU'LL NEVER FIND A BETTER RABBIT-CHASING DAY THAN THIS!
THE SUN IS SHINING...THE MEADOWS ARE GREEN...THE RABBITS AWAIT!
I CAN'T STAND IT!
DON'T COME BACK UNTIL YOU HAVE PURSUED YOUR QUOTA!
THE WHOLE TROUBLE WITH HIM IS HE'S NEVER DEVELOPED HIS INBORN ABILITIES...
I THINK IF HE ONCE SAW A FEW RABBITS, HE'D REALIZE WHAT HE'S BEEN MISSING...
AFTER ALL, THE THRILL OF THE CHASE IS IN HIS BLOOD, AND HE...
5-5
!
THIS WAY, LITTLE FRIEND...
SCHULZ

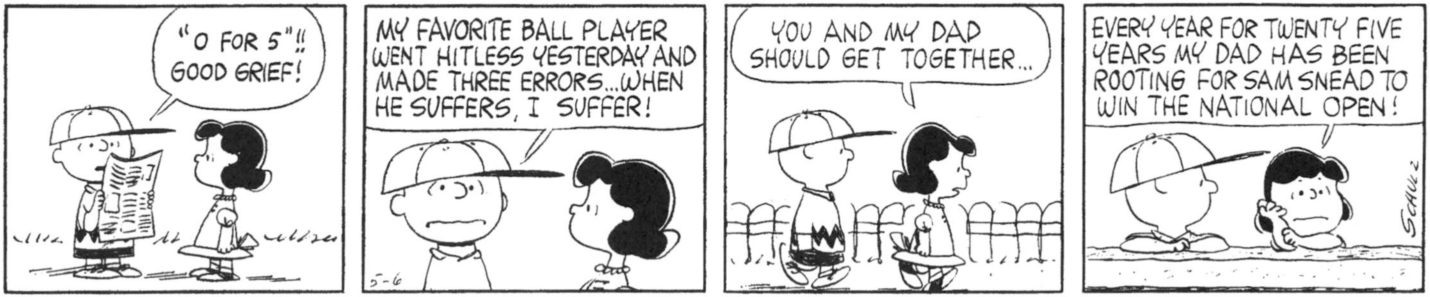
"O FOR 5"!! GOOD GRIEF!
MY FAVORITE BALL PLAYER WENT HITLESS YESTERDAY AND MADE THREE ERRORS...WHEN HE SUFFERS, I SUFFER!
5-6
YOU AND MY DAD SHOULD GET TOGETHER...
EVERY YEAR FOR TWENTY FIVE YEARS MY DAD HAS BEEN ROOTING FOR SAM SNEAD TO WIN THE NATIONAL OPEN!
SCHULZ

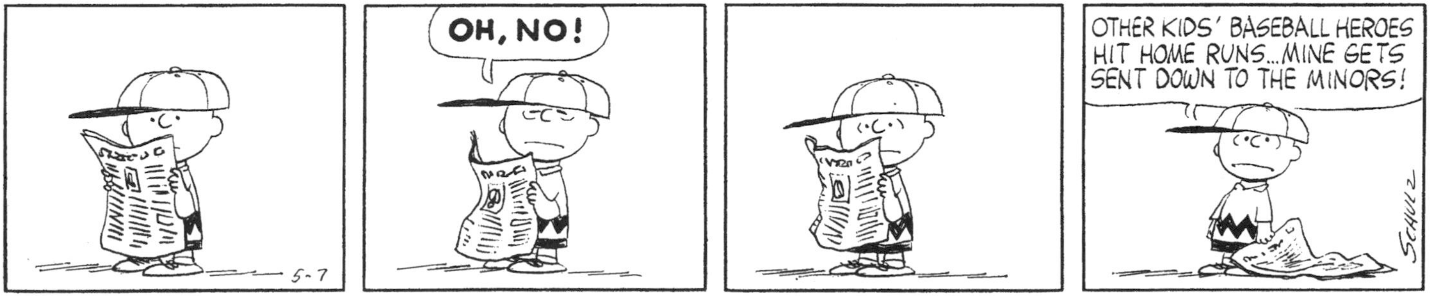
5-7
OH, NO!
OTHER KIDS' BASEBALL HEROES HIT HOME RUNS...MINE GETS SENT DOWN TO THE MINORS!
SCHULZ

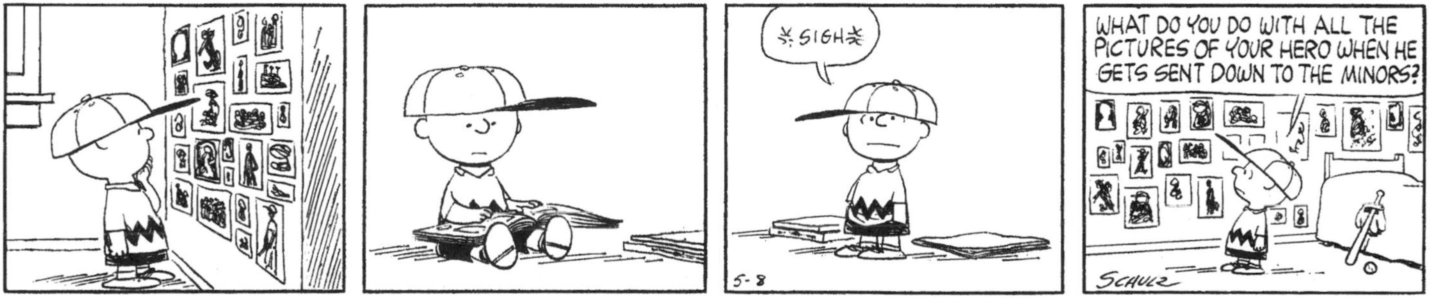
SIGH
5-8
WHAT DO YOU DO WITH ALL THE PICTURES OF YOUR HERO WHEN HE GETS SENT DOWN TO THE MINORS?
SCHULZ

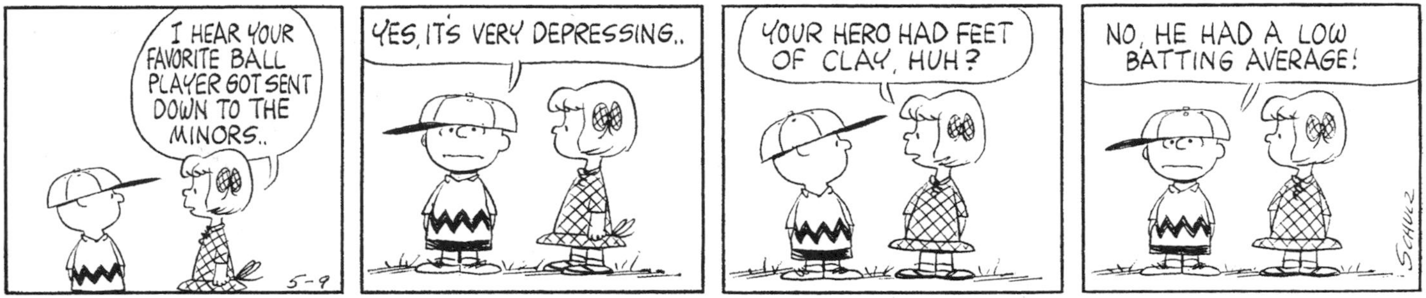
I HEAR YOUR FAVORITE BALL PLAYER GOT SENT DOWN TO THE MINORS..
5-9
YES, IT'S VERY DEPRESSING..
YOUR HERO HAD FEET OF CLAY, HUH?
NO, HE HAD A LOW BATTING AVERAGE!
SCHULZ

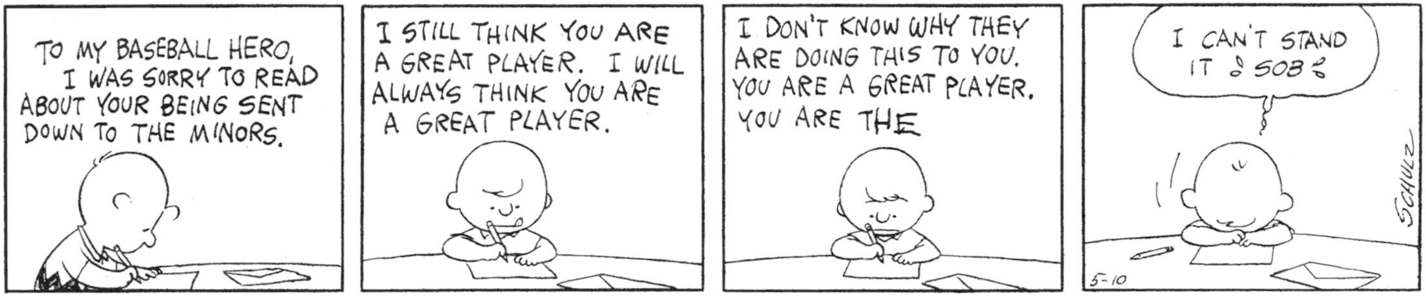
TO MY BASEBALL HERO, I WAS SORRY TO READ ABOUT YOUR BEING SENT DOWN TO THE MINORS.
I STILL THINK YOU ARE A GREAT PLAYER. I WILL ALWAYS THINK YOU ARE A GREAT PLAYER.
I DON'T KNOW WHY THEY ARE DOING THIS TO YOU. YOU ARE A GREAT PLAYER. YOU ARE THE
I CAN'T STAND IT SOB
SCHULZ
5-10

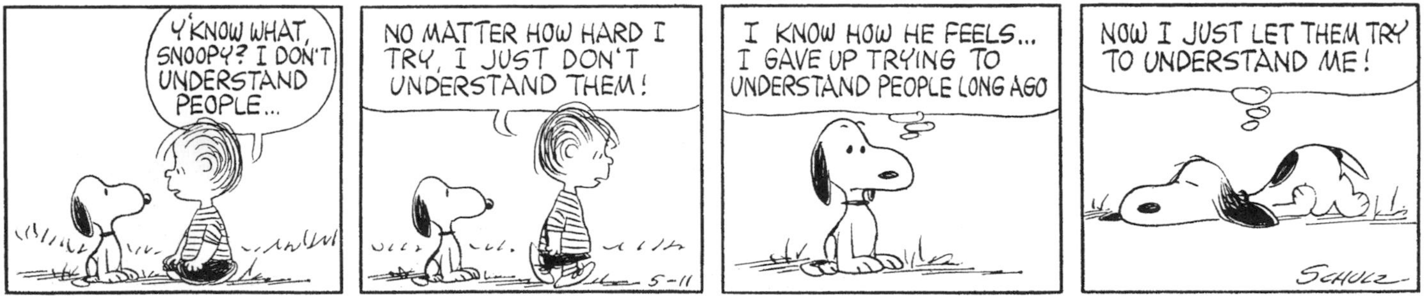
Y'KNOW WHAT, SNOOPY? I DON'T UNDERSTAND PEOPLE...
NO MATTER HOW HARD I TRY, I JUST DON'T UNDERSTAND THEM!
5-11
I KNOW HOW HE FEELS... I GAVE UP TRYING TO UNDERSTAND PEOPLE LONG AGO
NOW I JUST LET THEM TRY TO UNDERSTAND ME!
SCHULZ

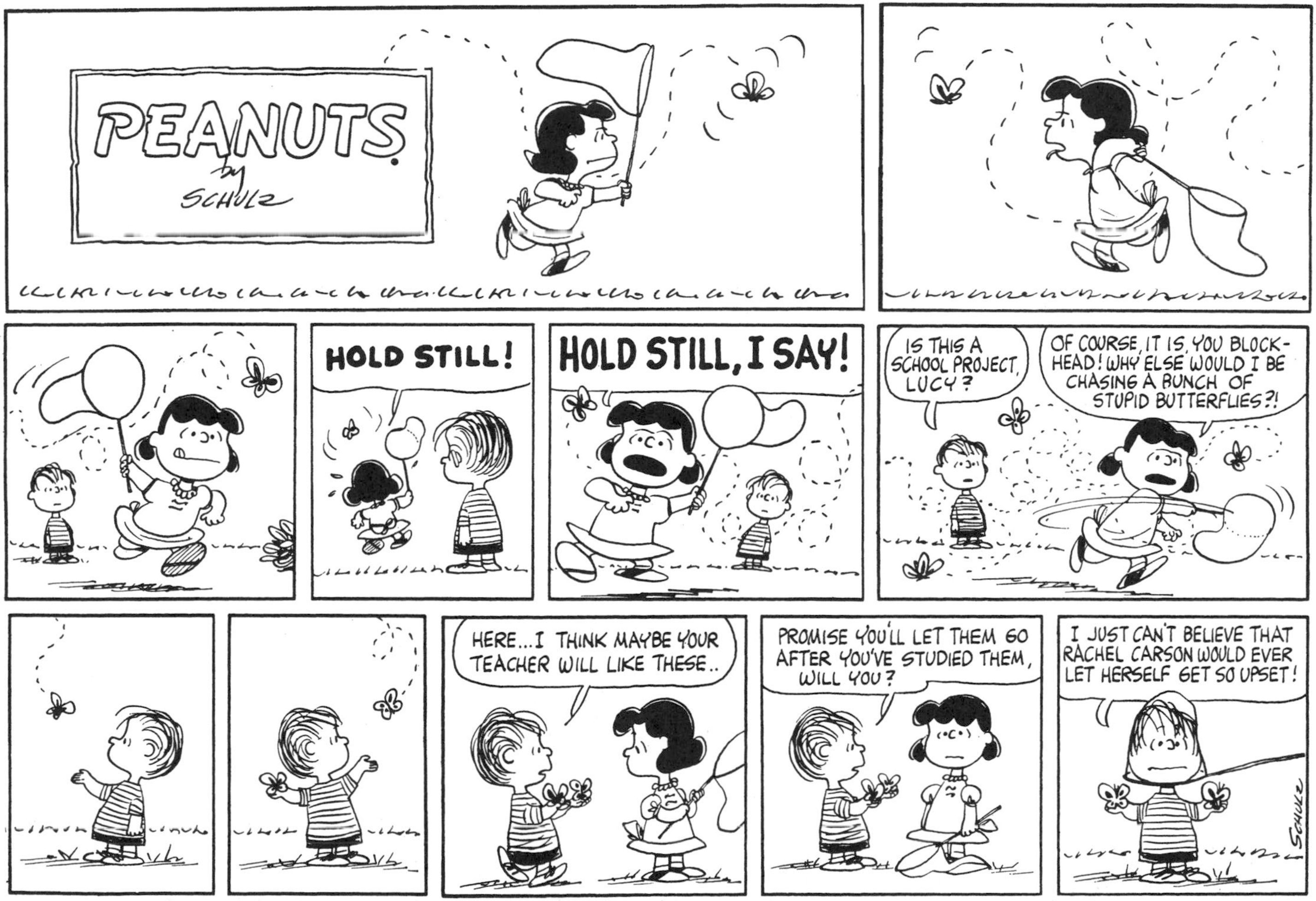
PEANUTS
by SCHULZ
HOLD STILL!
HOLD STILL, I SAY!
IS THIS A SCHOOL PROJECT, LUCY?
OF COURSE, IT IS, YOU BLOCKHEAD! WHY ELSE WOULD I BE CHASING A BUNCH OF STUPID BUTTERFLIES?!
HERE...I THINK MAYBE YOUR TEACHER WILL LIKE THESE..
PROMISE YOU'LL LET THEM GO AFTER YOU'VE STUDIED THEM, WILL YOU?
I JUST CAN'T BELIEVE THAT RACHEL CARSON WOULD EVER LET HERSELF GET SO UPSET!
SCHULZ

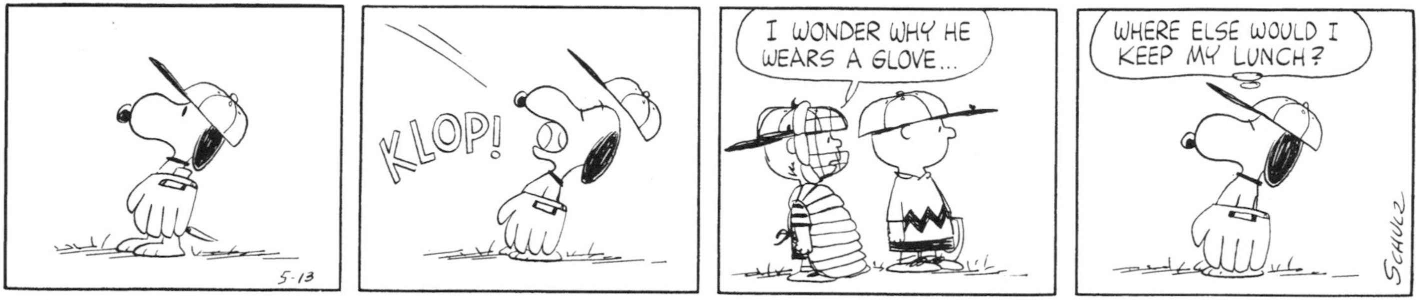
5-13
KLOP!
I WONDER WHY HE WEARS A GLOVE...
WHERE ELSE WOULD I KEEP MY LUNCH?
SCHULZ

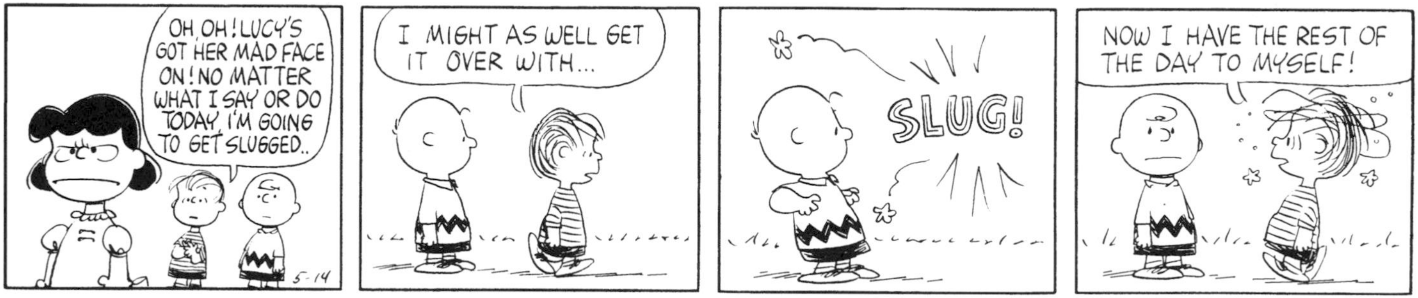
OH, OH! LUCY'S GOT HER MAD FACE ON! NO MATTER WHAT I SAY OR DO TODAY, I'M GOING TO GET SLUGGED..
5-14
I MIGHT AS WELL GET IT OVER WITH...
SLUG!
NOW I HAVE THE REST OF THE DAY TO MYSELF!

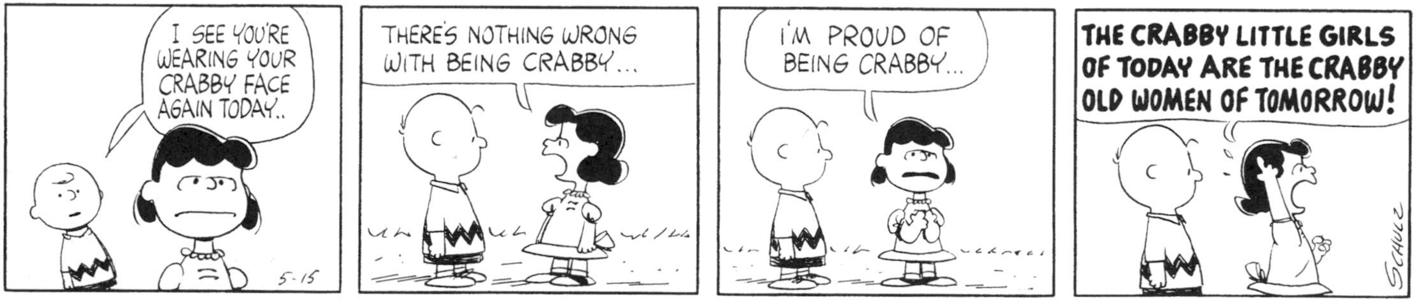
I SEE YOU'RE WEARING YOUR CRABBY FACE AGAIN TODAY..
5-15
THERE'S NOTHING WRONG WITH BEING CRABBY...
I'M PROUD OF BEING CRABBY...
THE CRABBY LITTLE GIRLS OF TODAY ARE THE CRABBY OLD WOMEN OF TOMORROW!
SCHULZ

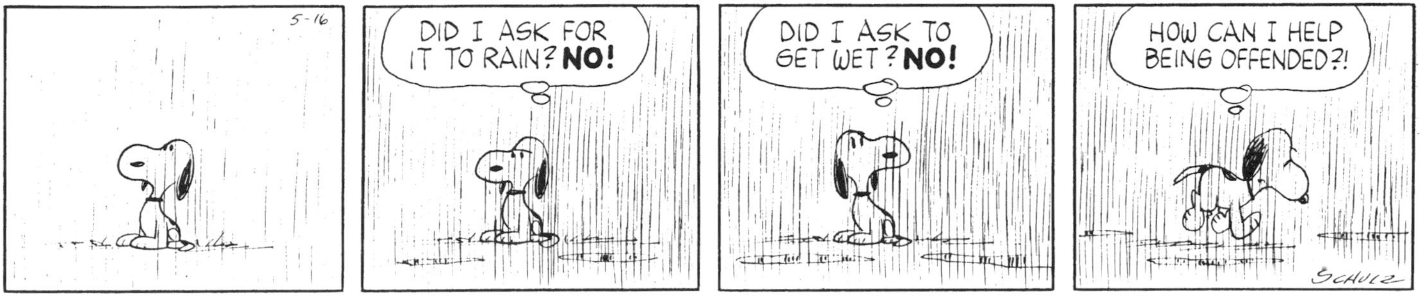
5-16
DID I ASK FOR IT TO RAIN? NO!
DID I ASK TO GET WET? NO!
HOW CAN I HELP BEING OFFENDED?!
SCHULZ

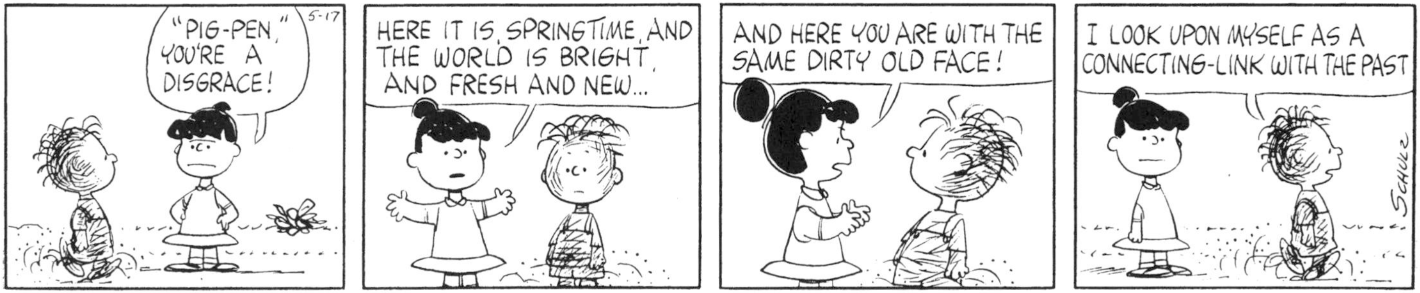
"PIG-PEN," YOU'RE A DISGRACE!
5-17
HERE IT IS, SPRINGTIME, AND THE WORLD IS BRIGHT, AND FRESH AND NEW...
AND HERE YOU ARE WITH THE SAME DIRTY OLD FACE!
I LOOK UPON MYSELF AS A CONNECTING-LINK WITH THE PAST
SCHULZ

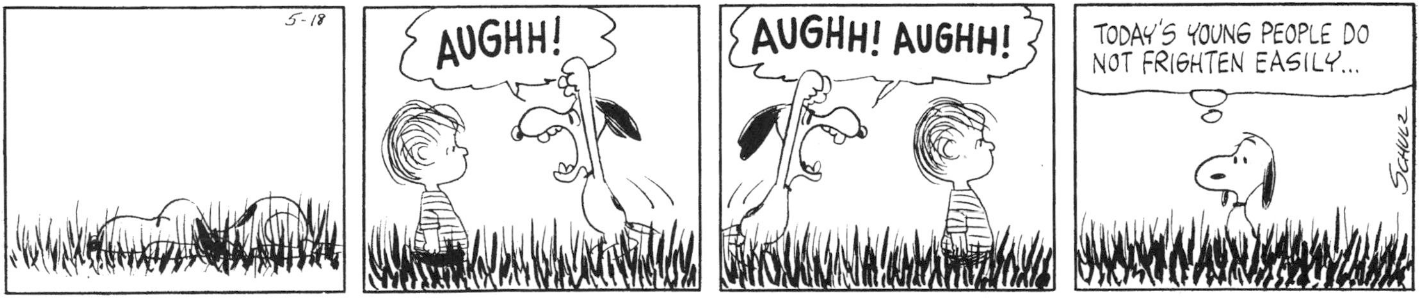
5-18
AUGHH!
AUGHH! AUGHH!
TODAY'S YOUNG PEOPLE DO NOT FRIGHTEN EASILY...
SCHULZ

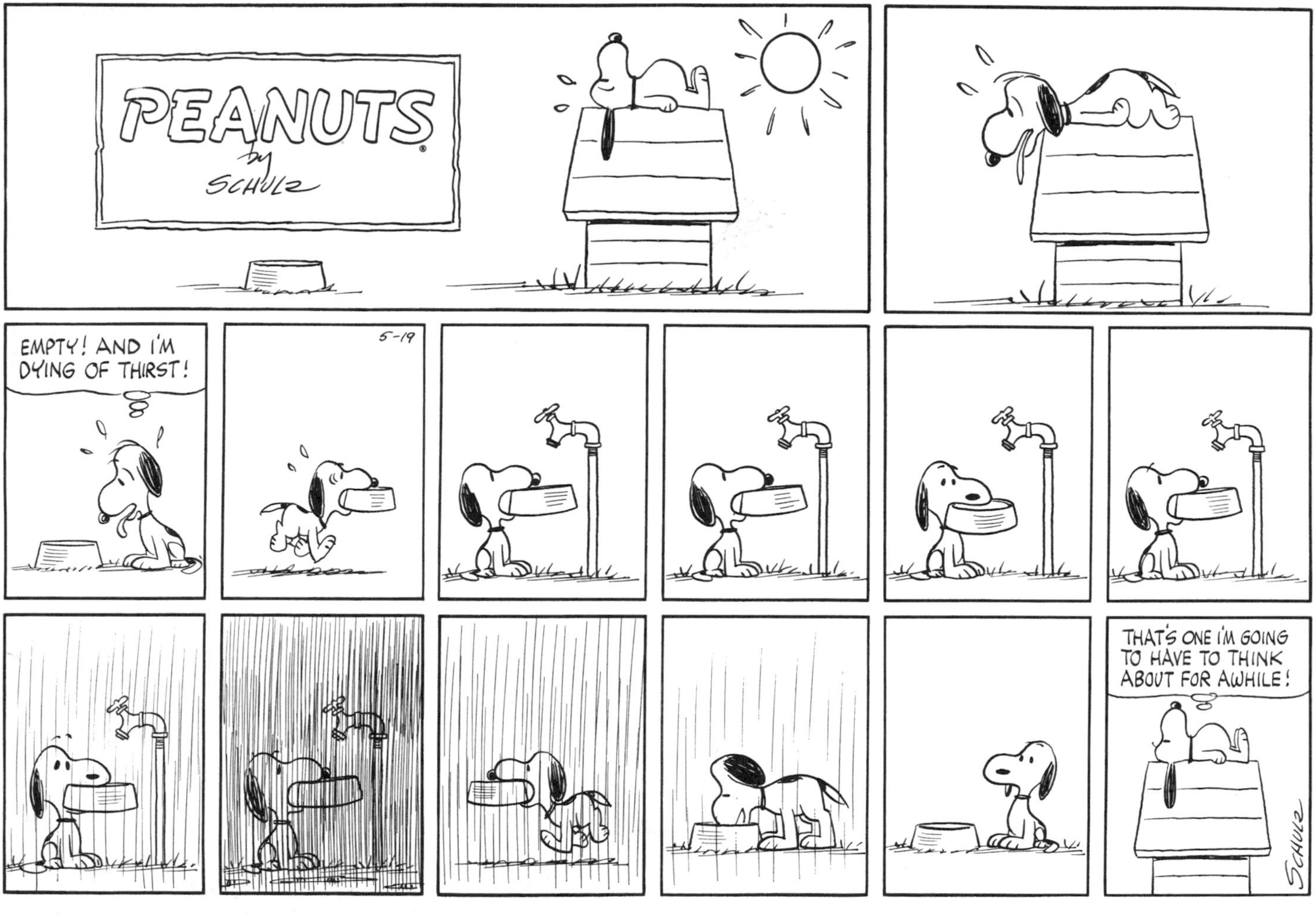
PEANUTS
by SCHULZ
EMPTY! AND I'M DYING OF THIRST!
5-19
THAT'S ONE I'M GOING TO HAVE TO THINK ABOUT FOR AWHILE!
SCHULZ

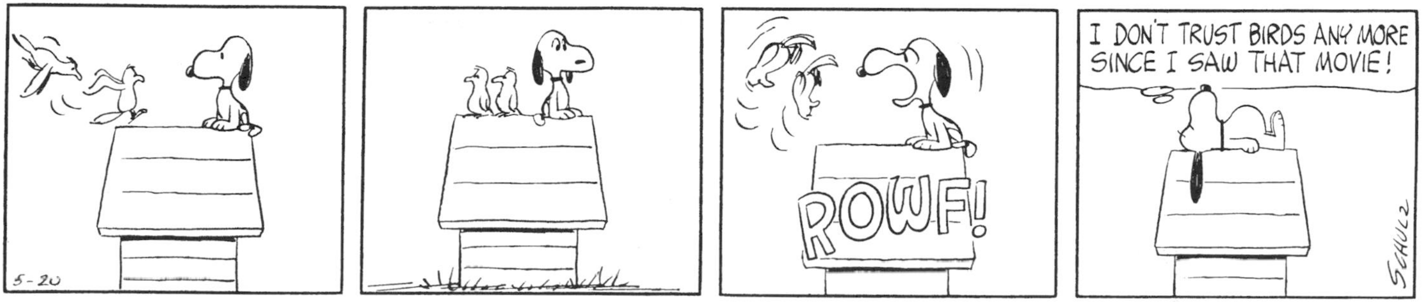
5-20
ROWF!
I DON'T TRUST BIRDS ANY MORE SINCE I SAW THAT MOVIE!
SCHULZ

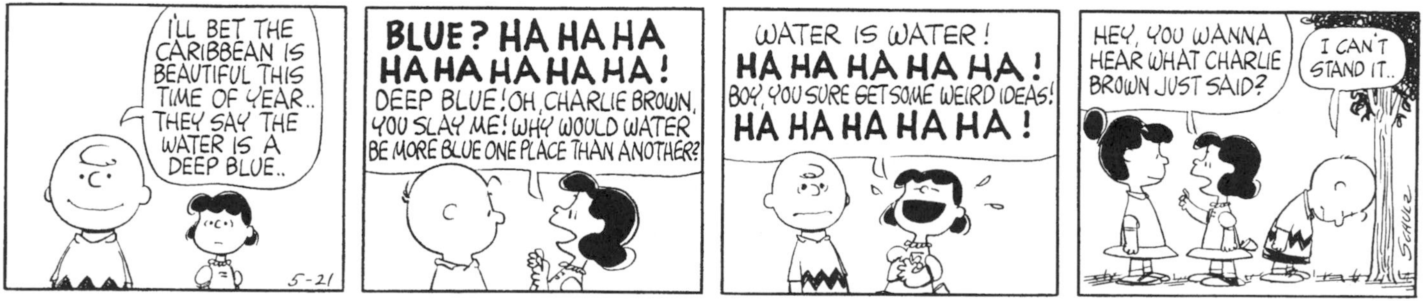
I'LL BET THE CARIBBEAN IS BEAUTIFUL THIS TIME OF YEAR.. THEY SAY THE WATER IS A DEEP BLUE..
5-21
BLUE? HA HA HA HA HA HA HA HA!
DEEP BLUE! OH, CHARLIE BROWN, YOU SLAY ME! WHY WOULD WATER BE MORE BLUE ONE PLACE THAN ANOTHER?
WATER IS WATER!
HA HA HA HA HA!
BOY, YOU SURE GET SOME WEIRD IDEAS!
HA HA HA HA HA!
HEY, YOU WANNA HEAR WHAT CHARLIE BROWN JUST SAID?
I CAN'T STAND IT..
SCHULZ

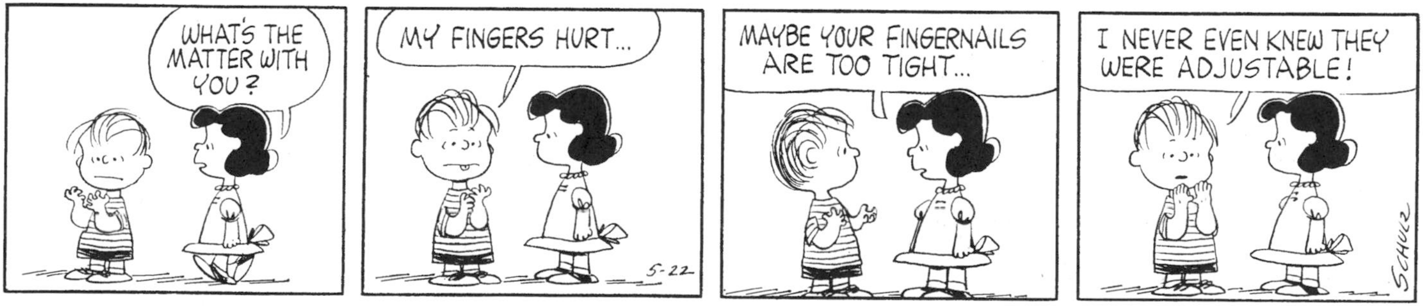
WHAT'S THE MATTER WITH YOU?
MY FINGERS HURT...
5-22
MAYBE YOUR FINGERNAILS ARE TOO TIGHT...
I NEVER EVEN KNEW THEY WERE ADJUSTABLE!
SCHULZ

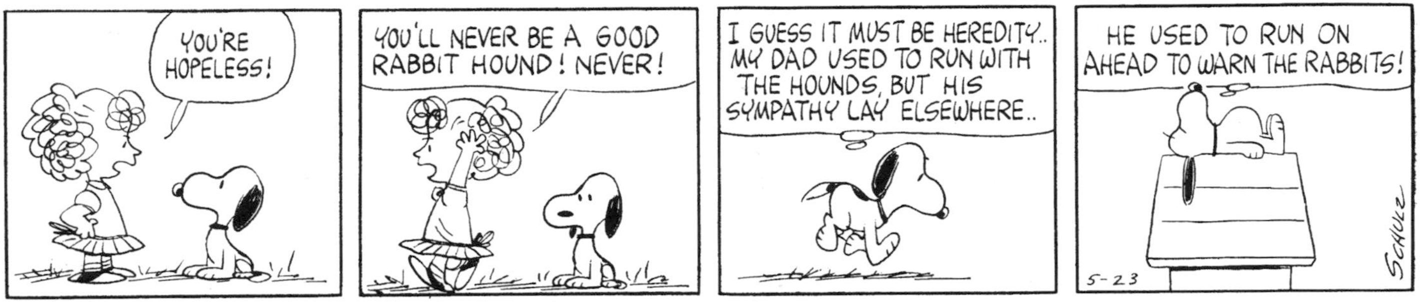
YOU'RE HOPELESS!
YOU'LL NEVER BE A GOOD RABBIT HOUND! NEVER!
I GUESS IT MUST BE HEREDITY.. MY DAD USED TO RUN WITH THE HOUNDS, BUT HIS SYMPATHY LAY ELSEWHERE..
HE USED TO RUN ON AHEAD TO WARN THE RABBITS!
5-23
SCHULZ

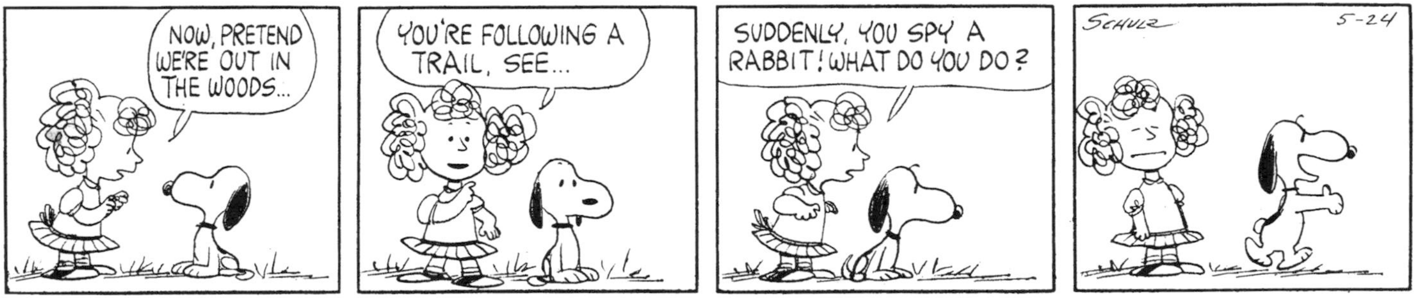
NOW, PRETEND WE'RE OUT IN THE WOODS...
YOU'RE FOLLOWING A TRAIL, SEE...
SUDDENLY, YOU SPY A RABBIT! WHAT DO YOU DO?
SCHULZ
5-24

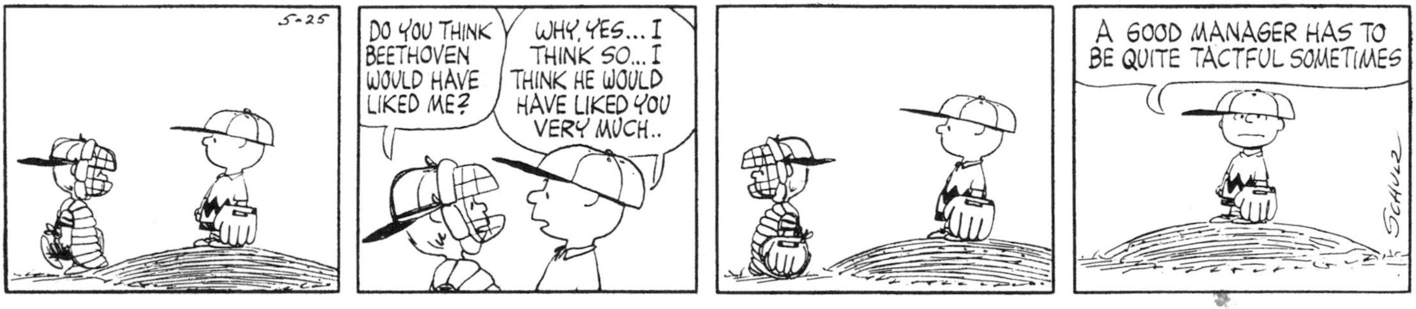
5-25
DO YOU THINK BEETHOVEN WOULD HAVE LIKED ME?
WHY, YES... I THINK SO... I THINK HE WOULD HAVE LIKED YOU VERY MUCH..
A GOOD MANAGER HAS TO BE QUITE TACTFUL SOMETIMES
SCHULZ

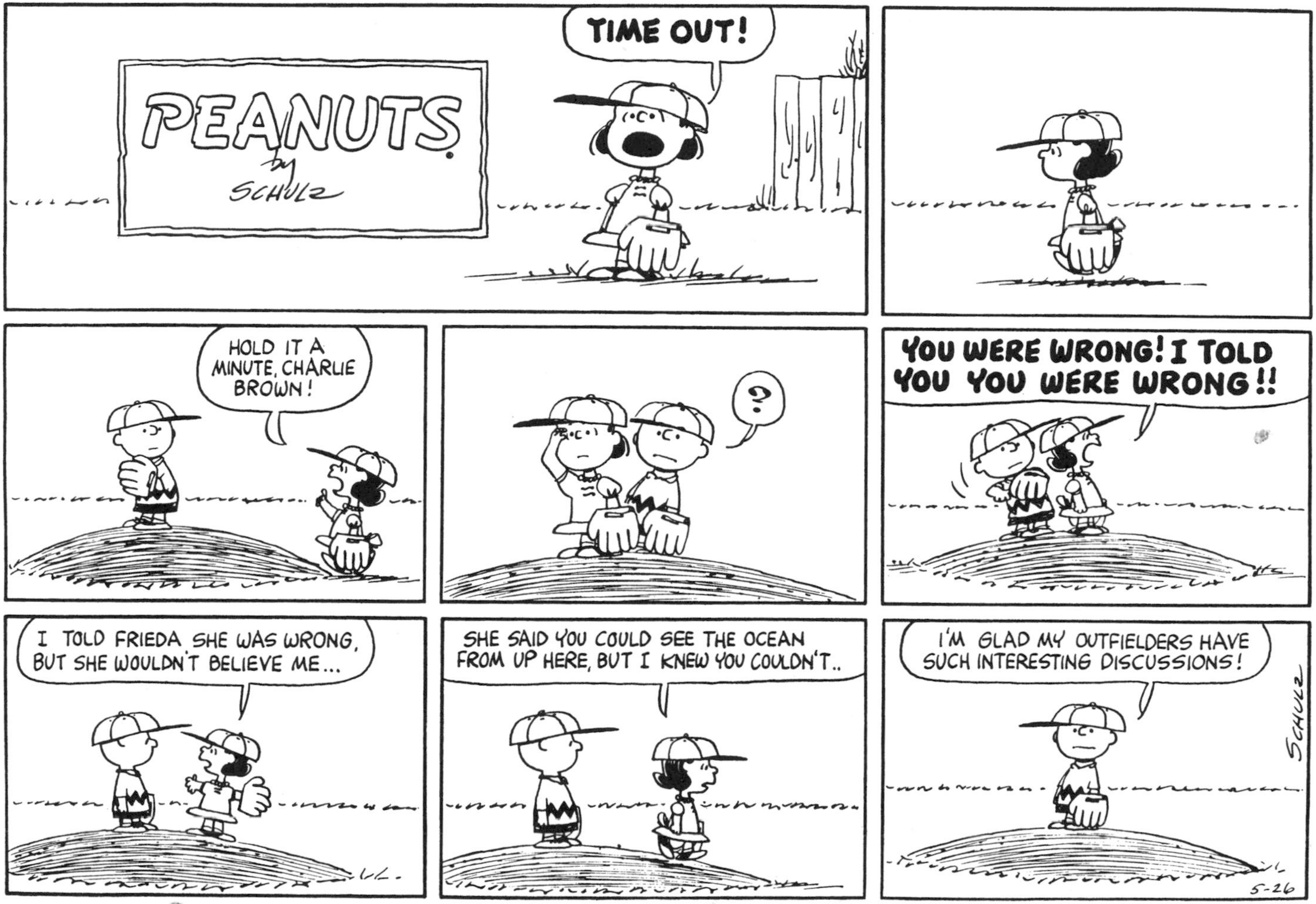
PEANUTS
by SCHULZ
TIME OUT!
HOLD IT A MINUTE, CHARLIE BROWN!
?
YOU WERE WRONG! I TOLD YOU YOU WERE WRONG!!
I TOLD FRIEDA SHE WAS WRONG, BUT SHE WOULDN'T BELIEVE ME...
SHE SAID YOU COULD SEE THE OCEAN FROM UP HERE, BUT I KNEW YOU COULDN'T..
I'M GLAD MY OUTFIELDERS HAVE SUCH INTERESTING DISCUSSIONS!
SCHULZ
5-26

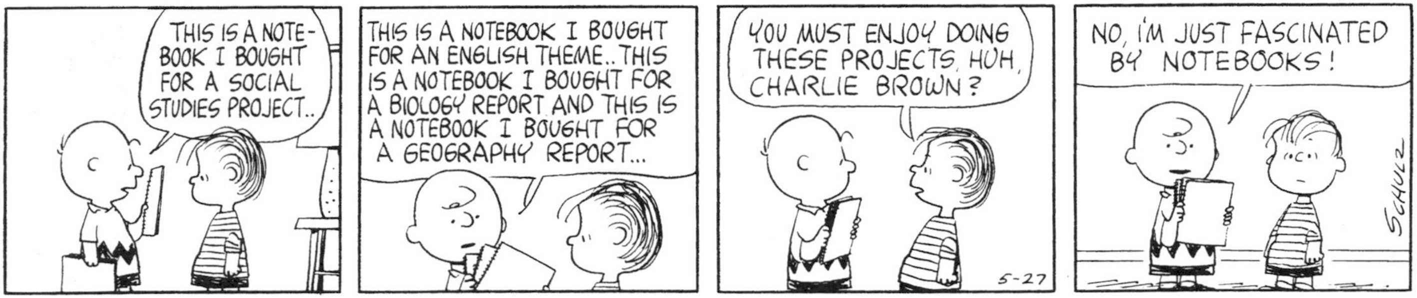
THIS IS A NOTE-BOOK I BOUGHT FOR A SOCIAL STUDIES PROJECT..
THIS IS A NOTEBOOK I BOUGHT FOR AN ENGLISH THEME.. THIS IS A NOTEBOOK I BOUGHT FOR A BIOLOGY REPORT AND THIS IS A NOTEBOOK I BOUGHT FOR A GEOGRAPHY REPORT...
YOU MUST ENJOY DOING THESE PROJECTS, HUH, CHARLIE BROWN?
5-27
NO, I'M JUST FASCINATED BY NOTEBOOKS!
SCHULZ

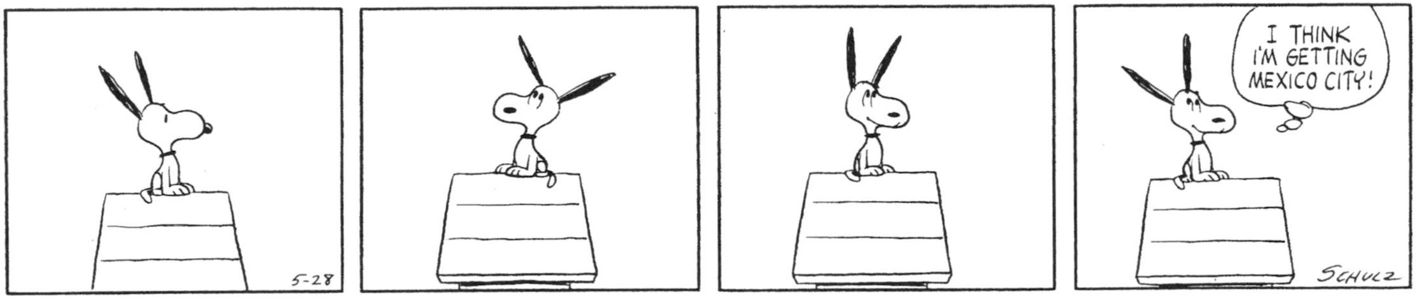
5-28
I THINK I'M GETTING MEXICO CITY!
SCHULZ

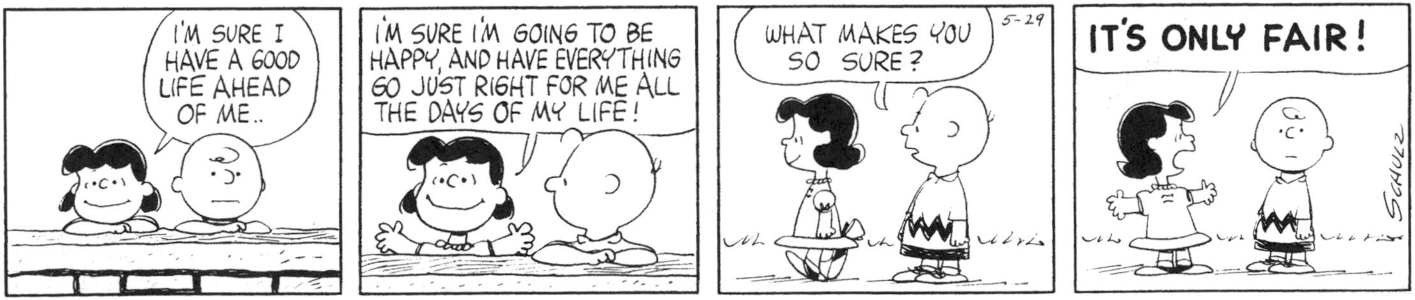
I'M SURE I HAVE A GOOD LIFE AHEAD OF ME..
I'M SURE I'M GOING TO BE HAPPY, AND HAVE EVERYTHING GO JUST RIGHT FOR ME ALL THE DAYS OF MY LIFE!
5-29
WHAT MAKES YOU SO SURE?
IT'S ONLY FAIR!
SCHULZ

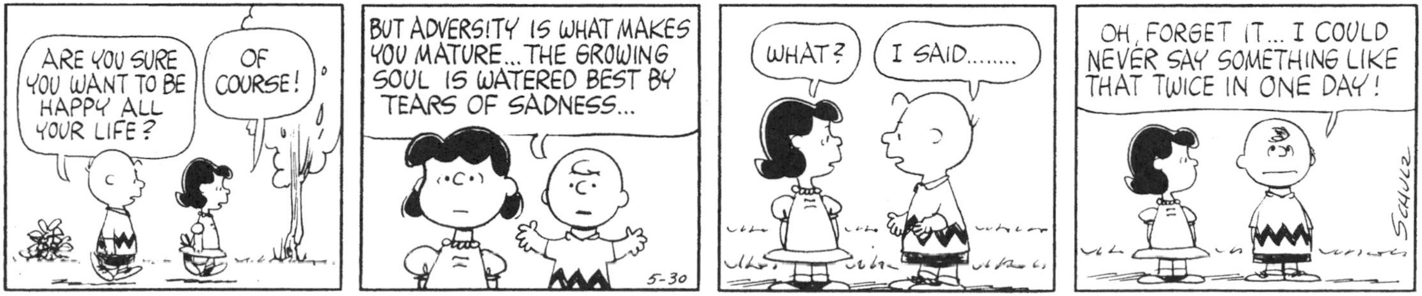
ARE YOU SURE YOU WANT TO BE HAPPY ALL YOUR LIFE?
OF COURSE!
BUT ADVERSITY IS WHAT MAKES YOU MATURE... THE GROWING SOUL IS WATERED BEST BY TEARS OF SADNESS...
5-30
WHAT?
I SAID........
OH, FORGET IT... I COULD NEVER SAY SOMETHING LIKE THAT TWICE IN ONE DAY!
SCHULZ

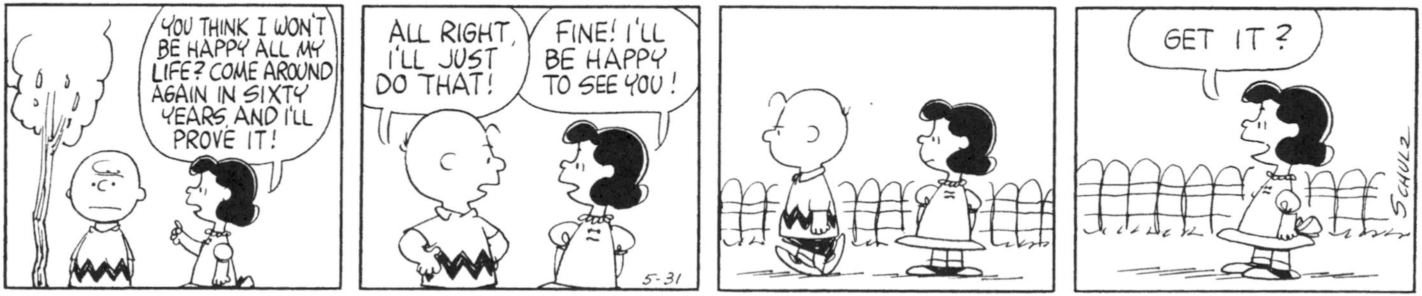
YOU THINK I WON'T BE HAPPY ALL MY LIFE? COME AROUND AGAIN IN SIXTY YEARS, AND I'LL PROVE IT!
ALL RIGHT, I'LL JUST DO THAT!
FINE! I'LL BE HAPPY TO SEE YOU!
5-31
GET IT?
SCHULZ

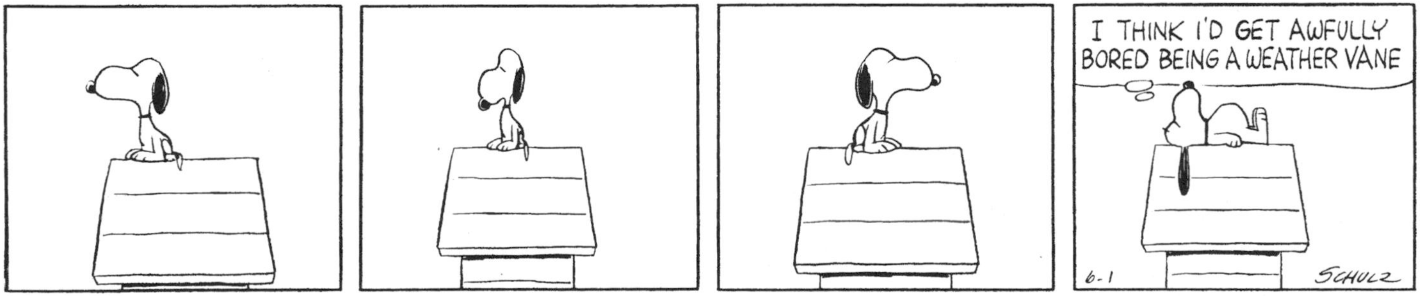
I THINK I'D GET AWFULLY BORED BEING A WEATHER VANE
6-1
SCHULZ

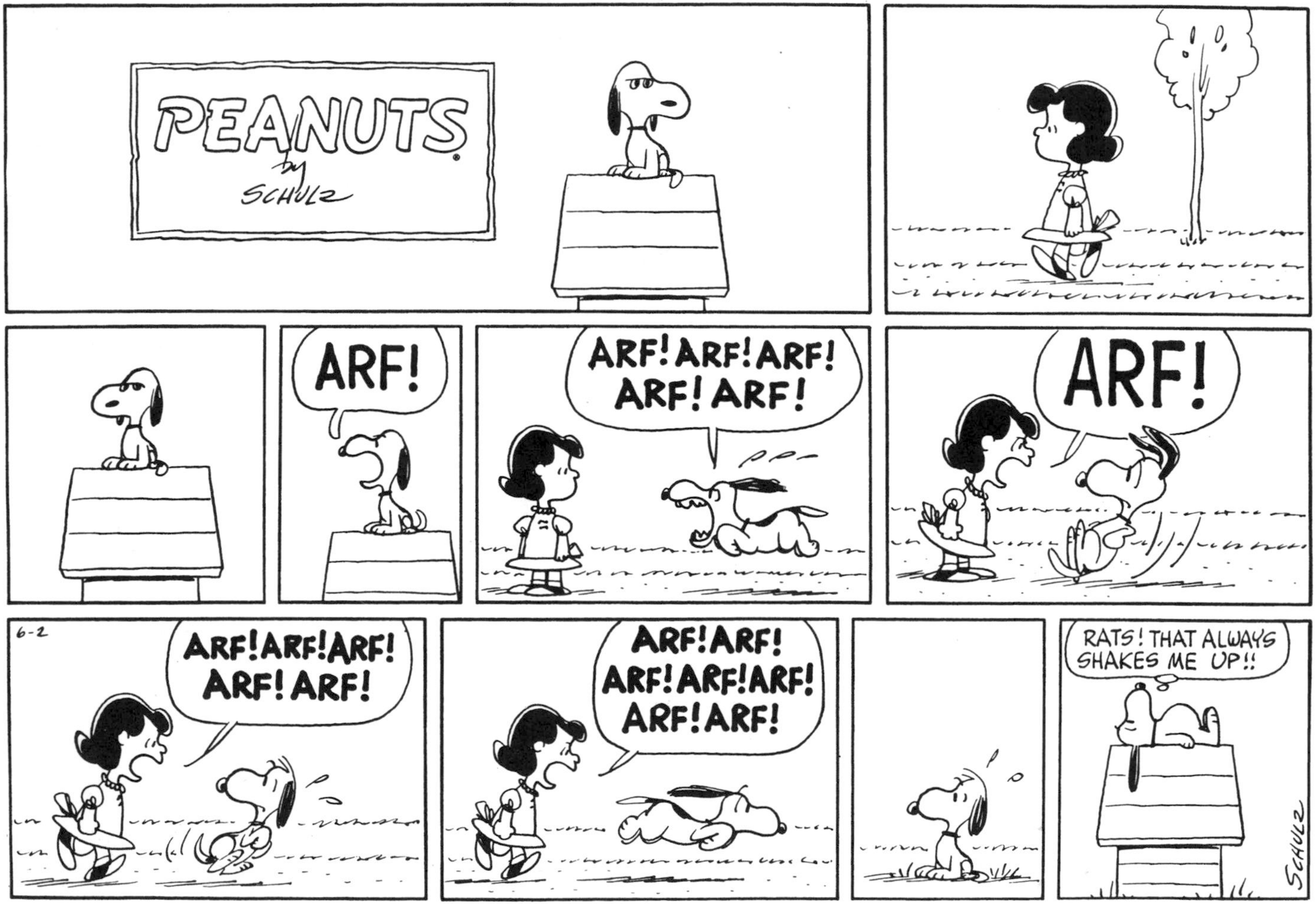
PEANUTS
by SCHULZ
ARF!
ARF! ARF! ARF! ARF! ARF!
ARF!
6-2
ARF! ARF! ARF! ARF! ARF!
ARF! ARF! ARF! ARF! ARF! ARF! ARF!
RATS! THAT ALWAYS SHAKES ME UP!!
SCHULZ

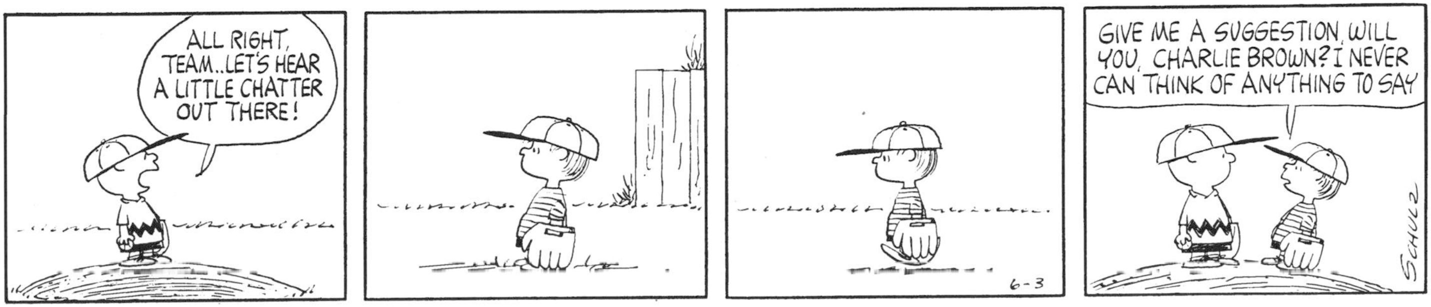
ALL RIGHT, TEAM..LET'S HEAR A LITTLE CHATTER OUT THERE!
6-3
GIVE ME A SUGGESTION, WILL YOU, CHARLIE BROWN? I NEVER CAN THINK OF ANYTHING TO SAY
SCHULZ

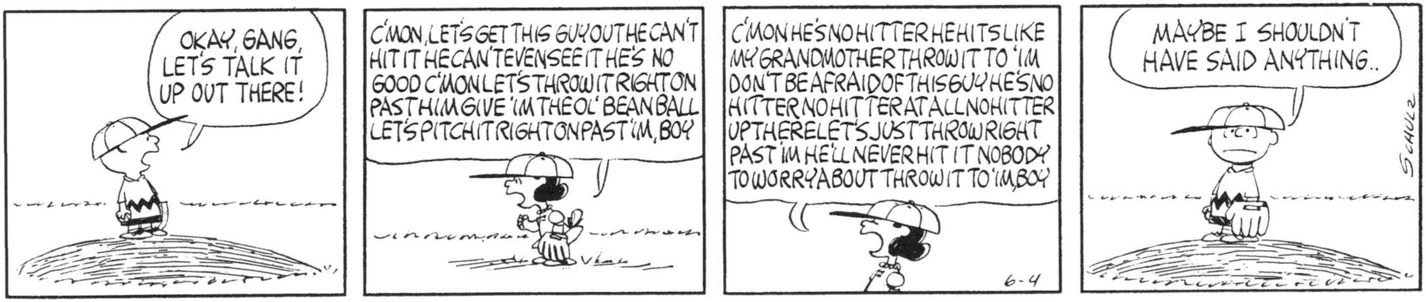
OKAY, GANG, LET'S TALK IT UP OUT THERE!
C'MON, LET'S GET THIS GUY OUT HE CAN'T HIT IT HE CAN'T EVEN SEE IT HE'S NO GOOD C'MON LET'S THROW IT RIGHT ON PAST HIM GIVE 'IM THE OL' BEAN BALL LET'S PITCH IT RIGHT ON PAST 'IM, BOY
C'MON HE'S NO HITTER HE HITS LIKE MY GRANDMOTHER THROW IT TO 'IM DON'T BE AFRAID OF THIS GUY HE'S NO HITTER NO HITTER AT ALL NO HITTER UP THERE LET'S JUST THROW RIGHT PAST 'IM HE'LL NEVER HIT IT NOBODY TO WORRY ABOUT THROW IT TO 'IM, BOY
6-4
MAYBE I SHOULDN'T HAVE SAID ANYTHING..
SCHULZ

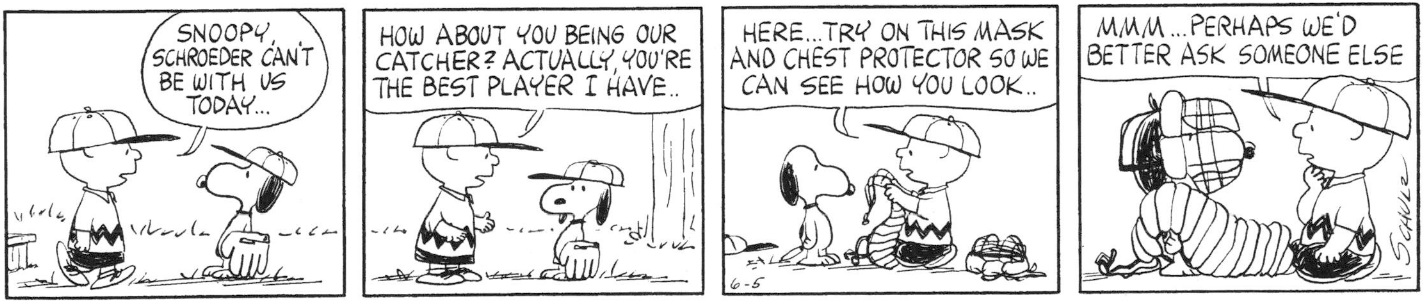
SNOOPY, SCHROEDER CAN'T BE WITH US TODAY...
HOW ABOUT YOU BEING OUR CATCHER? ACTUALLY, YOU'RE THE BEST PLAYER I HAVE..
HERE...TRY ON THIS MASK AND CHEST PROTECTOR SO WE CAN SEE HOW YOU LOOK..
6-5
MMM...PERHAPS WE'D BETTER ASK SOMEONE ELSE
SCHULZ

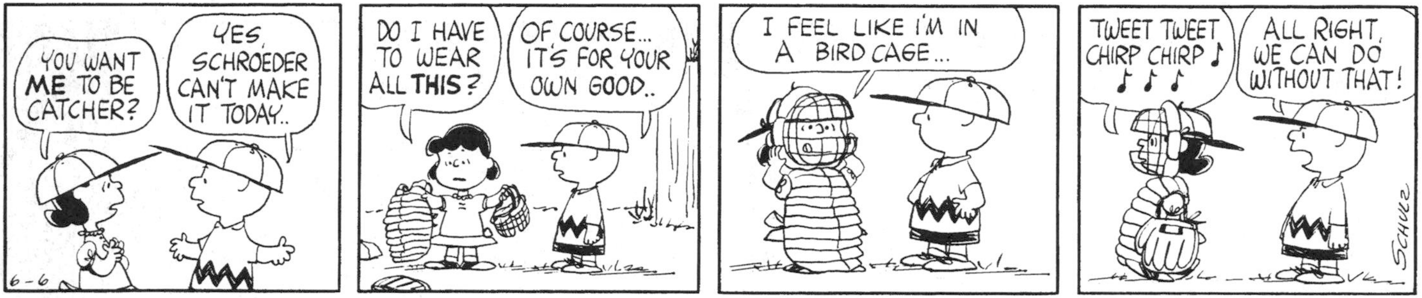
YOU WANT **ME** TO BE CATCHER?
YES, SCHROEDER CAN'T MAKE IT TODAY..
6-6
DO I HAVE TO WEAR ALL **THIS**?
OF COURSE... IT'S FOR YOUR OWN GOOD..
I FEEL LIKE I'M IN A BIRD CAGE...
TWEET TWEET CHIRP CHIRP ♪ ♪ ♪ ♪
ALL RIGHT, WE CAN DO WITHOUT THAT!
SCHULZ

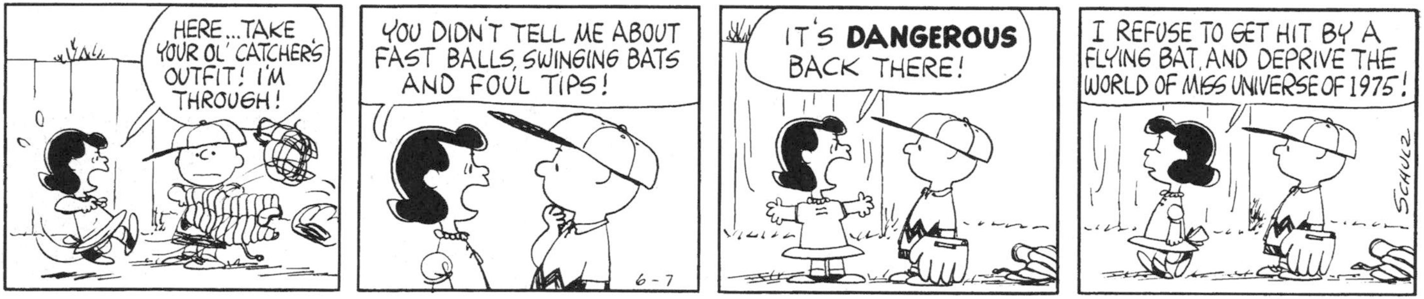
HERE...TAKE YOUR OL' CATCHER'S OUTFIT! I'M THROUGH!
YOU DIDN'T TELL ME ABOUT FAST BALLS, SWINGING BATS AND FOUL TIPS!
6-7
IT'S **DANGEROUS** BACK THERE!
I REFUSE TO GET HIT BY A FLYING BAT, AND DEPRIVE THE WORLD OF MISS UNIVERSE OF 1975!
SCHULZ

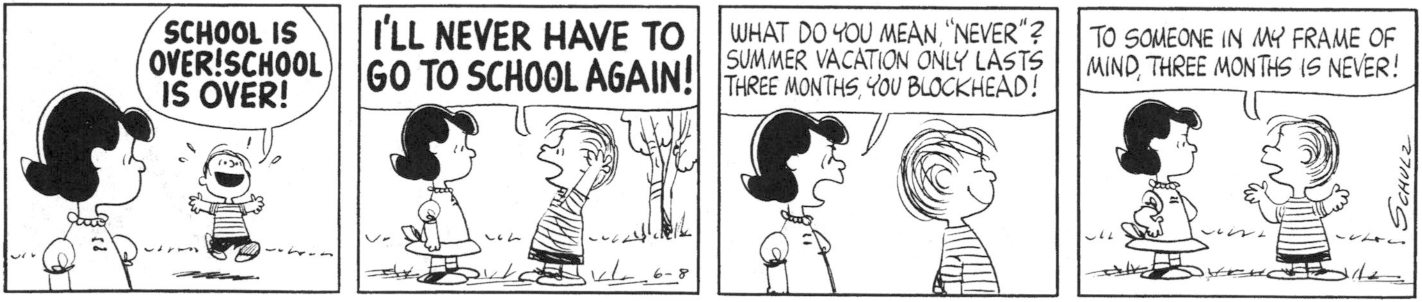
SCHOOL IS OVER! SCHOOL IS OVER!
I'LL NEVER HAVE TO GO TO SCHOOL AGAIN!
6-8
WHAT DO YOU MEAN, "NEVER"? SUMMER VACATION ONLY LASTS THREE MONTHS, YOU BLOCKHEAD!
TO SOMEONE IN MY FRAME OF MIND, THREE MONTHS IS NEVER!
SCHULZ

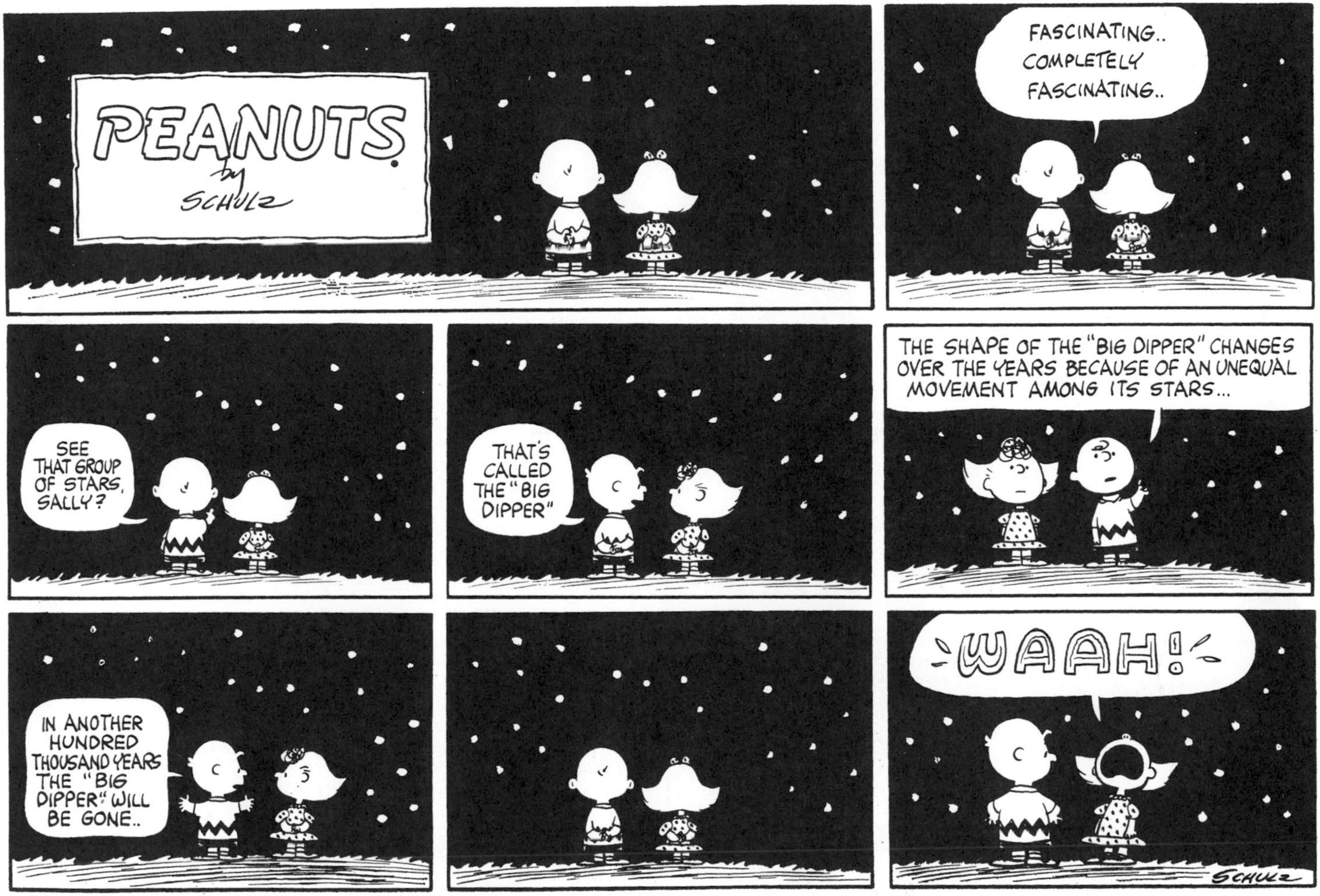
PEANUTS
by SCHULZ
FASCINATING.. COMPLETELY FASCINATING..
SEE THAT GROUP OF STARS, SALLY?
THAT'S CALLED THE "BIG DIPPER"
THE SHAPE OF THE "BIG DIPPER" CHANGES OVER THE YEARS BECAUSE OF AN UNEQUAL MOVEMENT AMONG ITS STARS...
IN ANOTHER HUNDRED THOUSAND YEARS THE "BIG DIPPER" WILL BE GONE..
WAAH!
SCHULZ

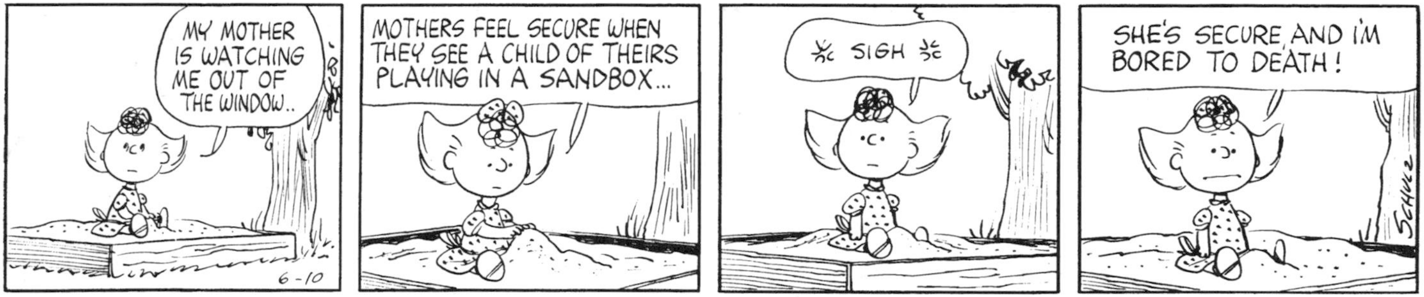
MY MOTHER IS WATCHING ME OUT OF THE WINDOW..
MOTHERS FEEL SECURE WHEN THEY SEE A CHILD OF THEIRS PLAYING IN A SANDBOX...
SIGH
SHE'S SECURE, AND I'M BORED TO DEATH!
SCHULZ
6-10

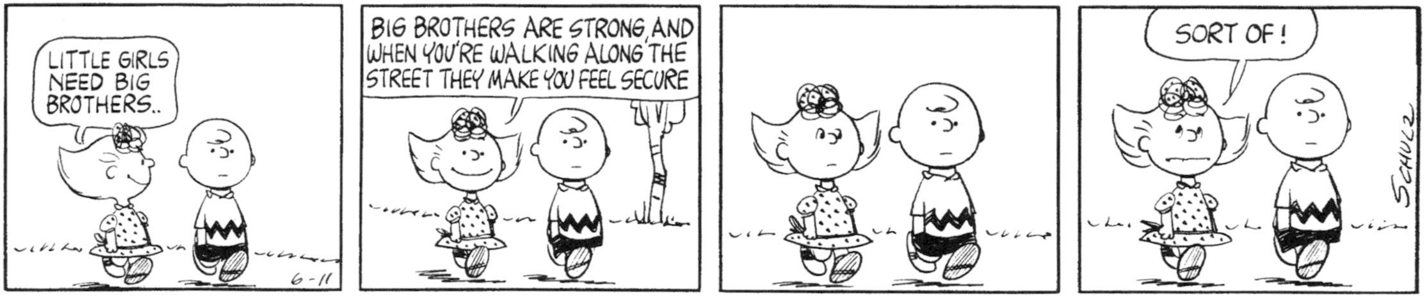
LITTLE GIRLS NEED BIG BROTHERS..
BIG BROTHERS ARE STRONG, AND WHEN YOU'RE WALKING ALONG THE STREET THEY MAKE YOU FEEL SECURE
SORT OF!
SCHULZ
6-11

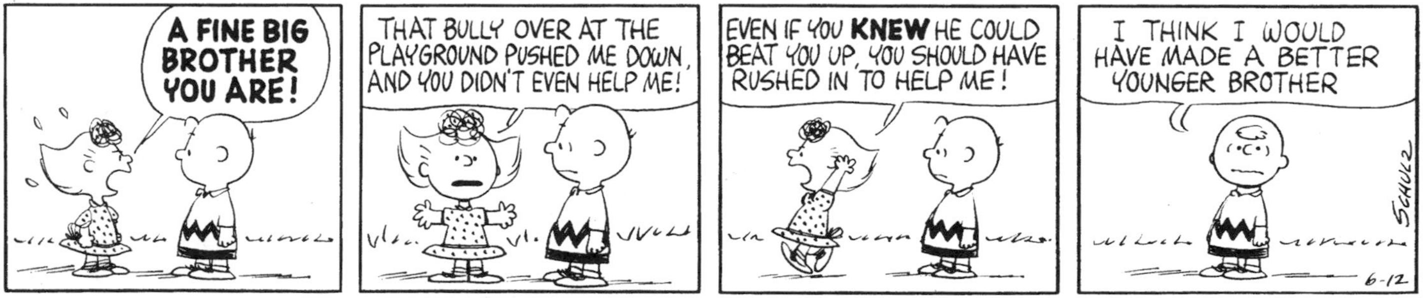
A FINE BIG BROTHER YOU ARE!
THAT BULLY OVER AT THE PLAYGROUND PUSHED ME DOWN, AND YOU DIDN'T EVEN HELP ME!
EVEN IF YOU KNEW HE COULD BEAT YOU UP, YOU SHOULD HAVE RUSHED IN TO HELP ME!
I THINK I WOULD HAVE MADE A BETTER YOUNGER BROTHER
SCHULZ
6-12

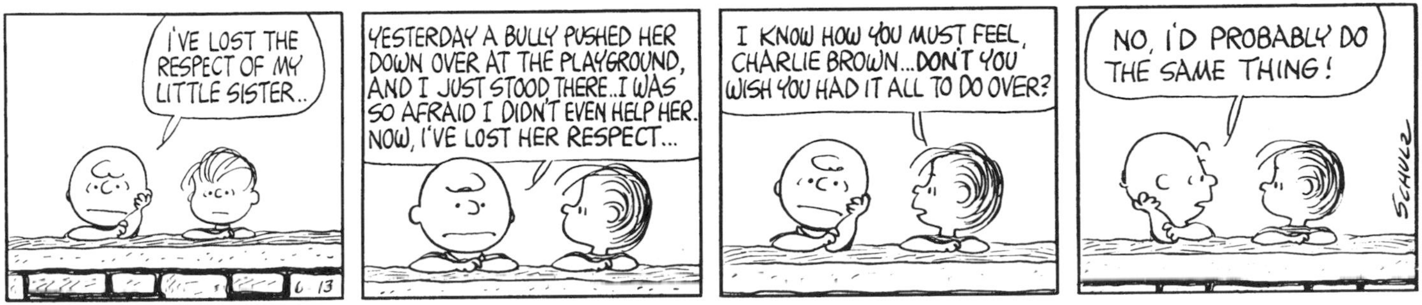
I'VE LOST THE RESPECT OF MY LITTLE SISTER..
YESTERDAY A BULLY PUSHED HER DOWN OVER AT THE PLAYGROUND, AND I JUST STOOD THERE..I WAS SO AFRAID I DIDN'T EVEN HELP HER. NOW, I'VE LOST HER RESPECT...
I KNOW HOW YOU MUST FEEL, CHARLIE BROWN...DON'T YOU WISH YOU HAD IT ALL TO DO OVER?
NO, I'D PROBABLY DO THE SAME THING!
SCHULZ
6-13

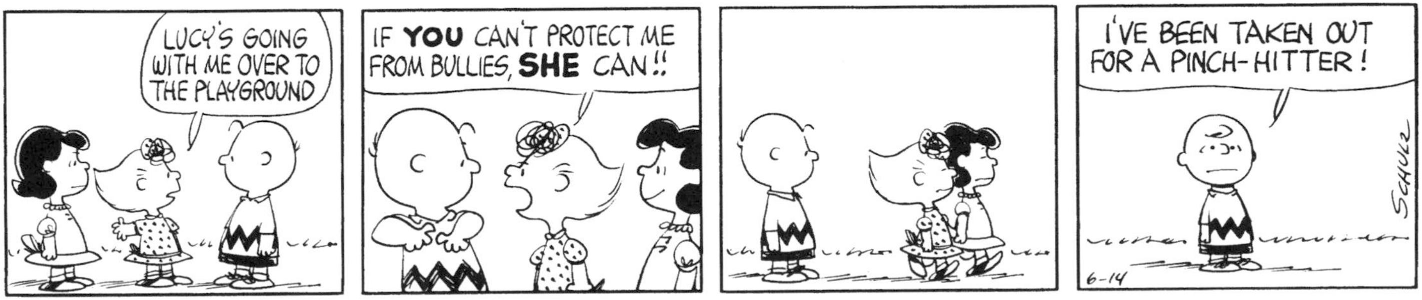
LUCY'S GOING WITH ME OVER TO THE PLAYGROUND
IF **YOU** CAN'T PROTECT ME FROM BULLIES, **SHE** CAN!!
I'VE BEEN TAKEN OUT FOR A PINCH-HITTER!
SCHULZ
6-14

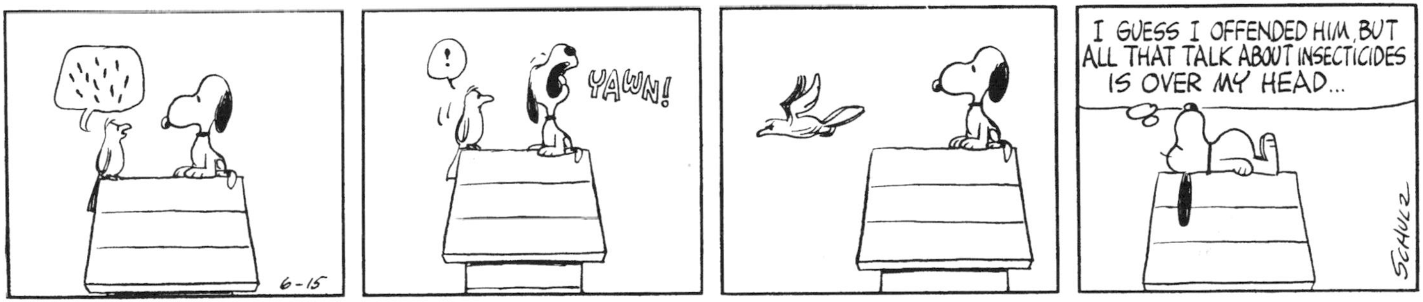
!
YAWN!
I GUESS I OFFENDED HIM, BUT ALL THAT TALK ABOUT INSECTICIDES IS OVER MY HEAD...
SCHULZ
6-15

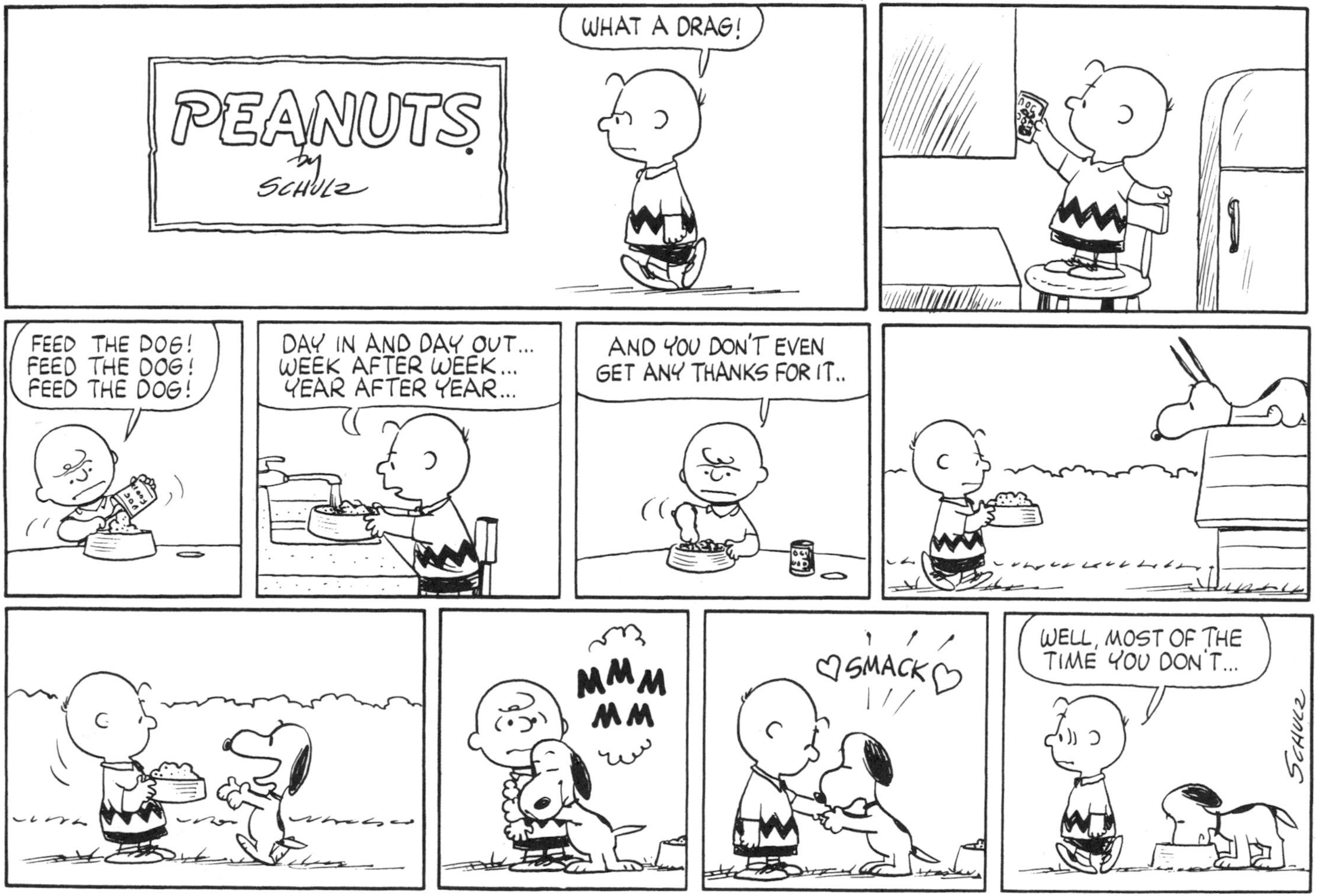
PEANUTS
by SCHULZ
WHAT A DRAG!
FEED THE DOG! FEED THE DOG! FEED THE DOG!
DAY IN AND DAY OUT... WEEK AFTER WEEK... YEAR AFTER YEAR...
AND YOU DON'T EVEN GET ANY THANKS FOR IT..
MMM MM
SMACK
WELL, MOST OF THE TIME YOU DON'T...
SCHULZ

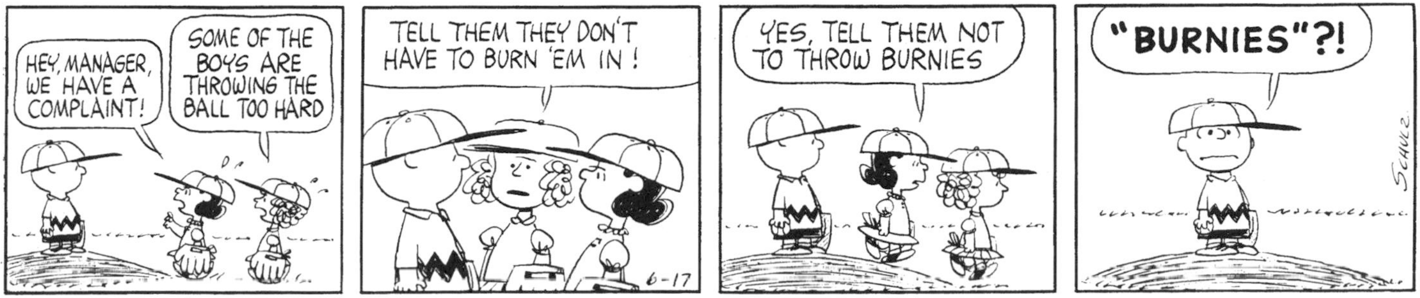
HEY, MANAGER, WE HAVE A COMPLAINT!
SOME OF THE BOYS ARE THROWING THE BALL TOO HARD
TELL THEM THEY DON'T HAVE TO BURN 'EM IN!
YES, TELL THEM NOT TO THROW BURNIES
"BURNIES"?!
6-17
SCHULZ

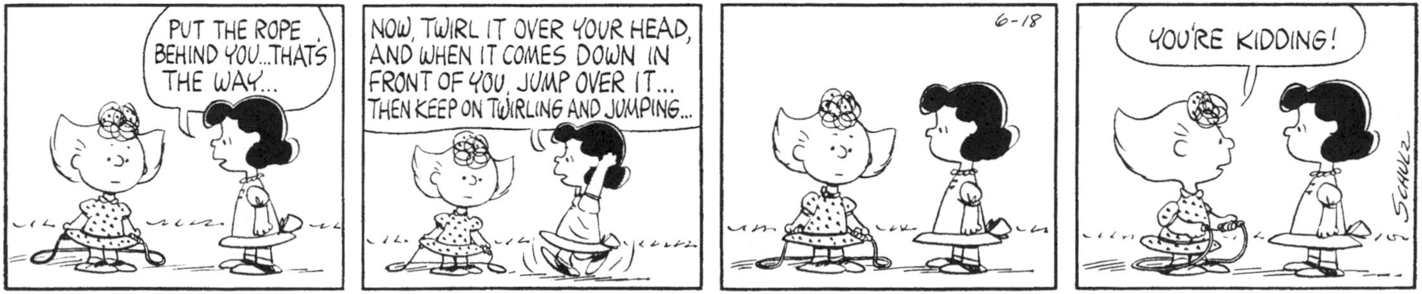
PUT THE ROPE BEHIND YOU...THAT'S THE WAY...
NOW, TWIRL IT OVER YOUR HEAD, AND WHEN IT COMES DOWN IN FRONT OF YOU, JUMP OVER IT... THEN KEEP ON TWIRLING AND JUMPING...
6-18
YOU'RE KIDDING!
SCHULZ

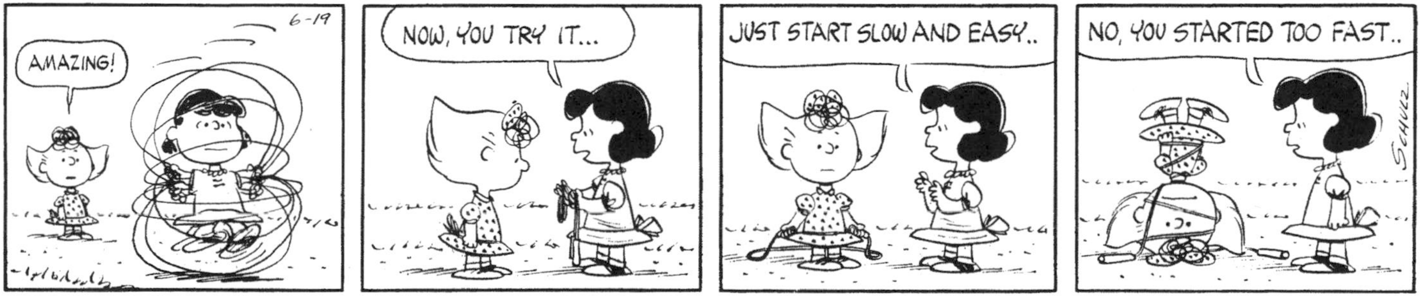
6-19
AMAZING!
NOW, YOU TRY IT...
JUST START SLOW AND EASY..
NO, YOU STARTED TOO FAST..
SCHULZ

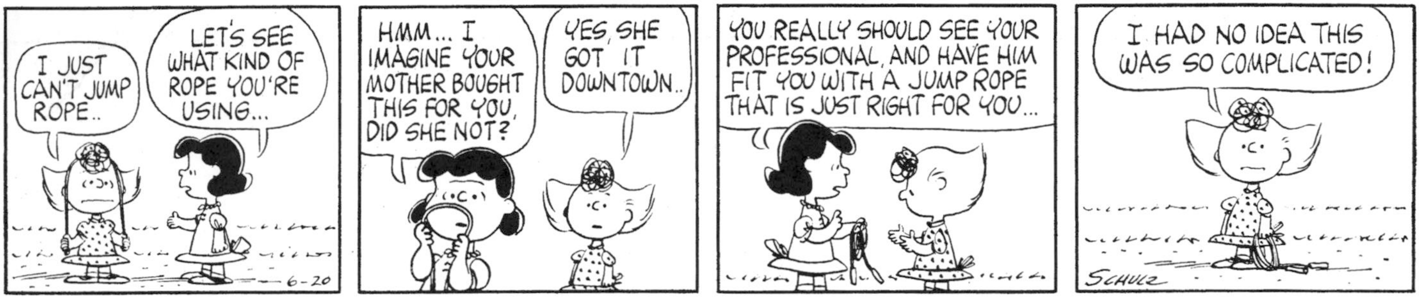
I JUST CAN'T JUMP ROPE..
LET'S SEE WHAT KIND OF ROPE YOU'RE USING...
HMM... I IMAGINE YOUR MOTHER BOUGHT THIS FOR YOU, DID SHE NOT?
YES, SHE GOT IT DOWNTOWN..
YOU REALLY SHOULD SEE YOUR PROFESSIONAL, AND HAVE HIM FIT YOU WITH A JUMP ROPE THAT IS JUST RIGHT FOR YOU...
I HAD NO IDEA THIS WAS SO COMPLICATED!
6-20
SCHULZ

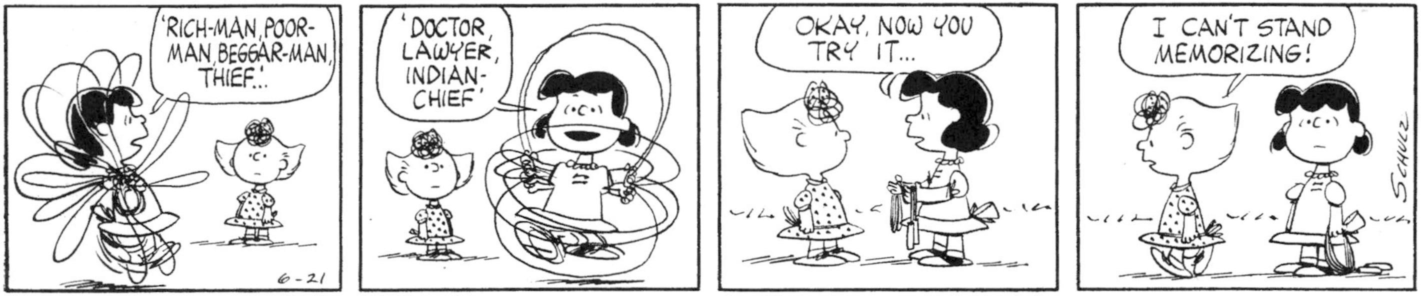
'RICH-MAN, POOR-MAN, BEGGAR-MAN, THIEF.'..
6-21
'DOCTOR, LAWYER, INDIAN-CHIEF'
OKAY, NOW YOU TRY IT...
I CAN'T STAND MEMORIZING!
SCHULZ

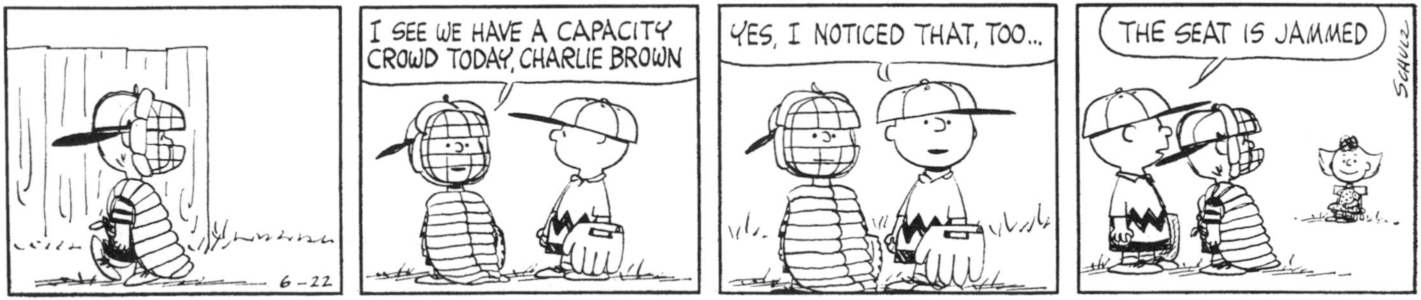
6-22
I SEE WE HAVE A CAPACITY CROWD TODAY, CHARLIE BROWN
YES, I NOTICED THAT, TOO...
THE SEAT IS JAMMED
SCHULZ

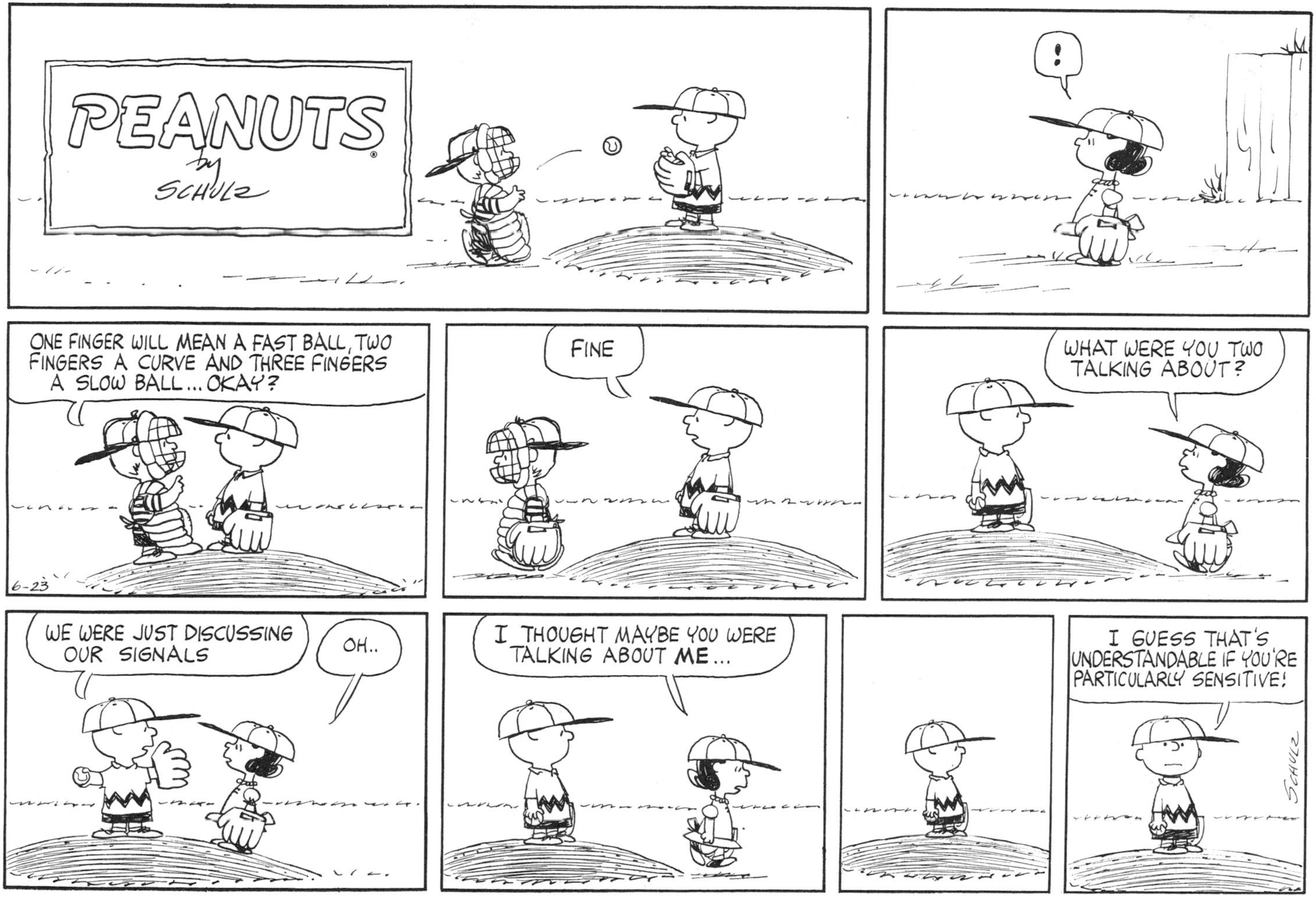
PEANUTS
by SCHULZ
!
ONE FINGER WILL MEAN A FAST BALL, TWO FINGERS A CURVE AND THREE FINGERS A SLOW BALL... OKAY?
6-23
FINE
WHAT WERE YOU TWO TALKING ABOUT?
WE WERE JUST DISCUSSING OUR SIGNALS
OH..
I THOUGHT MAYBE YOU WERE TALKING ABOUT ME...
I GUESS THAT'S UNDERSTANDABLE IF YOU'RE PARTICULARLY SENSITIVE!
SCHULZ

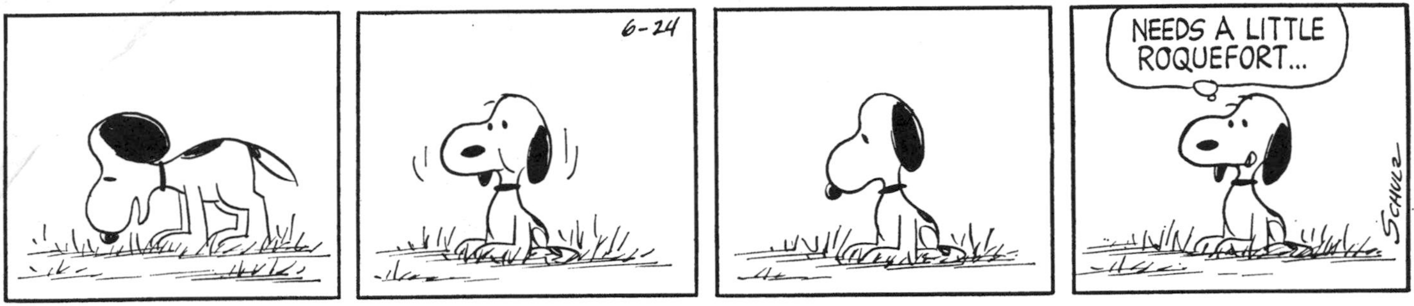
6-24
NEEDS A LITTLE ROQUEFORT...
SCHULZ

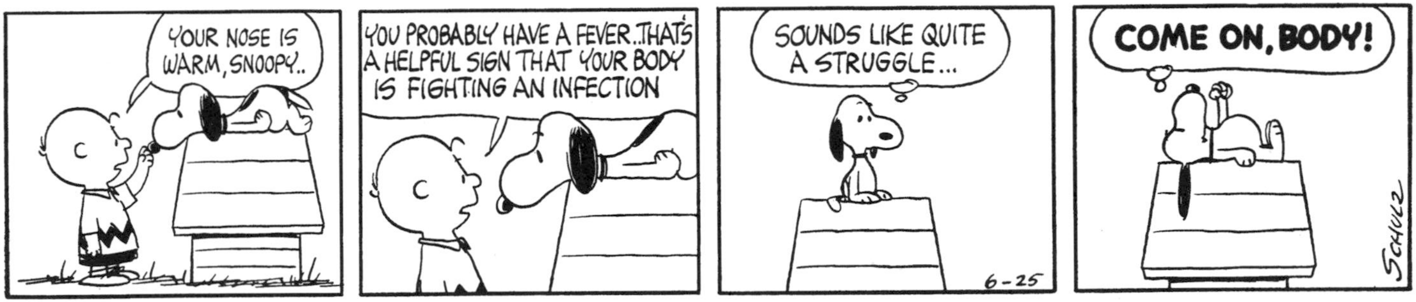
YOUR NOSE IS WARM, SNOOPY..
YOU PROBABLY HAVE A FEVER..THAT'S A HELPFUL SIGN THAT YOUR BODY IS FIGHTING AN INFECTION
SOUNDS LIKE QUITE A STRUGGLE...
6-25
COME ON, BODY!
SCHULZ

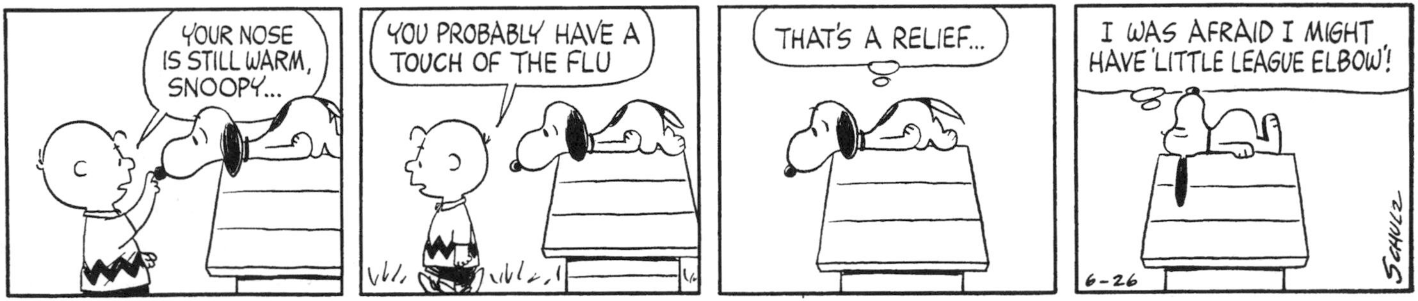
YOUR NOSE IS STILL WARM, SNOOPY...
YOU PROBABLY HAVE A TOUCH OF THE FLU
THAT'S A RELIEF...
I WAS AFRAID I MIGHT HAVE 'LITTLE LEAGUE ELBOW'!
6-26
SCHULZ

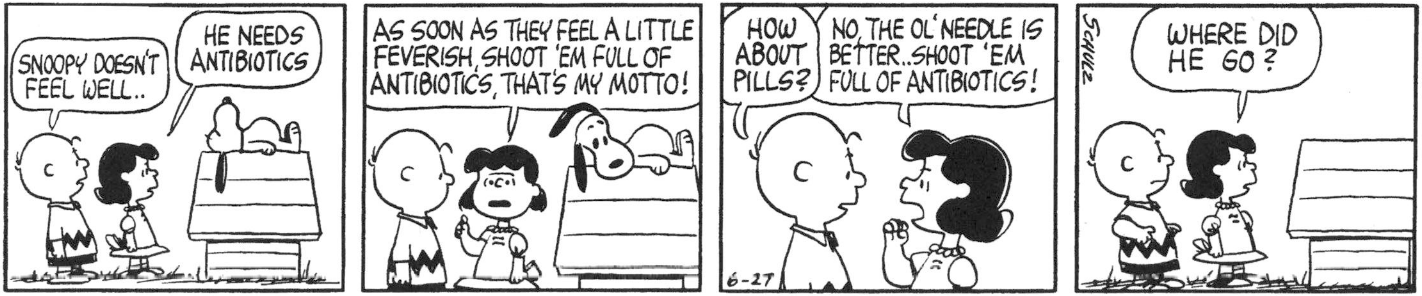
SNOOPY DOESN'T FEEL WELL..
HE NEEDS ANTIBIOTICS
AS SOON AS THEY FEEL A LITTLE FEVERISH, SHOOT 'EM FULL OF ANTIBIOTICS, THAT'S MY MOTTO!
HOW ABOUT PILLS?
NO, THE OL' NEEDLE IS BETTER..SHOOT 'EM FULL OF ANTIBIOTICS!
6-27
SCHULZ
WHERE DID HE GO?

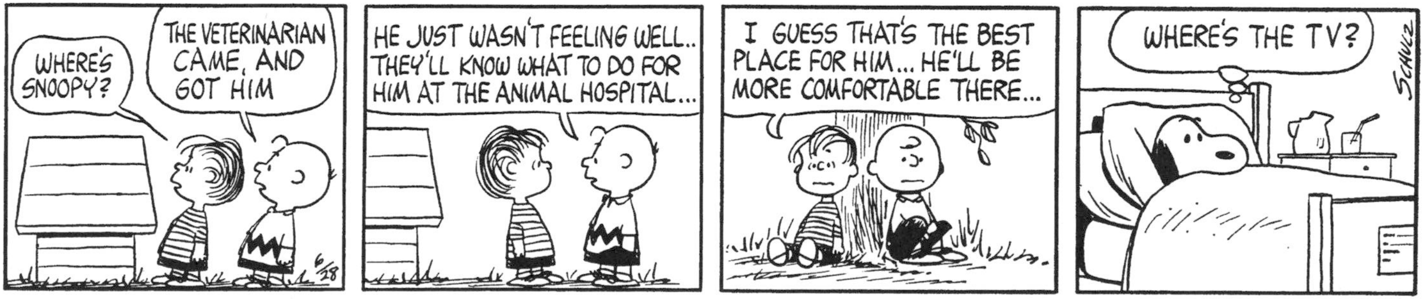
WHERE'S SNOOPY?
THE VETERINARIAN CAME, AND GOT HIM
6/28
HE JUST WASN'T FEELING WELL.. THEY'LL KNOW WHAT TO DO FOR HIM AT THE ANIMAL HOSPITAL...
I GUESS THAT'S THE BEST PLACE FOR HIM... HE'LL BE MORE COMFORTABLE THERE...
WHERE'S THE TV?
SCHULZ

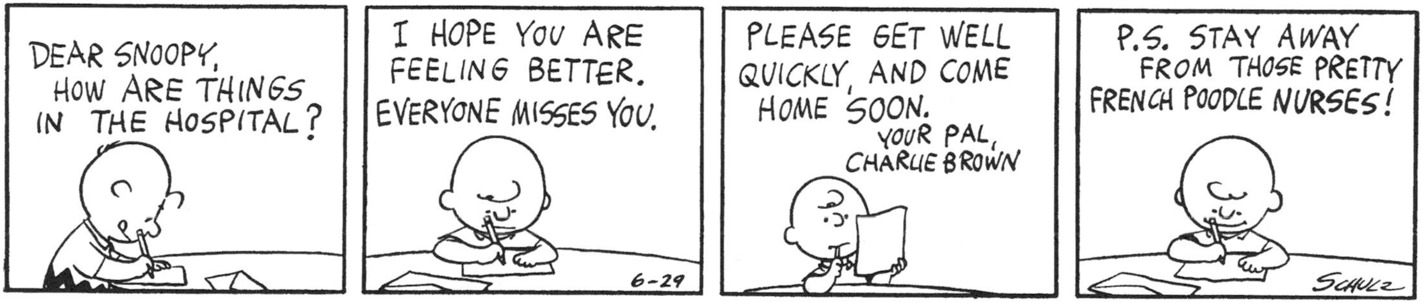
DEAR SNOOPY, HOW ARE THINGS IN THE HOSPITAL?
I HOPE YOU ARE FEELING BETTER.
EVERYONE MISSES YOU.
6-29
PLEASE GET WELL QUICKLY, AND COME HOME SOON.
YOUR PAL, CHARLIE BROWN
P.S. STAY AWAY FROM THOSE PRETTY FRENCH POODLE NURSES!
SCHULZ

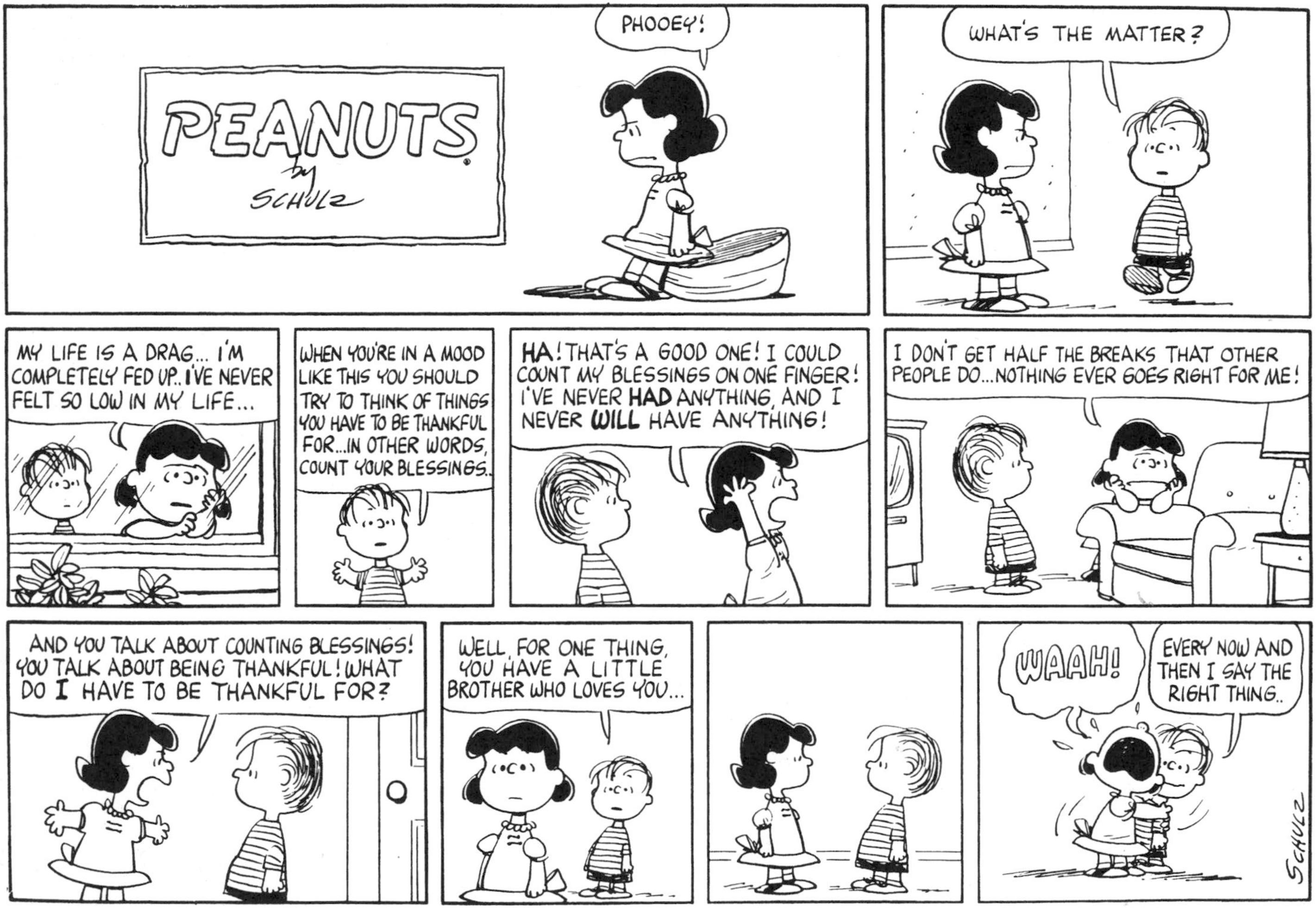
PEANUTS
by SCHULZ
PHOOEY!
WHAT'S THE MATTER?
MY LIFE IS A DRAG... I'M COMPLETELY FED UP.. I'VE NEVER FELT SO LOW IN MY LIFE...
WHEN YOU'RE IN A MOOD LIKE THIS YOU SHOULD TRY TO THINK OF THINGS YOU HAVE TO BE THANKFUL FOR...IN OTHER WORDS, COUNT YOUR BLESSINGS..
HA! THAT'S A GOOD ONE! I COULD COUNT MY BLESSINGS ON ONE FINGER! I'VE NEVER HAD ANYTHING, AND I NEVER WILL HAVE ANYTHING!
I DON'T GET HALF THE BREAKS THAT OTHER PEOPLE DO...NOTHING EVER GOES RIGHT FOR ME!
AND YOU TALK ABOUT COUNTING BLESSINGS! YOU TALK ABOUT BEING THANKFUL! WHAT DO I HAVE TO BE THANKFUL FOR?
WELL, FOR ONE THING, YOU HAVE A LITTLE BROTHER WHO LOVES YOU...
WAAH!
EVERY NOW AND THEN I SAY THE RIGHT THING..
SCHULZ

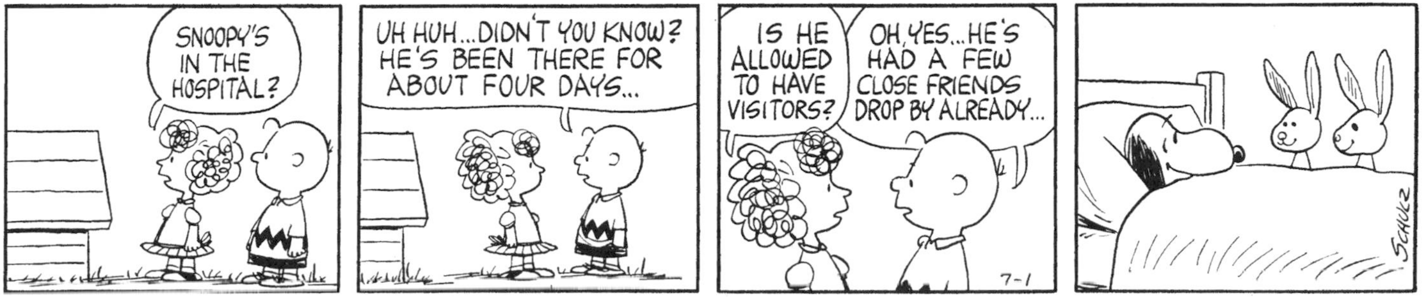
SNOOPY'S IN THE HOSPITAL?
UH HUH...DIDN'T YOU KNOW? HE'S BEEN THERE FOR ABOUT FOUR DAYS...
IS HE ALLOWED TO HAVE VISITORS?
OH, YES...HE'S HAD A FEW CLOSE FRIENDS DROP BY ALREADY...
7-1
SCHULZ

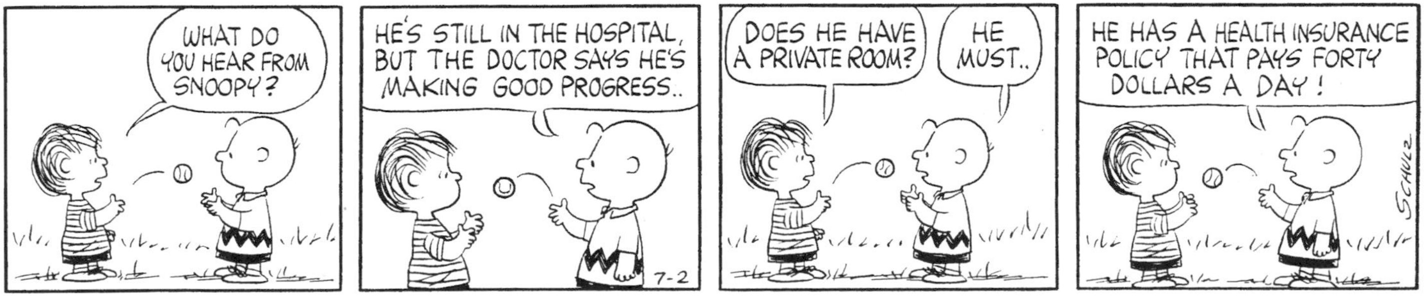
WHAT DO YOU HEAR FROM SNOOPY?
HE'S STILL IN THE HOSPITAL, BUT THE DOCTOR SAYS HE'S MAKING GOOD PROGRESS..
7-2
DOES HE HAVE A PRIVATE ROOM?
HE MUST..
HE HAS A HEALTH INSURANCE POLICY THAT PAYS FORTY DOLLARS A DAY!
SCHULZ

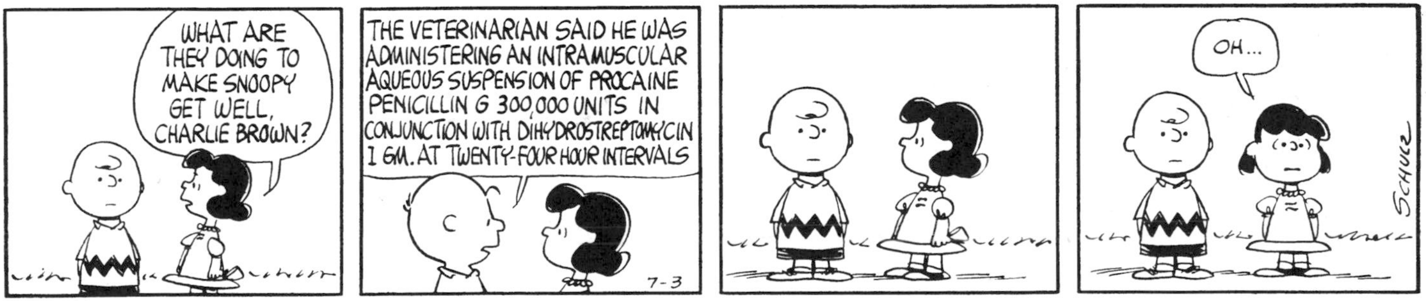
WHAT ARE THEY DOING TO MAKE SNOOPY GET WELL, CHARLIE BROWN?
THE VETERINARIAN SAID HE WAS ADMINISTERING AN INTRAMUSCULAR AQUEOUS SUSPENSION OF PROCAINE PENICILLIN G 300,000 UNITS IN CONJUNCTION WITH DIHYDROSTREPTOMYCIN 1 GM. AT TWENTY-FOUR HOUR INTERVALS
7-3
OH...
SCHULZ

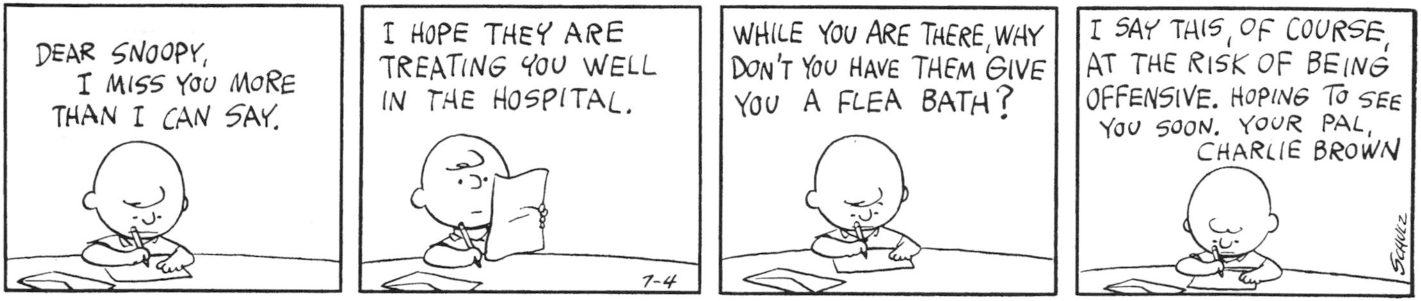
DEAR SNOOPY,
I MISS YOU MORE THAN I CAN SAY.
I HOPE THEY ARE TREATING YOU WELL IN THE HOSPITAL.
7-4
WHILE YOU ARE THERE, WHY DON'T YOU HAVE THEM GIVE YOU A FLEA BATH?
I SAY THIS, OF COURSE, AT THE RISK OF BEING OFFENSIVE. HOPING TO SEE YOU SOON. YOUR PAL, CHARLIE BROWN
SCHULZ

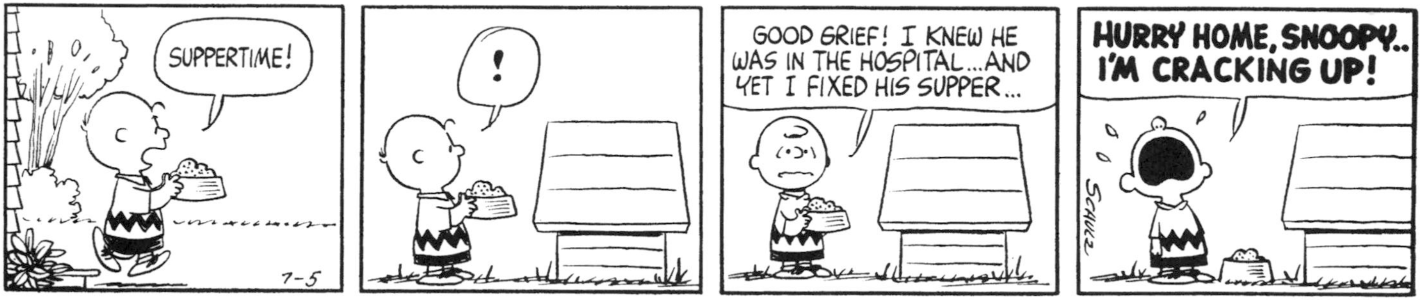
SUPPERTIME!
7-5
!
GOOD GRIEF! I KNEW HE WAS IN THE HOSPITAL...AND YET I FIXED HIS SUPPER...
HURRY HOME, SNOOPY.. I'M CRACKING UP!
SCHULZ

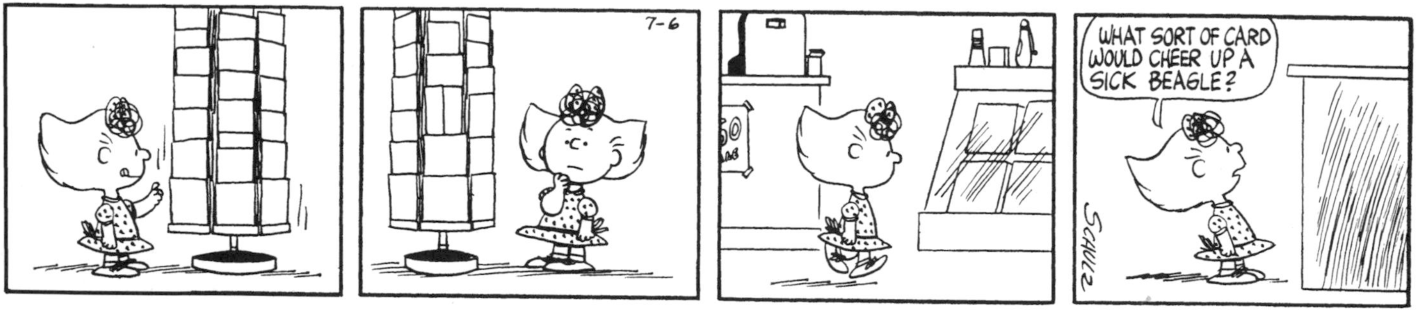
7-6
WHAT SORT OF CARD WOULD CHEER UP A SICK BEAGLE?
SCHULZ

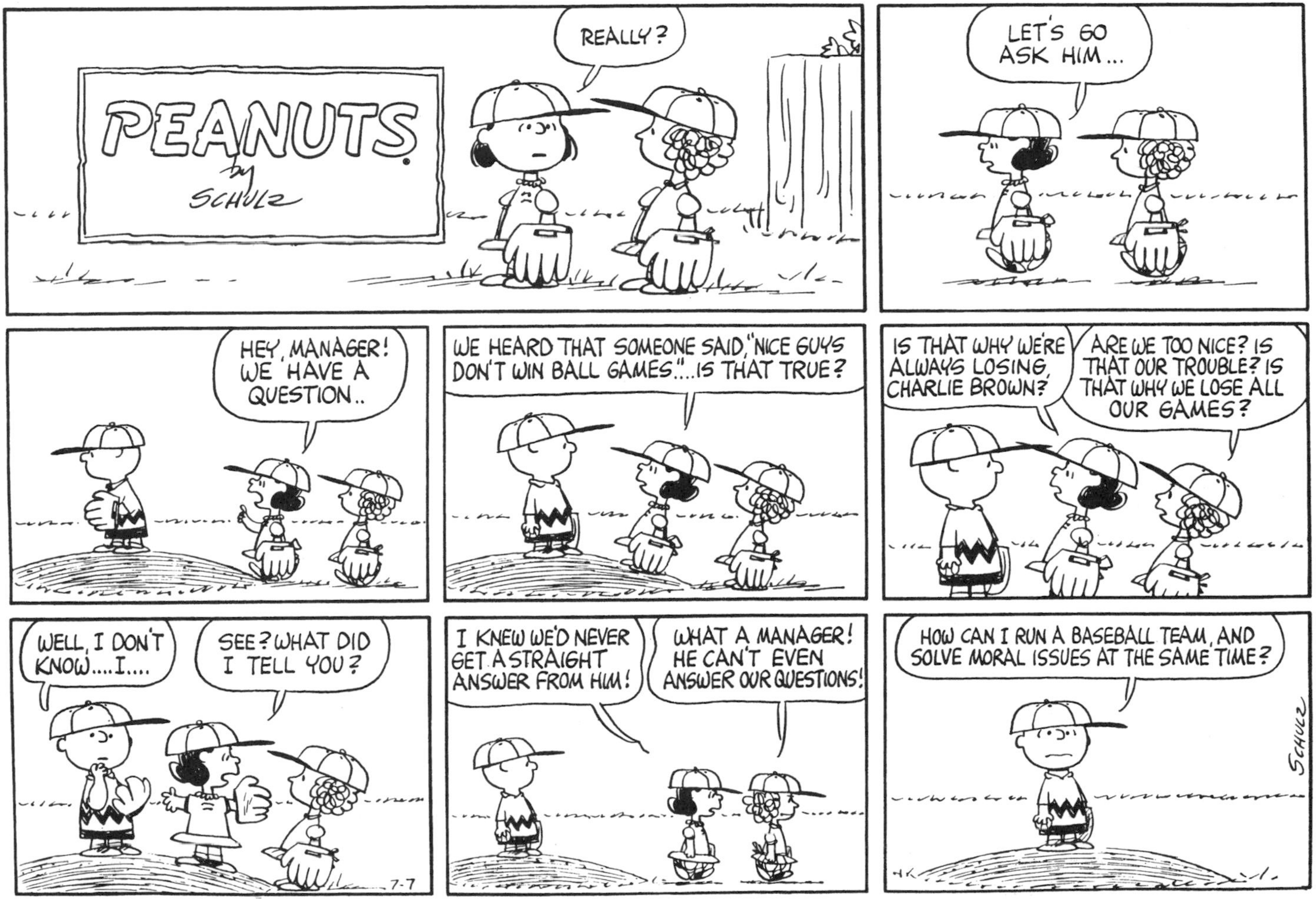
PEANUTS
by SCHULZ
REALLY?
LET'S GO ASK HIM...
HEY, MANAGER! WE HAVE A QUESTION..
WE HEARD THAT SOMEONE SAID, "NICE GUYS DON'T WIN BALL GAMES."...IS THAT TRUE?
IS THAT WHY WE'RE ALWAYS LOSING, CHARLIE BROWN?
ARE WE TOO NICE? IS THAT OUR TROUBLE? IS THAT WHY WE LOSE ALL OUR GAMES?
WELL, I DON'T KNOW....I....
SEE? WHAT DID I TELL YOU?
7-7
I KNEW WE'D NEVER GET A STRAIGHT ANSWER FROM HIM!
WHAT A MANAGER! HE CAN'T EVEN ANSWER OUR QUESTIONS!
HOW CAN I RUN A BASEBALL TEAM, AND SOLVE MORAL ISSUES AT THE SAME TIME?
SCHULZ

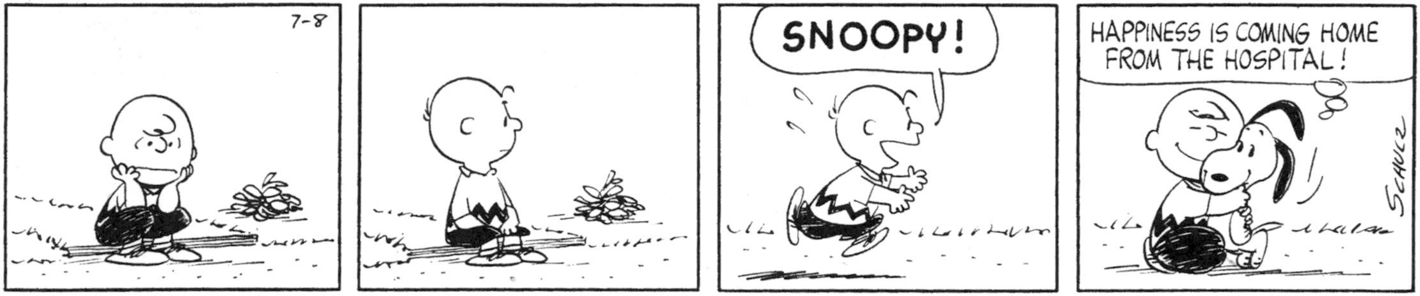
7-8
SNOOPY!
HAPPINESS IS COMING HOME FROM THE HOSPITAL!
SCHULZ

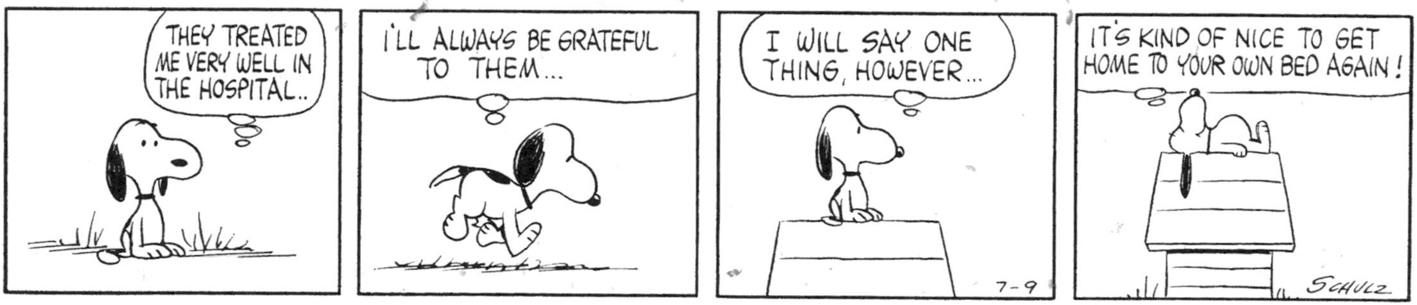
THEY TREATED ME VERY WELL IN THE HOSPITAL..
I'LL ALWAYS BE GRATEFUL TO THEM...
I WILL SAY ONE THING, HOWEVER...
7-9
IT'S KIND OF NICE TO GET HOME TO YOUR OWN BED AGAIN!
SCHULZ

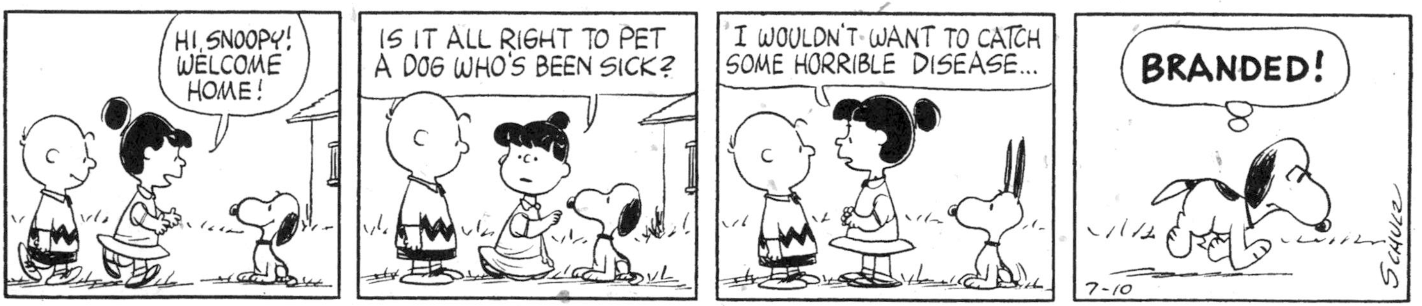
HI, SNOOPY! WELCOME HOME!
IS IT ALL RIGHT TO PET A DOG WHO'S BEEN SICK?
I WOULDN'T WANT TO CATCH SOME HORRIBLE DISEASE...
BRANDED!
7-10
SCHULZ

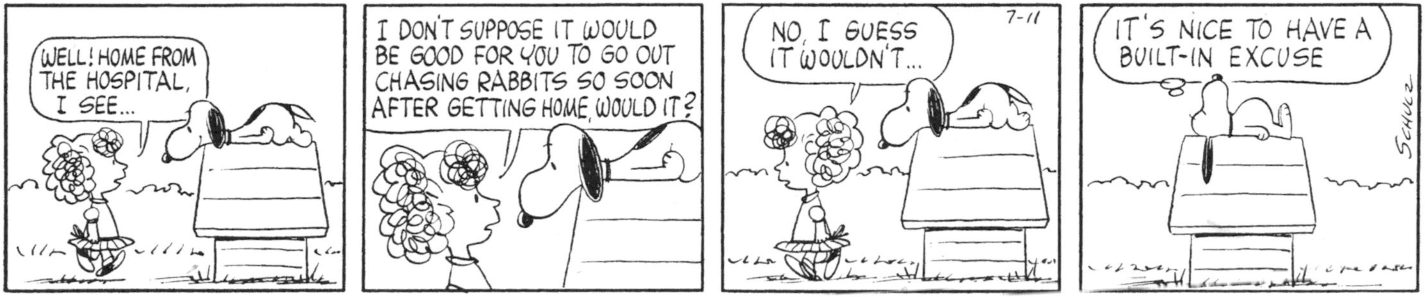
WELL! HOME FROM THE HOSPITAL, I SEE...
I DON'T SUPPOSE IT WOULD BE GOOD FOR YOU TO GO OUT CHASING RABBITS SO SOON AFTER GETTING HOME, WOULD IT?
NO, I GUESS IT WOULDN'T...
7-11
IT'S NICE TO HAVE A BUILT-IN EXCUSE
SCHULZ

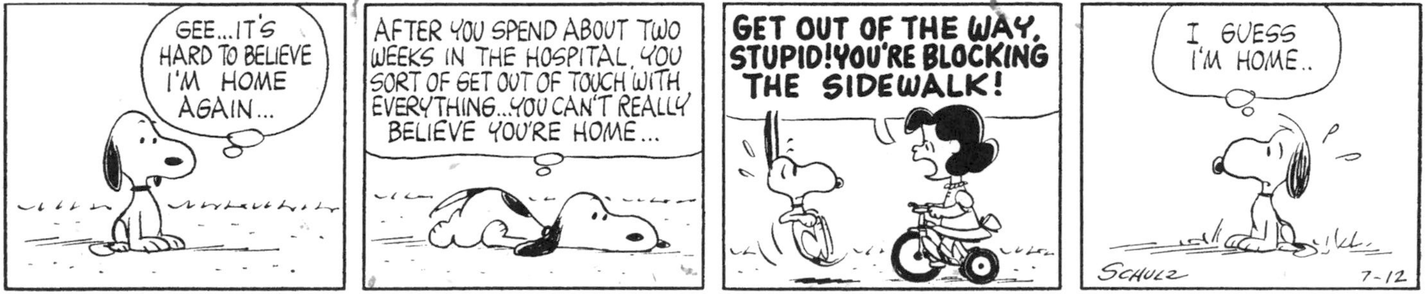
GEE...IT'S HARD TO BELIEVE I'M HOME AGAIN...
AFTER YOU SPEND ABOUT TWO WEEKS IN THE HOSPITAL, YOU SORT OF GET OUT OF TOUCH WITH EVERYTHING...YOU CAN'T REALLY BELIEVE YOU'RE HOME...
GET OUT OF THE WAY, STUPID! YOU'RE BLOCKING THE SIDEWALK!
I GUESS I'M HOME..
SCHULZ
7-12

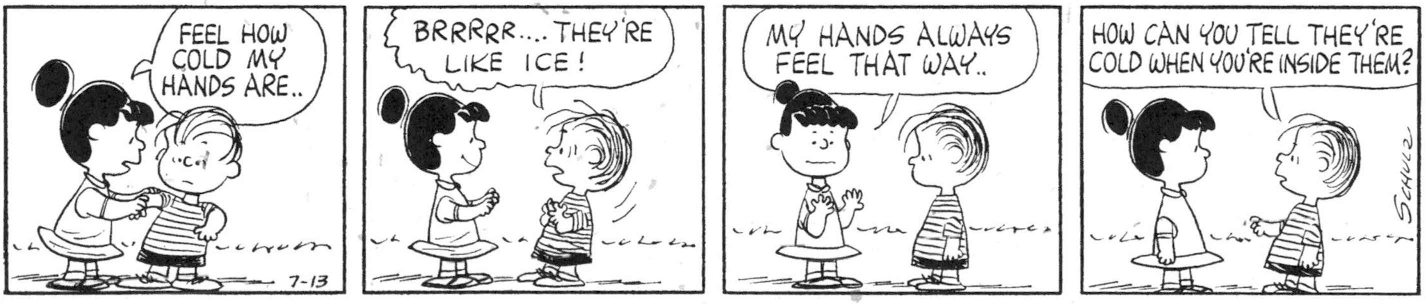
FEEL HOW COLD MY HANDS ARE..
7-13
BRRRRR.... THEY'RE LIKE ICE!
MY HANDS ALWAYS FEEL THAT WAY..
HOW CAN YOU TELL THEY'RE COLD WHEN YOU'RE INSIDE THEM?
SCHULZ

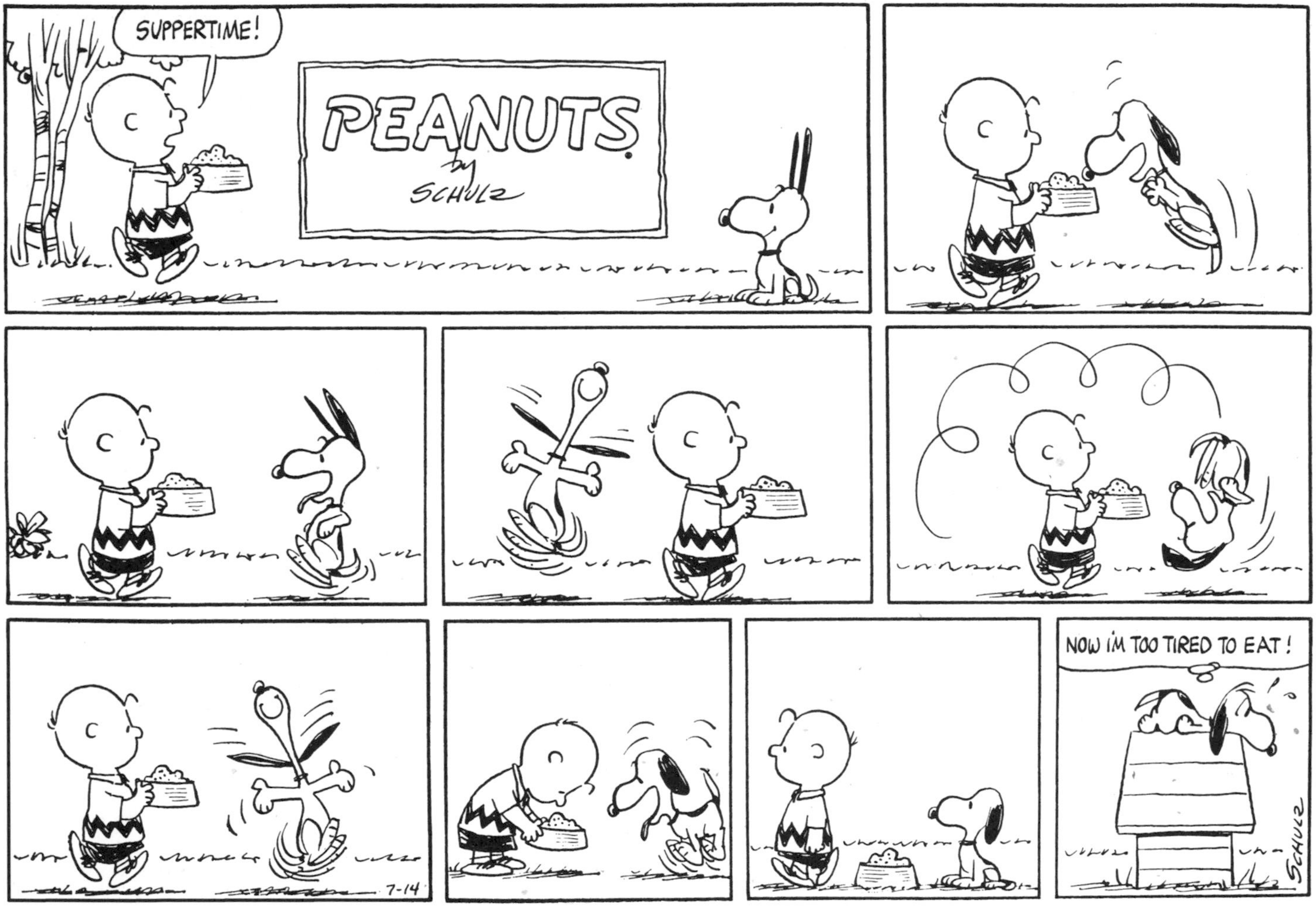
SUPPERTIME!
PEANUTS
by SCHULZ
7-14
NOW I'M TOO TIRED TO EAT!
SCHULZ

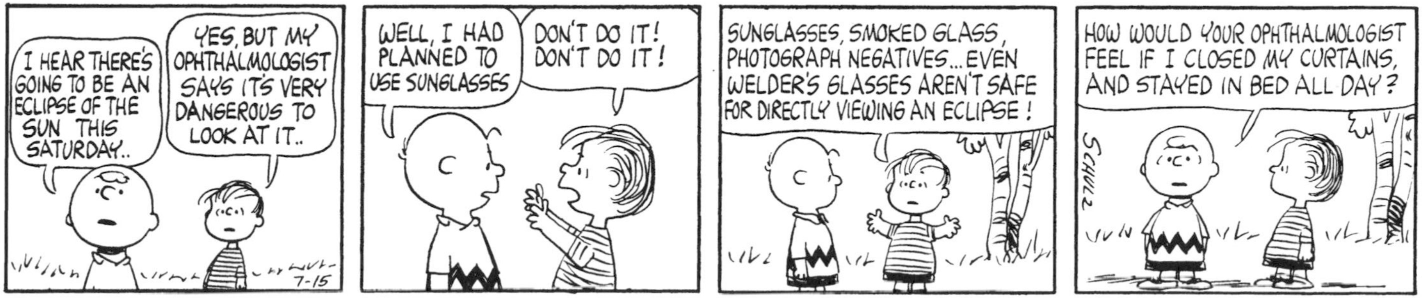
I HEAR THERE'S GOING TO BE AN ECLIPSE OF THE SUN THIS SATURDAY..
YES, BUT MY OPHTHALMOLOGIST SAYS IT'S VERY DANGEROUS TO LOOK AT IT..
7-15
WELL, I HAD PLANNED TO USE SUNGLASSES
DON'T DO IT! DON'T DO IT!
SUNGLASSES, SMOKED GLASS, PHOTOGRAPH NEGATIVES...EVEN WELDER'S GLASSES AREN'T SAFE FOR DIRECTLY VIEWING AN ECLIPSE!
HOW WOULD YOUR OPHTHALMOLOGIST FEEL IF I CLOSED MY CURTAINS, AND STAYED IN BED ALL DAY?
SCHULZ

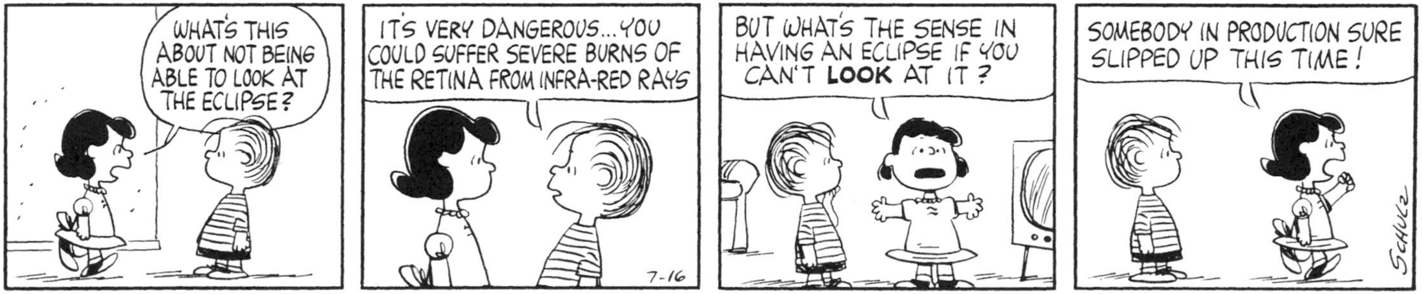
WHAT'S THIS ABOUT NOT BEING ABLE TO LOOK AT THE ECLIPSE?
IT'S VERY DANGEROUS...YOU COULD SUFFER SEVERE BURNS OF THE RETINA FROM INFRA-RED RAYS
7-16
BUT WHAT'S THE SENSE IN HAVING AN ECLIPSE IF YOU CAN'T **LOOK** AT IT?
SOMEBODY IN PRODUCTION SURE SLIPPED UP THIS TIME!
SCHULZ

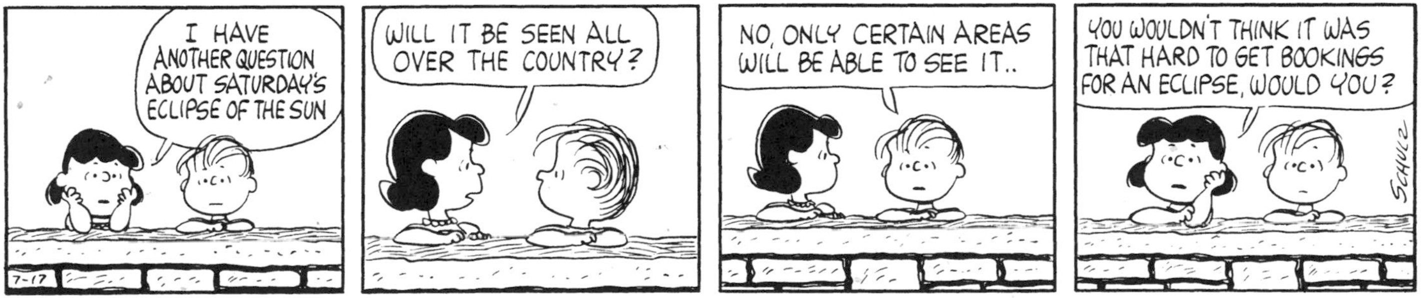
I HAVE ANOTHER QUESTION ABOUT SATURDAY'S ECLIPSE OF THE SUN
7-17
WILL IT BE SEEN ALL OVER THE COUNTRY?
NO, ONLY CERTAIN AREAS WILL BE ABLE TO SEE IT..
YOU WOULDN'T THINK IT WAS THAT HARD TO GET BOOKINGS FOR AN ECLIPSE, WOULD YOU?
SCHULZ

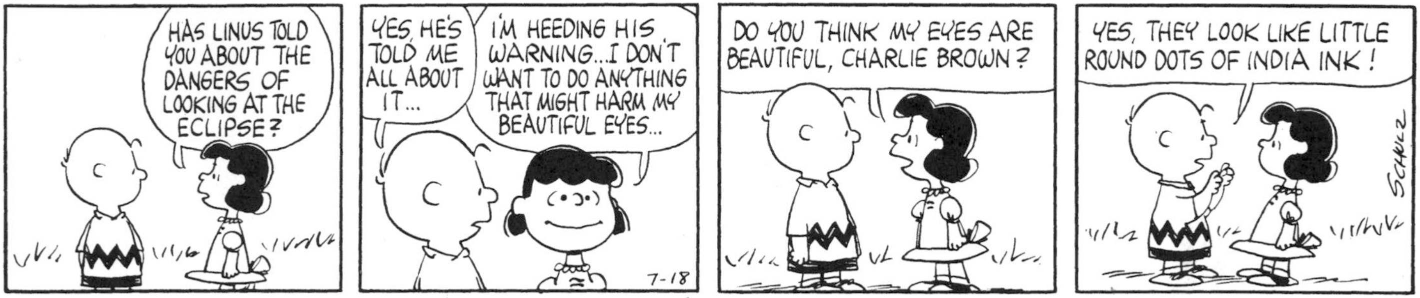
HAS LINUS TOLD YOU ABOUT THE DANGERS OF LOOKING AT THE ECLIPSE?
YES, HE'S TOLD ME ALL ABOUT IT...
I'M HEEDING HIS WARNING...I DON'T WANT TO DO ANYTHING THAT MIGHT HARM MY BEAUTIFUL EYES...
7-18
DO YOU THINK MY EYES ARE BEAUTIFUL, CHARLIE BROWN?
YES, THEY LOOK LIKE LITTLE ROUND DOTS OF INDIA INK!

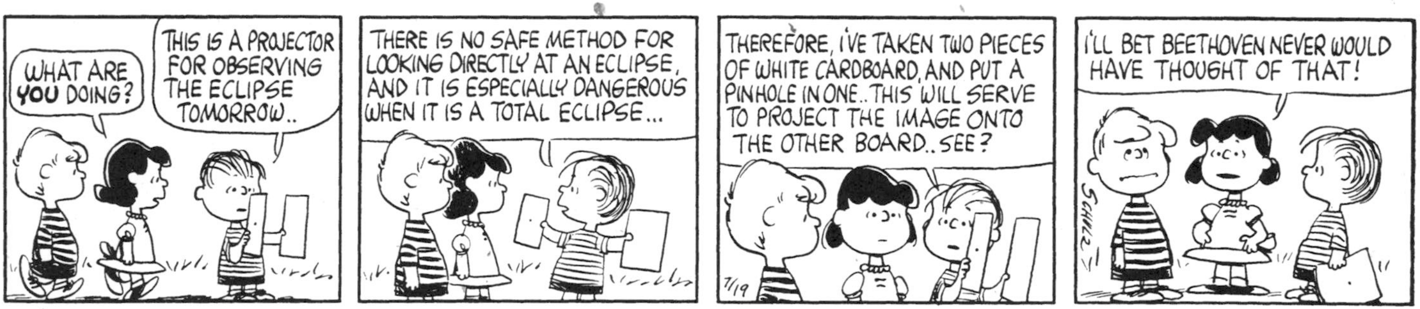
WHAT ARE **YOU** DOING?
THIS IS A PROJECTOR FOR OBSERVING THE ECLIPSE TOMORROW..
THERE IS NO SAFE METHOD FOR LOOKING DIRECTLY AT AN ECLIPSE, AND IT IS ESPECIALLY DANGEROUS WHEN IT IS A TOTAL ECLIPSE...
THEREFORE, I'VE TAKEN TWO PIECES OF WHITE CARDBOARD, AND PUT A PINHOLE IN ONE.. THIS WILL SERVE TO PROJECT THE IMAGE ONTO THE OTHER BOARD.. SEE?
7/19
I'LL BET BEETHOVEN NEVER WOULD HAVE THOUGHT OF THAT!

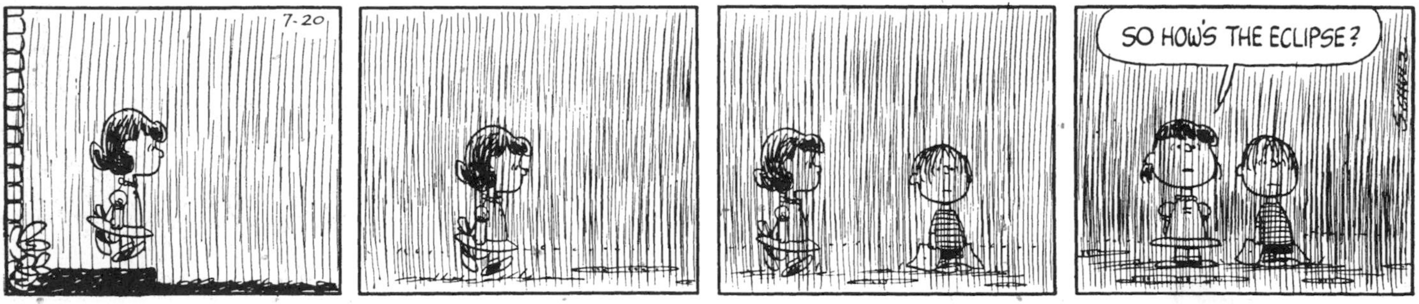
7-20
SO HOW'S THE ECLIPSE?

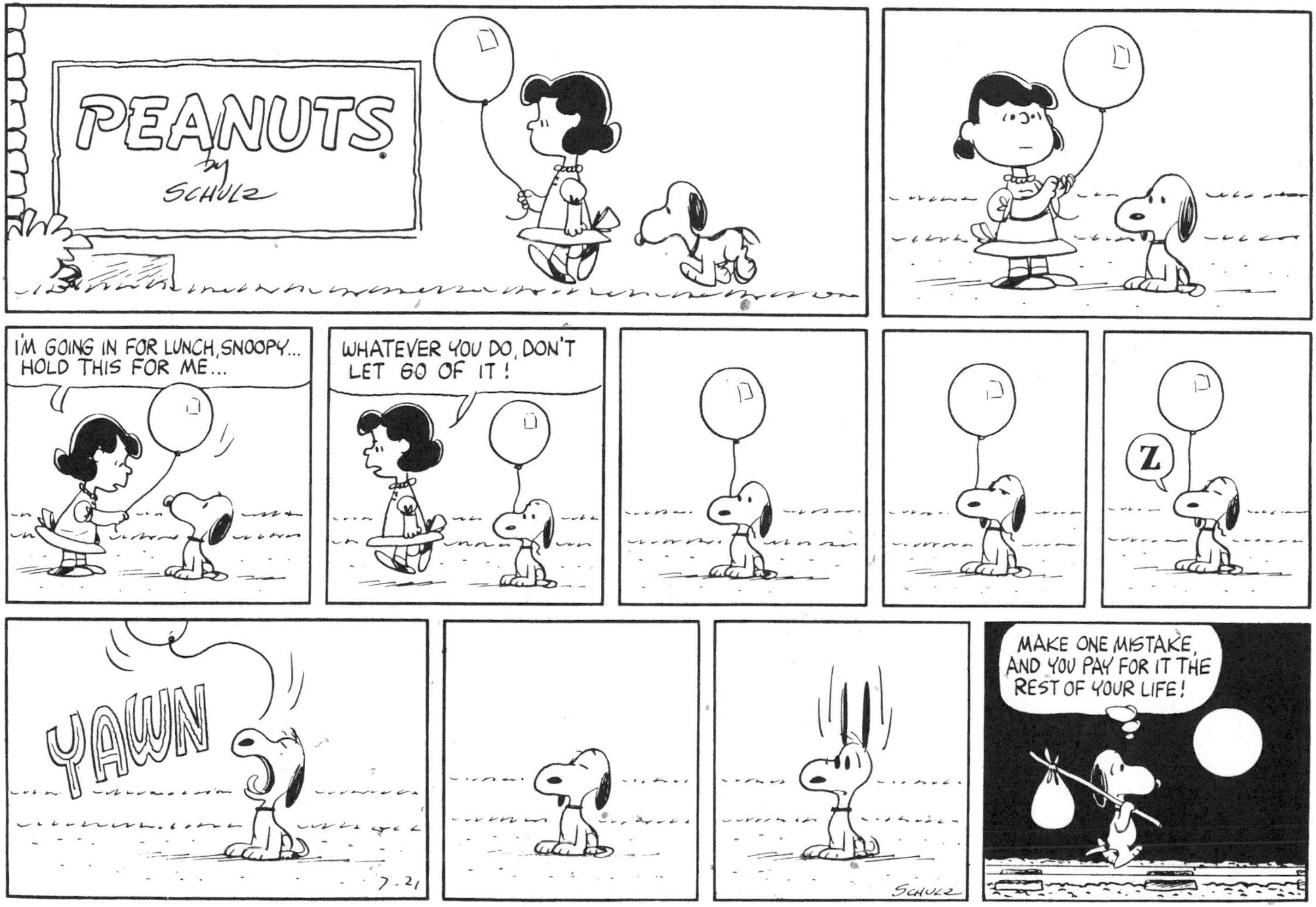
PEANUTS
by SCHULZ
I'M GOING IN FOR LUNCH, SNOOPY... HOLD THIS FOR ME...
WHATEVER YOU DO, DON'T LET GO OF IT!
Z
YAWN
7-21
SCHULZ
MAKE ONE MISTAKE, AND YOU PAY FOR IT THE REST OF YOUR LIFE!

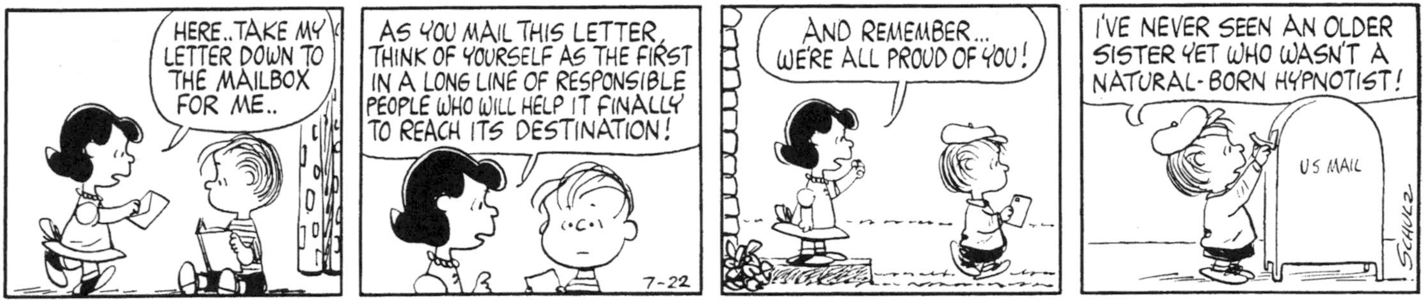
HERE..TAKE MY LETTER DOWN TO THE MAILBOX FOR ME..
AS YOU MAIL THIS LETTER, THINK OF YOURSELF AS THE FIRST IN A LONG LINE OF RESPONSIBLE PEOPLE WHO WILL HELP IT FINALLY TO REACH ITS DESTINATION!
AND REMEMBER... WE'RE ALL PROUD OF YOU!
I'VE NEVER SEEN AN OLDER SISTER YET WHO WASN'T A NATURAL-BORN HYPNOTIST!
US MAIL

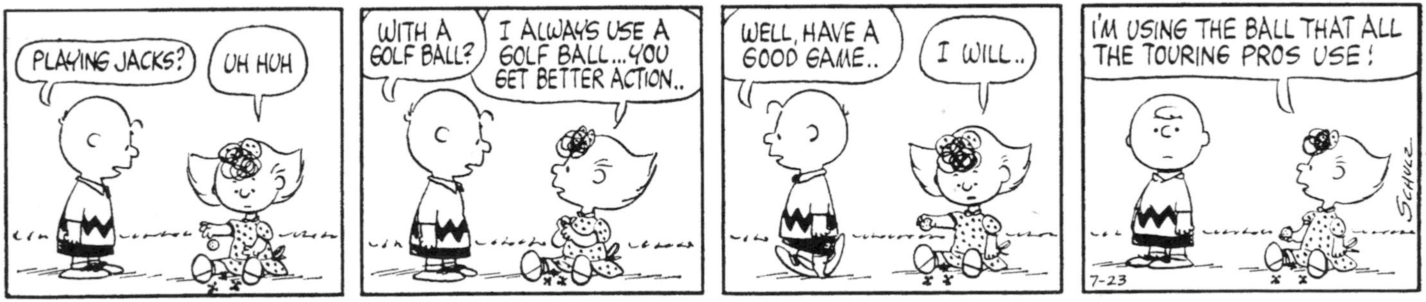
PLAYING JACKS?
UH HUH
WITH A GOLF BALL?
I ALWAYS USE A GOLF BALL...YOU GET BETTER ACTION..
WELL, HAVE A GOOD GAME..
I WILL..
I'M USING THE BALL THAT ALL THE TOURING PROS USE!

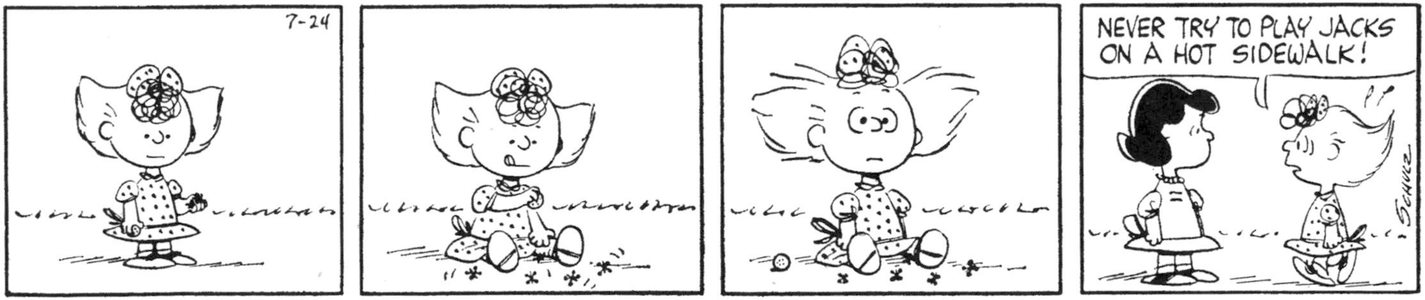
NEVER TRY TO PLAY JACKS ON A HOT SIDEWALK!

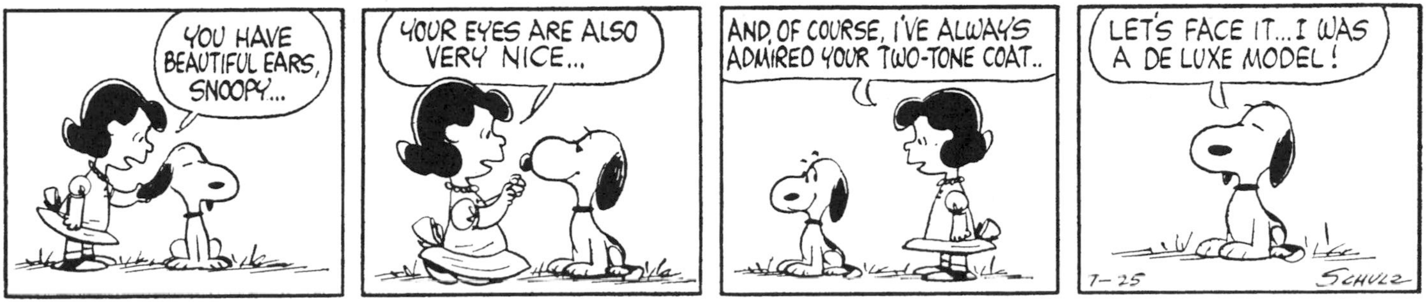
YOU HAVE BEAUTIFUL EARS, SNOOPY...
YOUR EYES ARE ALSO VERY NICE...
AND, OF COURSE, I'VE ALWAYS ADMIRED YOUR TWO-TONE COAT..
LET'S FACE IT... I WAS A DE LUXE MODEL!
7-25
SCHULZ

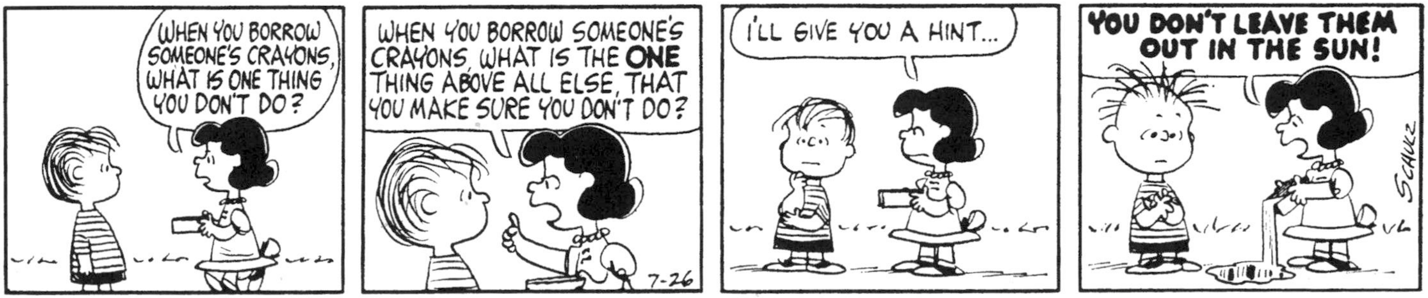
WHEN YOU BORROW SOMEONE'S CRAYONS, WHAT IS ONE THING YOU DON'T DO?
WHEN YOU BORROW SOMEONE'S CRAYONS, WHAT IS THE **ONE** THING ABOVE ALL ELSE, THAT YOU MAKE SURE YOU DON'T DO?
7-26
I'LL GIVE YOU A HINT...
YOU DON'T LEAVE THEM OUT IN THE SUN!
SCHULZ

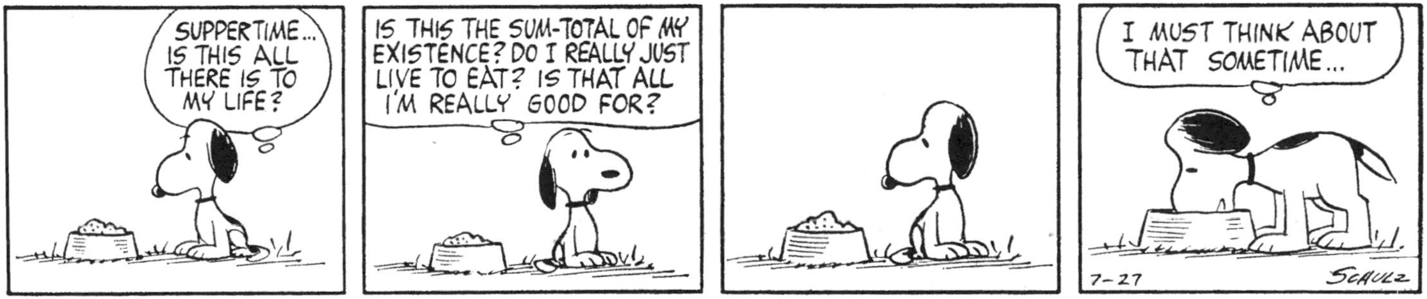
SUPPERTIME... IS THIS ALL THERE IS TO MY LIFE?
IS THIS THE SUM-TOTAL OF MY EXISTENCE? DO I REALLY JUST LIVE TO EAT? IS THAT ALL I'M REALLY GOOD FOR?
I MUST THINK ABOUT THAT SOMETIME...
7-27
SCHULZ

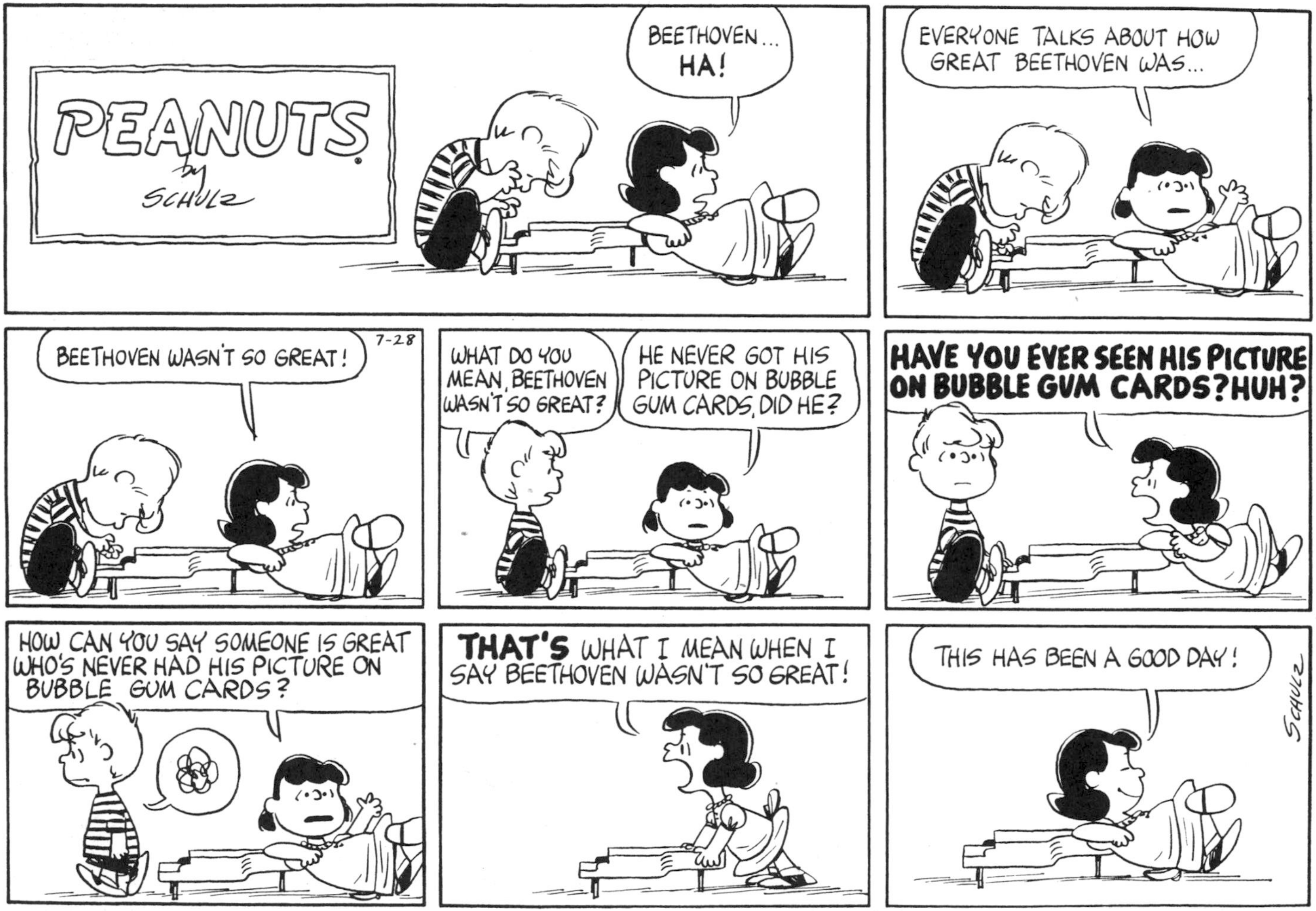
PEANUTS
by SCHULZ
BEETHOVEN... HA!
EVERYONE TALKS ABOUT HOW GREAT BEETHOVEN WAS...
BEETHOVEN WASN'T SO GREAT!
7-28
WHAT DO YOU MEAN, BEETHOVEN WASN'T SO GREAT?
HE NEVER GOT HIS PICTURE ON BUBBLE GUM CARDS, DID HE?
HAVE YOU EVER SEEN HIS PICTURE ON BUBBLE GUM CARDS? HUH?
HOW CAN YOU SAY SOMEONE IS GREAT WHO'S NEVER HAD HIS PICTURE ON BUBBLE GUM CARDS?
THAT'S WHAT I MEAN WHEN I SAY BEETHOVEN WASN'T SO GREAT!
THIS HAS BEEN A GOOD DAY!
SCHULZ

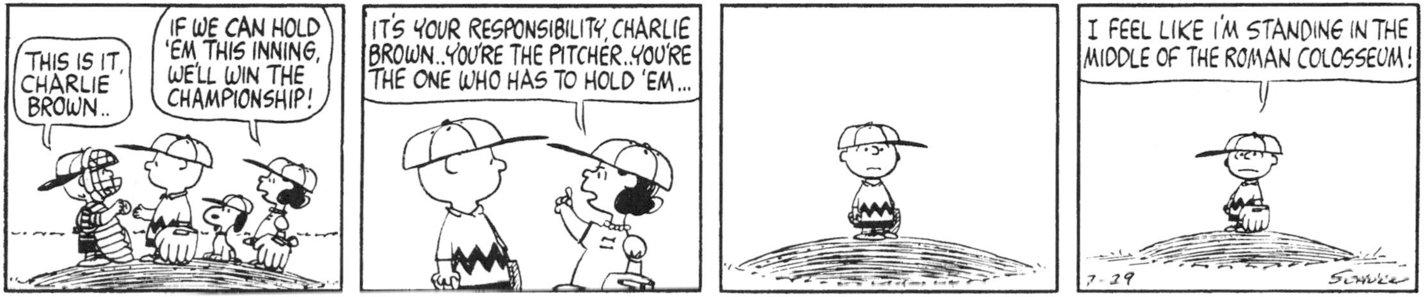
THIS IS IT, CHARLIE BROWN..
IF WE CAN HOLD 'EM THIS INNING, WE'LL WIN THE CHAMPIONSHIP!
IT'S YOUR RESPONSIBILITY, CHARLIE BROWN..YOU'RE THE PITCHER..YOU'RE THE ONE WHO HAS TO HOLD 'EM...
I FEEL LIKE I'M STANDING IN THE MIDDLE OF THE ROMAN COLOSSEUM!
7-29
SCHULZ

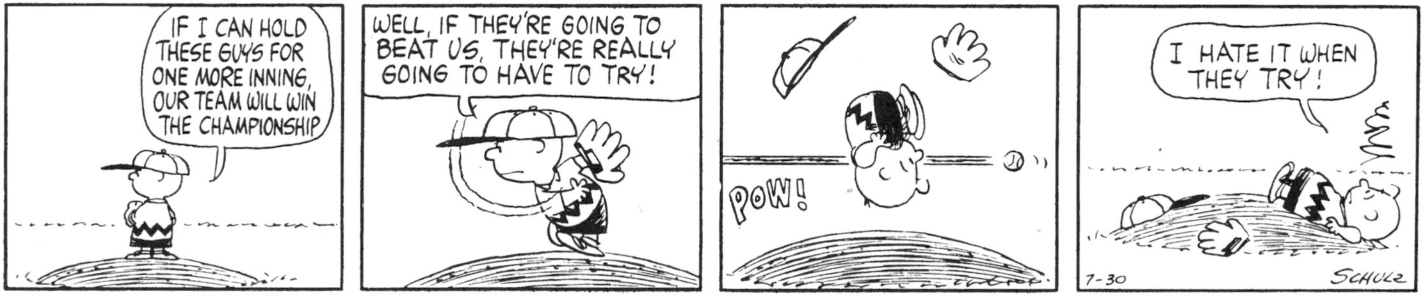
IF I CAN HOLD THESE GUYS FOR ONE MORE INNING, OUR TEAM WILL WIN THE CHAMPIONSHIP
WELL, IF THEY'RE GOING TO BEAT US, THEY'RE REALLY GOING TO HAVE TO TRY!
POW!
I HATE IT WHEN THEY TRY!
7-30
SCHULZ

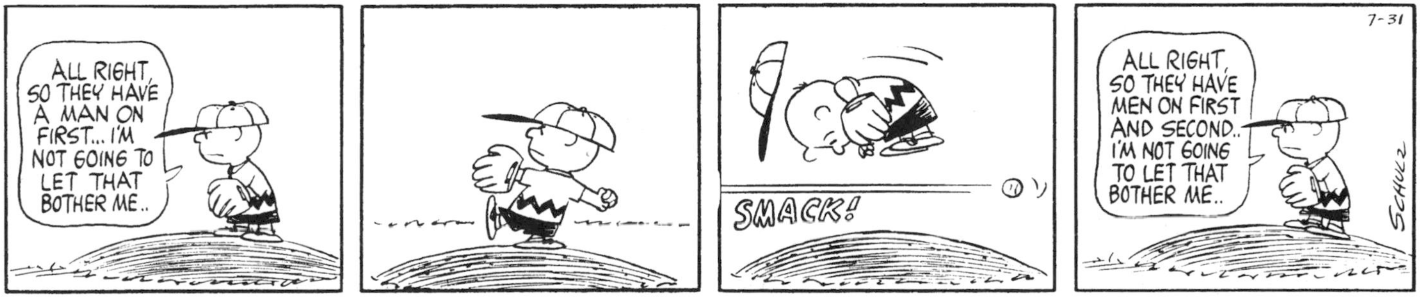
ALL RIGHT, SO THEY HAVE A MAN ON FIRST... I'M NOT GOING TO LET THAT BOTHER ME..
SMACK!
7-31
ALL RIGHT, SO THEY HAVE MEN ON FIRST AND SECOND.. I'M NOT GOING TO LET THAT BOTHER ME..
SCHULZ

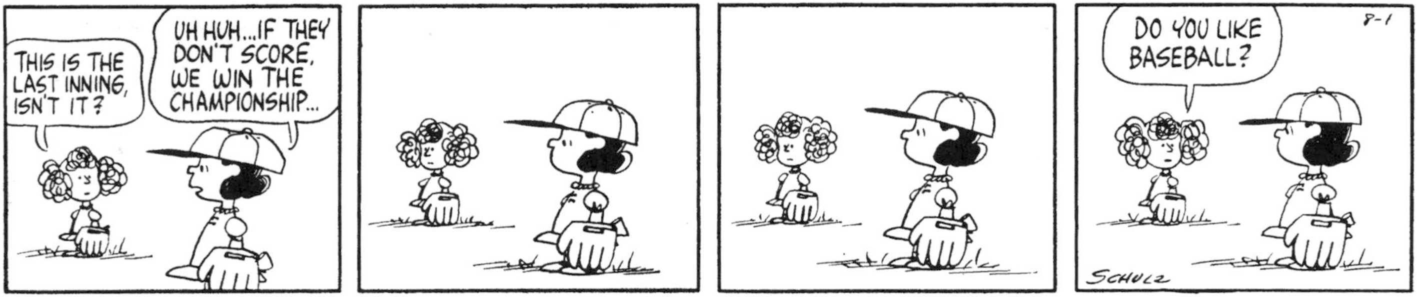
THIS IS THE LAST INNING, ISN'T IT?
UH HUH...IF THEY DON'T SCORE, WE WIN THE CHAMPIONSHIP...
DO YOU LIKE BASEBALL?
8-1
SCHULZ

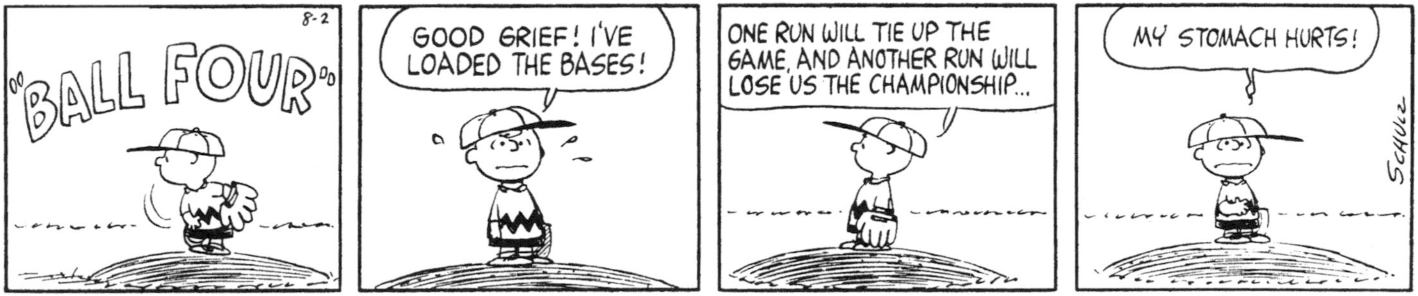
8-2
"BALL FOUR"
GOOD GRIEF! I'VE LOADED THE BASES!
ONE RUN WILL TIE UP THE GAME, AND ANOTHER RUN WILL LOSE US THE CHAMPIONSHIP...
MY STOMACH HURTS!
SCHULZ

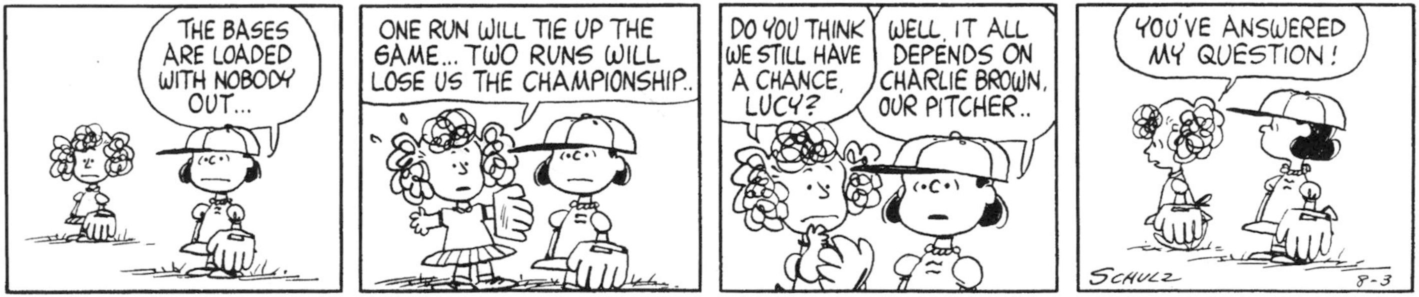
THE BASES ARE LOADED WITH NOBODY OUT...
ONE RUN WILL TIE UP THE GAME... TWO RUNS WILL LOSE US THE CHAMPIONSHIP..
DO YOU THINK WE STILL HAVE A CHANCE, LUCY?
WELL, IT ALL DEPENDS ON CHARLIE BROWN, OUR PITCHER..
YOU'VE ANSWERED MY QUESTION!
SCHULZ
8-3

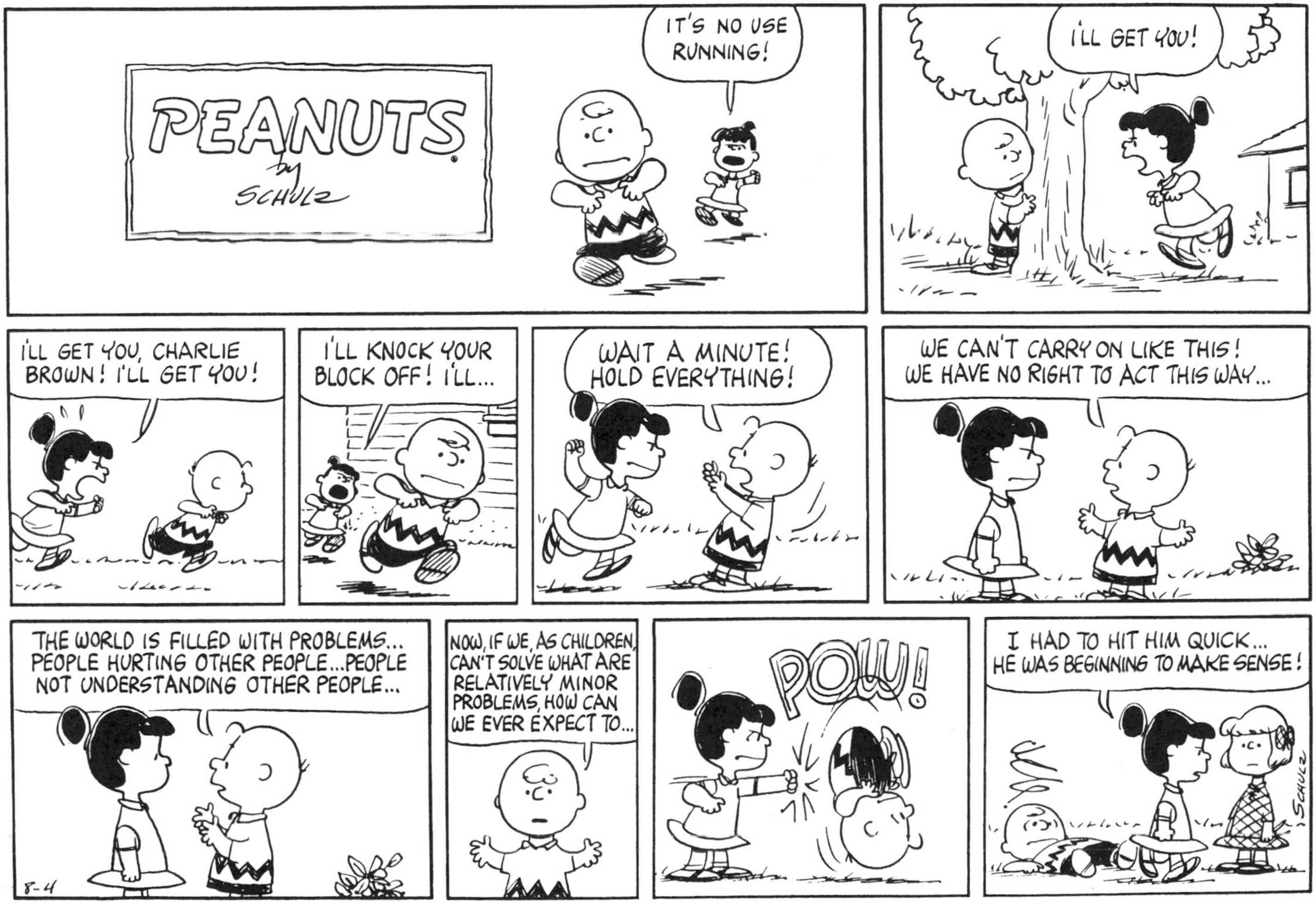
PEANUTS
by SCHULZ
IT'S NO USE RUNNING!
I'LL GET YOU!
I'LL GET YOU, CHARLIE BROWN! I'LL GET YOU!
I'LL KNOCK YOUR BLOCK OFF! I'LL...
WAIT A MINUTE! HOLD EVERYTHING!
WE CAN'T CARRY ON LIKE THIS! WE HAVE NO RIGHT TO ACT THIS WAY...
THE WORLD IS FILLED WITH PROBLEMS... PEOPLE HURTING OTHER PEOPLE...PEOPLE NOT UNDERSTANDING OTHER PEOPLE...
8-4
NOW, IF WE, AS CHILDREN, CAN'T SOLVE WHAT ARE RELATIVELY MINOR PROBLEMS, HOW CAN WE EVER EXPECT TO...
POW!
I HAD TO HIT HIM QUICK... HE WAS BEGINNING TO MAKE SENSE!
SCHULZ

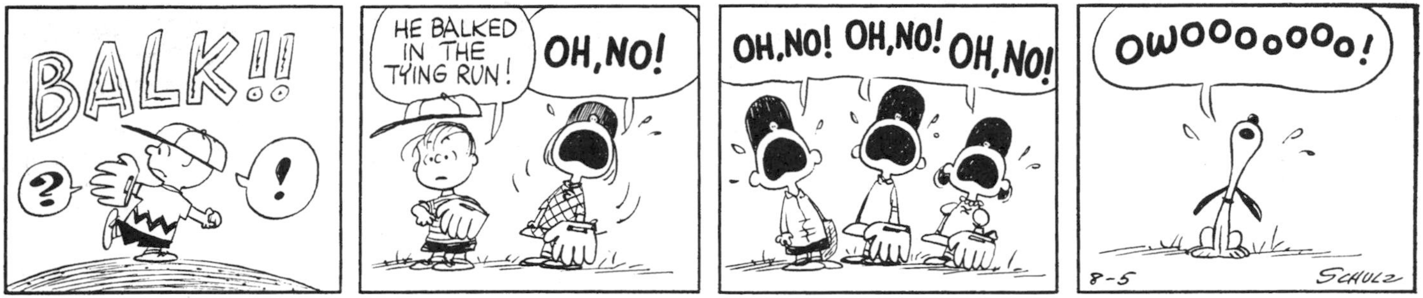
BALK!!
?
!
HE BALKED IN THE TYING RUN!
OH, NO!
OH, NO! OH, NO! OH, NO!
OWOOOOOOOo!
8-5
SCHULZ

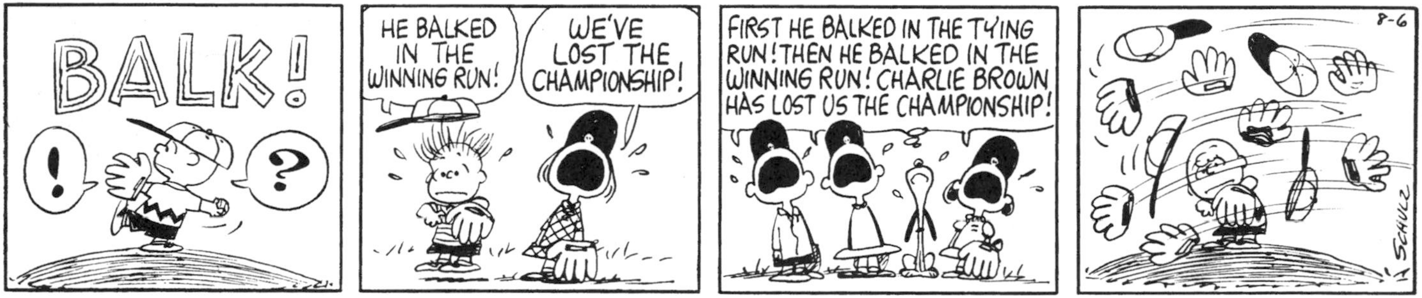
BALK!
!
?
HE BALKED IN THE WINNING RUN!
WE'VE LOST THE CHAMPIONSHIP!
FIRST HE BALKED IN THE TYING RUN! THEN HE BALKED IN THE WINNING RUN! CHARLIE BROWN HAS LOST US THE CHAMPIONSHIP!
8-6
SCHULZ

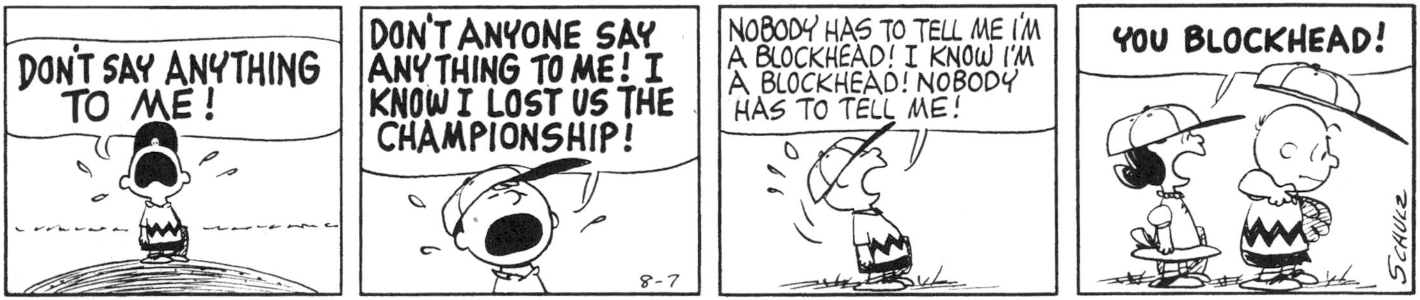
DON'T SAY ANYTHING TO ME!
DON'T ANYONE SAY ANYTHING TO ME! I KNOW I LOST US THE CHAMPIONSHIP!
8-7
NOBODY HAS TO TELL ME I'M A BLOCKHEAD! I KNOW I'M A BLOCKHEAD! NOBODY HAS TO TELL ME!
YOU BLOCKHEAD!
SCHULZ

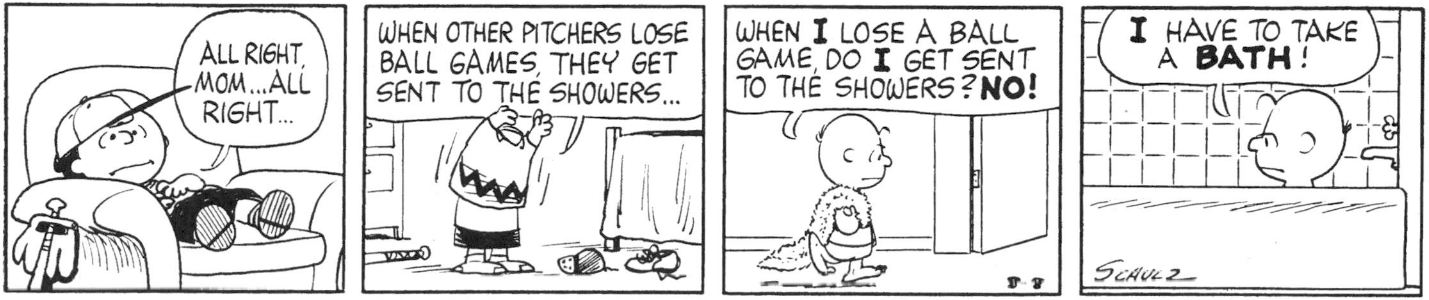
ALL RIGHT, MOM...ALL RIGHT...
WHEN OTHER PITCHERS LOSE BALL GAMES, THEY GET SENT TO THE SHOWERS...
WHEN I LOSE A BALL GAME, DO I GET SENT TO THE SHOWERS? NO!
I HAVE TO TAKE A BATH!
SCHULZ

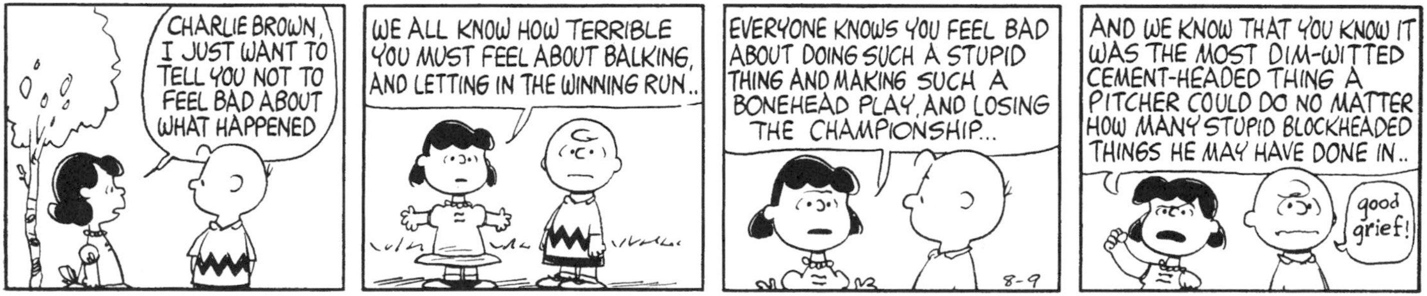
CHARLIE BROWN, I JUST WANT TO TELL YOU NOT TO FEEL BAD ABOUT WHAT HAPPENED
WE ALL KNOW HOW TERRIBLE YOU MUST FEEL ABOUT BALKING, AND LETTING IN THE WINNING RUN..
EVERYONE KNOWS YOU FEEL BAD ABOUT DOING SUCH A STUPID THING AND MAKING SUCH A BONEHEAD PLAY, AND LOSING THE CHAMPIONSHIP...
8-9
AND WE KNOW THAT YOU KNOW IT WAS THE MOST DIM-WITTED CEMENT-HEADED THING A PITCHER COULD DO NO MATTER HOW MANY STUPID BLOCKHEADED THINGS HE MAY HAVE DONE IN..
good grief!

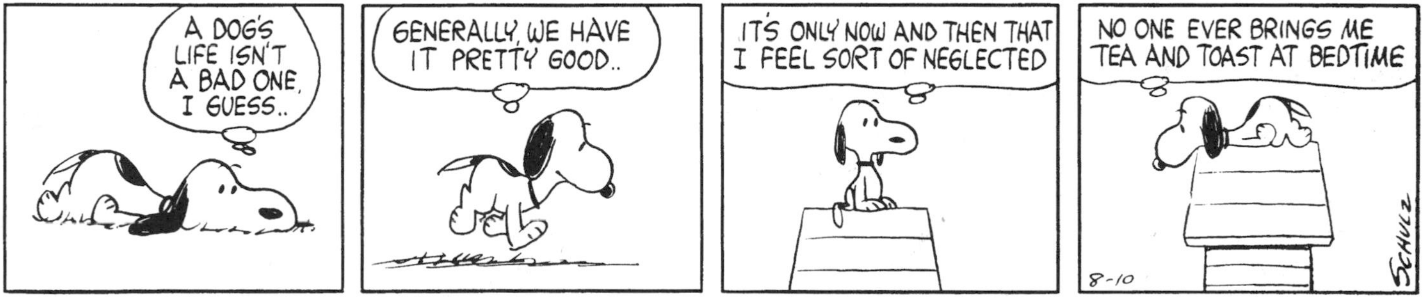
A DOG'S LIFE ISN'T A BAD ONE, I GUESS..
GENERALLY, WE HAVE IT PRETTY GOOD..
IT'S ONLY NOW AND THEN THAT I FEEL SORT OF NEGLECTED
NO ONE EVER BRINGS ME TEA AND TOAST AT BEDTIME
8-10
SCHULZ

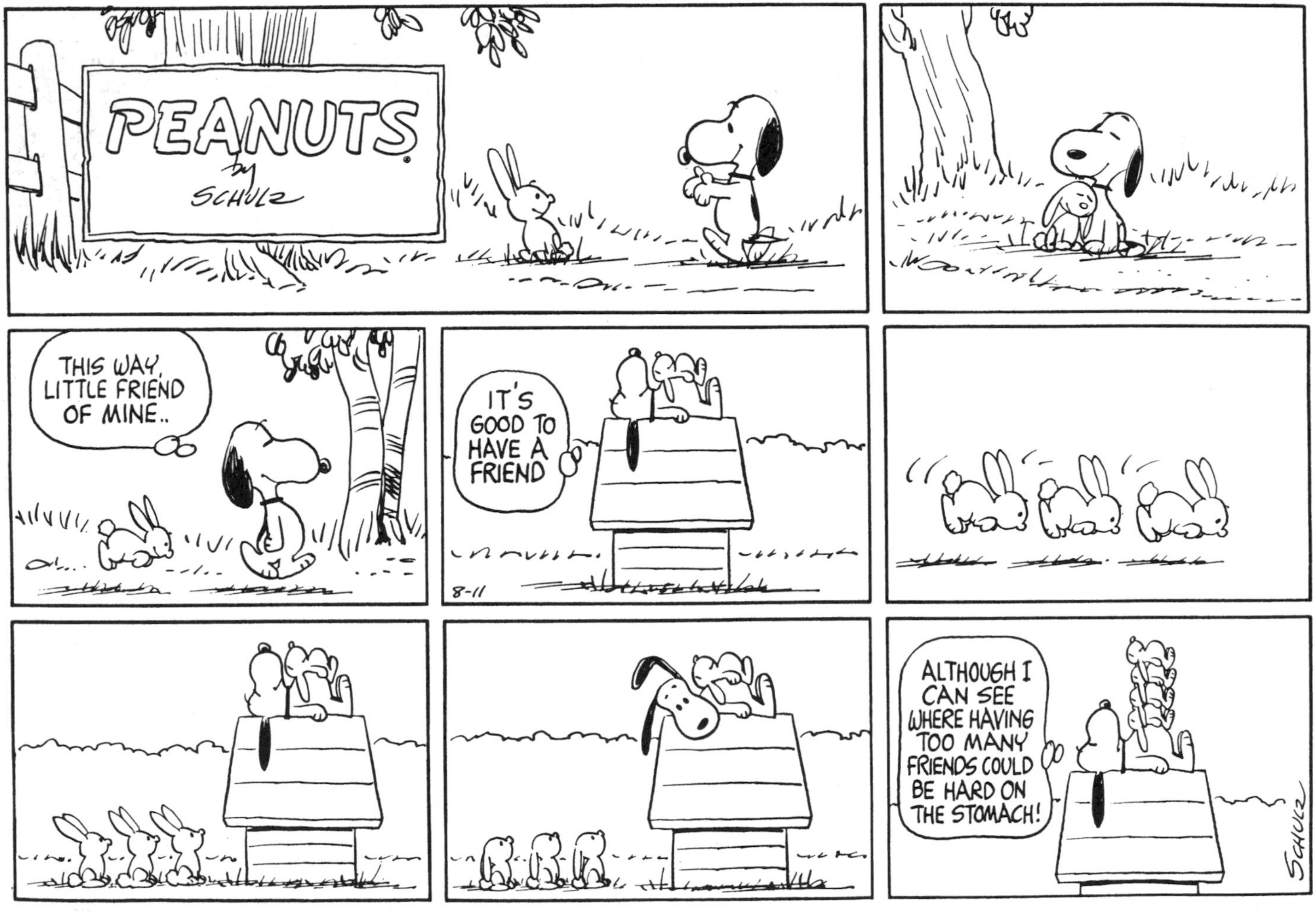
PEANUTS
by SCHULZ
THIS WAY, LITTLE FRIEND OF MINE..
IT'S GOOD TO HAVE A FRIEND
8-11
ALTHOUGH I CAN SEE WHERE HAVING TOO MANY FRIENDS COULD BE HARD ON THE STOMACH!
SCHULZ

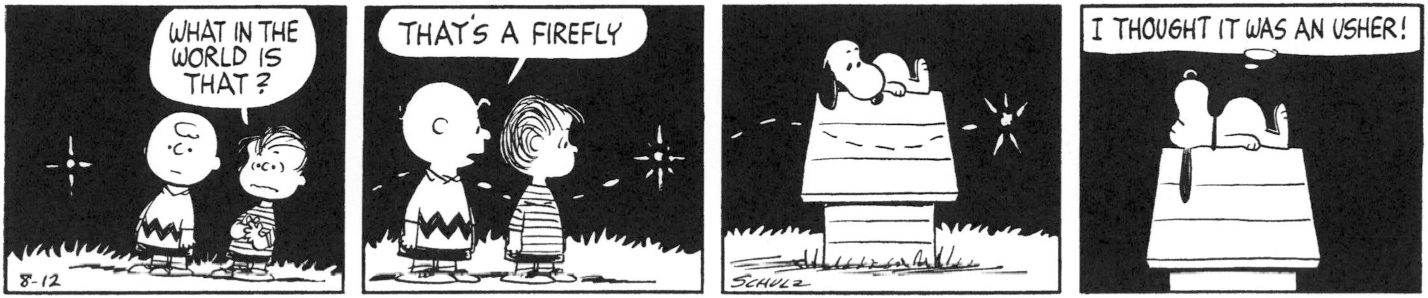
WHAT IN THE WORLD IS THAT?
THAT'S A FIREFLY
I THOUGHT IT WAS AN USHER!

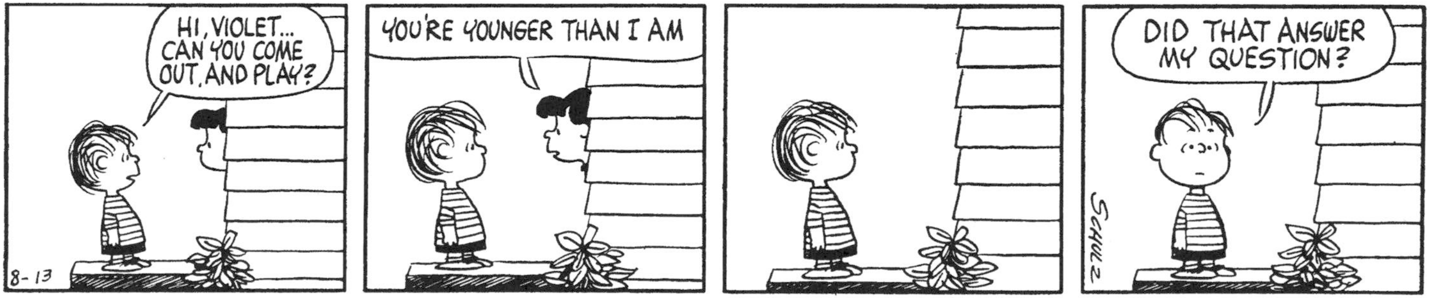
HI, VIOLET... CAN YOU COME OUT, AND PLAY?
YOU'RE YOUNGER THAN I AM
DID THAT ANSWER MY QUESTION?

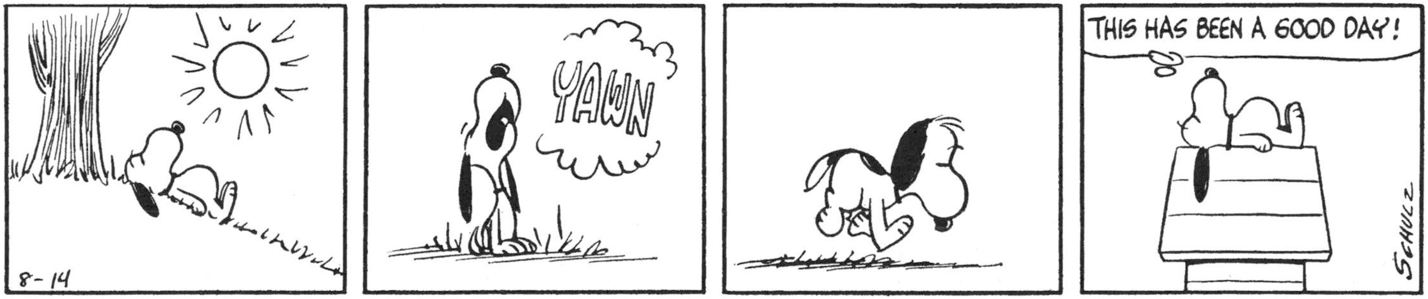
YAWN
THIS HAS BEEN A GOOD DAY!

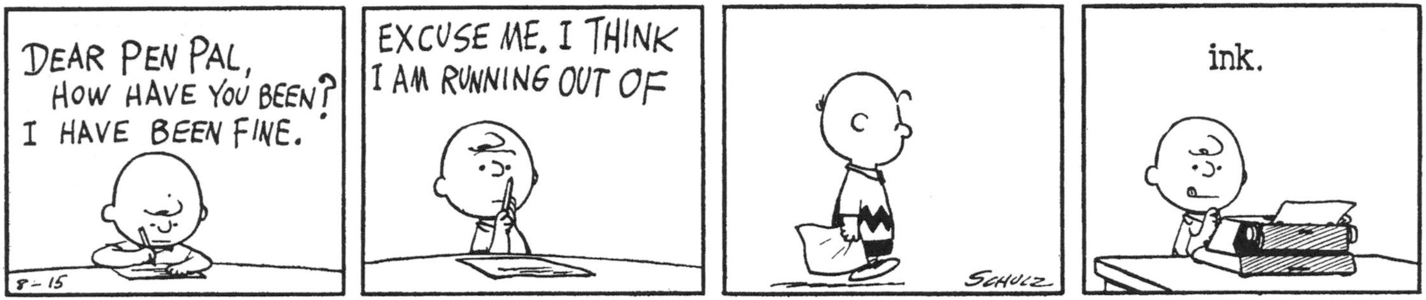
DEAR PEN PAL,
HOW HAVE YOU BEEN? I HAVE BEEN FINE.
8-15
EXCUSE ME. I THINK I AM RUNNING OUT OF
SCHULZ
ink.

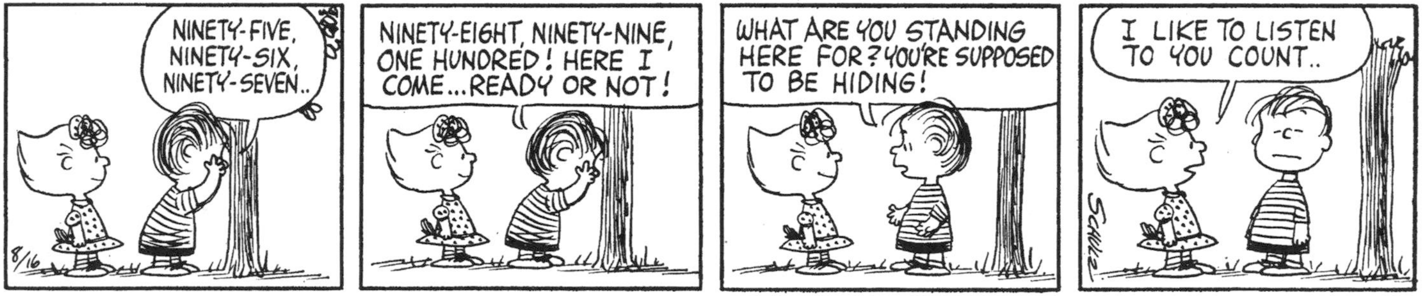
NINETY-FIVE, NINETY-SIX, NINETY-SEVEN..
8/16
NINETY-EIGHT, NINETY-NINE, ONE HUNDRED! HERE I COME...READY OR NOT!
WHAT ARE YOU STANDING HERE FOR? YOU'RE SUPPOSED TO BE HIDING!
I LIKE TO LISTEN TO YOU COUNT..
SCHULZ

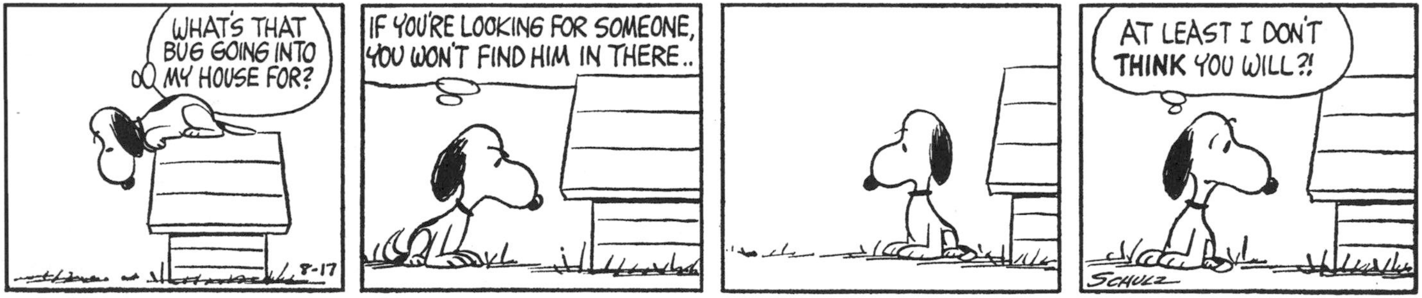
WHAT'S THAT BUG GOING INTO MY HOUSE FOR?
8-17
IF YOU'RE LOOKING FOR SOMEONE, YOU WON'T FIND HIM IN THERE..
AT LEAST I DON'T **THINK** YOU WILL?!
SCHULZ

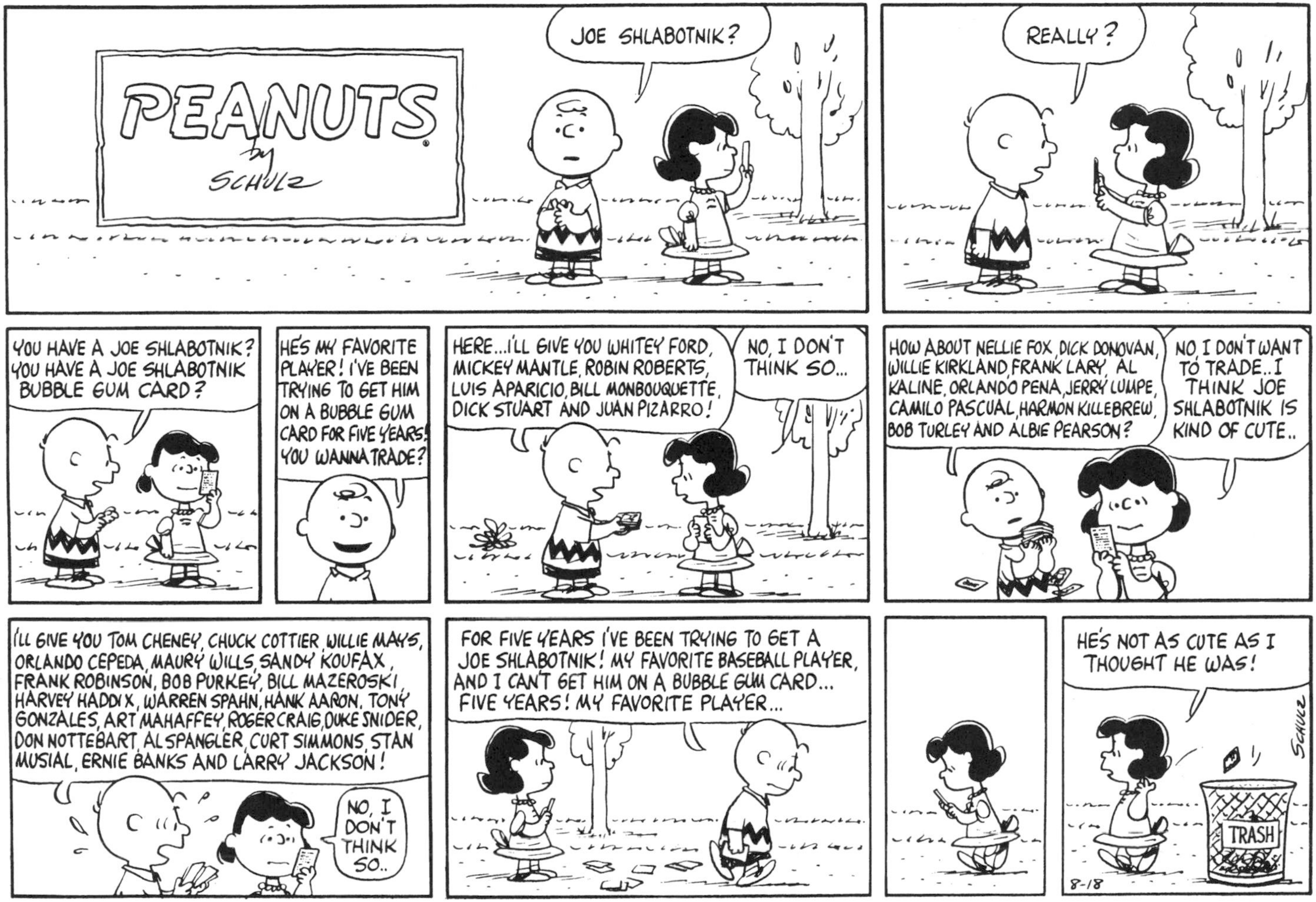
PEANUTS
by SCHULZ
JOE SHLABOTNIK?
REALLY?
YOU HAVE A JOE SHLABOTNIK? YOU HAVE A JOE SHLABOTNIK BUBBLE GUM CARD?
HE'S MY FAVORITE PLAYER! I'VE BEEN TRYING TO GET HIM ON A BUBBLE GUM CARD FOR FIVE YEARS! YOU WANNA TRADE?
HERE...I'LL GIVE YOU WHITEY FORD, MICKEY MANTLE, ROBIN ROBERTS, LUIS APARICIO, BILL MONBOUQUETTE, DICK STUART AND JUAN PIZARRO!
NO, I DON'T THINK SO...
HOW ABOUT NELLIE FOX, DICK DONOVAN, WILLIE KIRKLAND, FRANK LARY, AL KALINE, ORLANDO PENA, JERRY LUMPE, CAMILO PASCUAL, HARMON KILLEBREW, BOB TURLEY AND ALBIE PEARSON?
NO, I DON'T WANT TO TRADE.. I THINK JOE SHLABOTNIK IS KIND OF CUTE..
I'LL GIVE YOU TOM CHENEY, CHUCK COTTIER, WILLIE MAYS, ORLANDO CEPEDA, MAURY WILLS, SANDY KOUFAX, FRANK ROBINSON, BOB PURKEY, BILL MAZEROSKI, HARVEY HADDIX, WARREN SPAHN, HANK AARON, TONY GONZALES, ART MAHAFFEY, ROGER CRAIG, DUKE SNIDER, DON NOTTEBART, AL SPANGLER, CURT SIMMONS, STAN MUSIAL, ERNIE BANKS AND LARRY JACKSON!
NO, I DON'T THINK SO..
FOR FIVE YEARS I'VE BEEN TRYING TO GET A JOE SHLABOTNIK! MY FAVORITE BASEBALL PLAYER, AND I CAN'T GET HIM ON A BUBBLE GUM CARD... FIVE YEARS! MY FAVORITE PLAYER...
HE'S NOT AS CUTE AS I THOUGHT HE WAS!
TRASH
SCHULZ
8-18

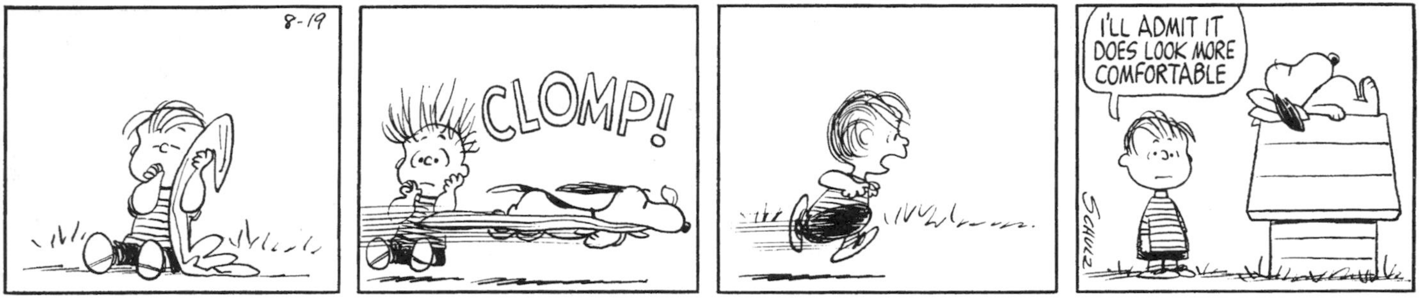
8-19
CLOMP!
I'LL ADMIT IT DOES LOOK MORE COMFORTABLE
SCHULZ

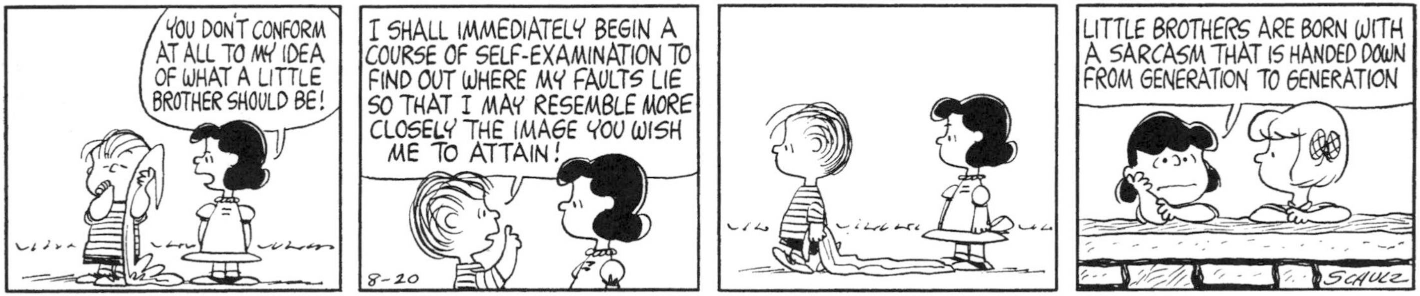
YOU DON'T CONFORM AT ALL TO MY IDEA OF WHAT A LITTLE BROTHER SHOULD BE!
I SHALL IMMEDIATELY BEGIN A COURSE OF SELF-EXAMINATION TO FIND OUT WHERE MY FAULTS LIE SO THAT I MAY RESEMBLE MORE CLOSELY THE IMAGE YOU WISH ME TO ATTAIN!
8-20
LITTLE BROTHERS ARE BORN WITH A SARCASM THAT IS HANDED DOWN FROM GENERATION TO GENERATION
SCHULZ

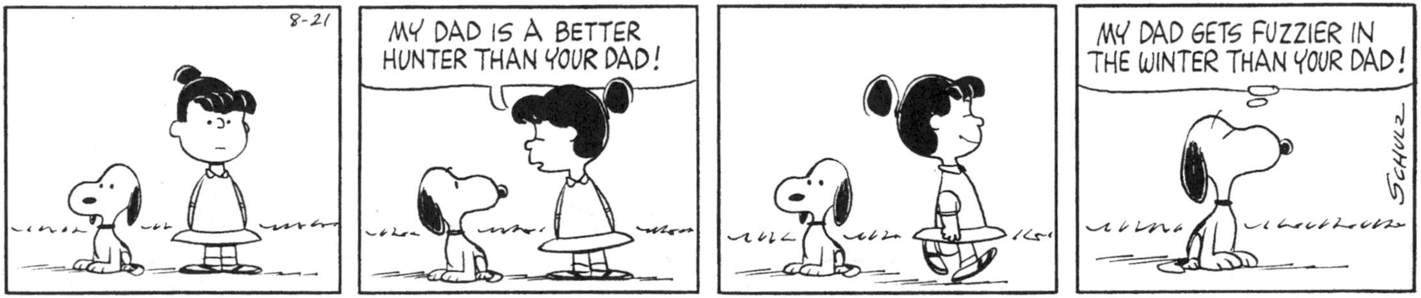
8-21
MY DAD IS A BETTER HUNTER THAN YOUR DAD!
MY DAD GETS FUZZIER IN THE WINTER THAN YOUR DAD!
SCHULZ

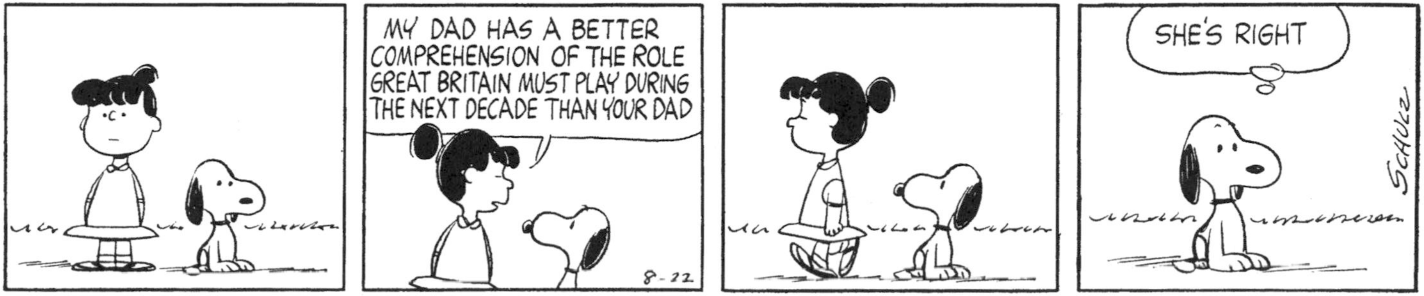
MY DAD HAS A BETTER COMPREHENSION OF THE ROLE GREAT BRITAIN MUST PLAY DURING THE NEXT DECADE THAN YOUR DAD
SHE'S RIGHT

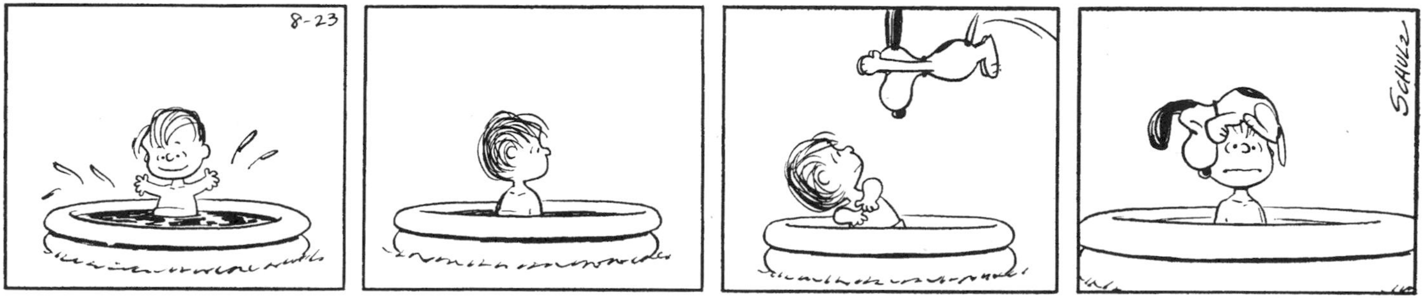

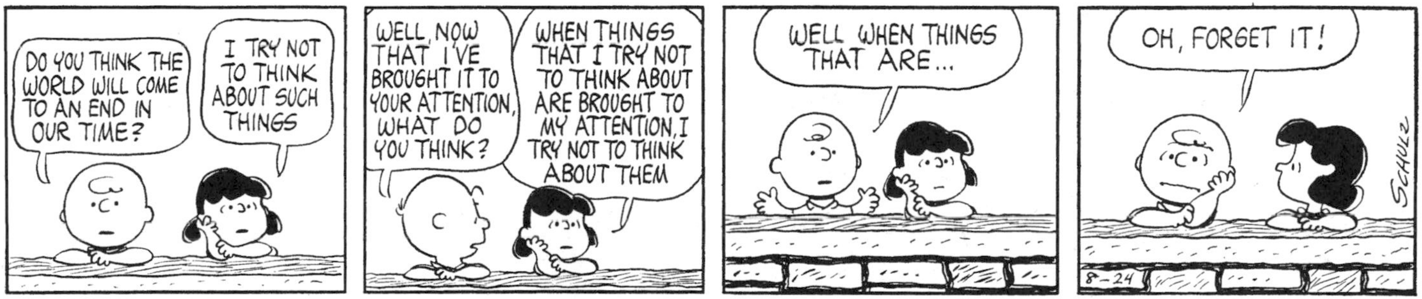
DO YOU THINK THE WORLD WILL COME TO AN END IN OUR TIME?
I TRY NOT TO THINK ABOUT SUCH THINGS
WELL, NOW THAT I'VE BROUGHT IT TO YOUR ATTENTION, WHAT DO YOU THINK?
WHEN THINGS THAT I TRY NOT TO THINK ABOUT ARE BROUGHT TO MY ATTENTION, I TRY NOT TO THINK ABOUT THEM
WELL WHEN THINGS THAT ARE...
OH, FORGET IT!

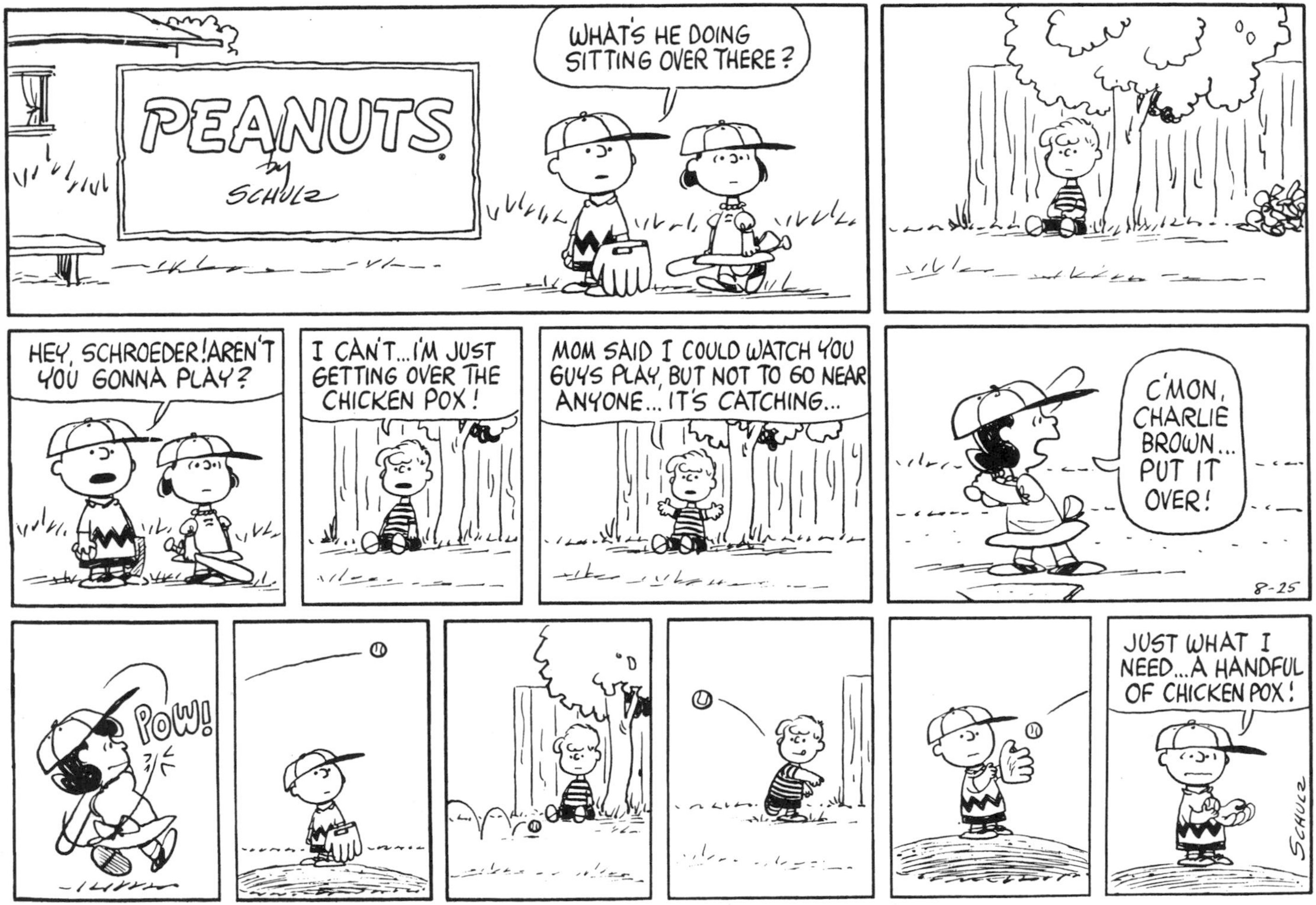
PEANUTS
by SCHULZ
WHAT'S HE DOING SITTING OVER THERE?
HEY, SCHROEDER! AREN'T YOU GONNA PLAY?
I CAN'T...I'M JUST GETTING OVER THE CHICKEN POX!
MOM SAID I COULD WATCH YOU GUYS PLAY, BUT NOT TO GO NEAR ANYONE... IT'S CATCHING...
C'MON, CHARLIE BROWN... PUT IT OVER!
8-25
POW!
JUST WHAT I NEED...A HANDFUL OF CHICKEN POX!
SCHULZ

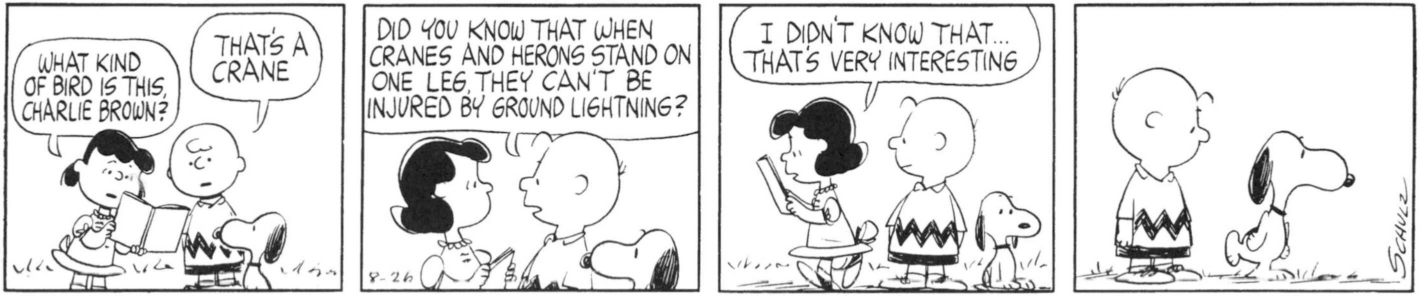
WHAT KIND OF BIRD IS THIS, CHARLIE BROWN?
THAT'S A CRANE
DID YOU KNOW THAT WHEN CRANES AND HERONS STAND ON ONE LEG, THEY CAN'T BE INJURED BY GROUND LIGHTNING?
8-26
I DIDN'T KNOW THAT... THAT'S VERY INTERESTING
SCHULZ

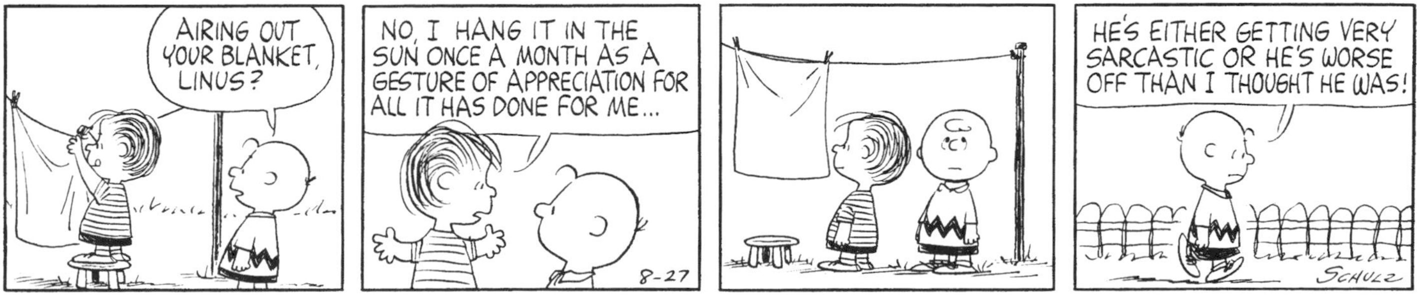
AIRING OUT YOUR BLANKET, LINUS?
NO, I HANG IT IN THE SUN ONCE A MONTH AS A GESTURE OF APPRECIATION FOR ALL IT HAS DONE FOR ME...
8-27
HE'S EITHER GETTING VERY SARCASTIC OR HE'S WORSE OFF THAN I THOUGHT HE WAS!
SCHULZ

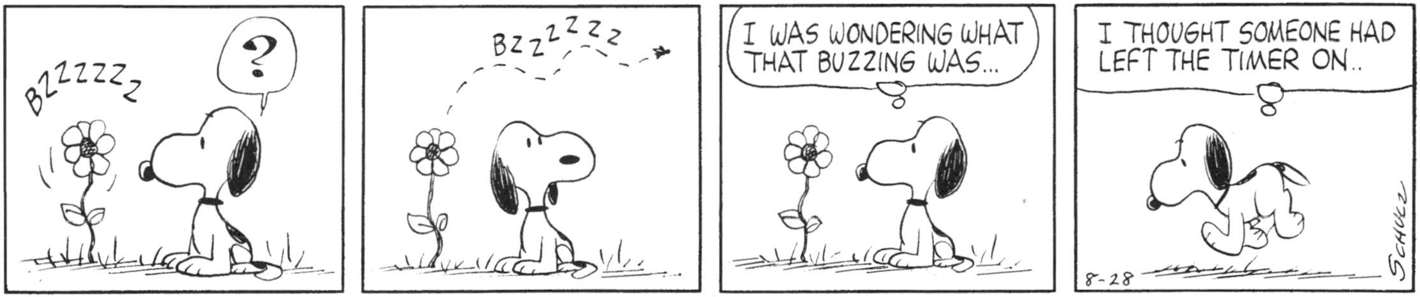
BZZZZZZ
?
BZZZZZZ
I WAS WONDERING WHAT THAT BUZZING WAS...
I THOUGHT SOMEONE HAD LEFT THE TIMER ON..
8-28
SCHULZ

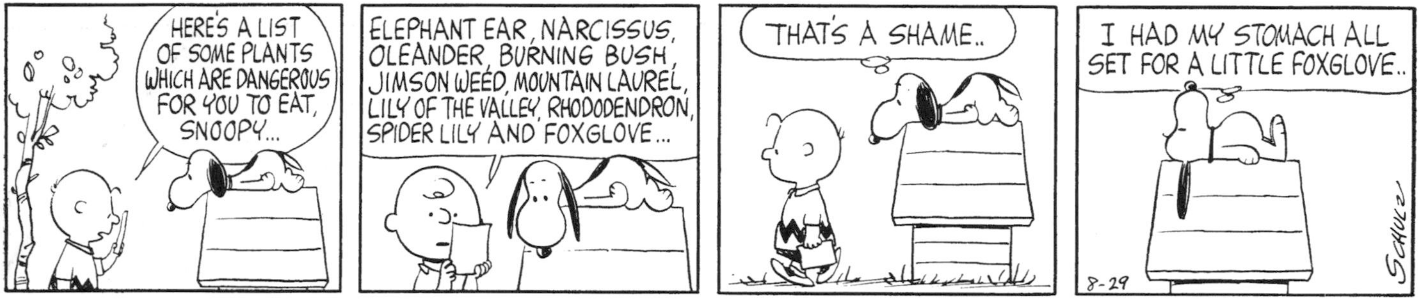
HERE'S A LIST OF SOME PLANTS WHICH ARE DANGEROUS FOR YOU TO EAT, SNOOPY...
ELEPHANT EAR, NARCISSUS, OLEANDER, BURNING BUSH, JIMSON WEED, MOUNTAIN LAUREL, LILY OF THE VALLEY, RHODODENDRON, SPIDER LILY AND FOXGLOVE...
THAT'S A SHAME..
I HAD MY STOMACH ALL SET FOR A LITTLE FOXGLOVE..
8-29
SCHULZ

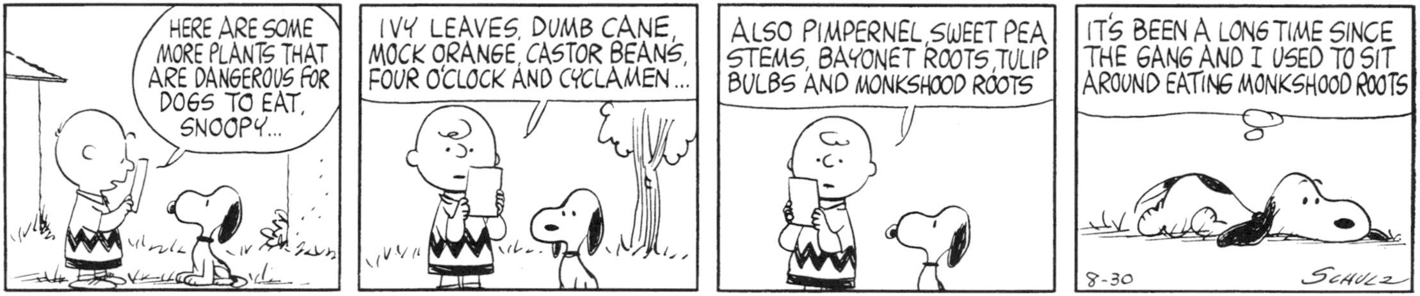
HERE ARE SOME MORE PLANTS THAT ARE DANGEROUS FOR DOGS TO EAT, SNOOPY...
IVY LEAVES, DUMB CANE, MOCK ORANGE, CASTOR BEANS, FOUR O'CLOCK AND CYCLAMEN...
ALSO PIMPERNEL, SWEET PEA STEMS, BAYONET ROOTS, TULIP BULBS AND MONKSHOOD ROOTS
IT'S BEEN A LONG TIME SINCE THE GANG AND I USED TO SIT AROUND EATING MONKSHOOD ROOTS
8-30
SCHULZ

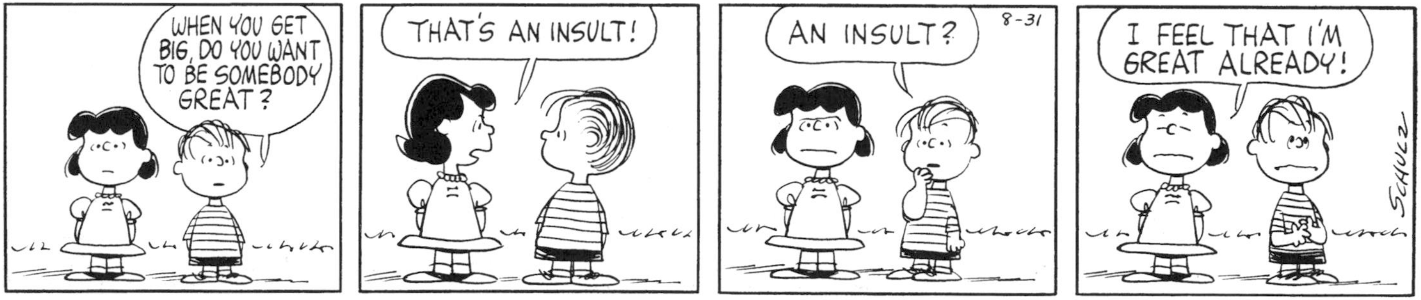
WHEN YOU GET BIG, DO YOU WANT TO BE SOMEBODY GREAT?
THAT'S AN INSULT!
AN INSULT?
8-31
I FEEL THAT I'M GREAT ALREADY!
SCHULZ

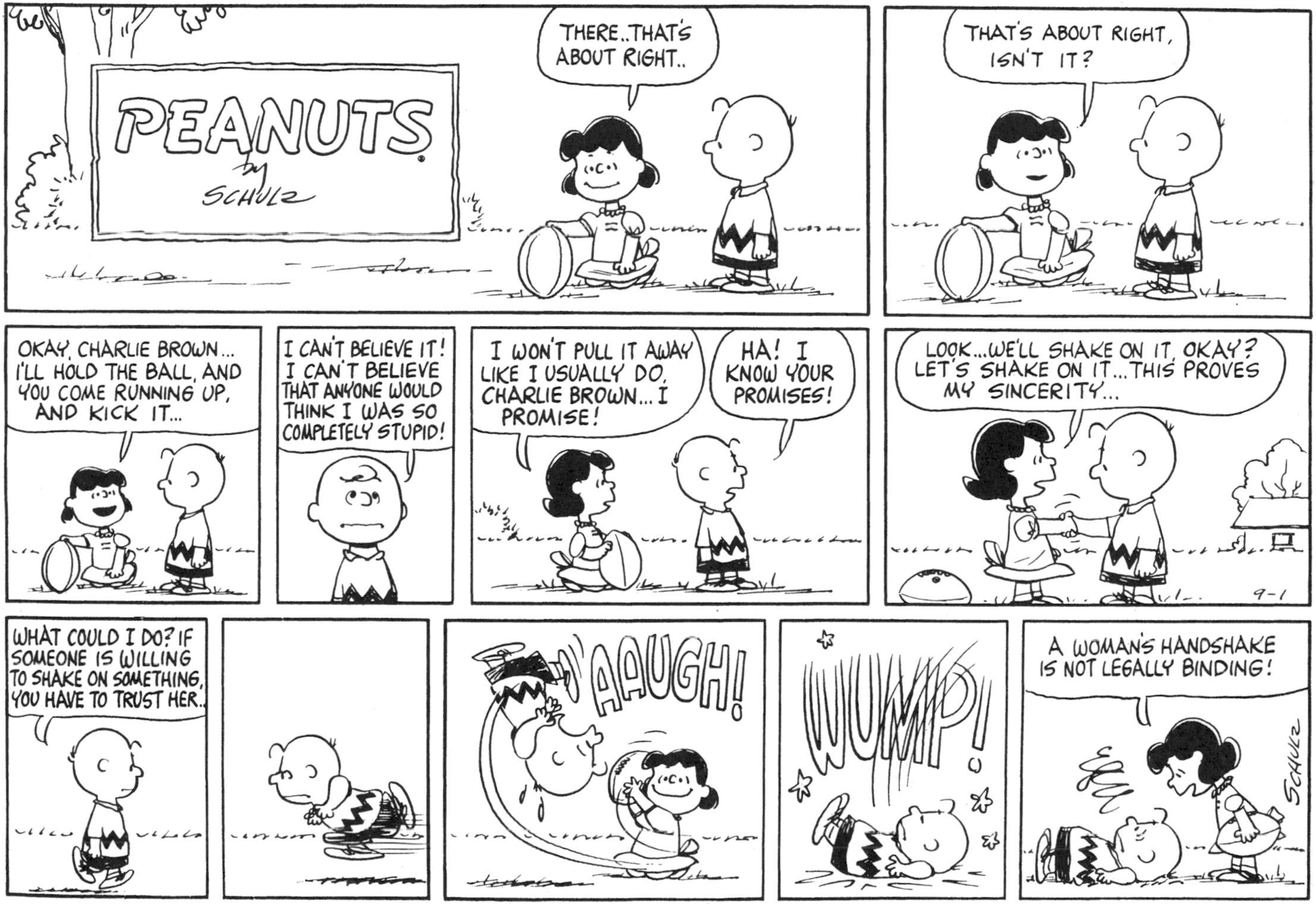
PEANUTS
by SCHULZ
THERE..THAT'S ABOUT RIGHT..
THAT'S ABOUT RIGHT, ISN'T IT?
OKAY, CHARLIE BROWN... I'LL HOLD THE BALL, AND YOU COME RUNNING UP, AND KICK IT...
I CAN'T BELIEVE IT! I CAN'T BELIEVE THAT ANYONE WOULD THINK I WAS SO COMPLETELY STUPID!
I WON'T PULL IT AWAY LIKE I USUALLY DO, CHARLIE BROWN... I PROMISE!
HA! I KNOW YOUR PROMISES!
LOOK...WE'LL SHAKE ON IT, OKAY? LET'S SHAKE ON IT... THIS PROVES MY SINCERITY...
9-1
WHAT COULD I DO? IF SOMEONE IS WILLING TO SHAKE ON SOMETHING, YOU HAVE TO TRUST HER..
AAUGH!
WUMP!
A WOMAN'S HANDSHAKE IS NOT LEGALLY BINDING!
SCHULZ

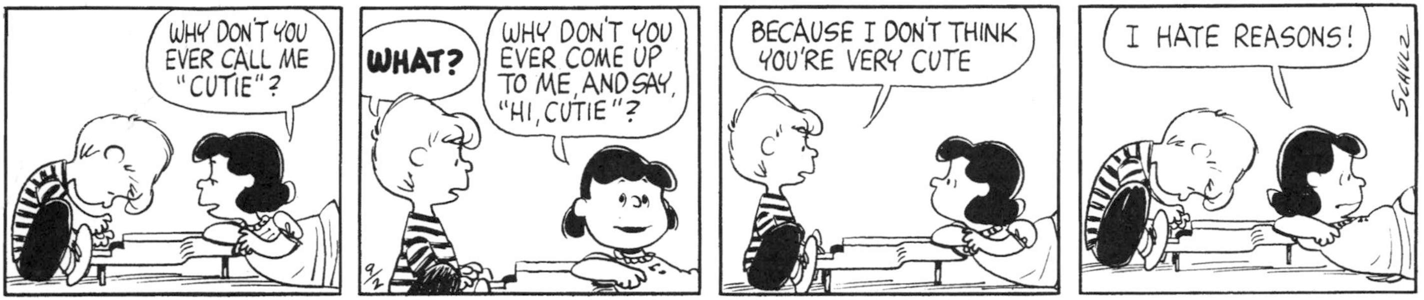
WHY DON'T YOU EVER CALL ME "CUTIE"?
WHAT?
WHY DON'T YOU EVER COME UP TO ME, AND SAY, "HI, CUTIE"?
BECAUSE I DON'T THINK YOU'RE VERY CUTE
I HATE REASONS!

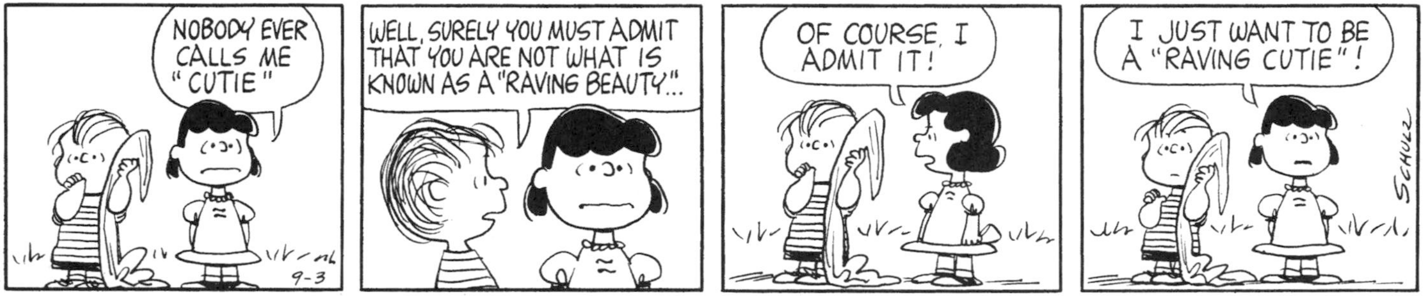
NOBODY EVER CALLS ME "CUTIE"
WELL, SURELY YOU MUST ADMIT THAT YOU ARE NOT WHAT IS KNOWN AS A "RAVING BEAUTY."...
OF COURSE, I ADMIT IT!
I JUST WANT TO BE A "RAVING CUTIE"!

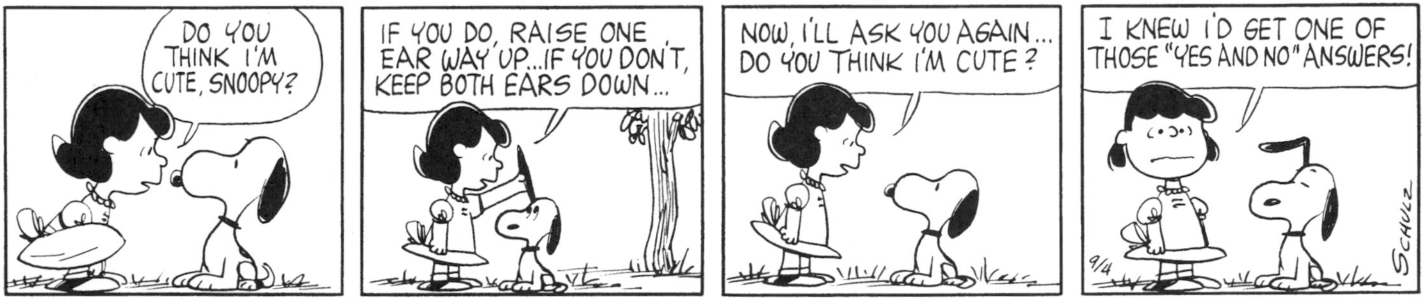
DO YOU THINK I'M CUTE, SNOOPY?
IF YOU DO, RAISE ONE EAR WAY UP...IF YOU DON'T, KEEP BOTH EARS DOWN...
NOW, I'LL ASK YOU AGAIN... DO YOU THINK I'M CUTE?
I KNEW I'D GET ONE OF THOSE "YES AND NO" ANSWERS!

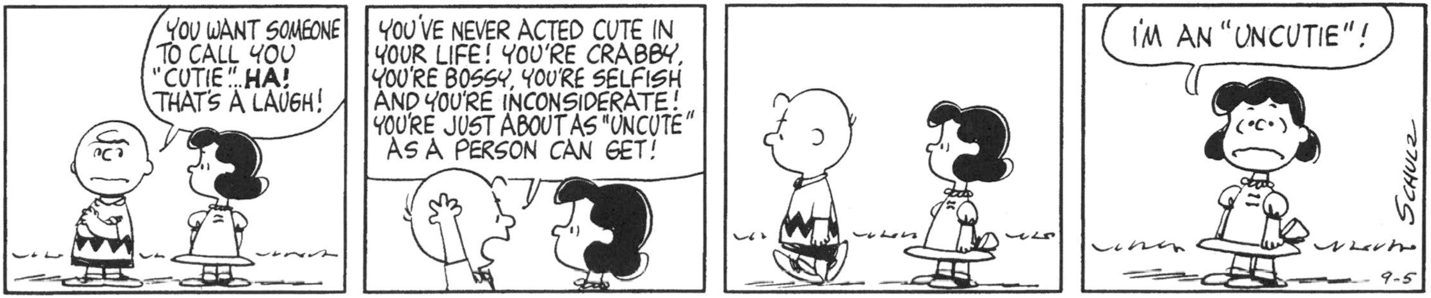
YOU WANT SOMEONE TO CALL YOU "CUTIE"... **HA!** THAT'S A LAUGH!
YOU'VE NEVER ACTED CUTE IN YOUR LIFE! YOU'RE CRABBY, YOU'RE BOSSY, YOU'RE SELFISH AND YOU'RE INCONSIDERATE! YOU'RE JUST ABOUT AS "UNCUTE" AS A PERSON CAN GET!
I'M AN "UNCUTIE"!
SCHULZ
9-5

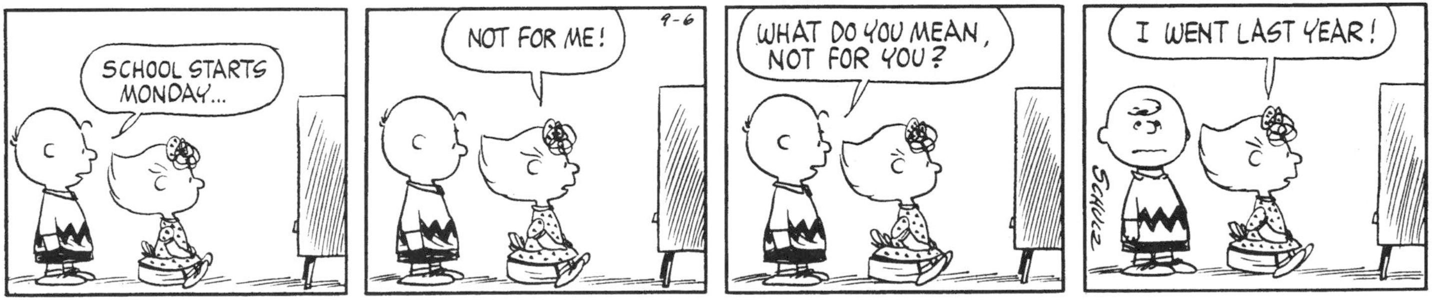
SCHOOL STARTS MONDAY...
NOT FOR ME!
9-6
WHAT DO YOU MEAN, NOT FOR YOU?
I WENT LAST YEAR!
SCHULZ

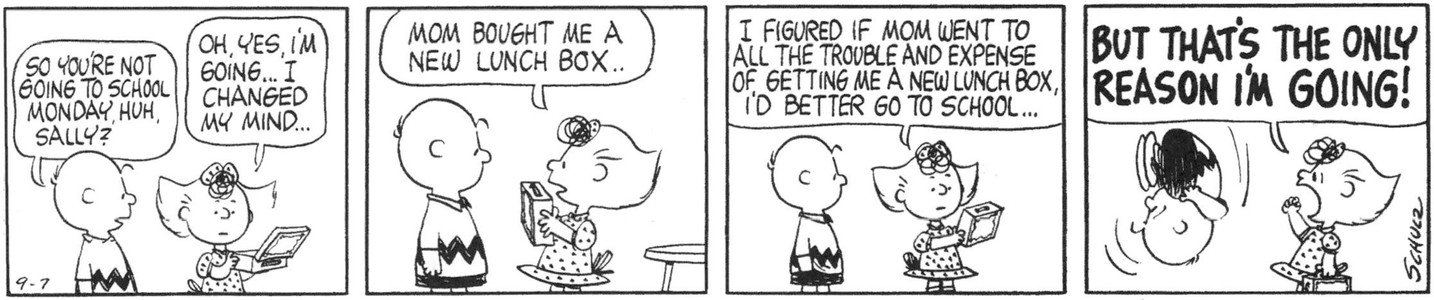
SO YOU'RE NOT GOING TO SCHOOL MONDAY, HUH, SALLY?
OH, YES, I'M GOING... I CHANGED MY MIND...
9-7
MOM BOUGHT ME A NEW LUNCH BOX..
I FIGURED IF MOM WENT TO ALL THE TROUBLE AND EXPENSE OF GETTING ME A NEW LUNCH BOX, I'D BETTER GO TO SCHOOL...
BUT THAT'S THE ONLY REASON I'M GOING!
SCHULZ

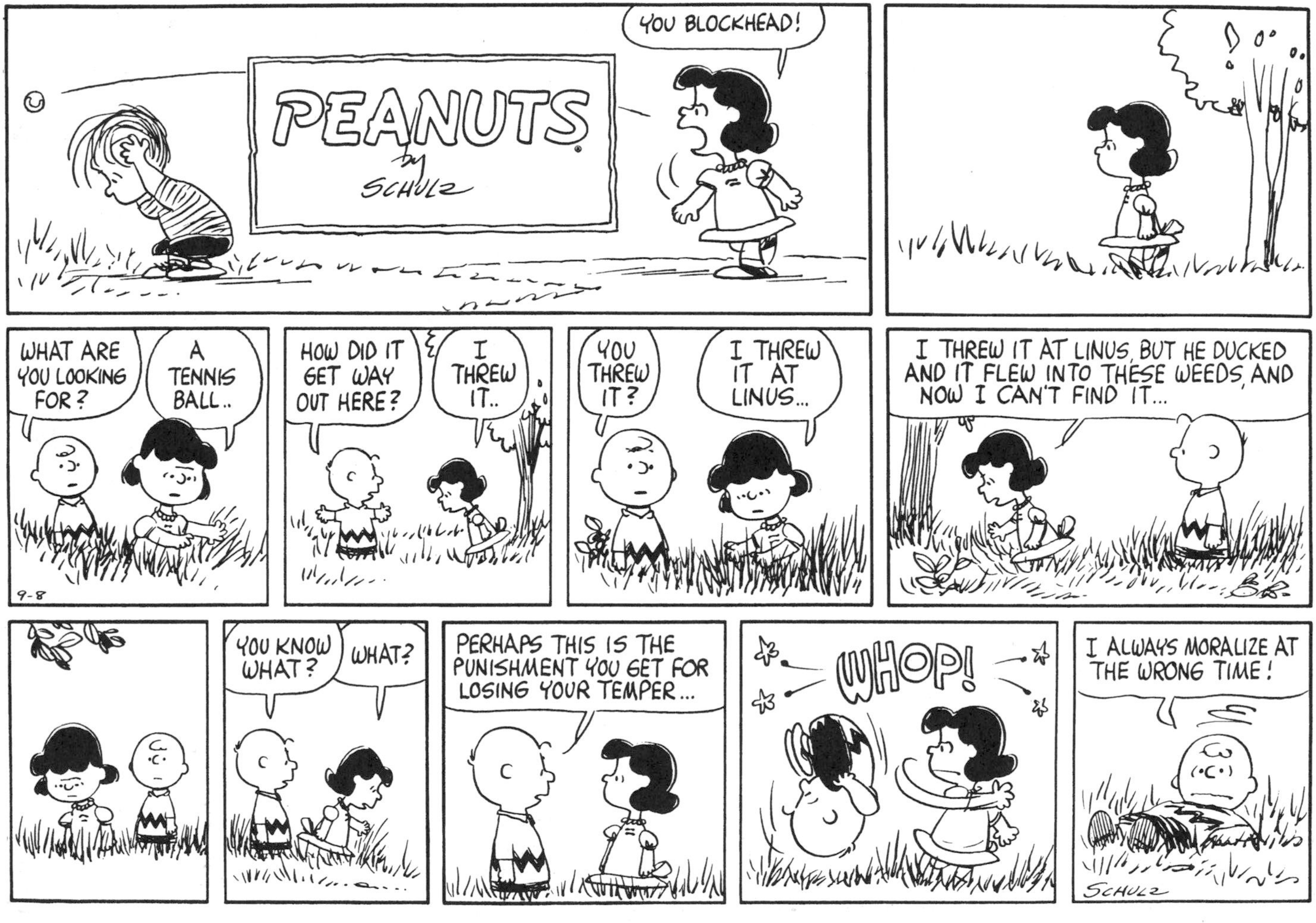
YOU BLOCKHEAD!
PEANUTS
by SCHULZ
WHAT ARE YOU LOOKING FOR?
A TENNIS BALL..
HOW DID IT GET WAY OUT HERE?
I THREW IT..
YOU THREW IT?
I THREW IT AT LINUS...
I THREW IT AT LINUS, BUT HE DUCKED AND IT FLEW INTO THESE WEEDS, AND NOW I CAN'T FIND IT...
9-8
YOU KNOW WHAT?
WHAT?
PERHAPS THIS IS THE PUNISHMENT YOU GET FOR LOSING YOUR TEMPER...
WHOP!
I ALWAYS MORALIZE AT THE WRONG TIME!
SCHULZ

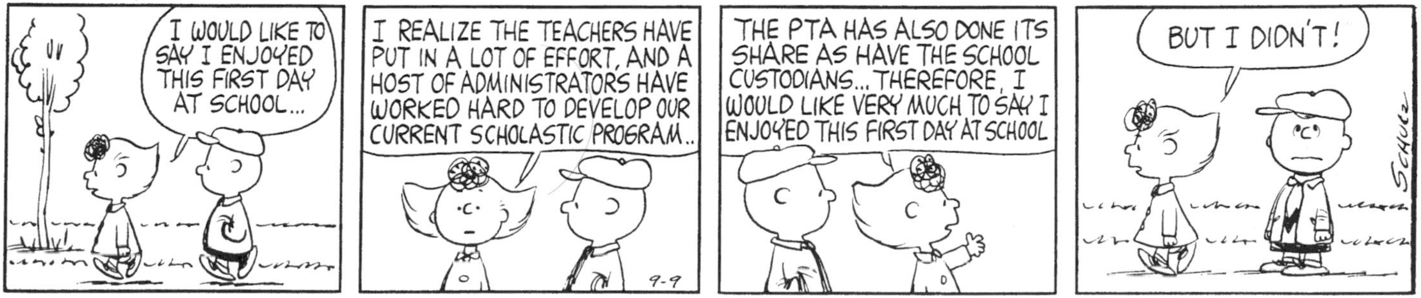
I WOULD LIKE TO SAY I ENJOYED THIS FIRST DAY AT SCHOOL...
I REALIZE THE TEACHERS HAVE PUT IN A LOT OF EFFORT, AND A HOST OF ADMINISTRATORS HAVE WORKED HARD TO DEVELOP OUR CURRENT SCHOLASTIC PROGRAM..
THE PTA HAS ALSO DONE ITS SHARE AS HAVE THE SCHOOL CUSTODIANS... THEREFORE, I WOULD LIKE VERY MUCH TO SAY I ENJOYED THIS FIRST DAY AT SCHOOL
BUT I DIDN'T!

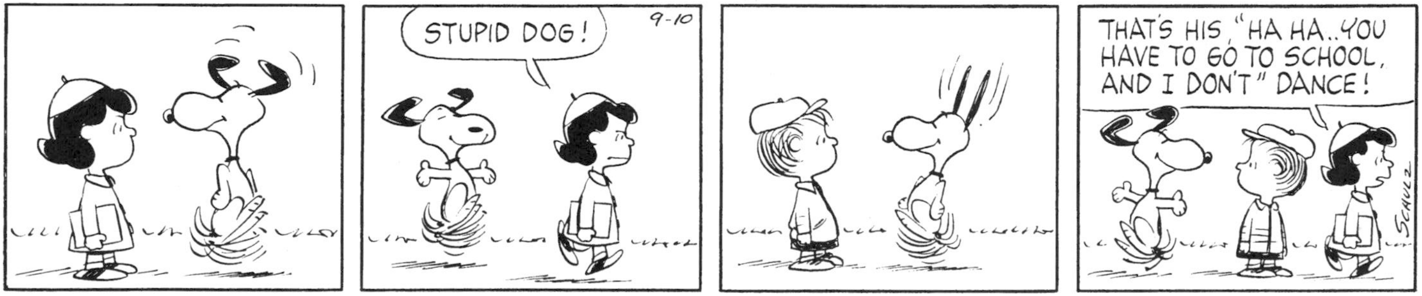
STUPID DOG!
THAT'S HIS, "HA HA..YOU HAVE TO GO TO SCHOOL, AND I DON'T" DANCE!

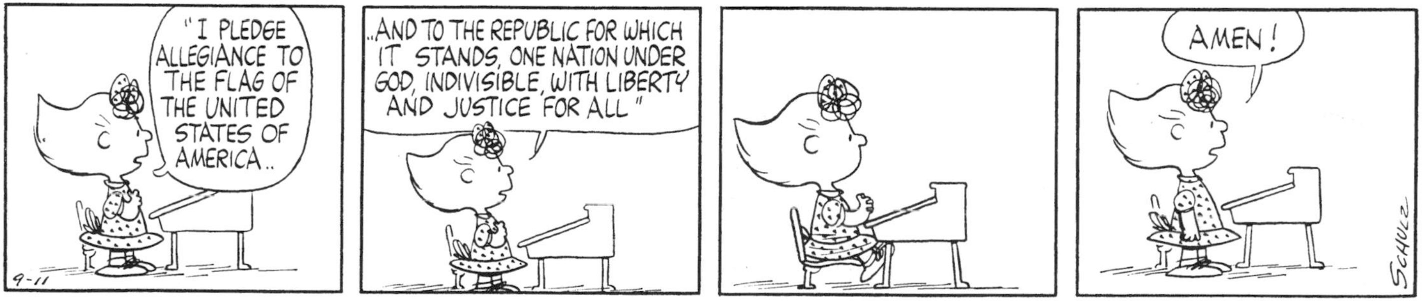
"I PLEDGE ALLEGIANCE TO THE FLAG OF THE UNITED STATES OF AMERICA..
..AND TO THE REPUBLIC FOR WHICH IT STANDS, ONE NATION UNDER GOD, INDIVISIBLE, WITH LIBERTY AND JUSTICE FOR ALL"
AMEN!

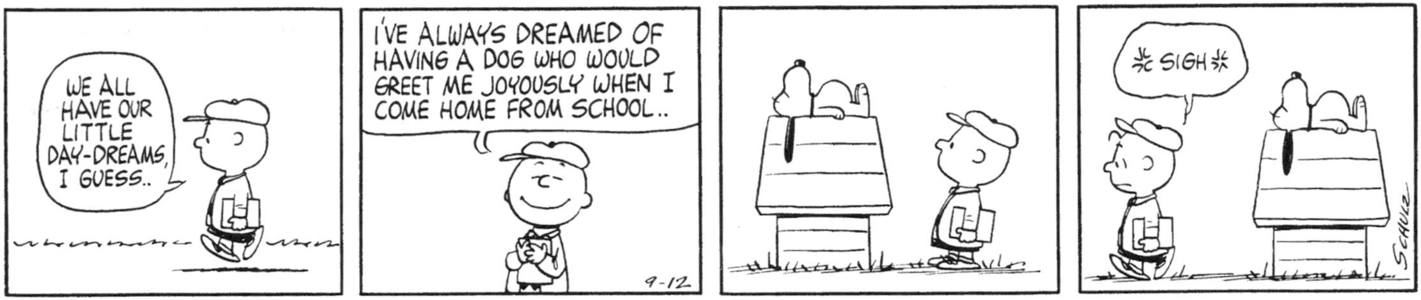
WE ALL HAVE OUR LITTLE DAY-DREAMS, I GUESS..
I'VE ALWAYS DREAMED OF HAVING A DOG WHO WOULD GREET ME JOYOUSLY WHEN I COME HOME FROM SCHOOL..
9-12
SIGH
SCHULZ

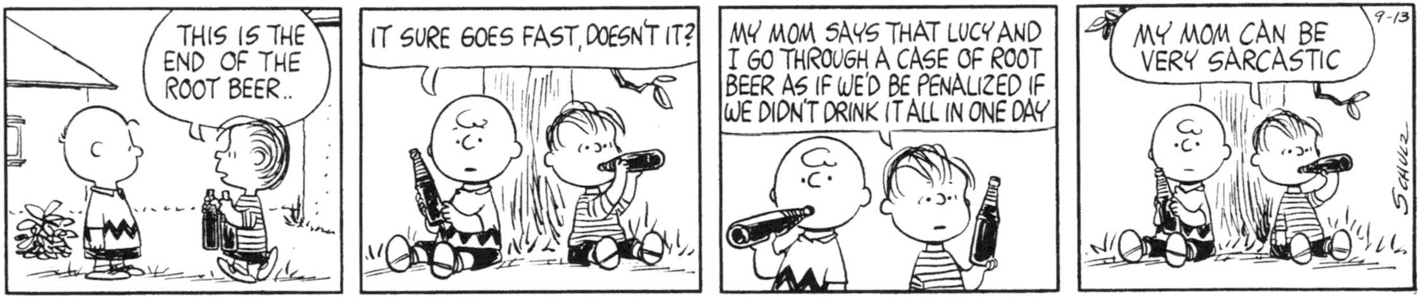
THIS IS THE END OF THE ROOT BEER..
IT SURE GOES FAST, DOESN'T IT?
MY MOM SAYS THAT LUCY AND I GO THROUGH A CASE OF ROOT BEER AS IF WE'D BE PENALIZED IF WE DIDN'T DRINK IT ALL IN ONE DAY
9-13
MY MOM CAN BE VERY SARCASTIC
SCHULZ

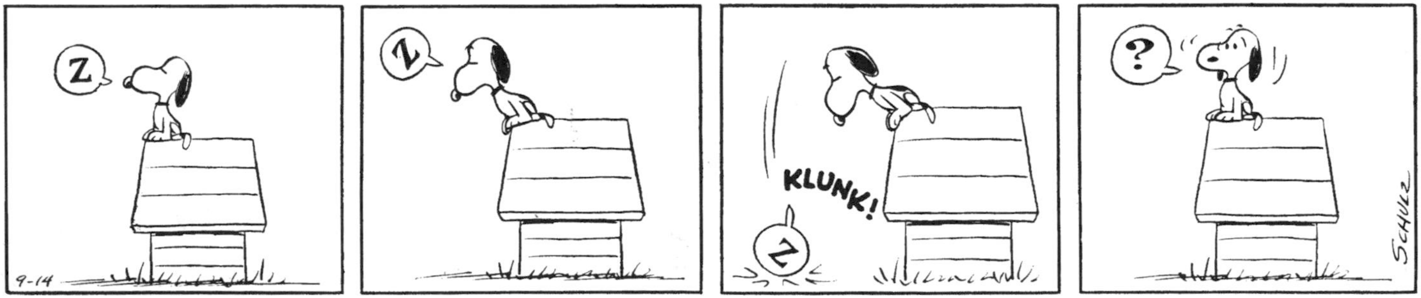
Z
9-14
Z
KLUNK!
Z
?
SCHULZ

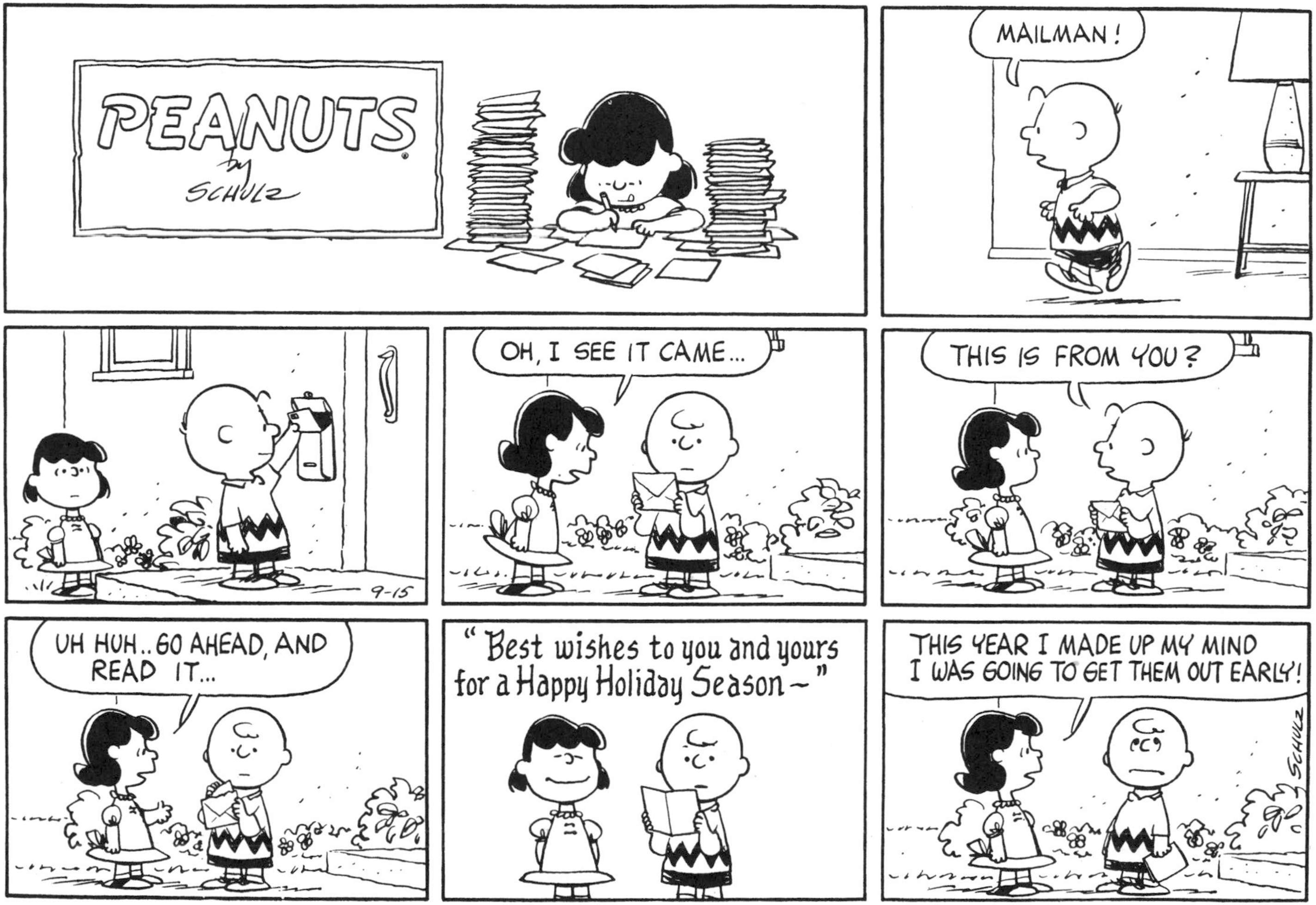
PEANUTS
by SCHULZ
MAILMAN!
9-15
OH, I SEE IT CAME...
THIS IS FROM YOU?
UH HUH.. GO AHEAD, AND READ IT...
"Best wishes to you and yours for a Happy Holiday Season ~"
THIS YEAR I MADE UP MY MIND I WAS GOING TO GET THEM OUT EARLY!
SCHULZ

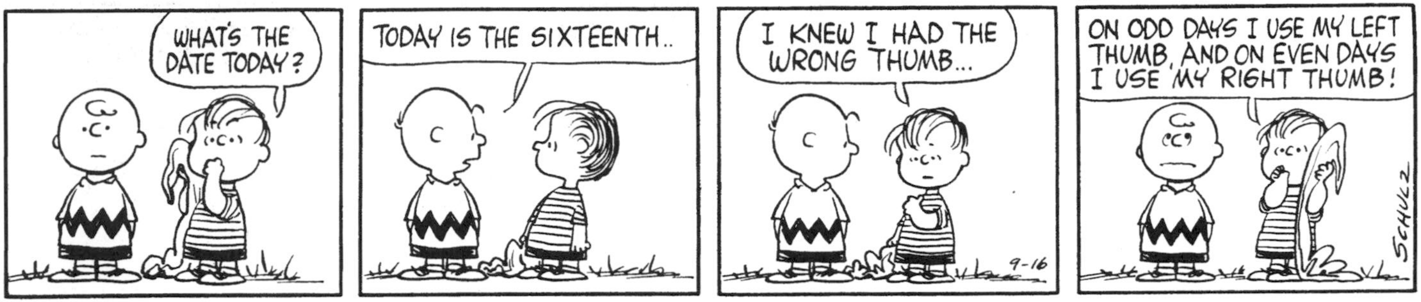
WHAT'S THE DATE TODAY?
TODAY IS THE SIXTEENTH..
I KNEW I HAD THE WRONG THUMB...
9-16
ON ODD DAYS I USE MY LEFT THUMB, AND ON EVEN DAYS I USE MY RIGHT THUMB!
SCHULZ

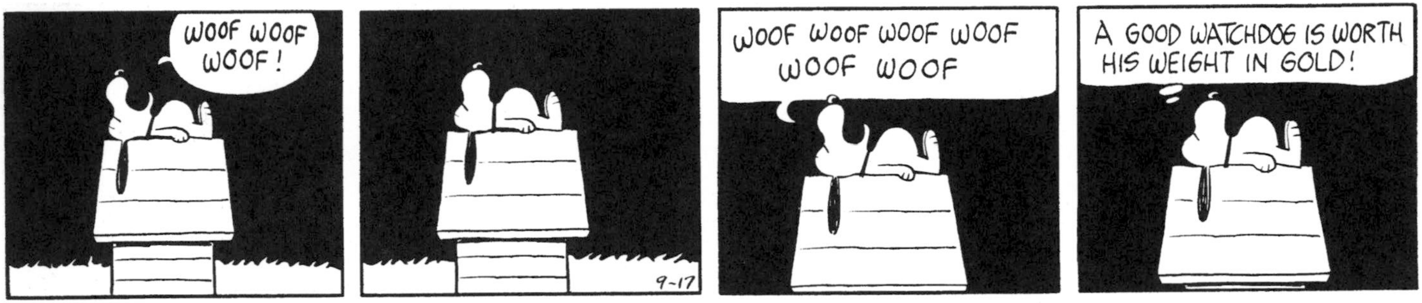
WOOF WOOF WOOF!
9-17
WOOF WOOF WOOF WOOF WOOF WOOF
A GOOD WATCHDOG IS WORTH HIS WEIGHT IN GOLD!

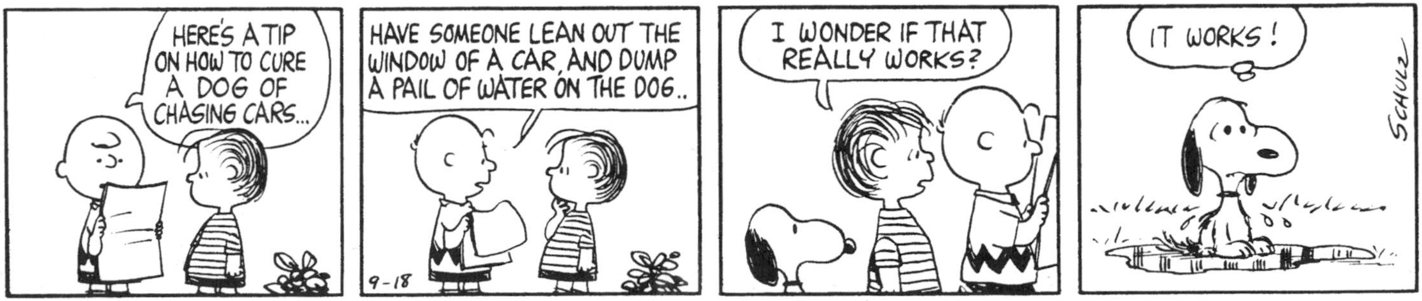
HERE'S A TIP ON HOW TO CURE A DOG OF CHASING CARS...
HAVE SOMEONE LEAN OUT THE WINDOW OF A CAR, AND DUMP A PAIL OF WATER ON THE DOG..
9-18
I WONDER IF THAT REALLY WORKS?
IT WORKS!
SCHULZ

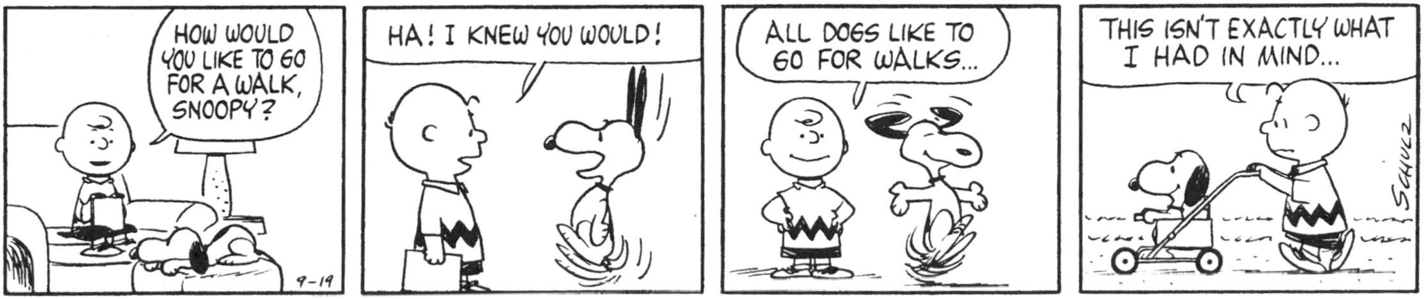
HOW WOULD YOU LIKE TO GO FOR A WALK, SNOOPY?
9-19
HA! I KNEW YOU WOULD!
ALL DOGS LIKE TO GO FOR WALKS...
THIS ISN'T EXACTLY WHAT I HAD IN MIND...
SCHULZ

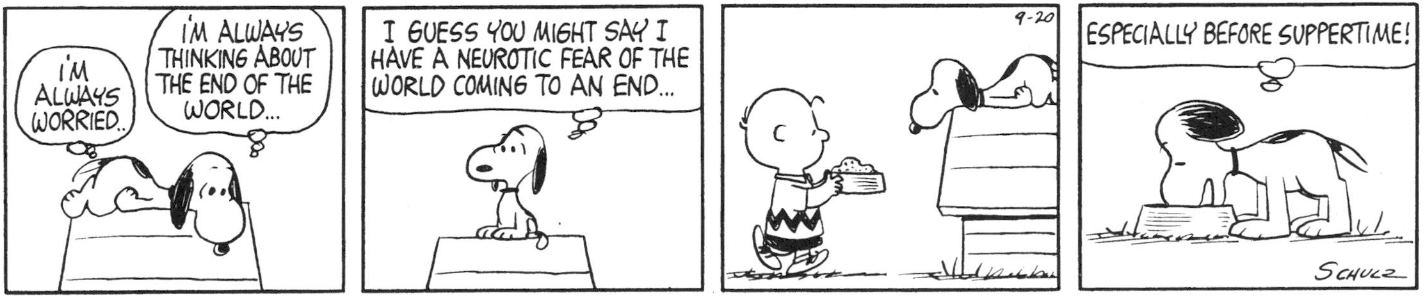
I'M ALWAYS WORRIED..
I'M ALWAYS THINKING ABOUT THE END OF THE WORLD...
I GUESS YOU MIGHT SAY I HAVE A NEUROTIC FEAR OF THE WORLD COMING TO AN END...
9-20
ESPECIALLY BEFORE SUPPERTIME!
SCHULZ

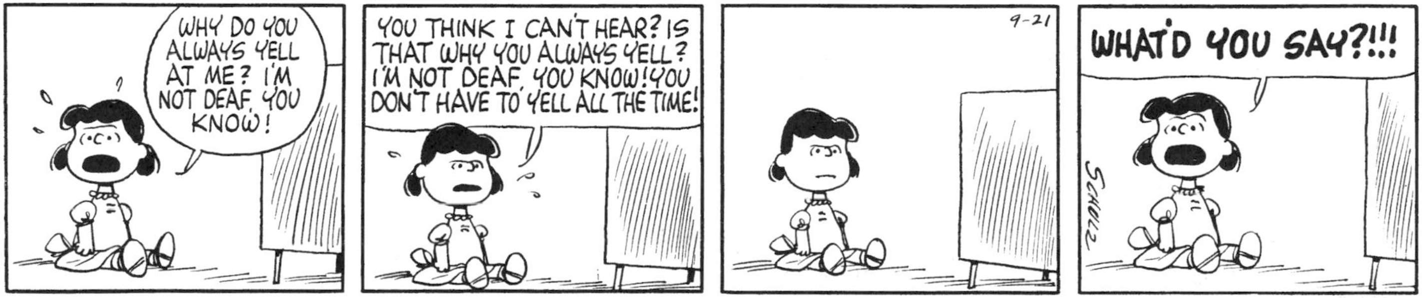
WHY DO YOU ALWAYS YELL AT ME? I'M NOT DEAF, YOU KNOW!
YOU THINK I CAN'T HEAR? IS THAT WHY YOU ALWAYS YELL? I'M NOT DEAF, YOU KNOW! YOU DON'T HAVE TO YELL ALL THE TIME!
9-21
WHAT'D YOU SAY?!!!
SCHULZ

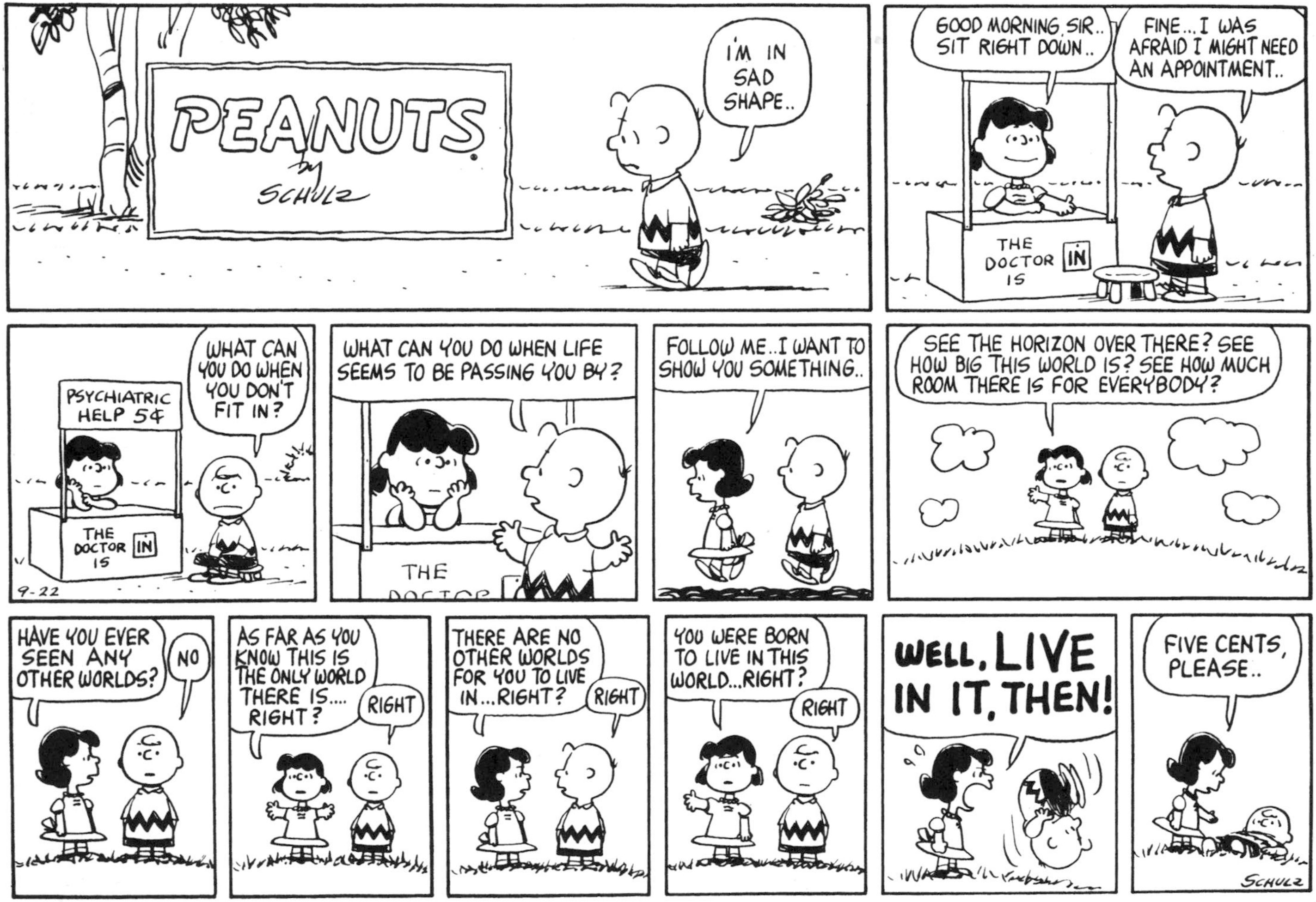
PEANUTS
by SCHULZ
I'M IN SAD SHAPE..
GOOD MORNING, SIR.. SIT RIGHT DOWN..
FINE... I WAS AFRAID I MIGHT NEED AN APPOINTMENT..
THE DOCTOR IS IN
PSYCHIATRIC HELP 5¢
WHAT CAN YOU DO WHEN YOU DON'T FIT IN?
9-22
WHAT CAN YOU DO WHEN LIFE SEEMS TO BE PASSING YOU BY?
FOLLOW ME..I WANT TO SHOW YOU SOMETHING..
SEE THE HORIZON OVER THERE? SEE HOW BIG THIS WORLD IS? SEE HOW MUCH ROOM THERE IS FOR EVERYBODY?
HAVE YOU EVER SEEN ANY OTHER WORLDS?
NO
AS FAR AS YOU KNOW THIS IS THE ONLY WORLD THERE IS.... RIGHT?
RIGHT
THERE ARE NO OTHER WORLDS FOR YOU TO LIVE IN...RIGHT?
RIGHT
YOU WERE BORN TO LIVE IN THIS WORLD...RIGHT?
RIGHT
WELL, LIVE IN IT, THEN!
FIVE CENTS, PLEASE..
SCHULZ

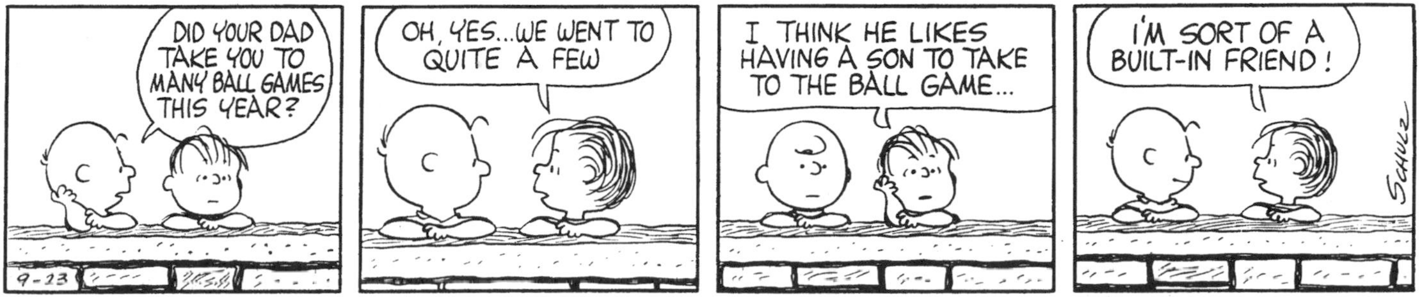
DID YOUR DAD TAKE YOU TO MANY BALL GAMES THIS YEAR?
OH, YES...WE WENT TO QUITE A FEW
I THINK HE LIKES HAVING A SON TO TAKE TO THE BALL GAME...
I'M SORT OF A BUILT-IN FRIEND!
9-23
SCHULZ

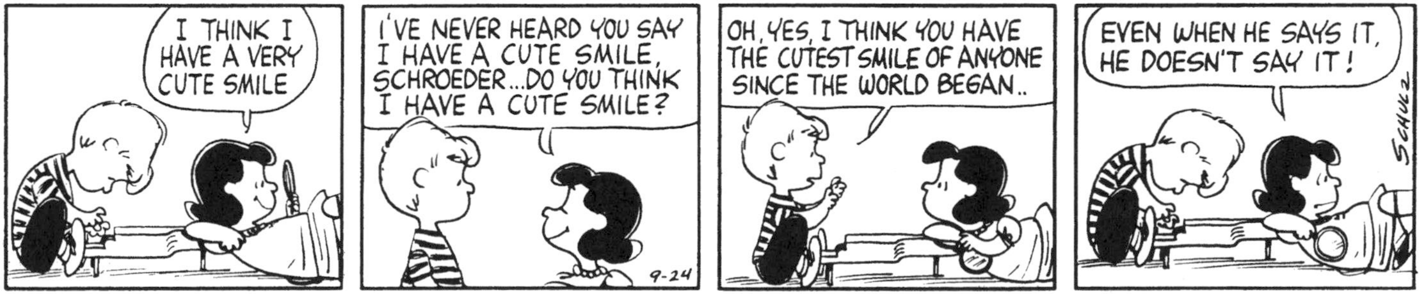
I THINK I HAVE A VERY CUTE SMILE
I'VE NEVER HEARD YOU SAY I HAVE A CUTE SMILE, SCHROEDER...DO YOU THINK I HAVE A CUTE SMILE?
OH, YES, I THINK YOU HAVE THE CUTEST SMILE OF ANYONE SINCE THE WORLD BEGAN..
EVEN WHEN HE SAYS IT, HE DOESN'T SAY IT!
9-24
SCHULZ

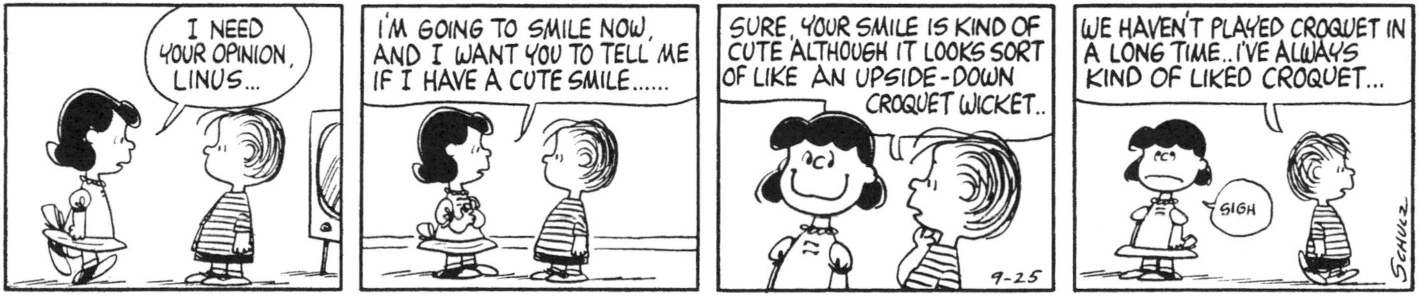
I NEED YOUR OPINION, LINUS...
I'M GOING TO SMILE NOW, AND I WANT YOU TO TELL ME IF I HAVE A CUTE SMILE......
SURE, YOUR SMILE IS KIND OF CUTE ALTHOUGH IT LOOKS SORT OF LIKE AN UPSIDE-DOWN CROQUET WICKET..
WE HAVEN'T PLAYED CROQUET IN A LONG TIME..I'VE ALWAYS KIND OF LIKED CROQUET...
SIGH
9-25
SCHULZ

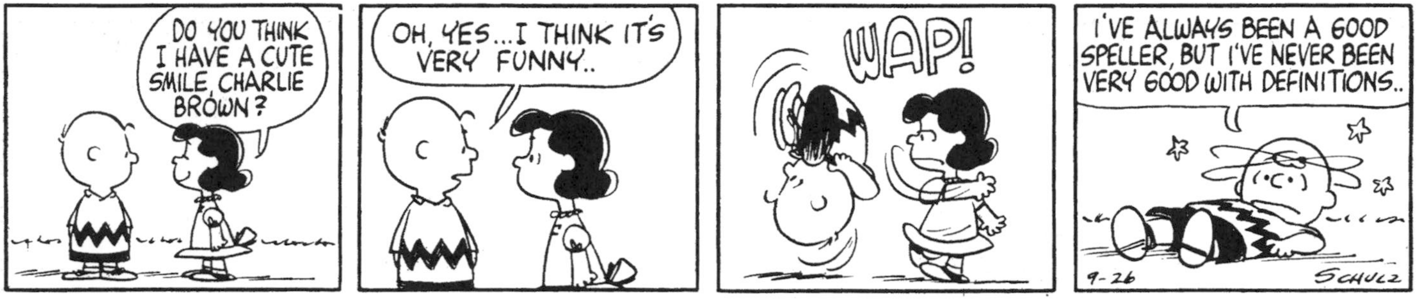
DO YOU THINK I HAVE A CUTE SMILE, CHARLIE BROWN?
OH, YES...I THINK IT'S VERY FUNNY..
WAP!
I'VE ALWAYS BEEN A GOOD SPELLER, BUT I'VE NEVER BEEN VERY GOOD WITH DEFINITIONS..
9-26
SCHULZ

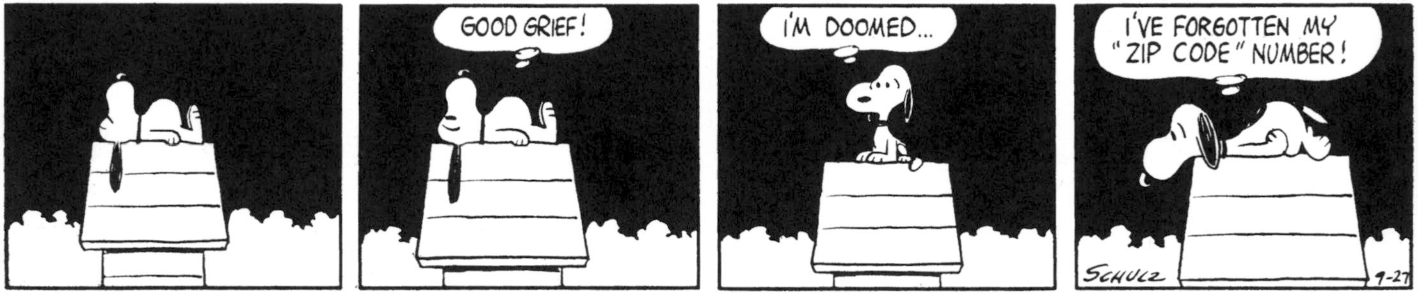
GOOD GRIEF!
I'M DOOMED...
I'VE FORGOTTEN MY "ZIP CODE" NUMBER!
SCHULZ
9-27

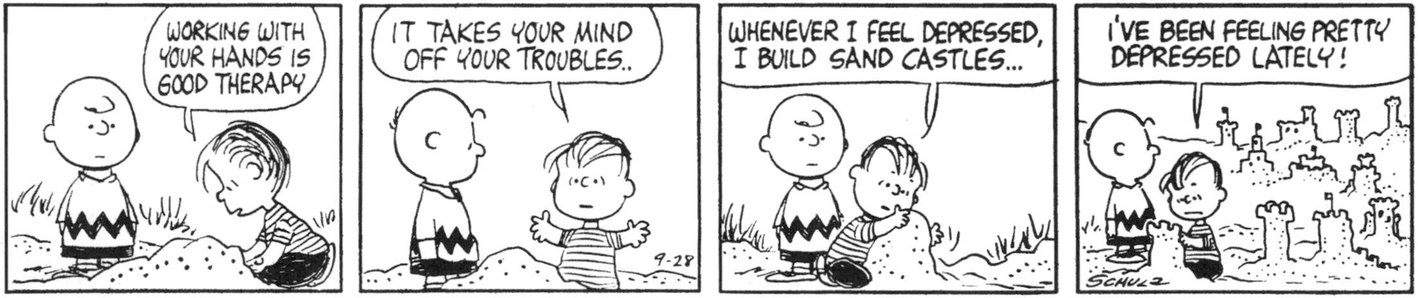
WORKING WITH YOUR HANDS IS GOOD THERAPY
IT TAKES YOUR MIND OFF YOUR TROUBLES..
9-28
WHENEVER I FEEL DEPRESSED, I BUILD SAND CASTLES...
I'VE BEEN FEELING PRETTY DEPRESSED LATELY!
SCHULZ

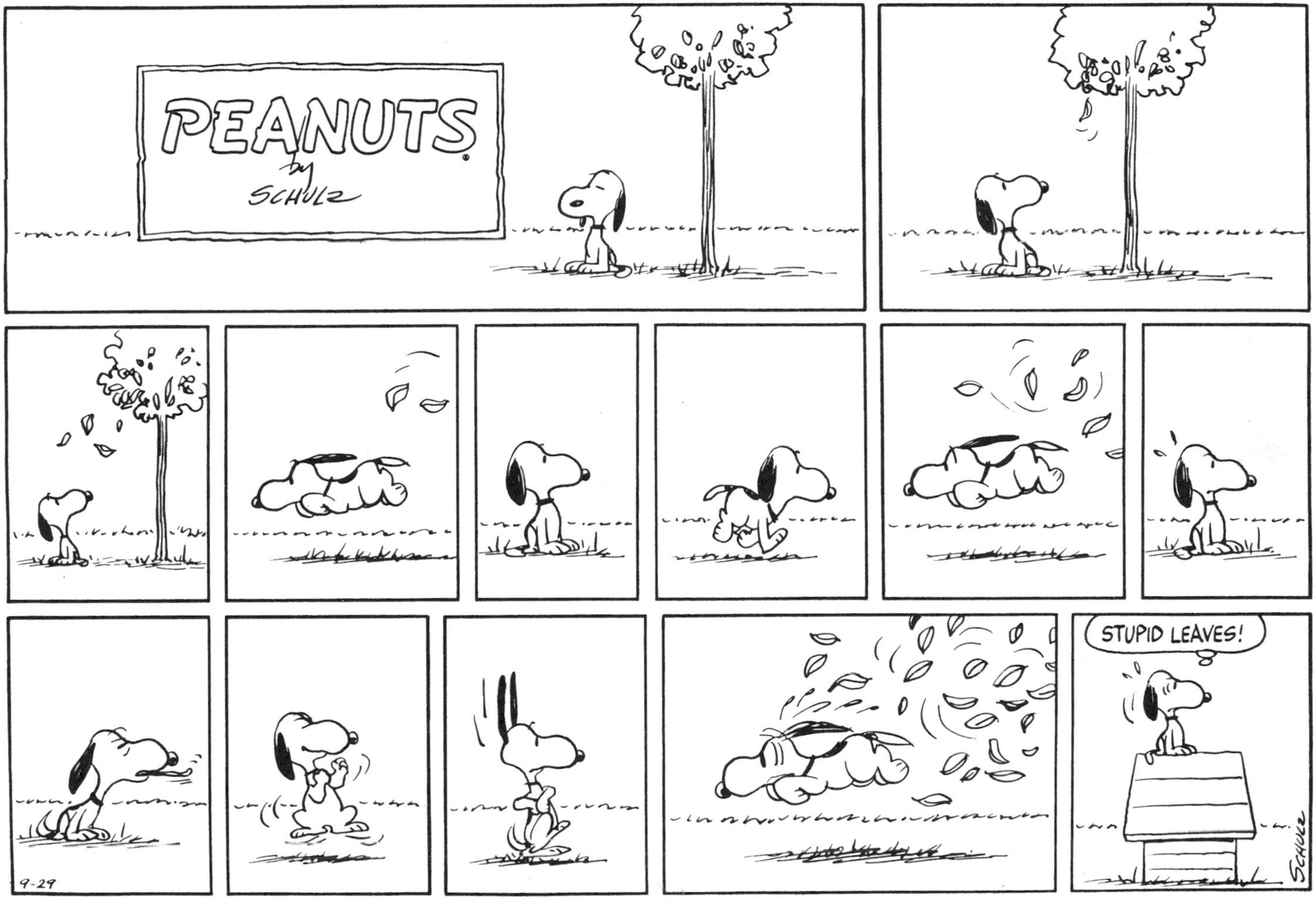
PEANUTS
by
SCHULZ
9-29
STUPID LEAVES!
SCHULZ

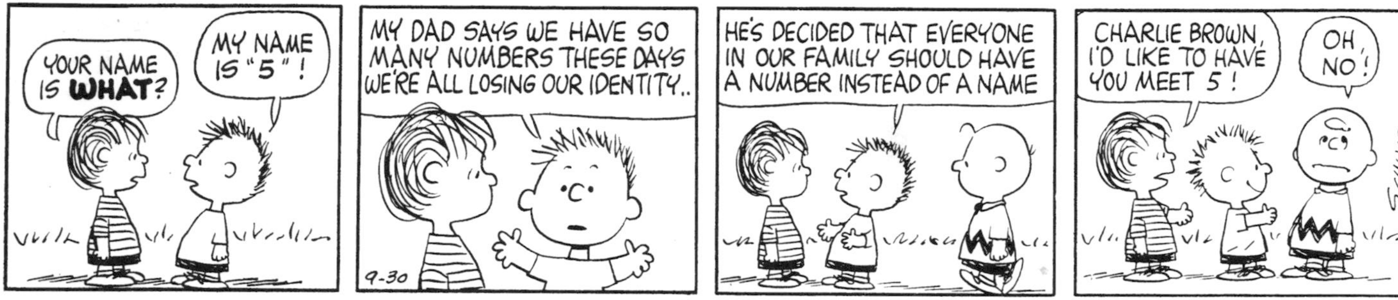
YOUR NAME IS **WHAT**?
MY NAME IS "5"!
MY DAD SAYS WE HAVE SO MANY NUMBERS THESE DAYS WE'RE ALL LOSING OUR IDENTITY..
9-30
HE'S DECIDED THAT EVERYONE IN OUR FAMILY SHOULD HAVE A NUMBER INSTEAD OF A NAME
CHARLIE BROWN, I'D LIKE TO HAVE YOU MEET 5!
OH, NO!
SCHULZ

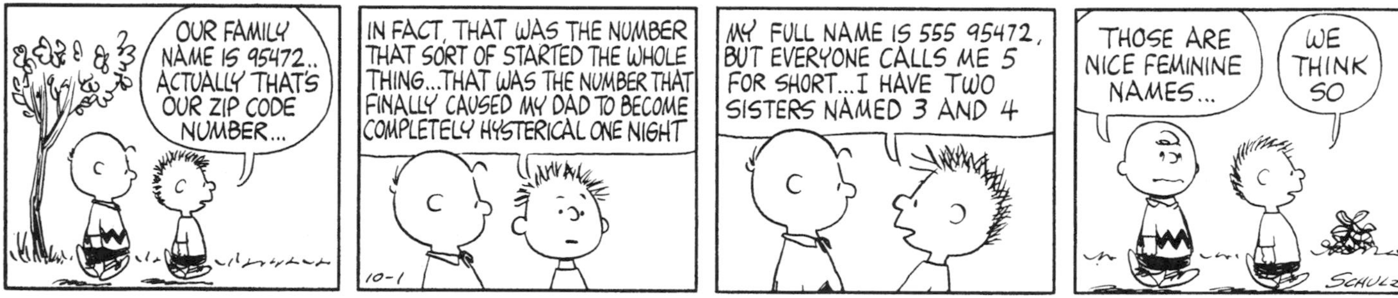
OUR FAMILY NAME IS 95472.. ACTUALLY THAT'S OUR ZIP CODE NUMBER...
IN FACT, THAT WAS THE NUMBER THAT SORT OF STARTED THE WHOLE THING...THAT WAS THE NUMBER THAT FINALLY CAUSED MY DAD TO BECOME COMPLETELY HYSTERICAL ONE NIGHT
10-1
MY FULL NAME IS 555 95472, BUT EVERYONE CALLS ME 5 FOR SHORT...I HAVE TWO SISTERS NAMED 3 AND 4
THOSE ARE NICE FEMININE NAMES...
WE THINK SO
SCHULZ

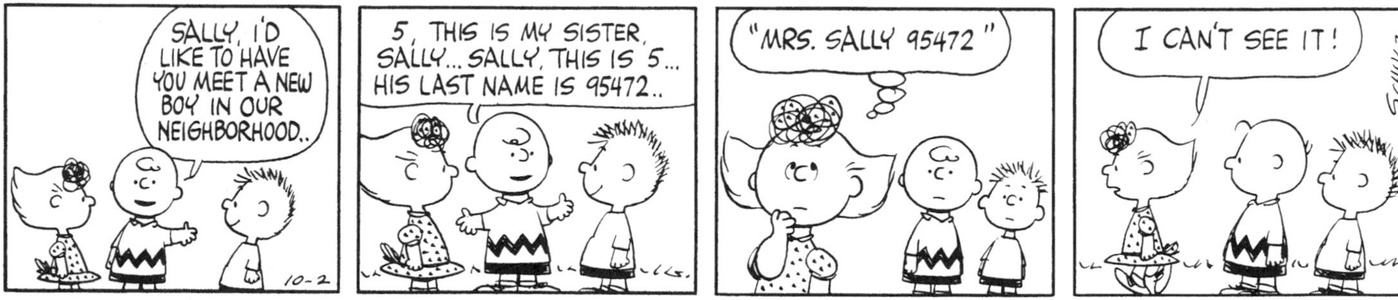
SALLY, I'D LIKE TO HAVE YOU MEET A NEW BOY IN OUR NEIGHBORHOOD..
10-2
5, THIS IS MY SISTER, SALLY... SALLY, THIS IS 5... HIS LAST NAME IS 95472..
"MRS. SALLY 95472"
I CAN'T SEE IT!
SCHULZ

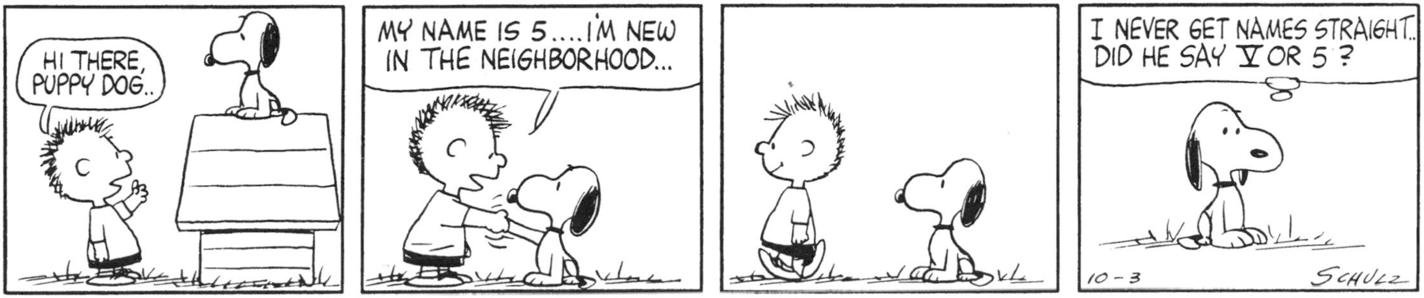
HI THERE, PUPPY DOG..
MY NAME IS 5....I'M NEW IN THE NEIGHBORHOOD...
I NEVER GET NAMES STRAIGHT.. DID HE SAY V OR 5 ?
10-3
SCHULZ

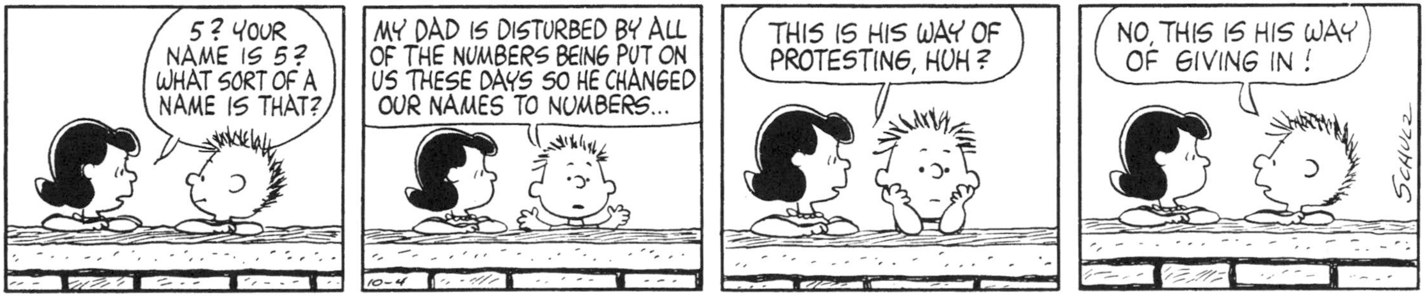
5? YOUR NAME IS 5? WHAT SORT OF A NAME IS THAT?
MY DAD IS DISTURBED BY ALL OF THE NUMBERS BEING PUT ON US THESE DAYS SO HE CHANGED OUR NAMES TO NUMBERS...
10-4
THIS IS HIS WAY OF PROTESTING, HUH?
NO, THIS IS HIS WAY OF GIVING IN!
SCHULZ

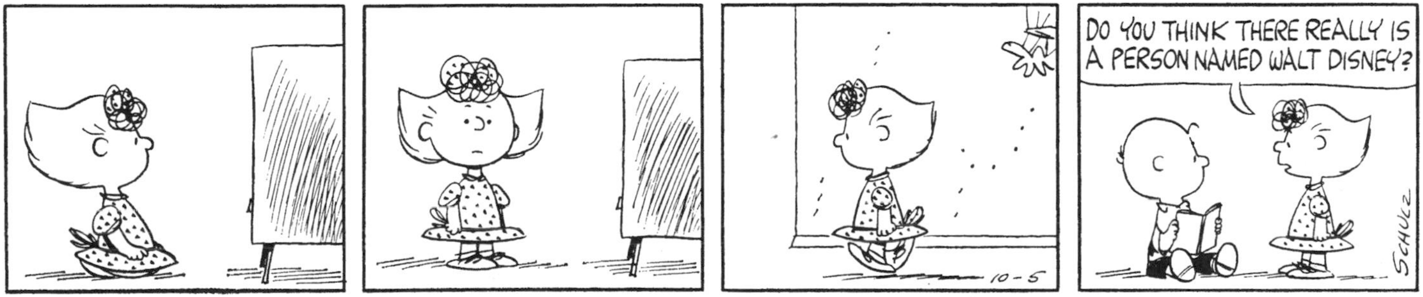
10-5
DO YOU THINK THERE REALLY IS A PERSON NAMED WALT DISNEY?
SCHULZ

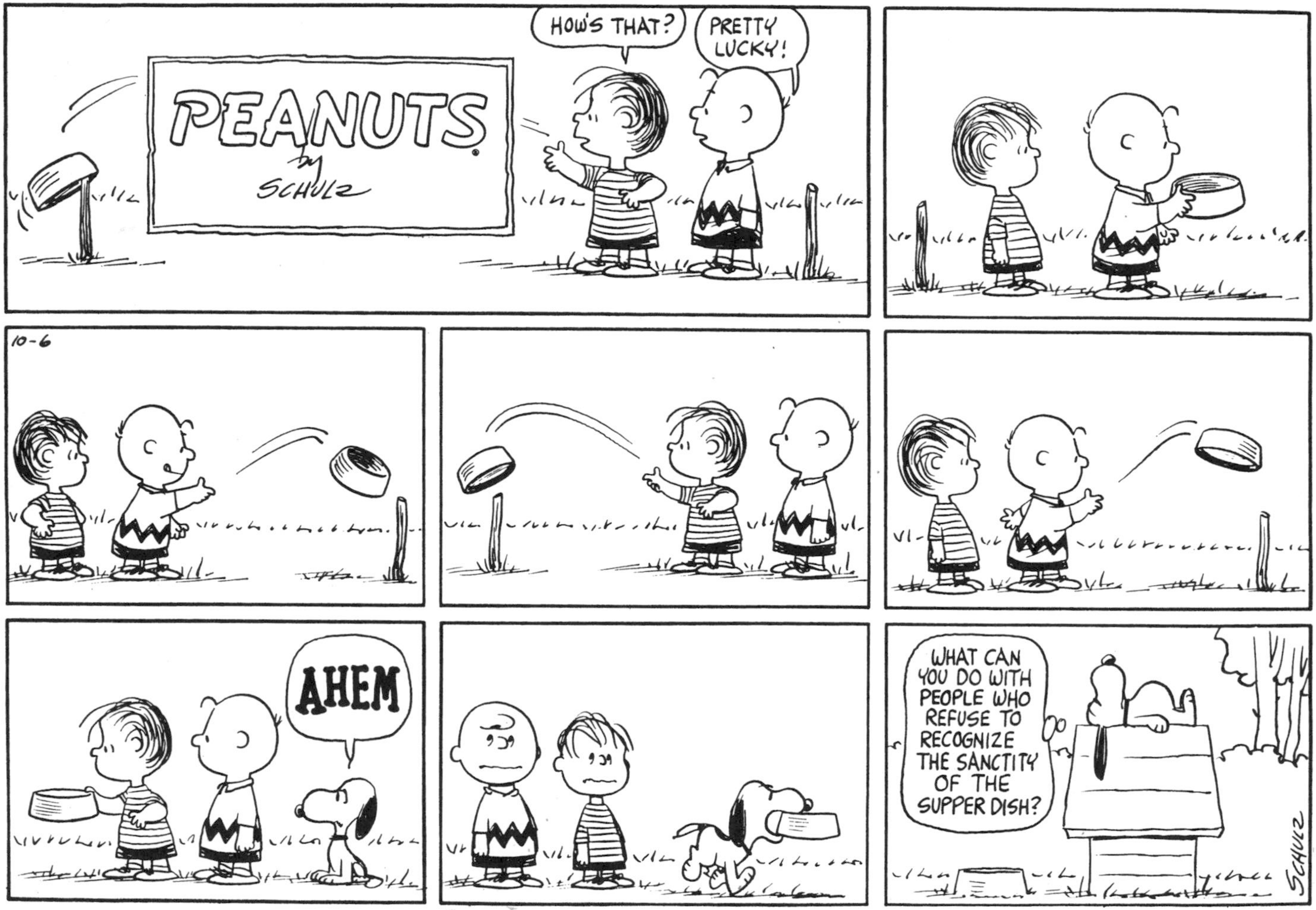
PEANUTS
by SCHULZ
HOW'S THAT?
PRETTY LUCKY!
10-6
AHEM
WHAT CAN YOU DO WITH PEOPLE WHO REFUSE TO RECOGNIZE THE SANCTITY OF THE SUPPER DISH?
SCHULZ

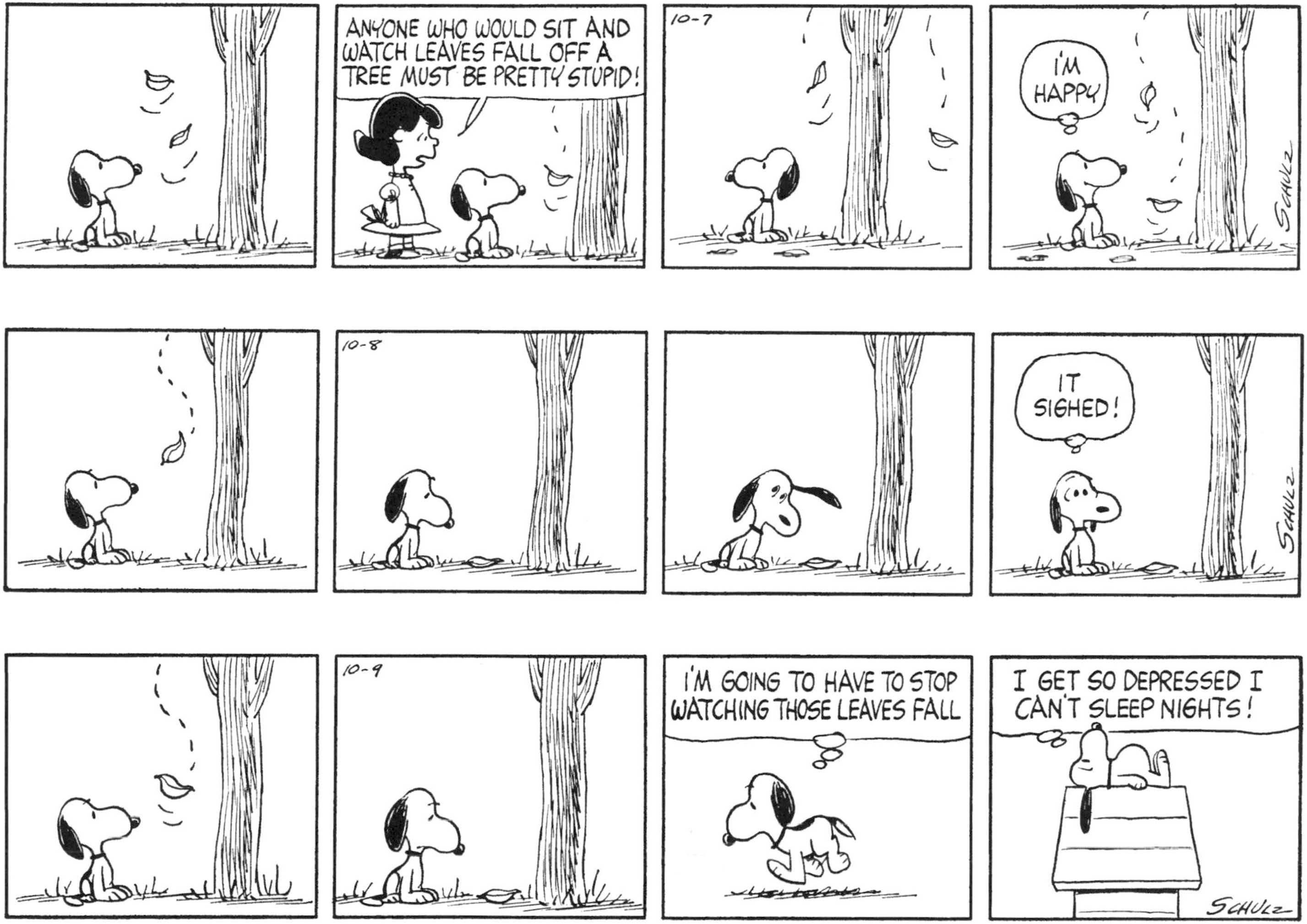
ANYONE WHO WOULD SIT AND WATCH LEAVES FALL OFF A TREE MUST BE PRETTY STUPID!
10-7
I'M HAPPY
SCHULZ
10-8
IT SIGHED!
SCHULZ
10-9
I'M GOING TO HAVE TO STOP WATCHING THOSE LEAVES FALL
I GET SO DEPRESSED I CAN'T SLEEP NIGHTS!
SCHULZ

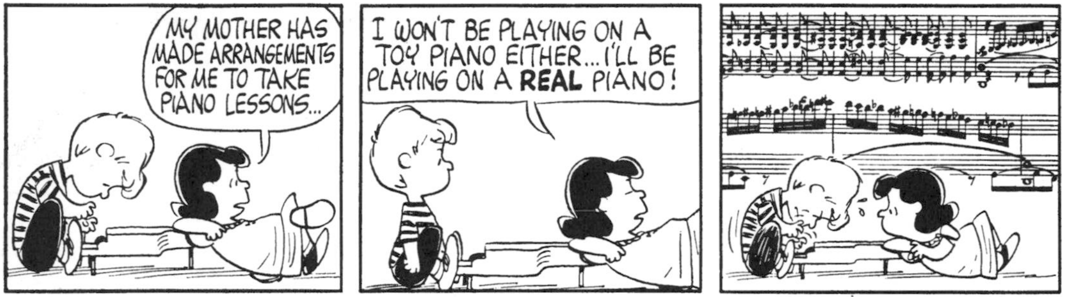
MY MOTHER HAS MADE ARRANGEMENTS FOR ME TO TAKE PIANO LESSONS...
I WON'T BE PLAYING ON A TOY PIANO EITHER... I'LL BE PLAYING ON A **REAL** PIANO!
10-10
YOU'RE CUTE WHEN YOU GET MAD...
SCHULZ

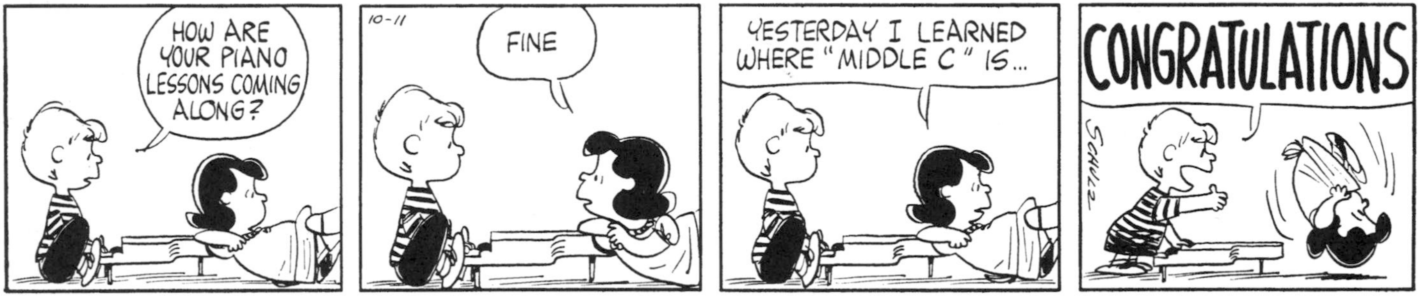
HOW ARE YOUR PIANO LESSONS COMING ALONG?
10-11
FINE
YESTERDAY I LEARNED WHERE "MIDDLE C" IS...
CONGRATULATIONS
SCHULZ

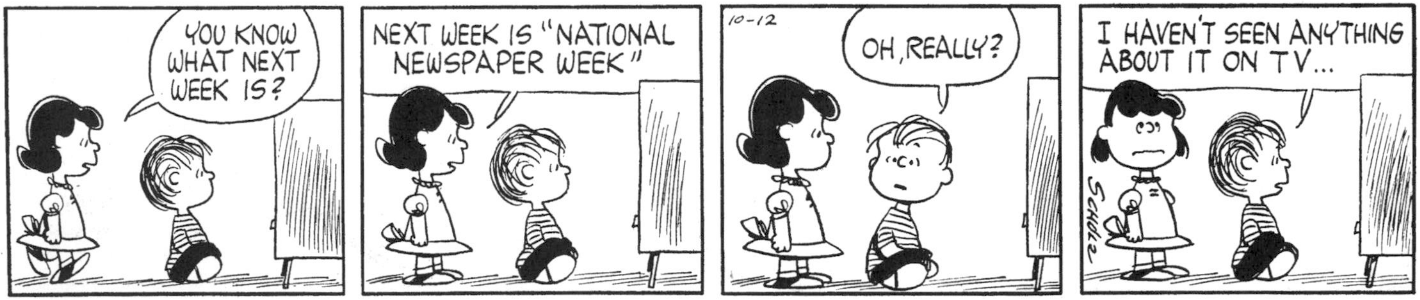
YOU KNOW WHAT NEXT WEEK IS?
NEXT WEEK IS "NATIONAL NEWSPAPER WEEK"
10-12
OH, REALLY?
I HAVEN'T SEEN ANYTHING ABOUT IT ON TV...
SCHULZ

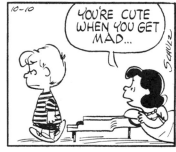

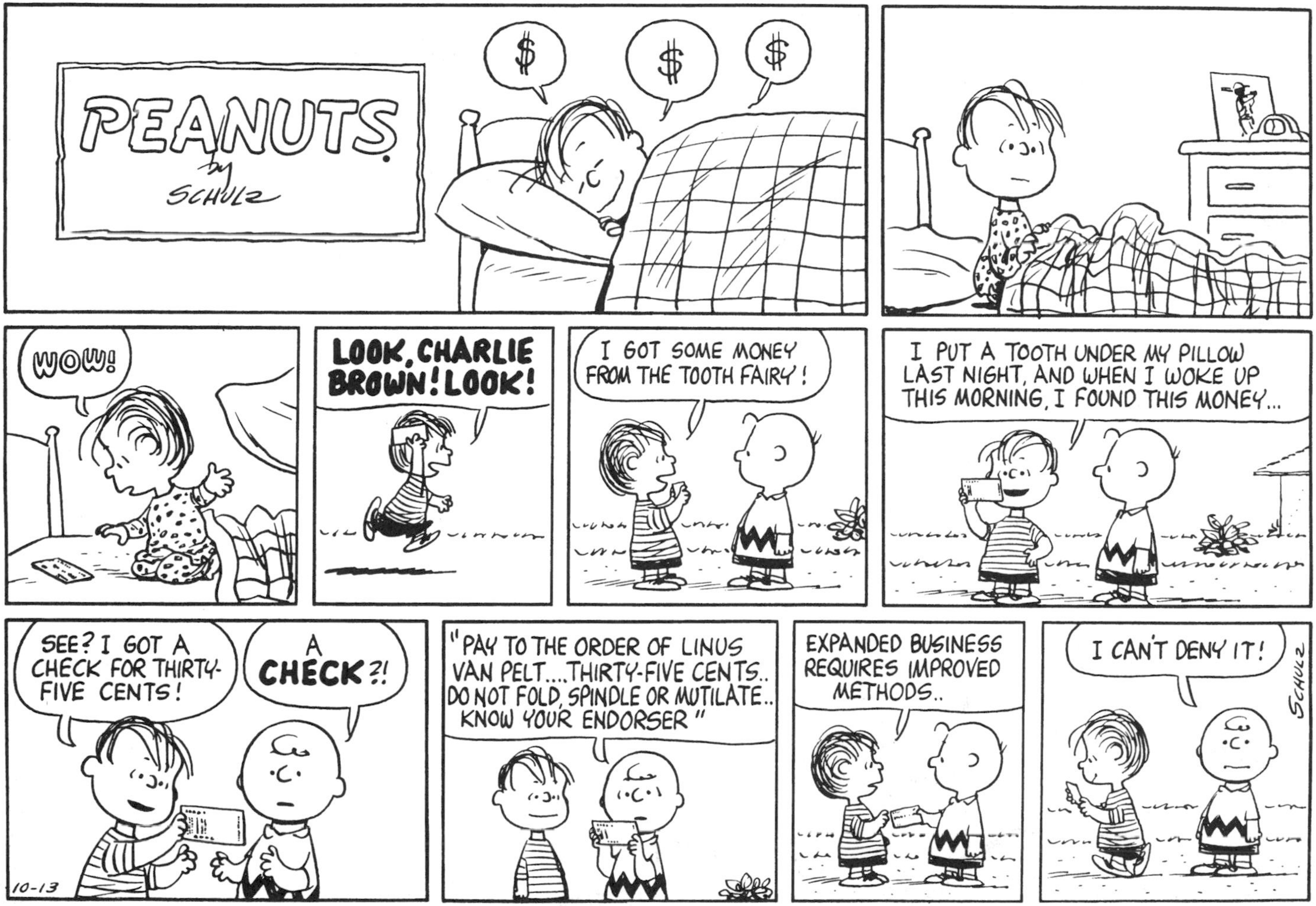
PEANUTS
by SCHULZ
$
$
$
WOW!
LOOK, CHARLIE BROWN! LOOK!
I GOT SOME MONEY FROM THE TOOTH FAIRY!
I PUT A TOOTH UNDER MY PILLOW LAST NIGHT, AND WHEN I WOKE UP THIS MORNING, I FOUND THIS MONEY...
SEE? I GOT A CHECK FOR THIRTY-FIVE CENTS!
A CHECK?!
"PAY TO THE ORDER OF LINUS VAN PELT....THIRTY-FIVE CENTS.. DO NOT FOLD, SPINDLE OR MUTILATE.. KNOW YOUR ENDORSER"
EXPANDED BUSINESS REQUIRES IMPROVED METHODS..
I CAN'T DENY IT!
SCHULZ
10-13

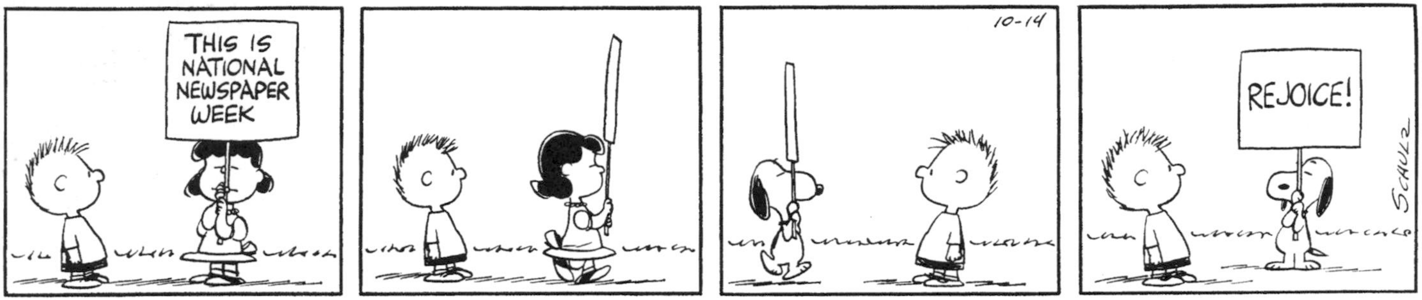
THIS IS NATIONAL NEWSPAPER WEEK
10-14
REJOICE!
SCHULZ

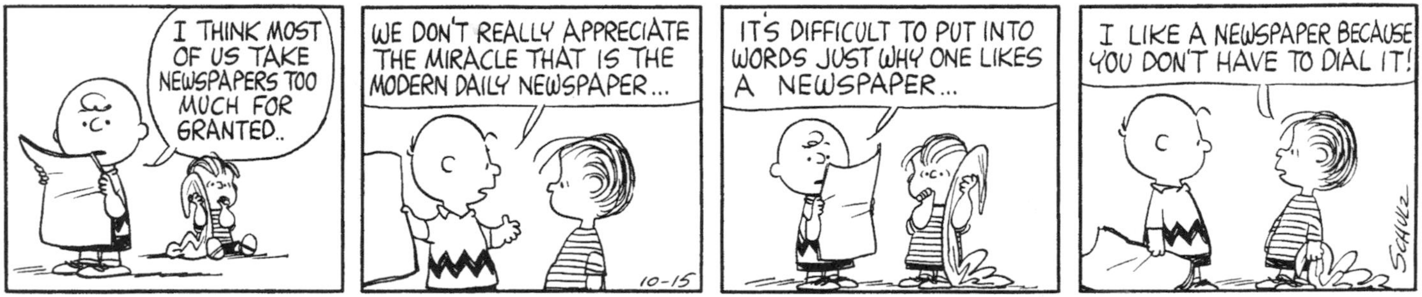
I THINK MOST OF US TAKE NEWSPAPERS TOO MUCH FOR GRANTED..
WE DON'T REALLY APPRECIATE THE MIRACLE THAT IS THE MODERN DAILY NEWSPAPER...
10-15
IT'S DIFFICULT TO PUT INTO WORDS JUST WHY ONE LIKES A NEWSPAPER...
I LIKE A NEWSPAPER BECAUSE YOU DON'T HAVE TO DIAL IT!
SCHULZ

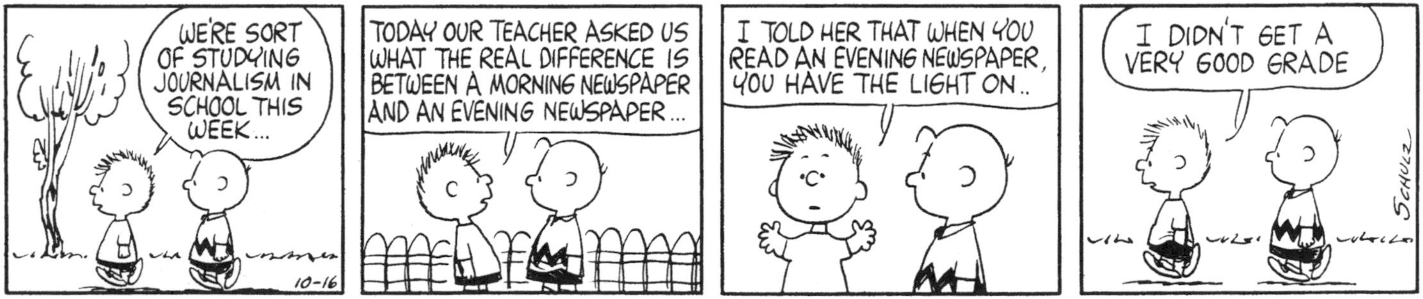
WE'RE SORT OF STUDYING JOURNALISM IN SCHOOL THIS WEEK...
10-16
TODAY OUR TEACHER ASKED US WHAT THE REAL DIFFERENCE IS BETWEEN A MORNING NEWSPAPER AND AN EVENING NEWSPAPER...
I TOLD HER THAT WHEN YOU READ AN EVENING NEWSPAPER, YOU HAVE THE LIGHT ON..
I DIDN'T GET A VERY GOOD GRADE
SCHULZ

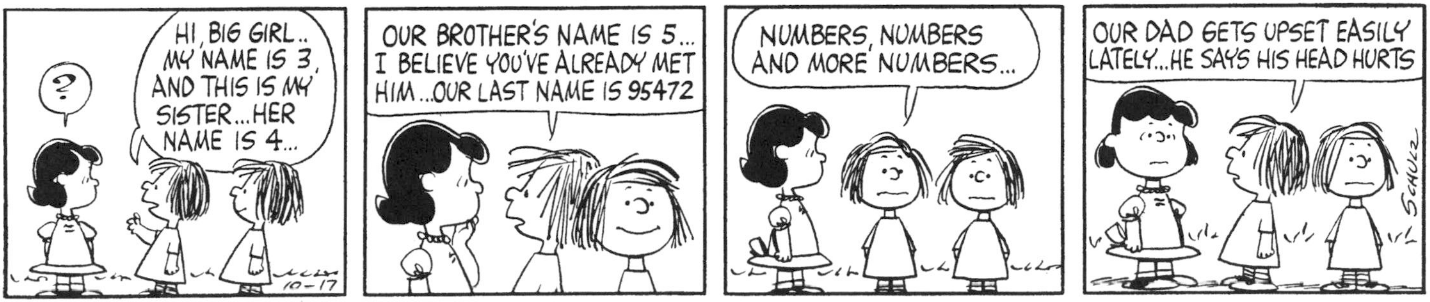
?
HI, BIG GIRL.. MY NAME IS 3, AND THIS IS MY SISTER...HER NAME IS 4...
10-17
OUR BROTHER'S NAME IS 5... I BELIEVE YOU'VE ALREADY MET HIM...OUR LAST NAME IS 95472
NUMBERS, NUMBERS AND MORE NUMBERS...
OUR DAD GETS UPSET EASILY LATELY...HE SAYS HIS HEAD HURTS
SCHULZ

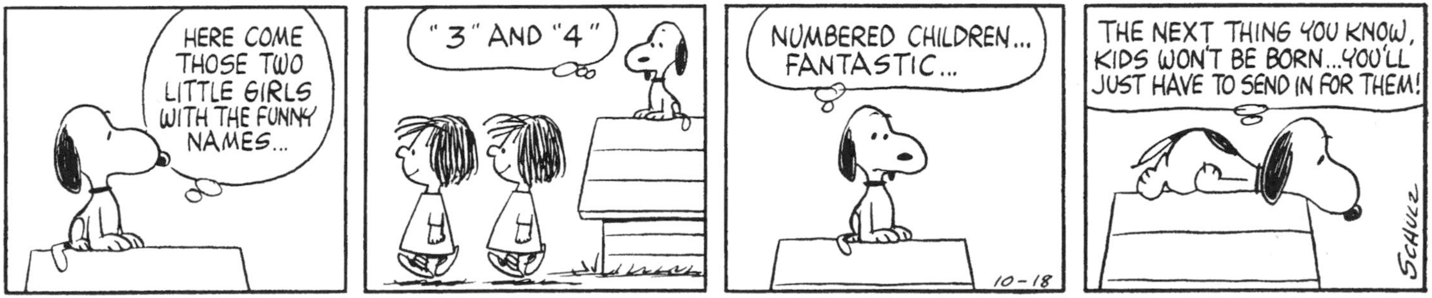
HERE COME THOSE TWO LITTLE GIRLS WITH THE FUNNY NAMES...
"3" AND "4"
NUMBERED CHILDREN... FANTASTIC...
10-18
THE NEXT THING YOU KNOW, KIDS WON'T BE BORN...YOU'LL JUST HAVE TO SEND IN FOR THEM!
SCHULZ

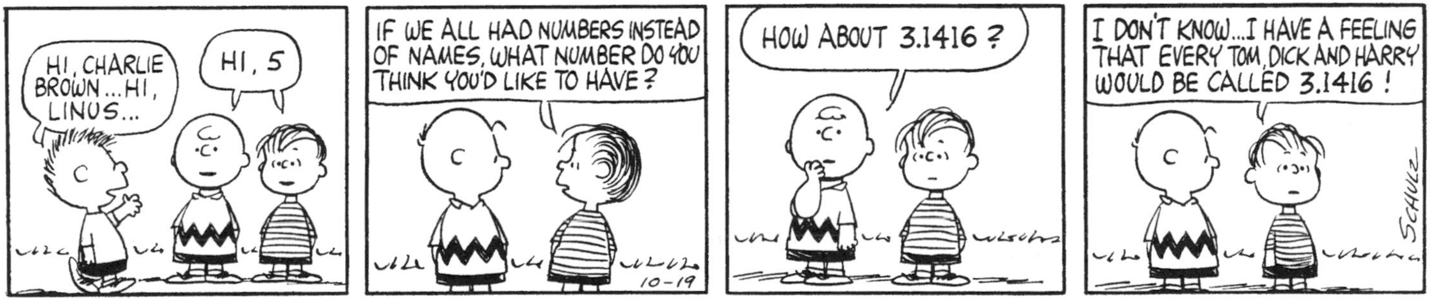
HI, CHARLIE BROWN...HI, LINUS...
HI, 5
IF WE ALL HAD NUMBERS INSTEAD OF NAMES, WHAT NUMBER DO YOU THINK YOU'D LIKE TO HAVE?
10-19
HOW ABOUT 3.1416 ?
I DON'T KNOW...I HAVE A FEELING THAT EVERY TOM, DICK AND HARRY WOULD BE CALLED 3.1416 !
SCHULZ

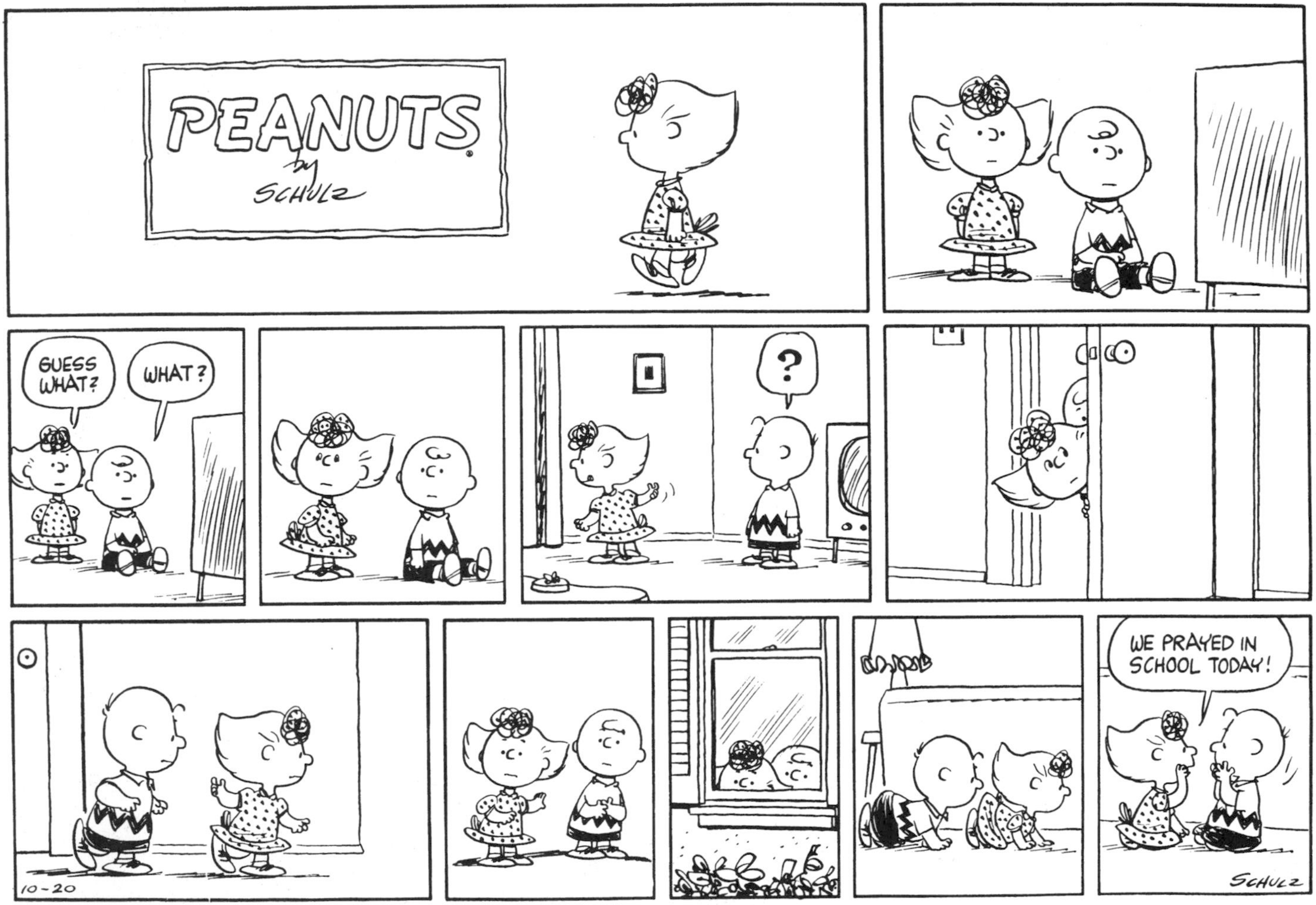
PEANUTS
by
SCHULZ
GUESS WHAT?
WHAT?
?
10-20
WE PRAYED IN SCHOOL TODAY!
SCHULZ

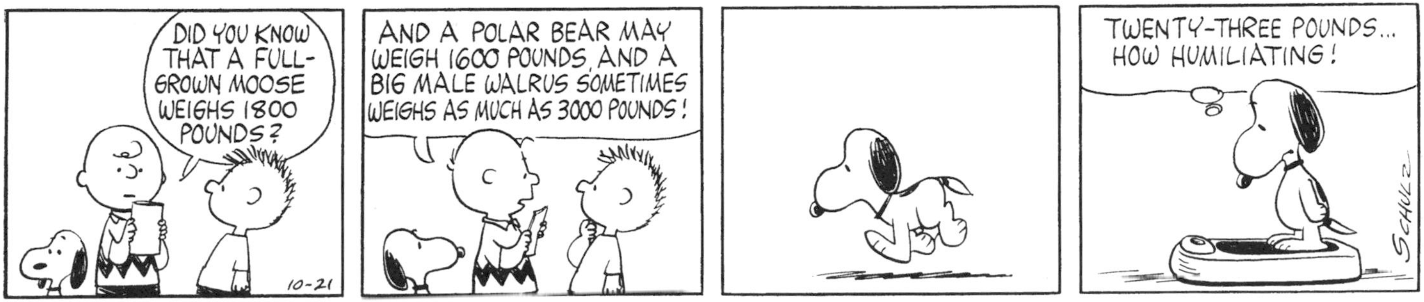
DID YOU KNOW THAT A FULL-GROWN MOOSE WEIGHS 1800 POUNDS?
AND A POLAR BEAR MAY WEIGH 1600 POUNDS, AND A BIG MALE WALRUS SOMETIMES WEIGHS AS MUCH AS 3000 POUNDS!
TWENTY-THREE POUNDS... HOW HUMILIATING!

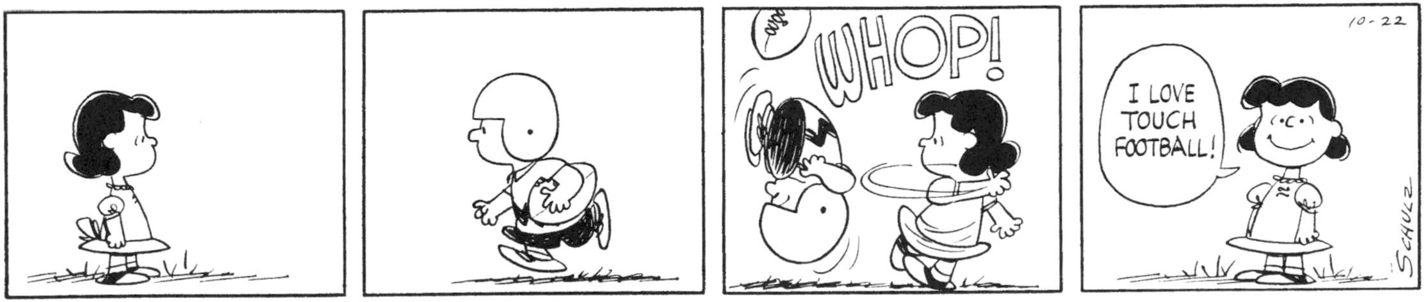
WHOP!
I LOVE TOUCH FOOTBALL!

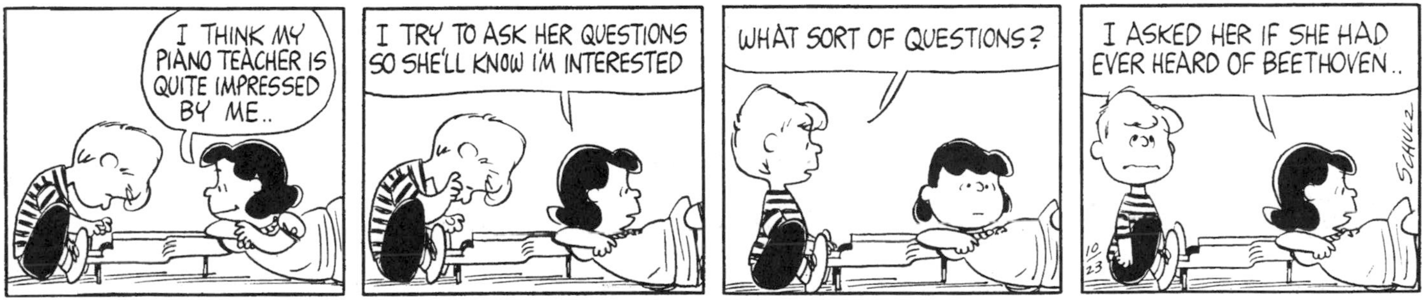
I THINK MY PIANO TEACHER IS QUITE IMPRESSED BY ME..
I TRY TO ASK HER QUESTIONS SO SHE'LL KNOW I'M INTERESTED
WHAT SORT OF QUESTIONS?
I ASKED HER IF SHE HAD EVER HEARD OF BEETHOVEN..

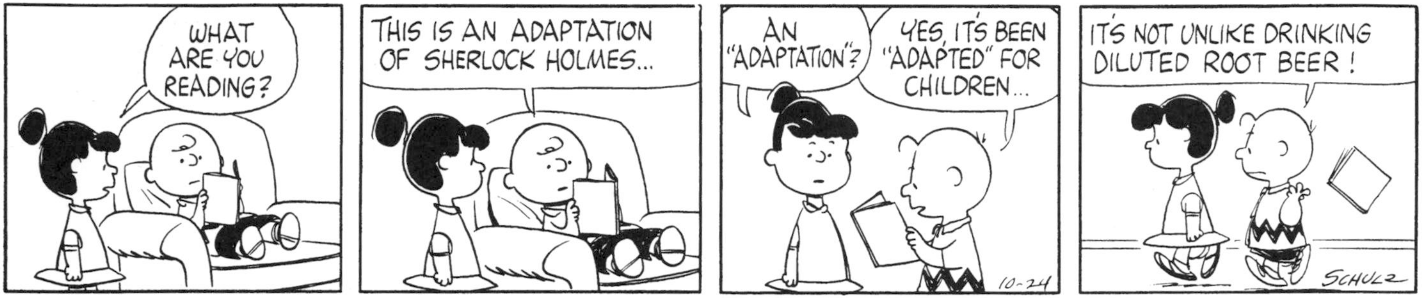
WHAT ARE YOU READING?
THIS IS AN ADAPTATION OF SHERLOCK HOLMES...
AN "ADAPTATION"?
YES, IT'S BEEN "ADAPTED" FOR CHILDREN...
IT'S NOT UNLIKE DRINKING DILUTED ROOT BEER!

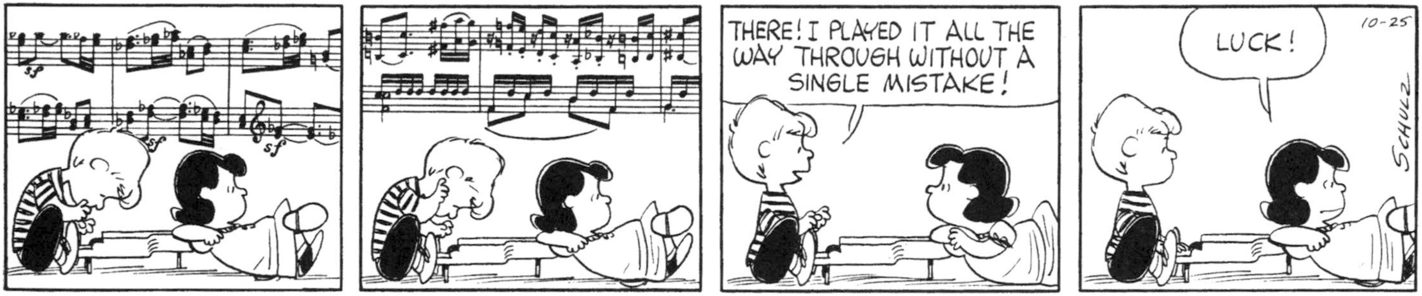
THERE! I PLAYED IT ALL THE WAY THROUGH WITHOUT A SINGLE MISTAKE!
LUCK!

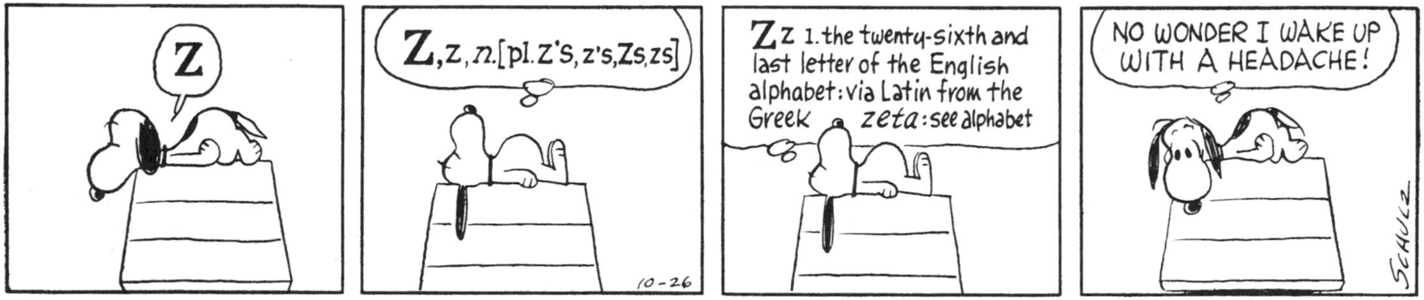
Z
Z, z, n. [pl. Z's, z's, Zs, zs]
Zz 1. the twenty-sixth and last letter of the English alphabet: via Latin from the Greek zeta: see alphabet
NO WONDER I WAKE UP WITH A HEADACHE!

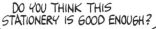

PEANUTS by Schulz

DO YOU THINK THIS STATIONERY IS GOOD ENOUGH?

I'D HATE TO INSULT HIM BY USING CHEAP STATIONERY...

DEAR GREAT PUMPKIN, OH, HOW I LOOK FORWARD TO YOUR ARRIVAL ON HALLOWEEN NIGHT.

10-27

WHEN YOU RISE OUT OF THE PUMPKIN PATCH, AND FLY THROUGH THE AIR, PLEASE BRING ME LOTS OF PRESENTS.

ARE YOU STILL PLANNING TO HELP ME MAIL THIS LETTER?

OF COURSE! I SAID I WOULD, AND I WILL!

MY SISTER LUCY IS GOING TO HELP ME MAIL THIS LETTER SO PLEASE BRING HER LOTS OF PRESENTS TOO.

HOW'S THAT?

FINE

GREED MAKES PEOPLE DO STRANGE THINGS..

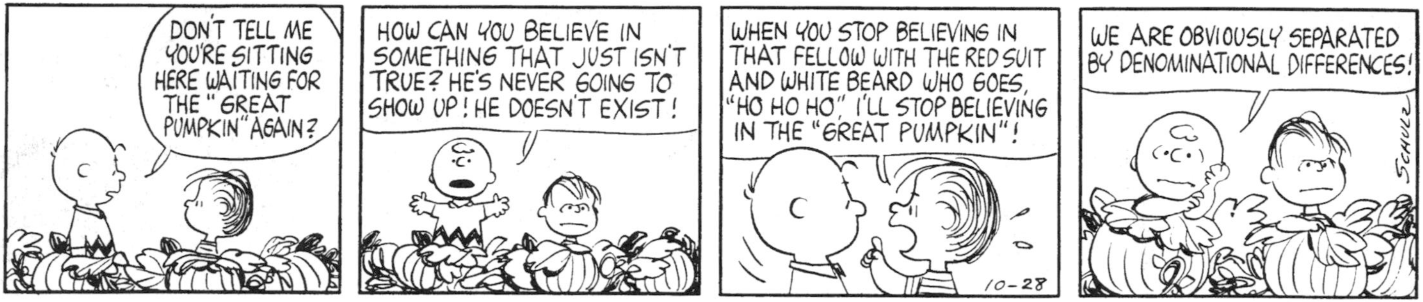
DON'T TELL ME YOU'RE SITTING HERE WAITING FOR THE "GREAT PUMPKIN" AGAIN?
HOW CAN YOU BELIEVE IN SOMETHING THAT JUST ISN'T TRUE? HE'S NEVER GOING TO SHOW UP! HE DOESN'T EXIST!
WHEN YOU STOP BELIEVING IN THAT FELLOW WITH THE RED SUIT AND WHITE BEARD WHO GOES, "HO HO HO," I'LL STOP BELIEVING IN THE "GREAT PUMPKIN"!
10-28
WE ARE OBVIOUSLY SEPARATED BY DENOMINATIONAL DIFFERENCES!
SCHULZ

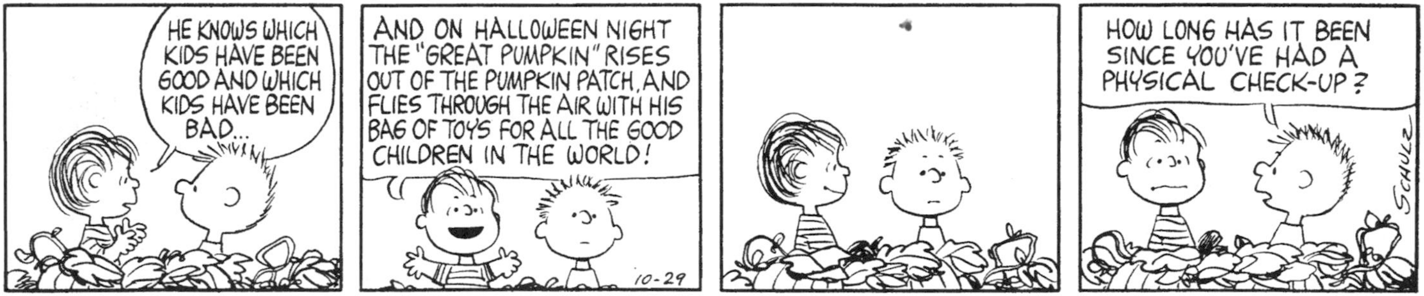
HE KNOWS WHICH KIDS HAVE BEEN GOOD AND WHICH KIDS HAVE BEEN BAD...
AND ON HALLOWEEN NIGHT THE "GREAT PUMPKIN" RISES OUT OF THE PUMPKIN PATCH, AND FLIES THROUGH THE AIR WITH HIS BAG OF TOYS FOR ALL THE GOOD CHILDREN IN THE WORLD!
10-29
HOW LONG HAS IT BEEN SINCE YOU'VE HAD A PHYSICAL CHECK-UP?
SCHULZ

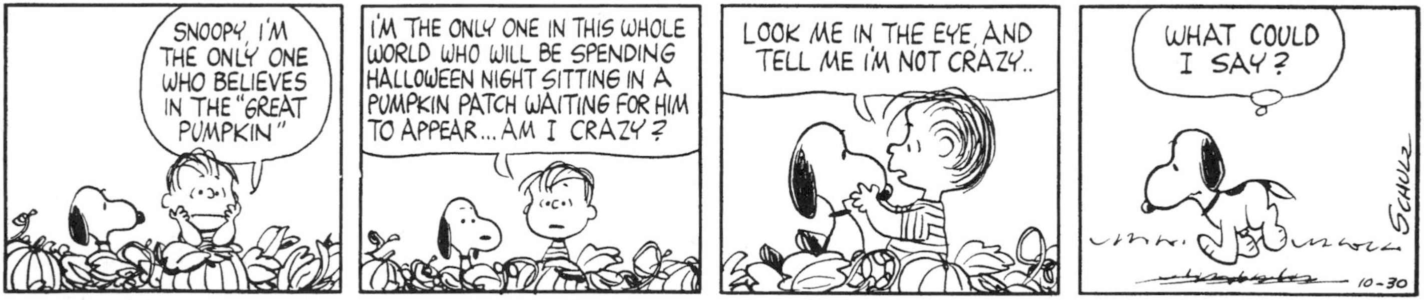
SNOOPY, I'M THE ONLY ONE WHO BELIEVES IN THE "GREAT PUMPKIN"
I'M THE ONLY ONE IN THIS WHOLE WORLD WHO WILL BE SPENDING HALLOWEEN NIGHT SITTING IN A PUMPKIN PATCH WAITING FOR HIM TO APPEAR... AM I CRAZY?
LOOK ME IN THE EYE, AND TELL ME I'M NOT CRAZY..
WHAT COULD I SAY?
SCHULZ
10-30

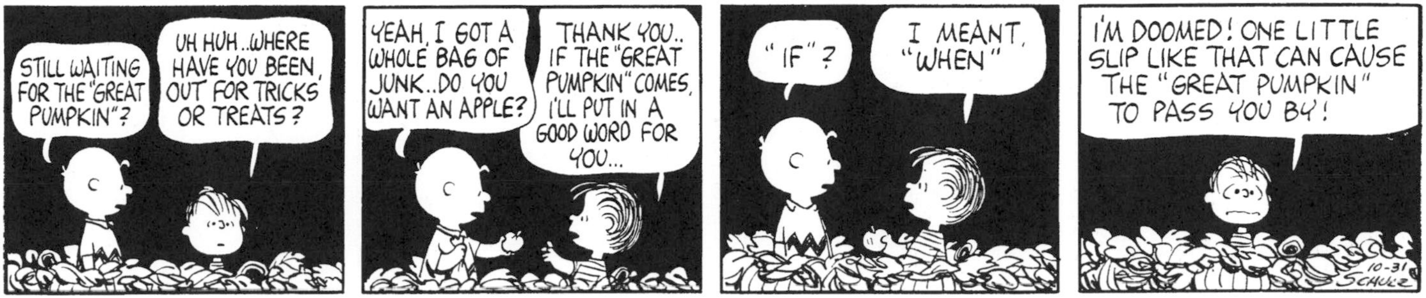
STILL WAITING FOR THE "GREAT PUMPKIN"?
UH HUH..WHERE HAVE YOU BEEN, OUT FOR TRICKS OR TREATS?
YEAH, I GOT A WHOLE BAG OF JUNK..DO YOU WANT AN APPLE?
THANK YOU.. IF THE "GREAT PUMPKIN" COMES, I'LL PUT IN A GOOD WORD FOR YOU...
"IF"?
I MEANT, "WHEN"
I'M DOOMED! ONE LITTLE SLIP LIKE THAT CAN CAUSE THE "GREAT PUMPKIN" TO PASS YOU BY!
10-31
SCHULZ

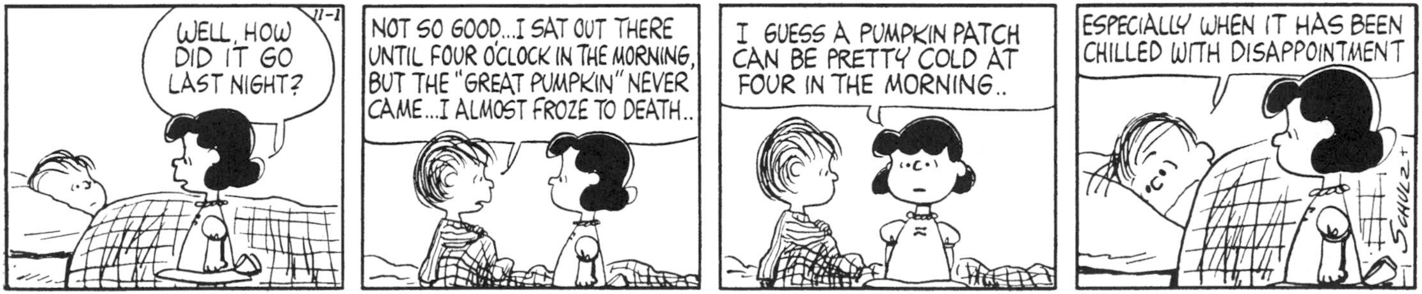
11-1
WELL, HOW DID IT GO LAST NIGHT?
NOT SO GOOD...I SAT OUT THERE UNTIL FOUR O'CLOCK IN THE MORNING, BUT THE "GREAT PUMPKIN" NEVER CAME...I ALMOST FROZE TO DEATH..
I GUESS A PUMPKIN PATCH CAN BE PRETTY COLD AT FOUR IN THE MORNING..
ESPECIALLY WHEN IT HAS BEEN CHILLED WITH DISAPPOINTMENT
SCHULZ

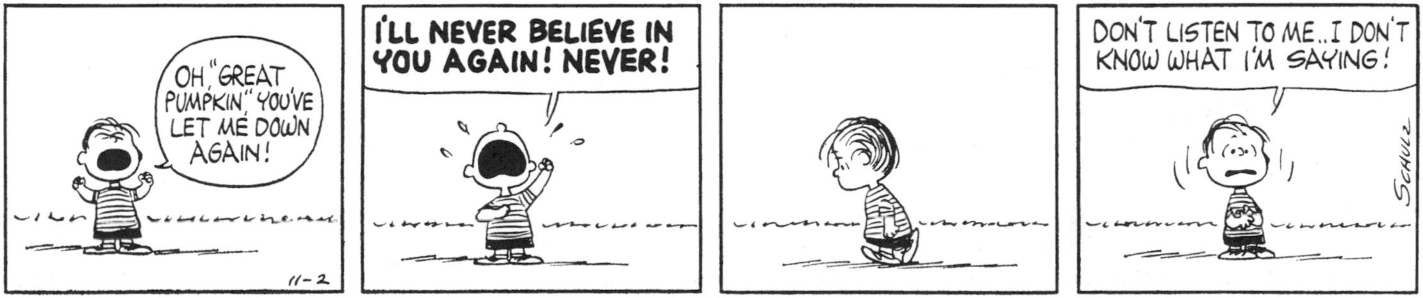
OH, "GREAT PUMPKIN," YOU'VE LET ME DOWN AGAIN!
11-2
I'LL NEVER BELIEVE IN YOU AGAIN! NEVER!
DON'T LISTEN TO ME..I DON'T KNOW WHAT I'M SAYING!
SCHULZ

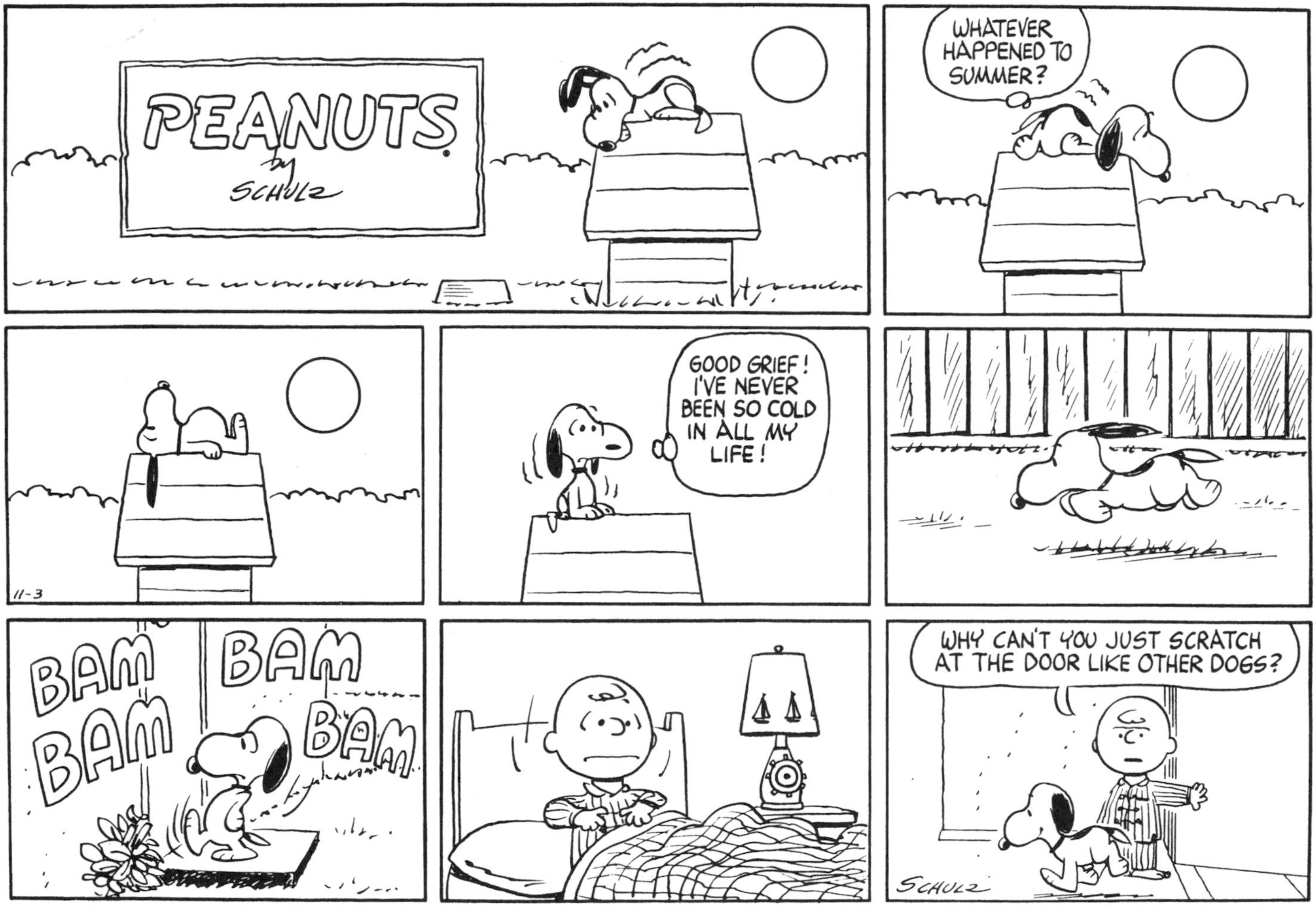
PEANUTS
by SCHULZ
WHATEVER HAPPENED TO SUMMER?
11-3
GOOD GRIEF! I'VE NEVER BEEN SO COLD IN ALL MY LIFE!
BAM BAM BAM BAM
WHY CAN'T YOU JUST SCRATCH AT THE DOOR LIKE OTHER DOGS?
SCHULZ

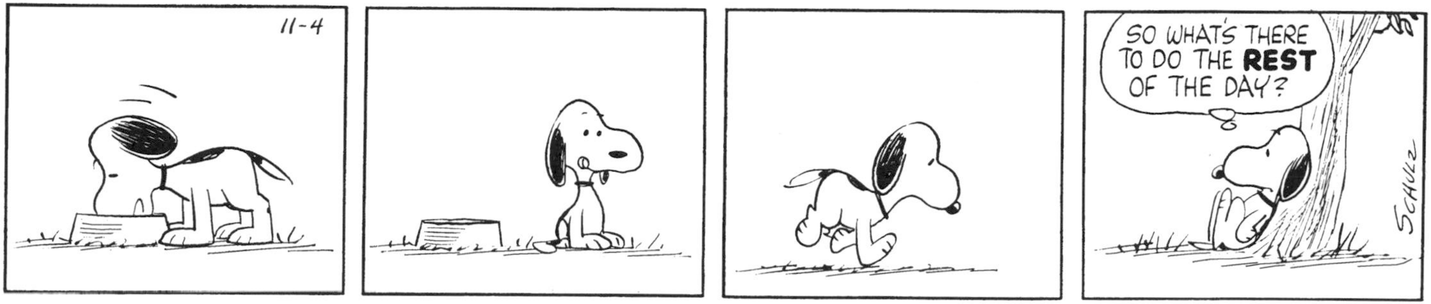
11-4
SO WHAT'S THERE TO DO THE **REST** OF THE DAY?
SCHULZ

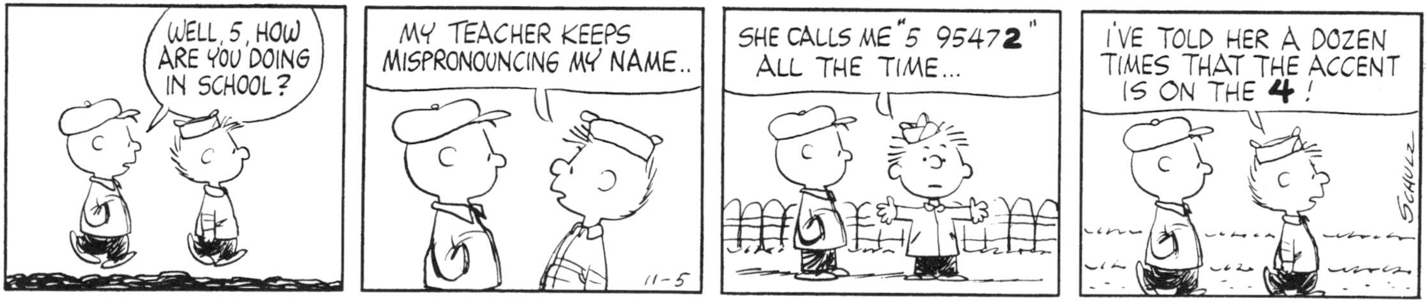
WELL, 5, HOW ARE YOU DOING IN SCHOOL?
MY TEACHER KEEPS MISPRONOUNCING MY NAME..
11-5
SHE CALLS ME "5 9547**2**" ALL THE TIME...
I'VE TOLD HER A DOZEN TIMES THAT THE ACCENT IS ON THE **4**!
SCHULZ

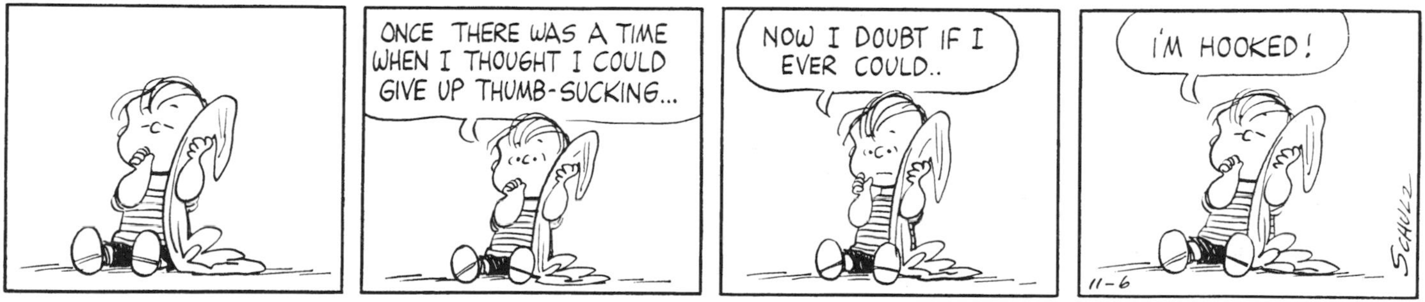
ONCE THERE WAS A TIME WHEN I THOUGHT I COULD GIVE UP THUMB-SUCKING...
NOW I DOUBT IF I EVER COULD..
I'M HOOKED!
11-6
SCHULZ

11-7

HOW NICE.. A SMALL DISH OF SHERBET!

NOBODY LIKES ME...EVERYBODY HATES ME...

WELL, CHARLIE BROWN, IF THE WHOLE WORLD IS EVER AGAINST YOU, I'D LIKE TO HAVE YOU KNOW HOW I'LL FEEL...
11-8

WILL YOU BE MY FRIEND?

NO, I'LL BE AGAINST YOU, TOO!

11-9

SUPPERTIME!

I WAS WRONG...IT ISN'T SUPPERTIME...

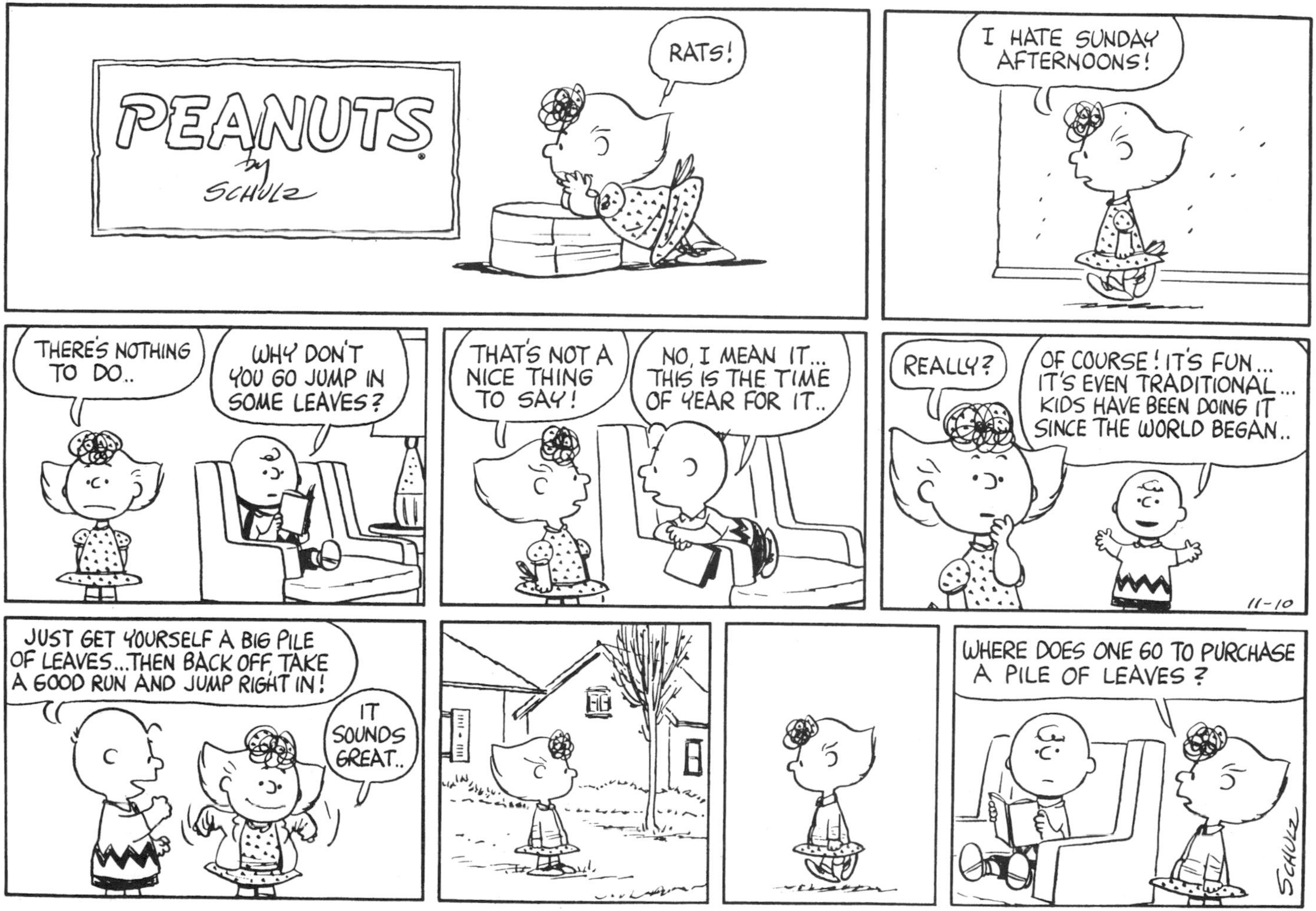
PEANUTS
by SCHULZ
RATS!
I HATE SUNDAY AFTERNOONS!
THERE'S NOTHING TO DO..
WHY DON'T YOU GO JUMP IN SOME LEAVES?
THAT'S NOT A NICE THING TO SAY!
NO, I MEAN IT... THIS IS THE TIME OF YEAR FOR IT..
REALLY?
OF COURSE! IT'S FUN... IT'S EVEN TRADITIONAL... KIDS HAVE BEEN DOING IT SINCE THE WORLD BEGAN..
11-10
JUST GET YOURSELF A BIG PILE OF LEAVES...THEN BACK OFF, TAKE A GOOD RUN AND JUMP RIGHT IN!
IT SOUNDS GREAT..
WHERE DOES ONE GO TO PURCHASE A PILE OF LEAVES?
SCHULZ

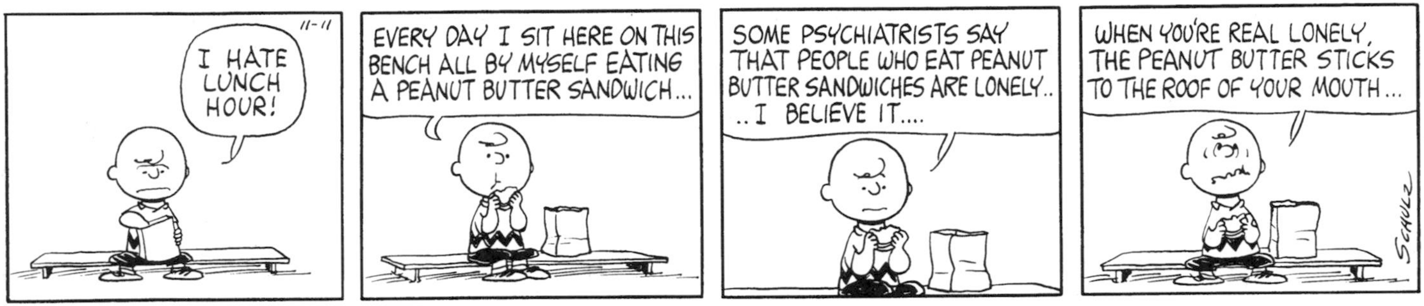
11-11
I HATE LUNCH HOUR!
EVERY DAY I SIT HERE ON THIS BENCH ALL BY MYSELF EATING A PEANUT BUTTER SANDWICH...
SOME PSYCHIATRISTS SAY THAT PEOPLE WHO EAT PEANUT BUTTER SANDWICHES ARE LONELY.. ..I BELIEVE IT....
WHEN YOU'RE REAL LONELY, THE PEANUT BUTTER STICKS TO THE ROOF OF YOUR MOUTH...
SCHULZ

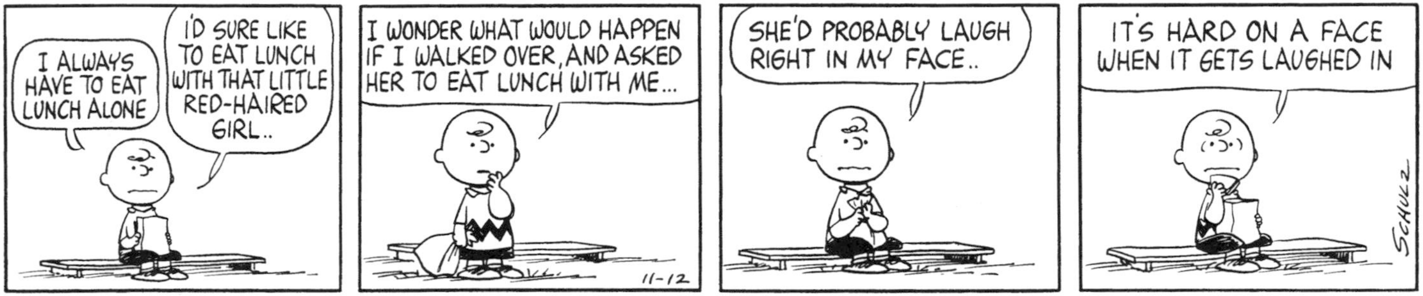
I ALWAYS HAVE TO EAT LUNCH ALONE
I'D SURE LIKE TO EAT LUNCH WITH THAT LITTLE RED-HAIRED GIRL..
I WONDER WHAT WOULD HAPPEN IF I WALKED OVER, AND ASKED HER TO EAT LUNCH WITH ME...
11-12
SHE'D PROBABLY LAUGH RIGHT IN MY FACE..
IT'S HARD ON A FACE WHEN IT GETS LAUGHED IN
SCHULZ

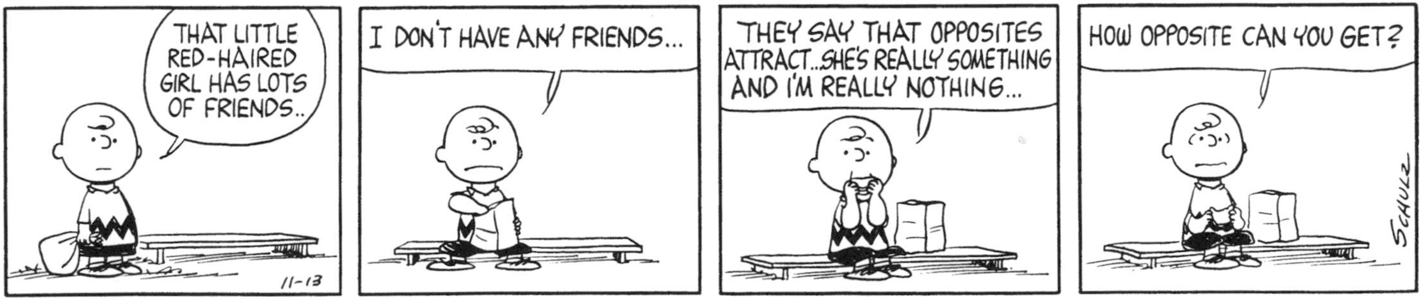
THAT LITTLE RED-HAIRED GIRL HAS LOTS OF FRIENDS..
11-13
I DON'T HAVE ANY FRIENDS...
THEY SAY THAT OPPOSITES ATTRACT...SHE'S REALLY SOMETHING AND I'M REALLY NOTHING...
HOW OPPOSITE CAN YOU GET?
SCHULZ

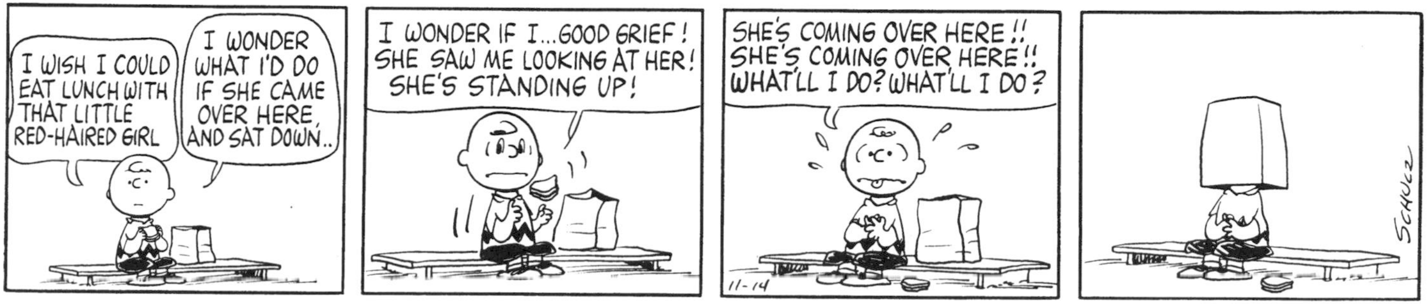
I WISH I COULD EAT LUNCH WITH THAT LITTLE RED-HAIRED GIRL
I WONDER WHAT I'D DO IF SHE CAME OVER HERE AND SAT DOWN..
I WONDER IF I...GOOD GRIEF! SHE SAW ME LOOKING AT HER! SHE'S STANDING UP!
SHE'S COMING OVER HERE!! SHE'S COMING OVER HERE!! WHAT'LL I DO? WHAT'LL I DO?

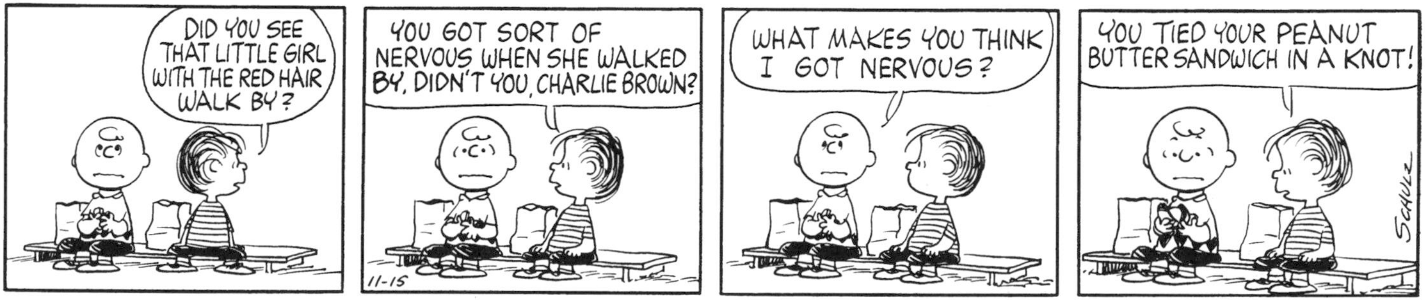
DID YOU SEE THAT LITTLE GIRL WITH THE RED HAIR WALK BY?
YOU GOT SORT OF NERVOUS WHEN SHE WALKED BY, DIDN'T YOU, CHARLIE BROWN?
WHAT MAKES YOU THINK I GOT NERVOUS?
YOU TIED YOUR PEANUT BUTTER SANDWICH IN A KNOT!

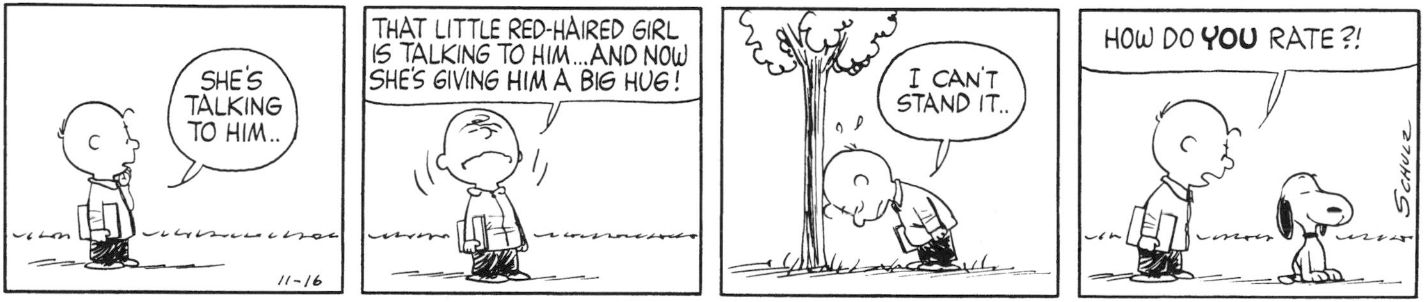
SHE'S TALKING TO HIM..
THAT LITTLE RED-HAIRED GIRL IS TALKING TO HIM...AND NOW SHE'S GIVING HIM A BIG HUG!
I CAN'T STAND IT..
HOW DO YOU RATE?!

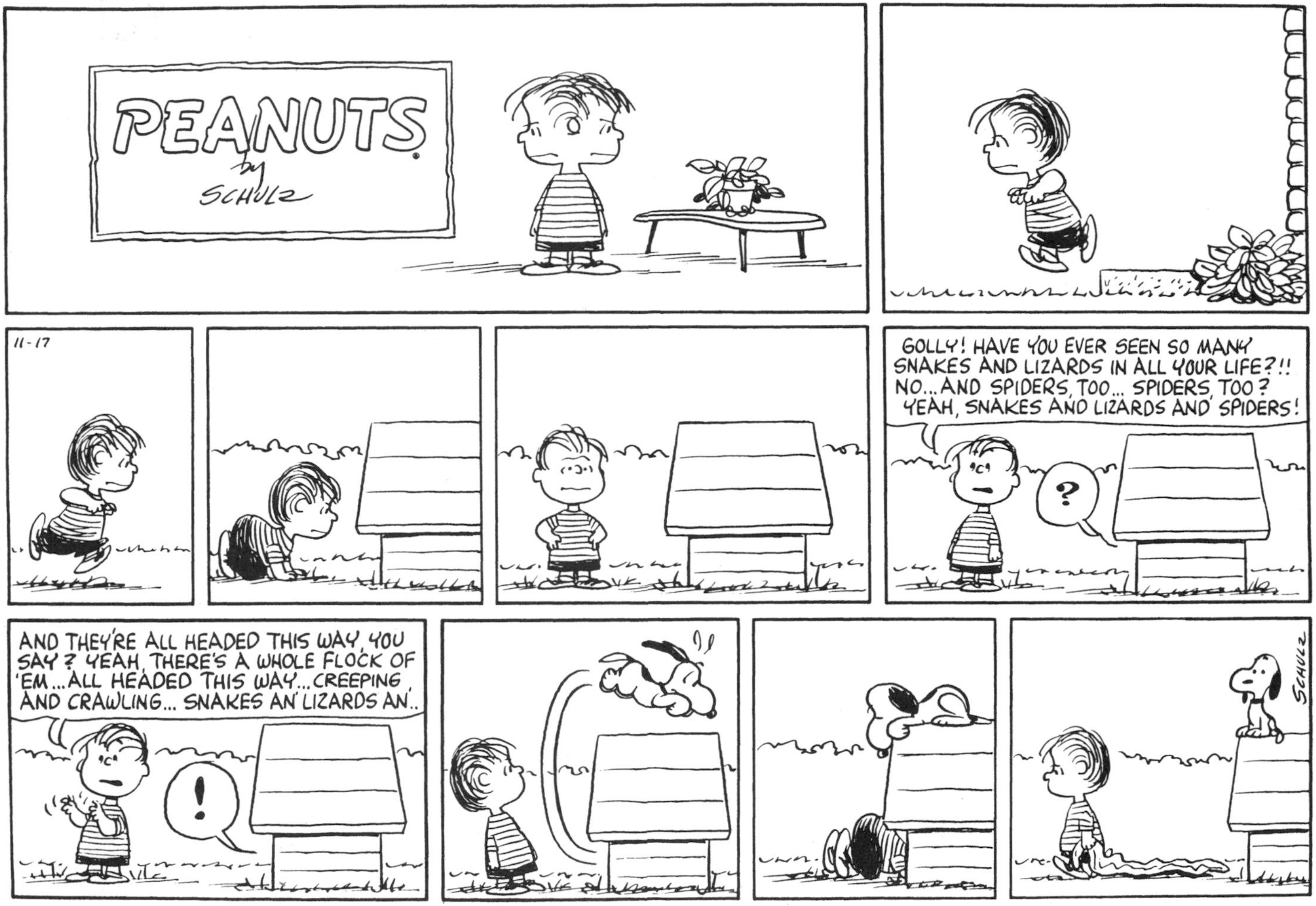
PEANUTS
by SCHULZ
11-17
GOLLY! HAVE YOU EVER SEEN SO MANY SNAKES AND LIZARDS IN ALL YOUR LIFE?!! NO...AND SPIDERS, TOO... SPIDERS, TOO? YEAH, SNAKES AND LIZARDS AND SPIDERS!
?
AND THEY'RE ALL HEADED THIS WAY, YOU SAY? YEAH, THERE'S A WHOLE FLOCK OF 'EM...ALL HEADED THIS WAY...CREEPING AND CRAWLING... SNAKES AN' LIZARDS AN'..
!
SCHULZ

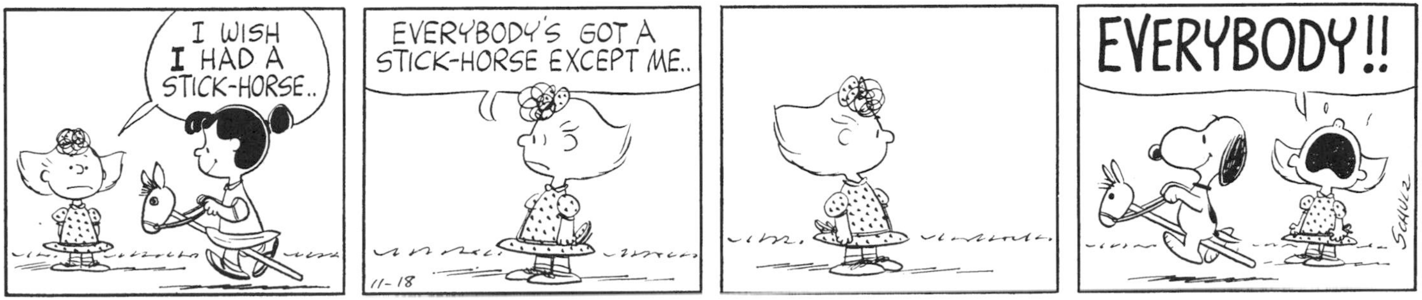
I WISH I HAD A STICK-HORSE..
EVERYBODY'S GOT A STICK-HORSE EXCEPT ME..
11-18
EVERYBODY!!
SCHULZ

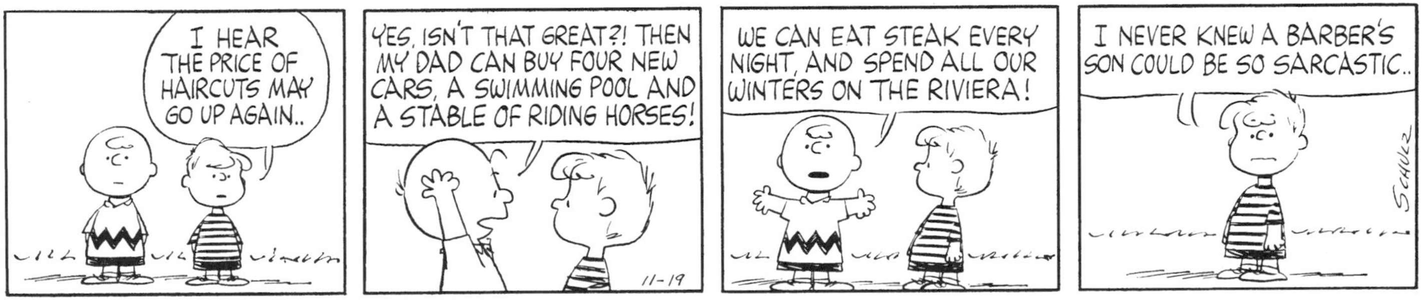
I HEAR THE PRICE OF HAIRCUTS MAY GO UP AGAIN..
YES, ISN'T THAT GREAT?! THEN MY DAD CAN BUY FOUR NEW CARS, A SWIMMING POOL AND A STABLE OF RIDING HORSES!
11-19
WE CAN EAT STEAK EVERY NIGHT, AND SPEND ALL OUR WINTERS ON THE RIVIERA!
I NEVER KNEW A BARBER'S SON COULD BE SO SARCASTIC..
SCHULZ

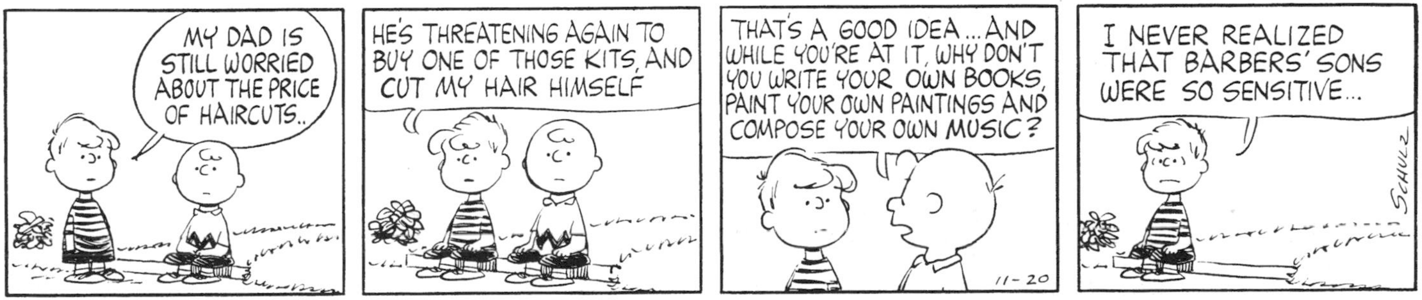
MY DAD IS STILL WORRIED ABOUT THE PRICE OF HAIRCUTS..
HE'S THREATENING AGAIN TO BUY ONE OF THOSE KITS, AND CUT MY HAIR HIMSELF
THAT'S A GOOD IDEA... AND WHILE YOU'RE AT IT, WHY DON'T YOU WRITE YOUR OWN BOOKS, PAINT YOUR OWN PAINTINGS AND COMPOSE YOUR OWN MUSIC?
11-20
I NEVER REALIZED THAT BARBERS' SONS WERE SO SENSITIVE...
SCHULZ

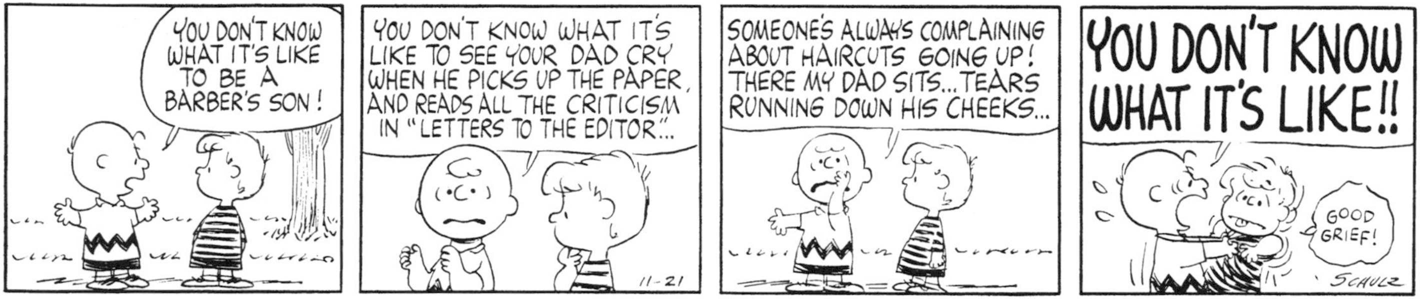
YOU DON'T KNOW WHAT IT'S LIKE TO BE A BARBER'S SON!
YOU DON'T KNOW WHAT IT'S LIKE TO SEE YOUR DAD CRY WHEN HE PICKS UP THE PAPER, AND READS ALL THE CRITICISM IN "LETTERS TO THE EDITOR"...
11-21
SOMEONE'S ALWAYS COMPLAINING ABOUT HAIRCUTS GOING UP! THERE MY DAD SITS...TEARS RUNNING DOWN HIS CHEEKS...
YOU DON'T KNOW WHAT IT'S LIKE!!
GOOD GRIEF!
SCHULZ

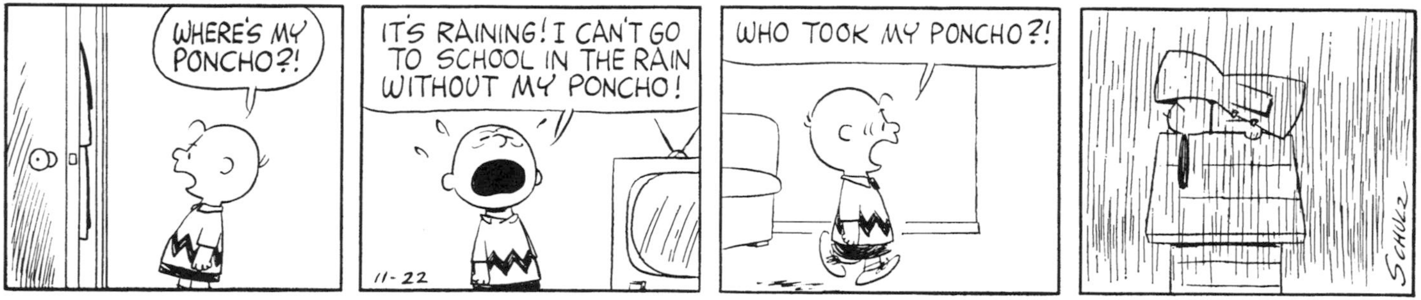
WHERE'S MY PONCHO?!
IT'S RAINING! I CAN'T GO TO SCHOOL IN THE RAIN WITHOUT MY PONCHO!
11-22
WHO TOOK MY PONCHO?!
SCHULZ

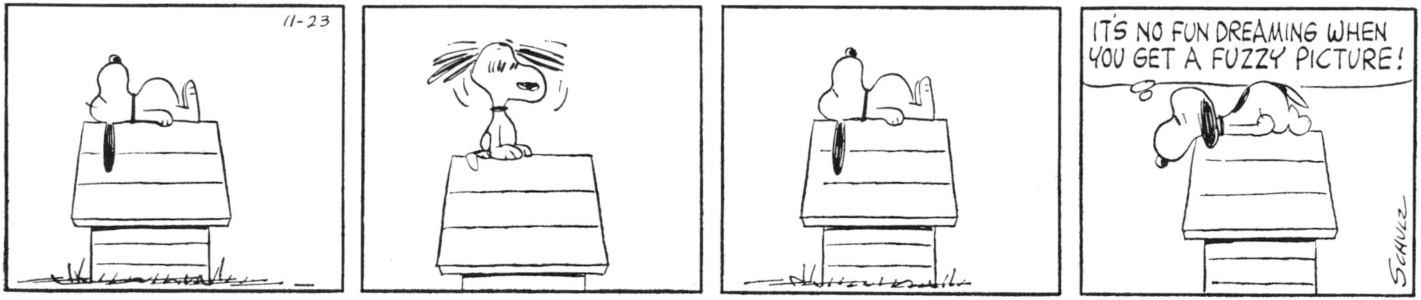
11-23
IT'S NO FUN DREAMING WHEN YOU GET A FUZZY PICTURE!
SCHULZ

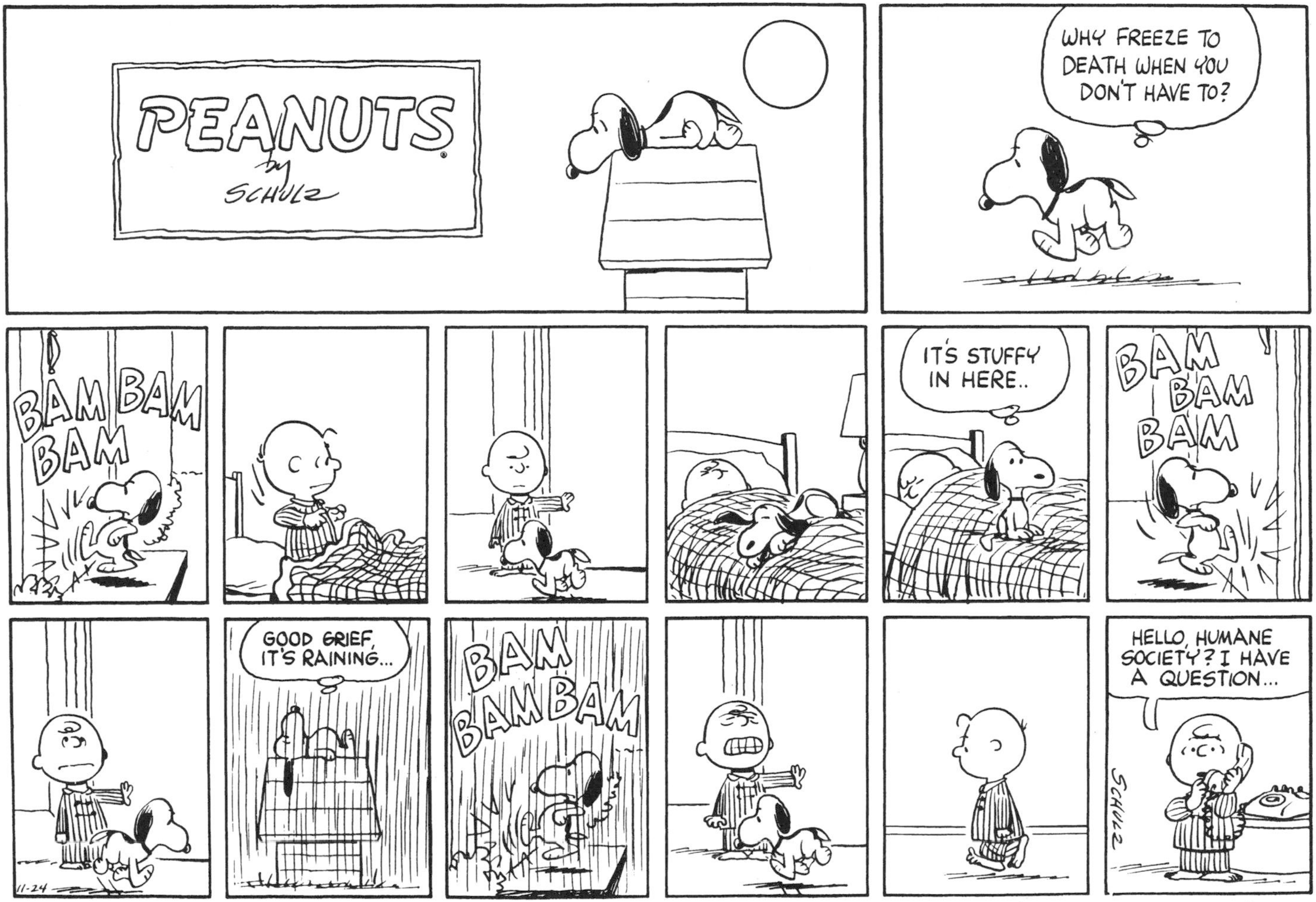
PEANUTS
by SCHULZ
WHY FREEZE TO DEATH WHEN YOU DON'T HAVE TO?
BAM BAM
BAM
IT'S STUFFY IN HERE..
BAM
BAM
BAM
11-24
GOOD GRIEF, IT'S RAINING...
BAM
BAM BAM
SCHULZ
HELLO, HUMANE SOCIETY? I HAVE A QUESTION...

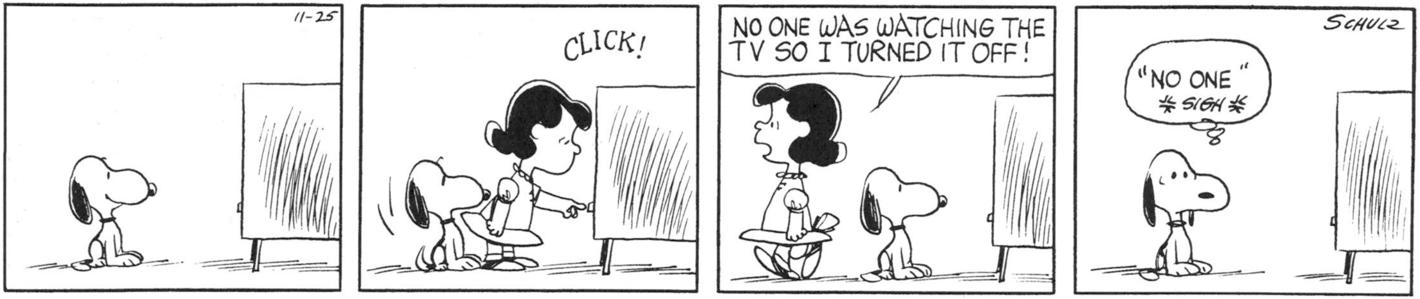
11-25
CLICK!
NO ONE WAS WATCHING THE TV SO I TURNED IT OFF!
SCHULZ
"NO ONE"
SIGH

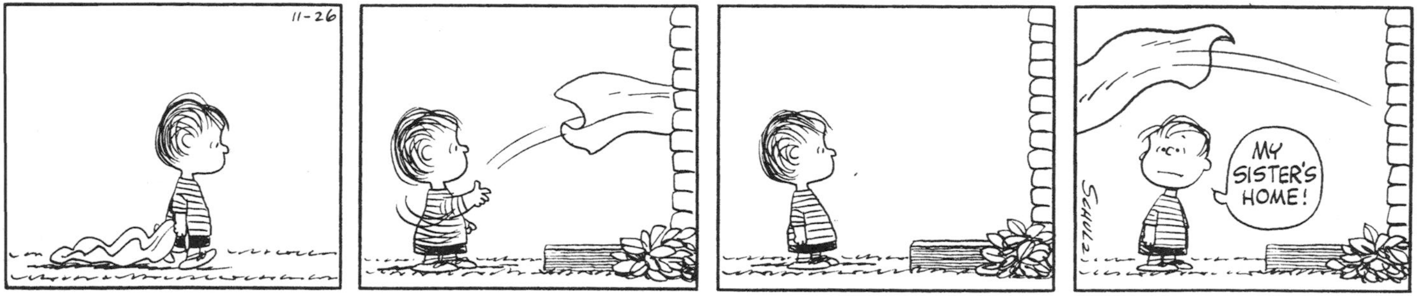
11-26
SCHULZ
MY SISTER'S HOME!

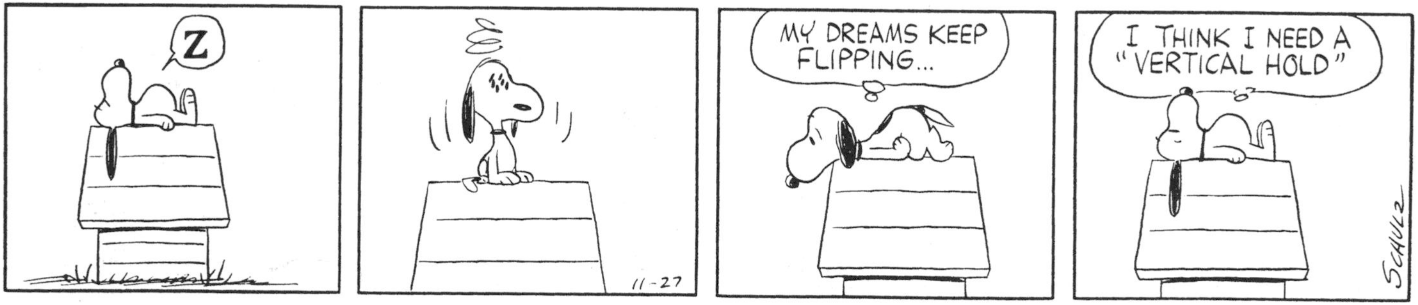
Z
11-27
MY DREAMS KEEP FLIPPING...
I THINK I NEED A "VERTICAL HOLD"
SCHULZ

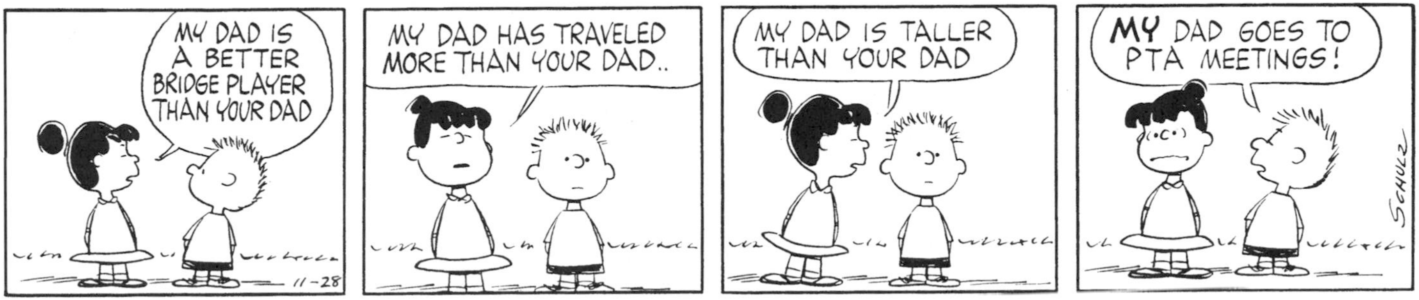
MY DAD IS A BETTER BRIDGE PLAYER THAN YOUR DAD
11-28
MY DAD HAS TRAVELED MORE THAN YOUR DAD..
MY DAD IS TALLER THAN YOUR DAD
MY DAD GOES TO PTA MEETINGS!
SCHULZ

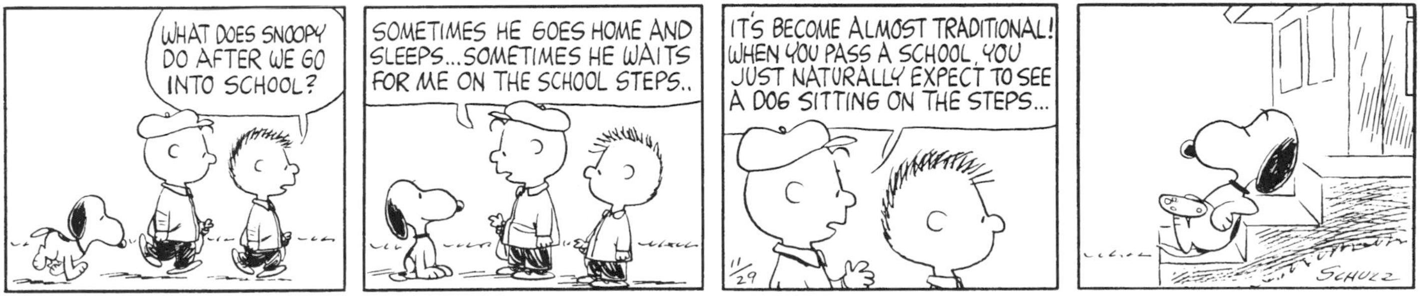
WHAT DOES SNOOPY DO AFTER WE GO INTO SCHOOL?
SOMETIMES HE GOES HOME AND SLEEPS...SOMETIMES HE WAITS FOR ME ON THE SCHOOL STEPS..
IT'S BECOME ALMOST TRADITIONAL! WHEN YOU PASS A SCHOOL, YOU JUST NATURALLY EXPECT TO SEE A DOG SITTING ON THE STEPS...
11/29
SCHULZ

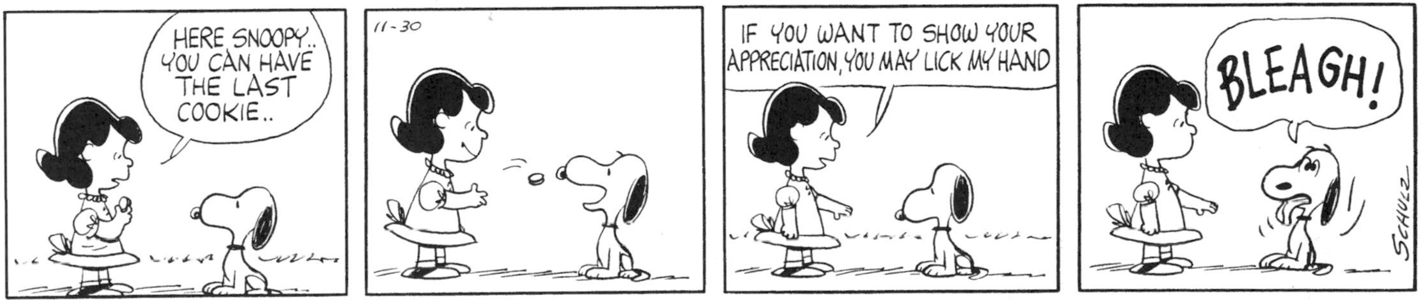
HERE SNOOPY.. YOU CAN HAVE THE LAST COOKIE..
11-30
IF YOU WANT TO SHOW YOUR APPRECIATION, YOU MAY LICK MY HAND
BLEAGH!
SCHULZ

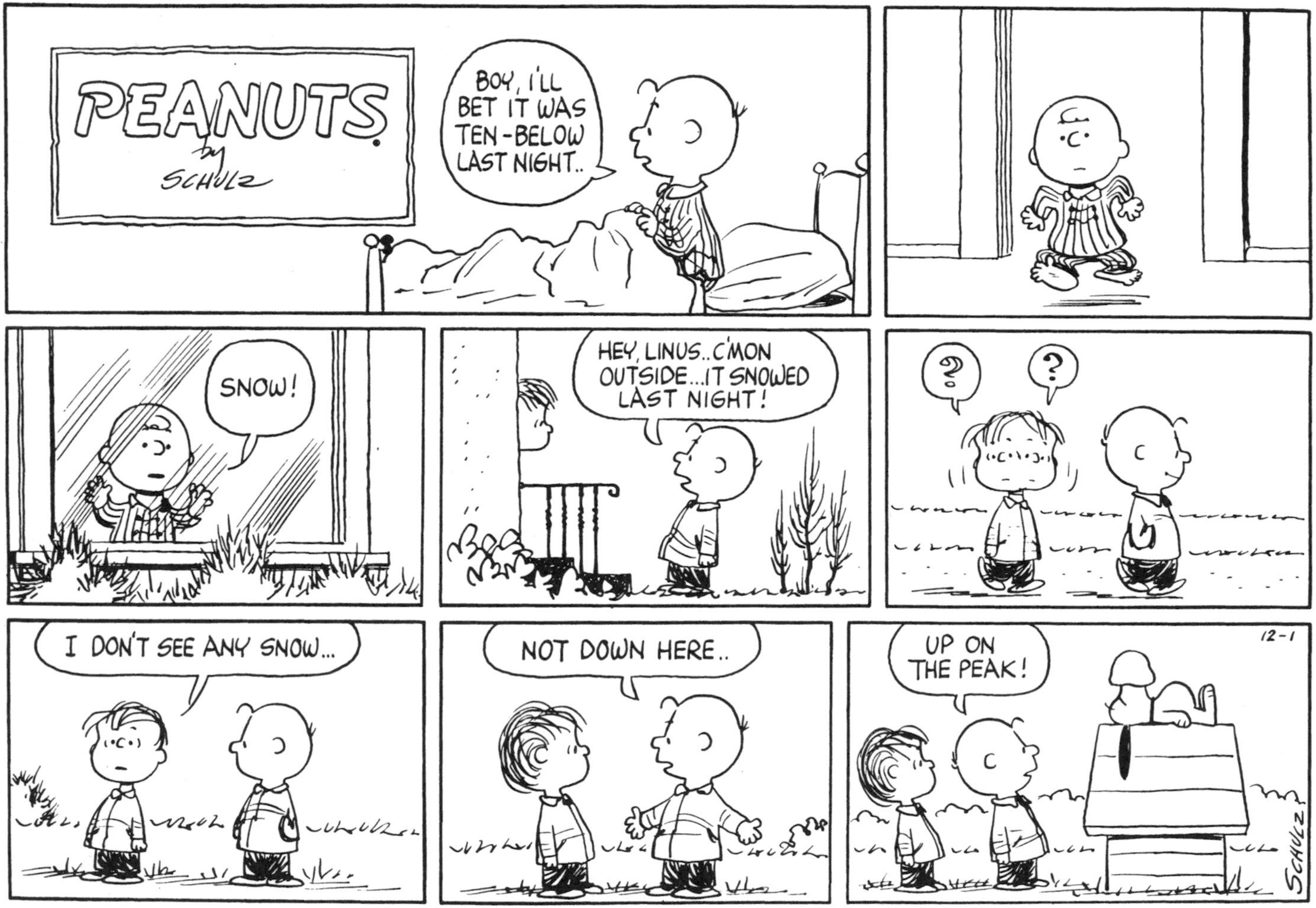
PEANUTS
by SCHULZ
BOY, I'LL BET IT WAS TEN-BELOW LAST NIGHT..
SNOW!
HEY, LINUS..C'MON OUTSIDE...IT SNOWED LAST NIGHT!
?
?
I DON'T SEE ANY SNOW...
NOT DOWN HERE..
UP ON THE PEAK!
12-1
SCHULZ

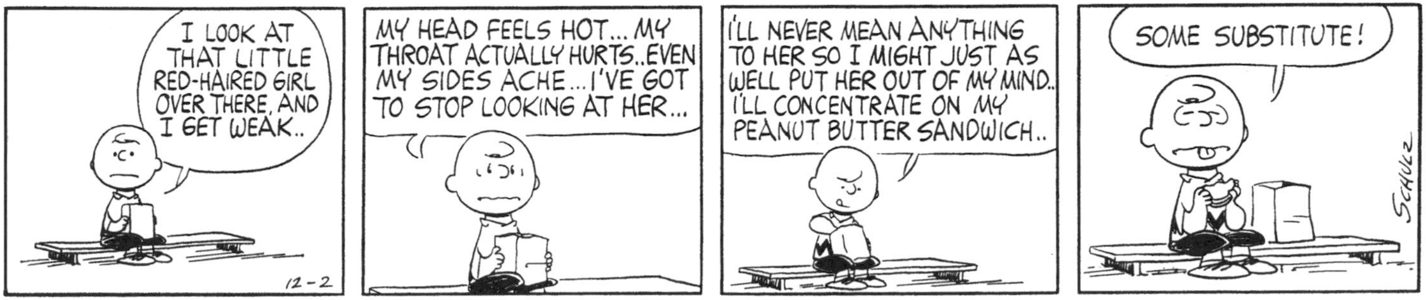
I LOOK AT THAT LITTLE RED-HAIRED GIRL OVER THERE, AND I GET WEAK..
MY HEAD FEELS HOT... MY THROAT ACTUALLY HURTS..EVEN MY SIDES ACHE...I'VE GOT TO STOP LOOKING AT HER...
I'LL NEVER MEAN ANYTHING TO HER SO I MIGHT JUST AS WELL PUT HER OUT OF MY MIND.. I'LL CONCENTRATE ON MY PEANUT BUTTER SANDWICH..
SOME SUBSTITUTE!
SCHULZ
12-2

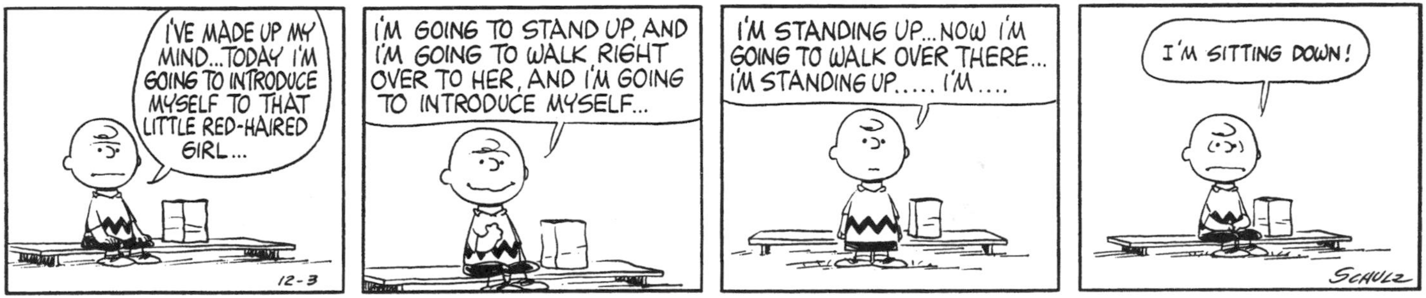
I'VE MADE UP MY MIND...TODAY I'M GOING TO INTRODUCE MYSELF TO THAT LITTLE RED-HAIRED GIRL...
I'M GOING TO STAND UP, AND I'M GOING TO WALK RIGHT OVER TO HER, AND I'M GOING TO INTRODUCE MYSELF...
I'M STANDING UP...NOW I'M GOING TO WALK OVER THERE... I'M STANDING UP..... I'M....
I'M SITTING DOWN!
SCHULZ
12-3

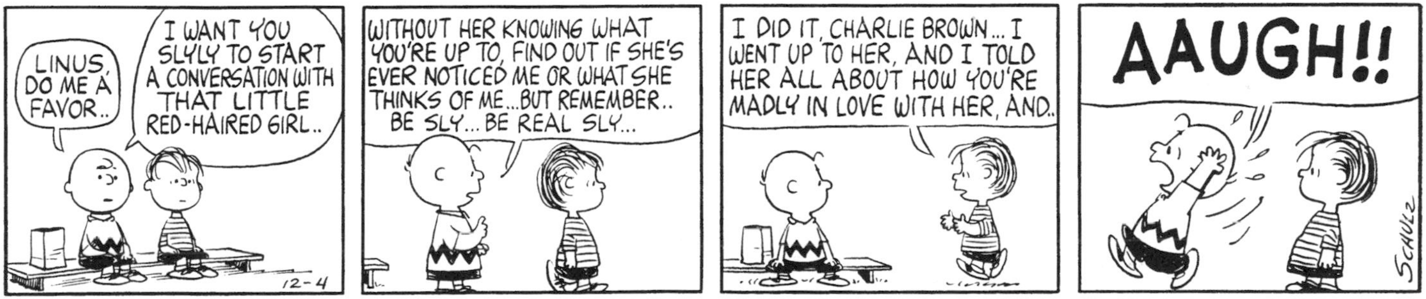
LINUS, DO ME A FAVOR..
I WANT YOU SLYLY TO START A CONVERSATION WITH THAT LITTLE RED-HAIRED GIRL..
WITHOUT HER KNOWING WHAT YOU'RE UP TO, FIND OUT IF SHE'S EVER NOTICED ME OR WHAT SHE THINKS OF ME...BUT REMEMBER.. BE SLY... BE REAL SLY...
I DID IT, CHARLIE BROWN... I WENT UP TO HER, AND I TOLD HER ALL ABOUT HOW YOU'RE MADLY IN LOVE WITH HER, AND..
AAUGH!!
SCHULZ
12-4

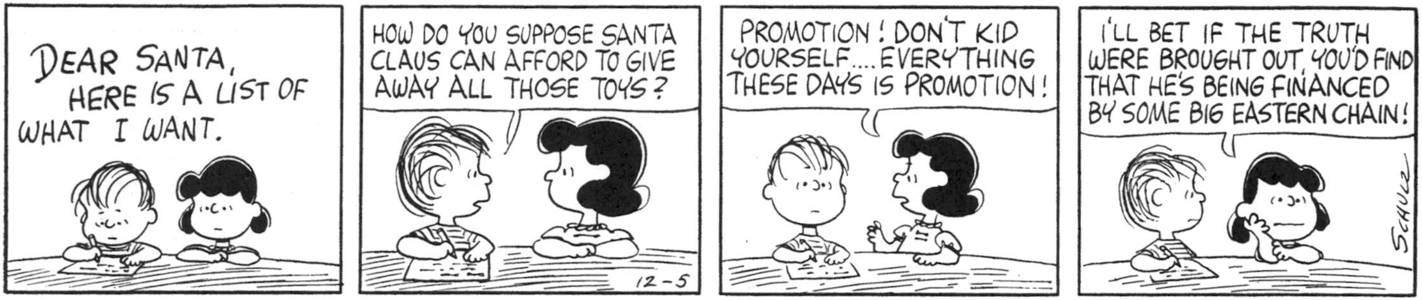
DEAR SANTA,
HERE IS A LIST OF WHAT I WANT.
HOW DO YOU SUPPOSE SANTA CLAUS CAN AFFORD TO GIVE AWAY ALL THOSE TOYS?
12-5
PROMOTION! DON'T KID YOURSELF.... EVERYTHING THESE DAYS IS PROMOTION!
I'LL BET IF THE TRUTH WERE BROUGHT OUT, YOU'D FIND THAT HE'S BEING FINANCED BY SOME BIG EASTERN CHAIN!
SCHULZ

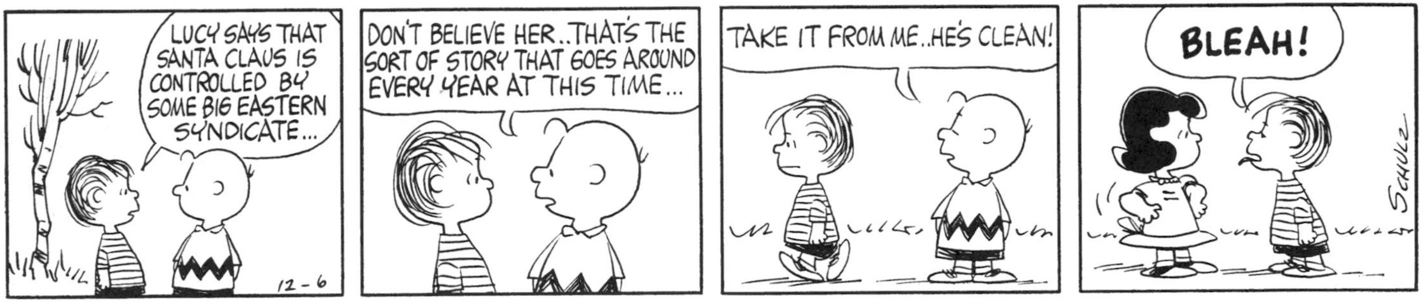
LUCY SAYS THAT SANTA CLAUS IS CONTROLLED BY SOME BIG EASTERN SYNDICATE...
12-6
DON'T BELIEVE HER..THAT'S THE SORT OF STORY THAT GOES AROUND EVERY YEAR AT THIS TIME...
TAKE IT FROM ME..HE'S CLEAN!
BLEAH!
SCHULZ

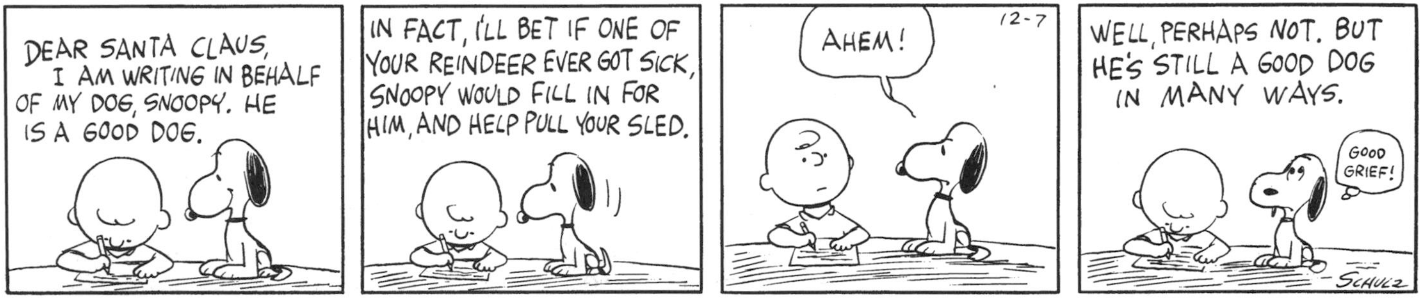
DEAR SANTA CLAUS,
I AM WRITING IN BEHALF OF MY DOG, SNOOPY. HE IS A GOOD DOG.
IN FACT, I'LL BET IF ONE OF YOUR REINDEER EVER GOT SICK, SNOOPY WOULD FILL IN FOR HIM, AND HELP PULL YOUR SLED.
12-7
AHEM!
WELL, PERHAPS NOT. BUT HE'S STILL A GOOD DOG IN MANY WAYS.
GOOD GRIEF!
SCHULZ

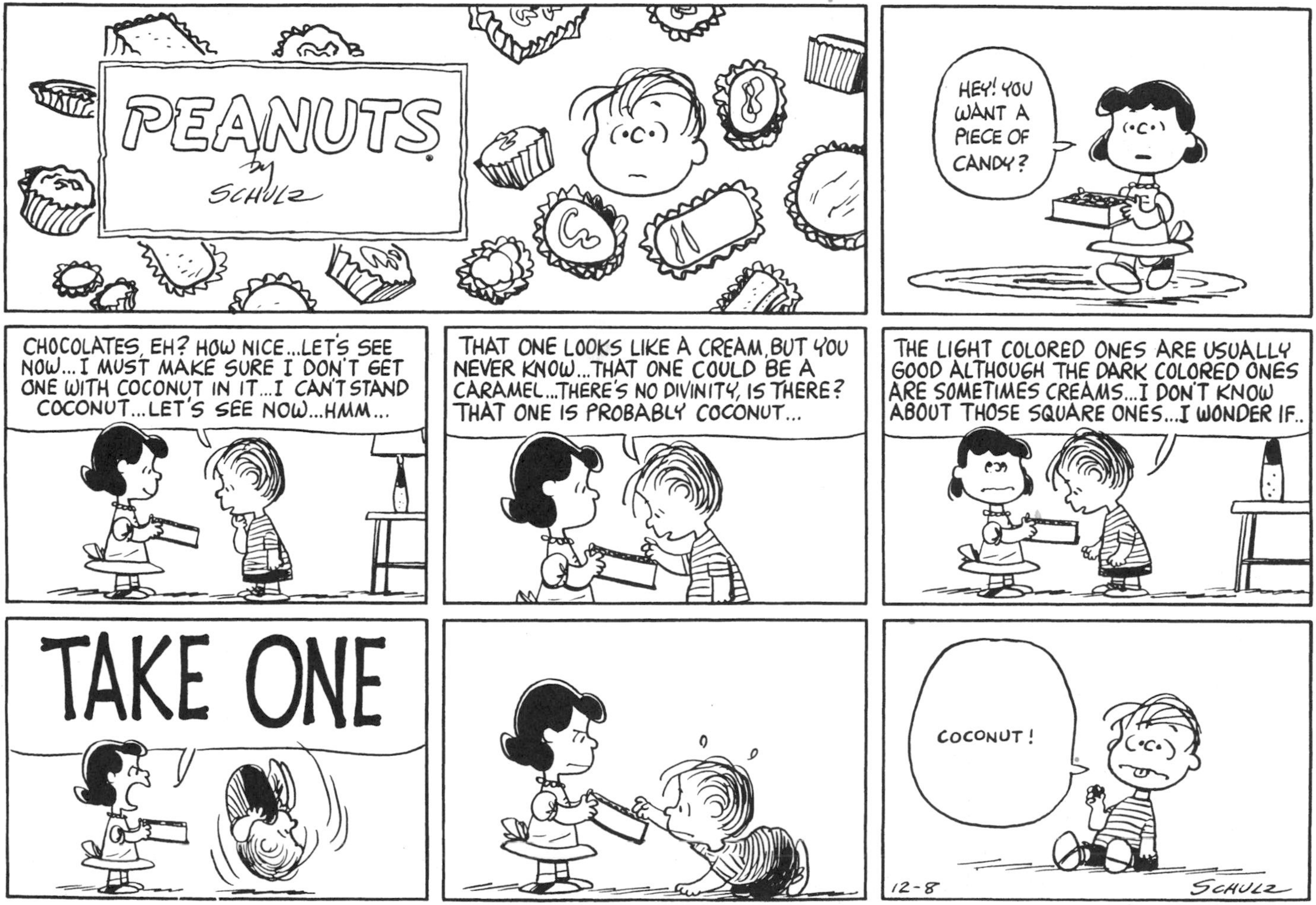
PEANUTS
by SCHULZ
HEY! YOU WANT A PIECE OF CANDY?
CHOCOLATES, EH? HOW NICE...LET'S SEE NOW...I MUST MAKE SURE I DON'T GET ONE WITH COCONUT IN IT...I CAN'T STAND COCONUT...LET'S SEE NOW...HMM...
THAT ONE LOOKS LIKE A CREAM, BUT YOU NEVER KNOW...THAT ONE COULD BE A CARAMEL...THERE'S NO DIVINITY, IS THERE? THAT ONE IS PROBABLY COCONUT...
THE LIGHT COLORED ONES ARE USUALLY GOOD ALTHOUGH THE DARK COLORED ONES ARE SOMETIMES CREAMS...I DON'T KNOW ABOUT THOSE SQUARE ONES...I WONDER IF..
TAKE ONE
COCONUT!
12-8
SCHULZ

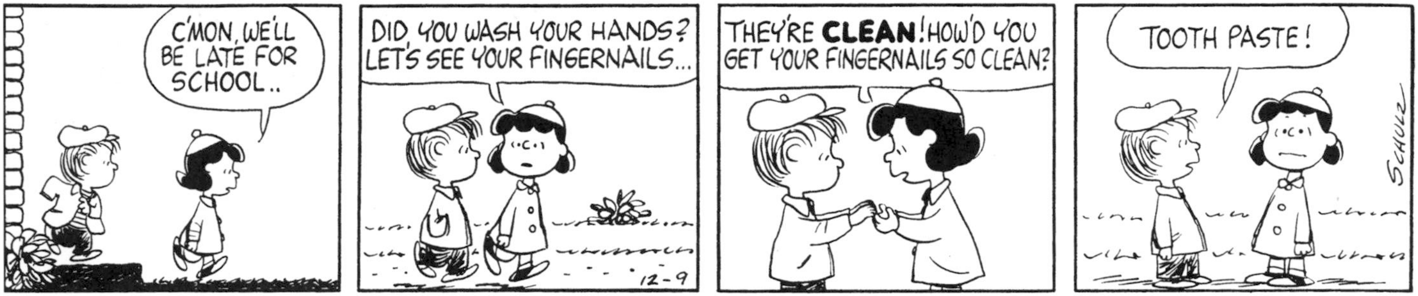
C'MON, WE'LL BE LATE FOR SCHOOL..
DID YOU WASH YOUR HANDS? LET'S SEE YOUR FINGERNAILS...
12-9
THEY'RE **CLEAN**! HOW'D YOU GET YOUR FINGERNAILS SO CLEAN?
TOOTH PASTE!
SCHULZ

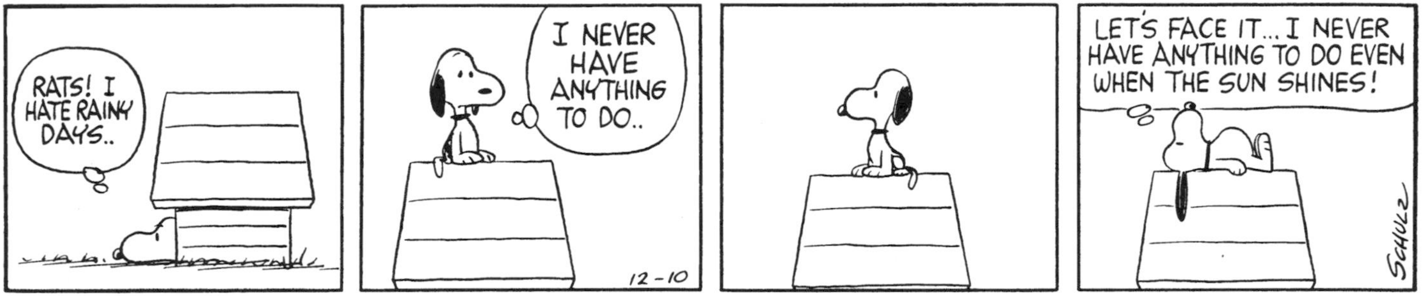
RATS! I HATE RAINY DAYS..
I NEVER HAVE ANYTHING TO DO..
12-10
LET'S FACE IT... I NEVER HAVE ANYTHING TO DO EVEN WHEN THE SUN SHINES!
SCHULZ

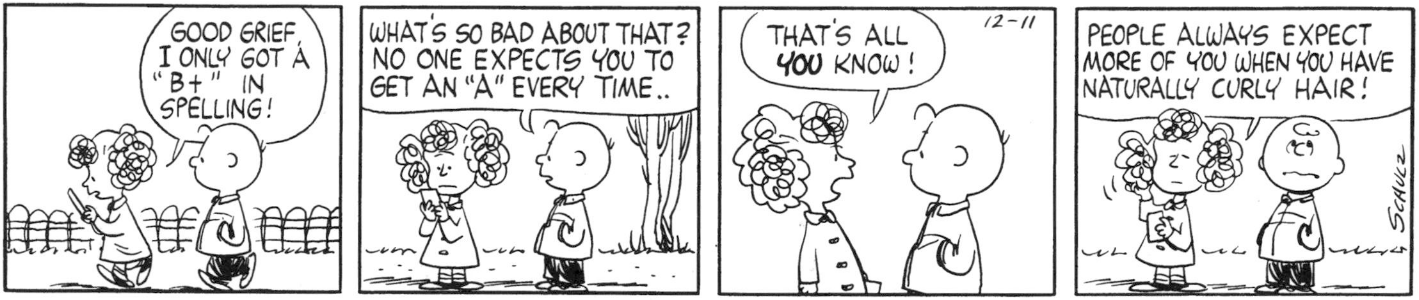
GOOD GRIEF, I ONLY GOT A "B+" IN SPELLING!
WHAT'S SO BAD ABOUT THAT? NO ONE EXPECTS YOU TO GET AN "A" EVERY TIME..
THAT'S ALL **YOU** KNOW!
12-11
PEOPLE ALWAYS EXPECT MORE OF YOU WHEN YOU HAVE NATURALLY CURLY HAIR!
SCHULZ

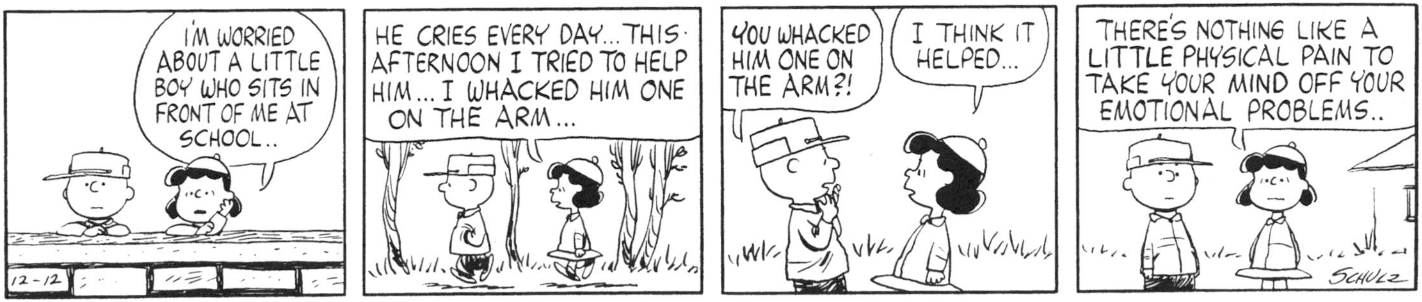
I'M WORRIED ABOUT A LITTLE BOY WHO SITS IN FRONT OF ME AT SCHOOL..
12-12
HE CRIES EVERY DAY... THIS AFTERNOON I TRIED TO HELP HIM... I WHACKED HIM ONE ON THE ARM...
YOU WHACKED HIM ONE ON THE ARM?!
I THINK IT HELPED...
THERE'S NOTHING LIKE A LITTLE PHYSICAL PAIN TO TAKE YOUR MIND OFF YOUR EMOTIONAL PROBLEMS..
SCHULZ

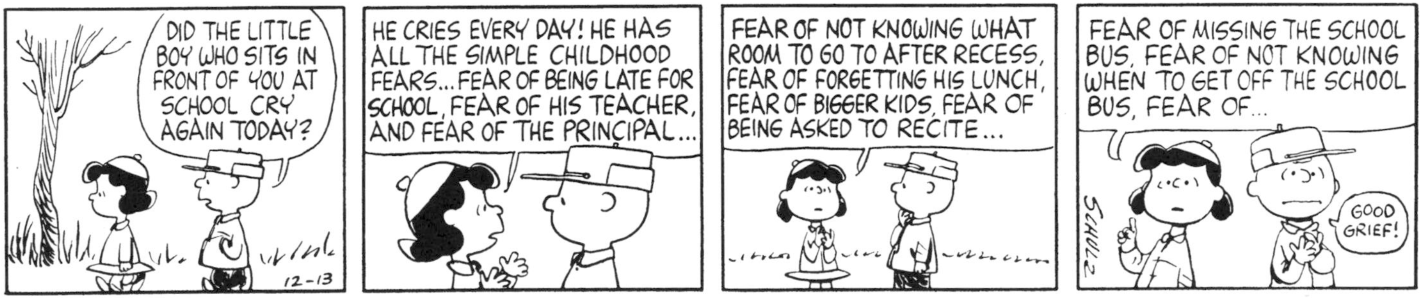
DID THE LITTLE BOY WHO SITS IN FRONT OF YOU AT SCHOOL CRY AGAIN TODAY?
12-13
HE CRIES EVERY DAY! HE HAS ALL THE SIMPLE CHILDHOOD FEARS...FEAR OF BEING LATE FOR SCHOOL, FEAR OF HIS TEACHER, AND FEAR OF THE PRINCIPAL...
FEAR OF NOT KNOWING WHAT ROOM TO GO TO AFTER RECESS, FEAR OF FORGETTING HIS LUNCH, FEAR OF BIGGER KIDS, FEAR OF BEING ASKED TO RECITE...
FEAR OF MISSING THE SCHOOL BUS, FEAR OF NOT KNOWING WHEN TO GET OFF THE SCHOOL BUS, FEAR OF...
SCHULZ
GOOD GRIEF!

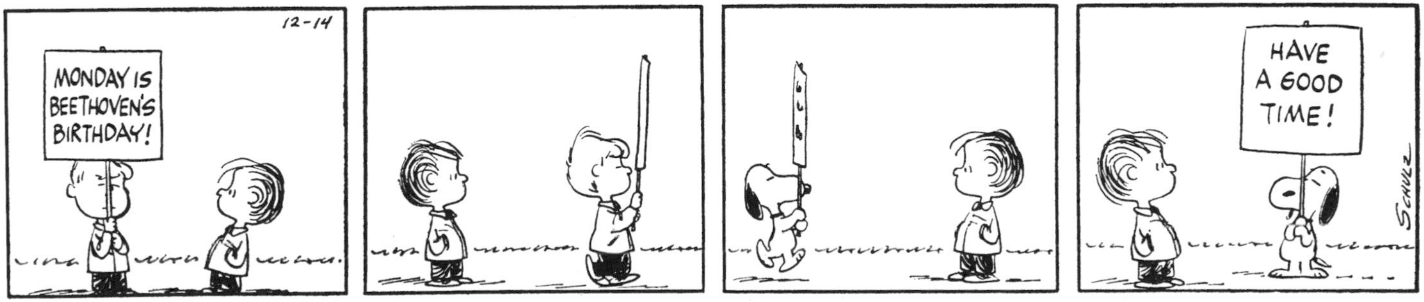
12-14
MONDAY IS BEETHOVEN'S BIRTHDAY!
HAVE A GOOD TIME!
SCHULZ

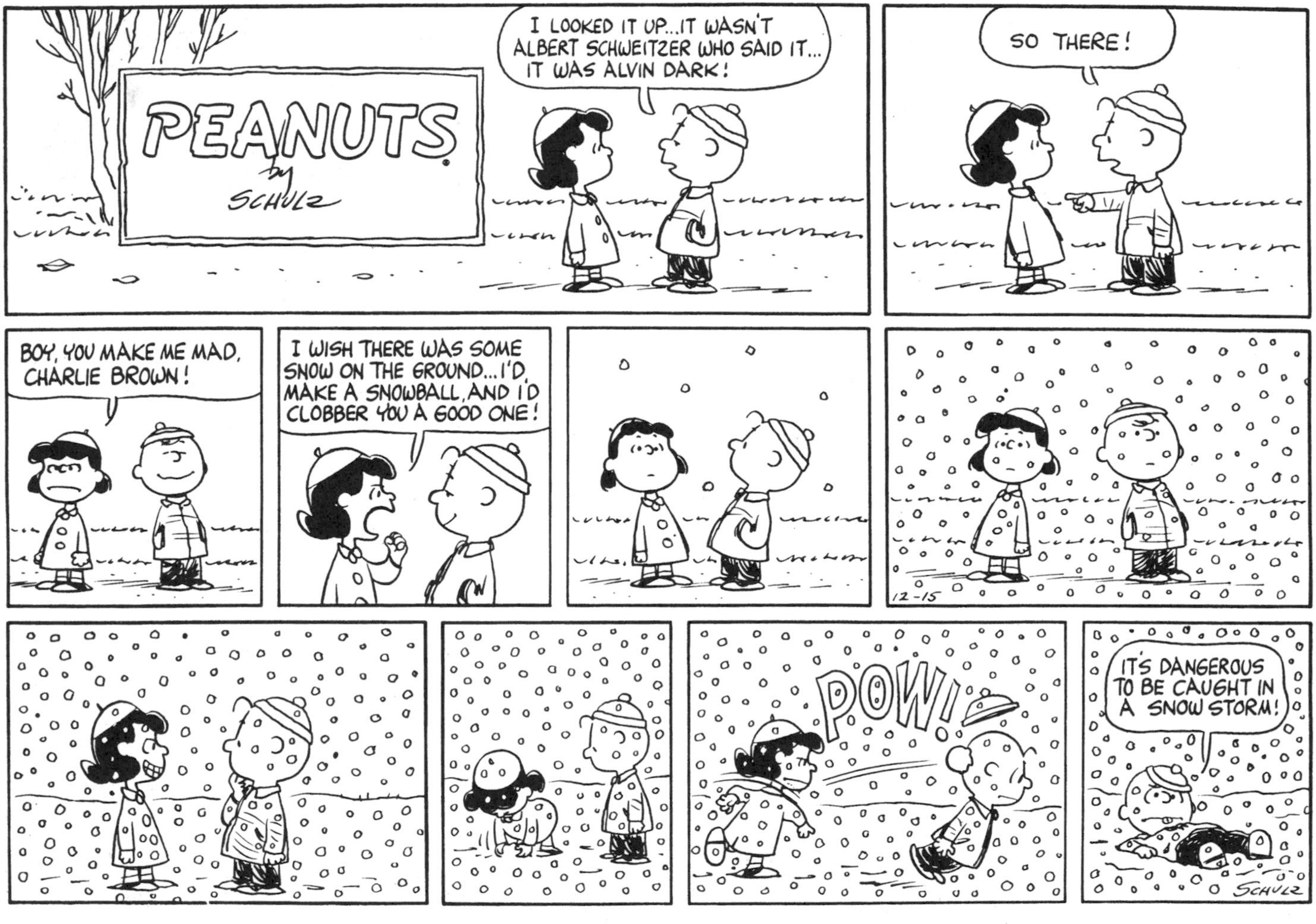
PEANUTS
by SCHULZ
I LOOKED IT UP...IT WASN'T ALBERT SCHWEITZER WHO SAID IT... IT WAS ALVIN DARK!
SO THERE!
BOY, YOU MAKE ME MAD, CHARLIE BROWN!
I WISH THERE WAS SOME SNOW ON THE GROUND...I'D MAKE A SNOWBALL, AND I'D CLOBBER YOU A GOOD ONE!
12-15
POW!
IT'S DANGEROUS TO BE CAUGHT IN A SNOW STORM!
SCHULZ

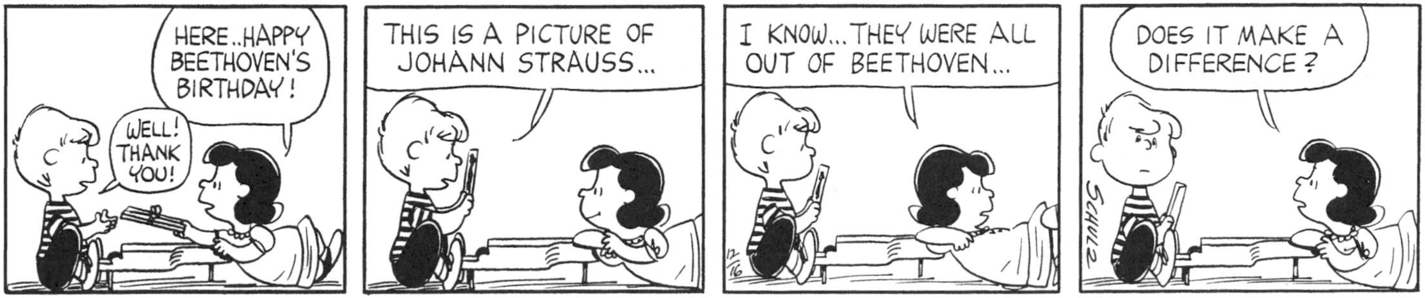
HERE..HAPPY BEETHOVEN'S BIRTHDAY!
WELL! THANK YOU!
THIS IS A PICTURE OF JOHANN STRAUSS...
I KNOW...THEY WERE ALL OUT OF BEETHOVEN...
DOES IT MAKE A DIFFERENCE?

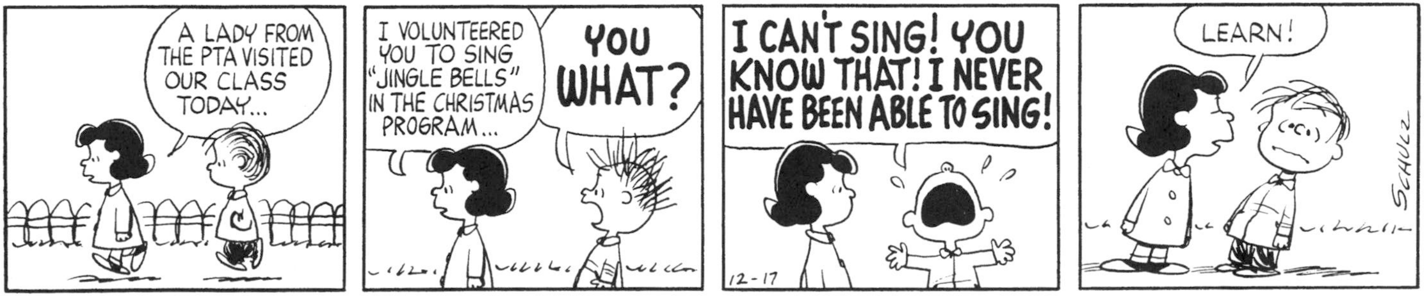
A LADY FROM THE PTA VISITED OUR CLASS TODAY...
I VOLUNTEERED YOU TO SING "JINGLE BELLS" IN THE CHRISTMAS PROGRAM...
YOU WHAT?
I CAN'T SING! YOU KNOW THAT! I NEVER HAVE BEEN ABLE TO SING!
LEARN!

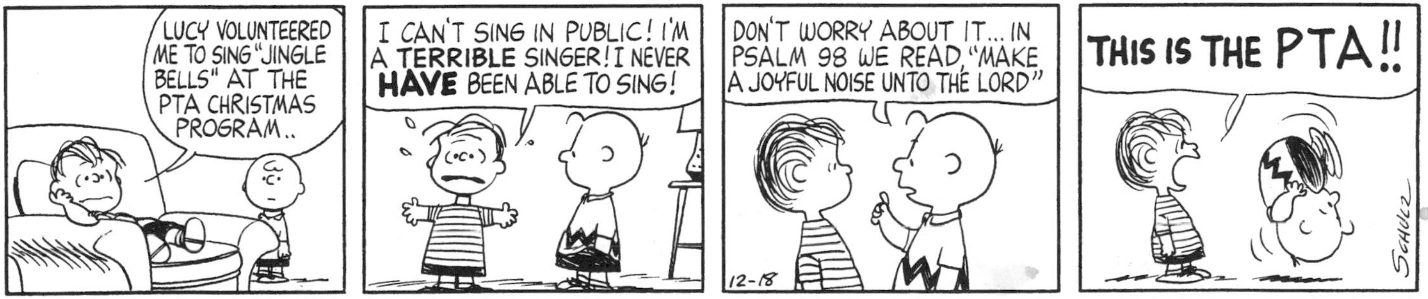
LUCY VOLUNTEERED ME TO SING "JINGLE BELLS" AT THE PTA CHRISTMAS PROGRAM..
I CAN'T SING IN PUBLIC! I'M A TERRIBLE SINGER! I NEVER HAVE BEEN ABLE TO SING!
DON'T WORRY ABOUT IT... IN PSALM 98 WE READ, "MAKE A JOYFUL NOISE UNTO THE LORD"
THIS IS THE PTA!!

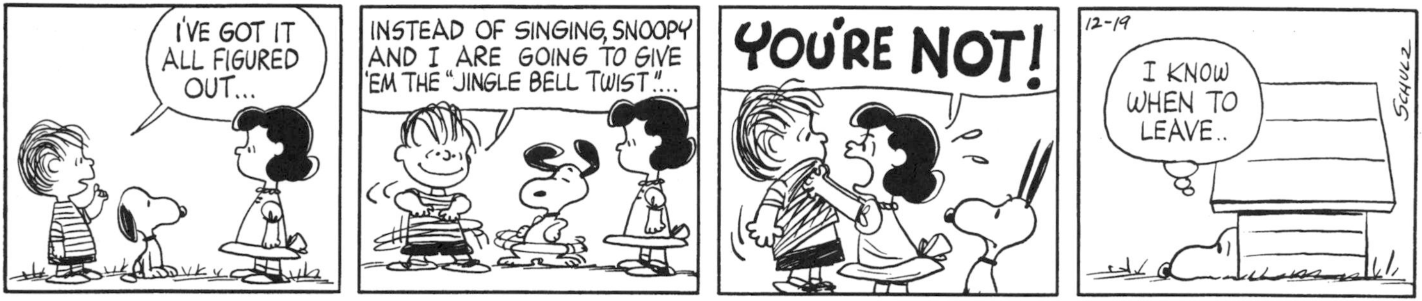
I'VE GOT IT ALL FIGURED OUT...
INSTEAD OF SINGING, SNOOPY AND I ARE GOING TO GIVE 'EM THE "JINGLE BELL TWIST"!...
YOU'RE NOT!
12-19
SCHULZ
I KNOW WHEN TO LEAVE..

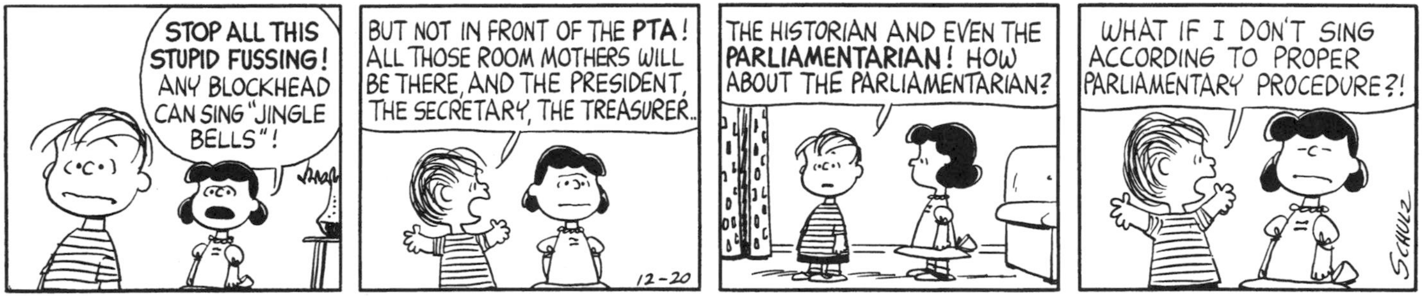
STOP ALL THIS STUPID FUSSING! ANY BLOCKHEAD CAN SING "JINGLE BELLS"!
BUT NOT IN FRONT OF THE PTA! ALL THOSE ROOM MOTHERS WILL BE THERE, AND THE PRESIDENT, THE SECRETARY, THE TREASURER..
12-20
THE HISTORIAN AND EVEN THE PARLIAMENTARIAN! HOW ABOUT THE PARLIAMENTARIAN?
WHAT IF I DON'T SING ACCORDING TO PROPER PARLIAMENTARY PROCEDURE?!
SCHULZ

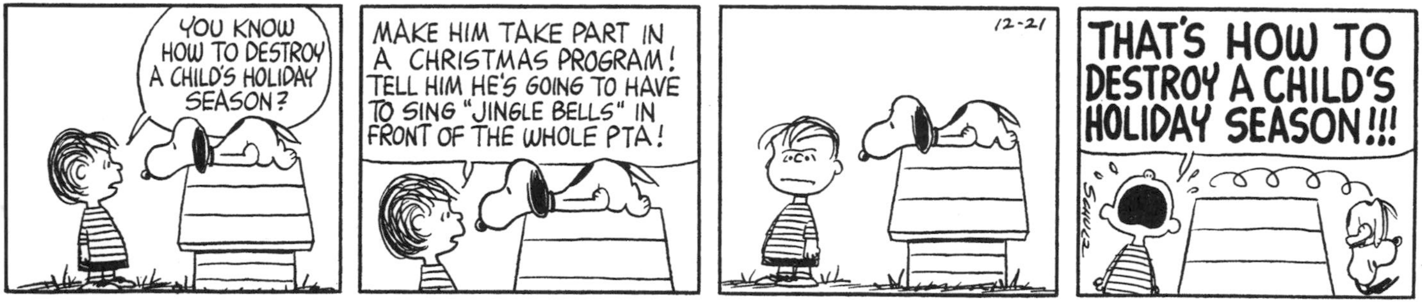
YOU KNOW HOW TO DESTROY A CHILD'S HOLIDAY SEASON?
MAKE HIM TAKE PART IN A CHRISTMAS PROGRAM! TELL HIM HE'S GOING TO HAVE TO SING "JINGLE BELLS" IN FRONT OF THE WHOLE PTA!
12-21
THAT'S HOW TO DESTROY A CHILD'S HOLIDAY SEASON!!!
SCHULZ

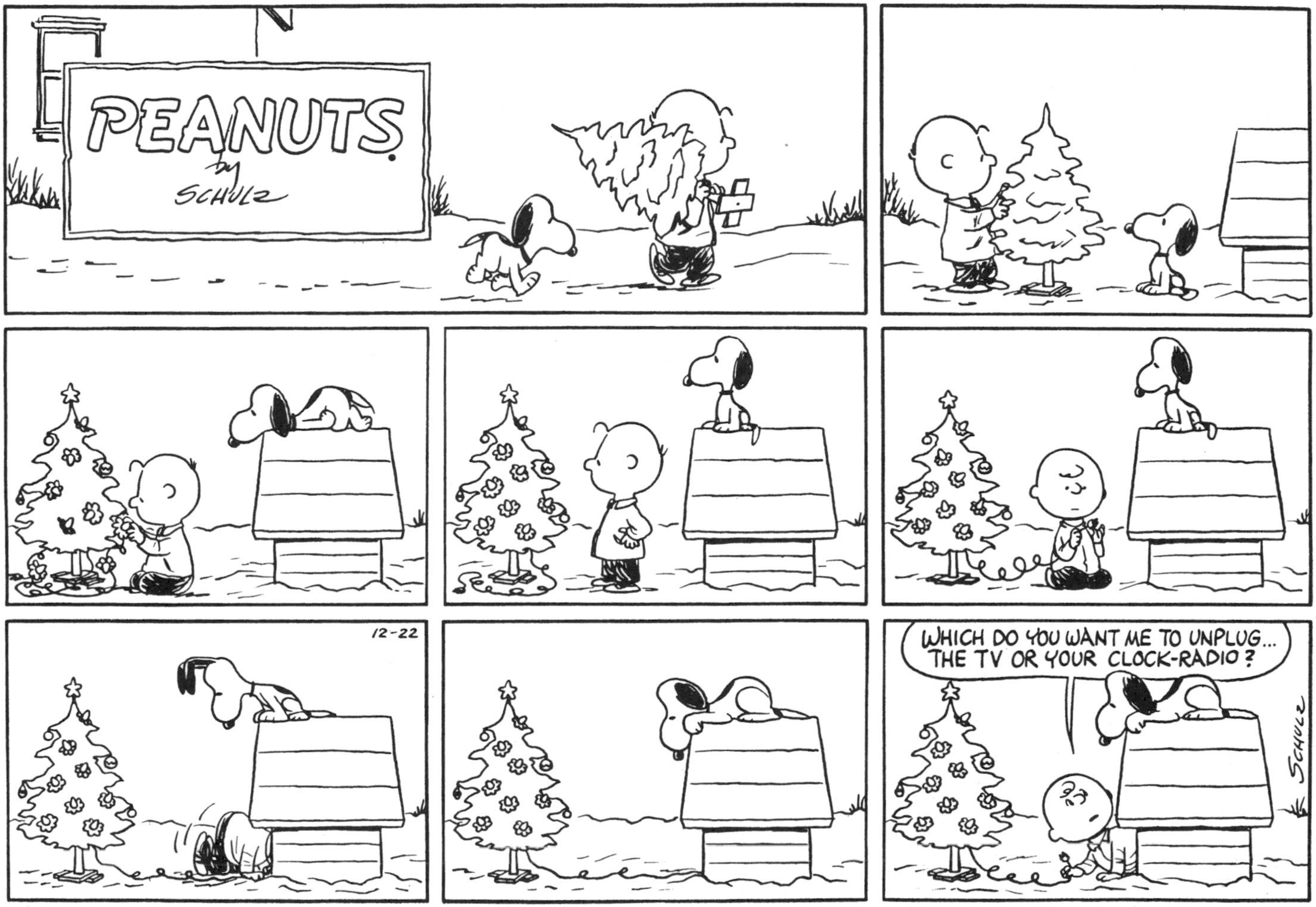
PEANUTS
by
SCHULZ
12-22
WHICH DO YOU WANT ME TO UNPLUG... THE TV OR YOUR CLOCK-RADIO?
SCHULZ

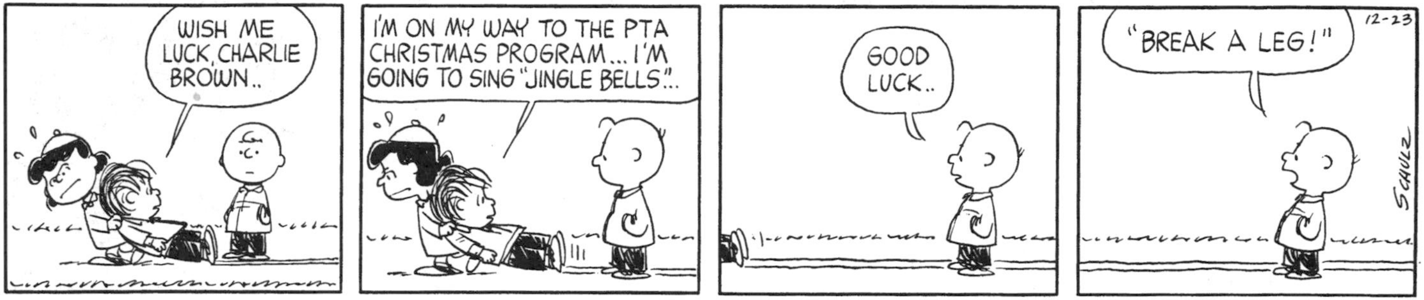
WISH ME LUCK, CHARLIE BROWN..
I'M ON MY WAY TO THE PTA CHRISTMAS PROGRAM... I'M GOING TO SING "JINGLE BELLS"..
GOOD LUCK..
"BREAK A LEG!"
12-23
SCHULZ

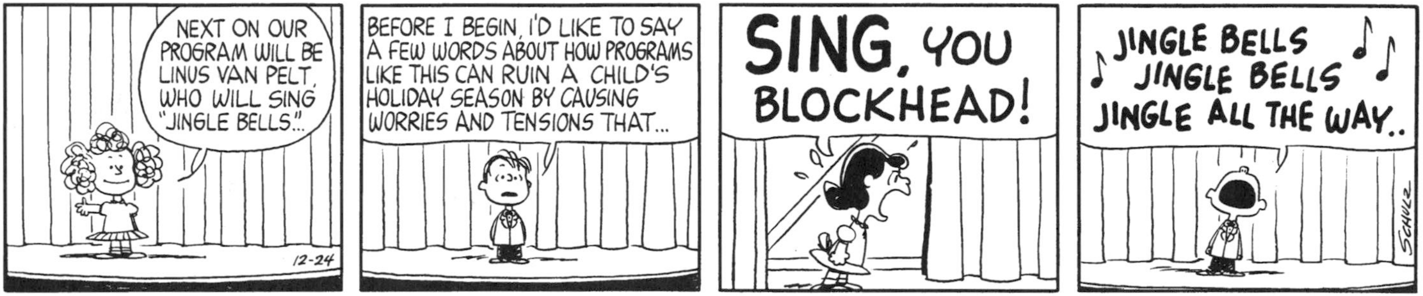
NEXT ON OUR PROGRAM WILL BE LINUS VAN PELT, WHO WILL SING "JINGLE BELLS"..
12-24
BEFORE I BEGIN, I'D LIKE TO SAY A FEW WORDS ABOUT HOW PROGRAMS LIKE THIS CAN RUIN A CHILD'S HOLIDAY SEASON BY CAUSING WORRIES AND TENSIONS THAT...
SING, YOU BLOCKHEAD!
JINGLE BELLS JINGLE BELLS JINGLE ALL THE WAY..
SCHULZ

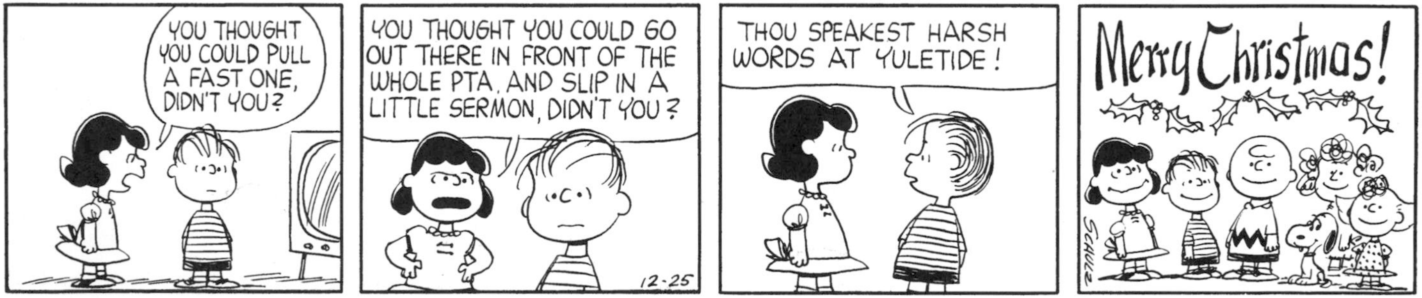
YOU THOUGHT YOU COULD PULL A FAST ONE, DIDN'T YOU?
YOU THOUGHT YOU COULD GO OUT THERE IN FRONT OF THE WHOLE PTA, AND SLIP IN A LITTLE SERMON, DIDN'T YOU?
12-25
THOU SPEAKEST HARSH WORDS AT YULETIDE!
Merry Christmas!
SCHULZ

NOW THAT CHRISTMAS IS OVER, I HEAR THE PTA IS PLANNING A NEW YEAR'S PROGRAM..
THEY NEED A LITTLE BOY TO PLAY THE PART OF THE NEW YEAR
BOY, I SURE PITY THAT POOR KID WHOEVER HE IS..
HAVEN'T YOU HEARD?
OH, NO!

AUGHHGHGH
GHHGAUGHH
PERHAPS YOU SHOULDN'T HAVE VOLUNTEERED HIM FOR ANOTHER PTA PROGRAM QUITE SO SOON..
THAT THOUGHT NEVER OCCURRED TO ME...
AUGH!

IT'S YOUR FAULT, YOU KNOW...
FIRST YOU VOLUNTEERED HIM FOR A PTA CHRISTMAS PROGRAM, AND WHEN HE SURVIVED THAT, YOU TURNED RIGHT AROUND, AND VOLUNTEERED HIM FOR THE PTA NEW YEAR'S PROGRAM!
IT'S YOUR FAULT HE'S UP IN THAT TREE... CAN'T YOU AT LEAST SAY SOMETHING TO HIM?
YOU BLOCKHEAD!

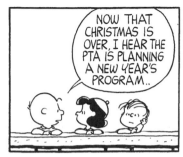

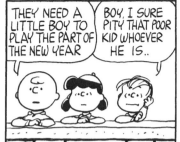

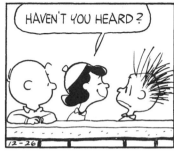

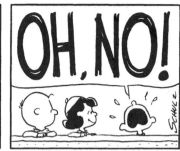

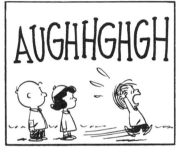

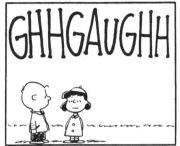

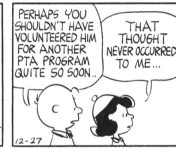

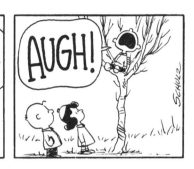

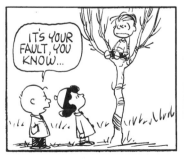

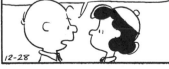

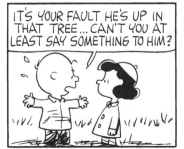

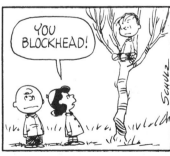

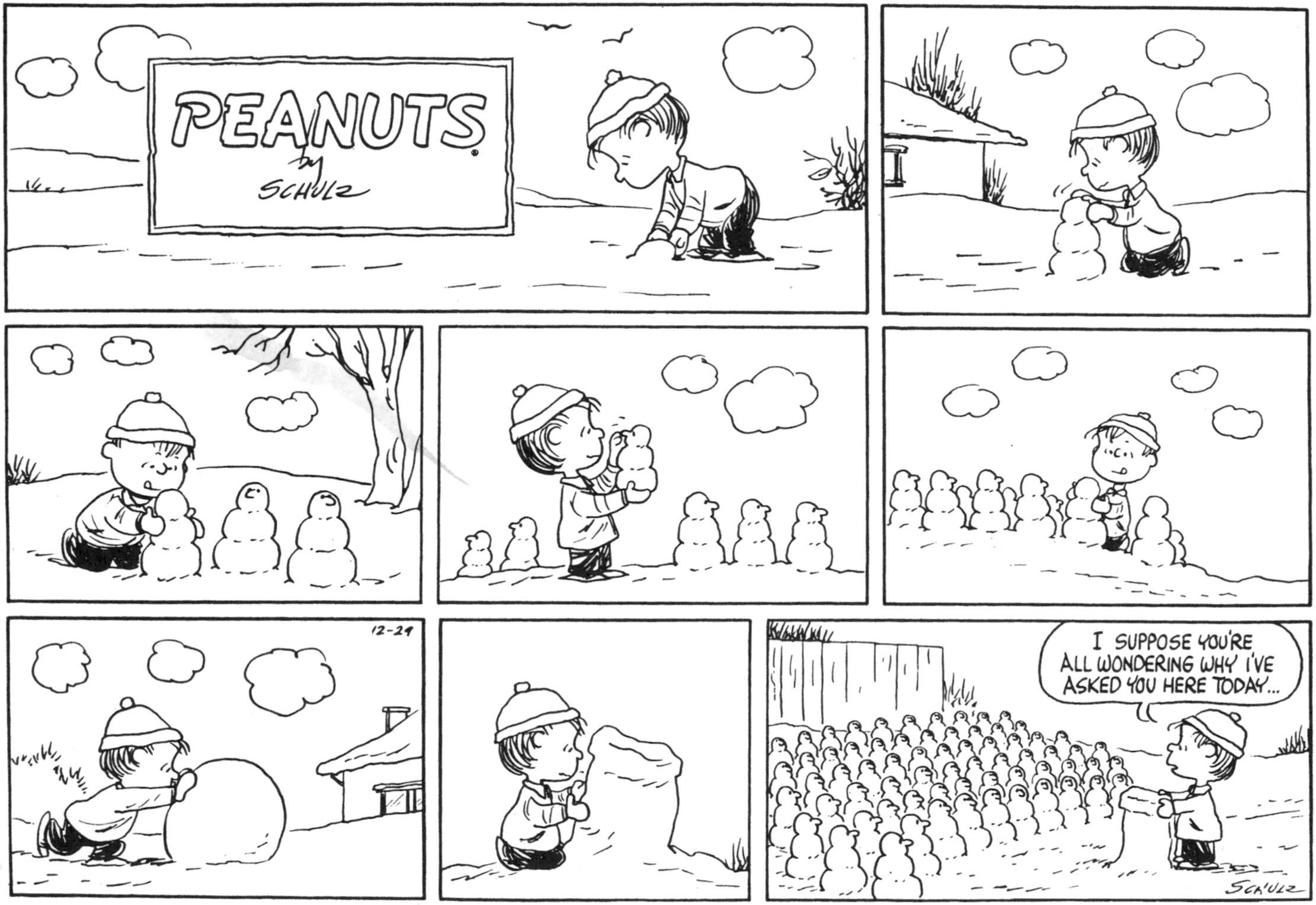
PEANUTS
by
SCHULZ
12-29
I SUPPOSE YOU'RE ALL WONDERING WHY I'VE ASKED YOU HERE TODAY...
SCHULZ

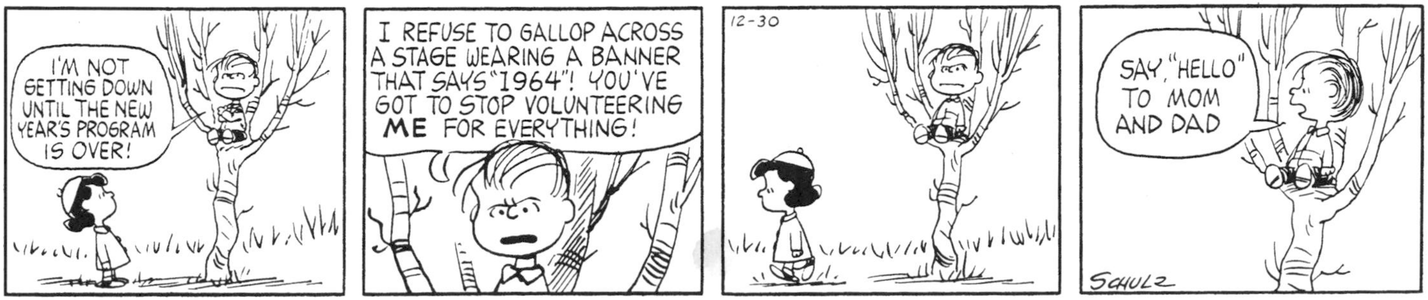
I'M NOT GETTING DOWN UNTIL THE NEW YEAR'S PROGRAM IS OVER!
I REFUSE TO GALLOP ACROSS A STAGE WEARING A BANNER THAT SAYS "1964"! YOU'VE GOT TO STOP VOLUNTEERING ME FOR EVERYTHING!
12-30
SAY, "HELLO" TO MOM AND DAD
SCHULZ

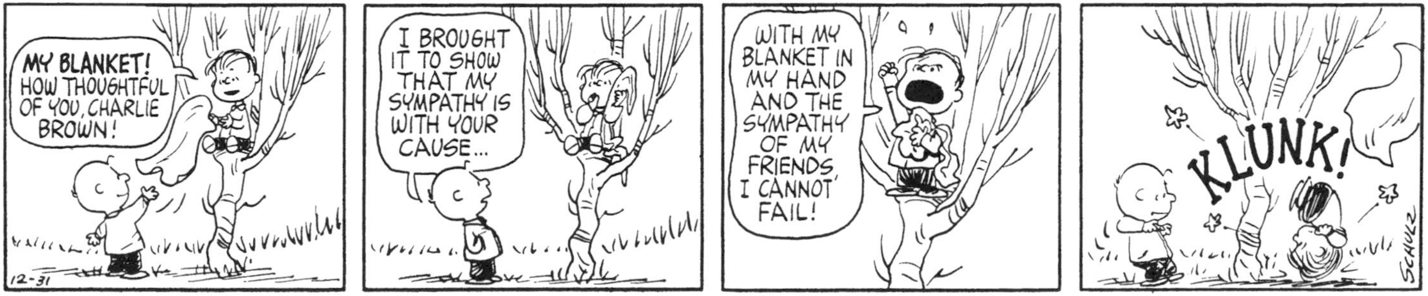
MY BLANKET! HOW THOUGHTFUL OF YOU, CHARLIE BROWN!
12-31
I BROUGHT IT TO SHOW THAT MY SYMPATHY IS WITH YOUR CAUSE...
WITH MY BLANKET IN MY HAND AND THE SYMPATHY OF MY FRIENDS, I CANNOT FAIL!
KLUNK!
SCHULZ

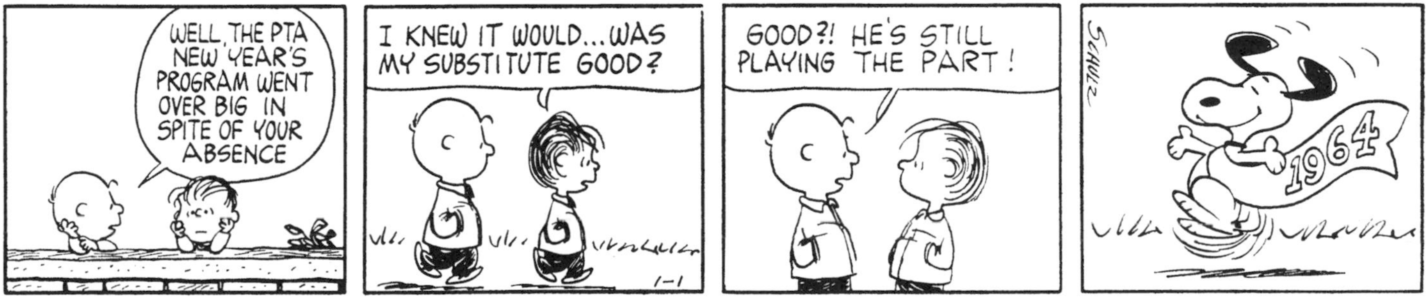
WELL, THE PTA NEW YEAR'S PROGRAM WENT OVER BIG IN SPITE OF YOUR ABSENCE
I KNEW IT WOULD... WAS MY SUBSTITUTE GOOD?
1-1
GOOD?! HE'S STILL PLAYING THE PART!
SCHULZ
1964

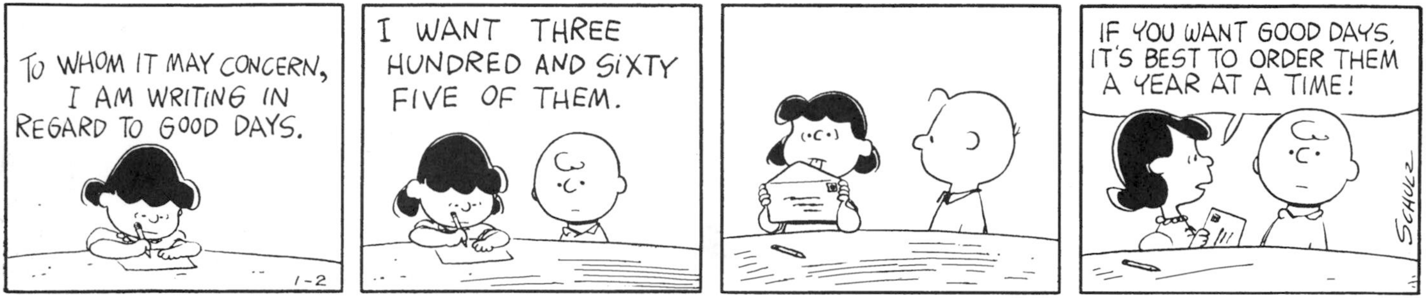
TO WHOM IT MAY CONCERN, I AM WRITING IN REGARD TO GOOD DAYS.
1-2
I WANT THREE HUNDRED AND SIXTY FIVE OF THEM.
IF YOU WANT GOOD DAYS, IT'S BEST TO ORDER THEM A YEAR AT A TIME!
SCHULZ

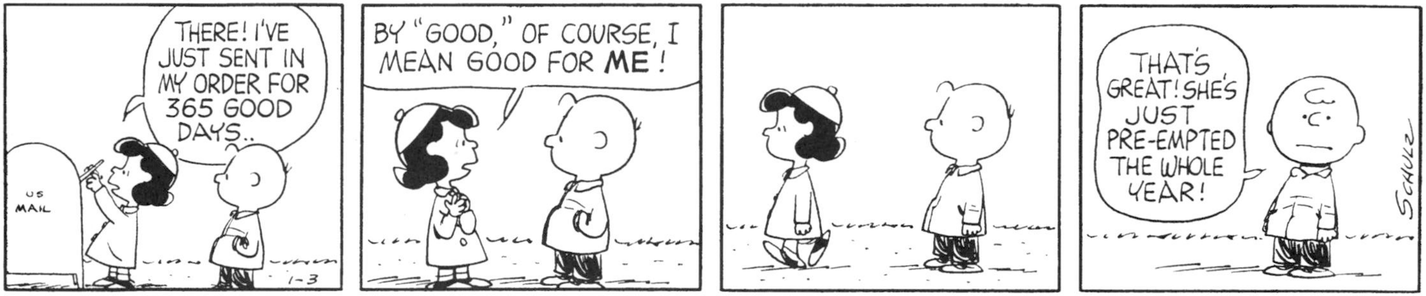
US MAIL
THERE! I'VE JUST SENT IN MY ORDER FOR 365 GOOD DAYS..
1-3
BY "GOOD," OF COURSE, I MEAN GOOD FOR **ME**!
THAT'S GREAT! SHE'S JUST PRE-EMPTED THE WHOLE YEAR!
SCHULZ

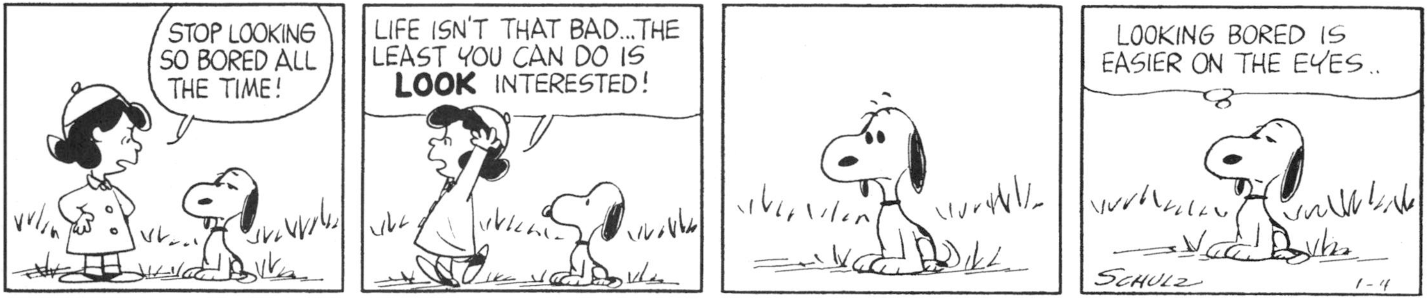
STOP LOOKING SO BORED ALL THE TIME!
LIFE ISN'T THAT BAD...THE LEAST YOU CAN DO IS **LOOK** INTERESTED!
LOOKING BORED IS EASIER ON THE EYES..
SCHULZ
1-4

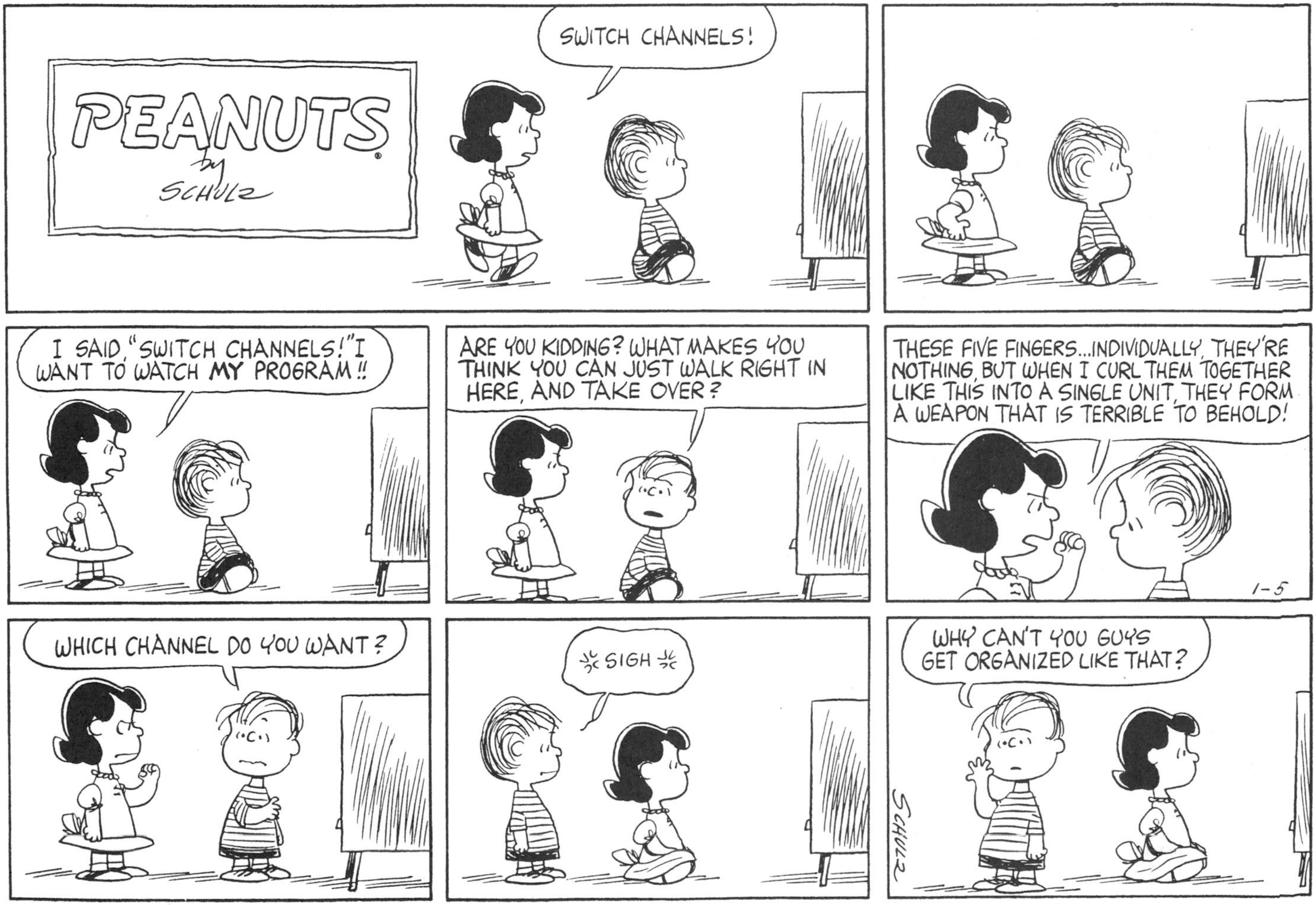
PEANUTS
by SCHULZ
SWITCH CHANNELS!
I SAID, "SWITCH CHANNELS!" I WANT TO WATCH MY PROGRAM!!
ARE YOU KIDDING? WHAT MAKES YOU THINK YOU CAN JUST WALK RIGHT IN HERE, AND TAKE OVER?
THESE FIVE FINGERS...INDIVIDUALLY, THEY'RE NOTHING, BUT WHEN I CURL THEM TOGETHER LIKE THIS INTO A SINGLE UNIT, THEY FORM A WEAPON THAT IS TERRIBLE TO BEHOLD!
1-5
WHICH CHANNEL DO YOU WANT?
SIGH
WHY CAN'T YOU GUYS GET ORGANIZED LIKE THAT?
SCHULZ

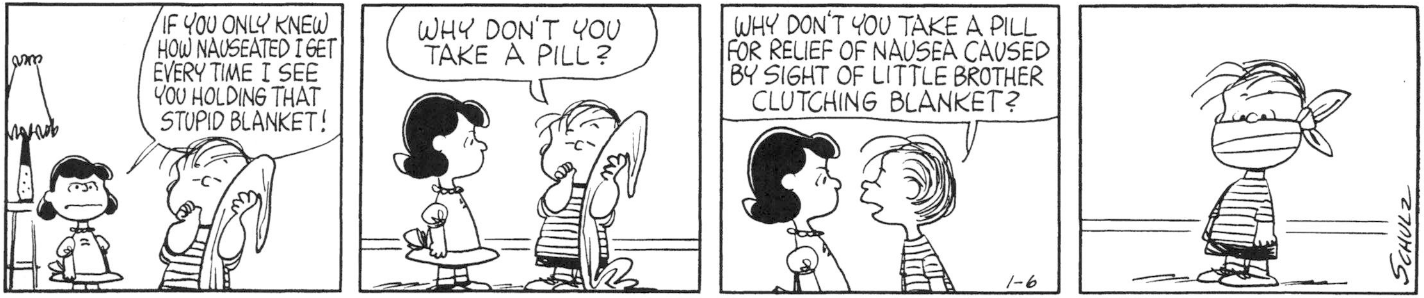
IF YOU ONLY KNEW HOW NAUSEATED I GET EVERY TIME I SEE YOU HOLDING THAT STUPID BLANKET!
WHY DON'T YOU TAKE A PILL?
WHY DON'T YOU TAKE A PILL FOR RELIEF OF NAUSEA CAUSED BY SIGHT OF LITTLE BROTHER CLUTCHING BLANKET?
1-6
SCHULZ

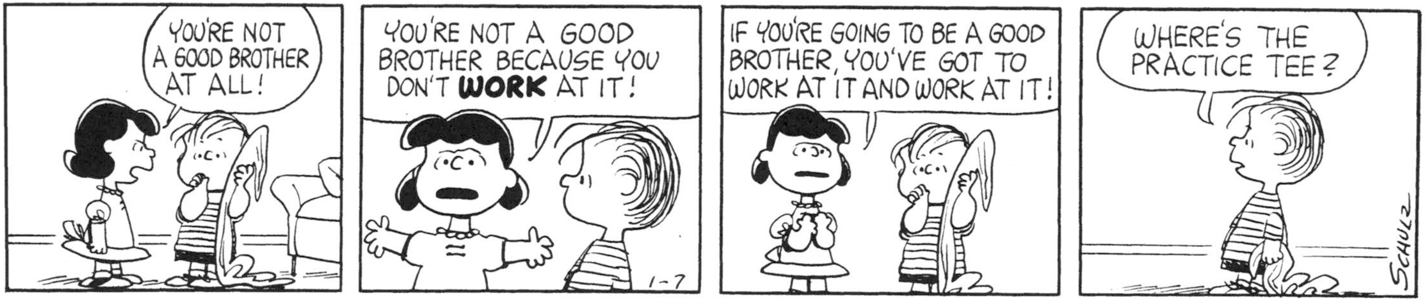
YOU'RE NOT A GOOD BROTHER AT ALL!
YOU'RE NOT A GOOD BROTHER BECAUSE YOU DON'T **WORK** AT IT!
1-7
IF YOU'RE GOING TO BE A GOOD BROTHER, YOU'VE GOT TO WORK AT IT AND WORK AT IT!
WHERE'S THE PRACTICE TEE?
SCHULZ

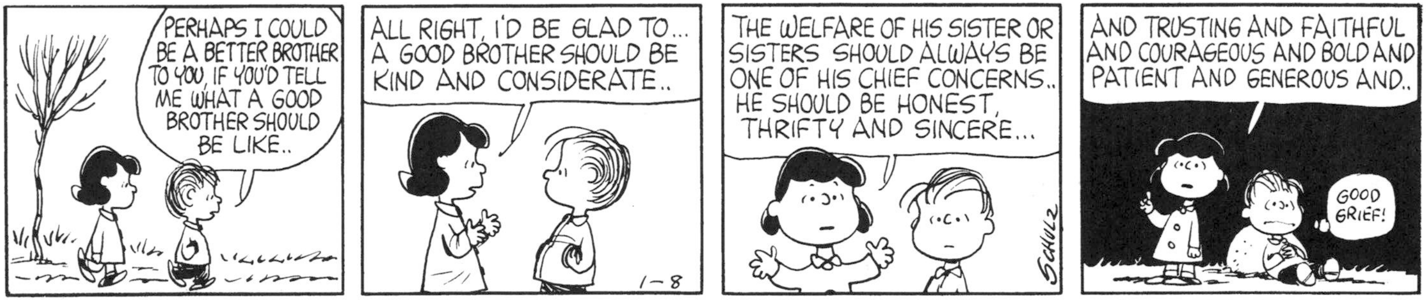
PERHAPS I COULD BE A BETTER BROTHER TO YOU, IF YOU'D TELL ME WHAT A GOOD BROTHER SHOULD BE LIKE..
ALL RIGHT, I'D BE GLAD TO... A GOOD BROTHER SHOULD BE KIND AND CONSIDERATE..
1-8
THE WELFARE OF HIS SISTER OR SISTERS SHOULD ALWAYS BE ONE OF HIS CHIEF CONCERNS.. HE SHOULD BE HONEST, THRIFTY AND SINCERE...
SCHULZ
AND TRUSTING AND FAITHFUL AND COURAGEOUS AND BOLD AND PATIENT AND GENEROUS AND..
GOOD GRIEF!

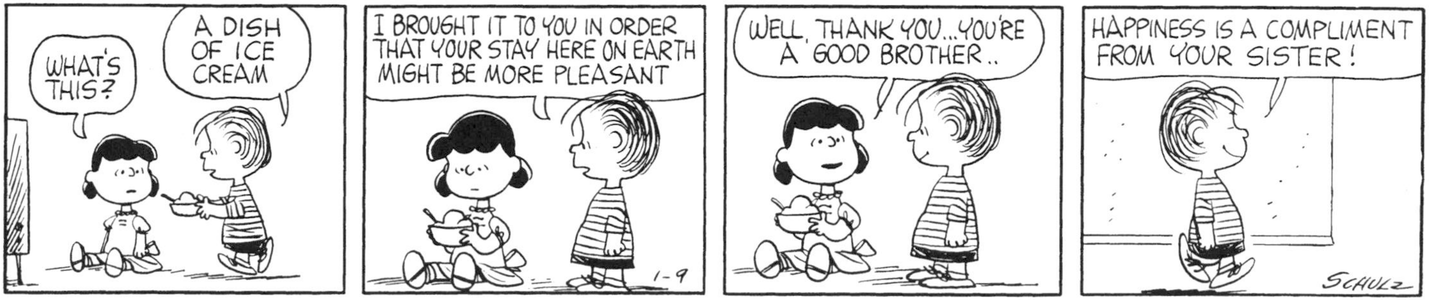
WHAT'S THIS?
A DISH OF ICE CREAM
I BROUGHT IT TO YOU IN ORDER THAT YOUR STAY HERE ON EARTH MIGHT BE MORE PLEASANT
WELL, THANK YOU...YOU'RE A GOOD BROTHER..
HAPPINESS IS A COMPLIMENT FROM YOUR SISTER!

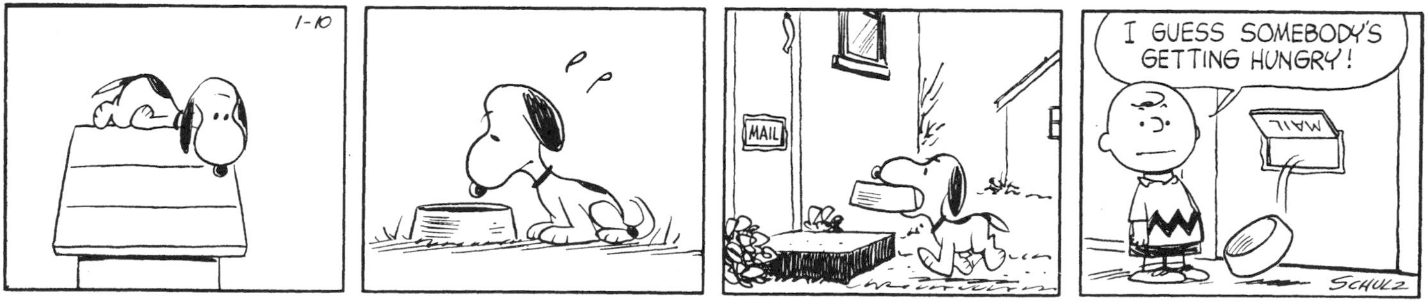
MAIL
I GUESS SOMEBODY'S GETTING HUNGRY!

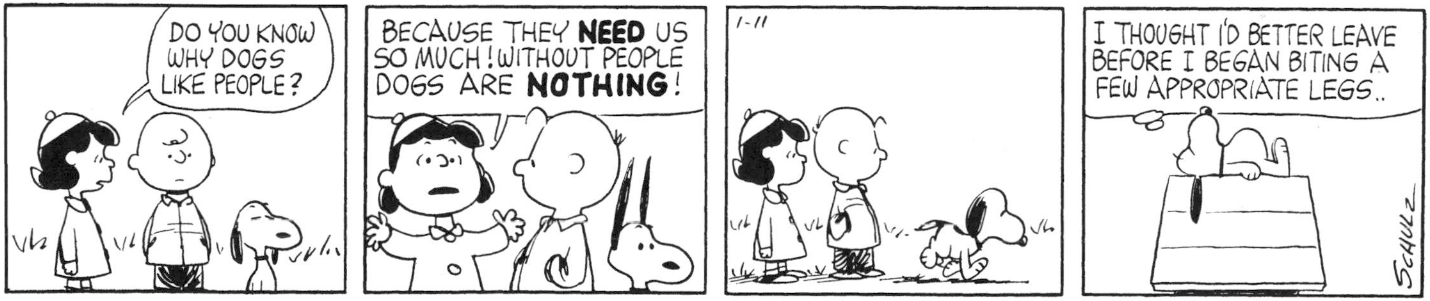
DO YOU KNOW WHY DOGS LIKE PEOPLE?
BECAUSE THEY **NEED** US SO MUCH! WITHOUT PEOPLE DOGS ARE **NOTHING**!
I THOUGHT I'D BETTER LEAVE BEFORE I BEGAN BITING A FEW APPROPRIATE LEGS..

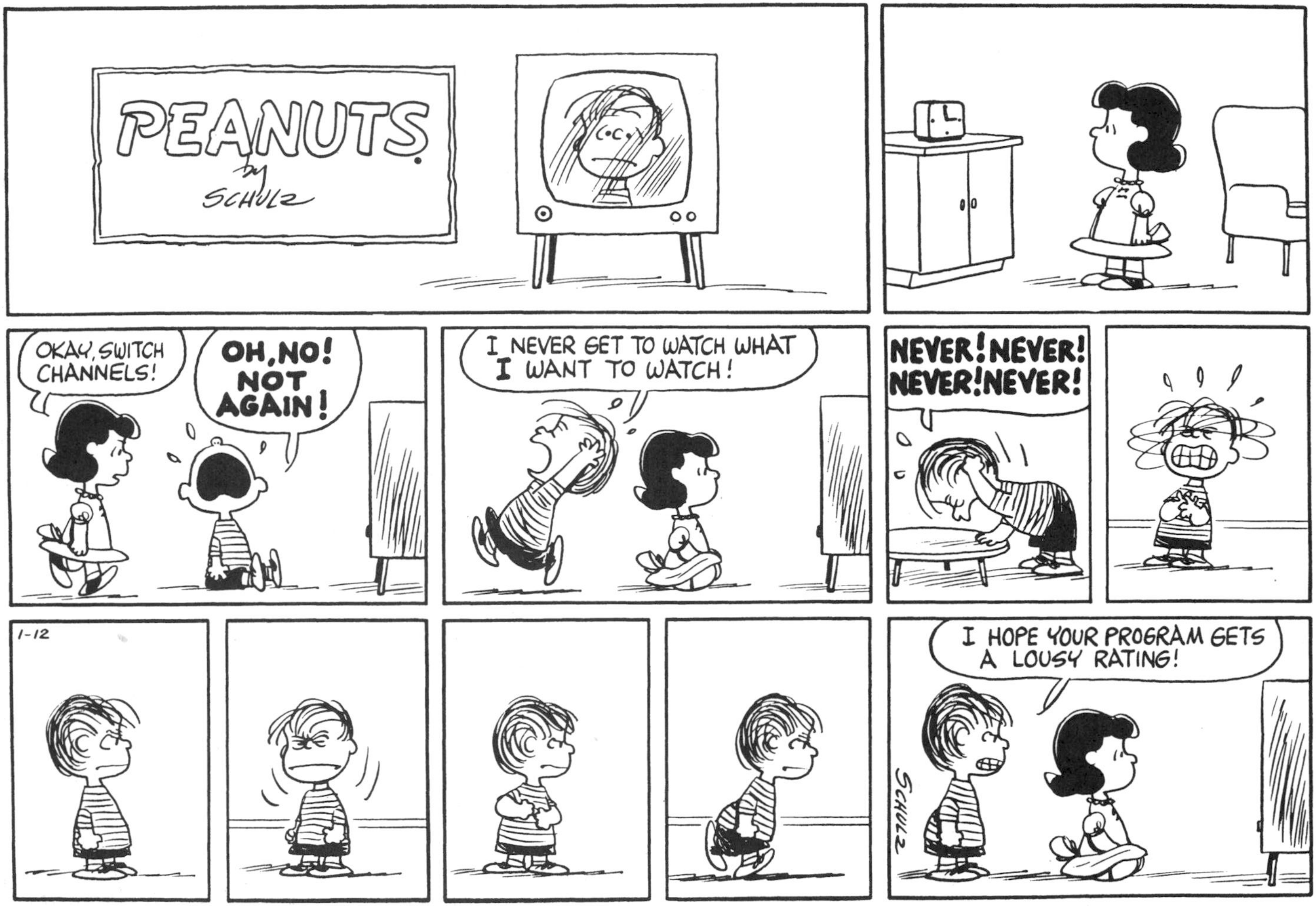
PEANUTS
by SCHULZ
OKAY, SWITCH CHANNELS!
OH, NO! NOT AGAIN!
I NEVER GET TO WATCH WHAT I WANT TO WATCH!
NEVER! NEVER! NEVER! NEVER!
1-12
I HOPE YOUR PROGRAM GETS A LOUSY RATING!
SCHULZ

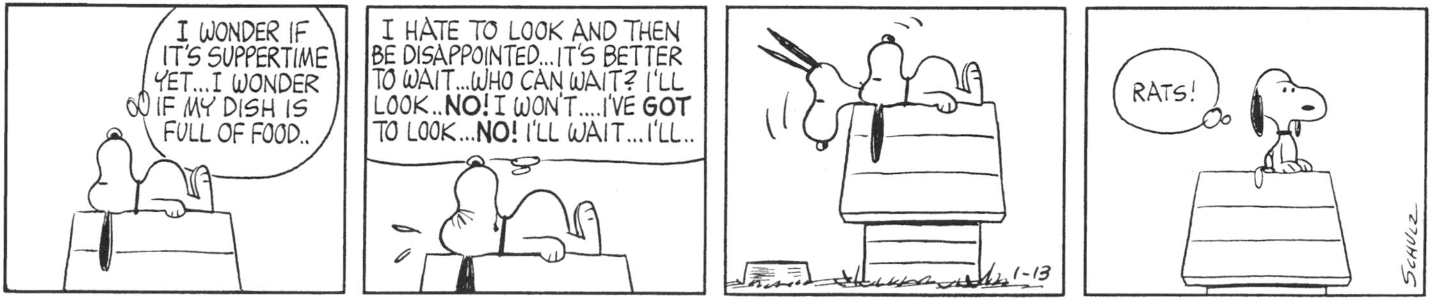
I WONDER IF IT'S SUPPERTIME YET...I WONDER IF MY DISH IS FULL OF FOOD..
I HATE TO LOOK AND THEN BE DISAPPOINTED...IT'S BETTER TO WAIT...WHO CAN WAIT? I'LL LOOK..NO! I WON'T....I'VE GOT TO LOOK...NO! I'LL WAIT...I'LL..
1-13
RATS!
SCHULZ

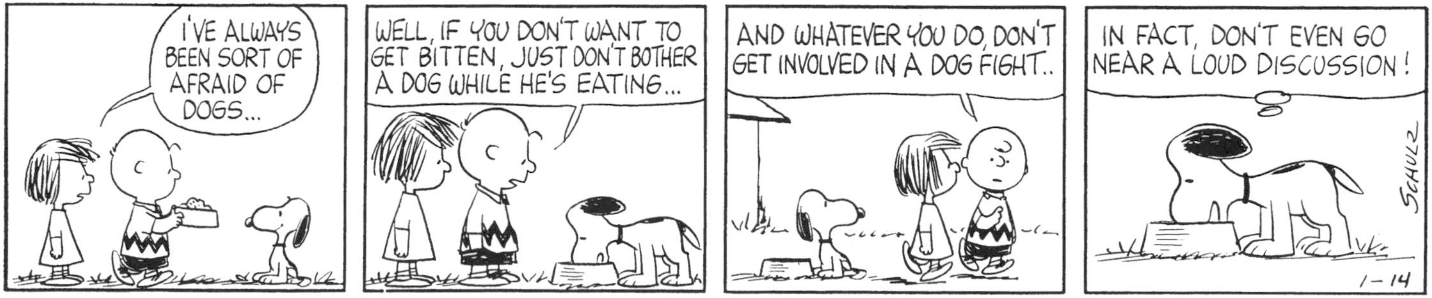
I'VE ALWAYS BEEN SORT OF AFRAID OF DOGS...
WELL, IF YOU DON'T WANT TO GET BITTEN, JUST DON'T BOTHER A DOG WHILE HE'S EATING...
AND WHATEVER YOU DO, DON'T GET INVOLVED IN A DOG FIGHT..
IN FACT, DON'T EVEN GO NEAR A LOUD DISCUSSION!
SCHULZ
1-14

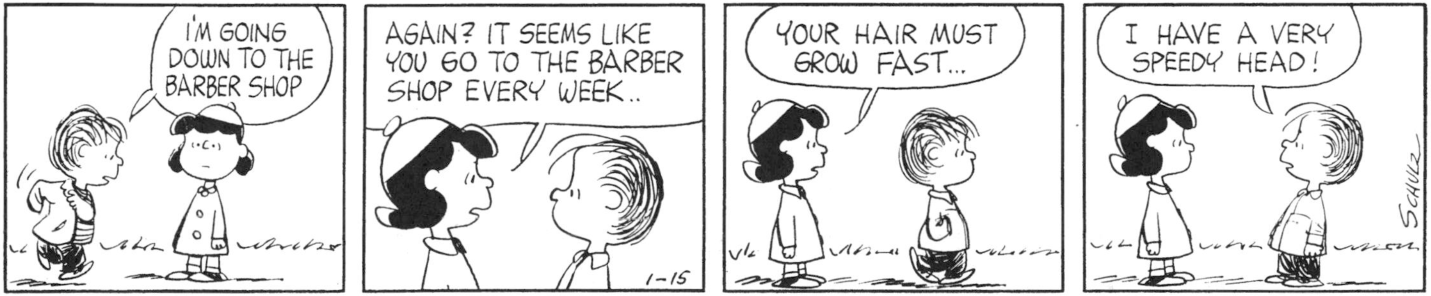
I'M GOING DOWN TO THE BARBER SHOP
AGAIN? IT SEEMS LIKE YOU GO TO THE BARBER SHOP EVERY WEEK..
1-15
YOUR HAIR MUST GROW FAST...
I HAVE A VERY SPEEDY HEAD!
SCHULZ

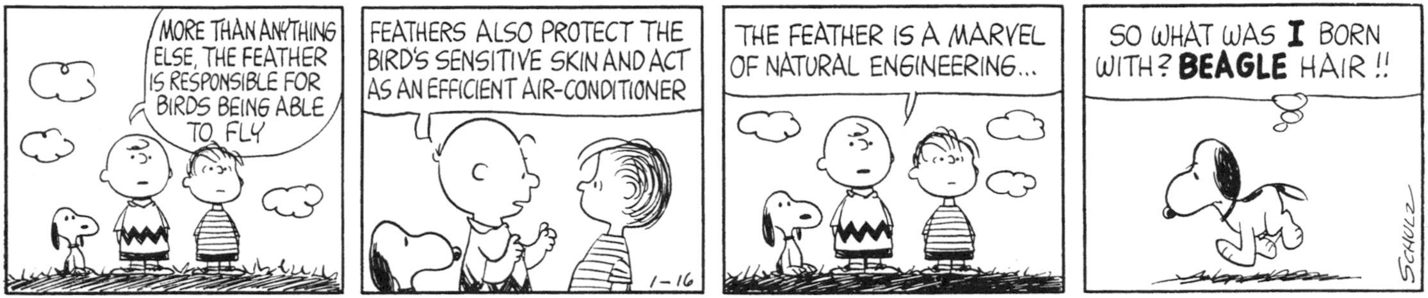
MORE THAN ANYTHING ELSE, THE FEATHER IS RESPONSIBLE FOR BIRDS BEING ABLE TO FLY
FEATHERS ALSO PROTECT THE BIRD'S SENSITIVE SKIN AND ACT AS AN EFFICIENT AIR-CONDITIONER
THE FEATHER IS A MARVEL OF NATURAL ENGINEERING...
SO WHAT WAS I BORN WITH? BEAGLE HAIR!!
1-16
SCHULZ

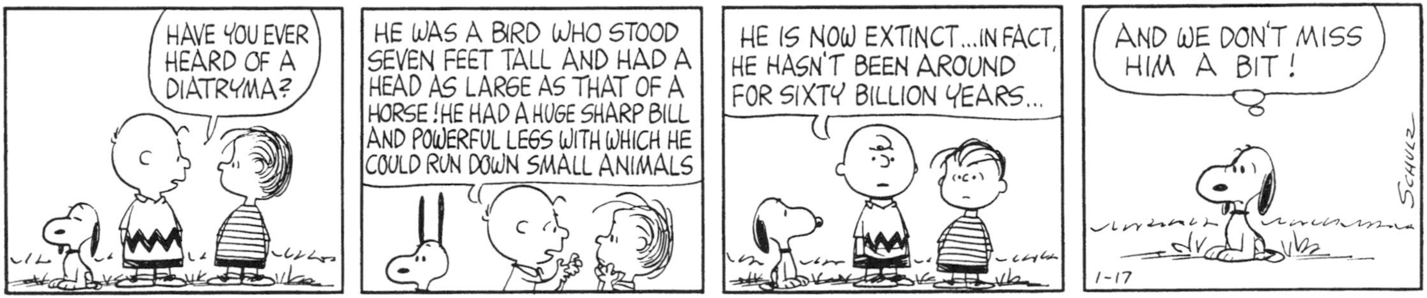
HAVE YOU EVER HEARD OF A DIATRYMA?
HE WAS A BIRD WHO STOOD SEVEN FEET TALL AND HAD A HEAD AS LARGE AS THAT OF A HORSE! HE HAD A HUGE SHARP BILL AND POWERFUL LEGS WITH WHICH HE COULD RUN DOWN SMALL ANIMALS
HE IS NOW EXTINCT...IN FACT, HE HASN'T BEEN AROUND FOR SIXTY BILLION YEARS...
AND WE DON'T MISS HIM A BIT!
SCHULZ
1-17

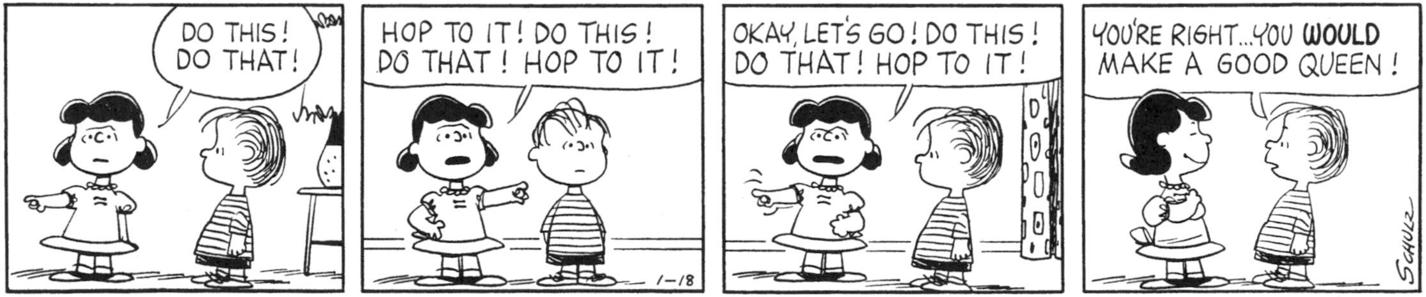
DO THIS! DO THAT!
HOP TO IT! DO THIS! DO THAT! HOP TO IT!
1-18
OKAY, LET'S GO! DO THIS! DO THAT! HOP TO IT!
YOU'RE RIGHT...YOU WOULD MAKE A GOOD QUEEN!
SCHULZ

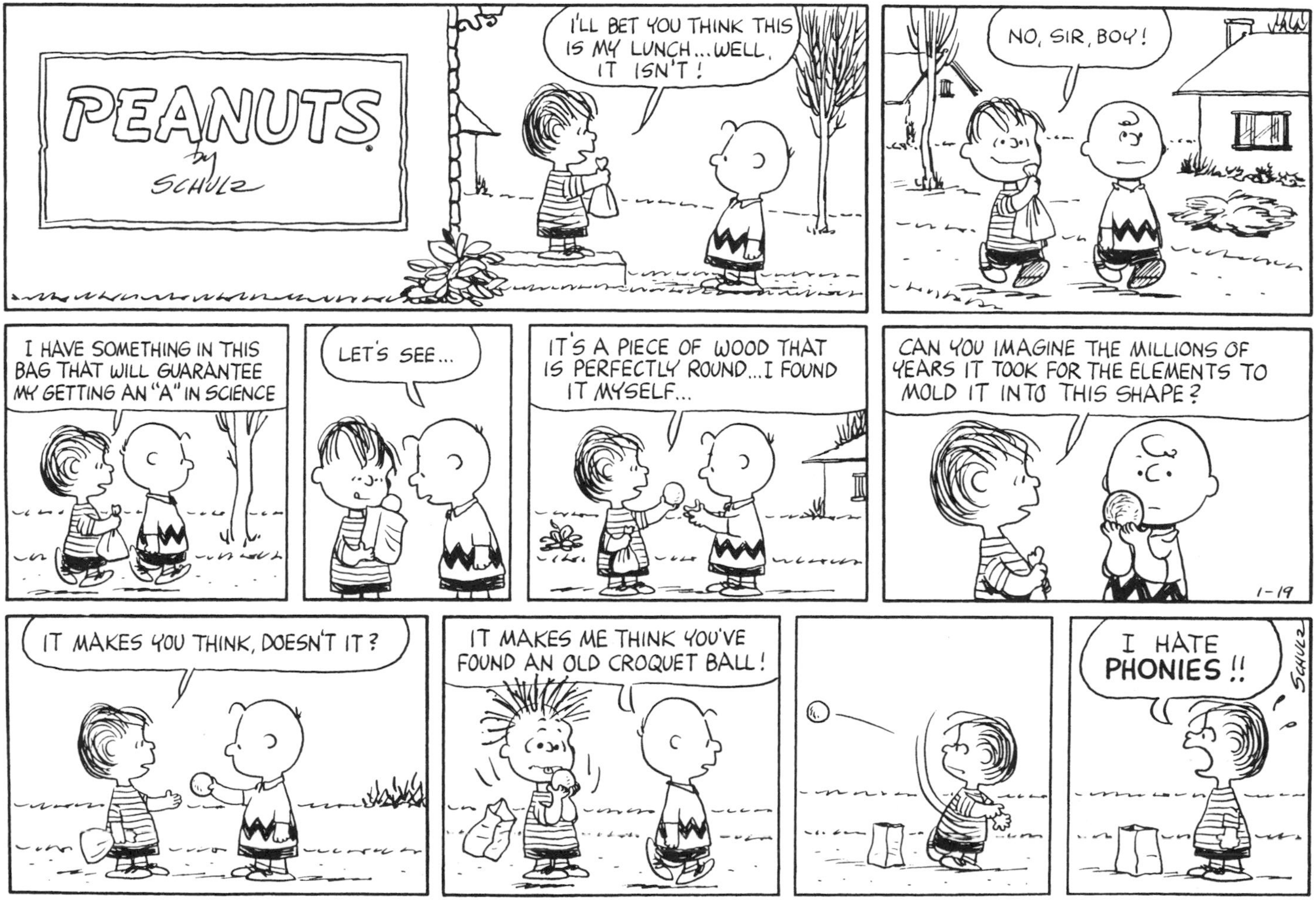
PEANUTS
by SCHULZ
I'LL BET YOU THINK THIS IS MY LUNCH... WELL, IT ISN'T!
NO, SIR, BOY!
I HAVE SOMETHING IN THIS BAG THAT WILL GUARANTEE MY GETTING AN "A" IN SCIENCE
LET'S SEE...
IT'S A PIECE OF WOOD THAT IS PERFECTLY ROUND... I FOUND IT MYSELF...
CAN YOU IMAGINE THE MILLIONS OF YEARS IT TOOK FOR THE ELEMENTS TO MOLD IT INTO THIS SHAPE?
1-19
IT MAKES YOU THINK, DOESN'T IT?
IT MAKES ME THINK YOU'VE FOUND AN OLD CROQUET BALL!
I HATE PHONIES!!
SCHULZ

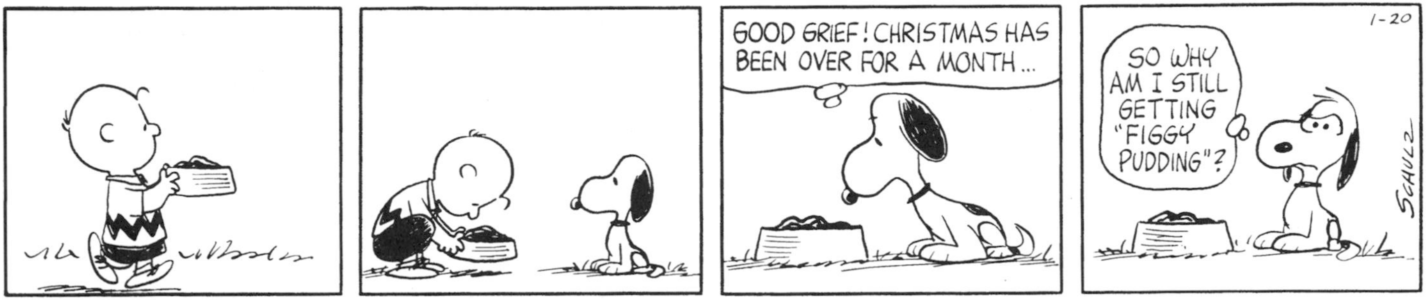
GOOD GRIEF! CHRISTMAS HAS BEEN OVER FOR A MONTH...
1-20
SO WHY AM I STILL GETTING "FIGGY PUDDING"?
SCHULZ

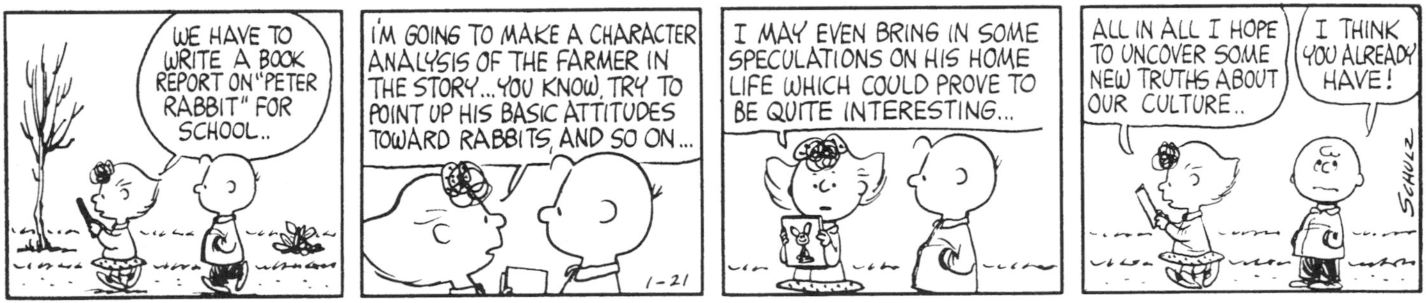
WE HAVE TO WRITE A BOOK REPORT ON "PETER RABBIT" FOR SCHOOL..
I'M GOING TO MAKE A CHARACTER ANALYSIS OF THE FARMER IN THE STORY...YOU KNOW, TRY TO POINT UP HIS BASIC ATTITUDES TOWARD RABBITS, AND SO ON...
1-21
I MAY EVEN BRING IN SOME SPECULATIONS ON HIS HOME LIFE WHICH COULD PROVE TO BE QUITE INTERESTING...
ALL IN ALL I HOPE TO UNCOVER SOME NEW TRUTHS ABOUT OUR CULTURE..
I THINK YOU ALREADY HAVE!
SCHULZ

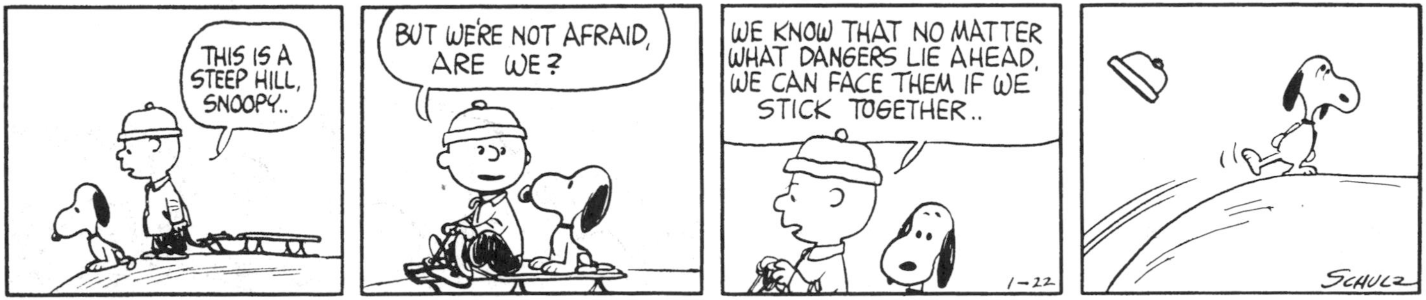
THIS IS A STEEP HILL, SNOOPY..
BUT WE'RE NOT AFRAID, ARE WE?
WE KNOW THAT NO MATTER WHAT DANGERS LIE AHEAD, WE CAN FACE THEM IF WE STICK TOGETHER..
1-22
SCHULZ

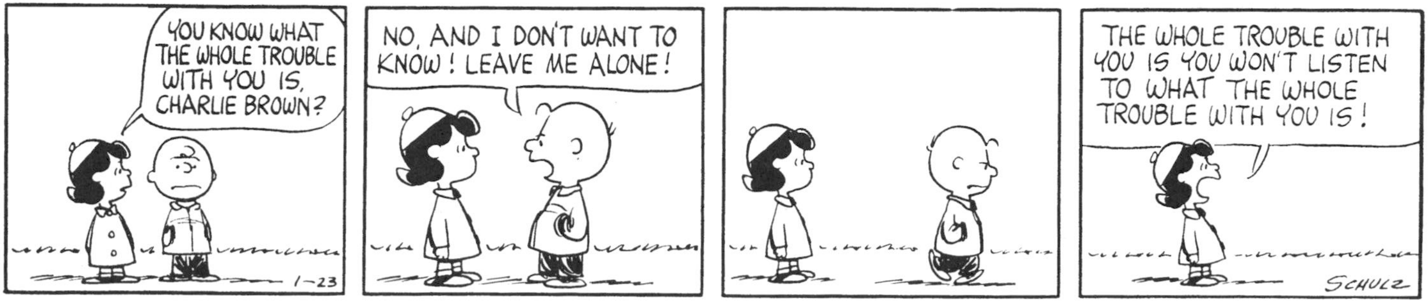
YOU KNOW WHAT THE WHOLE TROUBLE WITH YOU IS, CHARLIE BROWN?
1-23
NO, AND I DON'T WANT TO KNOW! LEAVE ME ALONE!
THE WHOLE TROUBLE WITH YOU IS YOU WON'T LISTEN TO WHAT THE WHOLE TROUBLE WITH YOU IS!
SCHULZ

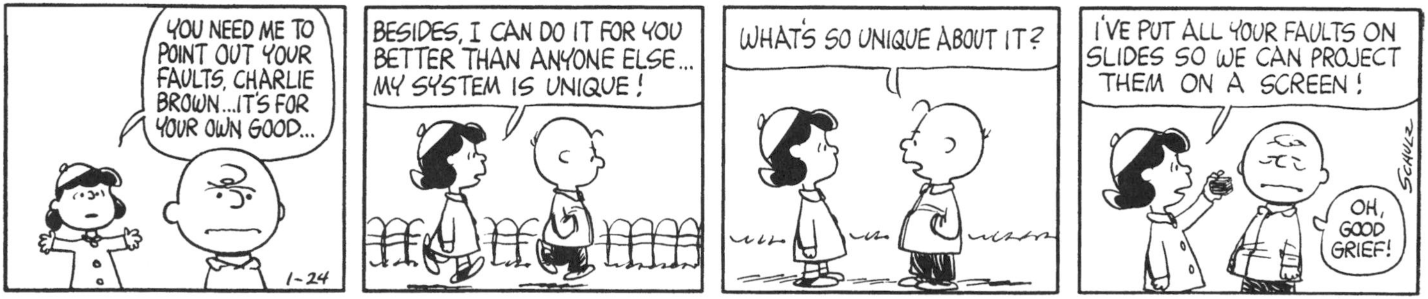
YOU NEED ME TO POINT OUT YOUR FAULTS, CHARLIE BROWN...IT'S FOR YOUR OWN GOOD...
1-24
BESIDES, I CAN DO IT FOR YOU BETTER THAN ANYONE ELSE... MY SYSTEM IS UNIQUE!
WHAT'S SO UNIQUE ABOUT IT?
I'VE PUT ALL YOUR FAULTS ON SLIDES SO WE CAN PROJECT THEM ON A SCREEN!
OH, GOOD GRIEF!
SCHULZ

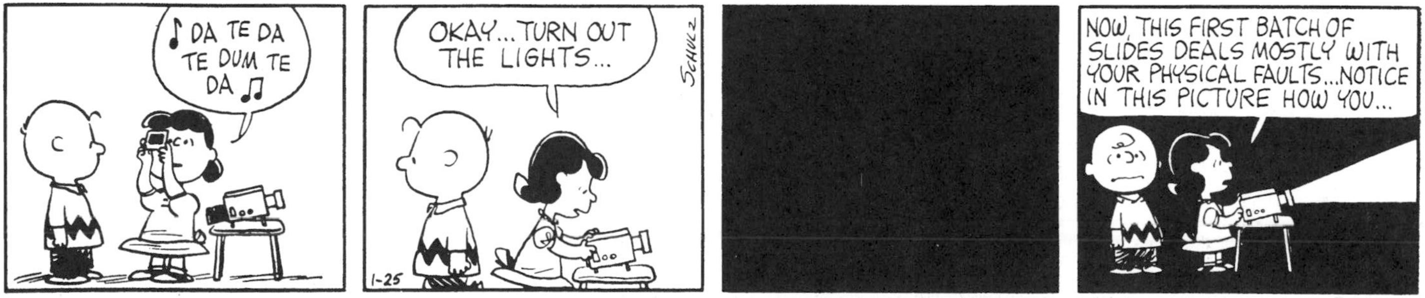
♪ DA TE DA TE DUM TE DA ♫
OKAY...TURN OUT THE LIGHTS...
SCHULZ
1-25
NOW, THIS FIRST BATCH OF SLIDES DEALS MOSTLY WITH YOUR PHYSICAL FAULTS...NOTICE IN THIS PICTURE HOW YOU...

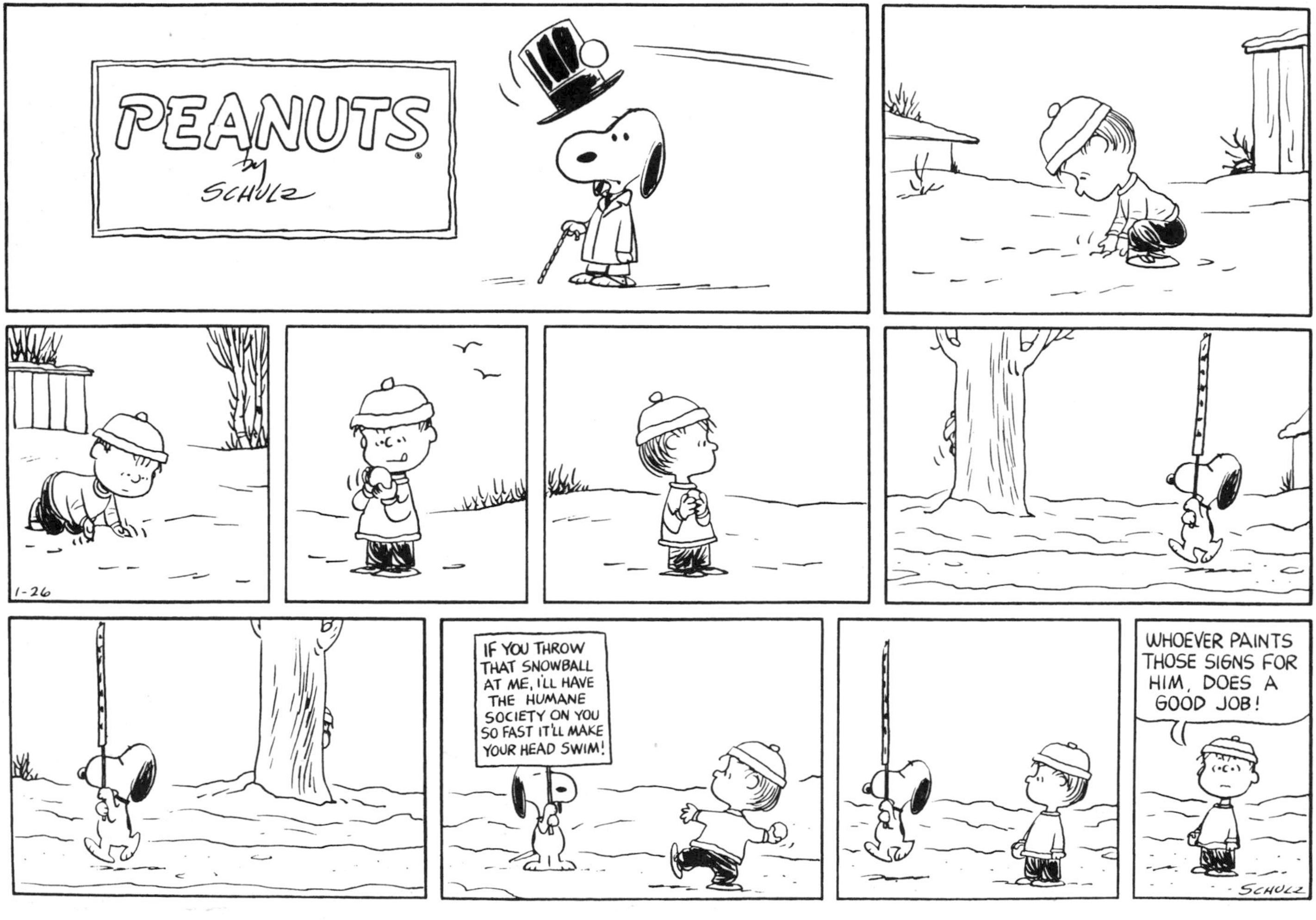
PEANUTS
by SCHULZ
1-26
IF YOU THROW THAT SNOWBALL AT ME, I'LL HAVE THE HUMANE SOCIETY ON YOU SO FAST IT'LL MAKE YOUR HEAD SWIM!
WHOEVER PAINTS THOSE SIGNS FOR HIM, DOES A GOOD JOB!
SCHULZ

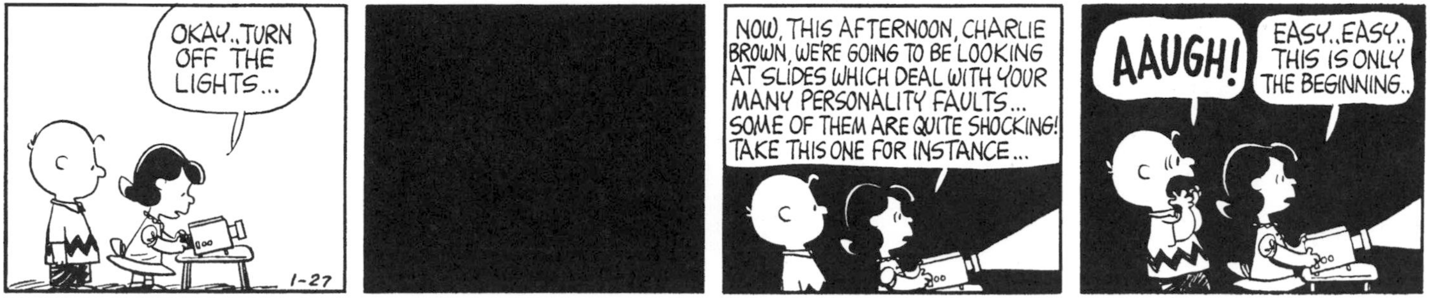
OKAY.. TURN OFF THE LIGHTS...
NOW, THIS AFTERNOON, CHARLIE BROWN, WE'RE GOING TO BE LOOKING AT SLIDES WHICH DEAL WITH YOUR MANY PERSONALITY FAULTS... SOME OF THEM ARE QUITE SHOCKING! TAKE THIS ONE FOR INSTANCE...
AAUGH!
EASY.. EASY.. THIS IS ONLY THE BEGINNING..

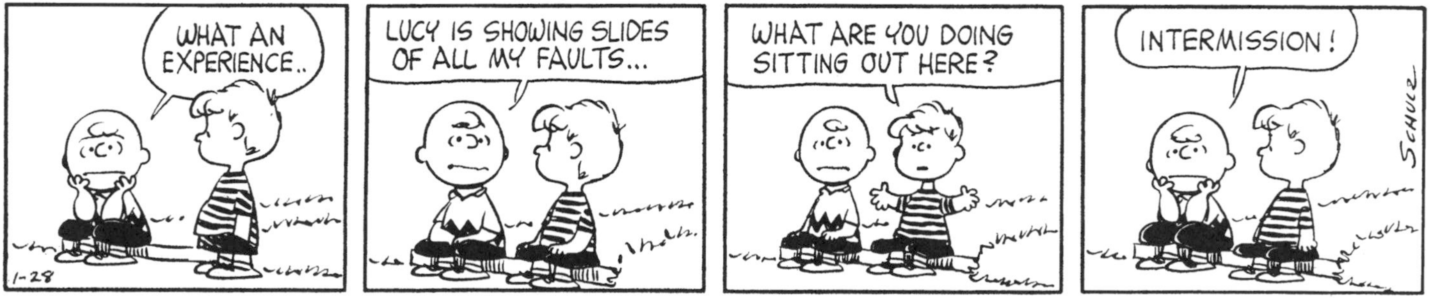
WHAT AN EXPERIENCE..
LUCY IS SHOWING SLIDES OF ALL MY FAULTS...
WHAT ARE YOU DOING SITTING OUT HERE?
INTERMISSION!

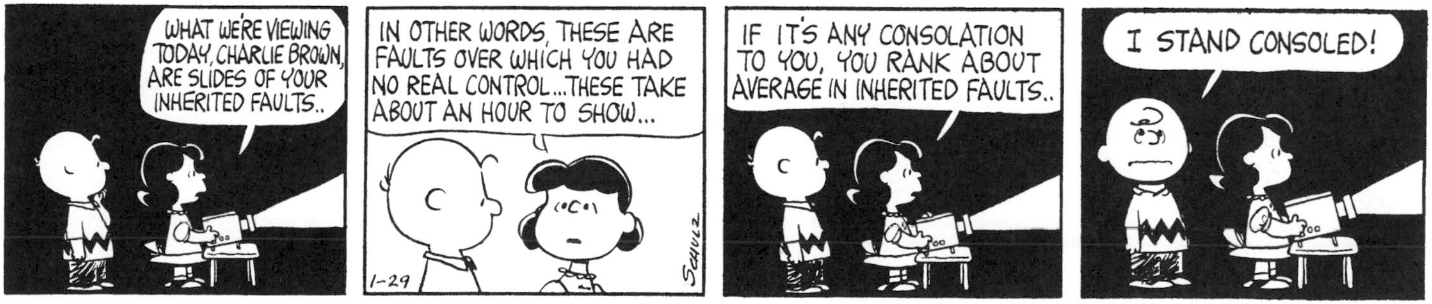
WHAT WE'RE VIEWING TODAY, CHARLIE BROWN, ARE SLIDES OF YOUR INHERITED FAULTS..
IN OTHER WORDS, THESE ARE FAULTS OVER WHICH YOU HAD NO REAL CONTROL... THESE TAKE ABOUT AN HOUR TO SHOW...
IF IT'S ANY CONSOLATION TO YOU, YOU RANK ABOUT AVERAGE IN INHERITED FAULTS..
I STAND CONSOLED!

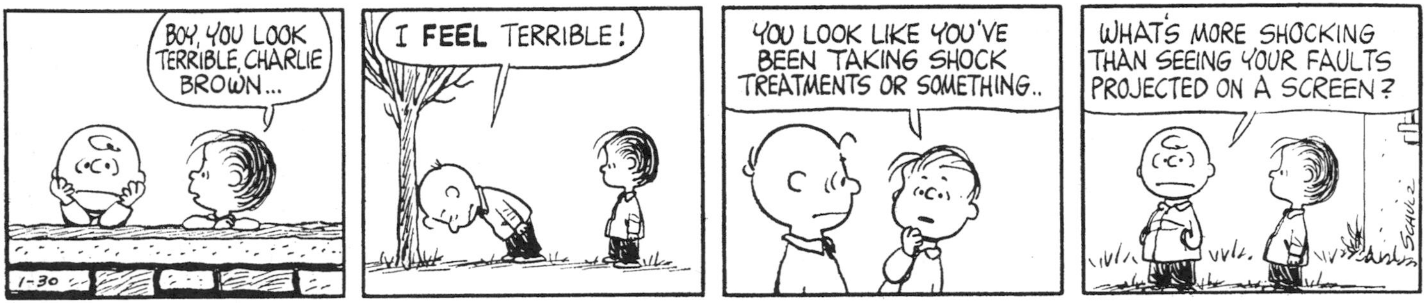
BOY, YOU LOOK TERRIBLE, CHARLIE BROWN...
1-30
I FEEL TERRIBLE!
YOU LOOK LIKE YOU'VE BEEN TAKING SHOCK TREATMENTS OR SOMETHING..
WHAT'S MORE SHOCKING THAN SEEING YOUR FAULTS PROJECTED ON A SCREEN?
SCHULZ

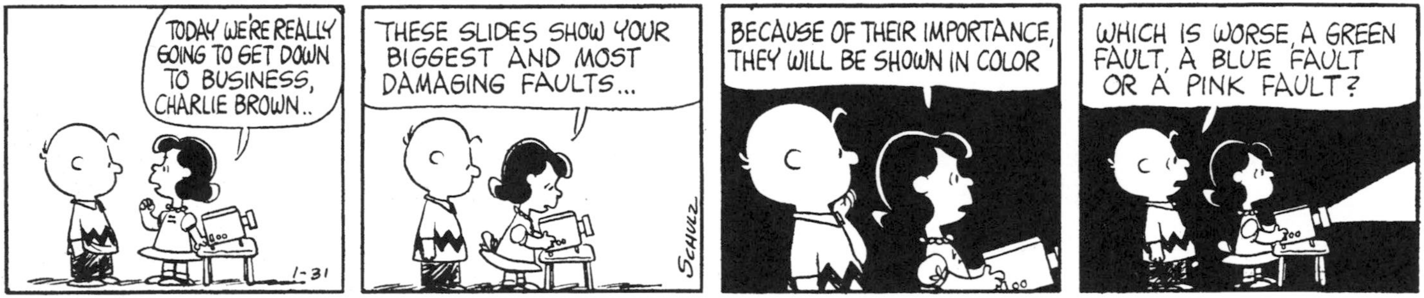
TODAY WE'RE REALLY GOING TO GET DOWN TO BUSINESS, CHARLIE BROWN..
1-31
THESE SLIDES SHOW YOUR BIGGEST AND MOST DAMAGING FAULTS...
SCHULZ
BECAUSE OF THEIR IMPORTANCE, THEY WILL BE SHOWN IN COLOR
WHICH IS WORSE, A GREEN FAULT, A BLUE FAULT OR A PINK FAULT?

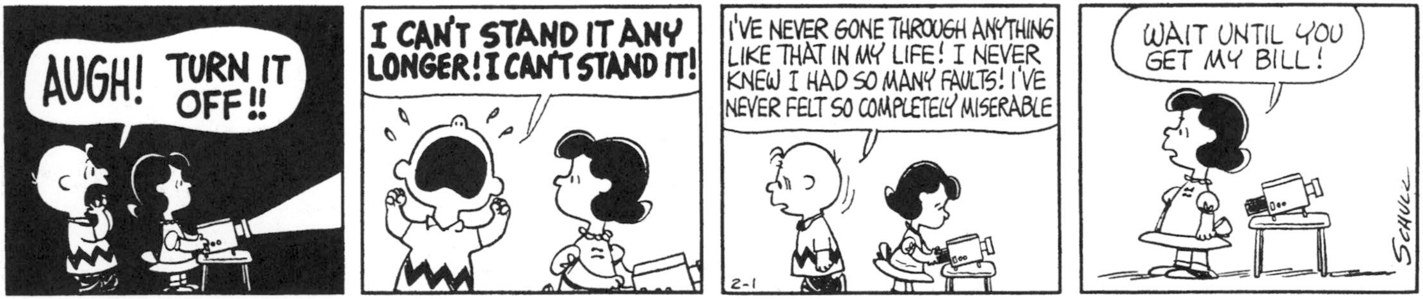
AUGH! TURN IT OFF!!
I CAN'T STAND IT ANY LONGER! I CAN'T STAND IT!
I'VE NEVER GONE THROUGH ANYTHING LIKE THAT IN MY LIFE! I NEVER KNEW I HAD SO MANY FAULTS! I'VE NEVER FELT SO COMPLETELY MISERABLE
2-1
WAIT UNTIL YOU GET MY BILL!
SCHULZ

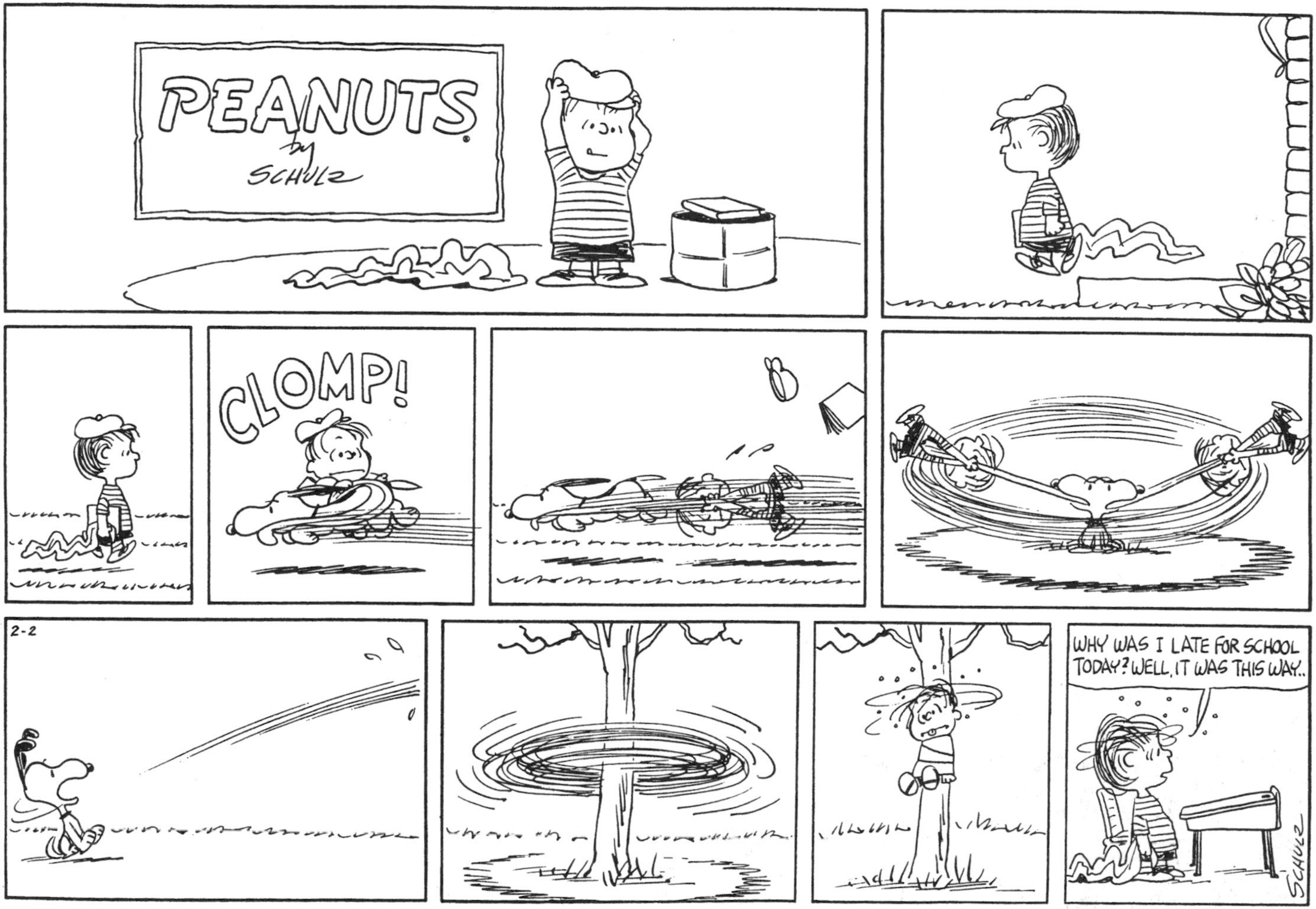
PEANUTS
by SCHULZ
CLOMP!
2-2
WHY WAS I LATE FOR SCHOOL TODAY? WELL, IT WAS THIS WAY..
SCHULZ

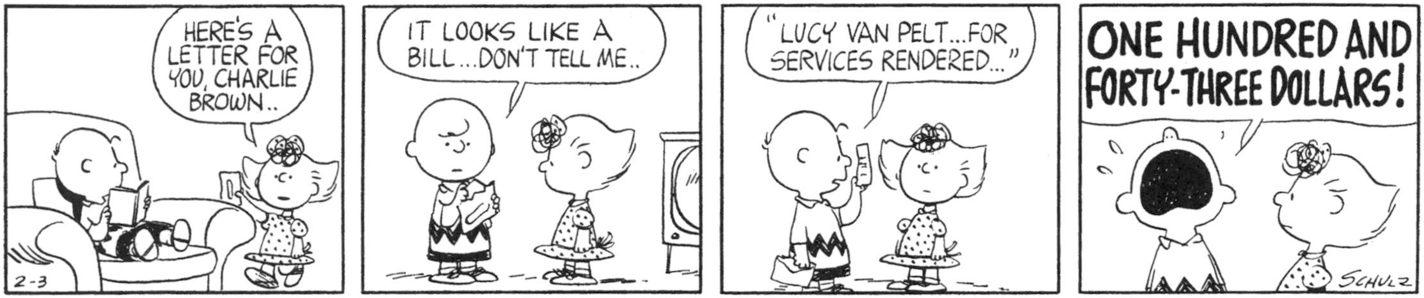
HERE'S A LETTER FOR YOU, CHARLIE BROWN..
2-3
IT LOOKS LIKE A BILL...DON'T TELL ME..
"LUCY VAN PELT...FOR SERVICES RENDERED..."
ONE HUNDRED AND FORTY-THREE DOLLARS!
SCHULZ

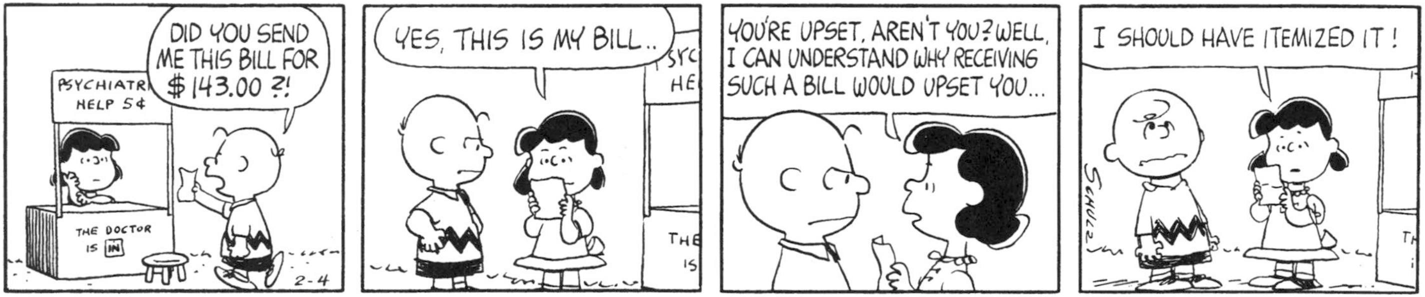
PSYCHIATR HELP 5¢
THE DOCTOR IS IN
DID YOU SEND ME THIS BILL FOR $143.00 ?!
2-4
YES, THIS IS MY BILL..
YOU'RE UPSET, AREN'T YOU? WELL, I CAN UNDERSTAND WHY RECEIVING SUCH A BILL WOULD UPSET YOU...
I SHOULD HAVE ITEMIZED IT!
SCHULZ

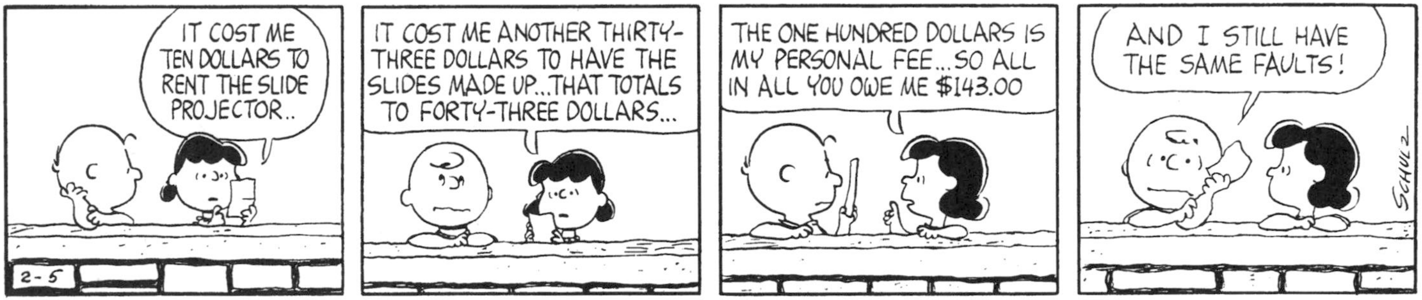
IT COST ME TEN DOLLARS TO RENT THE SLIDE PROJECTOR..
2-5
IT COST ME ANOTHER THIRTY-THREE DOLLARS TO HAVE THE SLIDES MADE UP...THAT TOTALS TO FORTY-THREE DOLLARS...
THE ONE HUNDRED DOLLARS IS MY PERSONAL FEE...SO ALL IN ALL YOU OWE ME $143.00
AND I STILL HAVE THE SAME FAULTS!
SCHULZ

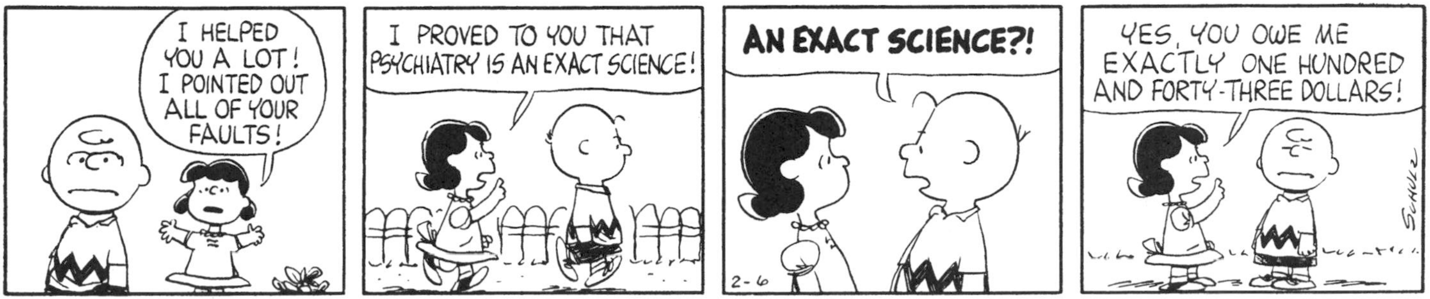
I HELPED YOU A LOT! I POINTED OUT ALL OF YOUR FAULTS!
I PROVED TO YOU THAT PSYCHIATRY IS AN EXACT SCIENCE!
AN EXACT SCIENCE?!
YES, YOU OWE ME EXACTLY ONE HUNDRED AND FORTY-THREE DOLLARS!
2-6
SCHULZ

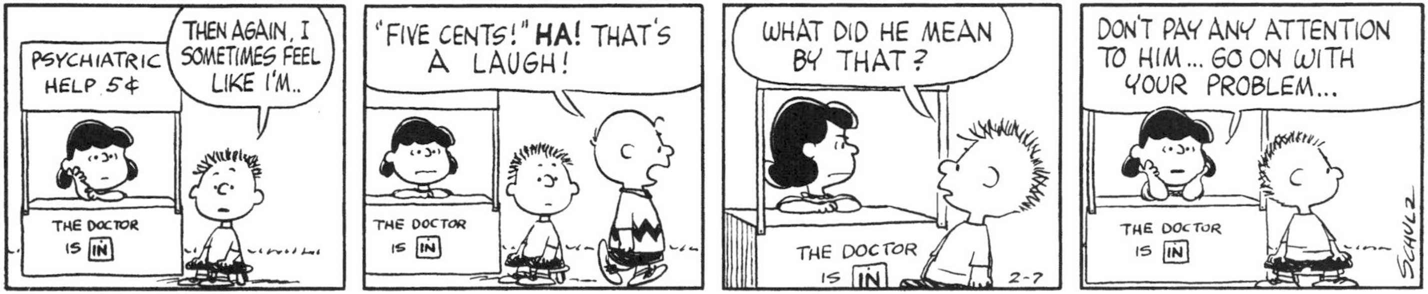
PSYCHIATRIC HELP 5¢
THEN AGAIN, I SOMETIMES FEEL LIKE I'M..
THE DOCTOR IS IN
"FIVE CENTS!" HA! THAT'S A LAUGH!
THE DOCTOR IS IN
WHAT DID HE MEAN BY THAT?
THE DOCTOR IS IN
2-7
DON'T PAY ANY ATTENTION TO HIM... GO ON WITH YOUR PROBLEM...
THE DOCTOR IS IN
SCHULZ

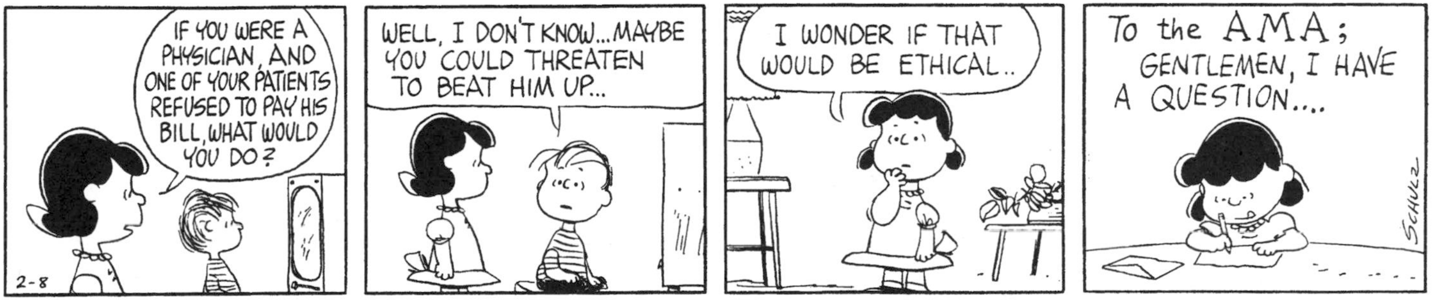
IF YOU WERE A PHYSICIAN, AND ONE OF YOUR PATIENTS REFUSED TO PAY HIS BILL, WHAT WOULD YOU DO?
2-8
WELL, I DON'T KNOW... MAYBE YOU COULD THREATEN TO BEAT HIM UP...
I WONDER IF THAT WOULD BE ETHICAL..
To the AMA;
GENTLEMEN, I HAVE A QUESTION....
SCHULZ

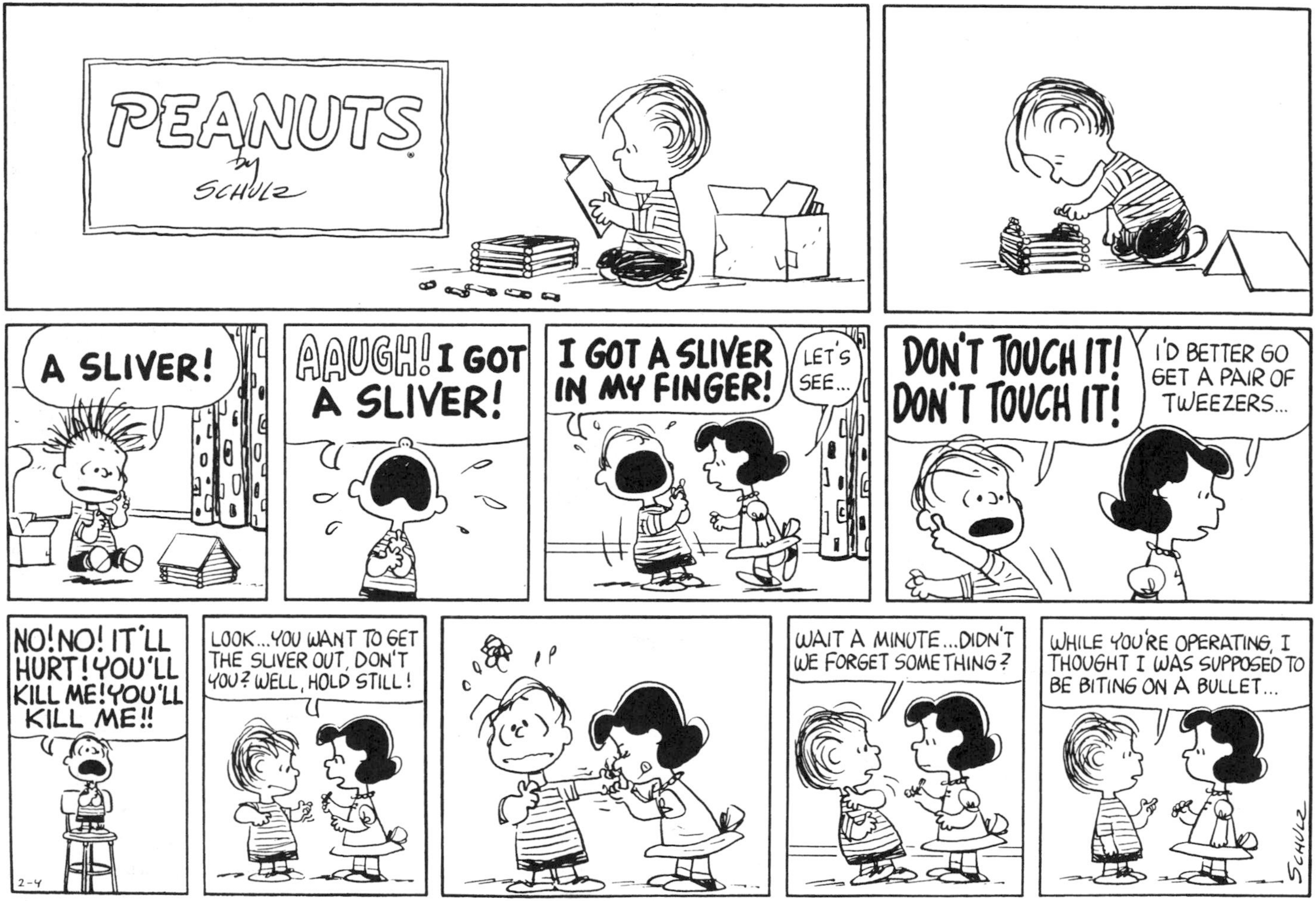
PEANUTS
by SCHULZ
A SLIVER!
AAUGH! I GOT A SLIVER!
I GOT A SLIVER IN MY FINGER!
LET'S SEE...
DON'T TOUCH IT! DON'T TOUCH IT!
I'D BETTER GO GET A PAIR OF TWEEZERS...
NO! NO! IT'LL HURT! YOU'LL KILL ME! YOU'LL KILL ME!!
2-4
LOOK...YOU WANT TO GET THE SLIVER OUT, DON'T YOU? WELL, HOLD STILL!
WAIT A MINUTE...DIDN'T WE FORGET SOMETHING?
WHILE YOU'RE OPERATING, I THOUGHT I WAS SUPPOSED TO BE BITING ON A BULLET...
SCHULZ

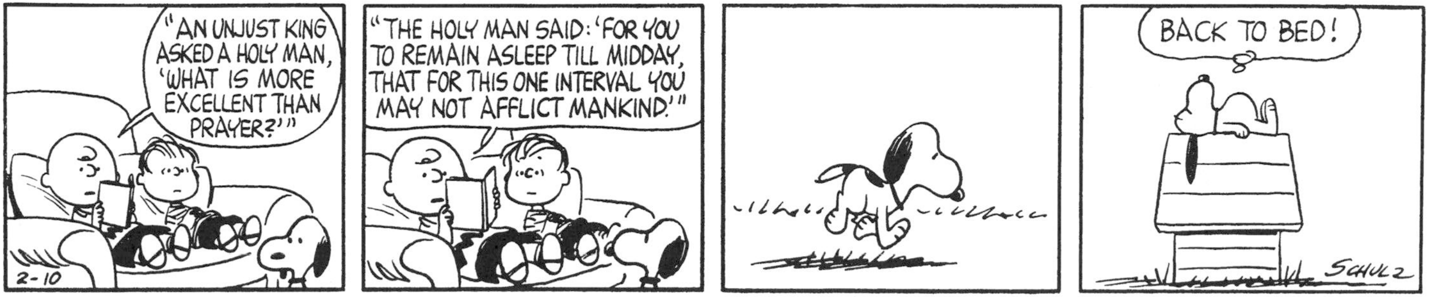
"AN UNJUST KING ASKED A HOLY MAN, 'WHAT IS MORE EXCELLENT THAN PRAYER?'"
"THE HOLY MAN SAID: 'FOR YOU TO REMAIN ASLEEP TILL MIDDAY, THAT FOR THIS ONE INTERVAL YOU MAY NOT AFFLICT MANKIND.'"
BACK TO BED!
2-10
SCHULZ

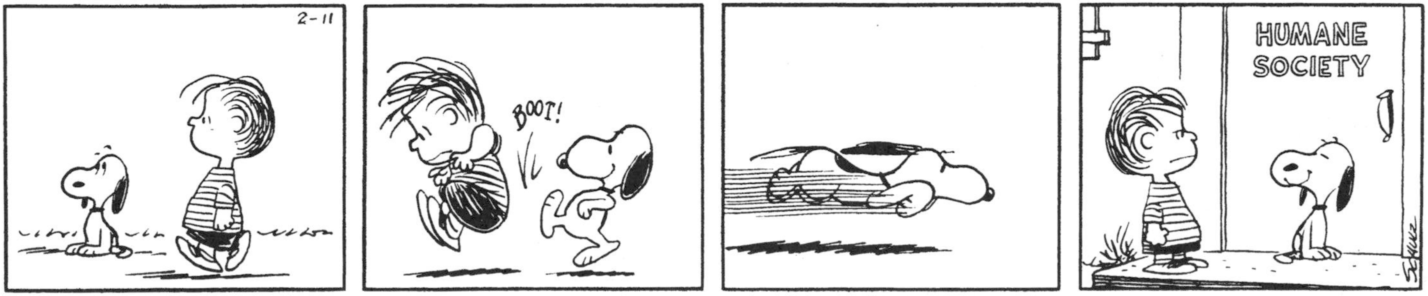
2-11
BOOT!
HUMANE SOCIETY
SCHULZ

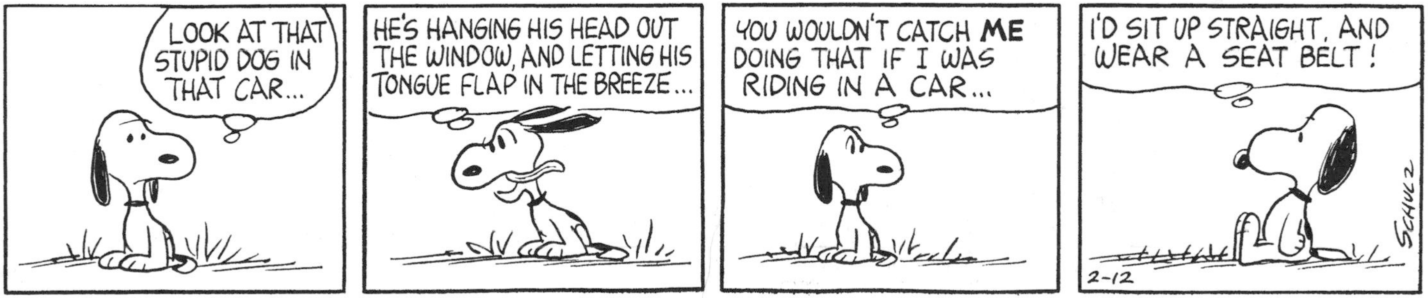
LOOK AT THAT STUPID DOG IN THAT CAR...
HE'S HANGING HIS HEAD OUT THE WINDOW, AND LETTING HIS TONGUE FLAP IN THE BREEZE...
YOU WOULDN'T CATCH **ME** DOING THAT IF I WAS RIDING IN A CAR...
I'D SIT UP STRAIGHT, AND WEAR A SEAT BELT!
2-12
SCHULZ

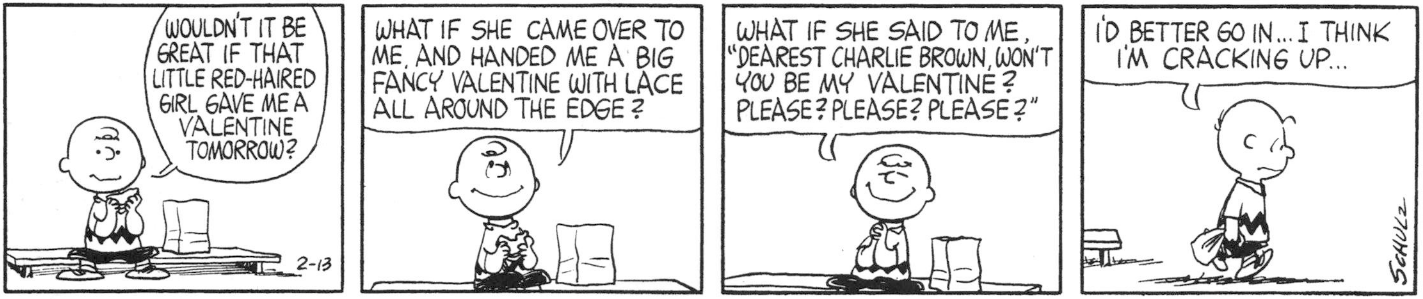
WOULDN'T IT BE GREAT IF THAT LITTLE RED-HAIRED GIRL GAVE ME A VALENTINE TOMORROW?
WHAT IF SHE CAME OVER TO ME, AND HANDED ME A BIG FANCY VALENTINE WITH LACE ALL AROUND THE EDGE?
WHAT IF SHE SAID TO ME, "DEAREST CHARLIE BROWN, WON'T YOU BE MY VALENTINE? PLEASE? PLEASE? PLEASE?"
I'D BETTER GO IN... I THINK I'M CRACKING UP...
SCHULZ
2-13

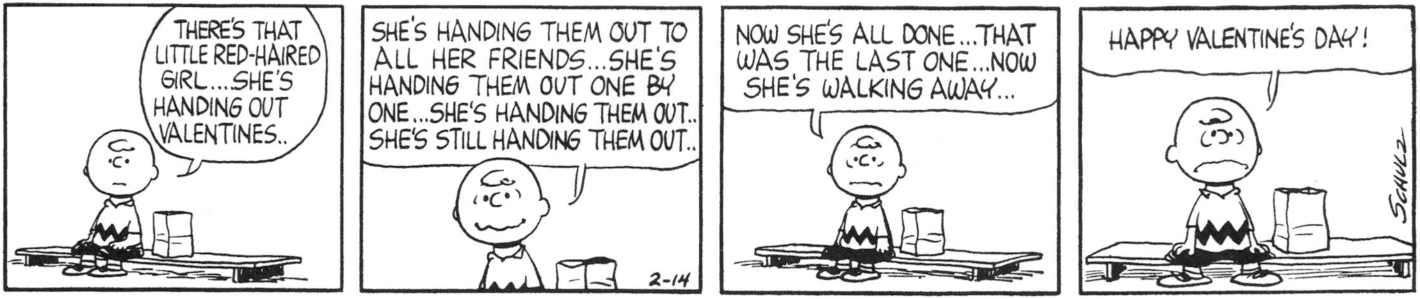
THERE'S THAT LITTLE RED-HAIRED GIRL....SHE'S HANDING OUT VALENTINES..
SHE'S HANDING THEM OUT TO ALL HER FRIENDS...SHE'S HANDING THEM OUT ONE BY ONE...SHE'S HANDING THEM OUT.. SHE'S STILL HANDING THEM OUT..
NOW SHE'S ALL DONE...THAT WAS THE LAST ONE...NOW SHE'S WALKING AWAY...
HAPPY VALENTINE'S DAY!
SCHULZ
2-14

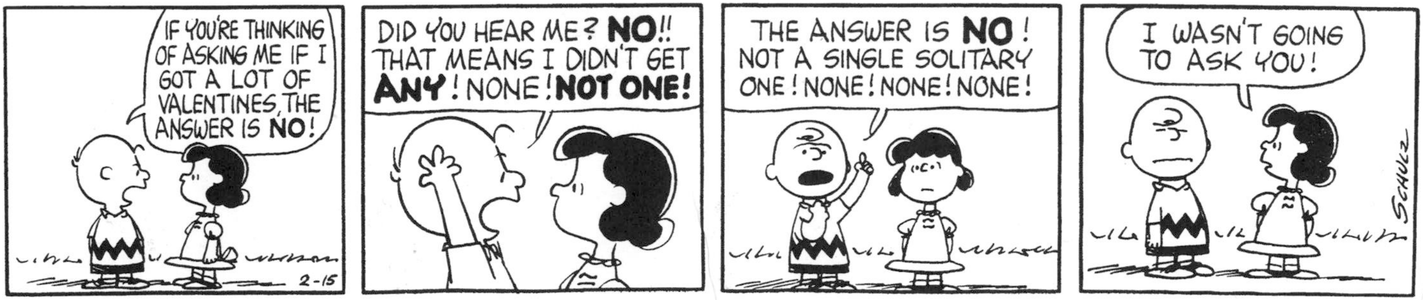
IF YOU'RE THINKING OF ASKING ME IF I GOT A LOT OF VALENTINES, THE ANSWER IS NO!
DID YOU HEAR ME? NO!! THAT MEANS I DIDN'T GET ANY! NONE! NOT ONE!
THE ANSWER IS NO! NOT A SINGLE SOLITARY ONE! NONE! NONE! NONE!
I WASN'T GOING TO ASK YOU!
SCHULZ
2-15

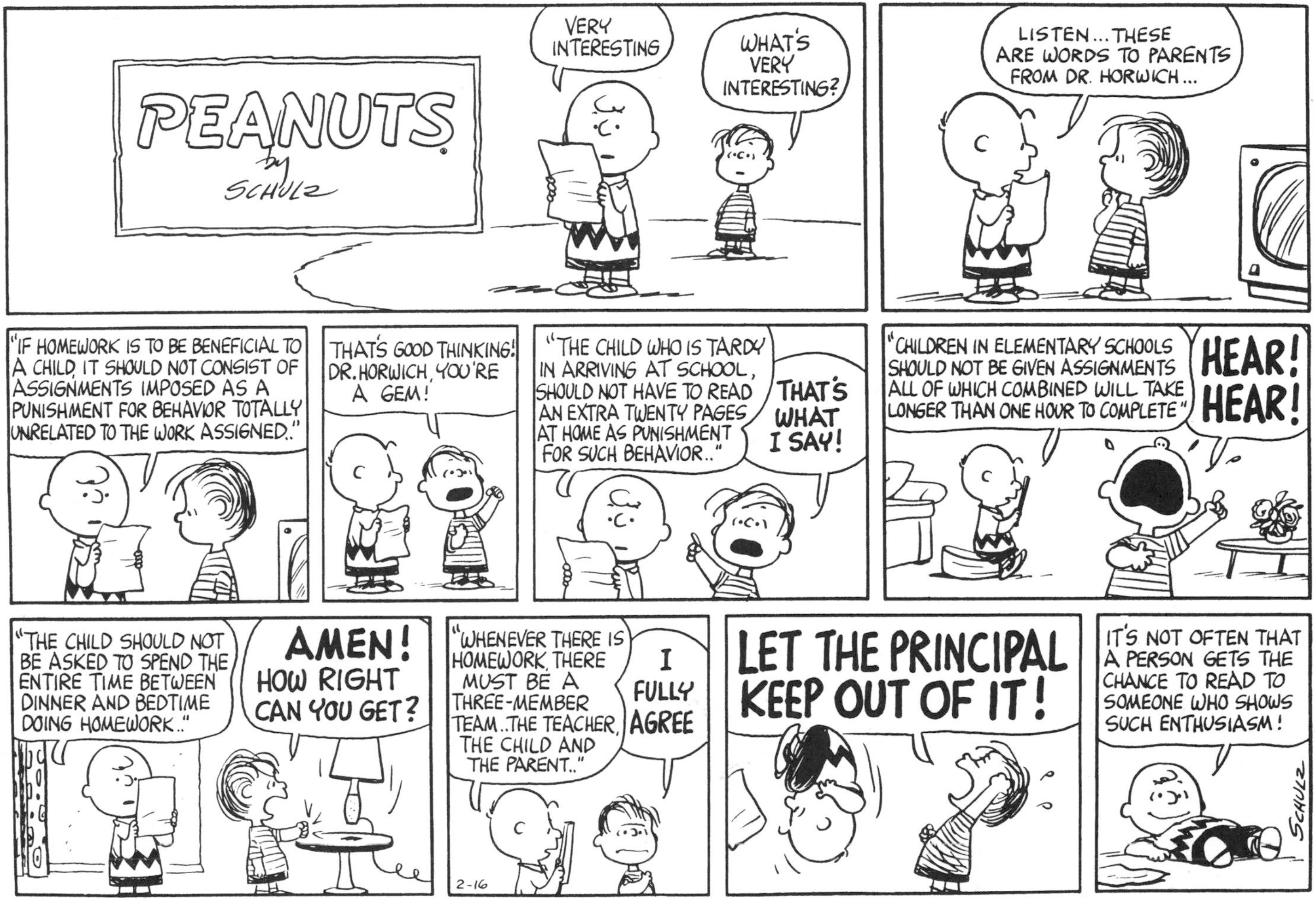
PEANUTS
by SCHULZ
VERY INTERESTING
WHAT'S VERY VERY INTERESTING?
LISTEN... THESE ARE WORDS TO PARENTS FROM DR. HORWICH...
"IF HOMEWORK IS TO BE BENEFICIAL TO A CHILD, IT SHOULD NOT CONSIST OF ASSIGNMENTS IMPOSED AS A PUNISHMENT FOR BEHAVIOR TOTALLY UNRELATED TO THE WORK ASSIGNED.."
THAT'S GOOD THINKING! DR. HORWICH, YOU'RE A GEM!
"THE CHILD WHO IS TARDY IN ARRIVING AT SCHOOL, SHOULD NOT HAVE TO READ AN EXTRA TWENTY PAGES AT HOME AS PUNISHMENT FOR SUCH BEHAVIOR.."
THAT'S WHAT I SAY!
"CHILDREN IN ELEMENTARY SCHOOLS SHOULD NOT BE GIVEN ASSIGNMENTS ALL OF WHICH COMBINED WILL TAKE LONGER THAN ONE HOUR TO COMPLETE"
HEAR! HEAR!
"THE CHILD SHOULD NOT BE ASKED TO SPEND THE ENTIRE TIME BETWEEN DINNER AND BEDTIME DOING HOMEWORK.."
AMEN! HOW RIGHT CAN YOU GET?
"WHENEVER THERE IS HOMEWORK, THERE MUST BE A THREE-MEMBER TEAM..THE TEACHER, THE CHILD AND THE PARENT.."
I FULLY AGREE
2-16
LET THE PRINCIPAL KEEP OUT OF IT!
IT'S NOT OFTEN THAT A PERSON GETS THE CHANCE TO READ TO SOMEONE WHO SHOWS SUCH ENTHUSIASM!
SCHULZ

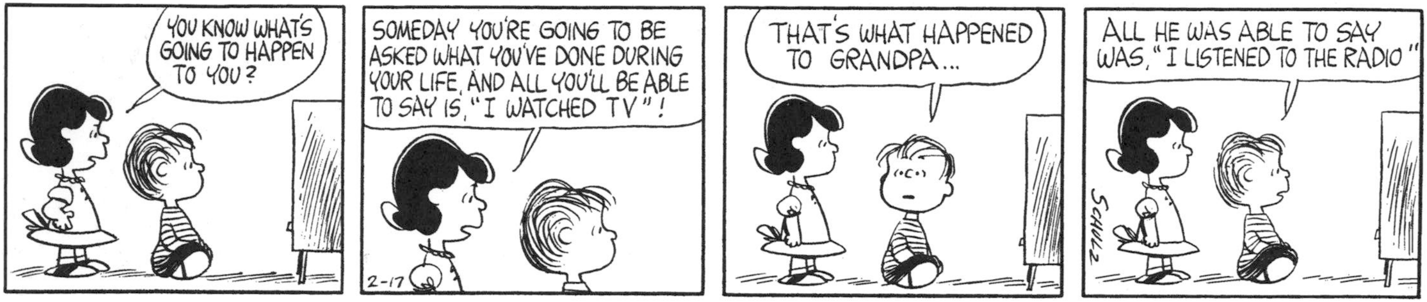
YOU KNOW WHAT'S GOING TO HAPPEN TO YOU?
SOMEDAY YOU'RE GOING TO BE ASKED WHAT YOU'VE DONE DURING YOUR LIFE, AND ALL YOU'LL BE ABLE TO SAY IS, "I WATCHED TV"!
THAT'S WHAT HAPPENED TO GRANDPA...
ALL HE WAS ABLE TO SAY WAS, "I LISTENED TO THE RADIO"

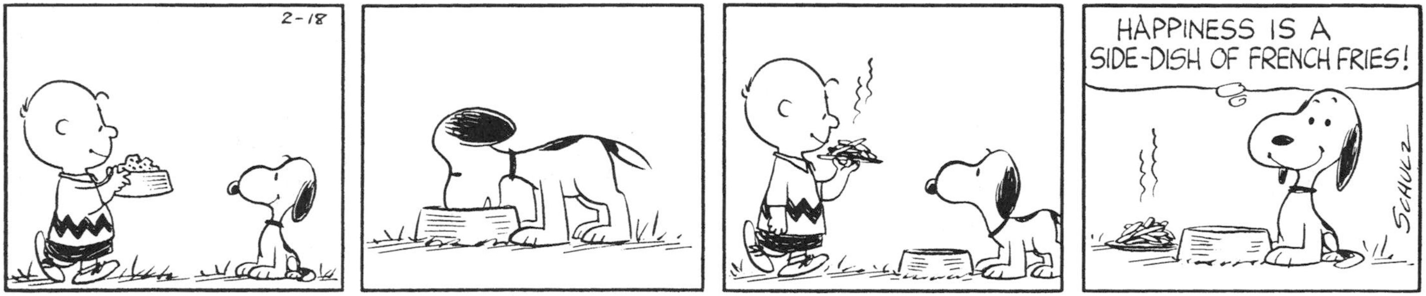
HAPPINESS IS A SIDE-DISH OF FRENCH FRIES!

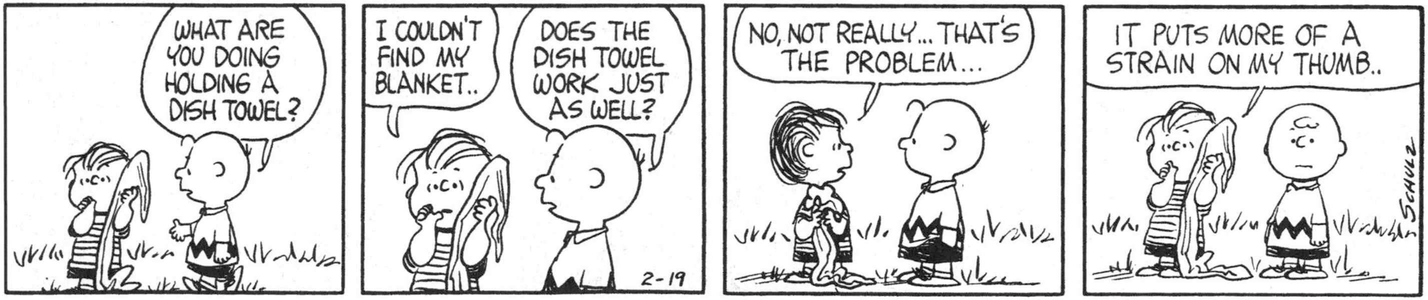
WHAT ARE YOU DOING HOLDING A DISH TOWEL?
I COULDN'T FIND MY BLANKET..
DOES THE DISH TOWEL WORK JUST AS WELL?
NO, NOT REALLY... THAT'S THE PROBLEM...
IT PUTS MORE OF A STRAIN ON MY THUMB..

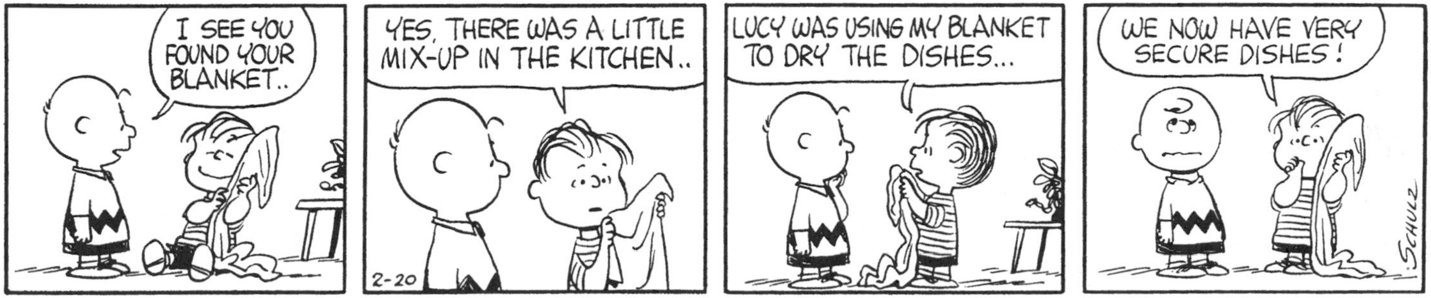
I SEE YOU FOUND YOUR BLANKET..
YES, THERE WAS A LITTLE MIX-UP IN THE KITCHEN..
2-20
LUCY WAS USING MY BLANKET TO DRY THE DISHES...
WE NOW HAVE VERY SECURE DISHES!
SCHULZ

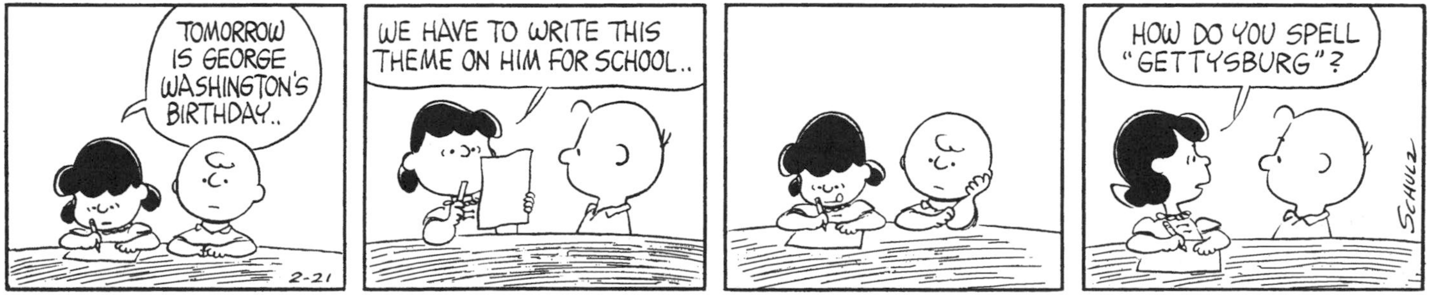
TOMORROW IS GEORGE WASHINGTON'S BIRTHDAY..
2-21
WE HAVE TO WRITE THIS THEME ON HIM FOR SCHOOL..
HOW DO YOU SPELL "GETTYSBURG"?
SCHULZ

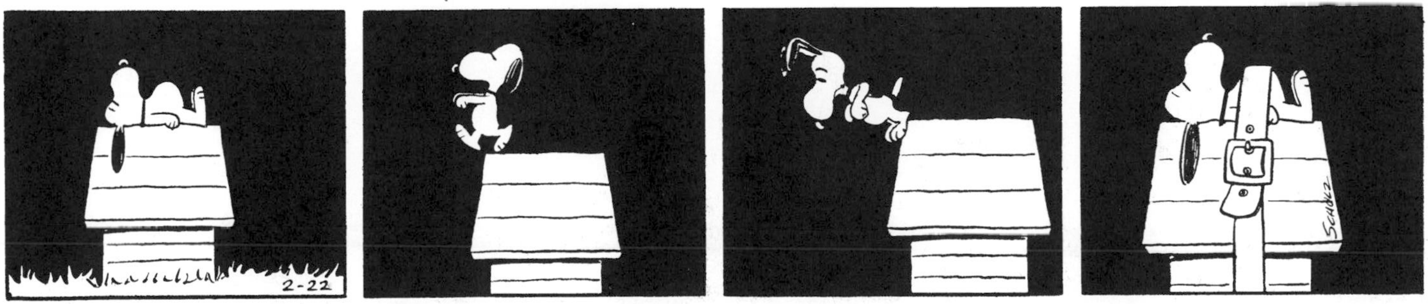
2-22
SCHULZ

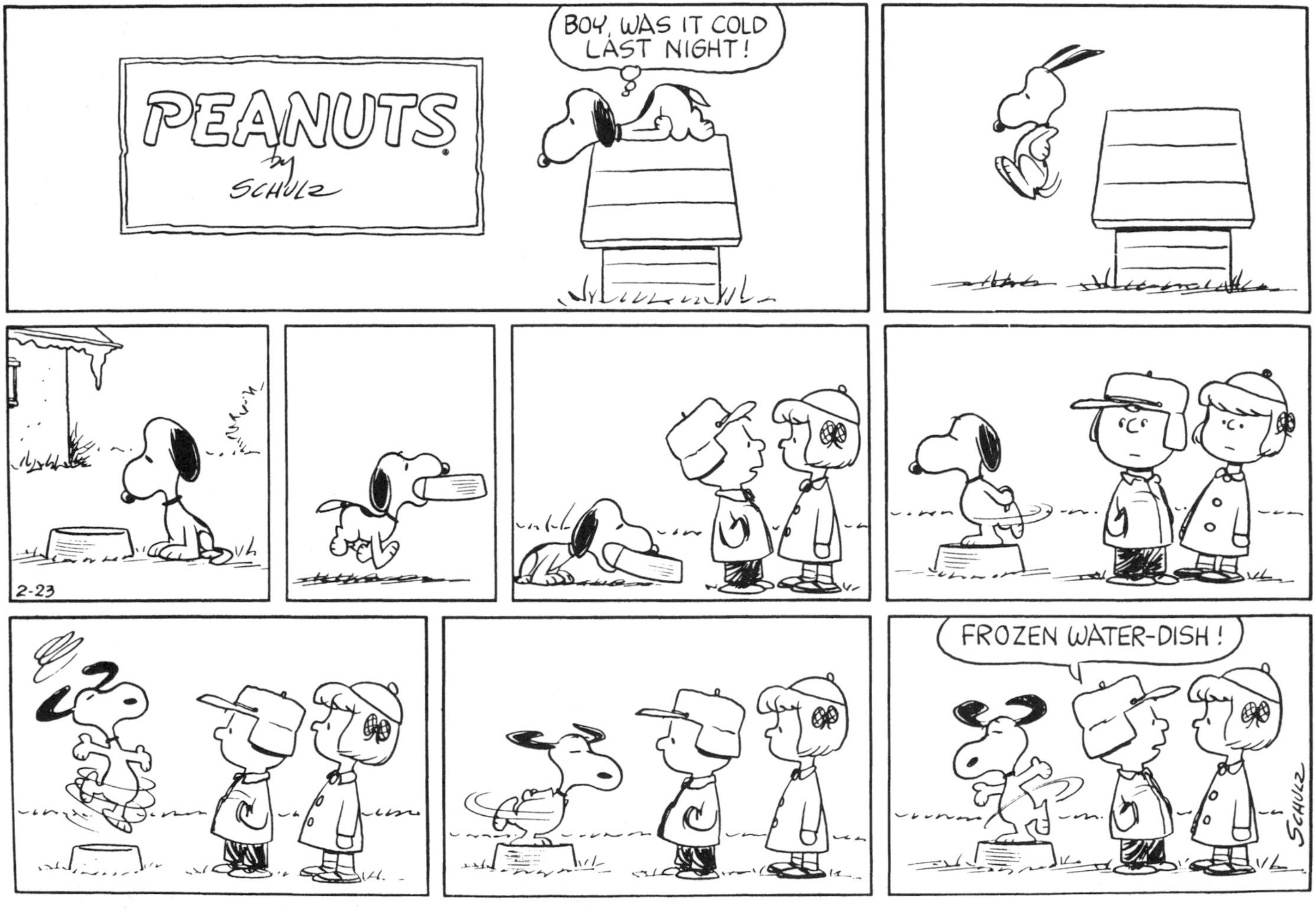
PEANUTS
by
SCHULZ
BOY, WAS IT COLD LAST NIGHT!
2-23
FROZEN WATER-DISH!
SCHULZ

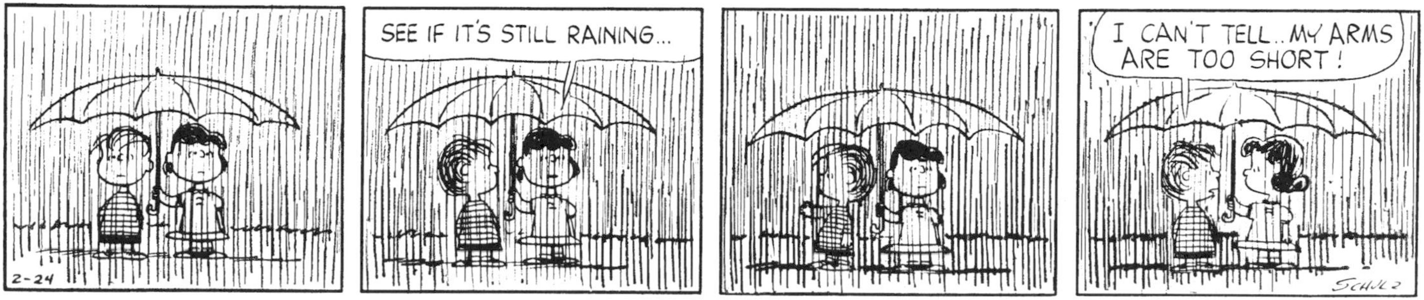
2-24
SEE IF IT'S STILL RAINING...
I CAN'T TELL.. MY ARMS ARE TOO SHORT!
SCHULZ

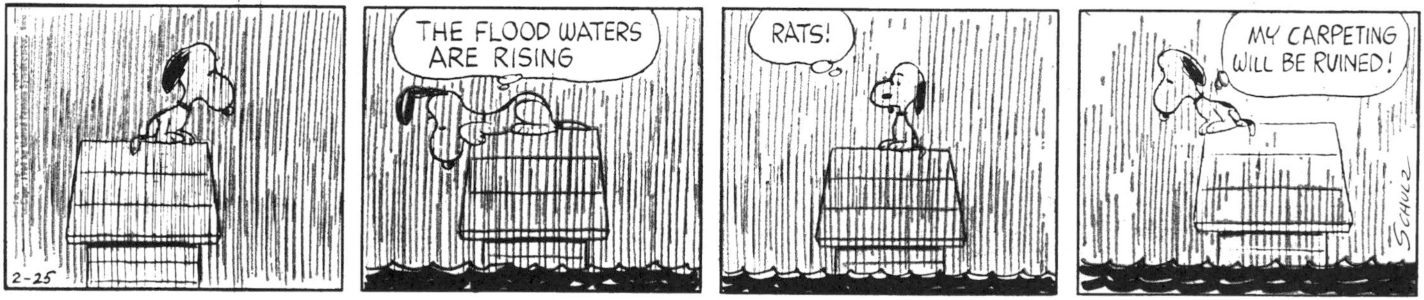
2-25
THE FLOOD WATERS ARE RISING
RATS!
MY CARPETING WILL BE RUINED!
SCHULZ

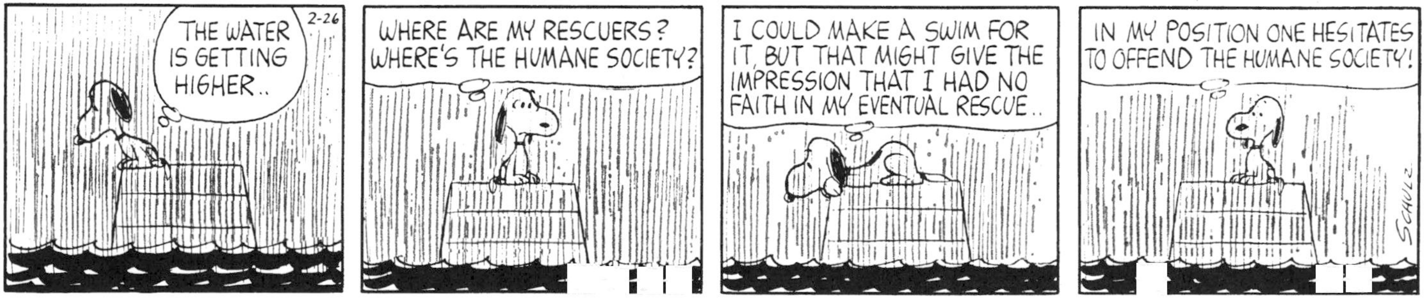
2-26
THE WATER IS GETTING HIGHER..
WHERE ARE MY RESCUERS? WHERE'S THE HUMANE SOCIETY?
I COULD MAKE A SWIM FOR IT, BUT THAT MIGHT GIVE THE IMPRESSION THAT I HAD NO FAITH IN MY EVENTUAL RESCUE..
IN MY POSITION ONE HESITATES TO OFFEND THE HUMANE SOCIETY!
SCHULZ

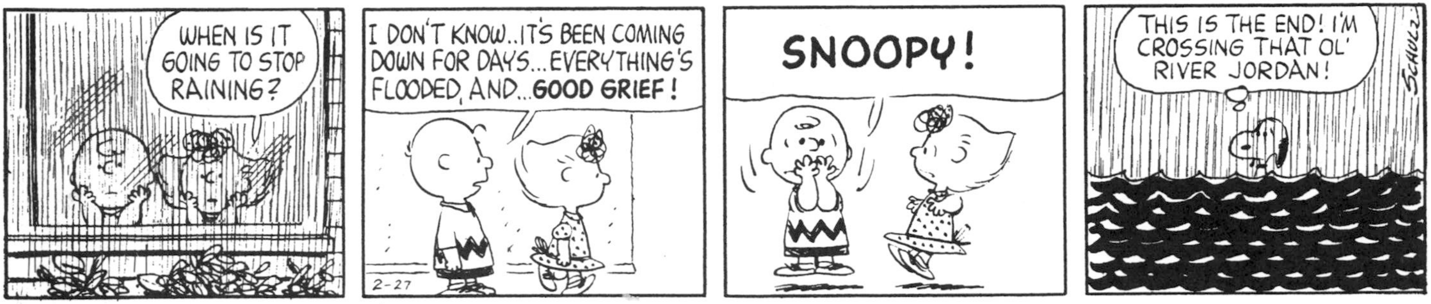
WHEN IS IT GOING TO STOP RAINING?
I DON'T KNOW..IT'S BEEN COMING DOWN FOR DAYS...EVERYTHING'S FLOODED, AND...GOOD GRIEF!
2-27
SNOOPY!
THIS IS THE END! I'M CROSSING THAT OL' RIVER JORDAN!
SCHULZ

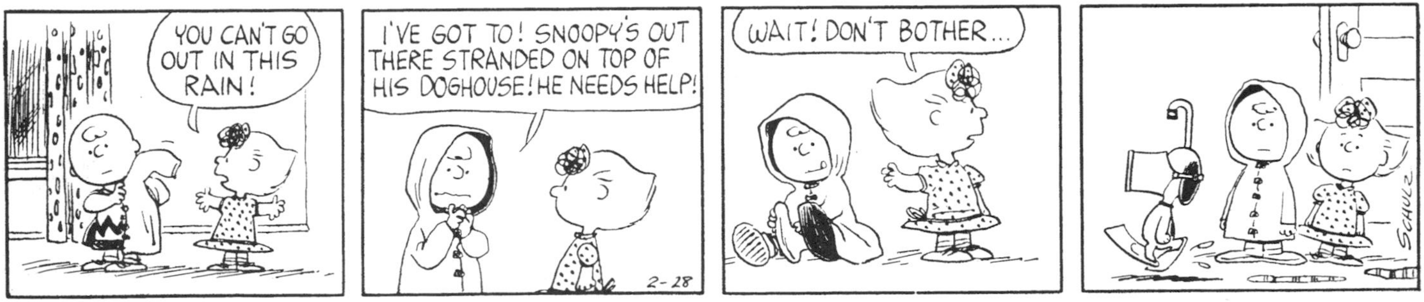
YOU CAN'T GO OUT IN THIS RAIN!
I'VE GOT TO! SNOOPY'S OUT THERE STRANDED ON TOP OF HIS DOGHOUSE! HE NEEDS HELP!
2-28
WAIT! DON'T BOTHER...
SCHULZ

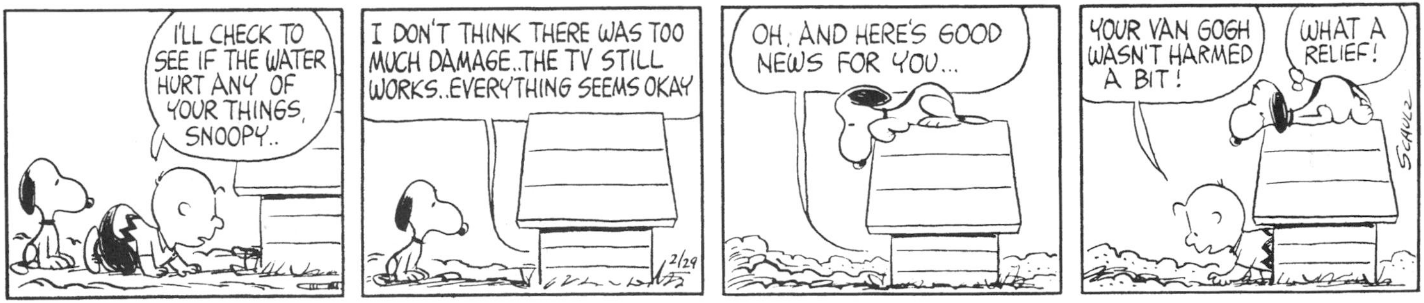
I'LL CHECK TO SEE IF THE WATER HURT ANY OF YOUR THINGS, SNOOPY..
I DON'T THINK THERE WAS TOO MUCH DAMAGE..THE TV STILL WORKS..EVERYTHING SEEMS OKAY
2/29
OH, AND HERE'S GOOD NEWS FOR YOU...
YOUR VAN GOGH WASN'T HARMED A BIT!
WHAT A RELIEF!
SCHULZ

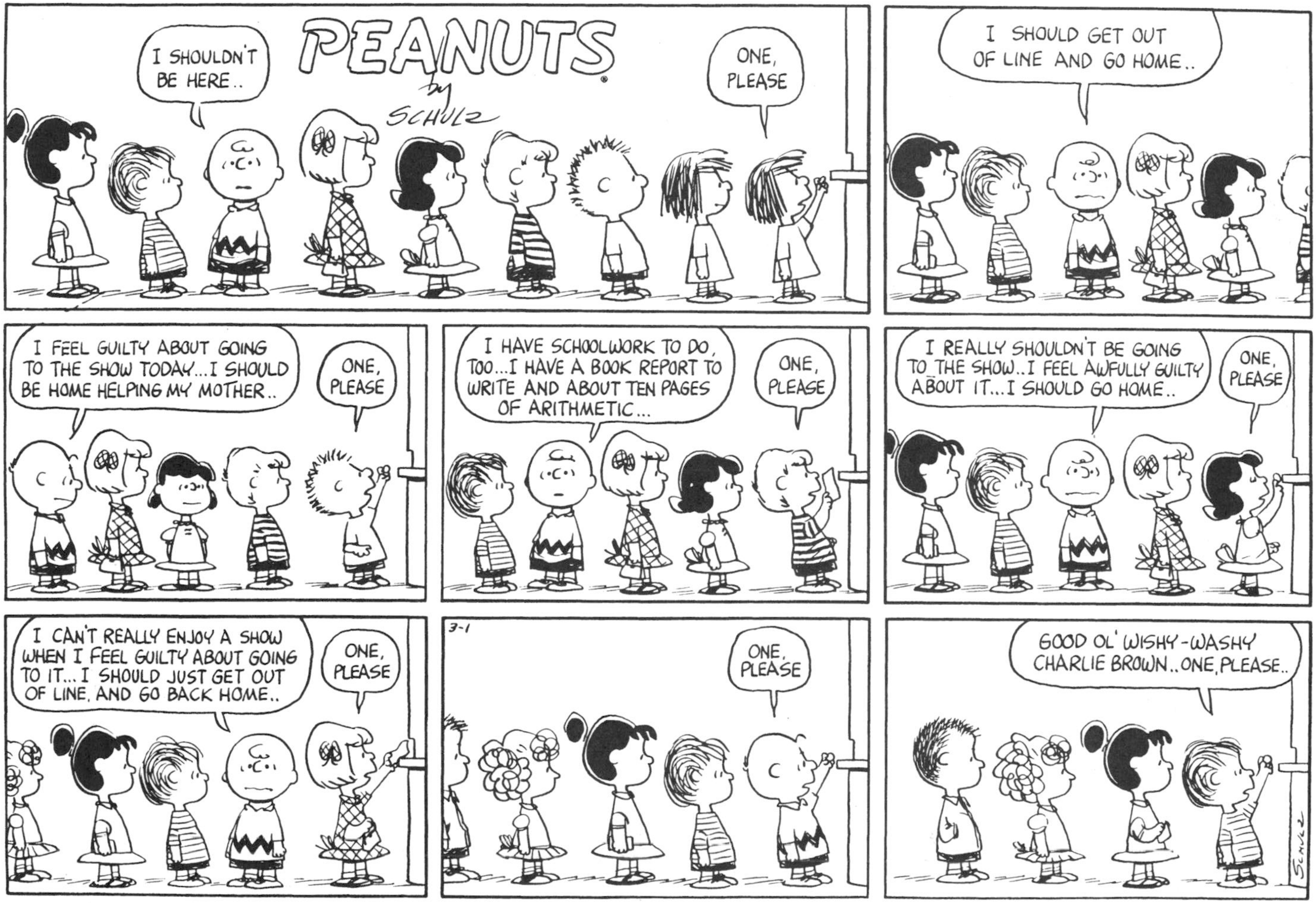

PEANUTS
by SCHULZ
I SHOULDN'T BE HERE..
ONE, PLEASE
I SHOULD GET OUT OF LINE AND GO HOME..
I FEEL GUILTY ABOUT GOING TO THE SHOW TODAY...I SHOULD BE HOME HELPING MY MOTHER..
ONE, PLEASE
I HAVE SCHOOLWORK TO DO, TOO...I HAVE A BOOK REPORT TO WRITE AND ABOUT TEN PAGES OF ARITHMETIC...
ONE, PLEASE
I REALLY SHOULDN'T BE GOING TO THE SHOW..I FEEL AWFULLY GUILTY ABOUT IT...I SHOULD GO HOME..
ONE, PLEASE
I CAN'T REALLY ENJOY A SHOW WHEN I FEEL GUILTY ABOUT GOING TO IT...I SHOULD JUST GET OUT OF LINE, AND GO BACK HOME..
ONE, PLEASE
3-1
ONE, PLEASE
GOOD OL' WISHY-WASHY CHARLIE BROWN..ONE, PLEASE..
SCHULZ

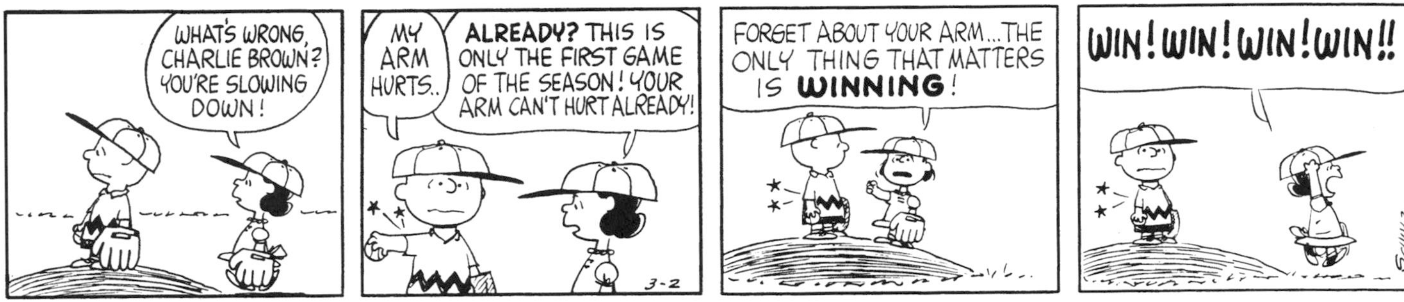
WHAT'S WRONG, CHARLIE BROWN? YOU'RE SLOWING DOWN!
MY ARM HURTS..
ALREADY? THIS IS ONLY THE FIRST GAME OF THE SEASON! YOUR ARM CAN'T HURT ALREADY!
3-2
FORGET ABOUT YOUR ARM... THE ONLY THING THAT MATTERS IS WINNING!
WIN! WIN! WIN! WIN!!
SCHULZ

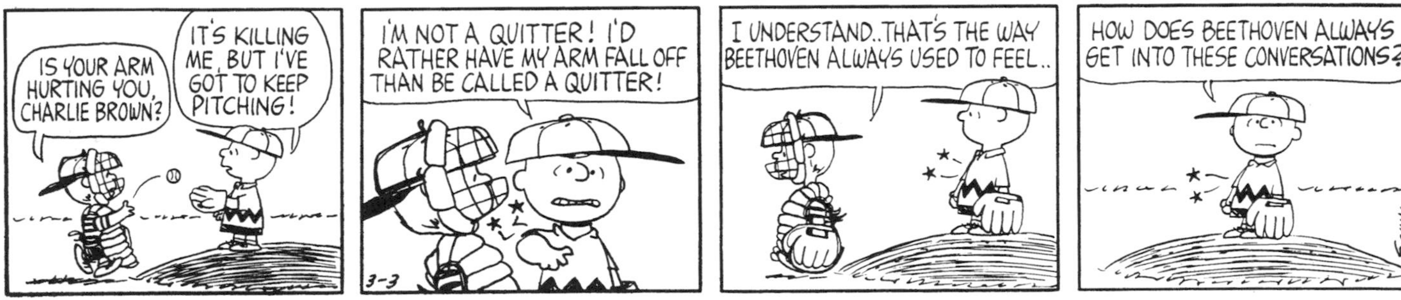
IS YOUR ARM HURTING YOU, CHARLIE BROWN?
IT'S KILLING ME, BUT I'VE GOT TO KEEP PITCHING!
I'M NOT A QUITTER! I'D RATHER HAVE MY ARM FALL OFF THAN BE CALLED A QUITTER!
3-3
I UNDERSTAND..THAT'S THE WAY BEETHOVEN ALWAYS USED TO FEEL..
HOW DOES BEETHOVEN ALWAYS GET INTO THESE CONVERSATIONS?
SCHULZ

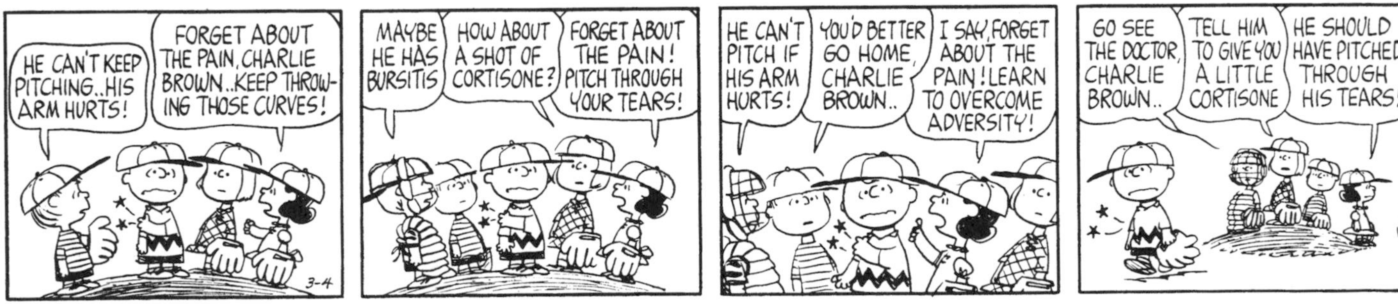
HE CAN'T KEEP PITCHING..HIS ARM HURTS!
FORGET ABOUT THE PAIN, CHARLIE BROWN..KEEP THROWING THOSE CURVES!
3-4
MAYBE HE HAS BURSITIS
HOW ABOUT A SHOT OF CORTISONE?
FORGET ABOUT THE PAIN! PITCH THROUGH YOUR TEARS!
HE CAN'T PITCH IF HIS ARM HURTS!
YOU'D BETTER GO HOME, CHARLIE BROWN..
I SAY, FORGET ABOUT THE PAIN! LEARN TO OVERCOME ADVERSITY!
GO SEE THE DOCTOR, CHARLIE BROWN..
TELL HIM TO GIVE YOU A LITTLE CORTISONE
HE SHOULD HAVE PITCHED THROUGH HIS TEARS!
SCHULZ

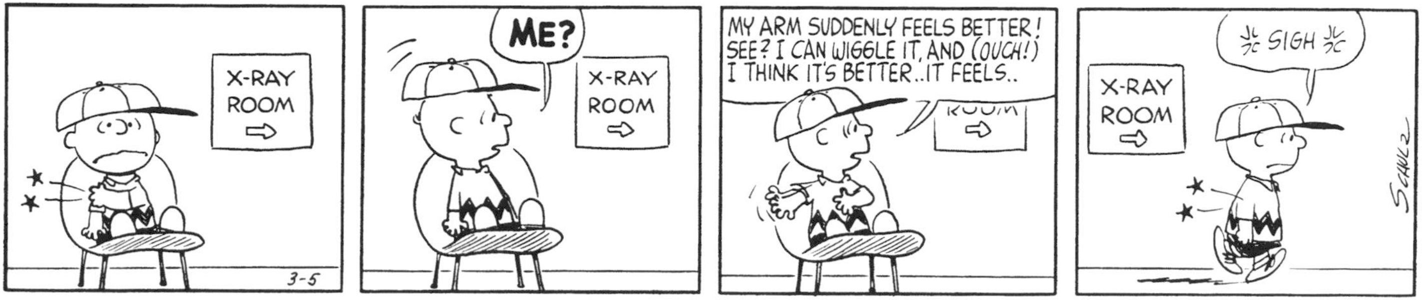
X-RAY ROOM
3-5
ME?
X-RAY ROOM
MY ARM SUDDENLY FEELS BETTER! SEE? I CAN WIGGLE IT, AND (OUCH!) I THINK IT'S BETTER..IT FEELS..
X-RAY ROOM
SIGH
SCHULZ

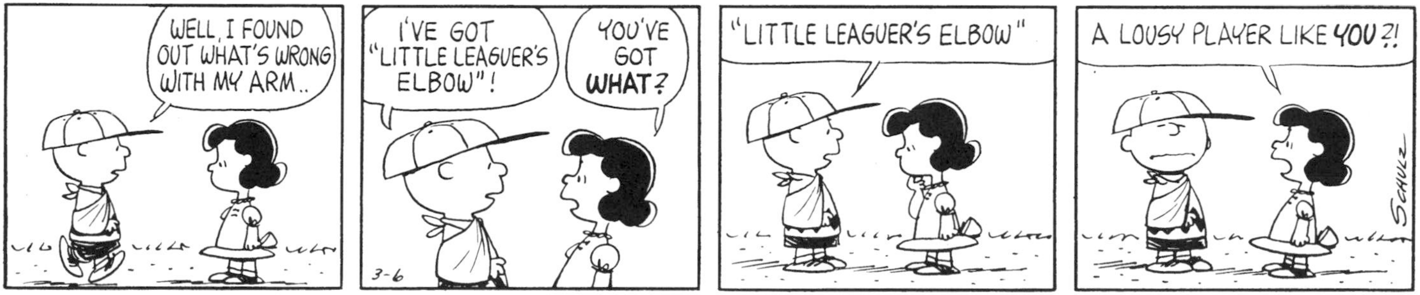
WELL, I FOUND OUT WHAT'S WRONG WITH MY ARM..
I'VE GOT "LITTLE LEAGUER'S ELBOW"!
YOU'VE GOT WHAT?
3-6
"LITTLE LEAGUER'S ELBOW"
A LOUSY PLAYER LIKE YOU?!
SCHULZ

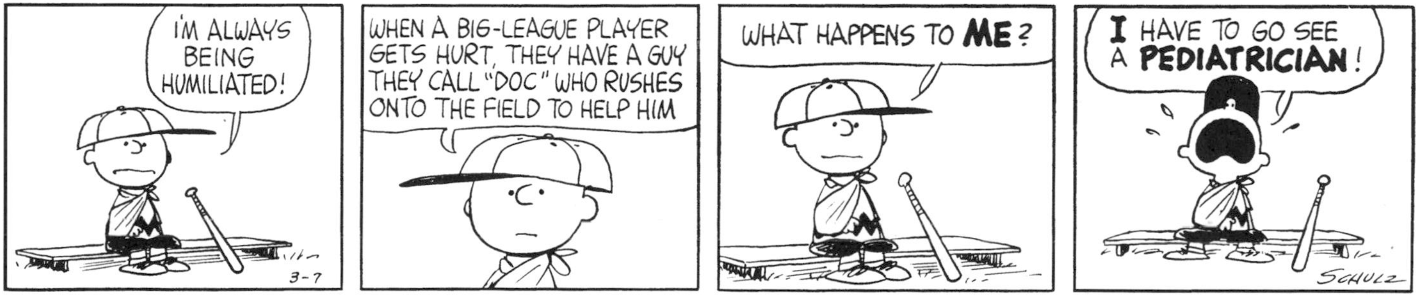
I'M ALWAYS BEING HUMILIATED!
3-7
WHEN A BIG-LEAGUE PLAYER GETS HURT, THEY HAVE A GUY THEY CALL "DOC" WHO RUSHES ONTO THE FIELD TO HELP HIM
WHAT HAPPENS TO ME?
I HAVE TO GO SEE A PEDIATRICIAN!
SCHULZ

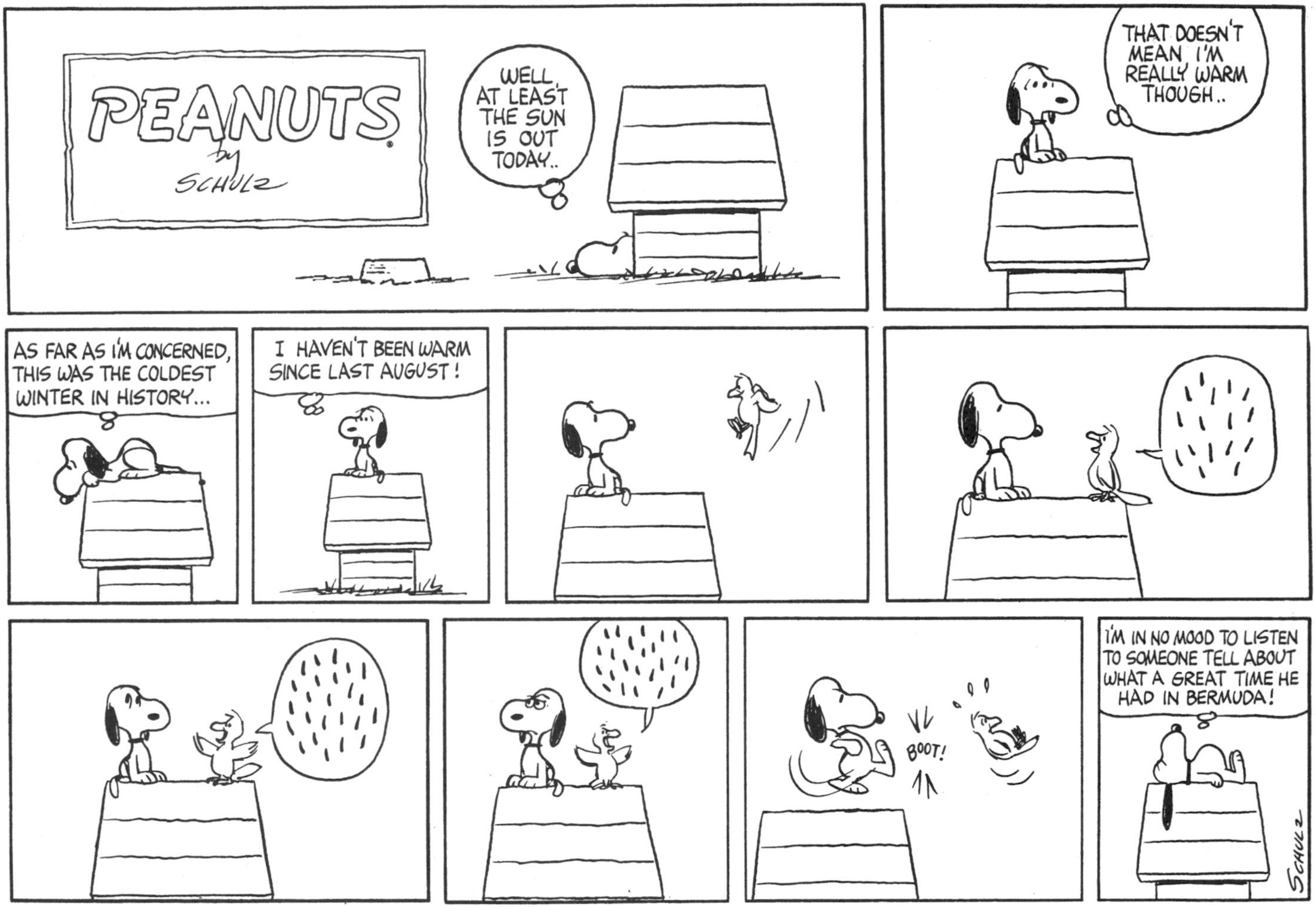
PEANUTS
by SCHULZ
WELL, AT LEAST THE SUN IS OUT TODAY..
THAT DOESN'T MEAN I'M REALLY WARM THOUGH..
AS FAR AS I'M CONCERNED, THIS WAS THE COLDEST WINTER IN HISTORY...
I HAVEN'T BEEN WARM SINCE LAST AUGUST!
BOOT!
I'M IN NO MOOD TO LISTEN TO SOMEONE TELL ABOUT WHAT A GREAT TIME HE HAD IN BERMUDA!
SCHULZ

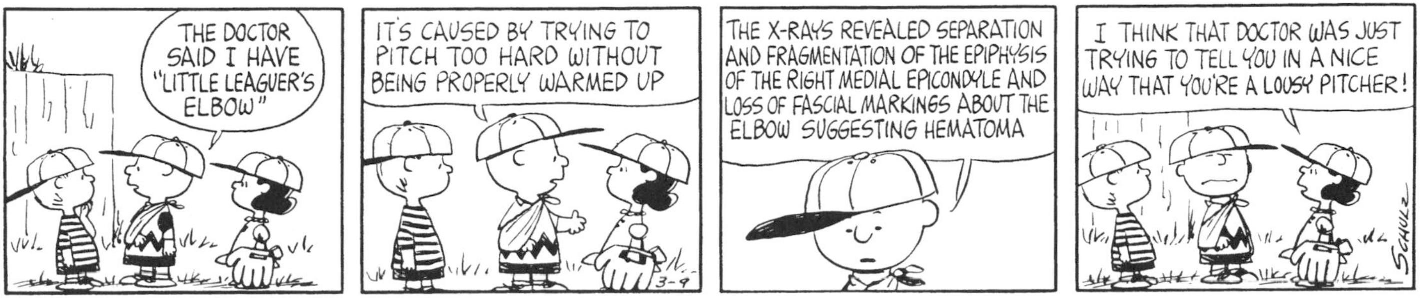
THE DOCTOR SAID I HAVE "LITTLE LEAGUER'S ELBOW"
IT'S CAUSED BY TRYING TO PITCH TOO HARD WITHOUT BEING PROPERLY WARMED UP
3-9
THE X-RAYS REVEALED SEPARATION AND FRAGMENTATION OF THE EPIPHYSIS OF THE RIGHT MEDIAL EPICONDYLE AND LOSS OF FASCIAL MARKINGS ABOUT THE ELBOW SUGGESTING HEMATOMA
I THINK THAT DOCTOR WAS JUST TRYING TO TELL YOU IN A NICE WAY THAT YOU'RE A LOUSY PITCHER!
SCHULZ

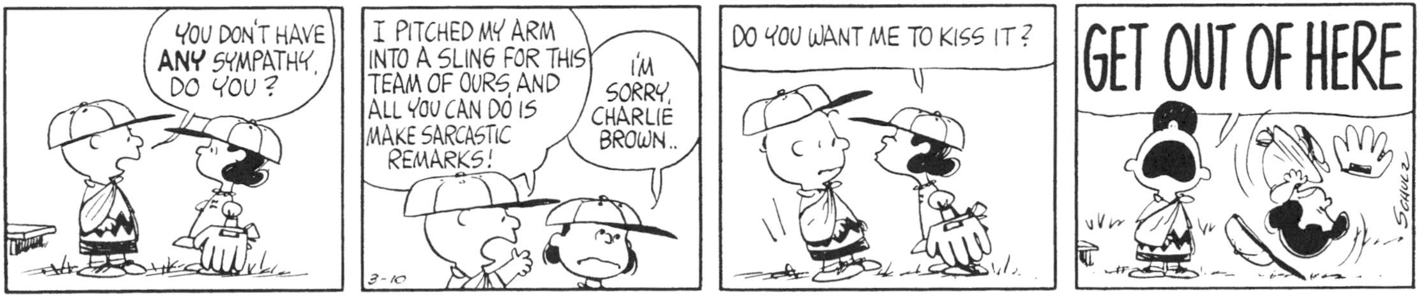
YOU DON'T HAVE **ANY** SYMPATHY, DO YOU?
I PITCHED MY ARM INTO A SLING FOR THIS TEAM OF OURS, AND ALL YOU CAN DO IS MAKE SARCASTIC REMARKS!
I'M SORRY, CHARLIE BROWN..
3-10
DO YOU WANT ME TO KISS IT?
GET OUT OF HERE
SCHULZ

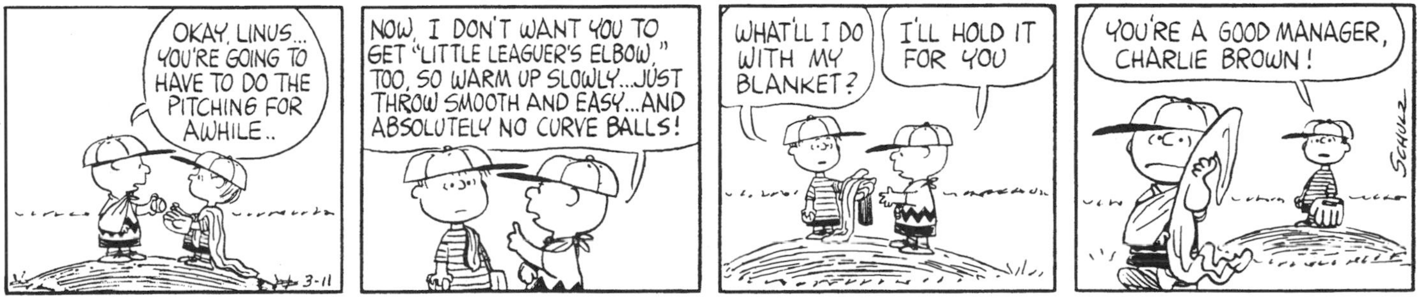
OKAY, LINUS... YOU'RE GOING TO HAVE TO DO THE PITCHING FOR AWHILE..
3-11
NOW, I DON'T WANT YOU TO GET "LITTLE LEAGUER'S ELBOW," TOO, SO WARM UP SLOWLY...JUST THROW SMOOTH AND EASY...AND ABSOLUTELY NO CURVE BALLS!
WHAT'LL I DO WITH MY BLANKET?
I'LL HOLD IT FOR YOU
YOU'RE A GOOD MANAGER, CHARLIE BROWN!
SCHULZ

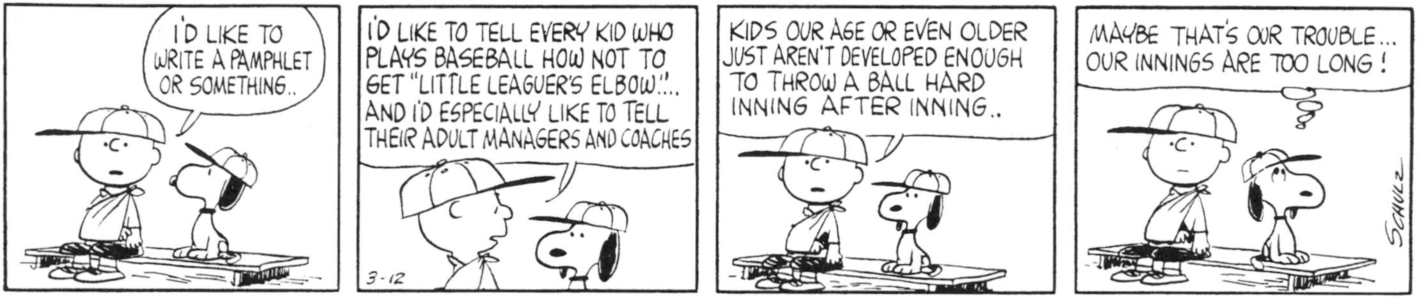
I'D LIKE TO WRITE A PAMPHLET OR SOMETHING..
I'D LIKE TO TELL EVERY KID WHO PLAYS BASEBALL HOW NOT TO GET "LITTLE LEAGUER'S ELBOW."... AND I'D ESPECIALLY LIKE TO TELL THEIR ADULT MANAGERS AND COACHES
3-12
KIDS OUR AGE OR EVEN OLDER JUST AREN'T DEVELOPED ENOUGH TO THROW A BALL HARD INNING AFTER INNING..
MAYBE THAT'S OUR TROUBLE... OUR INNINGS ARE TOO LONG!
SCHULZ

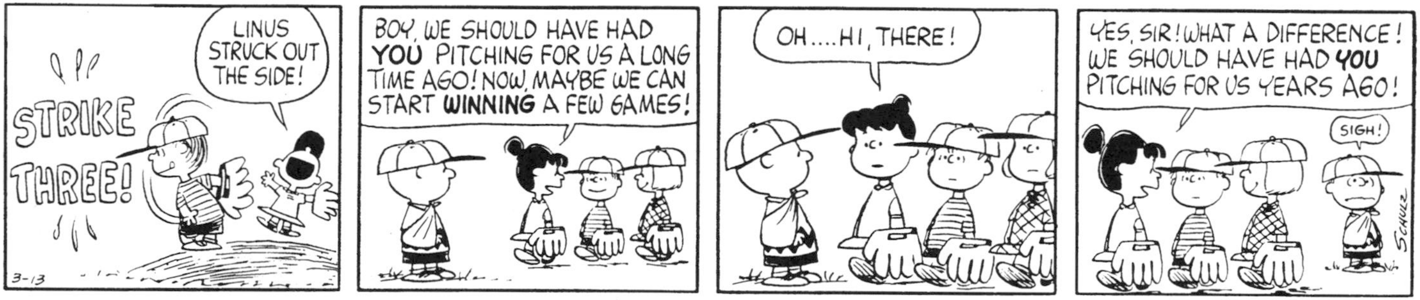
STRIKE THREE!
LINUS STRUCK OUT THE SIDE!
3-13
BOY, WE SHOULD HAVE HAD **YOU** PITCHING FOR US A LONG TIME AGO! NOW, MAYBE WE CAN START **WINNING** A FEW GAMES!
OH....HI, THERE!
YES, SIR! WHAT A DIFFERENCE! WE SHOULD HAVE HAD **YOU** PITCHING FOR US YEARS AGO!
SIGH!
SCHULZ

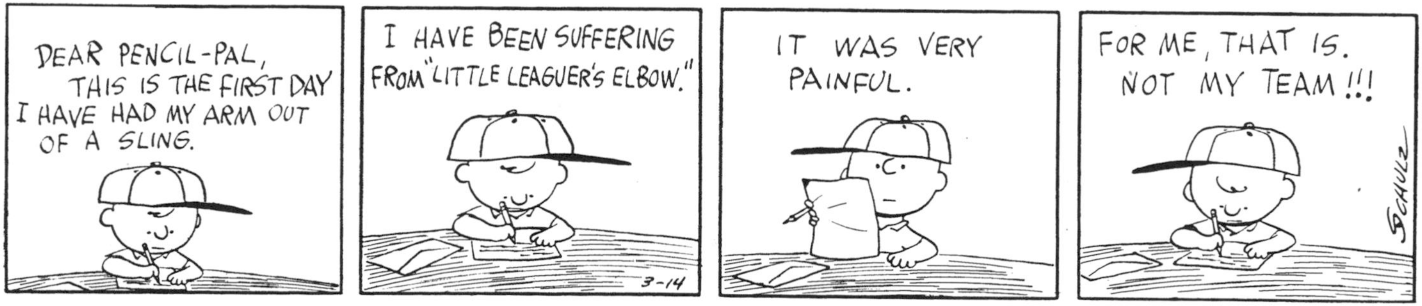
DEAR PENCIL-PAL, THIS IS THE FIRST DAY I HAVE HAD MY ARM OUT OF A SLING.
I HAVE BEEN SUFFERING FROM "LITTLE LEAGUER'S ELBOW."
3-14
IT WAS VERY PAINFUL.
FOR ME, THAT IS. NOT MY TEAM!!!
SCHULZ

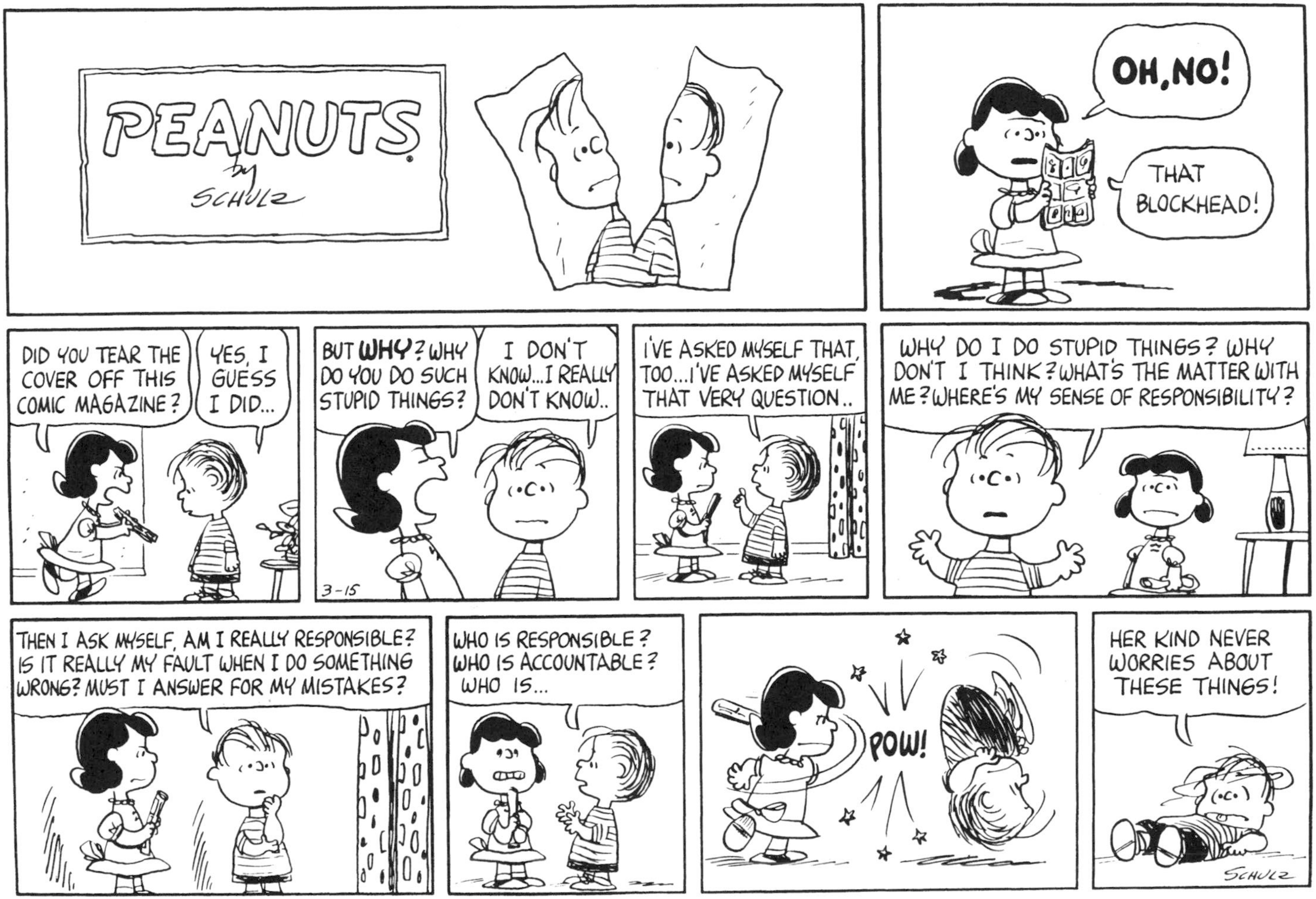
PEANUTS
by SCHULZ
OH, NO!
THAT BLOCKHEAD!
DID YOU TEAR THE COVER OFF THIS COMIC MAGAZINE?
YES, I GUESS I DID...
BUT WHY? WHY DO YOU DO SUCH STUPID THINGS?
I DON'T KNOW...I REALLY DON'T KNOW..
3-15
I'VE ASKED MYSELF THAT, TOO...I'VE ASKED MYSELF THAT VERY QUESTION..
WHY DO I DO STUPID THINGS? WHY DON'T I THINK? WHAT'S THE MATTER WITH ME? WHERE'S MY SENSE OF RESPONSIBILITY?
THEN I ASK MYSELF, AM I REALLY RESPONSIBLE? IS IT REALLY MY FAULT WHEN I DO SOMETHING WRONG? MUST I ANSWER FOR MY MISTAKES?
WHO IS RESPONSIBLE? WHO IS ACCOUNTABLE? WHO IS...
POW!
HER KIND NEVER WORRIES ABOUT THESE THINGS!
SCHULZ

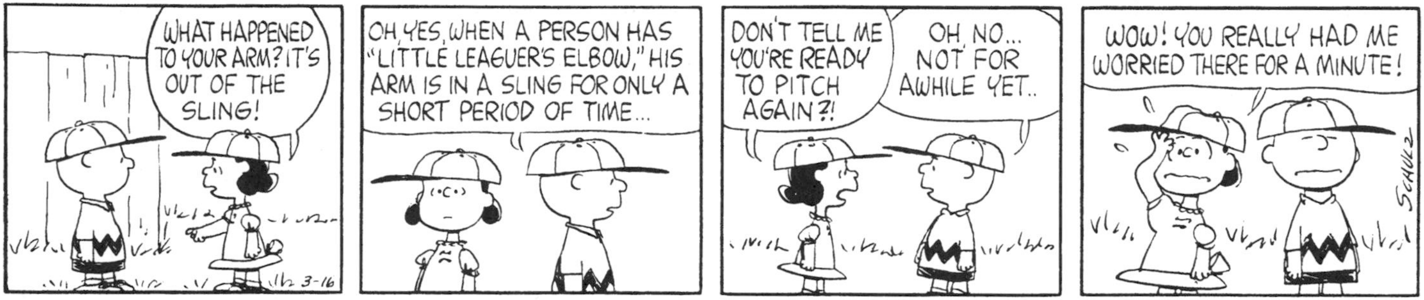
WHAT HAPPENED TO YOUR ARM? IT'S OUT OF THE SLING!
3-16
OH, YES, WHEN A PERSON HAS "LITTLE LEAGUER'S ELBOW," HIS ARM IS IN A SLING FOR ONLY A SHORT PERIOD OF TIME...
DON'T TELL ME YOU'RE READY TO PITCH AGAIN?!
OH, NO... NOT FOR AWHILE YET..
WOW! YOU REALLY HAD ME WORRIED THERE FOR A MINUTE!
SCHULZ

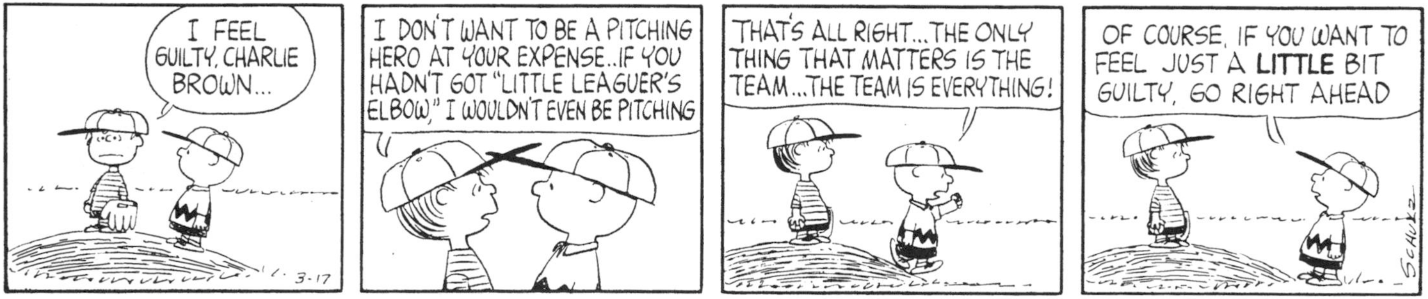
I FEEL GUILTY, CHARLIE BROWN...
3-17
I DON'T WANT TO BE A PITCHING HERO AT YOUR EXPENSE..IF YOU HADN'T GOT "LITTLE LEAGUER'S ELBOW," I WOULDN'T EVEN BE PITCHING
THAT'S ALL RIGHT...THE ONLY THING THAT MATTERS IS THE TEAM...THE TEAM IS EVERYTHING!
OF COURSE, IF YOU WANT TO FEEL JUST A **LITTLE** BIT GUILTY, GO RIGHT AHEAD
SCHULZ

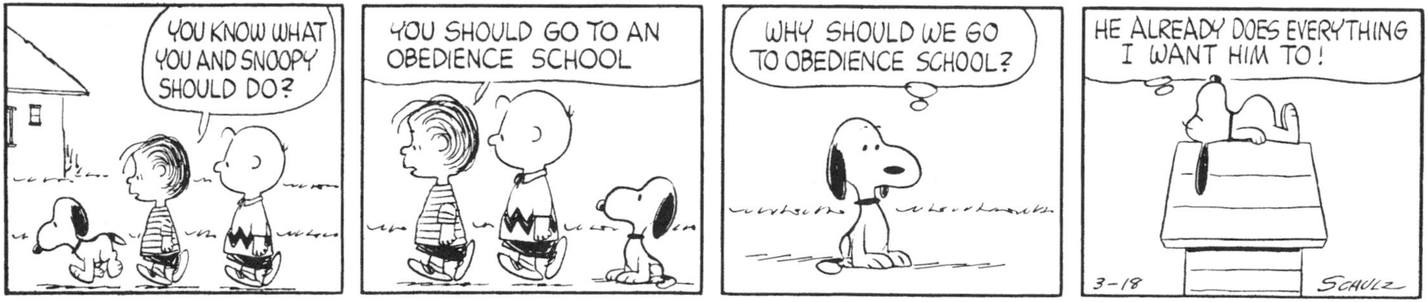
YOU KNOW WHAT YOU AND SNOOPY SHOULD DO?
YOU SHOULD GO TO AN OBEDIENCE SCHOOL
WHY SHOULD WE GO TO OBEDIENCE SCHOOL?
HE ALREADY DOES EVERYTHING I WANT HIM TO!
3-18
SCHULZ

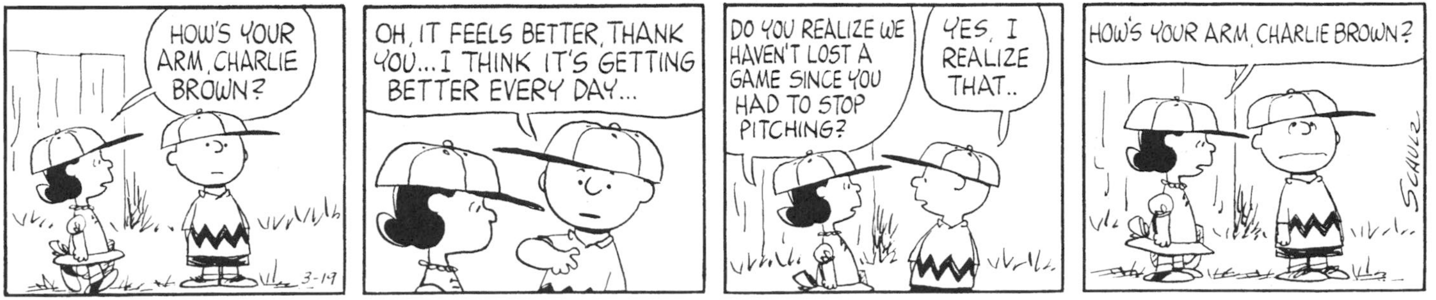
HOW'S YOUR ARM, CHARLIE BROWN?
OH, IT FEELS BETTER, THANK YOU...I THINK IT'S GETTING BETTER EVERY DAY...
DO YOU REALIZE WE HAVEN'T LOST A GAME SINCE YOU HAD TO STOP PITCHING?
YES, I REALIZE THAT..
HOW'S YOUR ARM, CHARLIE BROWN?

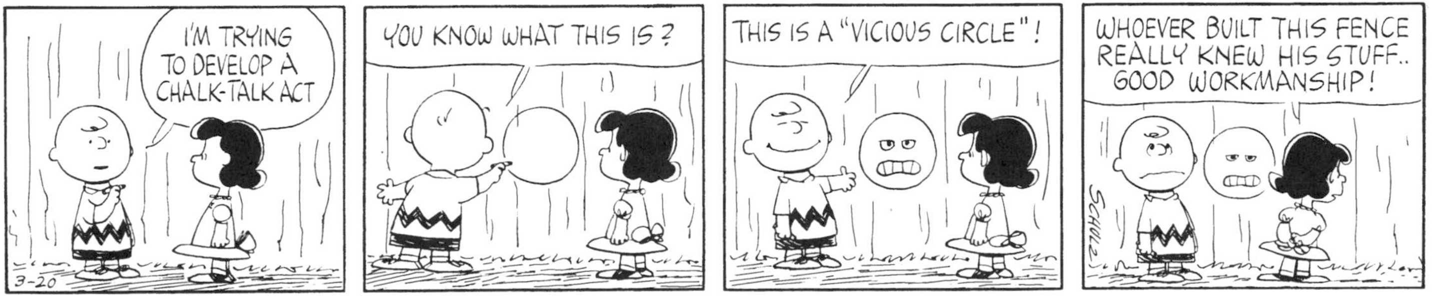
I'M TRYING TO DEVELOP A CHALK-TALK ACT
YOU KNOW WHAT THIS IS?
THIS IS A "VICIOUS CIRCLE"!
WHOEVER BUILT THIS FENCE REALLY KNEW HIS STUFF.. GOOD WORKMANSHIP!

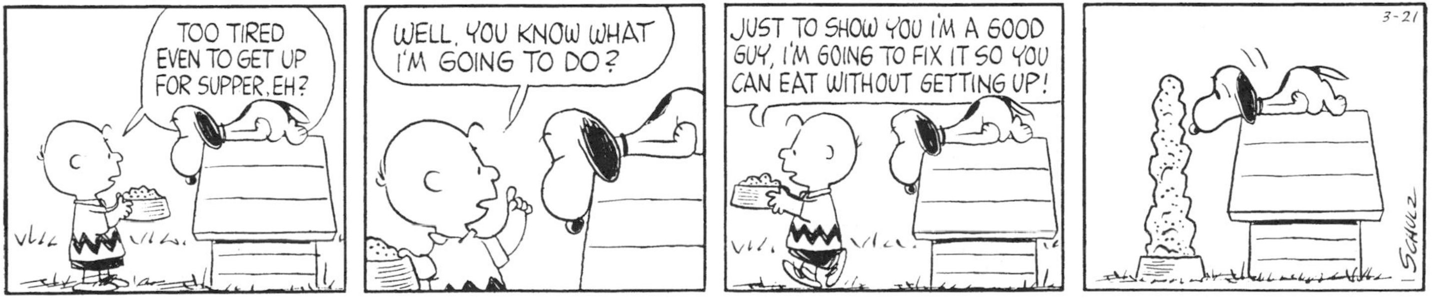
TOO TIRED EVEN TO GET UP FOR SUPPER, EH?
WELL, YOU KNOW WHAT I'M GOING TO DO?
JUST TO SHOW YOU I'M A GOOD GUY, I'M GOING TO FIX IT SO YOU CAN EAT WITHOUT GETTING UP!

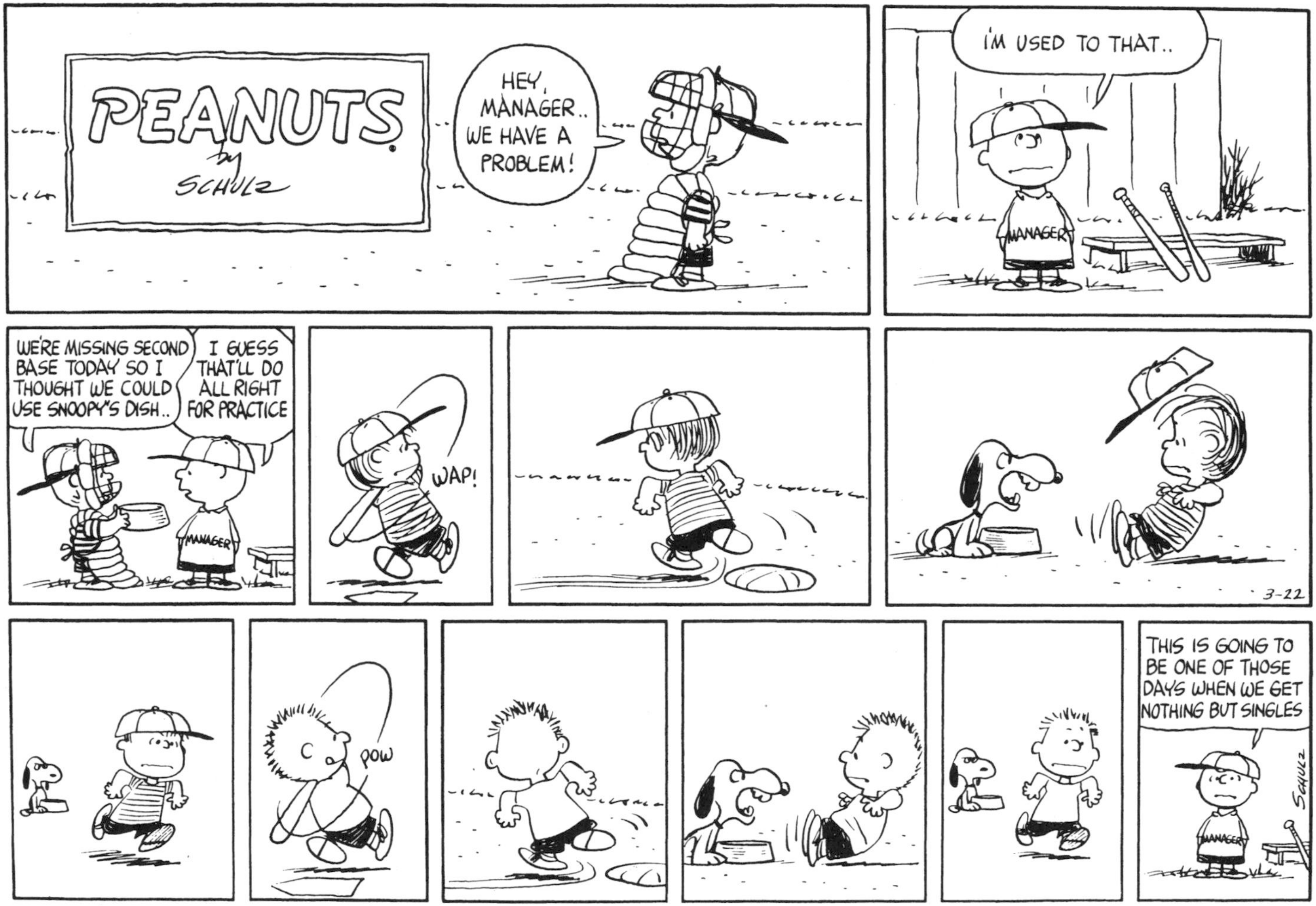
PEANUTS
by SCHULZ
HEY, MANAGER.. WE HAVE A PROBLEM!
I'M USED TO THAT..
WE'RE MISSING SECOND BASE TODAY SO I THOUGHT WE COULD USE SNOOPY'S DISH..
I GUESS THAT'LL DO ALL RIGHT FOR PRACTICE
MANAGER
WAP!
3-22
POW
THIS IS GOING TO BE ONE OF THOSE DAYS WHEN WE GET NOTHING BUT SINGLES
SCHULZ

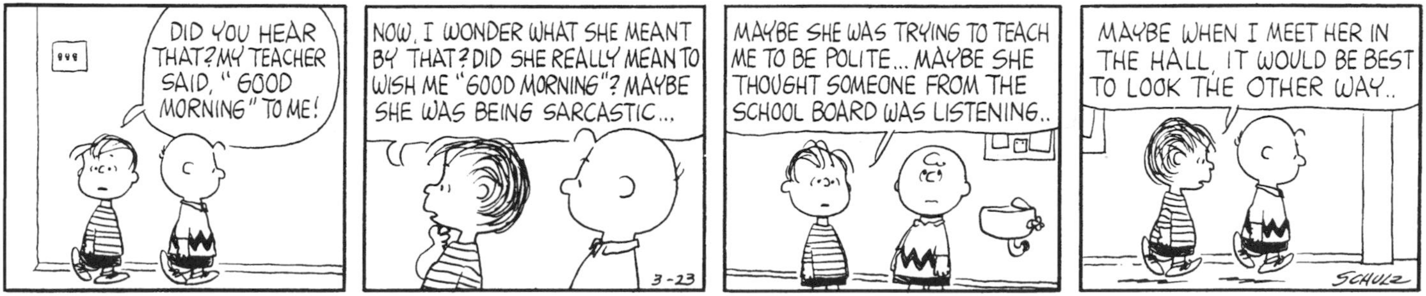
DID YOU HEAR THAT? MY TEACHER SAID, "GOOD MORNING" TO ME!
NOW, I WONDER WHAT SHE MEANT BY THAT? DID SHE REALLY MEAN TO WISH ME "GOOD MORNING"? MAYBE SHE WAS BEING SARCASTIC...
3-23
MAYBE SHE WAS TRYING TO TEACH ME TO BE POLITE... MAYBE SHE THOUGHT SOMEONE FROM THE SCHOOL BOARD WAS LISTENING..
MAYBE WHEN I MEET HER IN THE HALL, IT WOULD BE BEST TO LOOK THE OTHER WAY..
SCHULZ

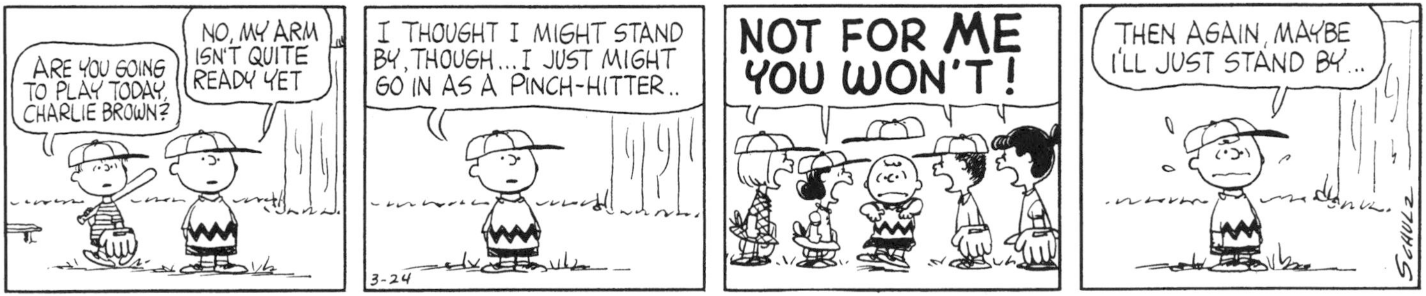
ARE YOU GOING TO PLAY TODAY, CHARLIE BROWN?
NO, MY ARM ISN'T QUITE READY YET
I THOUGHT I MIGHT STAND BY, THOUGH... I JUST MIGHT GO IN AS A PINCH-HITTER..
3-24
NOT FOR ME YOU WON'T!
THEN AGAIN, MAYBE I'LL JUST STAND BY...
SCHULZ

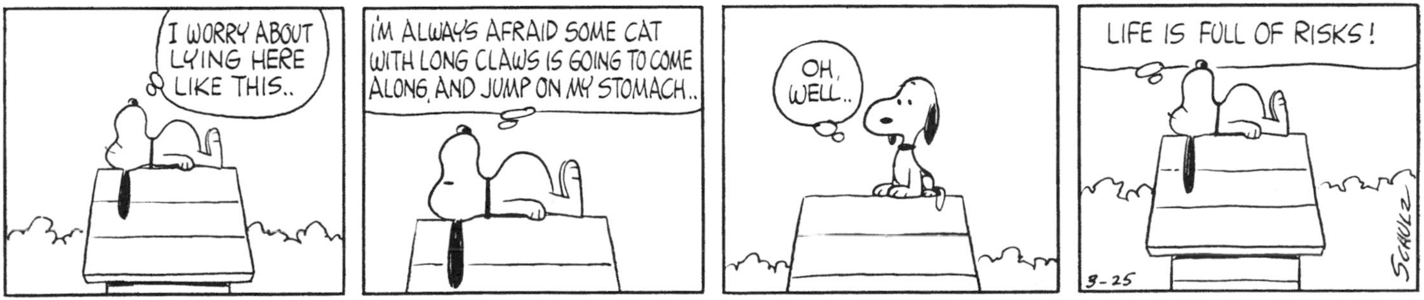
I WORRY ABOUT LYING HERE LIKE THIS..
I'M ALWAYS AFRAID SOME CAT WITH LONG CLAWS IS GOING TO COME ALONG, AND JUMP ON MY STOMACH..
OH, WELL..
LIFE IS FULL OF RISKS!
3-25
SCHULZ

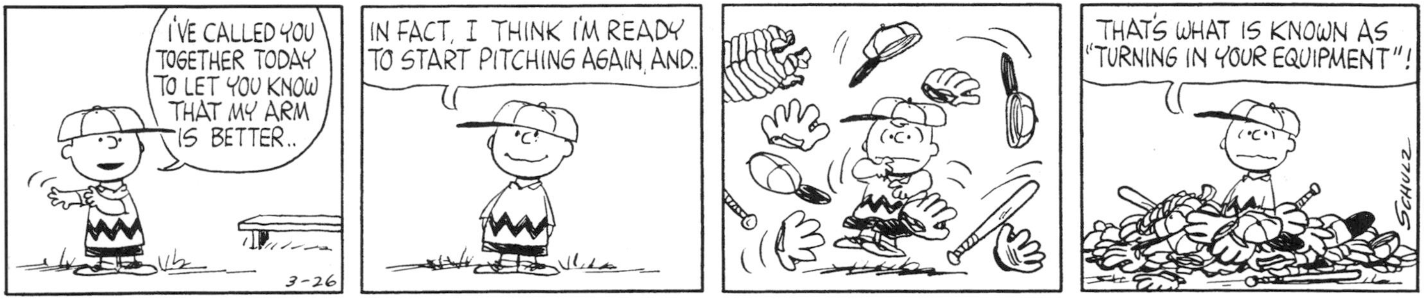
I'VE CALLED YOU TOGETHER TODAY TO LET YOU KNOW THAT MY ARM IS BETTER..
3-26
IN FACT, I THINK I'M READY TO START PITCHING AGAIN, AND..
THAT'S WHAT IS KNOWN AS "TURNING IN YOUR EQUIPMENT"!
SCHULZ

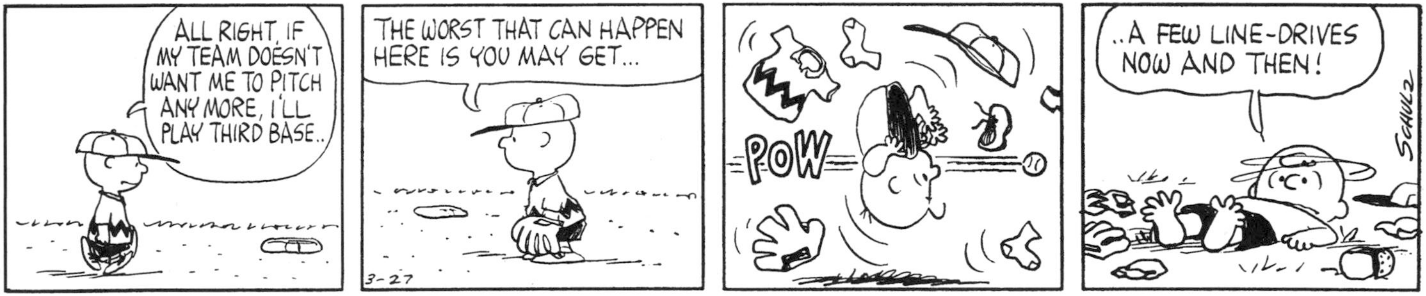
ALL RIGHT, IF MY TEAM DOESN'T WANT ME TO PITCH ANY MORE, I'LL PLAY THIRD BASE..
THE WORST THAT CAN HAPPEN HERE IS YOU MAY GET...
3-27
POW
..A FEW LINE-DRIVES NOW AND THEN!
SCHULZ

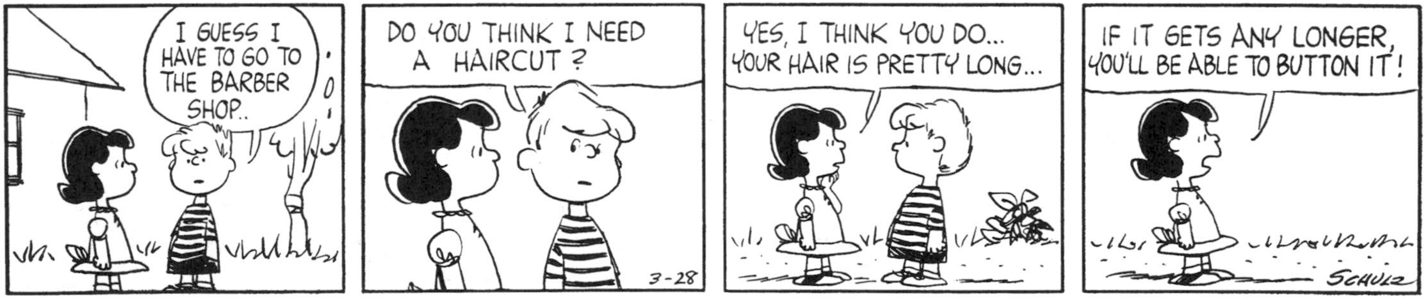
I GUESS I HAVE TO GO TO THE BARBER SHOP..
DO YOU THINK I NEED A HAIRCUT?
3-28
YES, I THINK YOU DO... YOUR HAIR IS PRETTY LONG...
IF IT GETS ANY LONGER, YOU'LL BE ABLE TO BUTTON IT!
SCHULZ

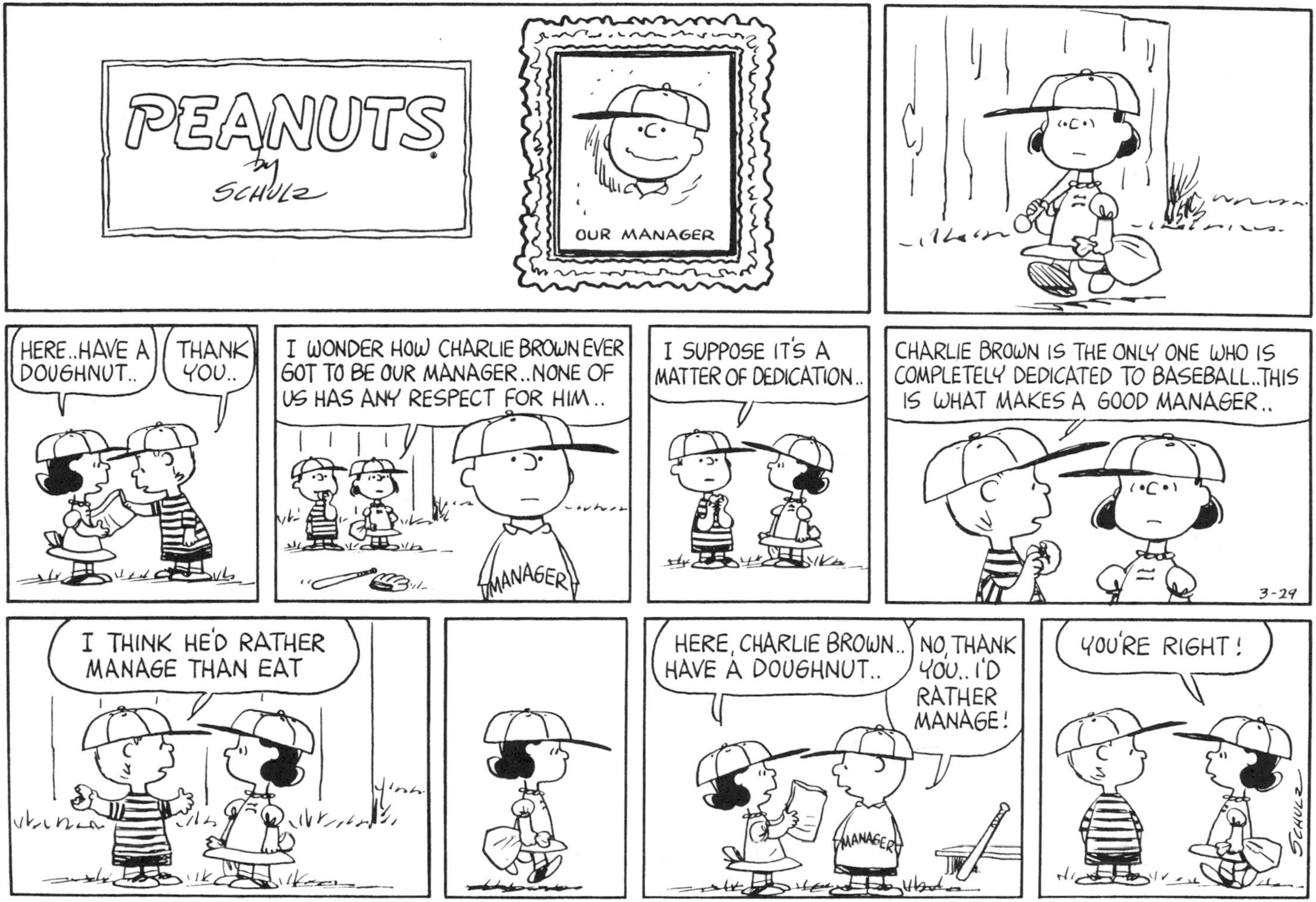
PEANUTS
by SCHULZ
OUR MANAGER
HERE..HAVE A DOUGHNUT..
THANK YOU..
I WONDER HOW CHARLIE BROWN EVER GOT TO BE OUR MANAGER..NONE OF US HAS ANY RESPECT FOR HIM..
MANAGER
I SUPPOSE IT'S A MATTER OF DEDICATION..
CHARLIE BROWN IS THE ONLY ONE WHO IS COMPLETELY DEDICATED TO BASEBALL..THIS IS WHAT MAKES A GOOD MANAGER..
3-29
I THINK HE'D RATHER MANAGE THAN EAT
HERE, CHARLIE BROWN.. HAVE A DOUGHNUT..
NO, THANK YOU..I'D RATHER MANAGE!
MANAGER
YOU'RE RIGHT!
SCHULZ

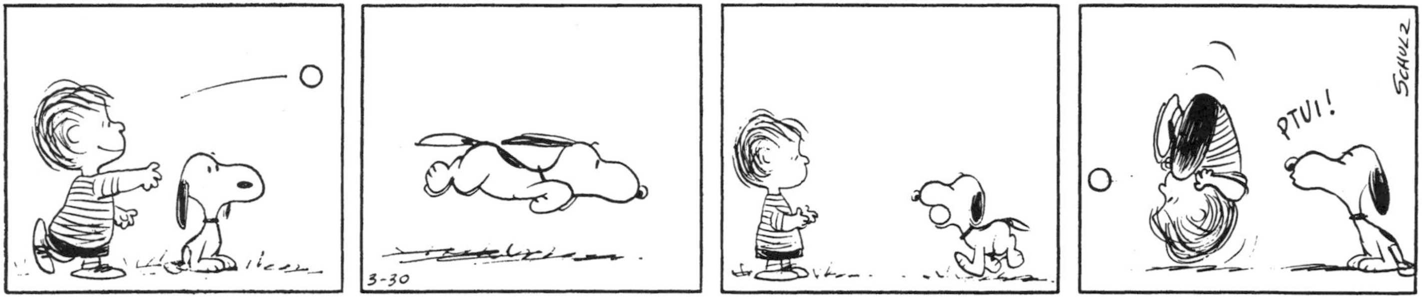
3-30
PTUI!
SCHULZ

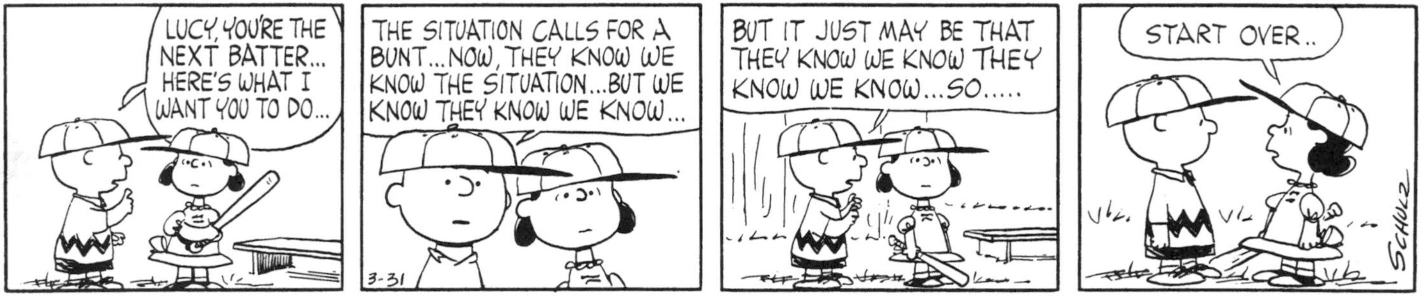
LUCY, YOU'RE THE NEXT BATTER... HERE'S WHAT I WANT YOU TO DO...
THE SITUATION CALLS FOR A BUNT...NOW, THEY KNOW WE KNOW THE SITUATION...BUT WE KNOW THEY KNOW WE KNOW...
3-31
BUT IT JUST MAY BE THAT THEY KNOW WE KNOW THEY KNOW WE KNOW...SO.....
START OVER..
SCHULZ

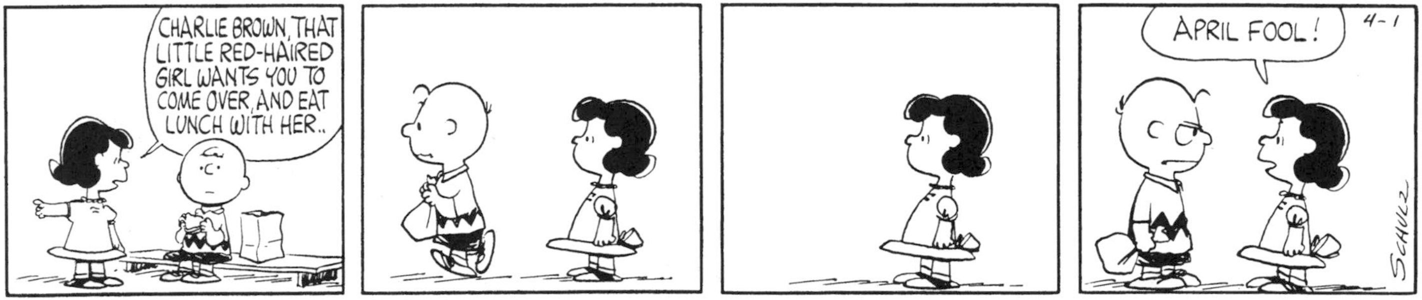
CHARLIE BROWN, THAT LITTLE RED-HAIRED GIRL WANTS YOU TO COME OVER, AND EAT LUNCH WITH HER..
APRIL FOOL!
4-1
SCHULZ

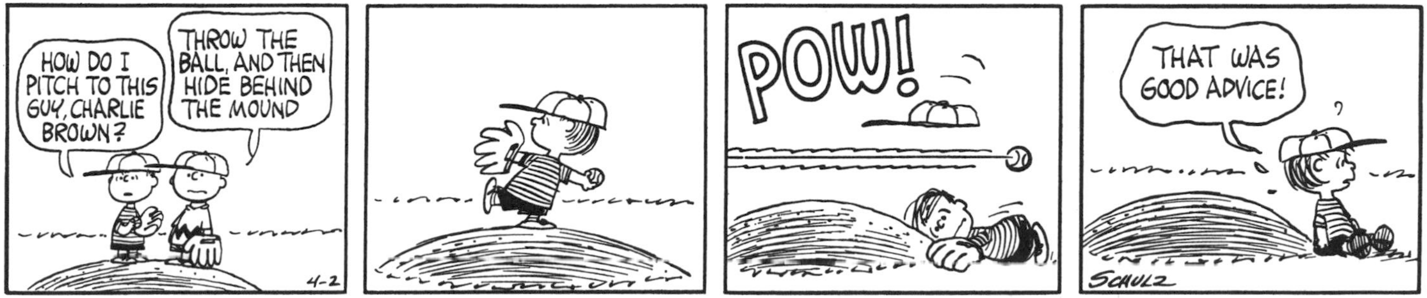
HOW DO I PITCH TO THIS GUY, CHARLIE BROWN?
THROW THE BALL, AND THEN HIDE BEHIND THE MOUND
4-2
POW!
THAT WAS GOOD ADVICE!
SCHULZ

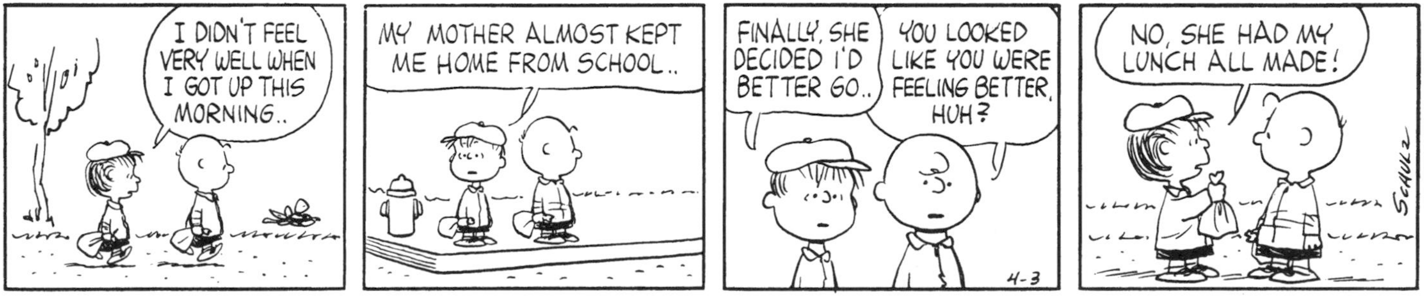
I DIDN'T FEEL VERY WELL WHEN I GOT UP THIS MORNING..
MY MOTHER ALMOST KEPT ME HOME FROM SCHOOL..
FINALLY, SHE DECIDED I'D BETTER GO..
YOU LOOKED LIKE YOU WERE FEELING BETTER, HUH?
4-3
NO, SHE HAD MY LUNCH ALL MADE!
SCHULZ

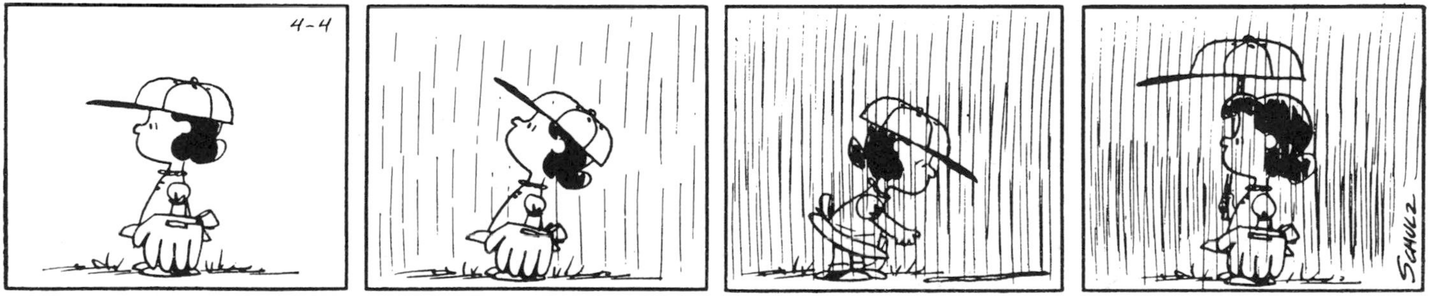
4-4
SCHULZ

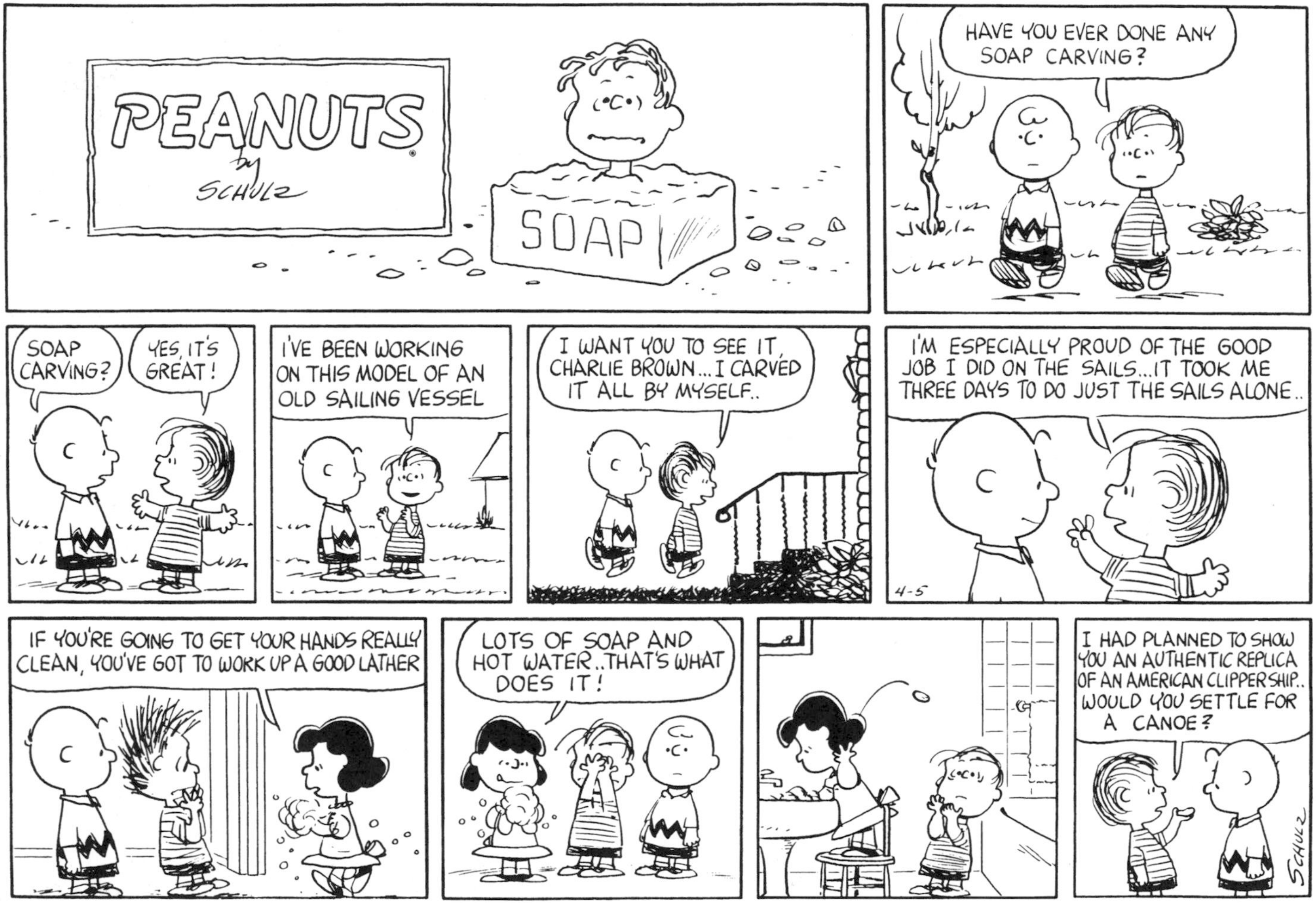
PEANUTS
by SCHULZ
SOAP
HAVE YOU EVER DONE ANY SOAP CARVING?
SOAP CARVING?
YES, IT'S GREAT!
I'VE BEEN WORKING ON THIS MODEL OF AN OLD SAILING VESSEL
I WANT YOU TO SEE IT, CHARLIE BROWN... I CARVED IT ALL BY MYSELF..
I'M ESPECIALLY PROUD OF THE GOOD JOB I DID ON THE SAILS... IT TOOK ME THREE DAYS TO DO JUST THE SAILS ALONE..
4-5
IF YOU'RE GOING TO GET YOUR HANDS REALLY CLEAN, YOU'VE GOT TO WORK UP A GOOD LATHER
LOTS OF SOAP AND HOT WATER.. THAT'S WHAT DOES IT!
I HAD PLANNED TO SHOW YOU AN AUTHENTIC REPLICA OF AN AMERICAN CLIPPERSHIP.. WOULD YOU SETTLE FOR A CANOE?
SCHULZ

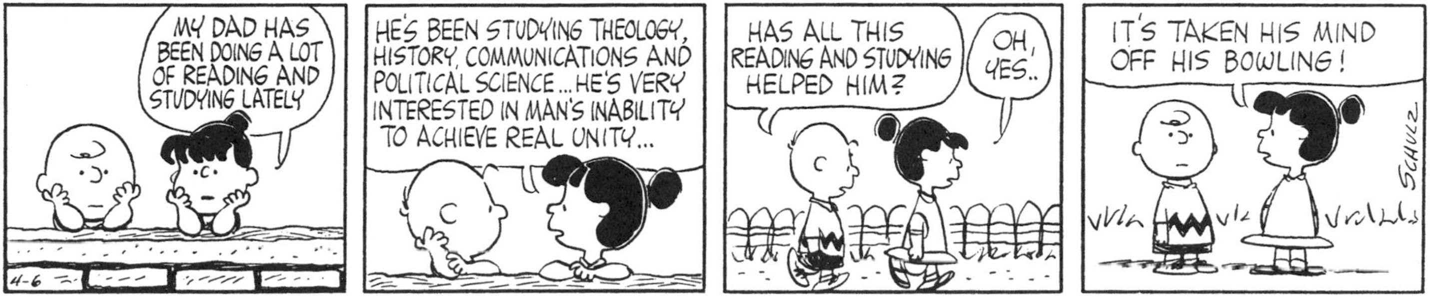
MY DAD HAS BEEN DOING A LOT OF READING AND STUDYING LATELY
4-6
HE'S BEEN STUDYING THEOLOGY, HISTORY, COMMUNICATIONS AND POLITICAL SCIENCE... HE'S VERY INTERESTED IN MAN'S INABILITY TO ACHIEVE REAL UNITY...
HAS ALL THIS READING AND STUDYING HELPED HIM?
OH, YES..
IT'S TAKEN HIS MIND OFF HIS BOWLING!
SCHULZ

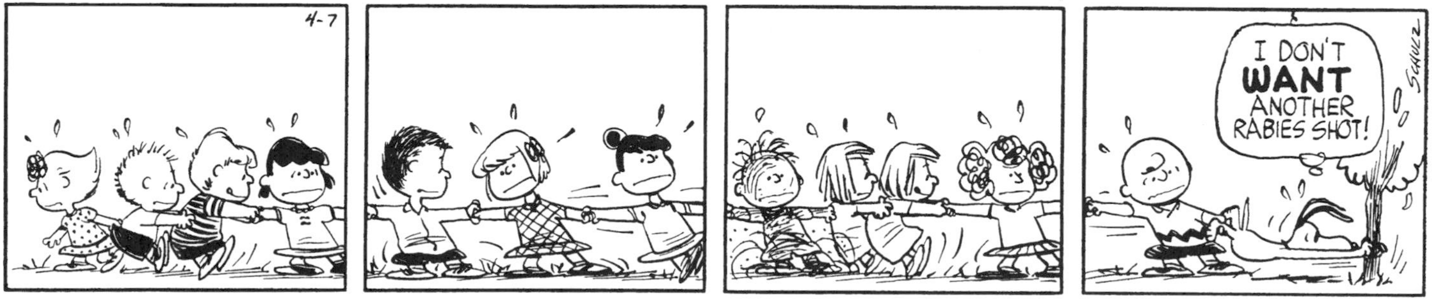
4-7
I DON'T **WANT** ANOTHER RABIES SHOT!
SCHULZ

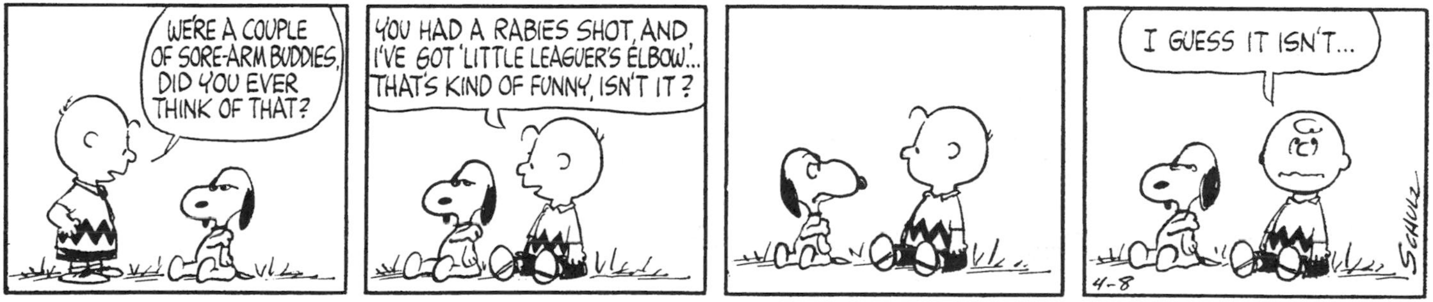
WE'RE A COUPLE OF SORE-ARM BUDDIES, DID YOU EVER THINK OF THAT?
YOU HAD A RABIES SHOT, AND I'VE GOT 'LITTLE LEAGUER'S ELBOW'... THAT'S KIND OF FUNNY, ISN'T IT?
I GUESS IT ISN'T...
SCHULZ
4-8

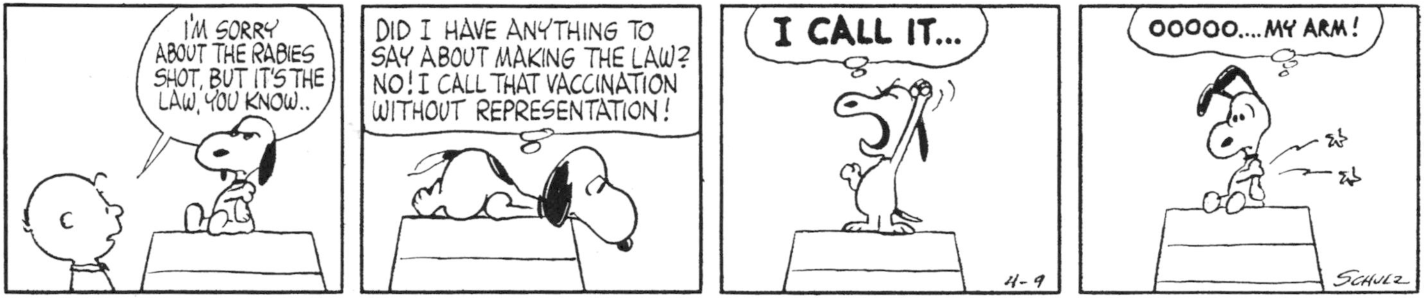
I'M SORRY ABOUT THE RABIES SHOT, BUT IT'S THE LAW, YOU KNOW..
DID I HAVE ANYTHING TO SAY ABOUT MAKING THE LAW? NO! I CALL THAT VACCINATION WITHOUT REPRESENTATION!
I CALL IT...
OOOOO....MY ARM!
4-9
SCHULZ

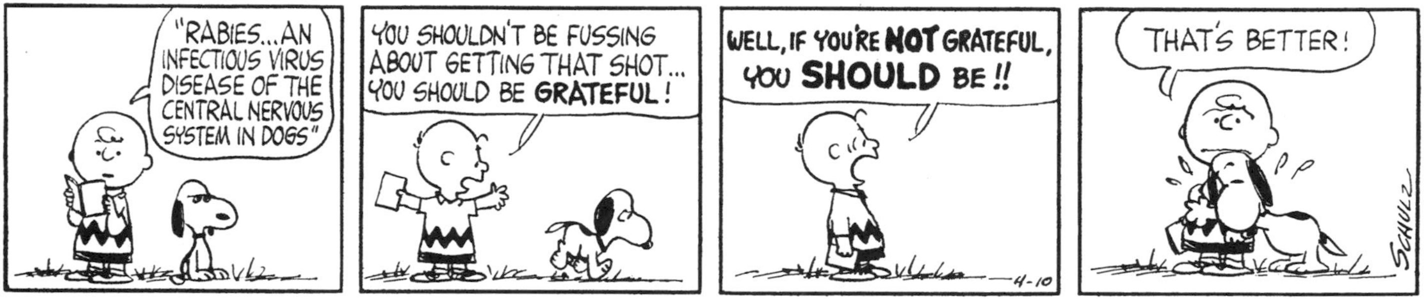
"RABIES...AN INFECTIOUS VIRUS DISEASE OF THE CENTRAL NERVOUS SYSTEM IN DOGS"
YOU SHOULDN'T BE FUSSING ABOUT GETTING THAT SHOT... YOU SHOULD BE GRATEFUL!
WELL, IF YOU'RE NOT GRATEFUL, YOU SHOULD BE!!
4-10
THAT'S BETTER!
SCHULZ

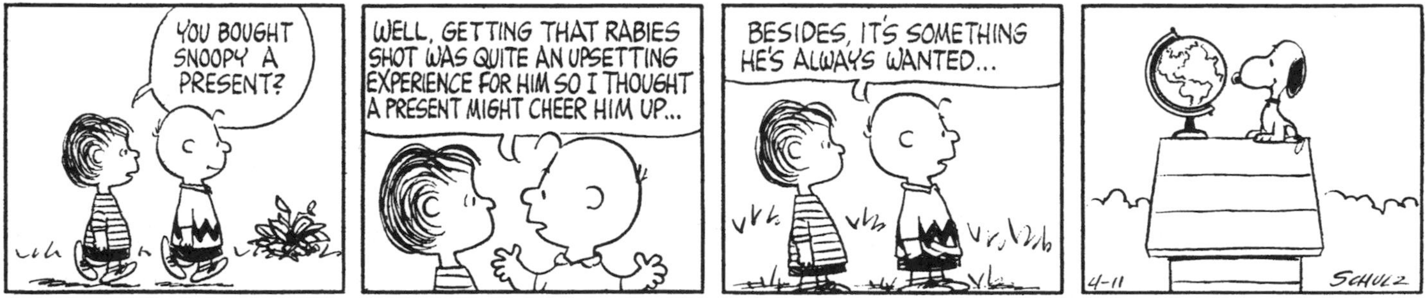
YOU BOUGHT SNOOPY A PRESENT?
WELL, GETTING THAT RABIES SHOT WAS QUITE AN UPSETTING EXPERIENCE FOR HIM SO I THOUGHT A PRESENT MIGHT CHEER HIM UP...
BESIDES, IT'S SOMETHING HE'S ALWAYS WANTED...
4-11
SCHULZ

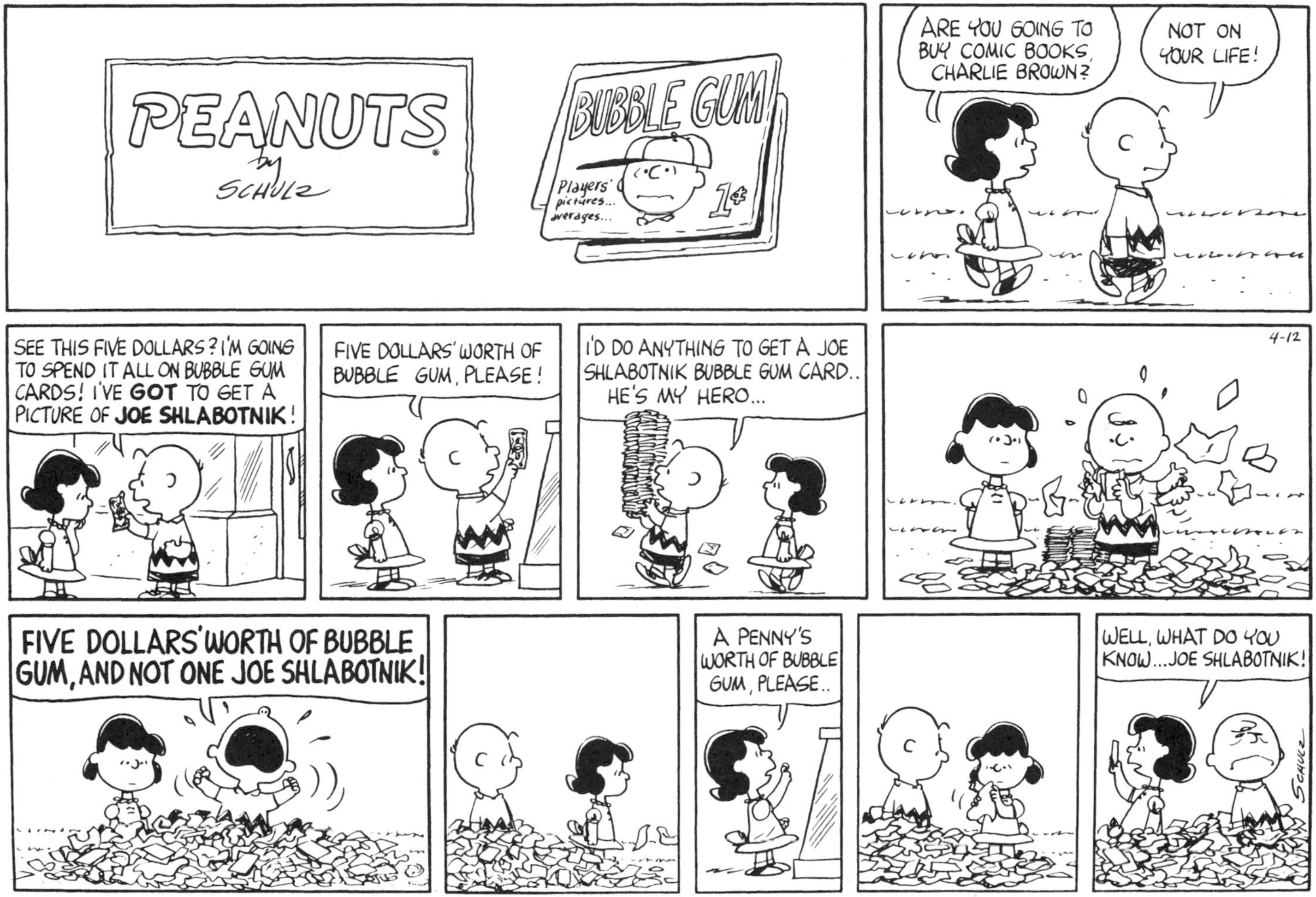
PEANUTS
by
SCHULZ
BUBBLE GUM
Players' pictures... averages...
1¢
ARE YOU GOING TO BUY COMIC BOOKS, CHARLIE BROWN?
NOT ON YOUR LIFE!
SEE THIS FIVE DOLLARS? I'M GOING TO SPEND IT ALL ON BUBBLE GUM CARDS! I'VE GOT TO GET A PICTURE OF JOE SHLABOTNIK!
FIVE DOLLARS' WORTH OF BUBBLE GUM, PLEASE!
I'D DO ANYTHING TO GET A JOE SHLABOTNIK BUBBLE GUM CARD.. HE'S MY HERO...
4-12
FIVE DOLLARS' WORTH OF BUBBLE GUM, AND NOT ONE JOE SHLABOTNIK!
A PENNY'S WORTH OF BUBBLE GUM, PLEASE..
WELL, WHAT DO YOU KNOW...JOE SHLABOTNIK!
SCHULZ

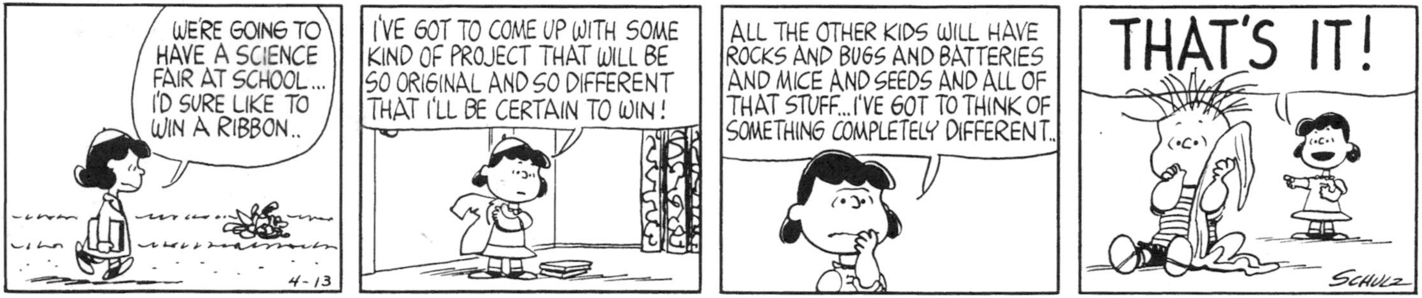
WE'RE GOING TO HAVE A SCIENCE FAIR AT SCHOOL... I'D SURE LIKE TO WIN A RIBBON..
4-13
I'VE GOT TO COME UP WITH SOME KIND OF PROJECT THAT WILL BE SO ORIGINAL AND SO DIFFERENT THAT I'LL BE CERTAIN TO WIN!
ALL THE OTHER KIDS WILL HAVE ROCKS AND BUGS AND BATTERIES AND MICE AND SEEDS AND ALL OF THAT STUFF...I'VE GOT TO THINK OF SOMETHING COMPLETELY DIFFERENT..
THAT'S IT!
SCHULZ

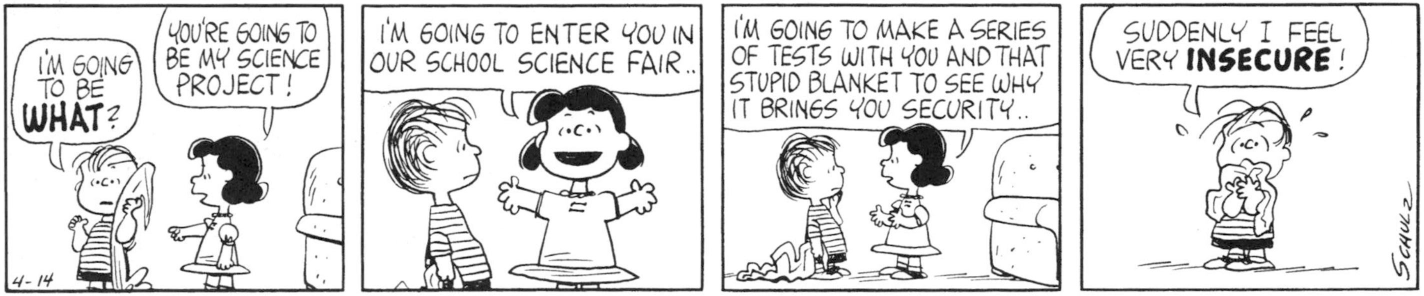
YOU'RE GOING TO BE MY SCIENCE PROJECT!
I'M GOING TO BE **WHAT**?
4-14
I'M GOING TO ENTER YOU IN OUR SCHOOL SCIENCE FAIR..
I'M GOING TO MAKE A SERIES OF TESTS WITH YOU AND THAT STUPID BLANKET TO SEE WHY IT BRINGS YOU SECURITY..
SUDDENLY I FEEL VERY **INSECURE**!
SCHULZ

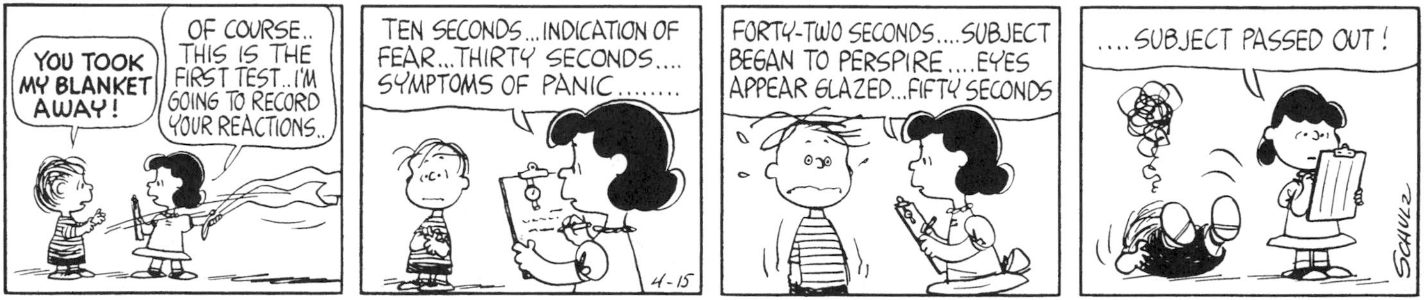
YOU TOOK MY BLANKET AWAY!
OF COURSE.. THIS IS THE FIRST TEST..I'M GOING TO RECORD YOUR REACTIONS..
TEN SECONDS...INDICATION OF FEAR...THIRTY SECONDS.... SYMPTOMS OF PANIC........
4-15
FORTY-TWO SECONDS....SUBJECT BEGAN TO PERSPIRE....EYES APPEAR GLAZED...FIFTY SECONDS
....SUBJECT PASSED OUT!
SCHULZ

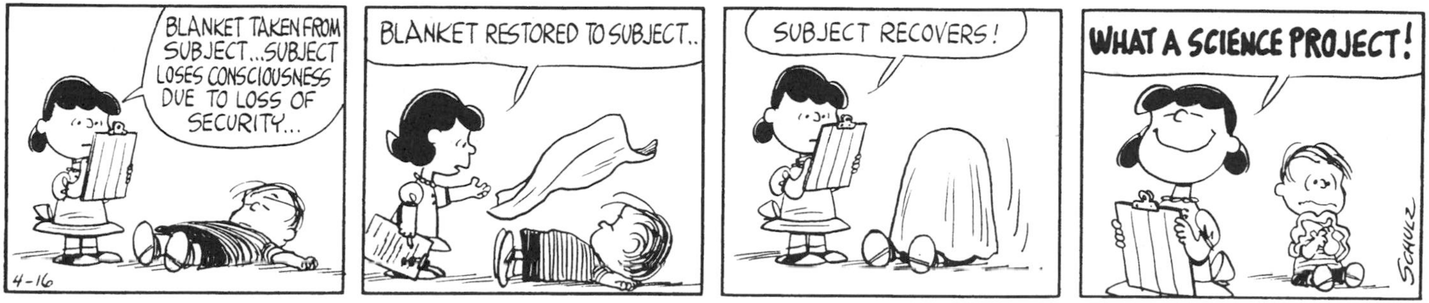
BLANKET TAKEN FROM SUBJECT...SUBJECT LOSES CONSCIOUSNESS DUE TO LOSS OF SECURITY...
BLANKET RESTORED TO SUBJECT..
SUBJECT RECOVERS!
WHAT A SCIENCE PROJECT!
4-16
SCHULZ

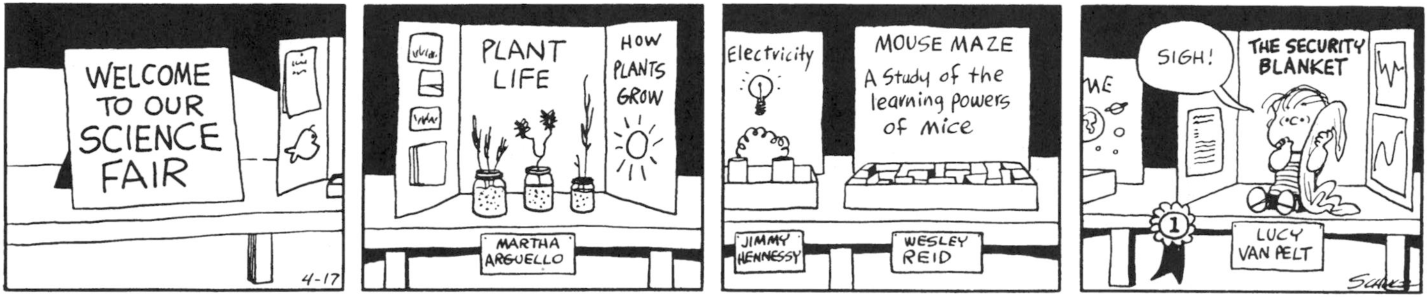
WELCOME TO OUR SCIENCE FAIR
4-17
PLANT LIFE
HOW PLANTS GROW
MARTHA ARGUELLO
Electricity
MOUSE MAZE
A Study of the learning powers of mice
JIMMY HENNESSY
WESLEY REID
SIGH!
THE SECURITY BLANKET
1
LUCY VAN PELT
SCHULZ

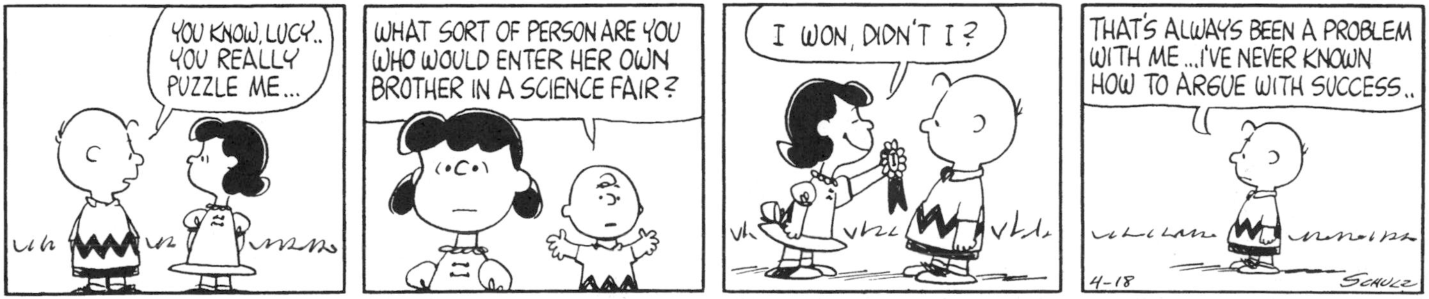
YOU KNOW, LUCY.. YOU REALLY PUZZLE ME...
WHAT SORT OF PERSON ARE YOU WHO WOULD ENTER HER OWN BROTHER IN A SCIENCE FAIR?
I WON, DIDN'T I?
THAT'S ALWAYS BEEN A PROBLEM WITH ME...I'VE NEVER KNOWN HOW TO ARGUE WITH SUCCESS..
4-18
SCHULZ

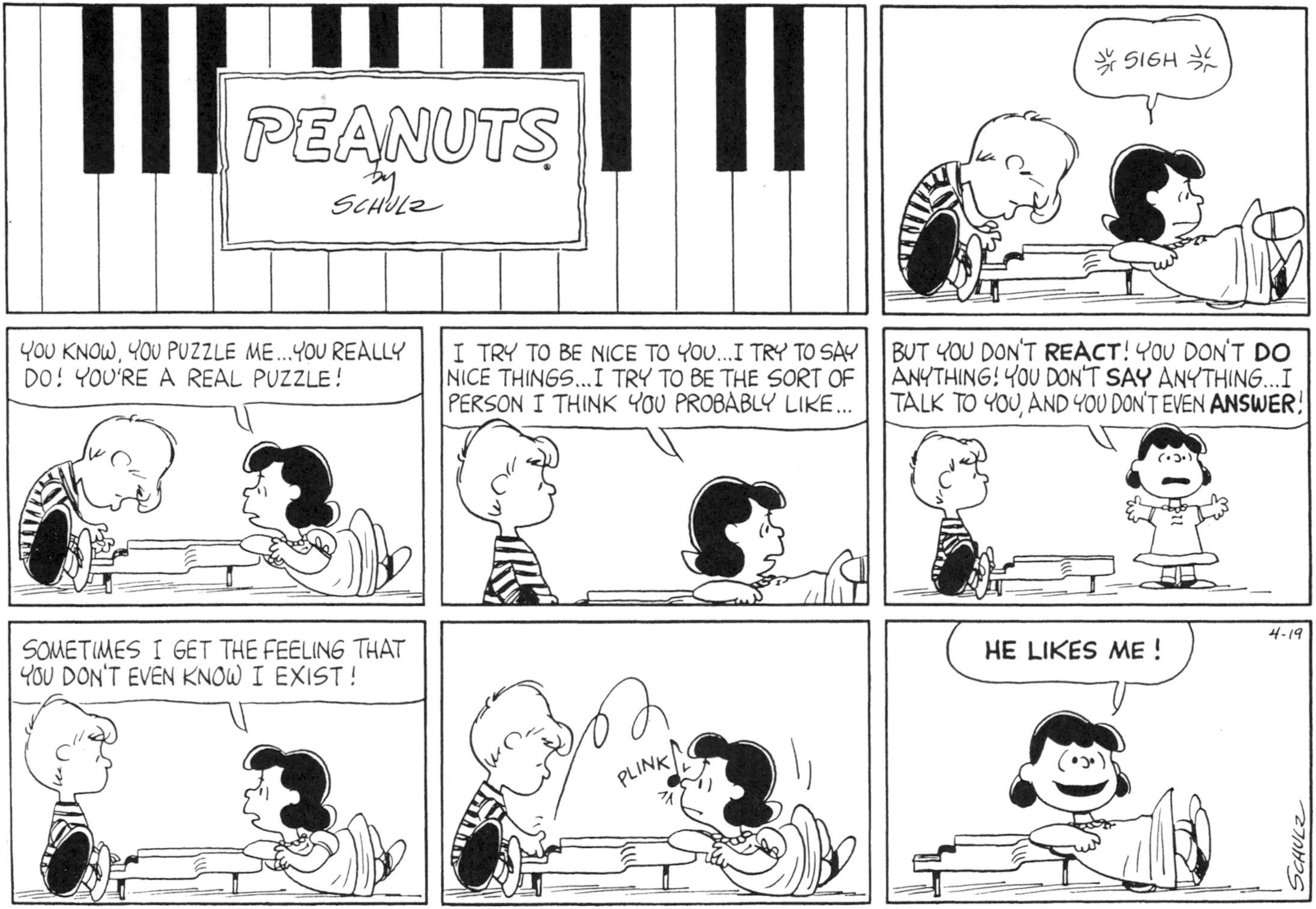
PEANUTS
by SCHULZ
SIGH
YOU KNOW, YOU PUZZLE ME...YOU REALLY DO! YOU'RE A REAL PUZZLE!
I TRY TO BE NICE TO YOU...I TRY TO SAY NICE THINGS...I TRY TO BE THE SORT OF PERSON I THINK YOU PROBABLY LIKE...
BUT YOU DON'T REACT! YOU DON'T DO ANYTHING! YOU DON'T SAY ANYTHING...I TALK TO YOU, AND YOU DON'T EVEN ANSWER!
SOMETIMES I GET THE FEELING THAT YOU DON'T EVEN KNOW I EXIST!
PLINK
4-19
HE LIKES ME!
SCHULZ

WHERE HAVE **YOU** BEEN ALL DAY?

I'VE BEEN MEDITATING..

I DON'T THINK IT HELPED YOU... YOU DON'T LOOK ANY DIFFERENT..

4-20

I'M NEW AT IT!

4-21

DOGS ARE STUPID! HOW IN THE WORLD IS HE GOING TO REMEMBER WHERE HE BURIED THAT BONE?

DON'T WORRY ABOUT HIM...

4/21/64

THIS "NEW MATH" IS TOO MUCH FOR ME!

4-22

YOU'LL GET ON TO IT... IT JUST TAKES TIME..

NOT ME... I'LL NEVER GET ON TO IT!

HOW CAN YOU DO "NEW MATH" PROBLEMS WITH AN "OLD MATH" MIND?

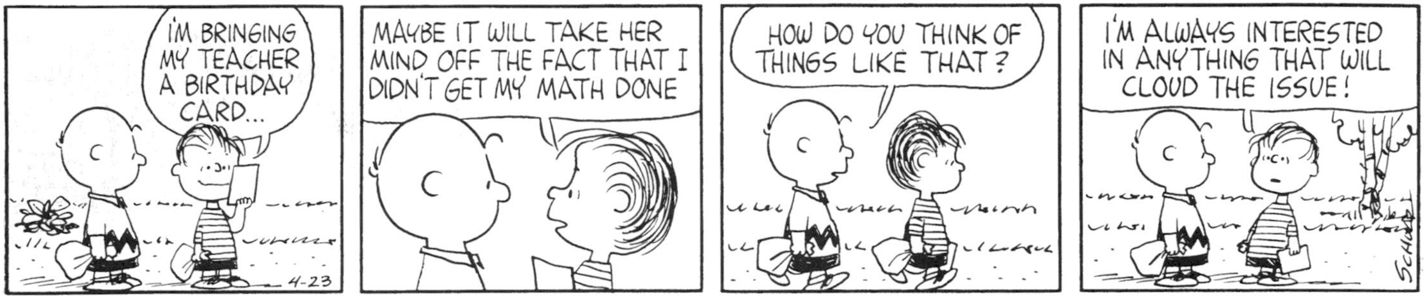
I'M BRINGING MY TEACHER A BIRTHDAY CARD...
MAYBE IT WILL TAKE HER MIND OFF THE FACT THAT I DIDN'T GET MY MATH DONE
HOW DO YOU THINK OF THINGS LIKE THAT?
I'M ALWAYS INTERESTED IN ANYTHING THAT WILL CLOUD THE ISSUE!
4-23
SCHULZ

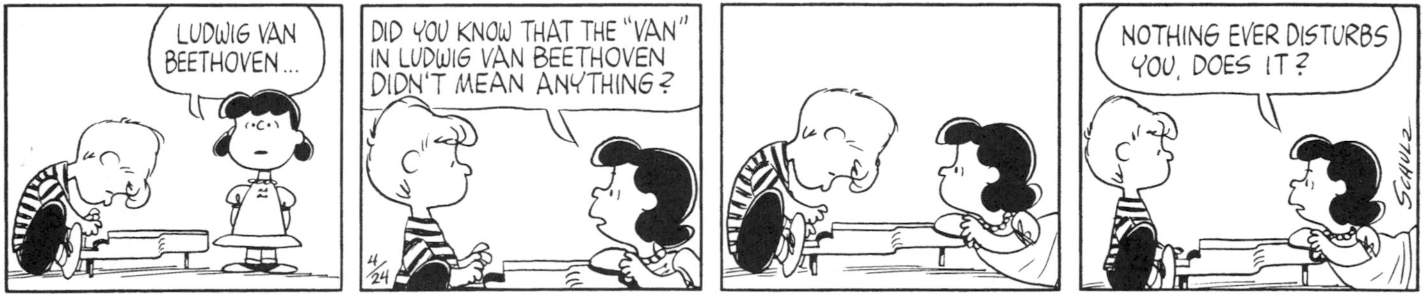
LUDWIG VAN BEETHOVEN...
DID YOU KNOW THAT THE "VAN" IN LUDWIG VAN BEETHOVEN DIDN'T MEAN ANYTHING?
4/24
NOTHING EVER DISTURBS YOU, DOES IT?
SCHULZ

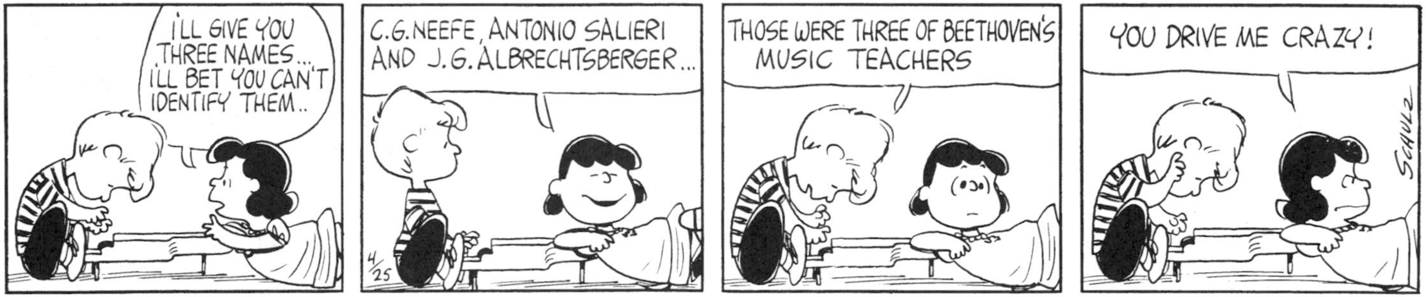
I'LL GIVE YOU THREE NAMES... I'LL BET YOU CAN'T IDENTIFY THEM..
C.G. NEEFE, ANTONIO SALIERI AND J.G. ALBRECHTSBERGER...
4/25
THOSE WERE THREE OF BEETHOVEN'S MUSIC TEACHERS
YOU DRIVE ME CRAZY!
SCHULZ

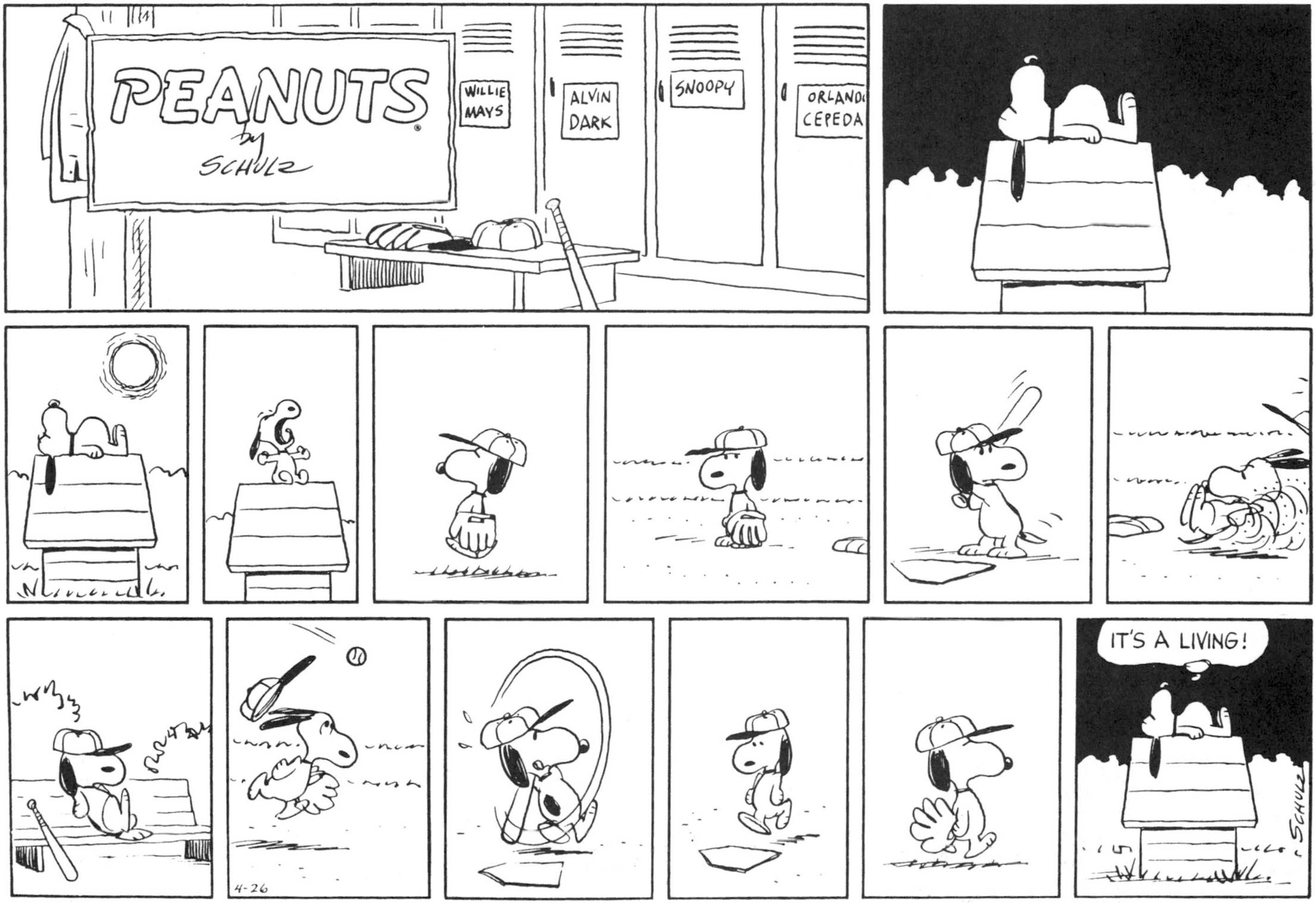
PEANUTS
by SCHULZ
WILLIE MAYS
ALVIN DARK
SNOOPY
ORLANDO CEPEDA
4-26
IT'S A LIVING!
SCHULZ

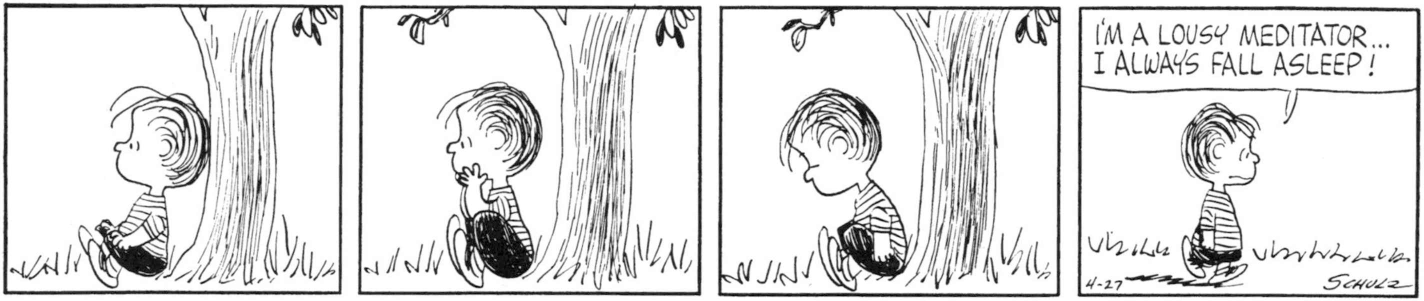
I'M A LOUSY MEDITATOR... I ALWAYS FALL ASLEEP!
4-27
SCHULZ

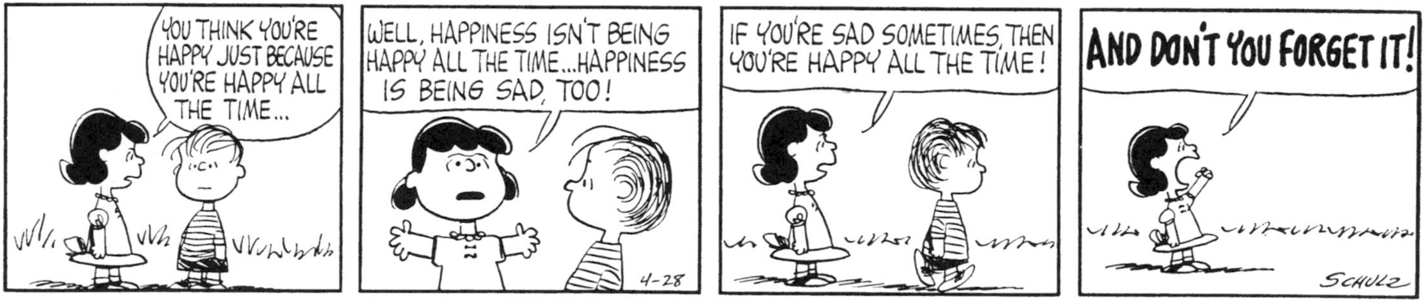
YOU THINK YOU'RE HAPPY JUST BECAUSE YOU'RE HAPPY ALL THE TIME...
WELL, HAPPINESS ISN'T BEING HAPPY ALL THE TIME...HAPPINESS IS BEING SAD, TOO!
4-28
IF YOU'RE SAD SOMETIMES, THEN YOU'RE HAPPY ALL THE TIME!
AND DON'T YOU FORGET IT!
SCHULZ

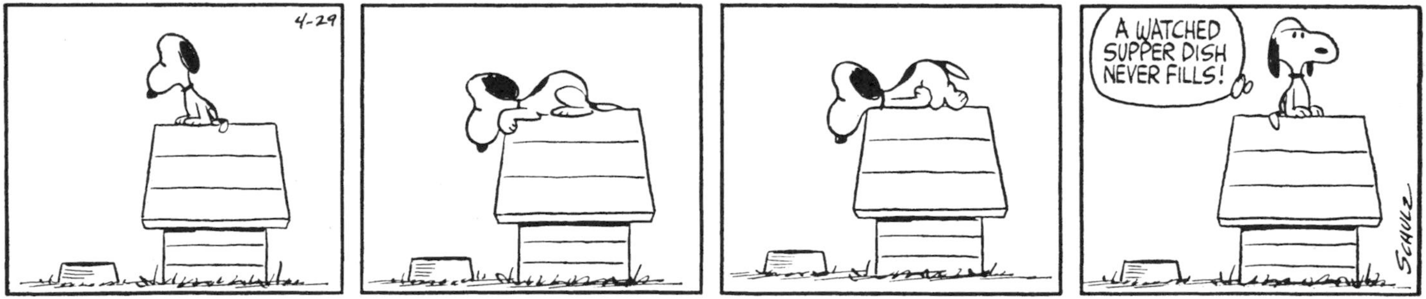
4-29
A WATCHED SUPPER DISH NEVER FILLS!
SCHULZ

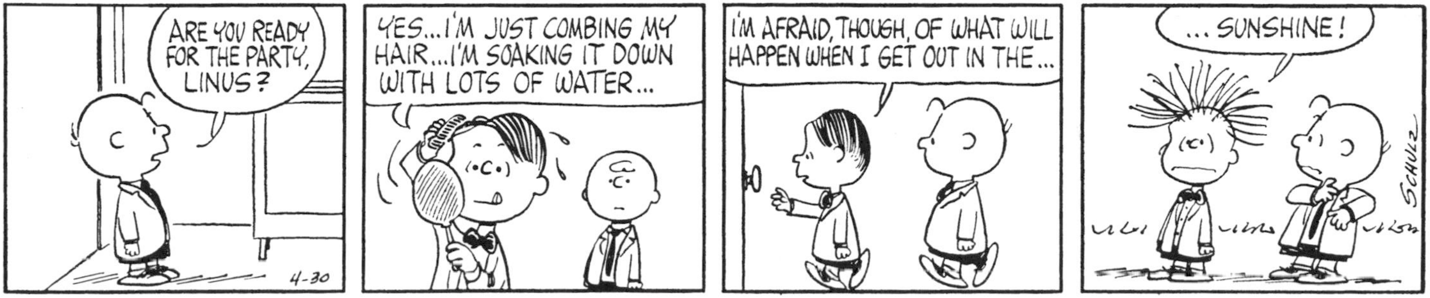
ARE YOU READY FOR THE PARTY, LINUS?
YES...I'M JUST COMBING MY HAIR...I'M SOAKING IT DOWN WITH LOTS OF WATER...
I'M AFRAID, THOUGH, OF WHAT WILL HAPPEN WHEN I GET OUT IN THE...
...SUNSHINE!

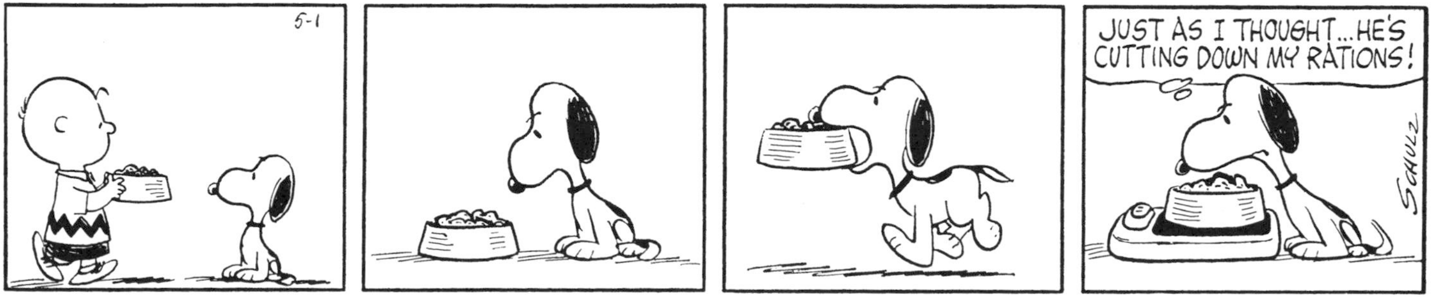
JUST AS I THOUGHT...HE'S CUTTING DOWN MY RATIONS!

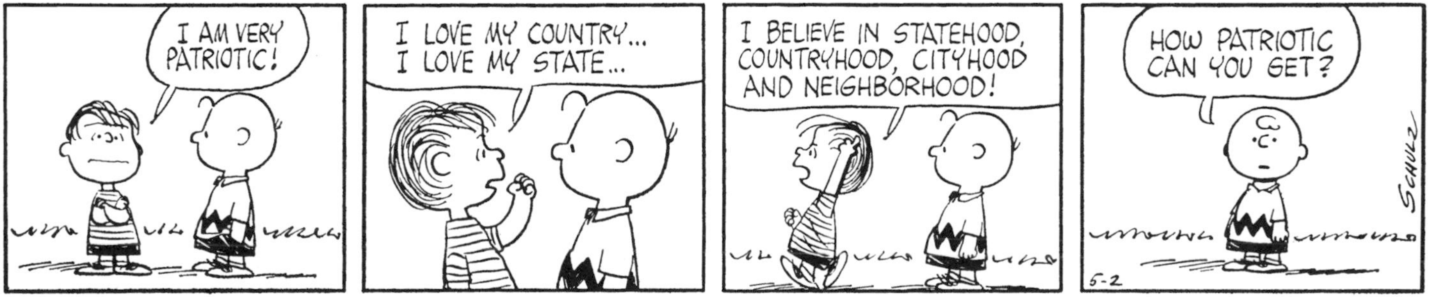
I AM VERY PATRIOTIC!
I LOVE MY COUNTRY... I LOVE MY STATE...
I BELIEVE IN STATEHOOD, COUNTRYHOOD, CITYHOOD AND NEIGHBORHOOD!
HOW PATRIOTIC CAN YOU GET?

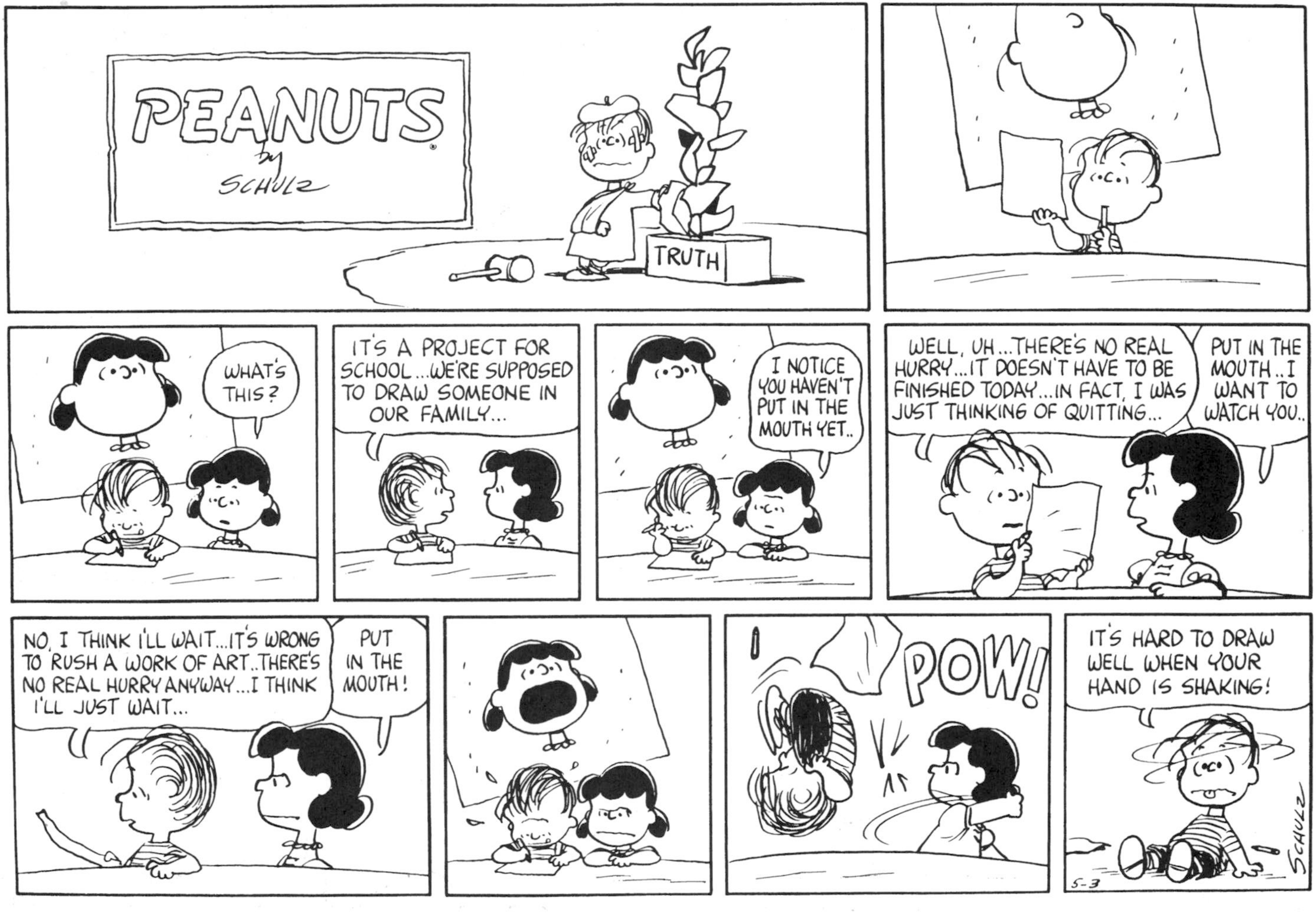
PEANUTS
by SCHULZ
TRUTH
WHAT'S THIS?
IT'S A PROJECT FOR SCHOOL...WE'RE SUPPOSED TO DRAW SOMEONE IN OUR FAMILY...
I NOTICE YOU HAVEN'T PUT IN THE MOUTH YET..
WELL, UH...THERE'S NO REAL HURRY...IT DOESN'T HAVE TO BE FINISHED TODAY...IN FACT, I WAS JUST THINKING OF QUITTING...
PUT IN THE MOUTH..I WANT TO WATCH YOU..
NO, I THINK I'LL WAIT...IT'S WRONG TO RUSH A WORK OF ART..THERE'S NO REAL HURRY ANYWAY...I THINK I'LL JUST WAIT...
PUT IN THE MOUTH!
POW!
5-3
SCHULZ
IT'S HARD TO DRAW WELL WHEN YOUR HAND IS SHAKING!

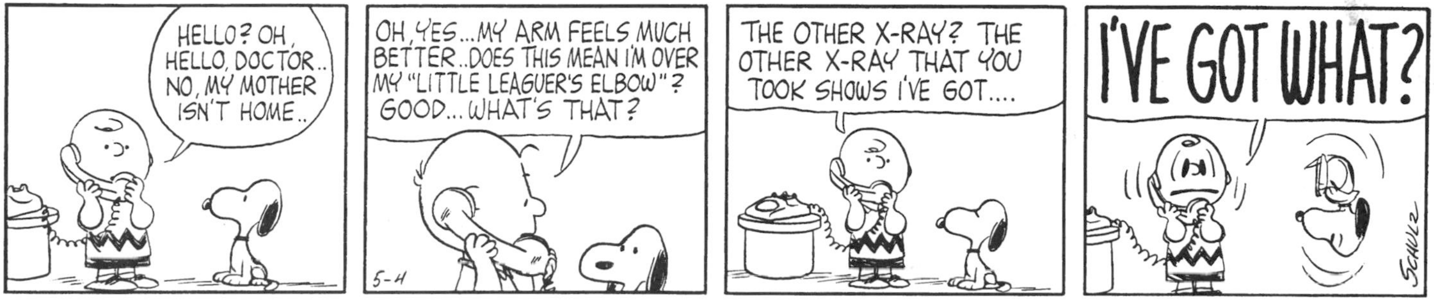
HELLO? OH, HELLO, DOCTOR.. NO, MY MOTHER ISN'T HOME..
OH, YES...MY ARM FEELS MUCH BETTER..DOES THIS MEAN I'M OVER MY "LITTLE LEAGUER'S ELBOW"? GOOD...WHAT'S THAT?
5-4
THE OTHER X-RAY? THE OTHER X-RAY THAT YOU TOOK SHOWS I'VE GOT....
I'VE GOT WHAT?
SCHULZ

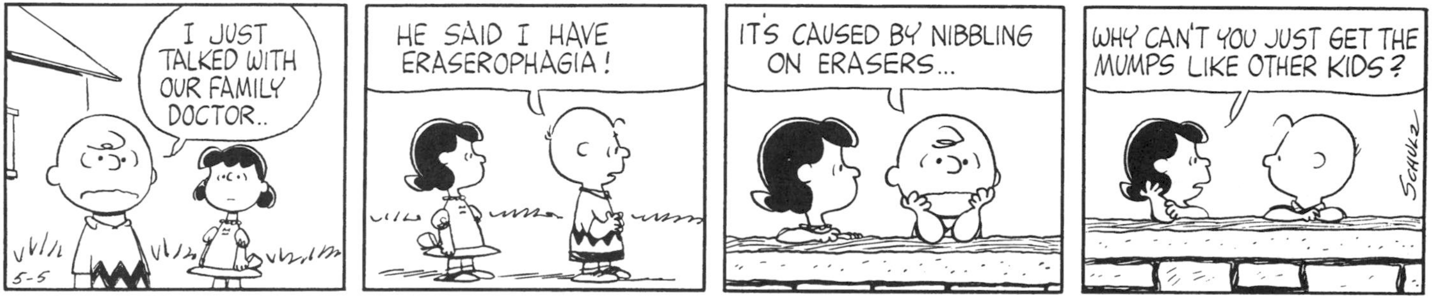
I JUST TALKED WITH OUR FAMILY DOCTOR..
5-5
HE SAID I HAVE ERASEROPHAGIA!
IT'S CAUSED BY NIBBLING ON ERASERS...
WHY CAN'T YOU JUST GET THE MUMPS LIKE OTHER KIDS?
SCHULZ

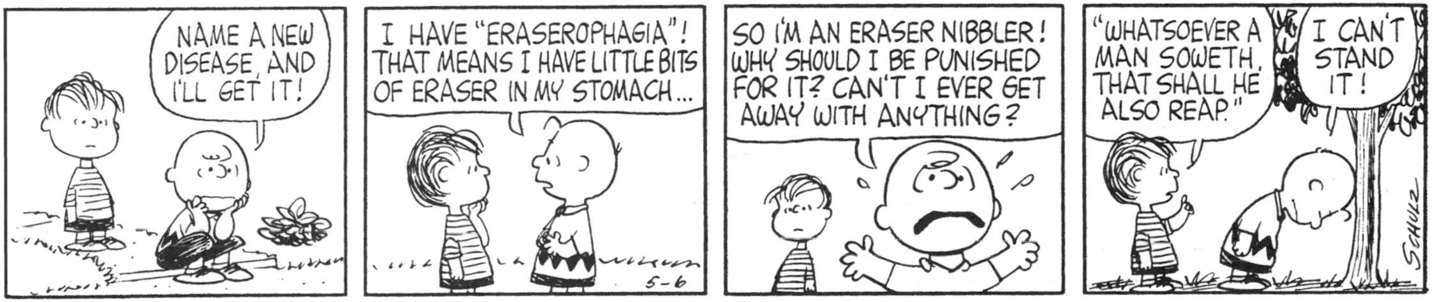
NAME A NEW DISEASE, AND I'LL GET IT!
I HAVE "ERASEROPHAGIA"! THAT MEANS I HAVE LITTLE BITS OF ERASER IN MY STOMACH...
5-6
SO I'M AN ERASER NIBBLER! WHY SHOULD I BE PUNISHED FOR IT? CAN'T I EVER GET AWAY WITH ANYTHING?
"WHATSOEVER A MAN SOWETH, THAT SHALL HE ALSO REAP."
I CAN'T STAND IT!
SCHULZ

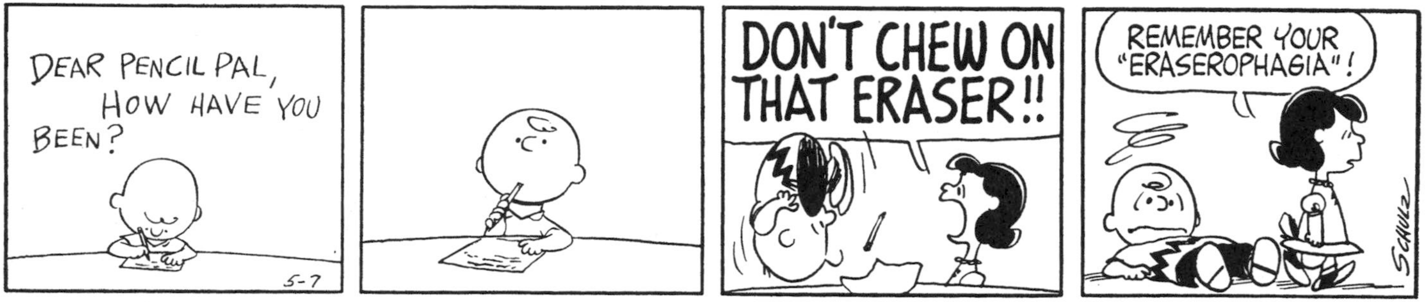
DEAR PENCIL PAL,
HOW HAVE YOU BEEN?
5-7
DON'T CHEW ON THAT ERASER!!
REMEMBER YOUR "ERASEROPHAGIA"!
SCHULZ

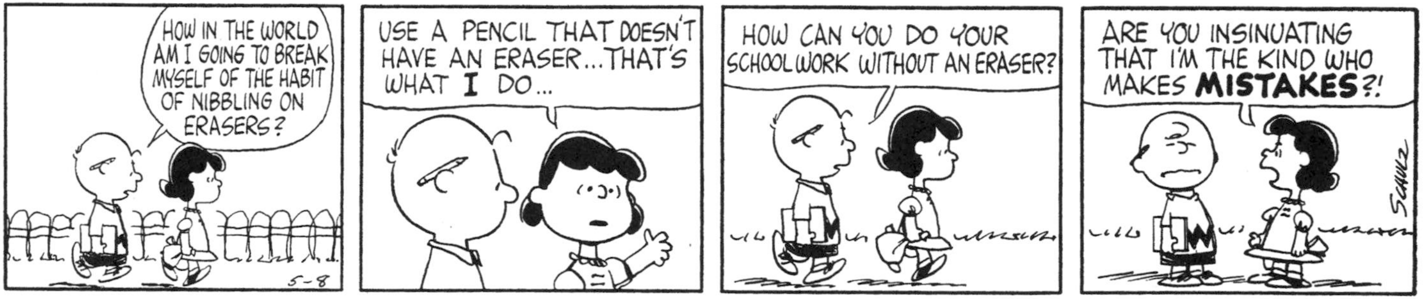
HOW IN THE WORLD AM I GOING TO BREAK MYSELF OF THE HABIT OF NIBBLING ON ERASERS?
5-8
USE A PENCIL THAT DOESN'T HAVE AN ERASER...THAT'S WHAT **I** DO...
HOW CAN YOU DO YOUR SCHOOLWORK WITHOUT AN ERASER?
ARE YOU INSINUATING THAT I'M THE KIND WHO MAKES **MISTAKES**?!
SCHULZ

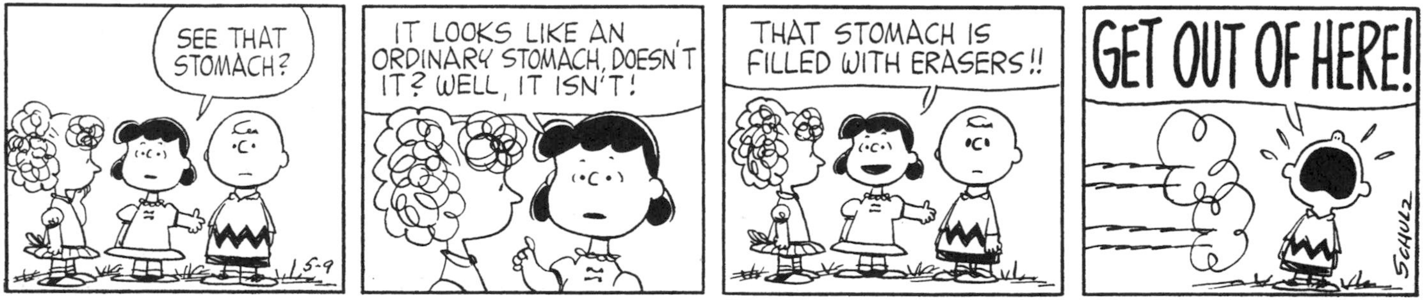
SEE THAT STOMACH?
5-9
IT LOOKS LIKE AN ORDINARY STOMACH, DOESN'T IT? WELL, IT ISN'T!
THAT STOMACH IS FILLED WITH ERASERS!!
GET OUT OF HERE!
SCHULZ

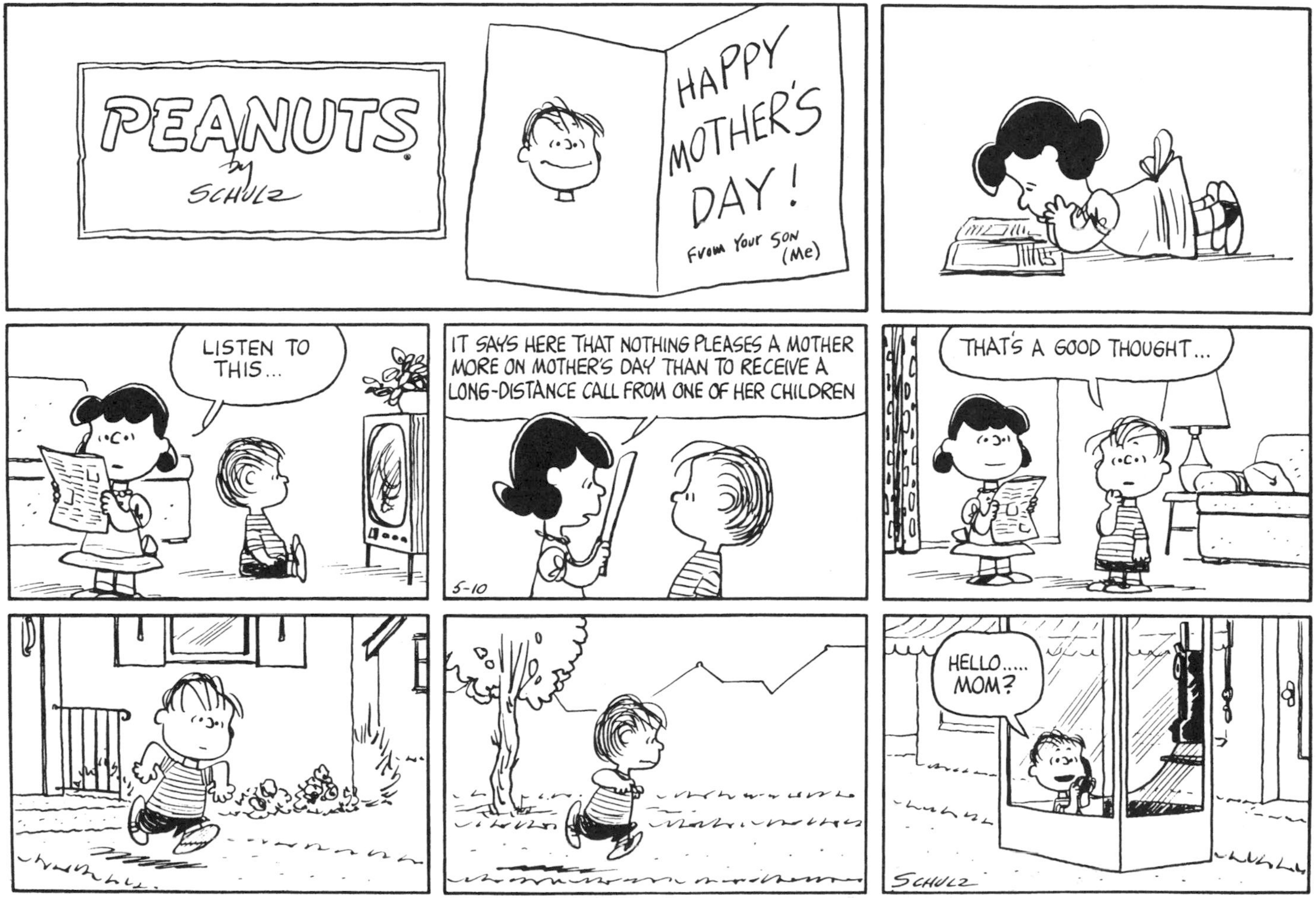
PEANUTS
by SCHULZ
HAPPY MOTHER'S DAY!
From Your Son (Me)
LISTEN TO THIS...
IT SAYS HERE THAT NOTHING PLEASES A MOTHER MORE ON MOTHER'S DAY THAN TO RECEIVE A LONG-DISTANCE CALL FROM ONE OF HER CHILDREN
5-10
THAT'S A GOOD THOUGHT...
HELLO..... MOM?
SCHULZ

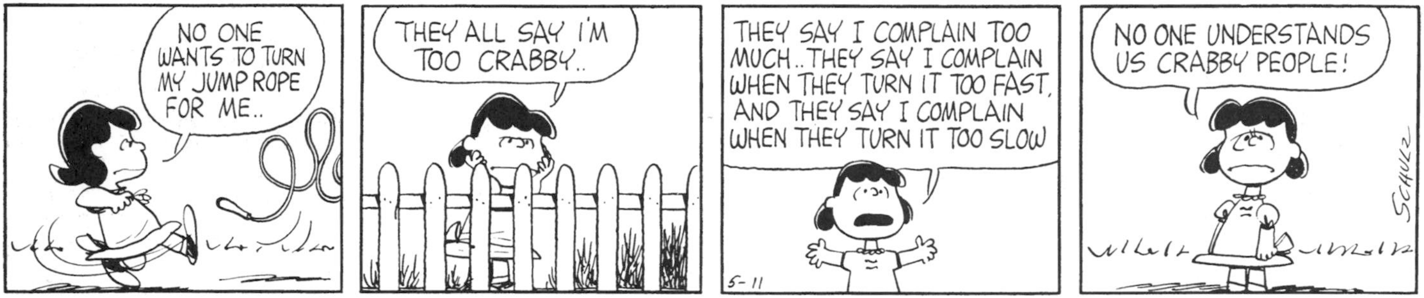
NO ONE WANTS TO TURN MY JUMP ROPE FOR ME..
THEY ALL SAY I'M TOO CRABBY..
THEY SAY I COMPLAIN TOO MUCH..THEY SAY I COMPLAIN WHEN THEY TURN IT TOO FAST, AND THEY SAY I COMPLAIN WHEN THEY TURN IT TOO SLOW
5-11
NO ONE UNDERSTANDS US CRABBY PEOPLE!
SCHULZ

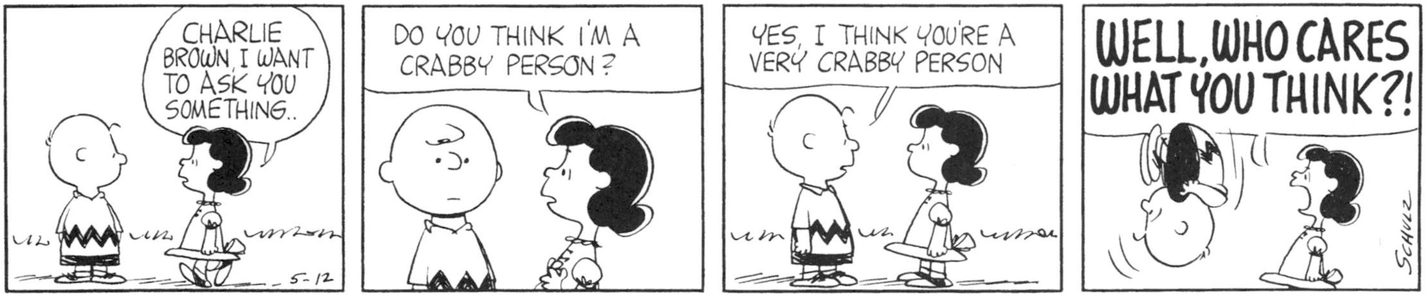
CHARLIE BROWN, I WANT TO ASK YOU SOMETHING..
5-12
DO YOU THINK I'M A CRABBY PERSON?
YES, I THINK YOU'RE A VERY CRABBY PERSON
WELL, WHO CARES WHAT YOU THINK?!
SCHULZ

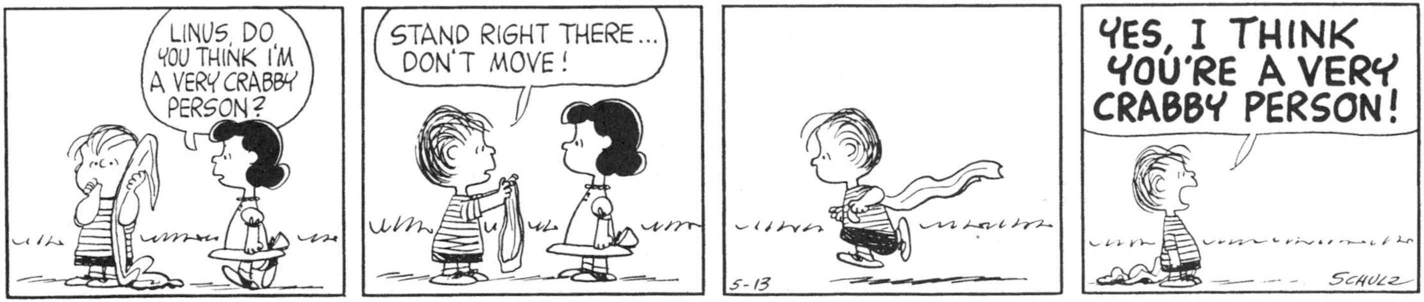
LINUS, DO YOU THINK I'M A VERY CRABBY PERSON?
STAND RIGHT THERE... DON'T MOVE!
5-13
YES, I THINK YOU'RE A VERY CRABBY PERSON!
SCHULZ

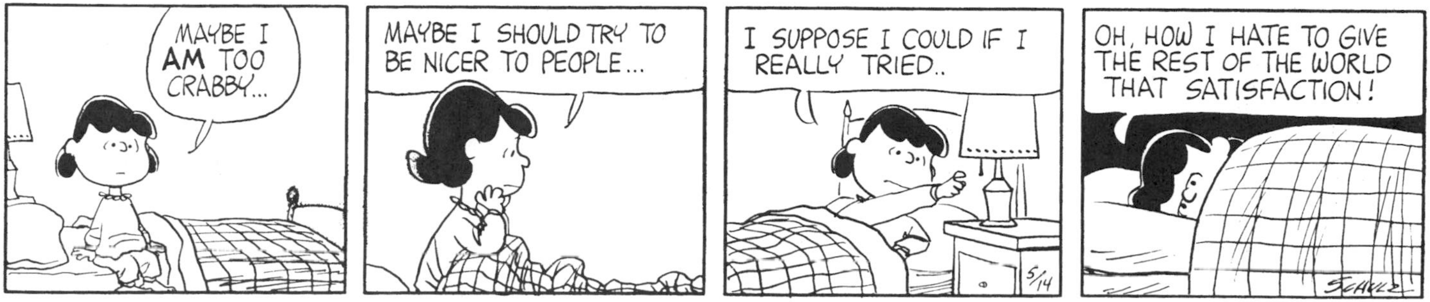
MAYBE I AM TOO CRABBY...
MAYBE I SHOULD TRY TO BE NICER TO PEOPLE...
I SUPPOSE I COULD IF I REALLY TRIED..
OH, HOW I HATE TO GIVE THE REST OF THE WORLD THAT SATISFACTION!

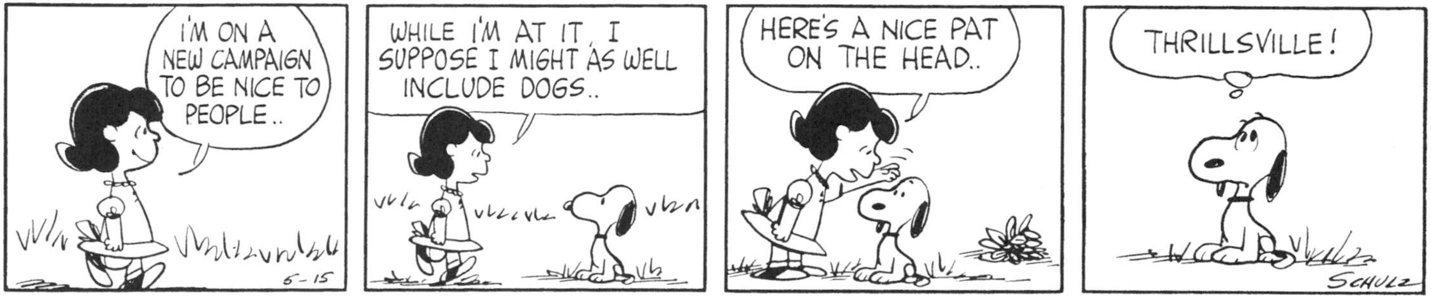
I'M ON A NEW CAMPAIGN TO BE NICE TO PEOPLE..
WHILE I'M AT IT, I SUPPOSE I MIGHT AS WELL INCLUDE DOGS..
HERE'S A NICE PAT ON THE HEAD..
THRILLSVILLE!

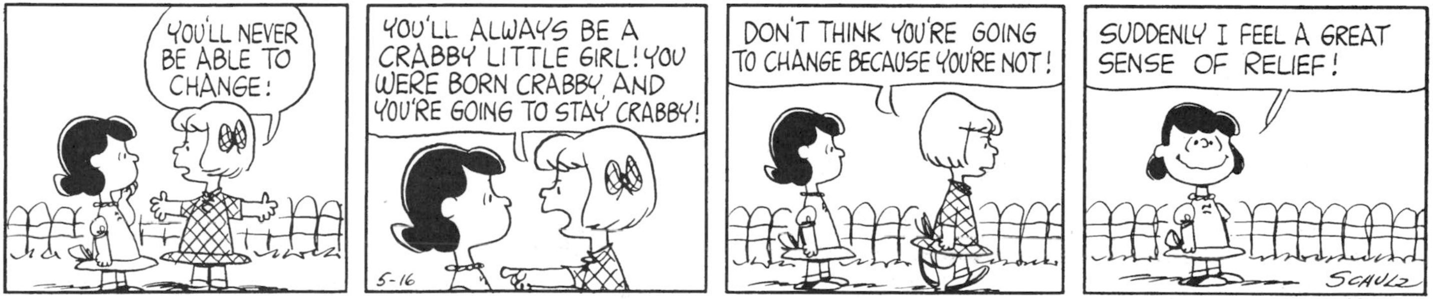
YOU'LL NEVER BE ABLE TO CHANGE!
YOU'LL ALWAYS BE A CRABBY LITTLE GIRL! YOU WERE BORN CRABBY AND YOU'RE GOING TO STAY CRABBY!
DON'T THINK YOU'RE GOING TO CHANGE BECAUSE YOU'RE NOT!
SUDDENLY I FEEL A GREAT SENSE OF RELIEF!

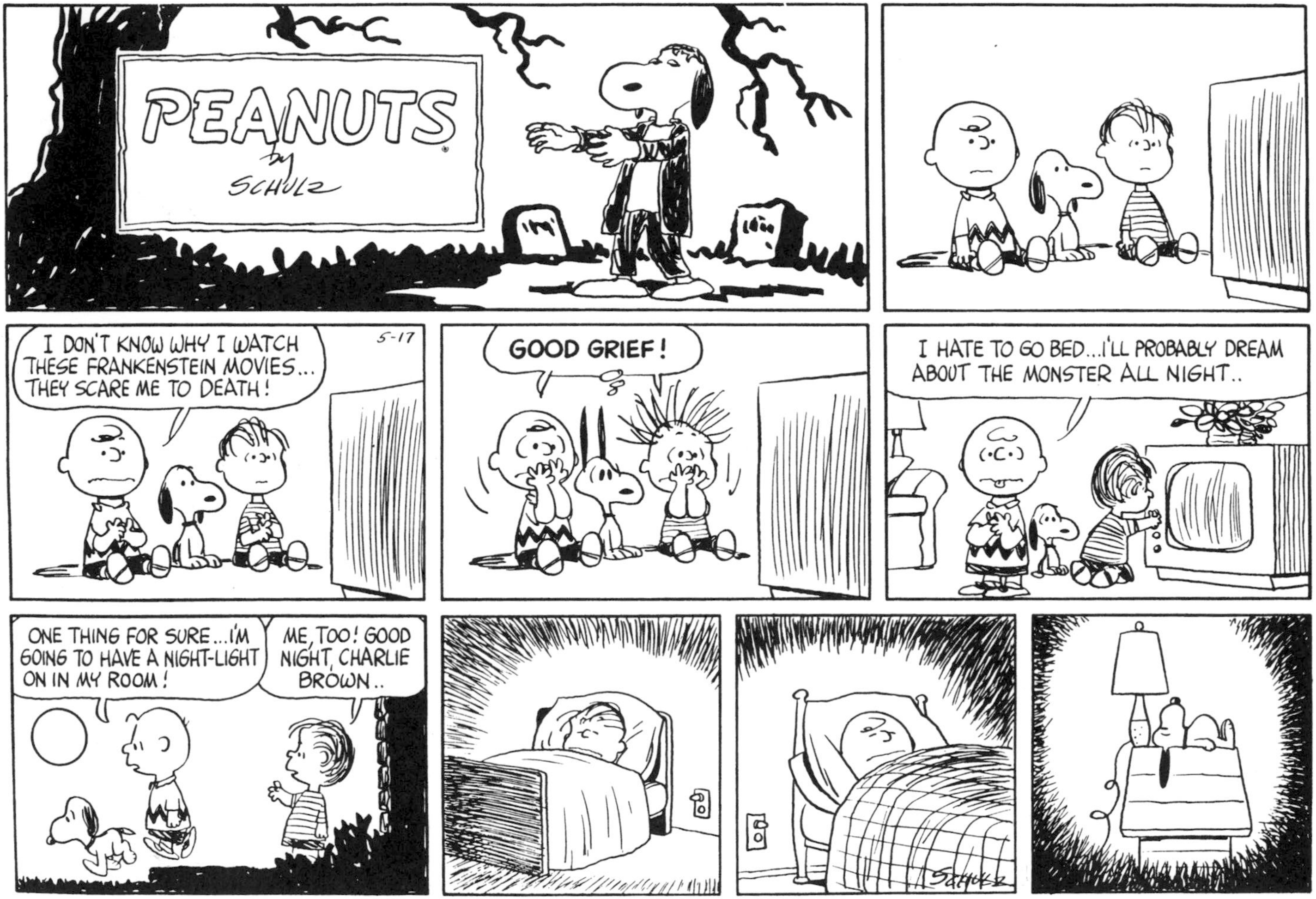
PEANUTS
by SCHULZ
5-17
I DON'T KNOW WHY I WATCH THESE FRANKENSTEIN MOVIES... THEY SCARE ME TO DEATH!
GOOD GRIEF!
I HATE TO GO BED...I'LL PROBABLY DREAM ABOUT THE MONSTER ALL NIGHT..
ONE THING FOR SURE...I'M GOING TO HAVE A NIGHT-LIGHT ON IN MY ROOM!
ME, TOO! GOOD NIGHT, CHARLIE BROWN..
SCHULZ

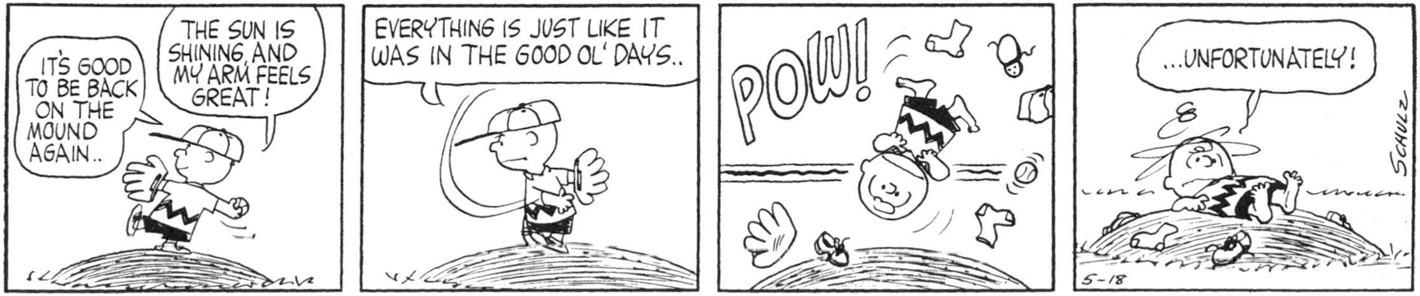
IT'S GOOD TO BE BACK ON THE MOUND AGAIN..
THE SUN IS SHINING, AND MY ARM FEELS GREAT!
EVERYTHING IS JUST LIKE IT WAS IN THE GOOD OL' DAYS..
POW!
...UNFORTUNATELY!
SCHULZ
5-18

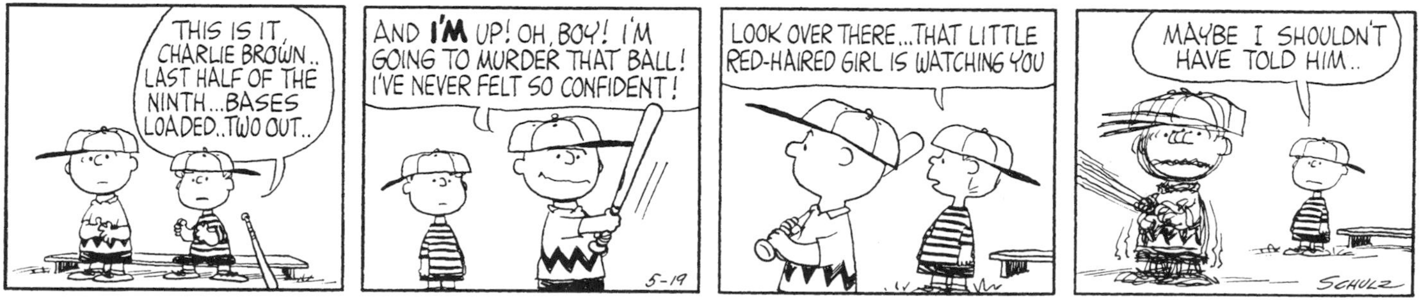
THIS IS IT, CHARLIE BROWN.. LAST HALF OF THE NINTH...BASES LOADED..TWO OUT..
AND I'M UP! OH, BOY! I'M GOING TO MURDER THAT BALL! I'VE NEVER FELT SO CONFIDENT!
5-19
LOOK OVER THERE...THAT LITTLE RED-HAIRED GIRL IS WATCHING YOU
MAYBE I SHOULDN'T HAVE TOLD HIM..
SCHULZ

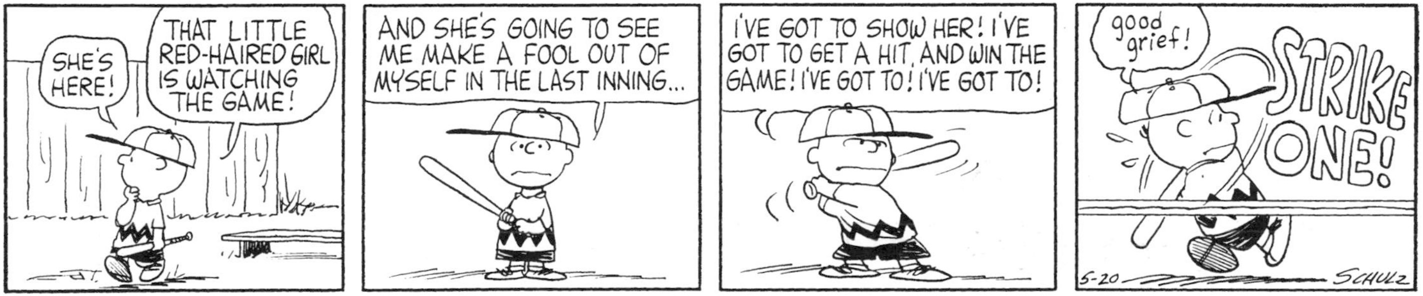
SHE'S HERE!
THAT LITTLE RED-HAIRED GIRL IS WATCHING THE GAME!
AND SHE'S GOING TO SEE ME MAKE A FOOL OUT OF MYSELF IN THE LAST INNING...
I'VE GOT TO SHOW HER! I'VE GOT TO GET A HIT, AND WIN THE GAME! I'VE GOT TO! I'VE GOT TO!
good grief!
STRIKE ONE!
5-20
SCHULZ

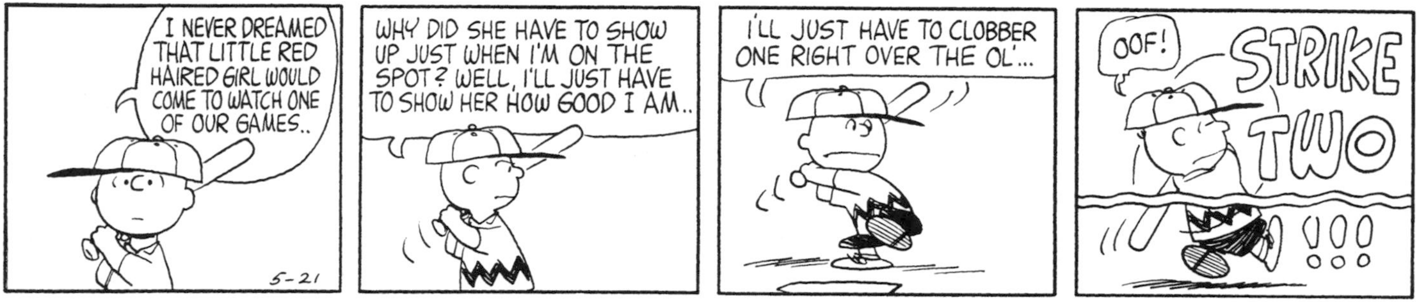
I NEVER DREAMED THAT LITTLE RED HAIRED GIRL WOULD COME TO WATCH ONE OF OUR GAMES..
5-21
WHY DID SHE HAVE TO SHOW UP JUST WHEN I'M ON THE SPOT? WELL, I'LL JUST HAVE TO SHOW HER HOW GOOD I AM..
I'LL JUST HAVE TO CLOBBER ONE RIGHT OVER THE OL'...
OOF!
STRIKE TWO
!!!

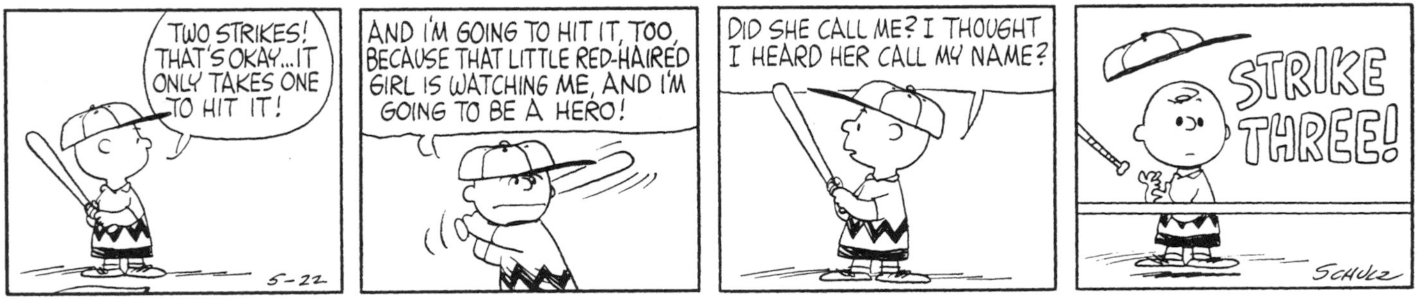
TWO STRIKES! THAT'S OKAY...IT ONLY TAKES ONE TO HIT IT!
5-22
AND I'M GOING TO HIT IT, TOO, BECAUSE THAT LITTLE RED-HAIRED GIRL IS WATCHING ME, AND I'M GOING TO BE A HERO!
DID SHE CALL ME? I THOUGHT I HEARD HER CALL MY NAME?
STRIKE THREE!
SCHULZ

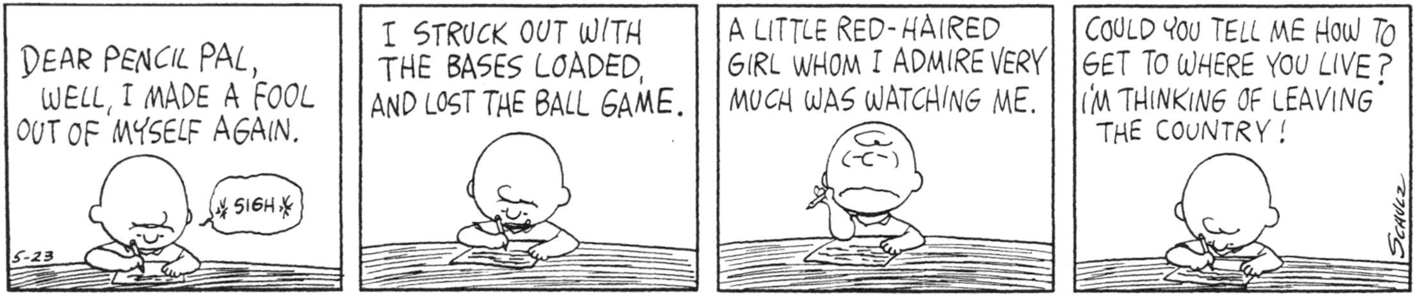
DEAR PENCIL PAL, WELL, I MADE A FOOL OUT OF MYSELF AGAIN.
SIGH
5-23
I STRUCK OUT WITH THE BASES LOADED, AND LOST THE BALL GAME.
A LITTLE RED-HAIRED GIRL WHOM I ADMIRE VERY MUCH WAS WATCHING ME.
COULD YOU TELL ME HOW TO GET TO WHERE YOU LIVE? I'M THINKING OF LEAVING THE COUNTRY!
SCHULZ

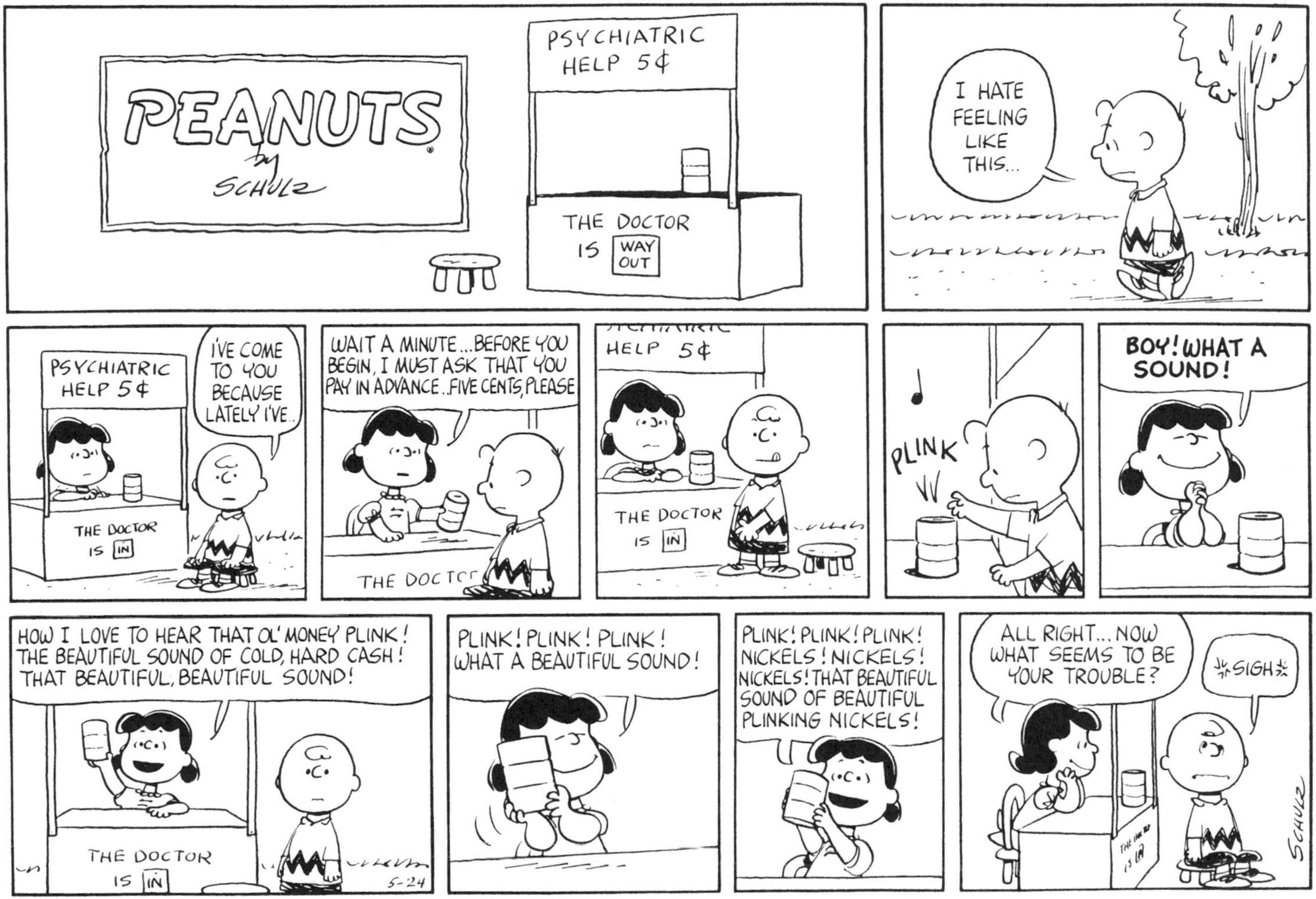
PEANUTS
by SCHULZ
PSYCHIATRIC HELP 5¢
THE DOCTOR IS WAY OUT
I HATE FEELING LIKE THIS...
PSYCHIATRIC HELP 5¢
THE DOCTOR IS IN
I'VE COME TO YOU BECAUSE LATELY I'VE..
WAIT A MINUTE...BEFORE YOU BEGIN, I MUST ASK THAT YOU PAY IN ADVANCE..FIVE CENTS, PLEASE
HELP 5¢
THE DOCTOR IS IN
PLINK
BOY! WHAT A SOUND!
HOW I LOVE TO HEAR THAT OL' MONEY PLINK! THE BEAUTIFUL SOUND OF COLD, HARD CASH! THAT BEAUTIFUL, BEAUTIFUL SOUND!
THE DOCTOR IS IN
5-24
PLINK! PLINK! PLINK! WHAT A BEAUTIFUL SOUND!
PLINK! PLINK! PLINK! NICKELS! NICKELS! NICKELS! THAT BEAUTIFUL SOUND OF BEAUTIFUL PLINKING NICKELS!
ALL RIGHT... NOW WHAT SEEMS TO BE YOUR TROUBLE?
SIGH
SCHULZ

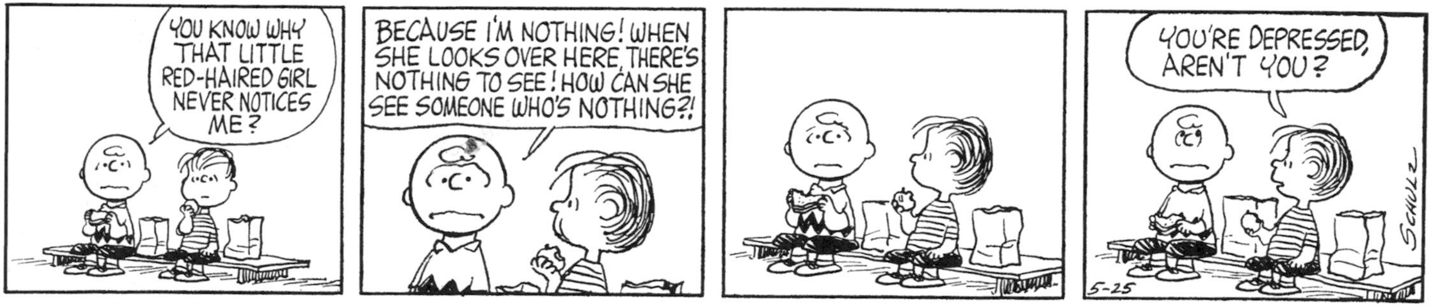
YOU KNOW WHY THAT LITTLE RED-HAIRED GIRL NEVER NOTICES ME?
BECAUSE I'M NOTHING! WHEN SHE LOOKS OVER HERE, THERE'S NOTHING TO SEE! HOW CAN SHE SEE SOMEONE WHO'S NOTHING?!
YOU'RE DEPRESSED, AREN'T YOU?
5-25
SCHULZ

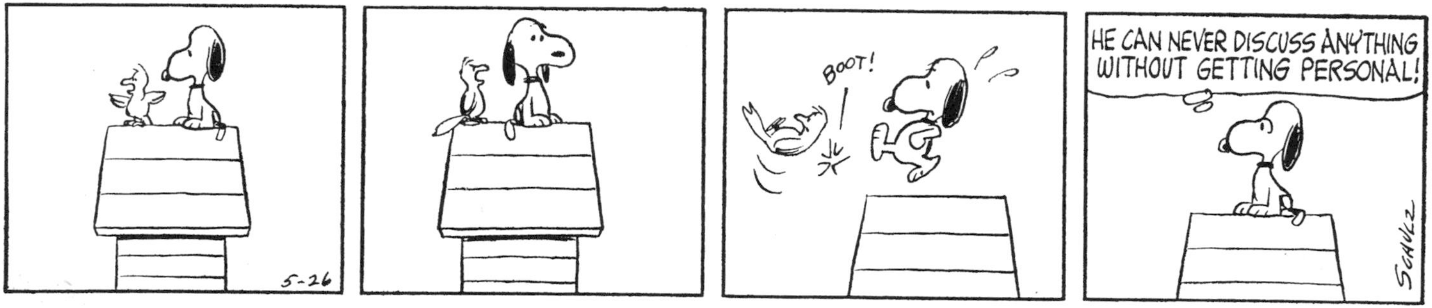
5-26
BOOT!
HE CAN NEVER DISCUSS ANYTHING WITHOUT GETTING PERSONAL!
SCHULZ

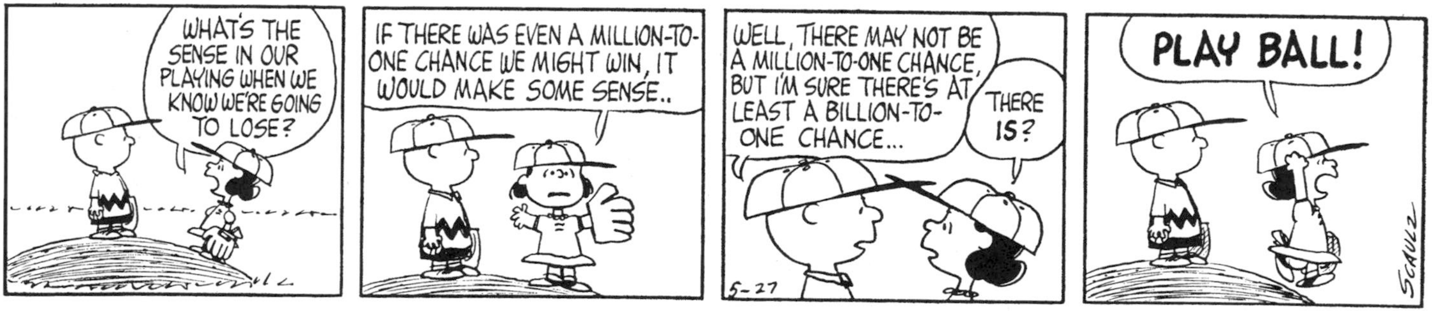
WHAT'S THE SENSE IN OUR PLAYING WHEN WE KNOW WE'RE GOING TO LOSE?
IF THERE WAS EVEN A MILLION-TO-ONE CHANCE WE MIGHT WIN, IT WOULD MAKE SOME SENSE..
WELL, THERE MAY NOT BE A MILLION-TO-ONE CHANCE, BUT I'M SURE THERE'S AT LEAST A BILLION-TO-ONE CHANCE...
THERE IS?
5-27
PLAY BALL!
SCHULZ

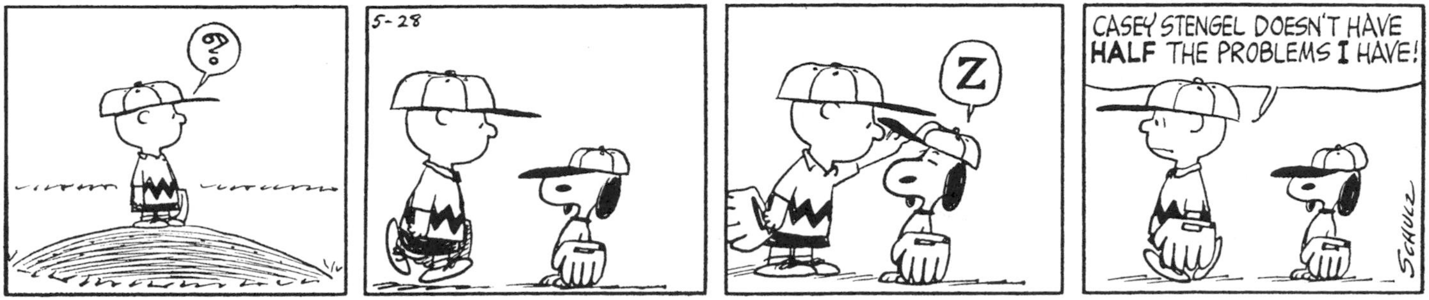
?
5-28
Z
CASEY STENGEL DOESN'T HAVE **HALF** THE PROBLEMS **I** HAVE!
SCHULZ

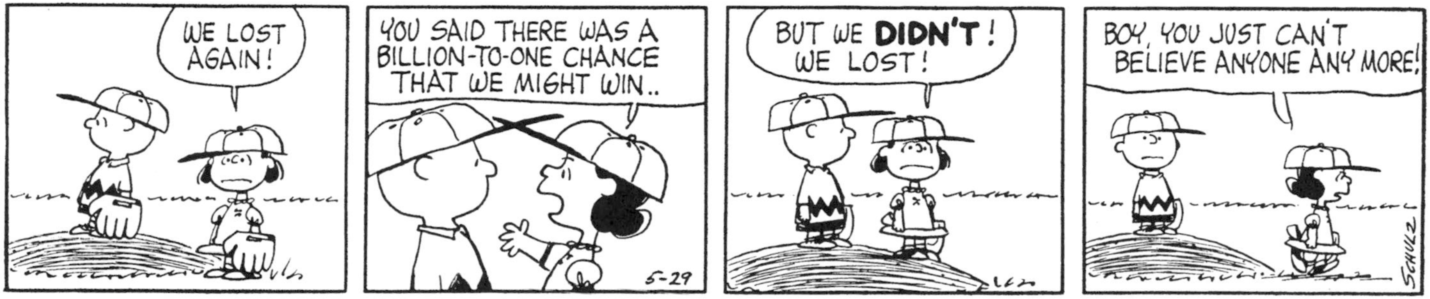
WE LOST AGAIN!
YOU SAID THERE WAS A BILLION-TO-ONE CHANCE THAT WE MIGHT WIN..
5-29
BUT WE **DIDN'T**! WE LOST!
BOY, YOU JUST CAN'T BELIEVE ANYONE ANY MORE!
SCHULZ

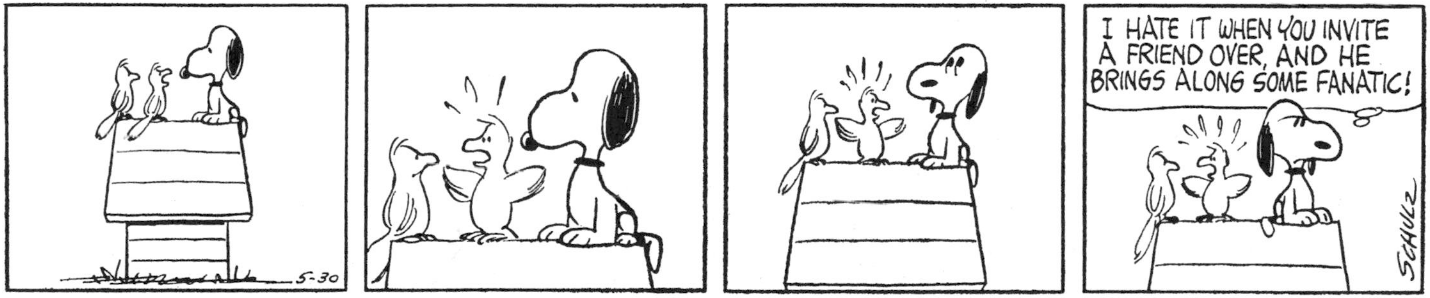
5-30
I HATE IT WHEN YOU INVITE A FRIEND OVER, AND HE BRINGS ALONG SOME FANATIC!
SCHULZ

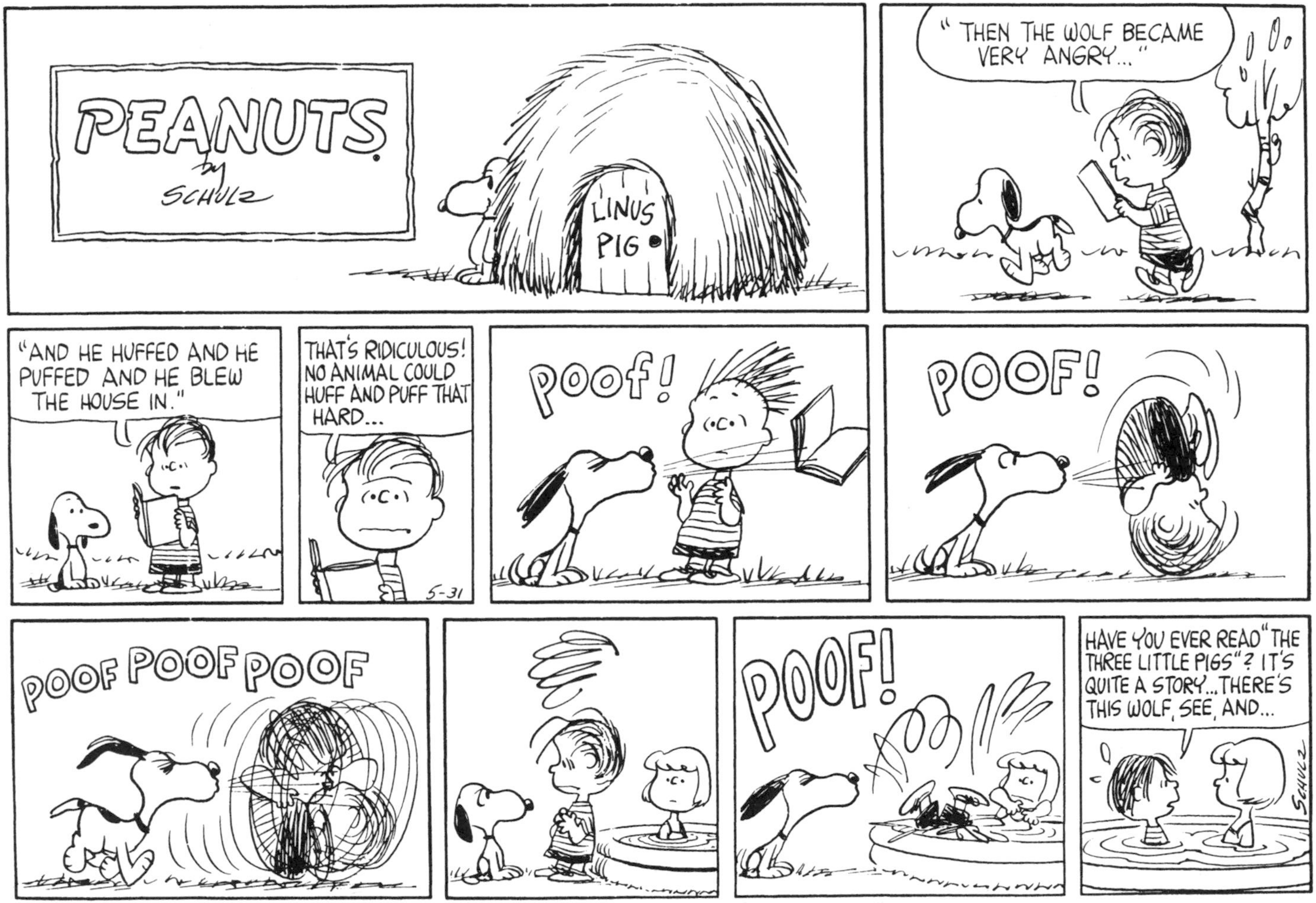
PEANUTS
by SCHULZ
LINUS PIG
" THEN THE WOLF BECAME VERY ANGRY..."
"AND HE HUFFED AND HE PUFFED AND HE BLEW THE HOUSE IN."
THAT'S RIDICULOUS! NO ANIMAL COULD HUFF AND PUFF THAT HARD...
5-31
POOF!
POOF!
POOF POOF POOF
POOF!
HAVE YOU EVER READ "THE THREE LITTLE PIGS"? IT'S QUITE A STORY... THERE'S THIS WOLF, SEE, AND...
SCHULZ

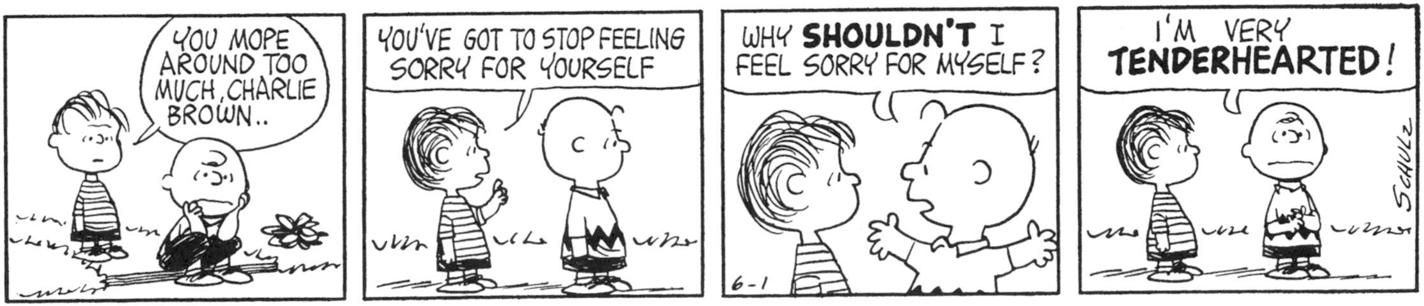
YOU MOPE AROUND TOO MUCH, CHARLIE BROWN..
YOU'VE GOT TO STOP FEELING SORRY FOR YOURSELF
WHY **SHOULDN'T** I FEEL SORRY FOR MYSELF?
I'M VERY **TENDERHEARTED**!
6-1
SCHULZ

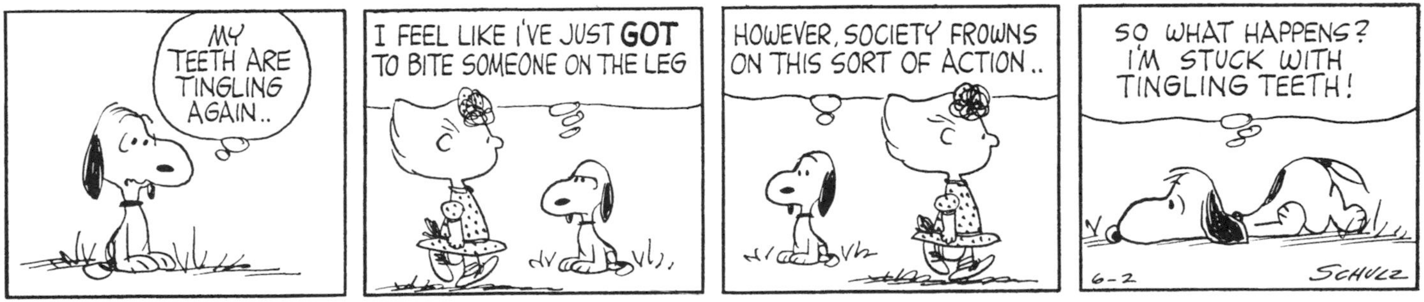
MY TEETH ARE TINGLING AGAIN..
I FEEL LIKE I'VE JUST **GOT** TO BITE SOMEONE ON THE LEG
HOWEVER, SOCIETY FROWNS ON THIS SORT OF ACTION..
SO WHAT HAPPENS? I'M STUCK WITH TINGLING TEETH!
6-2
SCHULZ

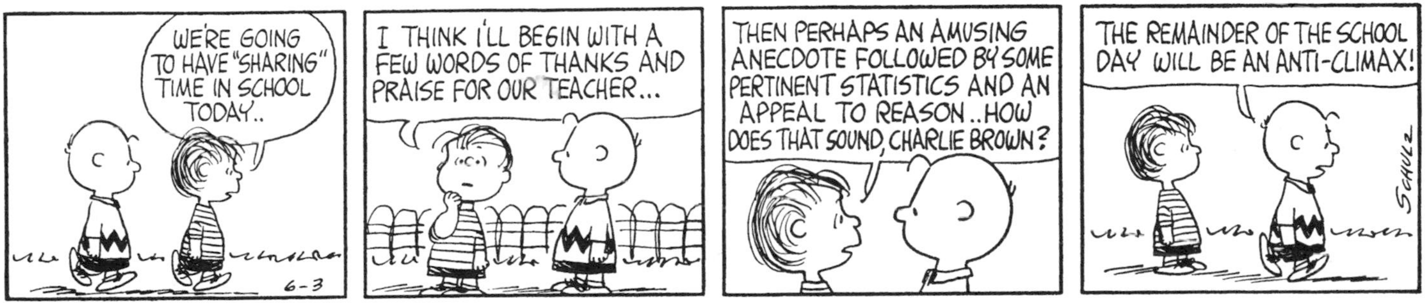
WE'RE GOING TO HAVE "SHARING" TIME IN SCHOOL TODAY..
I THINK I'LL BEGIN WITH A FEW WORDS OF THANKS AND PRAISE FOR OUR TEACHER...
THEN PERHAPS AN AMUSING ANECDOTE FOLLOWED BY SOME PERTINENT STATISTICS AND AN APPEAL TO REASON..HOW DOES THAT SOUND, CHARLIE BROWN?
THE REMAINDER OF THE SCHOOL DAY WILL BE AN ANTI-CLIMAX!
6-3
SCHULZ

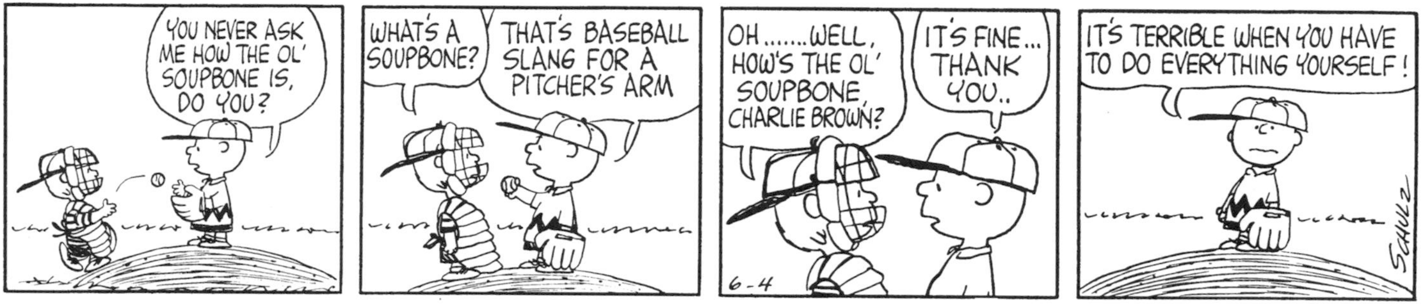
YOU NEVER ASK ME HOW THE OL' SOUPBONE IS, DO YOU?
WHAT'S A SOUPBONE?
THAT'S BASEBALL SLANG FOR A PITCHER'S ARM
OH.......WELL, HOW'S THE OL' SOUPBONE, CHARLIE BROWN?
IT'S FINE... THANK YOU..
6-4
IT'S TERRIBLE WHEN YOU HAVE TO DO EVERYTHING YOURSELF!
SCHULZ

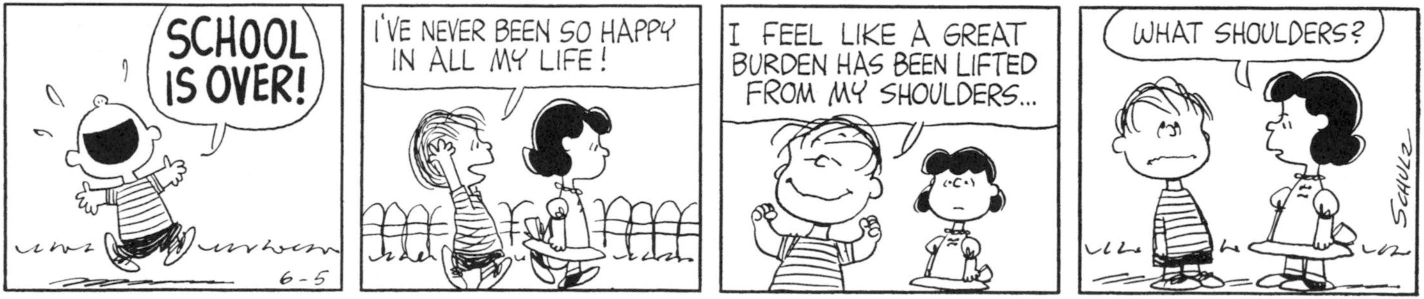
SCHOOL IS OVER!
6-5
I'VE NEVER BEEN SO HAPPY IN ALL MY LIFE!
I FEEL LIKE A GREAT BURDEN HAS BEEN LIFTED FROM MY SHOULDERS...
WHAT SHOULDERS?
SCHULZ

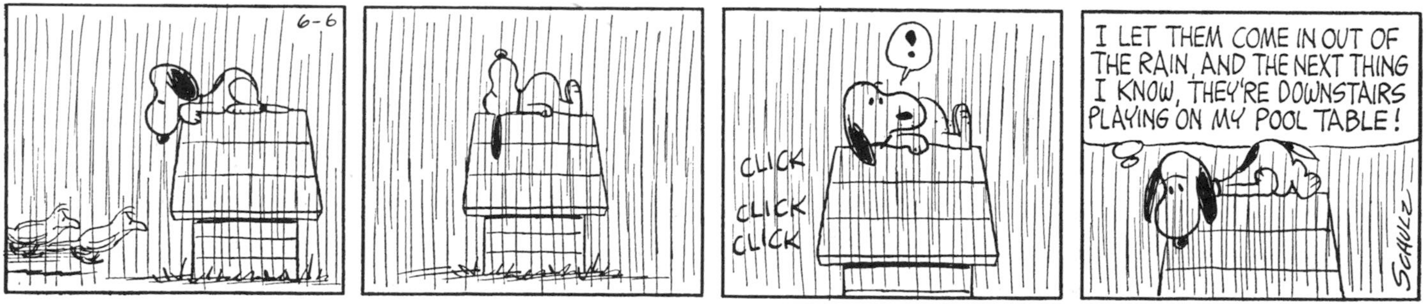
6-6
!
CLICK
CLICK
CLICK
I LET THEM COME IN OUT OF THE RAIN, AND THE NEXT THING I KNOW, THEY'RE DOWNSTAIRS PLAYING ON MY POOL TABLE!
SCHULZ

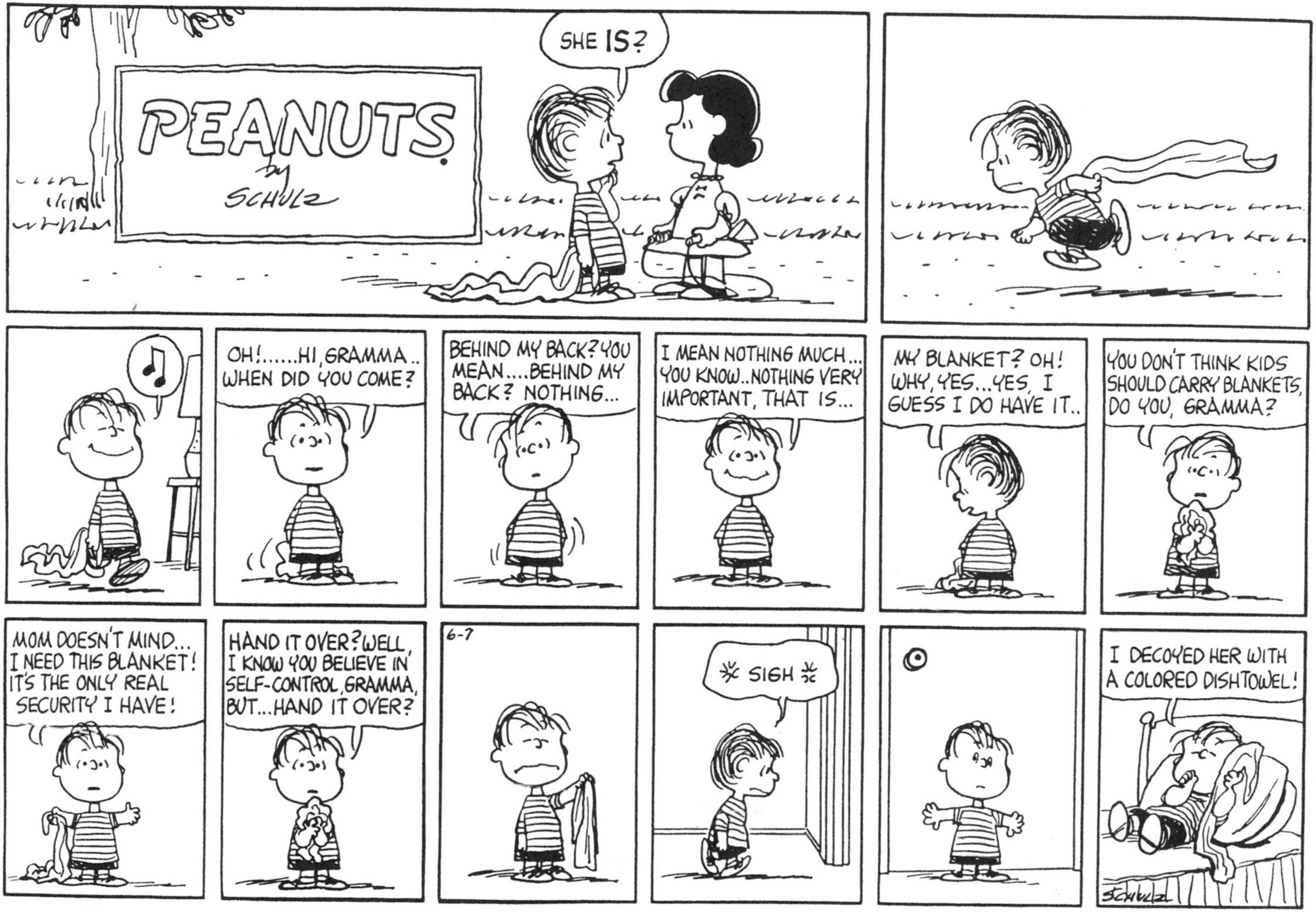
PEANUTS
by SCHULZ
SHE IS?
OH!......HI, GRAMMA.. WHEN DID YOU COME?
BEHIND MY BACK? YOU MEAN....BEHIND MY BACK? NOTHING...
I MEAN NOTHING MUCH... YOU KNOW..NOTHING VERY IMPORTANT, THAT IS...
MY BLANKET? OH! WHY, YES...YES, I GUESS I DO HAVE IT..
YOU DON'T THINK KIDS SHOULD CARRY BLANKETS, DO YOU, GRAMMA?
MOM DOESN'T MIND... I NEED THIS BLANKET! IT'S THE ONLY REAL SECURITY I HAVE!
HAND IT OVER? WELL, I KNOW YOU BELIEVE IN SELF-CONTROL, GRAMMA, BUT...HAND IT OVER?
6-7
SIGH
I DECOYED HER WITH A COLORED DISHTOWEL!
SCHULZ

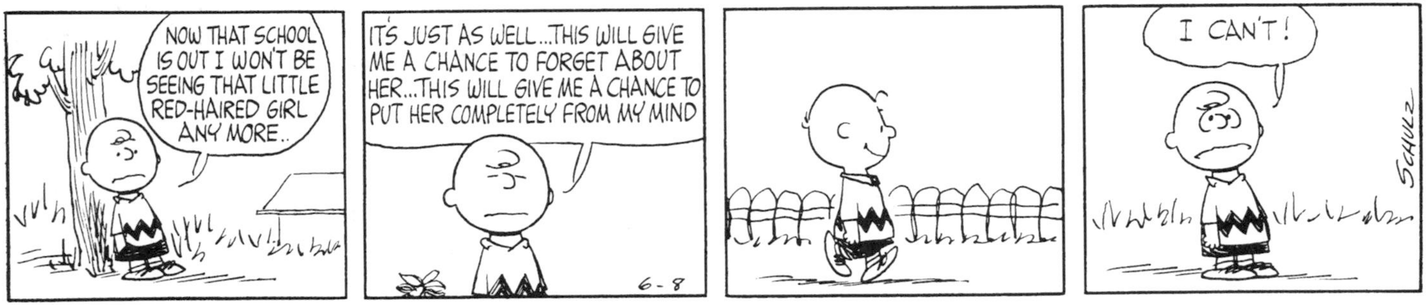
NOW THAT SCHOOL IS OUT I WON'T BE SEEING THAT LITTLE RED-HAIRED GIRL ANY MORE..
IT'S JUST AS WELL...THIS WILL GIVE ME A CHANCE TO FORGET ABOUT HER...THIS WILL GIVE ME A CHANCE TO PUT HER COMPLETELY FROM MY MIND
6-8
I CAN'T!
SCHULZ

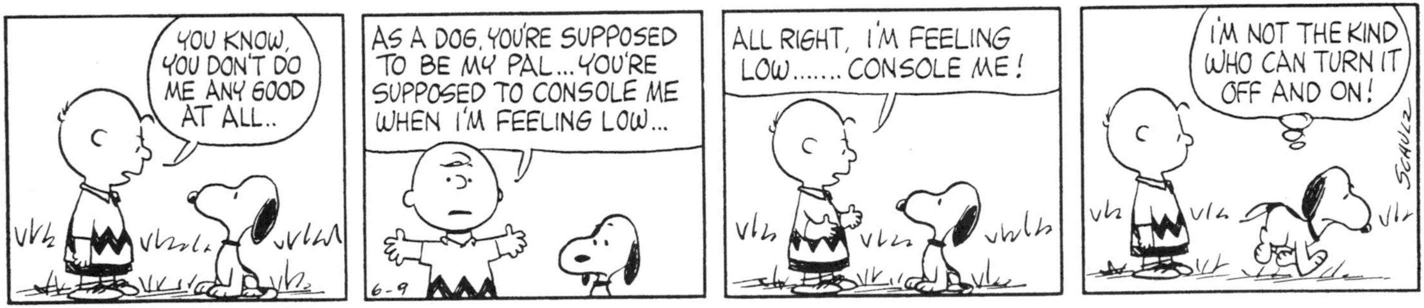
YOU KNOW, YOU DON'T DO ME ANY GOOD AT ALL..
AS A DOG, YOU'RE SUPPOSED TO BE MY PAL...YOU'RE SUPPOSED TO CONSOLE ME WHEN I'M FEELING LOW...
6-9
ALL RIGHT, I'M FEELING LOW....... CONSOLE ME!
I'M NOT THE KIND WHO CAN TURN IT OFF AND ON!
SCHULZ

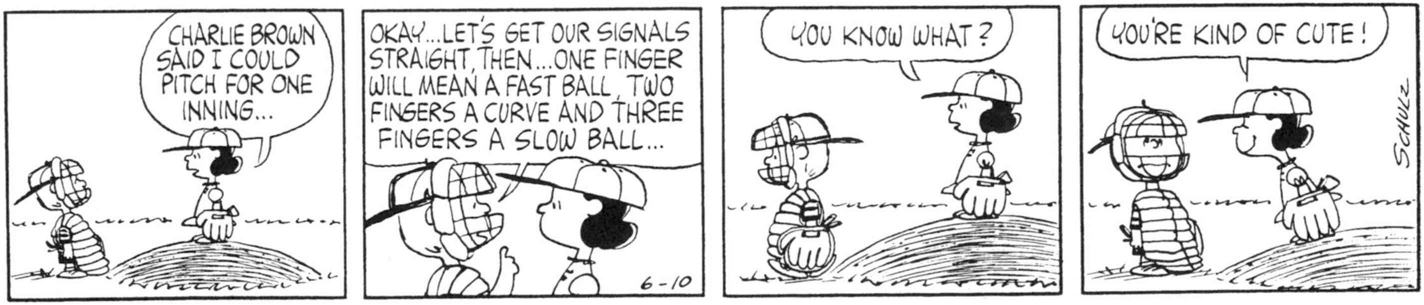
CHARLIE BROWN SAID I COULD PITCH FOR ONE INNING...
OKAY...LET'S GET OUR SIGNALS STRAIGHT, THEN...ONE FINGER WILL MEAN A FAST BALL, TWO FINGERS A CURVE AND THREE FINGERS A SLOW BALL...
6-10
YOU KNOW WHAT?
YOU'RE KIND OF CUTE!
SCHULZ

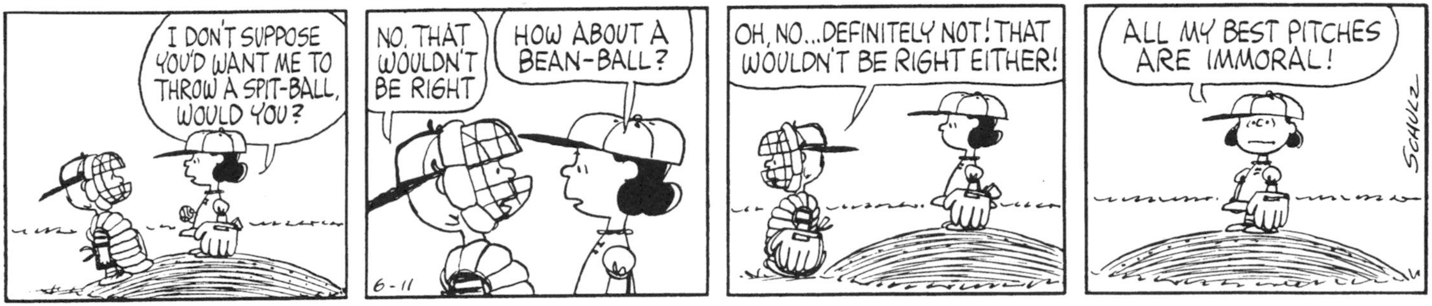
I DON'T SUPPOSE YOU'D WANT ME TO THROW A SPIT-BALL, WOULD YOU?
NO, THAT WOULDN'T BE RIGHT
HOW ABOUT A BEAN-BALL?
OH, NO...DEFINITELY NOT! THAT WOULDN'T BE RIGHT EITHER!
ALL MY BEST PITCHES ARE IMMORAL!
6-11
SCHULZ

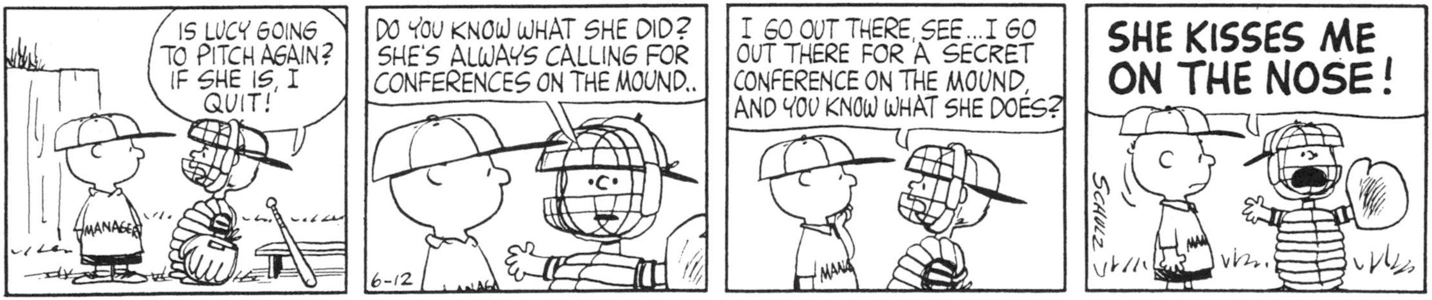
IS LUCY GOING TO PITCH AGAIN? IF SHE IS, I QUIT!
MANAGER
DO YOU KNOW WHAT SHE DID? SHE'S ALWAYS CALLING FOR CONFERENCES ON THE MOUND..
6-12
I GO OUT THERE, SEE...I GO OUT THERE FOR A SECRET CONFERENCE ON THE MOUND, AND YOU KNOW WHAT SHE DOES?
SHE KISSES ME ON THE NOSE!
SCHULZ

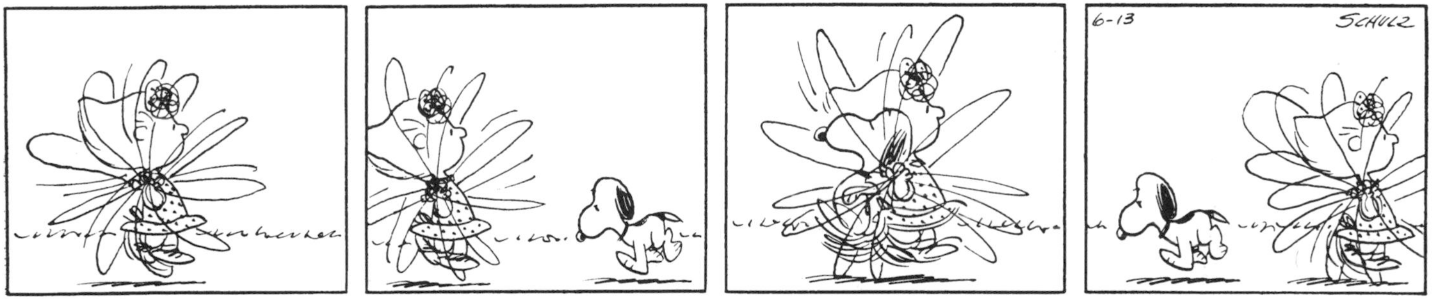
6-13
SCHULZ

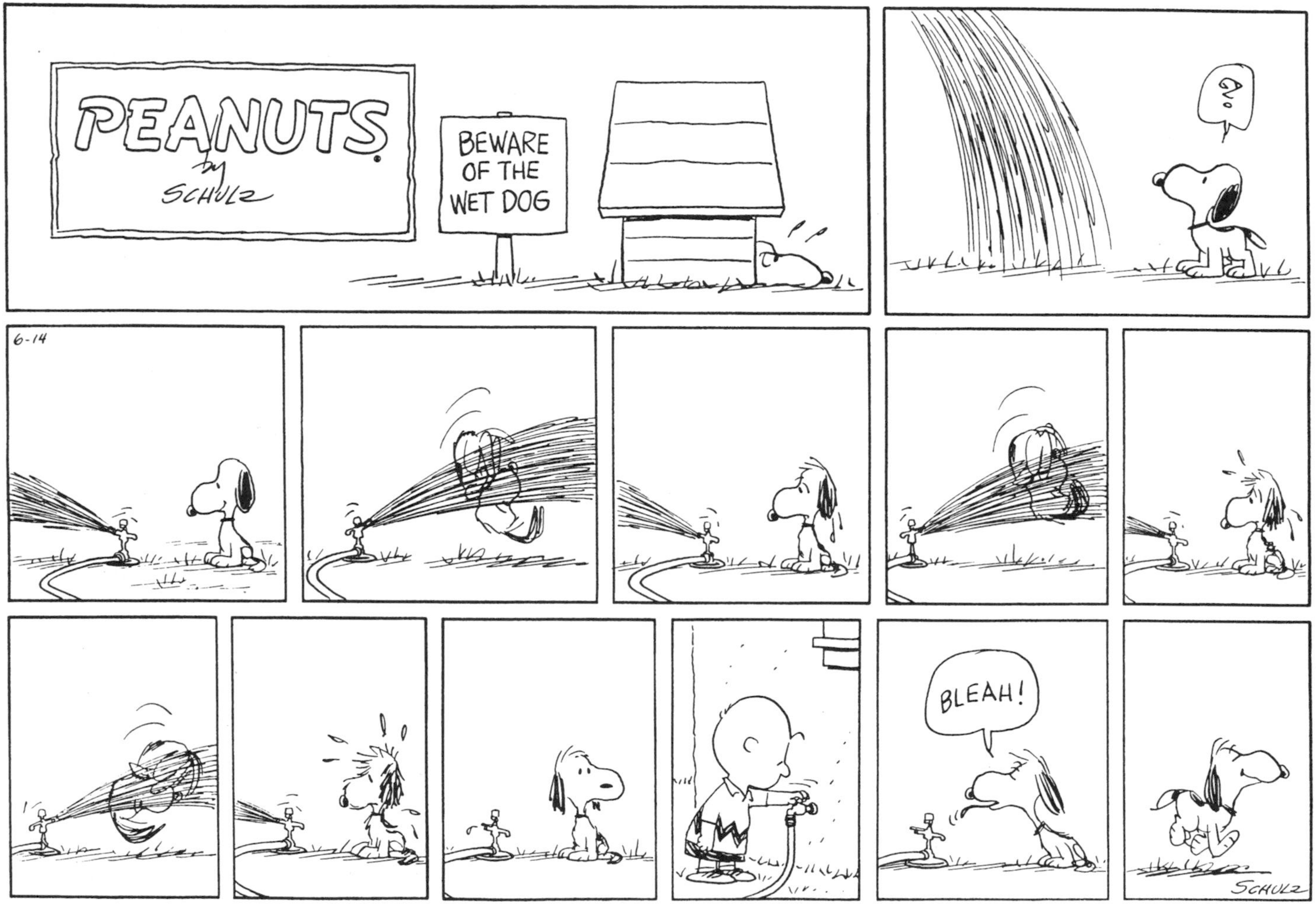
PEANUTS
by SCHULZ
BEWARE OF THE WET DOG
?
6-14
BLEAH!
SCHULZ

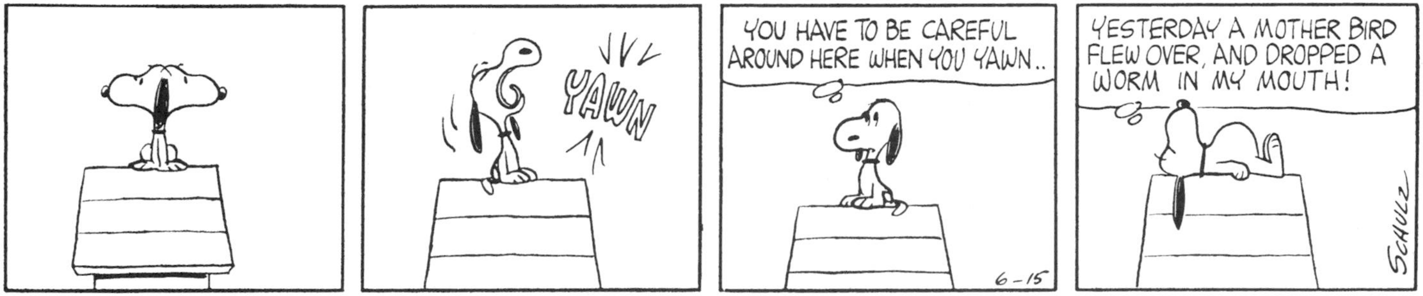
YAWN
YOU HAVE TO BE CAREFUL AROUND HERE WHEN YOU YAWN..
6-15
YESTERDAY A MOTHER BIRD FLEW OVER, AND DROPPED A WORM IN MY MOUTH!
SCHULZ

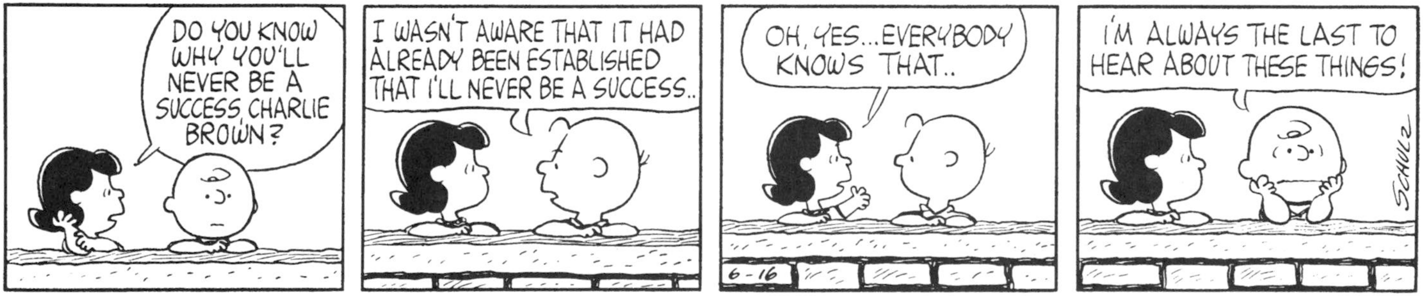
DO YOU KNOW WHY YOU'LL NEVER BE A SUCCESS CHARLIE BROWN?
I WASN'T AWARE THAT IT HAD ALREADY BEEN ESTABLISHED THAT I'LL NEVER BE A SUCCESS..
OH, YES...EVERYBODY KNOWS THAT..
6-16
I'M ALWAYS THE LAST TO HEAR ABOUT THESE THINGS!
SCHULZ

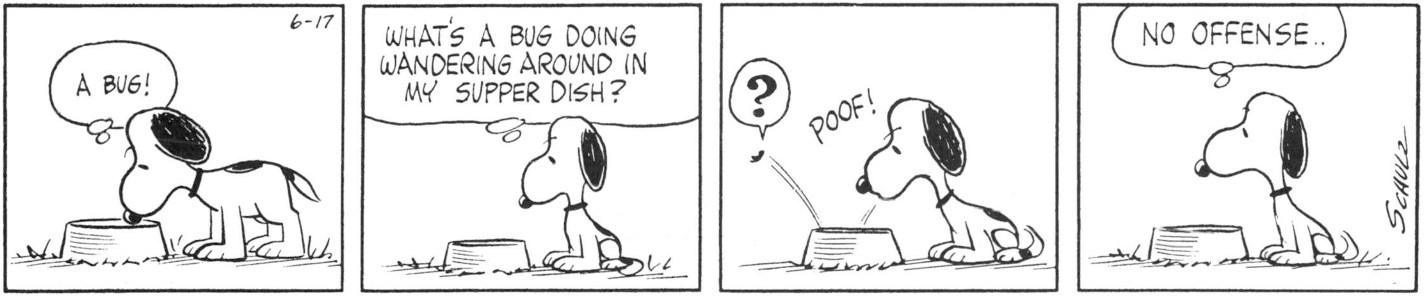
6-17
A BUG!
WHAT'S A BUG DOING WANDERING AROUND IN MY SUPPER DISH?
?
POOF!
NO OFFENSE..
SCHULZ

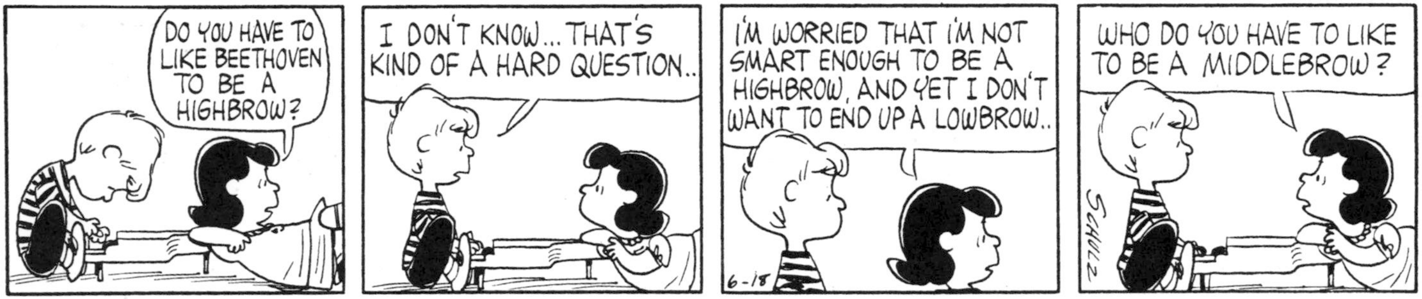
DO YOU HAVE TO LIKE BEETHOVEN TO BE A HIGHBROW?
I DON'T KNOW... THAT'S KIND OF A HARD QUESTION..
I'M WORRIED THAT I'M NOT SMART ENOUGH TO BE A HIGHBROW, AND YET I DON'T WANT TO END UP A LOWBROW..
6-18
WHO DO YOU HAVE TO LIKE TO BE A MIDDLEBROW?
SCHULZ

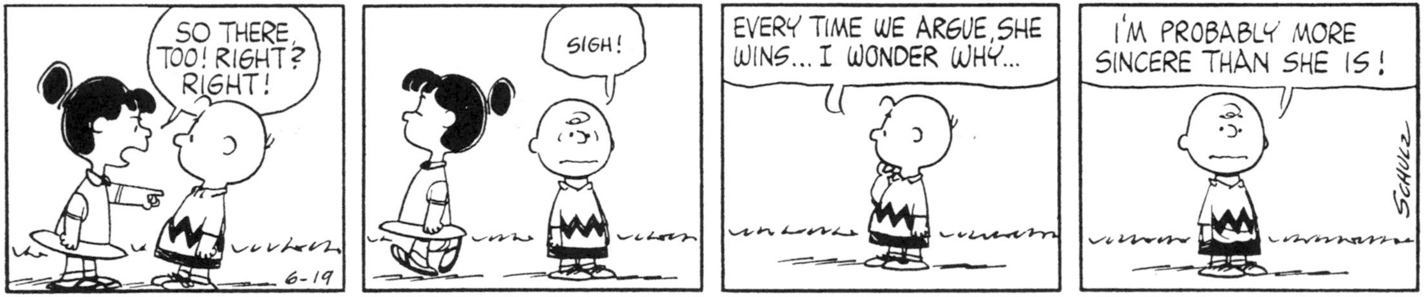
SO THERE, TOO! RIGHT? RIGHT!
6-19
SIGH!
EVERY TIME WE ARGUE, SHE WINS... I WONDER WHY...
I'M PROBABLY MORE SINCERE THAN SHE IS!
SCHULZ

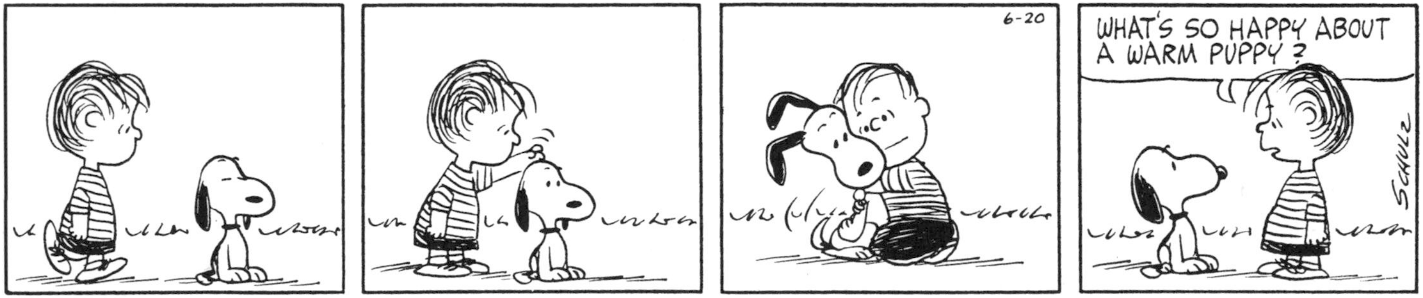
6-20
WHAT'S SO HAPPY ABOUT A WARM PUPPY?
SCHULZ

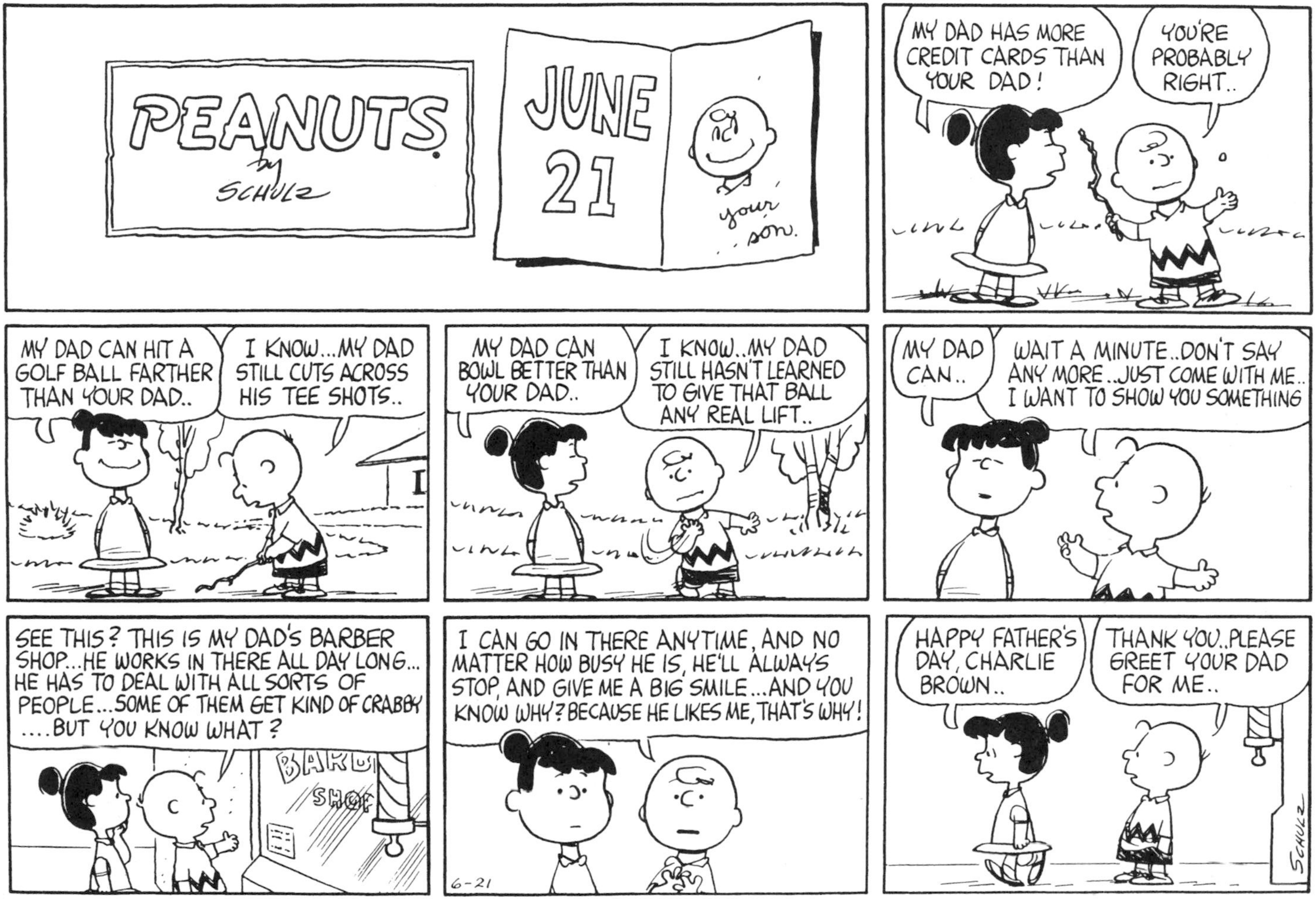
PEANUTS
by SCHULZ
JUNE 21
your son.
MY DAD HAS MORE CREDIT CARDS THAN YOUR DAD!
YOU'RE PROBABLY RIGHT..
MY DAD CAN HIT A GOLF BALL FARTHER THAN YOUR DAD..
I KNOW...MY DAD STILL CUTS ACROSS HIS TEE SHOTS..
MY DAD CAN BOWL BETTER THAN YOUR DAD..
I KNOW..MY DAD STILL HASN'T LEARNED TO GIVE THAT BALL ANY REAL LIFT..
MY DAD CAN..
WAIT A MINUTE..DON'T SAY ANY MORE..JUST COME WITH ME.. I WANT TO SHOW YOU SOMETHING
SEE THIS? THIS IS MY DAD'S BARBER SHOP...HE WORKS IN THERE ALL DAY LONG... HE HAS TO DEAL WITH ALL SORTS OF PEOPLE...SOME OF THEM GET KIND OF CRABBY ....BUT YOU KNOW WHAT?
BARB
SHOP
I CAN GO IN THERE ANYTIME, AND NO MATTER HOW BUSY HE IS, HE'LL ALWAYS STOP, AND GIVE ME A BIG SMILE...AND YOU KNOW WHY? BECAUSE HE LIKES ME, THAT'S WHY!
6-21
HAPPY FATHER'S DAY, CHARLIE BROWN..
THANK YOU..PLEASE GREET YOUR DAD FOR ME..
SCHULZ

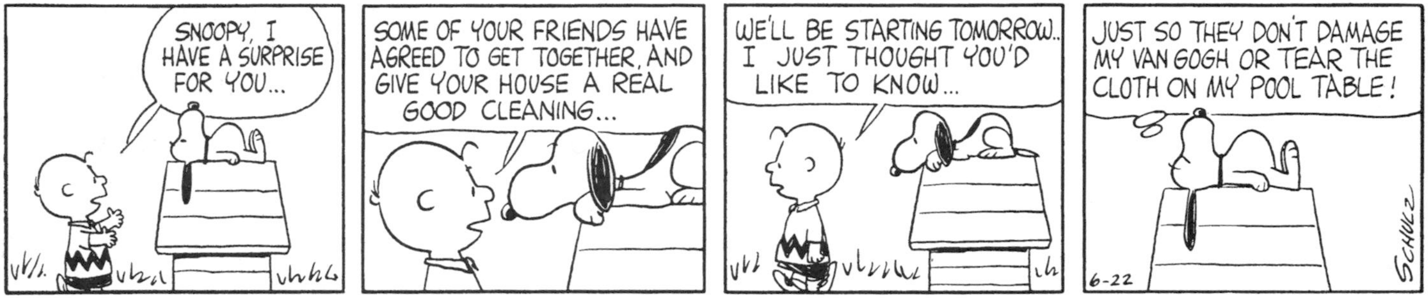
SNOOPY, I HAVE A SURPRISE FOR YOU...
SOME OF YOUR FRIENDS HAVE AGREED TO GET TOGETHER, AND GIVE YOUR HOUSE A REAL GOOD CLEANING...
WE'LL BE STARTING TOMORROW.. I JUST THOUGHT YOU'D LIKE TO KNOW...
JUST SO THEY DON'T DAMAGE MY VAN GOGH OR TEAR THE CLOTH ON MY POOL TABLE!
6-22
SCHULZ

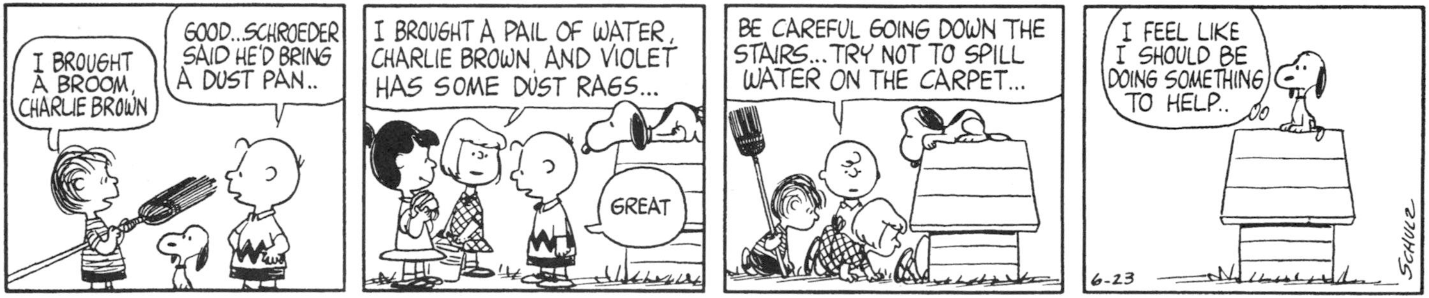
I BROUGHT A BROOM, CHARLIE BROWN
GOOD...SCHROEDER SAID HE'D BRING A DUST PAN..
I BROUGHT A PAIL OF WATER, CHARLIE BROWN, AND VIOLET HAS SOME DUST RAGS...
GREAT
BE CAREFUL GOING DOWN THE STAIRS...TRY NOT TO SPILL WATER ON THE CARPET...
I FEEL LIKE I SHOULD BE DOING SOMETHING TO HELP..
6-23
SCHULZ

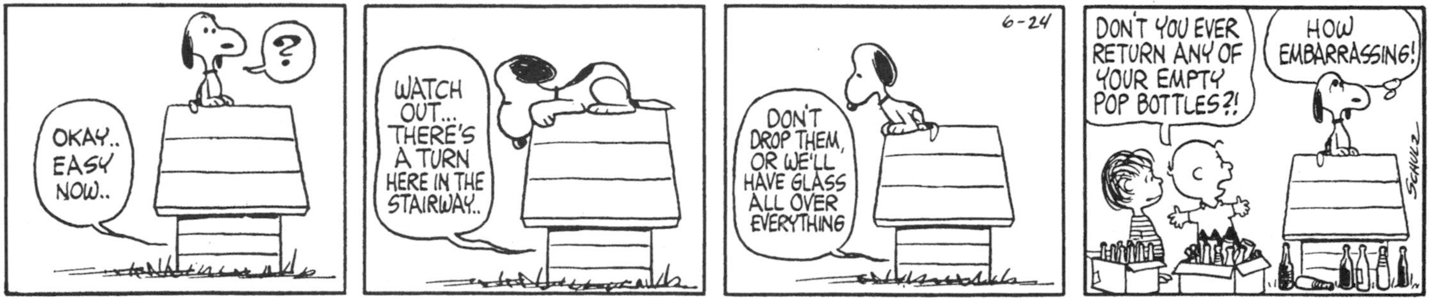
?
OKAY.. EASY NOW..
WATCH OUT... THERE'S A TURN HERE IN THE STAIRWAY..
6-24
DON'T DROP THEM, OR WE'LL HAVE GLASS ALL OVER EVERYTHING
DON'T YOU EVER RETURN ANY OF YOUR EMPTY POP BOTTLES?!
HOW EMBARRASSING!
SCHULZ

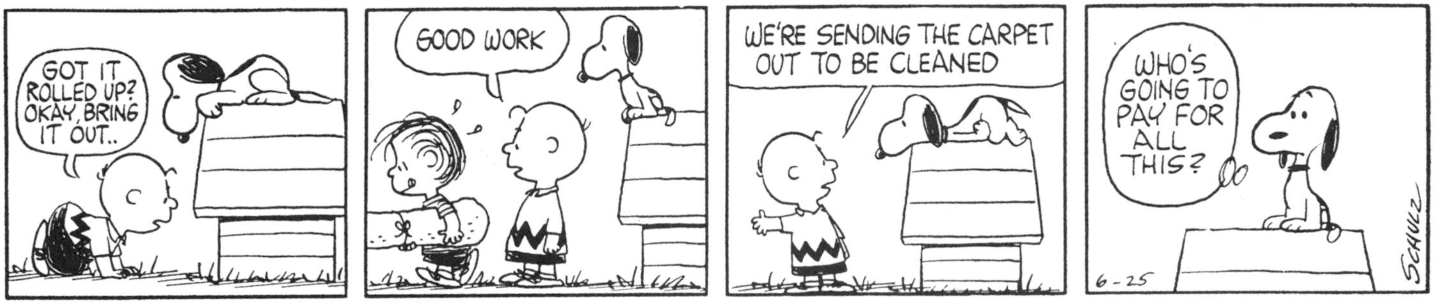
GOT IT ROLLED UP? OKAY, BRING IT OUT..
GOOD WORK
WE'RE SENDING THE CARPET OUT TO BE CLEANED
WHO'S GOING TO PAY FOR ALL THIS?
6-25
SCHULZ

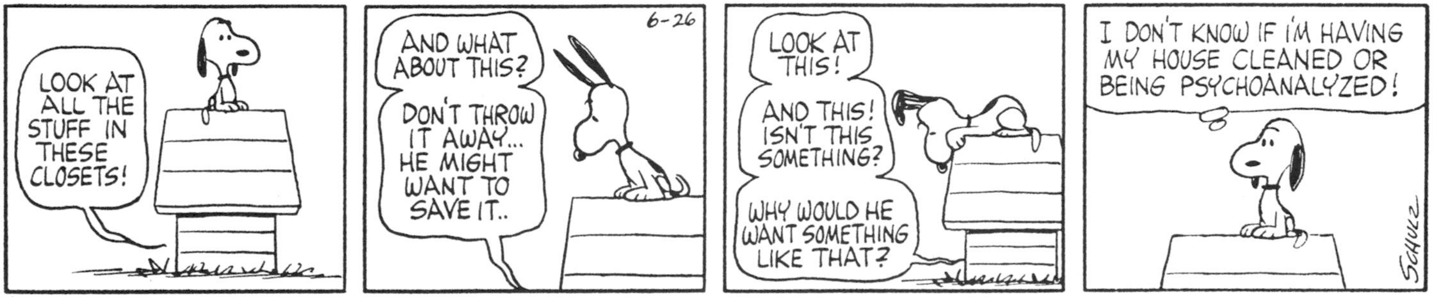
LOOK AT ALL THE STUFF IN THESE CLOSETS!
6-26
AND WHAT ABOUT THIS?
DON'T THROW IT AWAY... HE MIGHT WANT TO SAVE IT..
LOOK AT THIS!
AND THIS! ISN'T THIS SOMETHING?
WHY WOULD HE WANT SOMETHING LIKE THAT?
I DON'T KNOW IF I'M HAVING MY HOUSE CLEANED OR BEING PSYCHOANALYZED!
SCHULZ

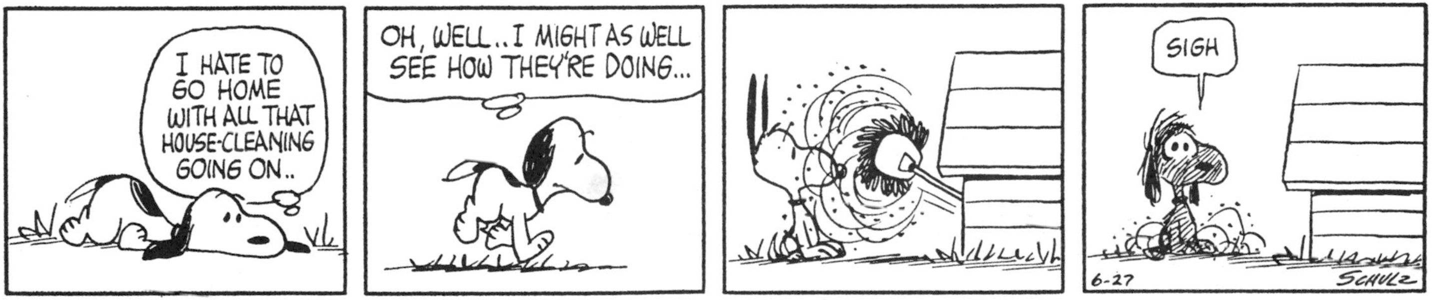
I HATE TO GO HOME WITH ALL THAT HOUSE-CLEANING GOING ON..
OH, WELL.. I MIGHT AS WELL SEE HOW THEY'RE DOING...
SIGH
6-27
SCHULZ

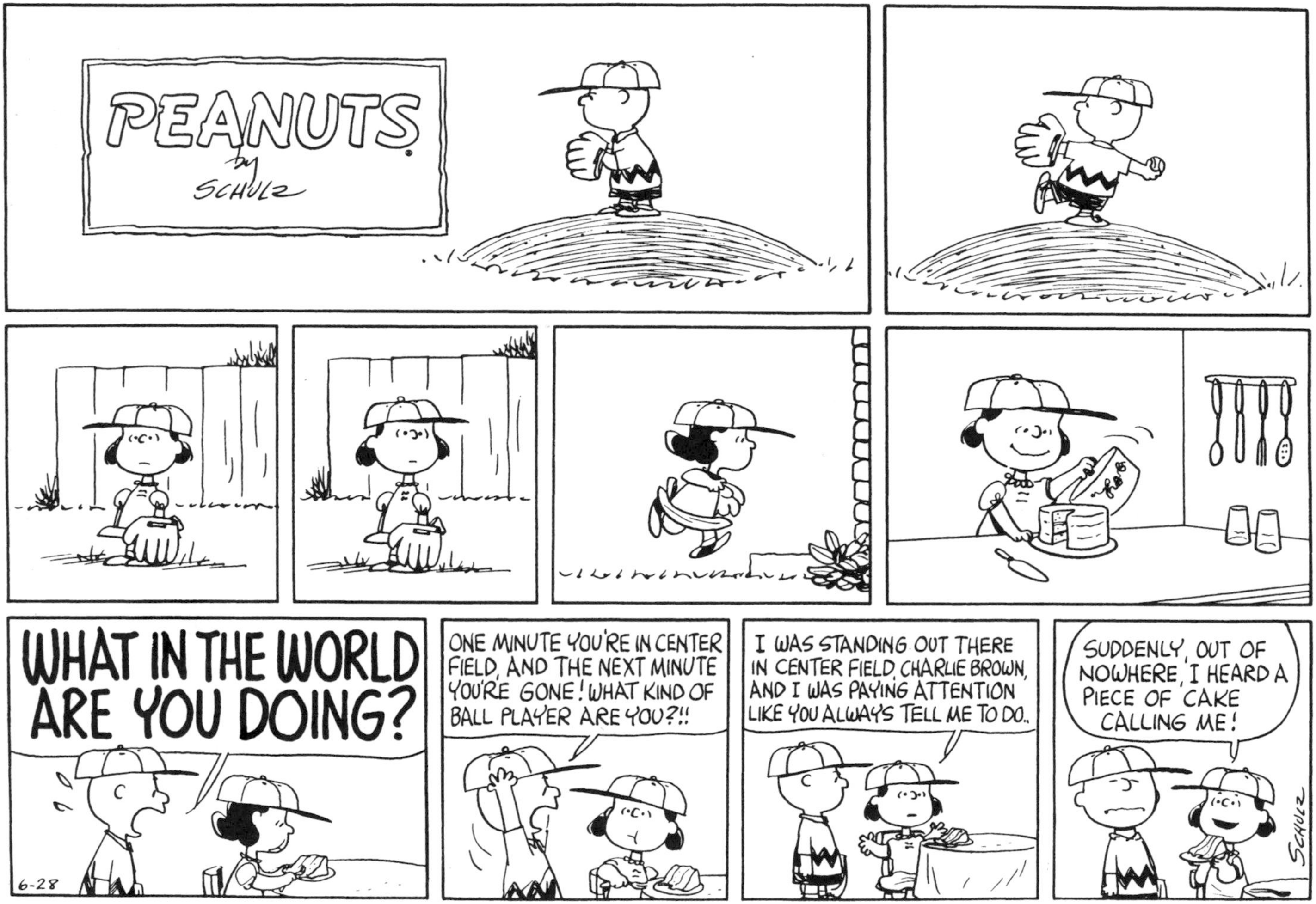
PEANUTS
by SCHULZ
WHAT IN THE WORLD ARE YOU DOING?
6-28
ONE MINUTE YOU'RE IN CENTER FIELD, AND THE NEXT MINUTE YOU'RE GONE! WHAT KIND OF BALL PLAYER ARE YOU?!!
I WAS STANDING OUT THERE IN CENTER FIELD, CHARLIE BROWN, AND I WAS PAYING ATTENTION LIKE YOU ALWAYS TELL ME TO DO..
SUDDENLY, OUT OF NOWHERE, I HEARD A PIECE OF CAKE CALLING ME!
SCHULZ

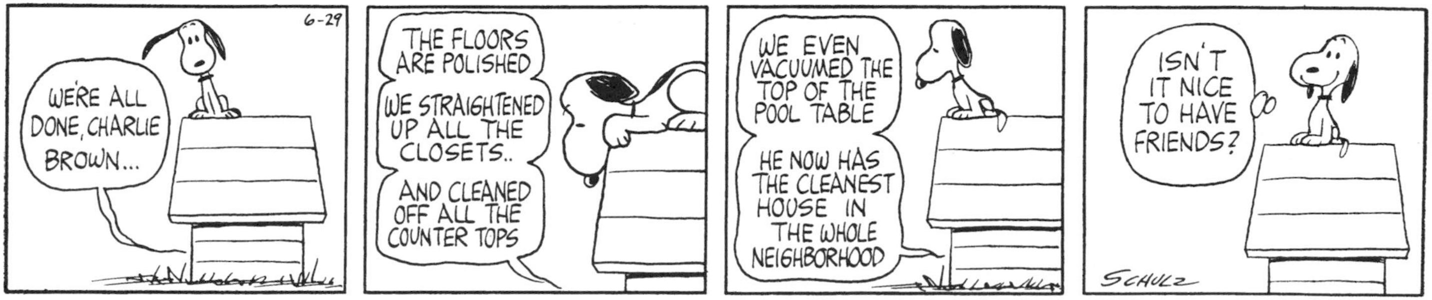
6-29
WE'RE ALL DONE, CHARLIE BROWN...
THE FLOORS ARE POLISHED
WE STRAIGHTENED UP ALL THE CLOSETS..
AND CLEANED OFF ALL THE COUNTER TOPS
WE EVEN VACUUMED THE TOP OF THE POOL TABLE
HE NOW HAS THE CLEANEST HOUSE IN THE WHOLE NEIGHBORHOOD
ISN'T IT NICE TO HAVE FRIENDS?
SCHULZ

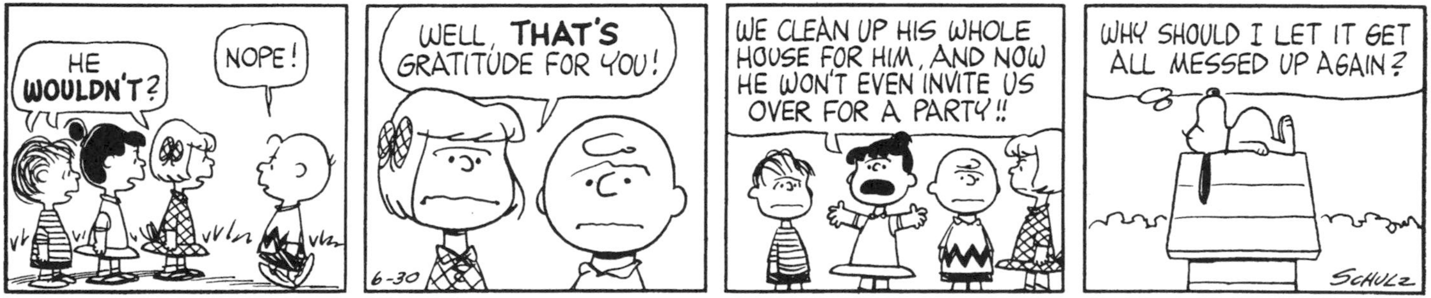
HE WOULDN'T?
NOPE!
WELL, THAT'S GRATITUDE FOR YOU!
6-30
WE CLEAN UP HIS WHOLE HOUSE FOR HIM, AND NOW HE WON'T EVEN INVITE US OVER FOR A PARTY!!
WHY SHOULD I LET IT GET ALL MESSED UP AGAIN?
SCHULZ

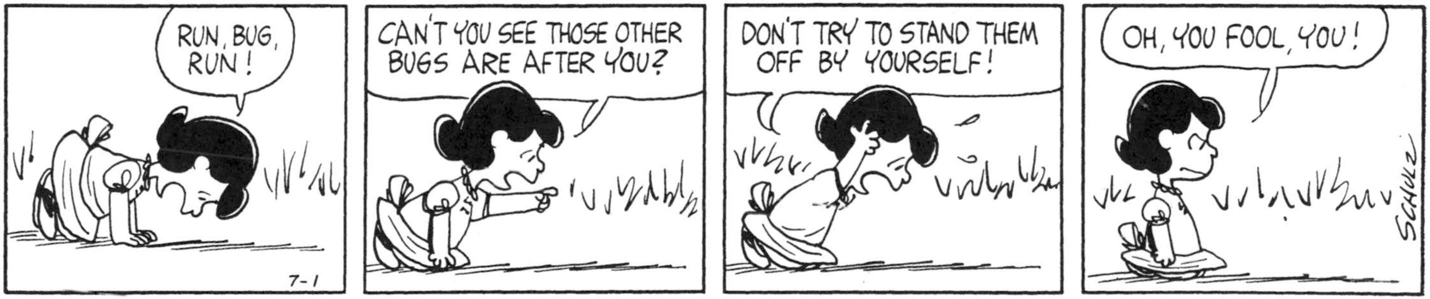
RUN, BUG, RUN!
7-1
CAN'T YOU SEE THOSE OTHER BUGS ARE AFTER YOU?
DON'T TRY TO STAND THEM OFF BY YOURSELF!
OH, YOU FOOL, YOU!
SCHULZ

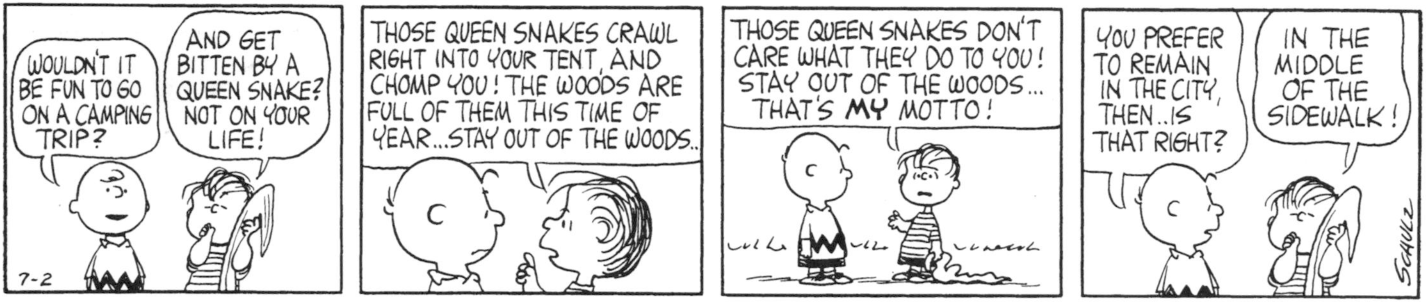
WOULDN'T IT BE FUN TO GO ON A CAMPING TRIP?
AND GET BITTEN BY A QUEEN SNAKE? NOT ON YOUR LIFE!
7-2
THOSE QUEEN SNAKES CRAWL RIGHT INTO YOUR TENT, AND CHOMP YOU! THE WOODS ARE FULL OF THEM THIS TIME OF YEAR...STAY OUT OF THE WOODS..
THOSE QUEEN SNAKES DON'T CARE WHAT THEY DO TO YOU! STAY OUT OF THE WOODS... THAT'S **MY** MOTTO!
YOU PREFER TO REMAIN IN THE CITY, THEN..IS THAT RIGHT?
IN THE MIDDLE OF THE SIDEWALK!
SCHULZ

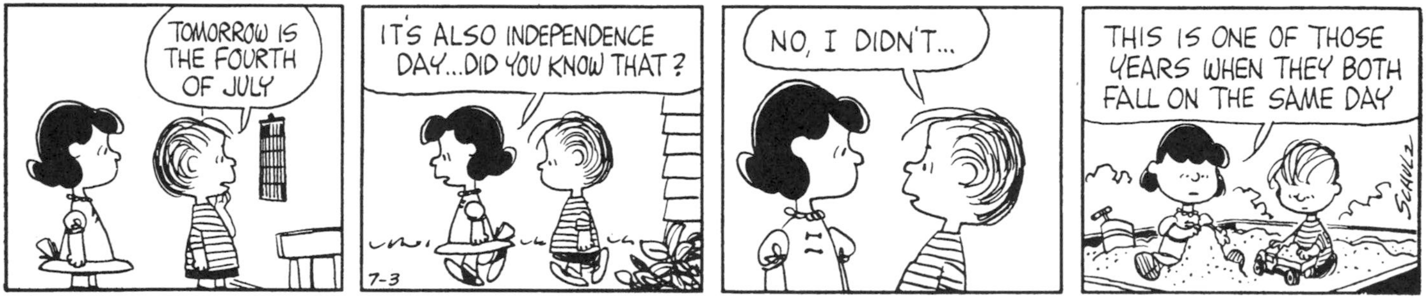
TOMORROW IS THE FOURTH OF JULY
IT'S ALSO INDEPENDENCE DAY...DID YOU KNOW THAT?
7-3
NO, I DIDN'T...
THIS IS ONE OF THOSE YEARS WHEN THEY BOTH FALL ON THE SAME DAY
SCHULZ

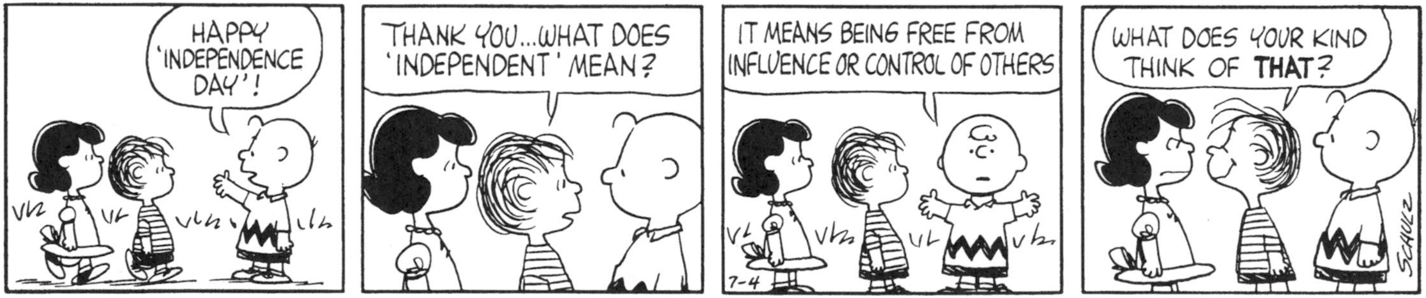
HAPPY 'INDEPENDENCE DAY'!
THANK YOU...WHAT DOES 'INDEPENDENT' MEAN?
IT MEANS BEING FREE FROM INFLUENCE OR CONTROL OF OTHERS
7-4
WHAT DOES YOUR KIND THINK OF **THAT**?
SCHULZ

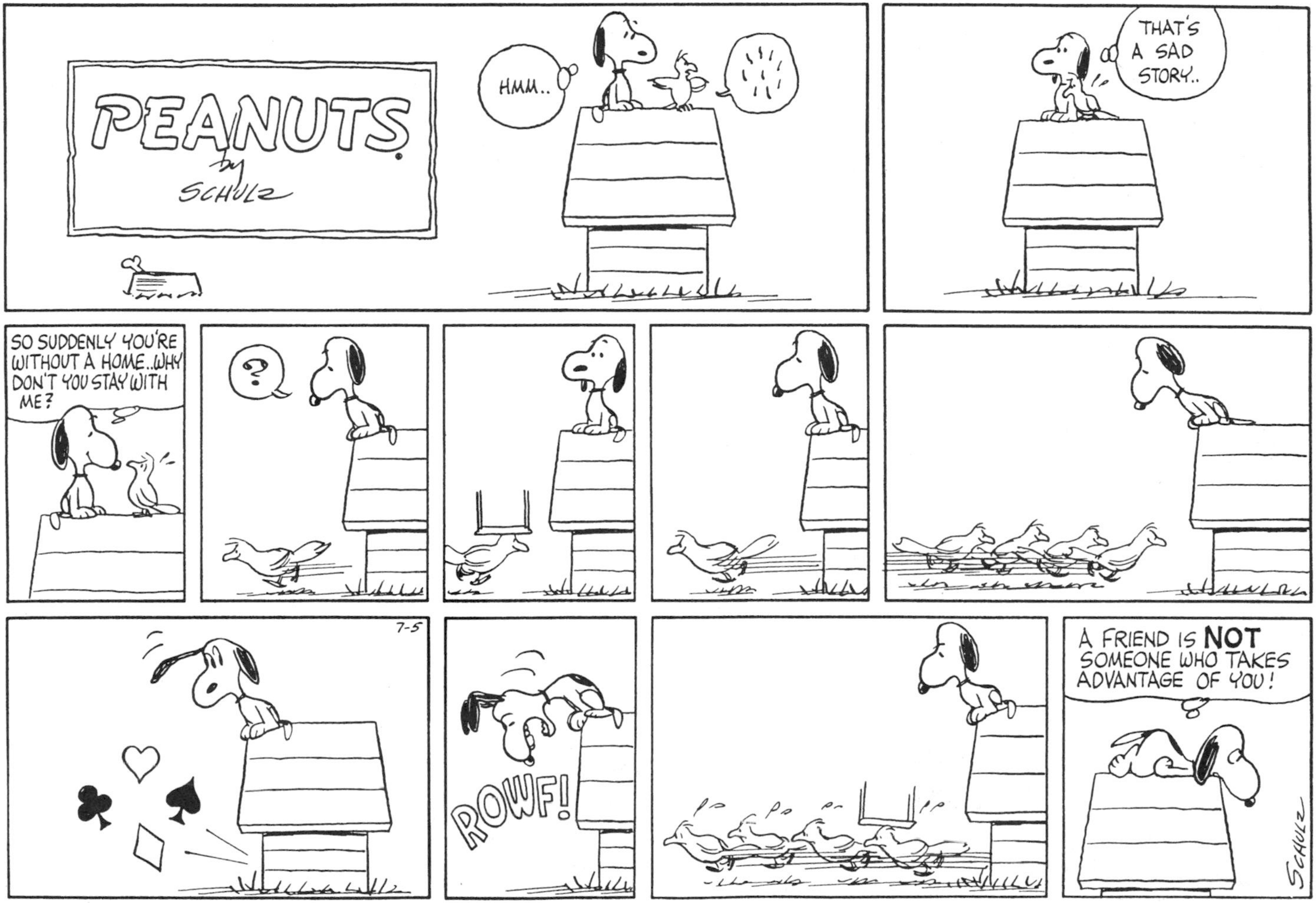
PEANUTS
by
SCHULZ
HMM..
THAT'S A SAD STORY..
SO SUDDENLY YOU'RE WITHOUT A HOME..WHY DON'T YOU STAY WITH ME?
?
7-5
ROWF!
A FRIEND IS NOT SOMEONE WHO TAKES ADVANTAGE OF YOU!
SCHULZ

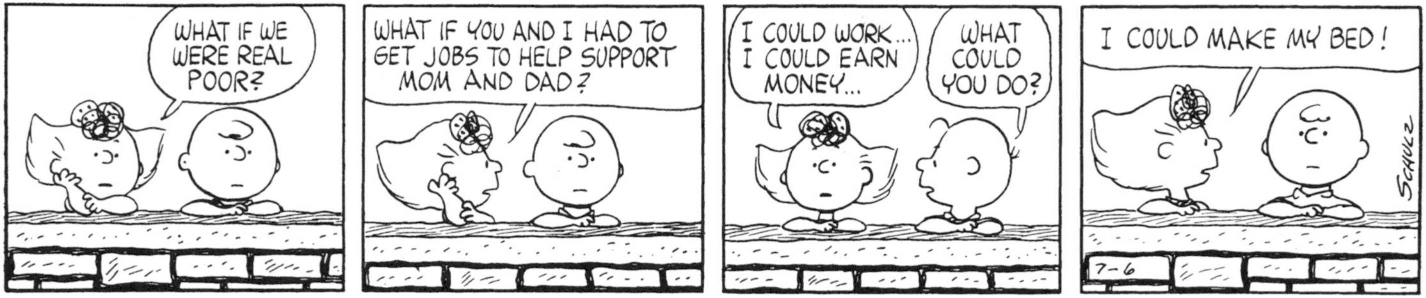
WHAT IF WE WERE REAL POOR?
WHAT IF YOU AND I HAD TO GET JOBS TO HELP SUPPORT MOM AND DAD?
I COULD WORK... I COULD EARN MONEY...
WHAT COULD YOU DO?
I COULD MAKE MY BED!
7-6
SCHULZ

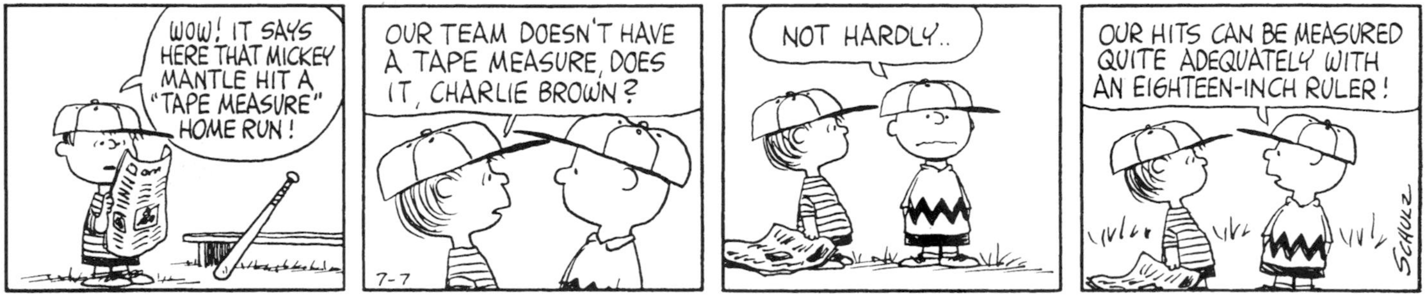
WOW! IT SAYS HERE THAT MICKEY MANTLE HIT A "TAPE MEASURE" HOME RUN!
OUR TEAM DOESN'T HAVE A TAPE MEASURE, DOES IT, CHARLIE BROWN?
7-7
NOT HARDLY..
OUR HITS CAN BE MEASURED QUITE ADEQUATELY WITH AN EIGHTEEN-INCH RULER!
SCHULZ

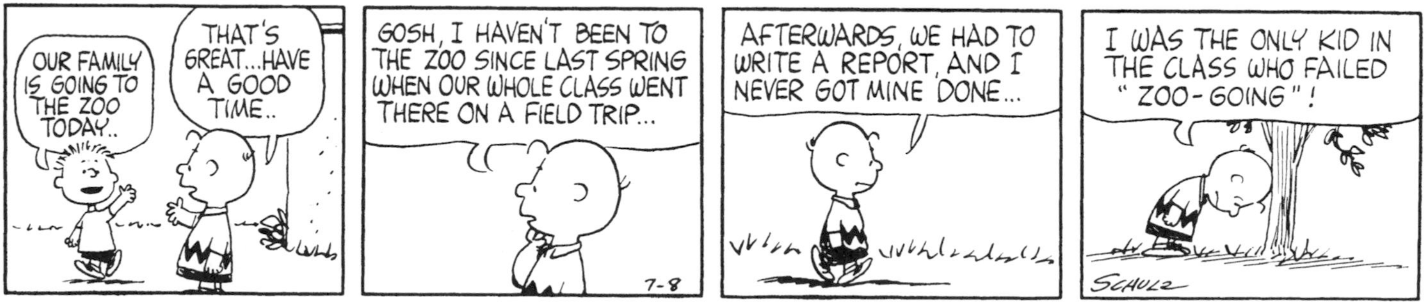
OUR FAMILY IS GOING TO THE ZOO TODAY..
THAT'S GREAT...HAVE A GOOD TIME..
GOSH, I HAVEN'T BEEN TO THE ZOO SINCE LAST SPRING WHEN OUR WHOLE CLASS WENT THERE ON A FIELD TRIP...
7-8
AFTERWARDS, WE HAD TO WRITE A REPORT, AND I NEVER GOT MINE DONE...
I WAS THE ONLY KID IN THE CLASS WHO FAILED "ZOO-GOING"!
SCHULZ

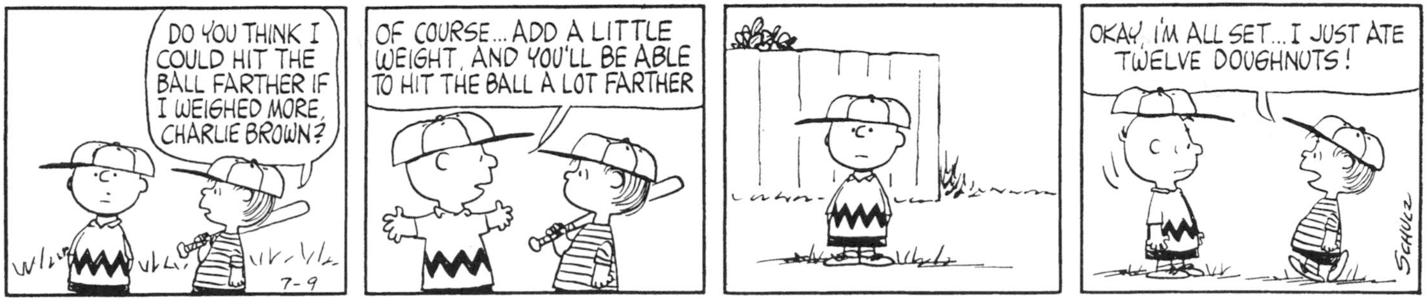
DO YOU THINK I COULD HIT THE BALL FARTHER IF I WEIGHED MORE, CHARLIE BROWN?
7-9
OF COURSE... ADD A LITTLE WEIGHT, AND YOU'LL BE ABLE TO HIT THE BALL A LOT FARTHER
OKAY, I'M ALL SET... I JUST ATE TWELVE DOUGHNUTS!
SCHULZ

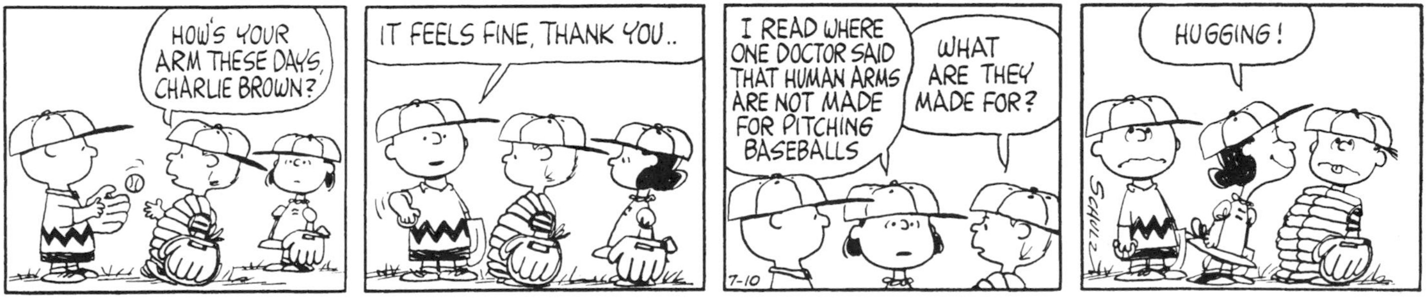
HOW'S YOUR ARM THESE DAYS, CHARLIE BROWN?
IT FEELS FINE, THANK YOU..
I READ WHERE ONE DOCTOR SAID THAT HUMAN ARMS ARE NOT MADE FOR PITCHING BASEBALLS
WHAT ARE THEY MADE FOR?
7-10
HUGGING!
SCHULZ

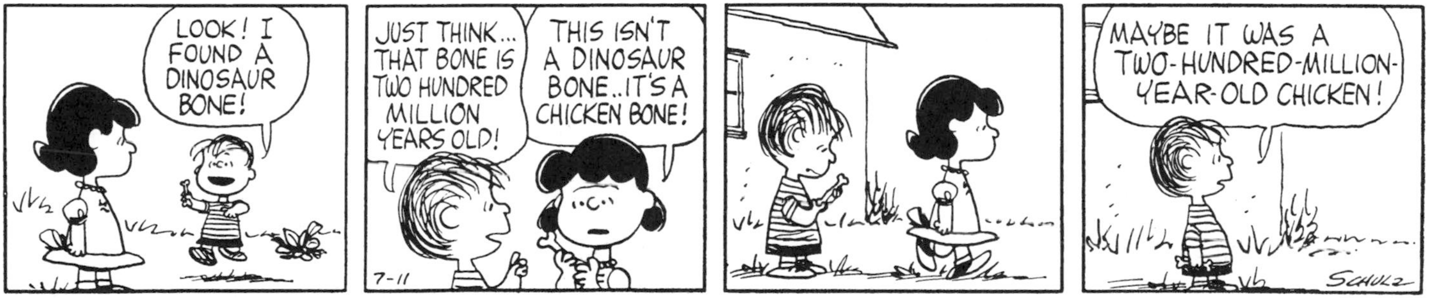
LOOK! I FOUND A DINOSAUR BONE!
JUST THINK... THAT BONE IS TWO HUNDRED MILLION YEARS OLD!
THIS ISN'T A DINOSAUR BONE.. IT'S A CHICKEN BONE!
7-11
MAYBE IT WAS A TWO-HUNDRED-MILLION-YEAR-OLD CHICKEN!
SCHULZ

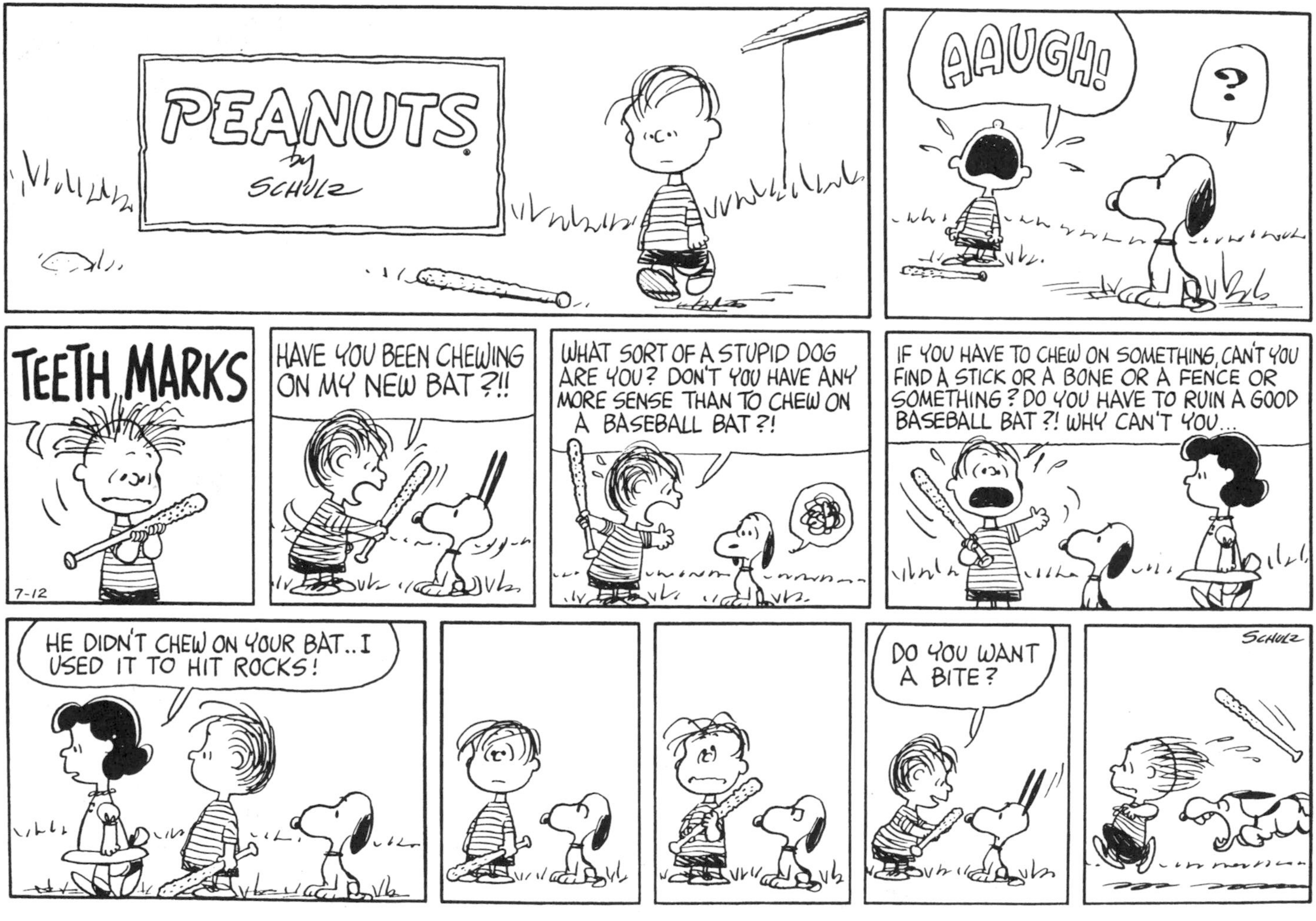
PEANUTS
by SCHULZ
AAUGH!
?
TEETH MARKS
7-12
HAVE YOU BEEN CHEWING ON MY NEW BAT ?!!
WHAT SORT OF A STUPID DOG ARE YOU? DON'T YOU HAVE ANY MORE SENSE THAN TO CHEW ON A BASEBALL BAT ?!
IF YOU HAVE TO CHEW ON SOMETHING, CAN'T YOU FIND A STICK OR A BONE OR A FENCE OR SOMETHING? DO YOU HAVE TO RUIN A GOOD BASEBALL BAT ?! WHY CAN'T YOU...
HE DIDN'T CHEW ON YOUR BAT.. I USED IT TO HIT ROCKS!
DO YOU WANT A BITE?
SCHULZ

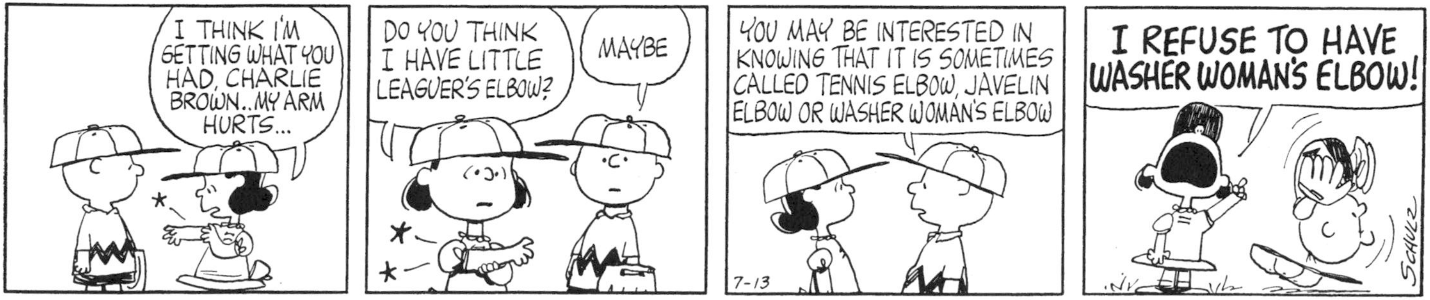
I THINK I'M GETTING WHAT YOU HAD, CHARLIE BROWN..MY ARM HURTS...
DO YOU THINK I HAVE LITTLE LEAGUER'S ELBOW?
MAYBE
YOU MAY BE INTERESTED IN KNOWING THAT IT IS SOMETIMES CALLED TENNIS ELBOW, JAVELIN ELBOW OR WASHER WOMAN'S ELBOW
7-13
I REFUSE TO HAVE WASHER WOMAN'S ELBOW!
SCHULZ

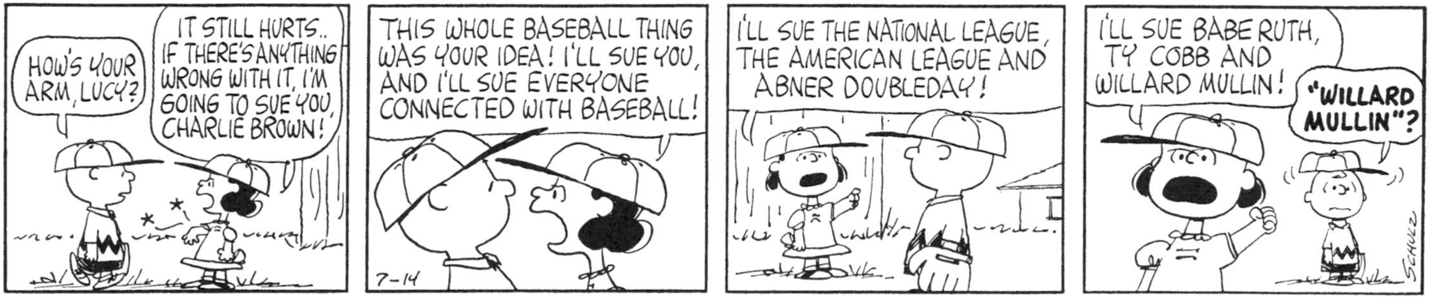
HOW'S YOUR ARM, LUCY?
IT STILL HURTS.. IF THERE'S ANYTHING WRONG WITH IT, I'M GOING TO SUE YOU, CHARLIE BROWN!
THIS WHOLE BASEBALL THING WAS YOUR IDEA! I'LL SUE YOU, AND I'LL SUE EVERYONE CONNECTED WITH BASEBALL!
7-14
I'LL SUE THE NATIONAL LEAGUE, THE AMERICAN LEAGUE AND ABNER DOUBLEDAY!
I'LL SUE BABE RUTH, TY COBB AND WILLARD MULLIN!
"WILLARD MULLIN"?
SCHULZ

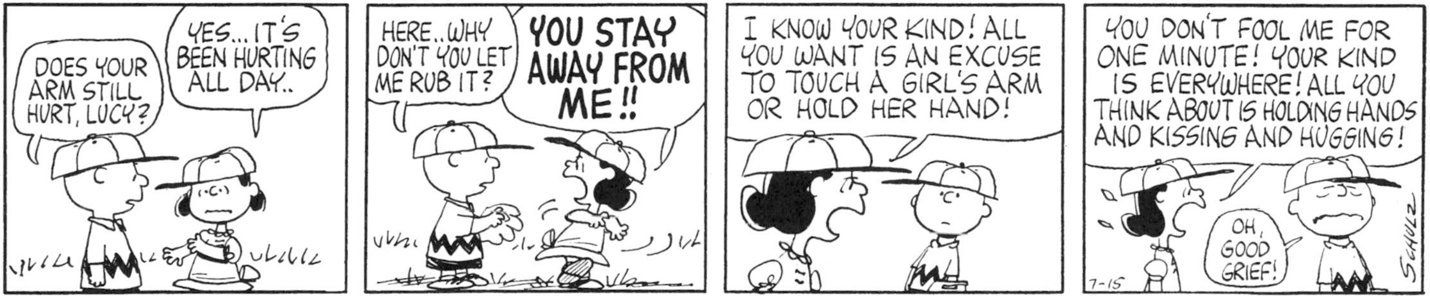
DOES YOUR ARM STILL HURT, LUCY?
YES...IT'S BEEN HURTING ALL DAY..
HERE..WHY DON'T YOU LET ME RUB IT?
YOU STAY AWAY FROM ME!!
I KNOW YOUR KIND! ALL YOU WANT IS AN EXCUSE TO TOUCH A GIRL'S ARM OR HOLD HER HAND!
YOU DON'T FOOL ME FOR ONE MINUTE! YOUR KIND IS EVERYWHERE! ALL YOU THINK ABOUT IS HOLDING HANDS AND KISSING AND HUGGING!
OH, GOOD GRIEF!
7-15
SCHULZ

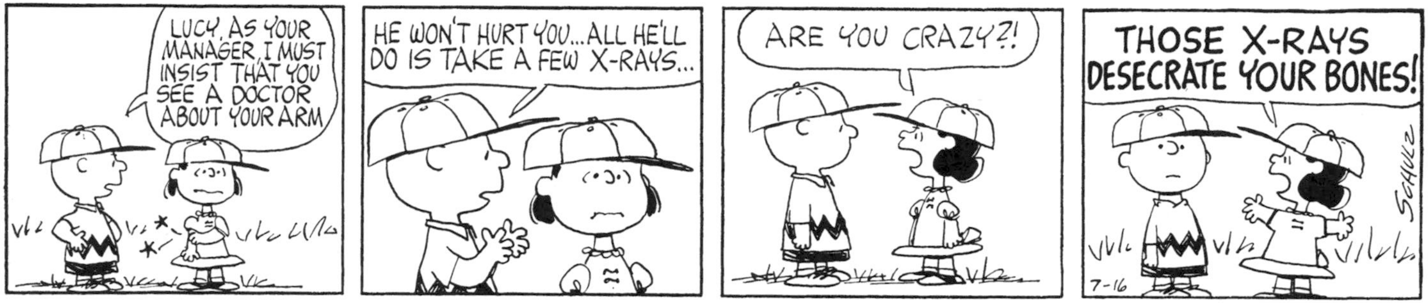
LUCY, AS YOUR MANAGER, I MUST INSIST THAT YOU SEE A DOCTOR ABOUT YOUR ARM
HE WON'T HURT YOU...ALL HE'LL DO IS TAKE A FEW X-RAYS...
ARE YOU CRAZY?!
THOSE X-RAYS DESECRATE YOUR BONES!
SCHULZ
7-16

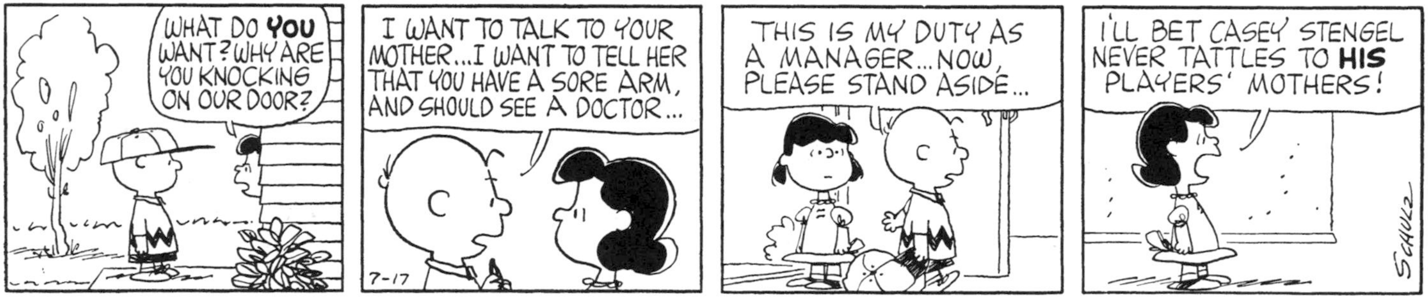
WHAT DO **YOU** WANT? WHY ARE YOU KNOCKING ON OUR DOOR?
I WANT TO TALK TO YOUR MOTHER...I WANT TO TELL HER THAT YOU HAVE A SORE ARM, AND SHOULD SEE A DOCTOR...
7-17
THIS IS MY DUTY AS A MANAGER...NOW, PLEASE STAND ASIDE...
I'LL BET CASEY STENGEL NEVER TATTLES TO **HIS** PLAYERS' MOTHERS!
SCHULZ

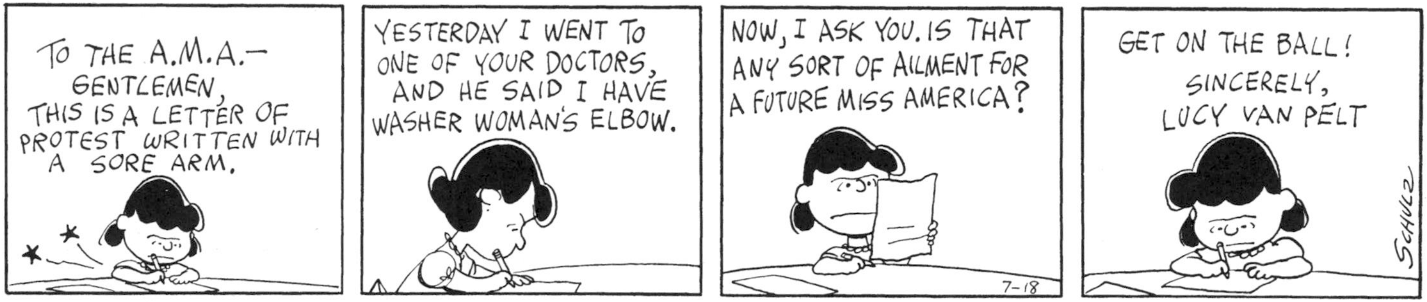
TO THE A.M.A.—
GENTLEMEN,
THIS IS A LETTER OF PROTEST WRITTEN WITH A SORE ARM.
YESTERDAY I WENT TO ONE OF YOUR DOCTORS, AND HE SAID I HAVE WASHER WOMAN'S ELBOW.
NOW, I ASK YOU. IS THAT ANY SORT OF AILMENT FOR A FUTURE MISS AMERICA?
7-18
GET ON THE BALL!
SINCERELY,
LUCY VAN PELT
SCHULZ

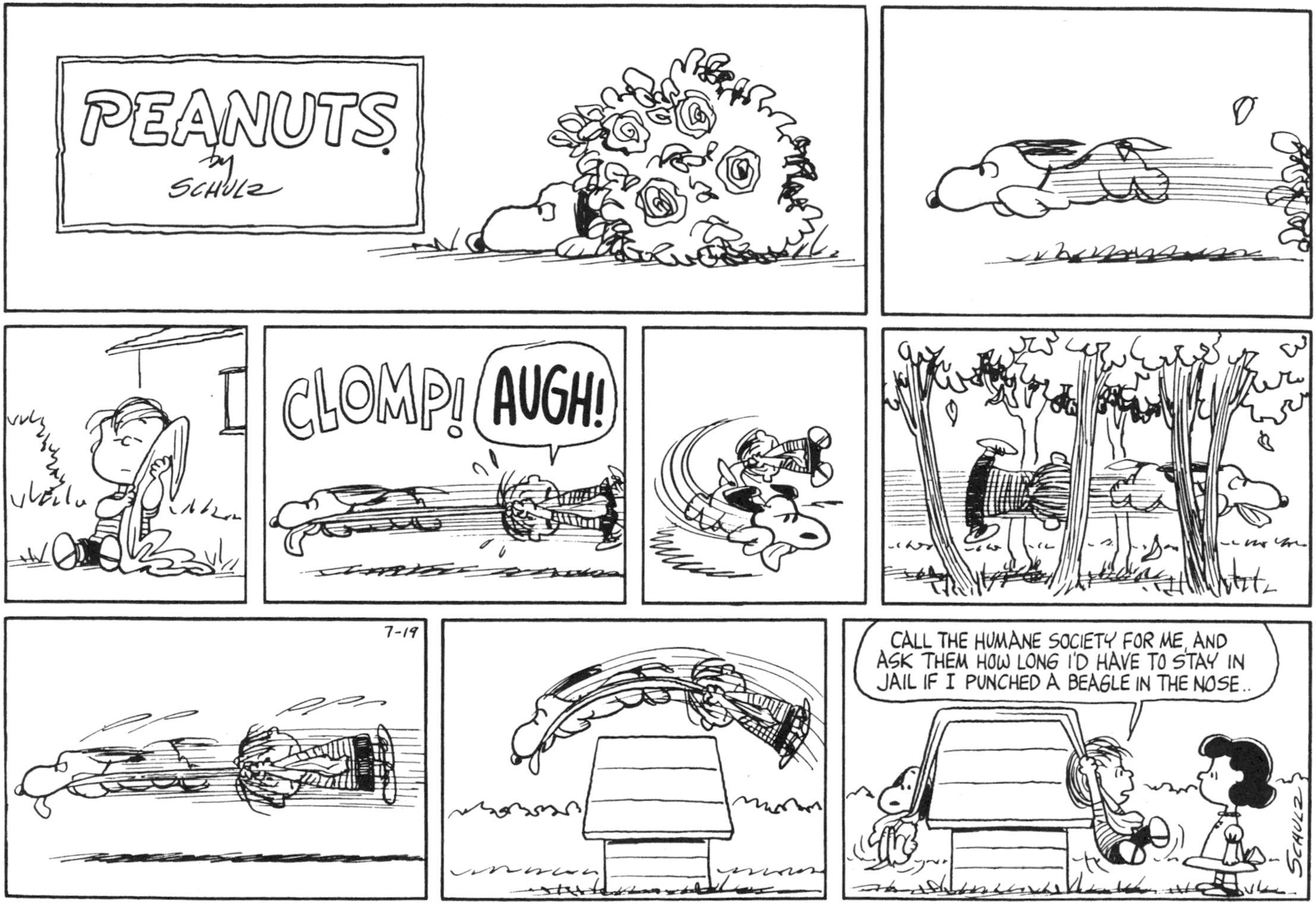
PEANUTS
by SCHULZ
CLOMP!
AUGH!
7-19
CALL THE HUMANE SOCIETY FOR ME, AND ASK THEM HOW LONG I'D HAVE TO STAY IN JAIL IF I PUNCHED A BEAGLE IN THE NOSE..
SCHULZ

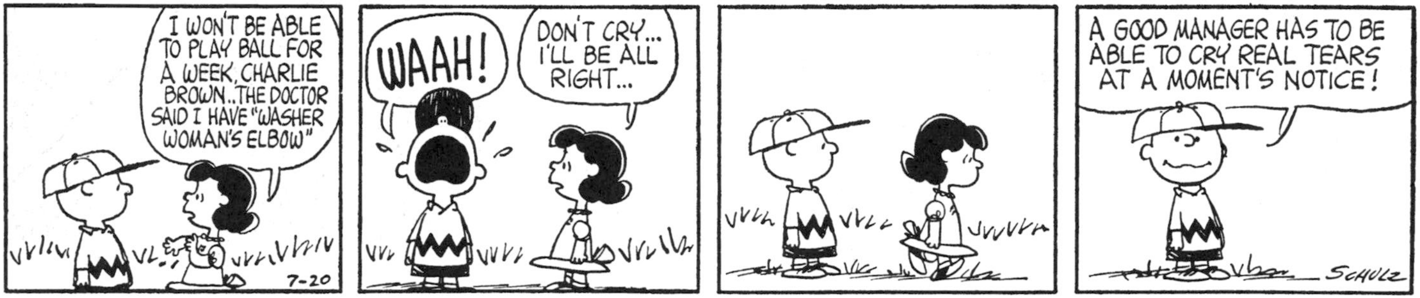
I WON'T BE ABLE TO PLAY BALL FOR A WEEK, CHARLIE BROWN..THE DOCTOR SAID I HAVE "WASHER WOMAN'S ELBOW"
7-20
WAAH!
DON'T CRY... I'LL BE ALL RIGHT...
A GOOD MANAGER HAS TO BE ABLE TO CRY REAL TEARS AT A MOMENT'S NOTICE!
SCHULZ

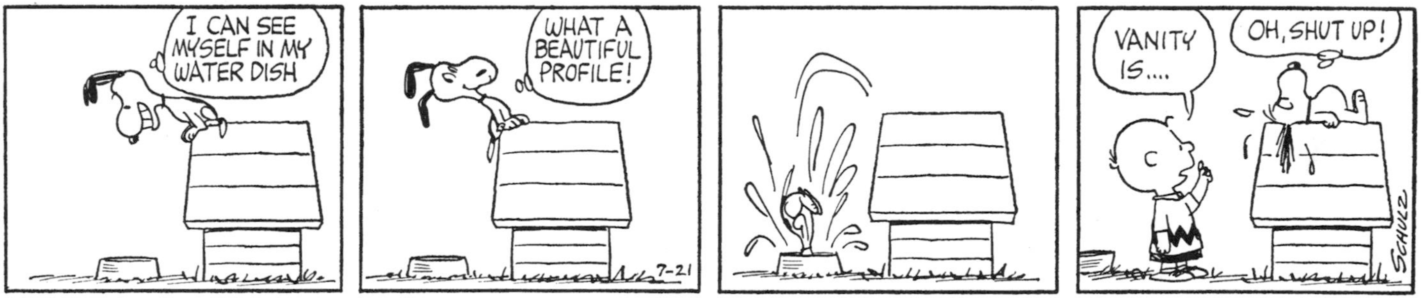
I CAN SEE MYSELF IN MY WATER DISH
WHAT A BEAUTIFUL PROFILE!
7-21
VANITY IS....
OH, SHUT UP!
SCHULZ

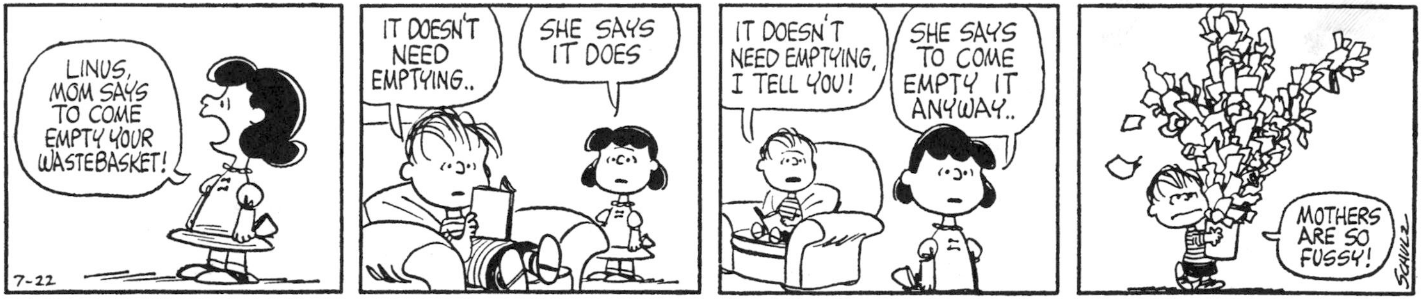
LINUS, MOM SAYS TO COME EMPTY YOUR WASTEBASKET!
7-22
IT DOESN'T NEED EMPTYING..
SHE SAYS IT DOES
IT DOESN'T NEED EMPTYING, I TELL YOU!
SHE SAYS TO COME EMPTY IT ANYWAY..
MOTHERS ARE SO FUSSY!
SCHULZ

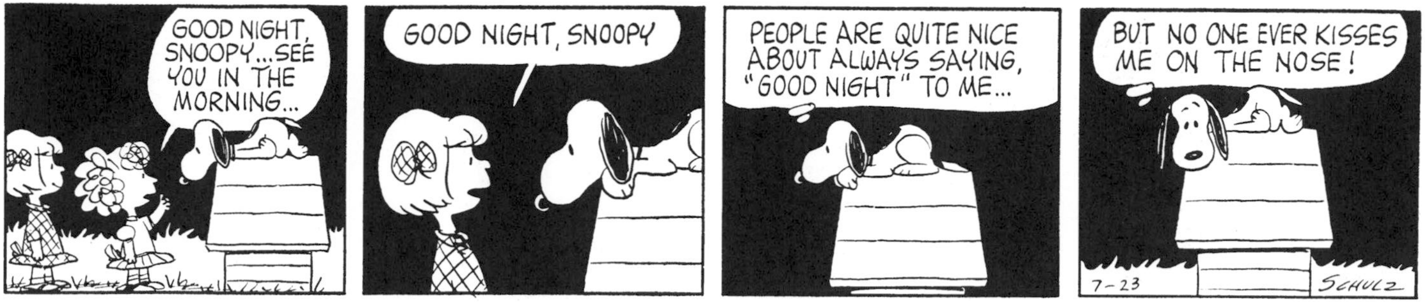
GOOD NIGHT, SNOOPY...SEE YOU IN THE MORNING...
GOOD NIGHT, SNOOPY
PEOPLE ARE QUITE NICE ABOUT ALWAYS SAYING, "GOOD NIGHT" TO ME...
BUT NO ONE EVER KISSES ME ON THE NOSE!
7-23
SCHULZ

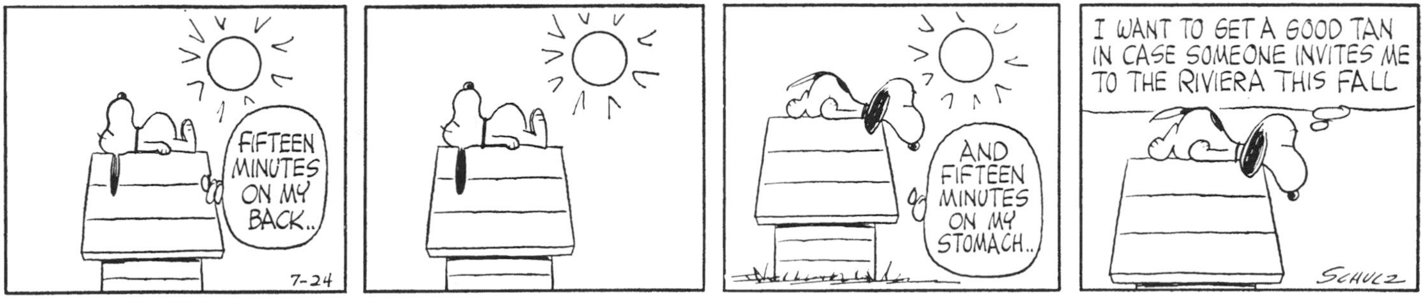
FIFTEEN MINUTES ON MY BACK..
7-24
AND FIFTEEN MINUTES ON MY STOMACH..
I WANT TO GET A GOOD TAN IN CASE SOMEONE INVITES ME TO THE RIVIERA THIS FALL
SCHULZ

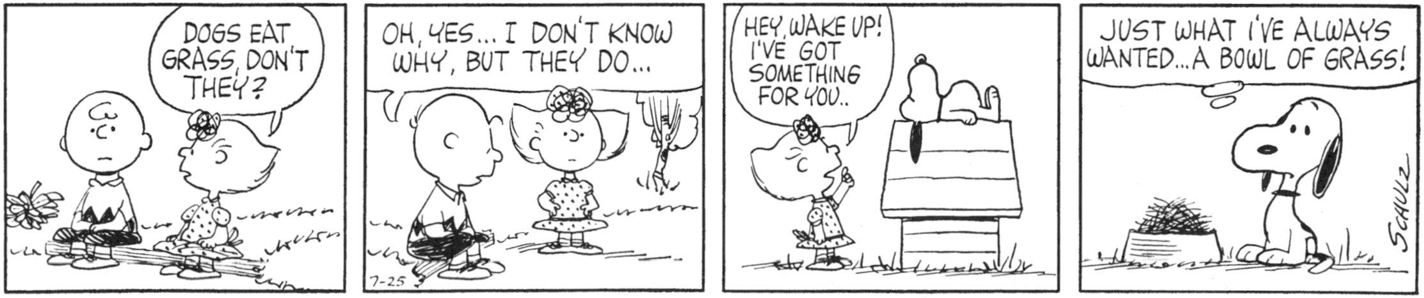
DOGS EAT GRASS, DON'T THEY?
OH, YES... I DON'T KNOW WHY, BUT THEY DO...
7-25
HEY, WAKE UP! I'VE GOT SOMETHING FOR YOU..
JUST WHAT I'VE ALWAYS WANTED...A BOWL OF GRASS!
SCHULZ

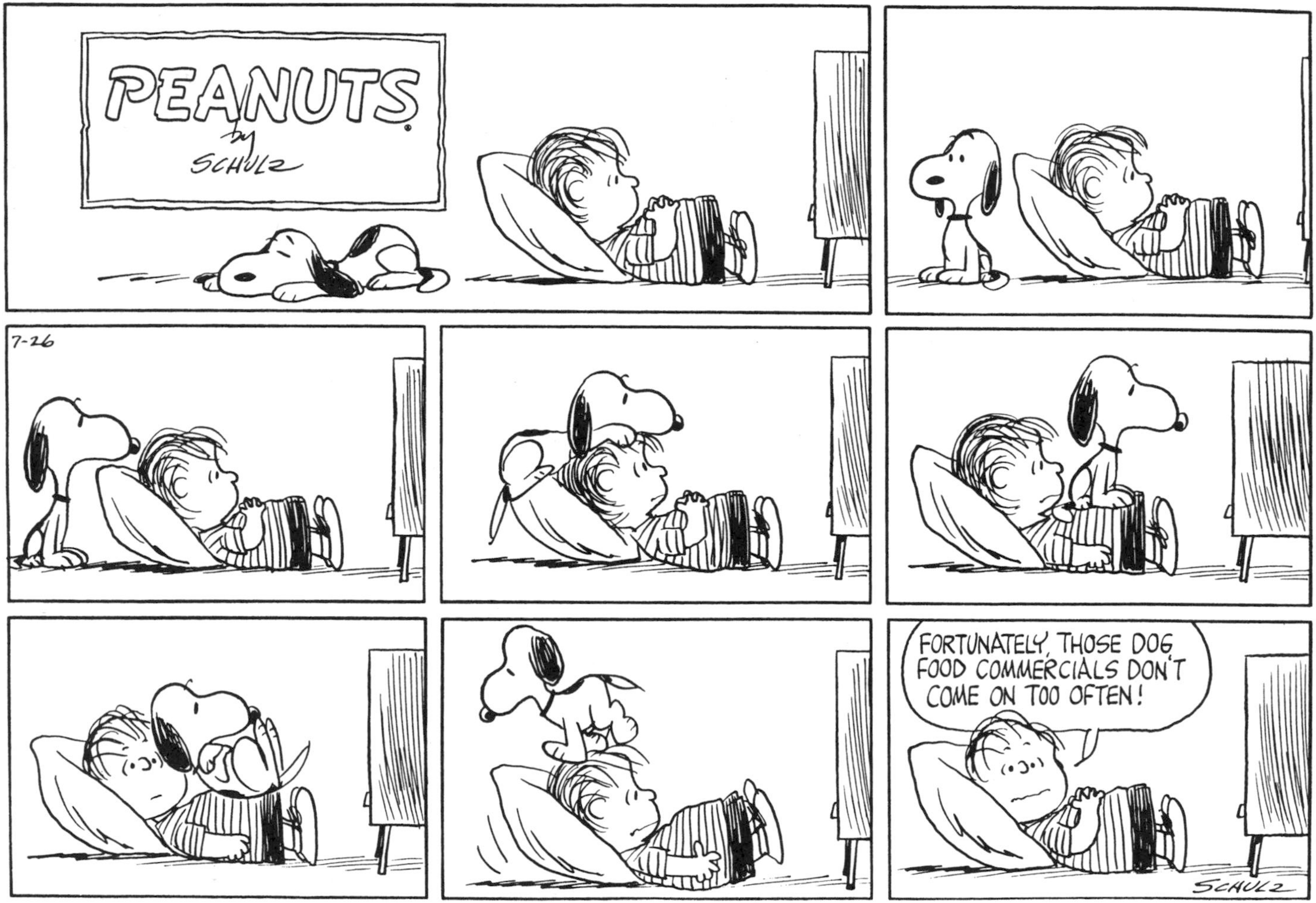
PEANUTS
by
SCHULZ
7-26
FORTUNATELY, THOSE DOG FOOD COMMERCIALS DON'T COME ON TOO OFTEN!
SCHULZ

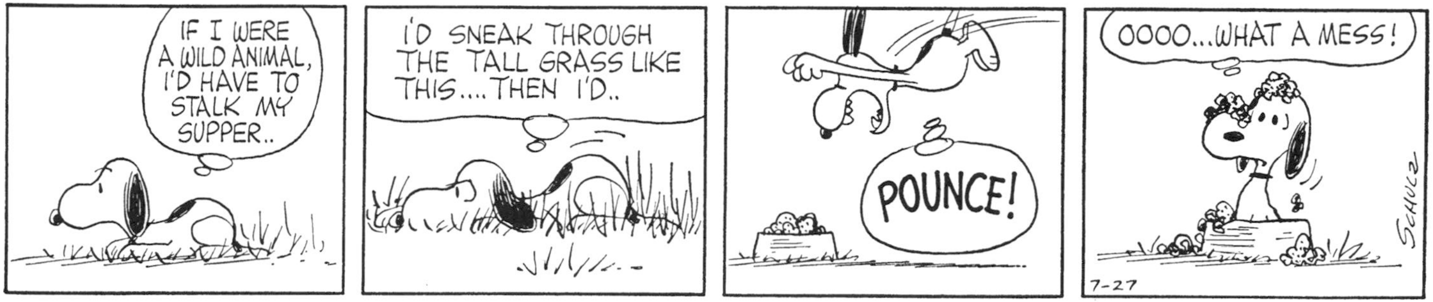
IF I WERE A WILD ANIMAL, I'D HAVE TO STALK MY SUPPER..
I'D SNEAK THROUGH THE TALL GRASS LIKE THIS.... THEN I'D..
POUNCE!
OOOO...WHAT A MESS!
SCHULZ
7-27

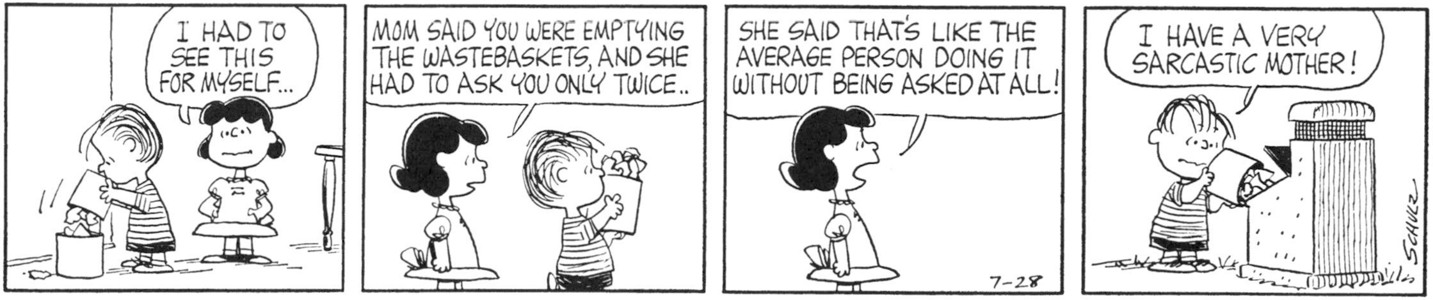
I HAD TO SEE THIS FOR MYSELF...
MOM SAID YOU WERE EMPTYING THE WASTEBASKETS, AND SHE HAD TO ASK YOU ONLY TWICE..
SHE SAID THAT'S LIKE THE AVERAGE PERSON DOING IT WITHOUT BEING ASKED AT ALL!
7-28
I HAVE A VERY SARCASTIC MOTHER!
SCHULZ

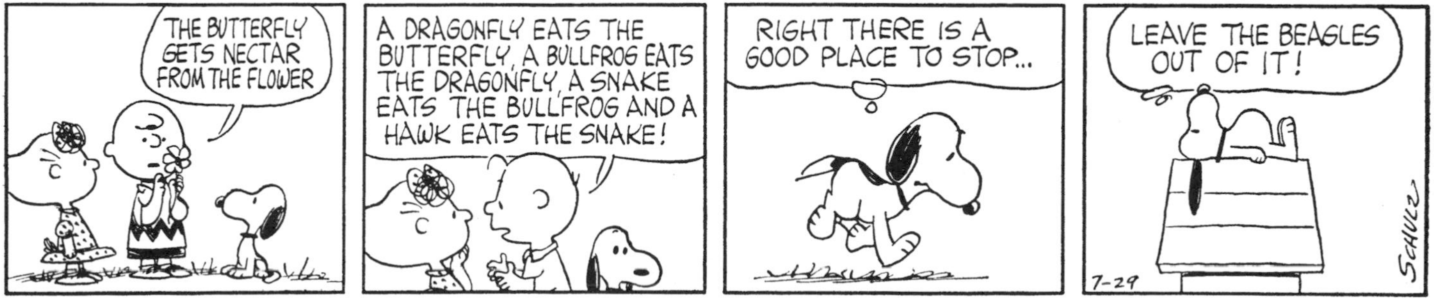
THE BUTTERFLY GETS NECTAR FROM THE FLOWER
A DRAGONFLY EATS THE BUTTERFLY, A BULLFROG EATS THE DRAGONFLY, A SNAKE EATS THE BULLFROG AND A HAWK EATS THE SNAKE!
RIGHT THERE IS A GOOD PLACE TO STOP...
LEAVE THE BEAGLES OUT OF IT!
SCHULZ
7-29

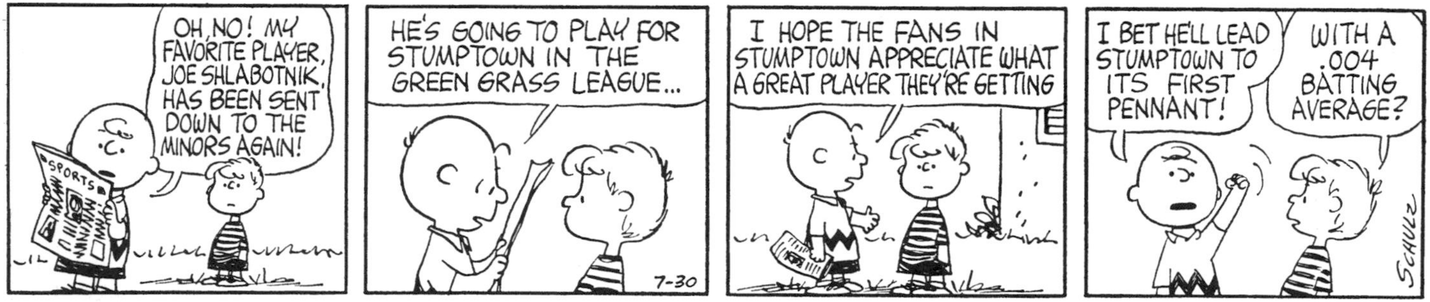
OH, NO! MY FAVORITE PLAYER, JOE SHLABOTNIK, HAS BEEN SENT DOWN TO THE MINORS AGAIN!
SPORTS
HE'S GOING TO PLAY FOR STUMPTOWN IN THE GREEN GRASS LEAGUE...
7-30
I HOPE THE FANS IN STUMPTOWN APPRECIATE WHAT A GREAT PLAYER THEY'RE GETTING
I BET HE'LL LEAD STUMPTOWN TO ITS FIRST PENNANT!
WITH A .004 BATTING AVERAGE?
SCHULZ

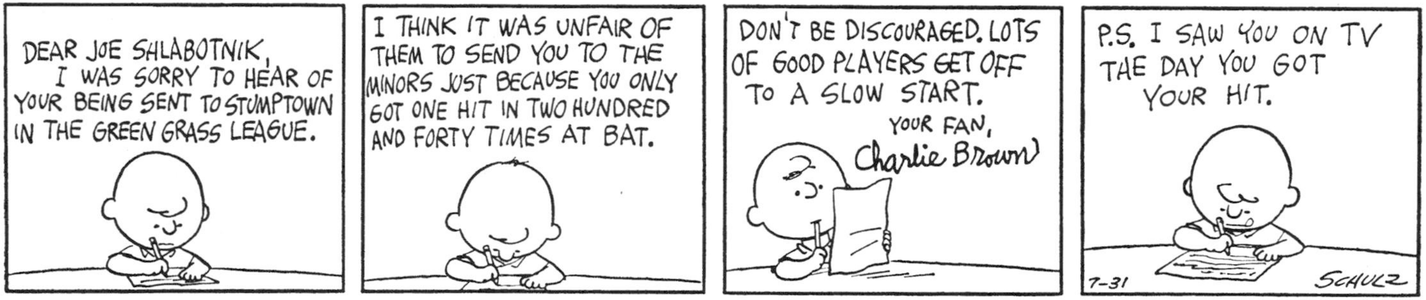
DEAR JOE SHLABOTNIK,
I WAS SORRY TO HEAR OF YOUR BEING SENT TO STUMPTOWN IN THE GREEN GRASS LEAGUE.
I THINK IT WAS UNFAIR OF THEM TO SEND YOU TO THE MINORS JUST BECAUSE YOU ONLY GOT ONE HIT IN TWO HUNDRED AND FORTY TIMES AT BAT.
DON'T BE DISCOURAGED. LOTS OF GOOD PLAYERS GET OFF TO A SLOW START.
YOUR FAN,
Charlie Brown
P.S. I SAW YOU ON TV THE DAY YOU GOT YOUR HIT.
7-31
SCHULZ

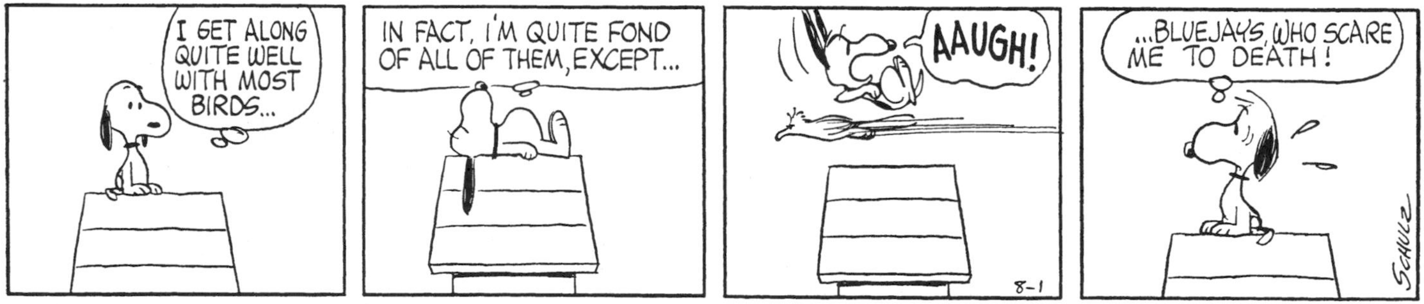
I GET ALONG QUITE WELL WITH MOST BIRDS...
IN FACT, I'M QUITE FOND OF ALL OF THEM, EXCEPT...
AAUGH!
8-1
...BLUEJAYS, WHO SCARE ME TO DEATH!
SCHULZ

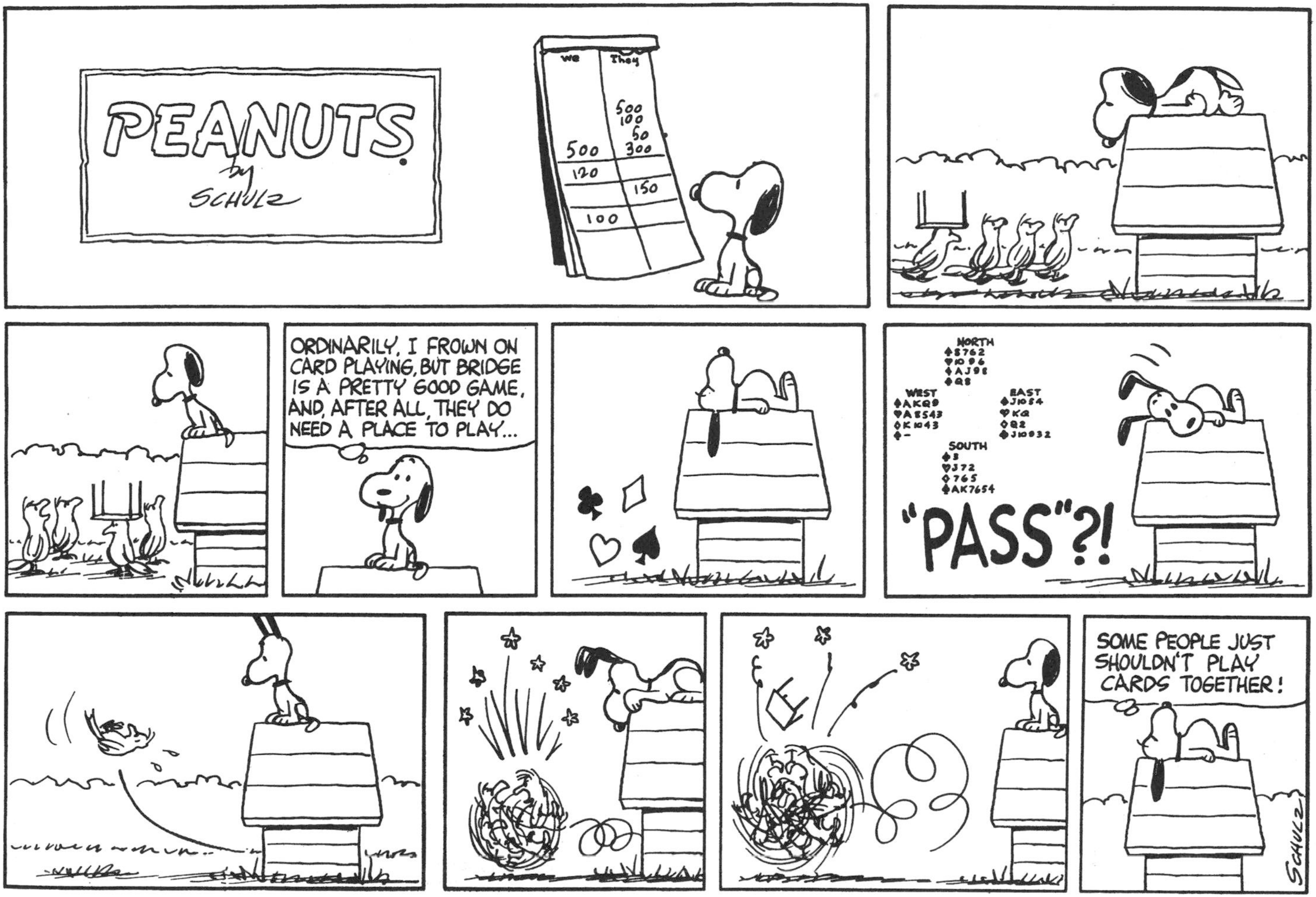
PEANUTS
by SCHULZ
WE THEY
500
100
50
500 300
120
150
100
ORDINARILY, I FROWN ON CARD PLAYING, BUT BRIDGE IS A PRETTY GOOD GAME, AND, AFTER ALL, THEY DO NEED A PLACE TO PLAY...
NORTH
♠8762
♥10 9 6
♦AJ98
♣Q8
WEST
♠AKQ9
♥A8543
♦K1043
♣—
EAST
♠J1054
♥KQ
♦Q2
♣J10932
SOUTH
♠3
♥J72
♦765
♣AK7654
"PASS"?!
SOME PEOPLE JUST SHOULDN'T PLAY CARDS TOGETHER!
SCHULZ

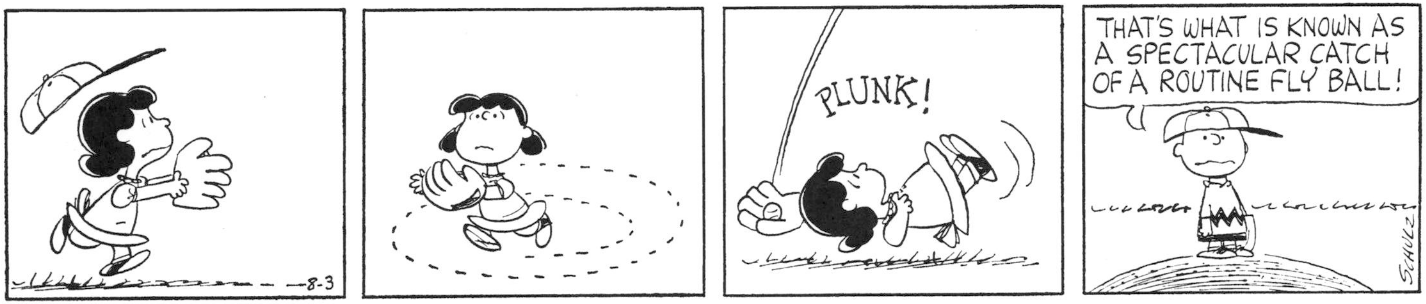
PLUNK!
THAT'S WHAT IS KNOWN AS A SPECTACULAR CATCH OF A ROUTINE FLY BALL!

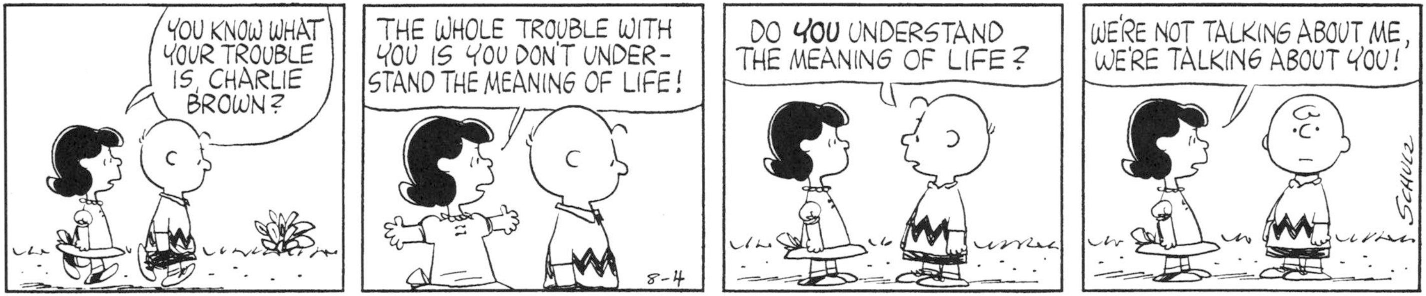
YOU KNOW WHAT YOUR TROUBLE IS, CHARLIE BROWN?
THE WHOLE TROUBLE WITH YOU IS YOU DON'T UNDERSTAND THE MEANING OF LIFE!
DO YOU UNDERSTAND THE MEANING OF LIFE?
WE'RE NOT TALKING ABOUT ME, WE'RE TALKING ABOUT YOU!

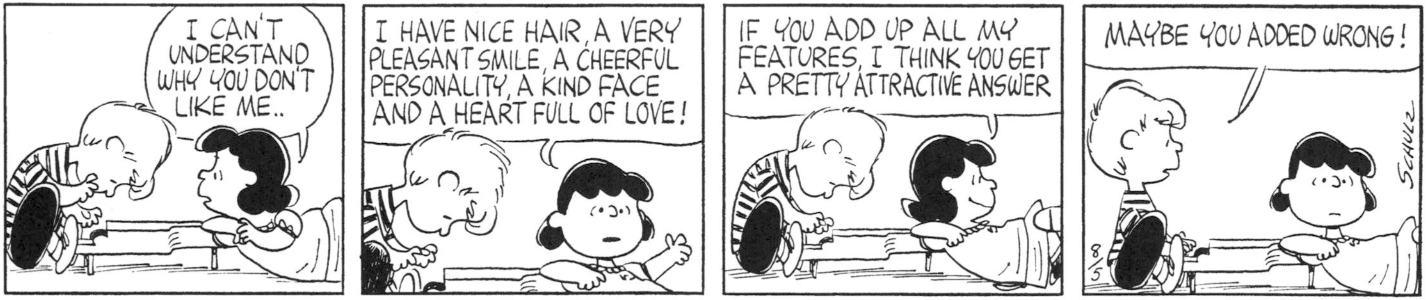
I CAN'T UNDERSTAND WHY YOU DON'T LIKE ME..
I HAVE NICE HAIR, A VERY PLEASANT SMILE, A CHEERFUL PERSONALITY, A KIND FACE AND A HEART FULL OF LOVE!
IF YOU ADD UP ALL MY FEATURES, I THINK YOU GET A PRETTY ATTRACTIVE ANSWER
MAYBE YOU ADDED WRONG!

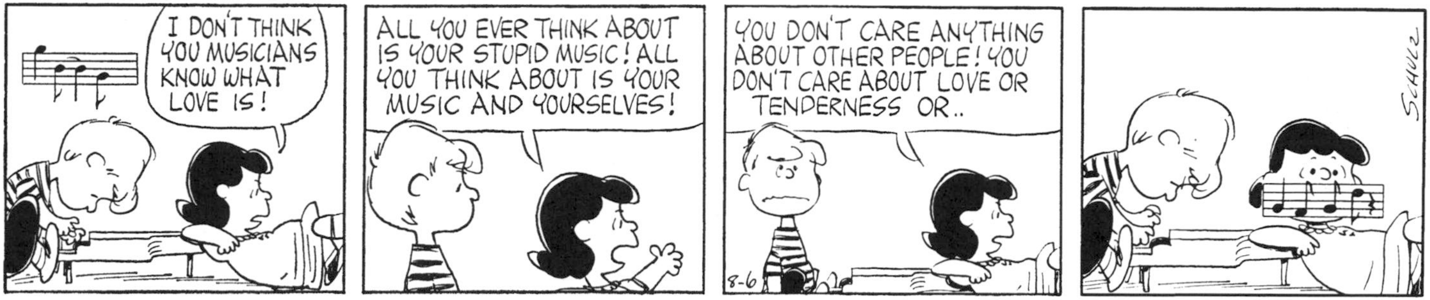
I DON'T THINK YOU MUSICIANS KNOW WHAT LOVE IS!
ALL YOU EVER THINK ABOUT IS YOUR STUPID MUSIC! ALL YOU THINK ABOUT IS YOUR MUSIC AND YOURSELVES!
YOU DON'T CARE ANYTHING ABOUT OTHER PEOPLE! YOU DON'T CARE ABOUT LOVE OR TENDERNESS OR..
SCHULZ

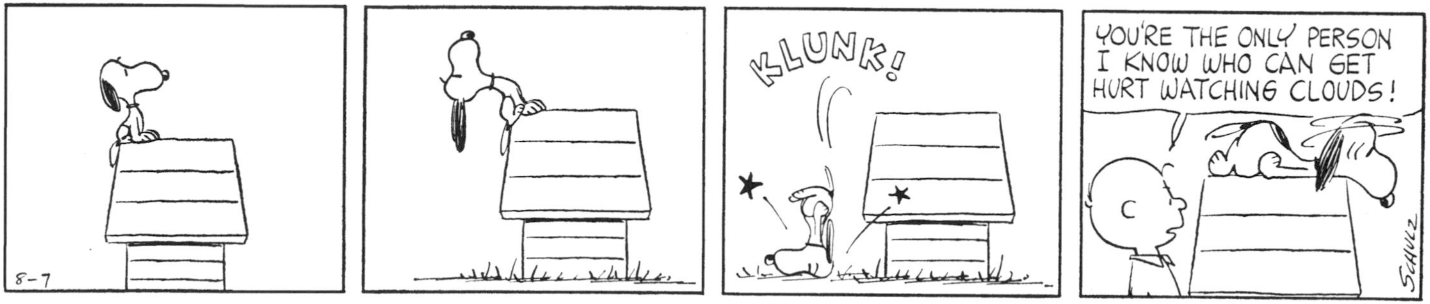
KLUNK!
YOU'RE THE ONLY PERSON I KNOW WHO CAN GET HURT WATCHING CLOUDS!
SCHULZ

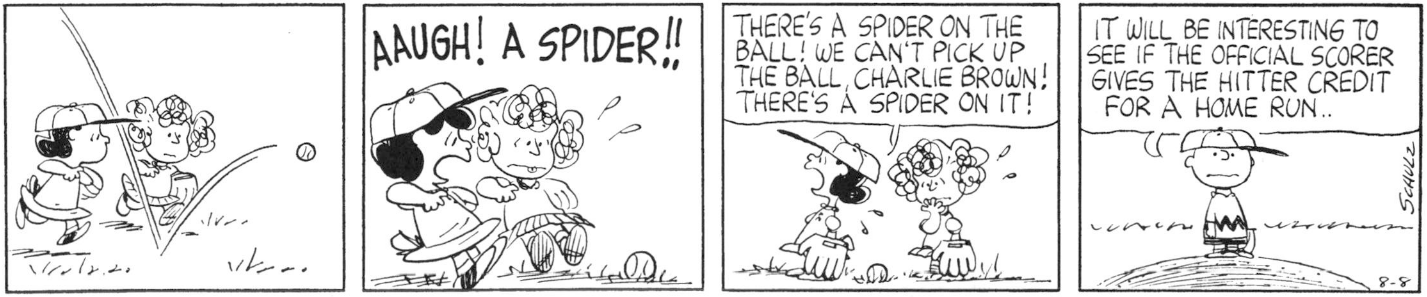
AAUGH! A SPIDER!!
THERE'S A SPIDER ON THE BALL! WE CAN'T PICK UP THE BALL, CHARLIE BROWN! THERE'S A SPIDER ON IT!
IT WILL BE INTERESTING TO SEE IF THE OFFICIAL SCORER GIVES THE HITTER CREDIT FOR A HOME RUN..
SCHULZ

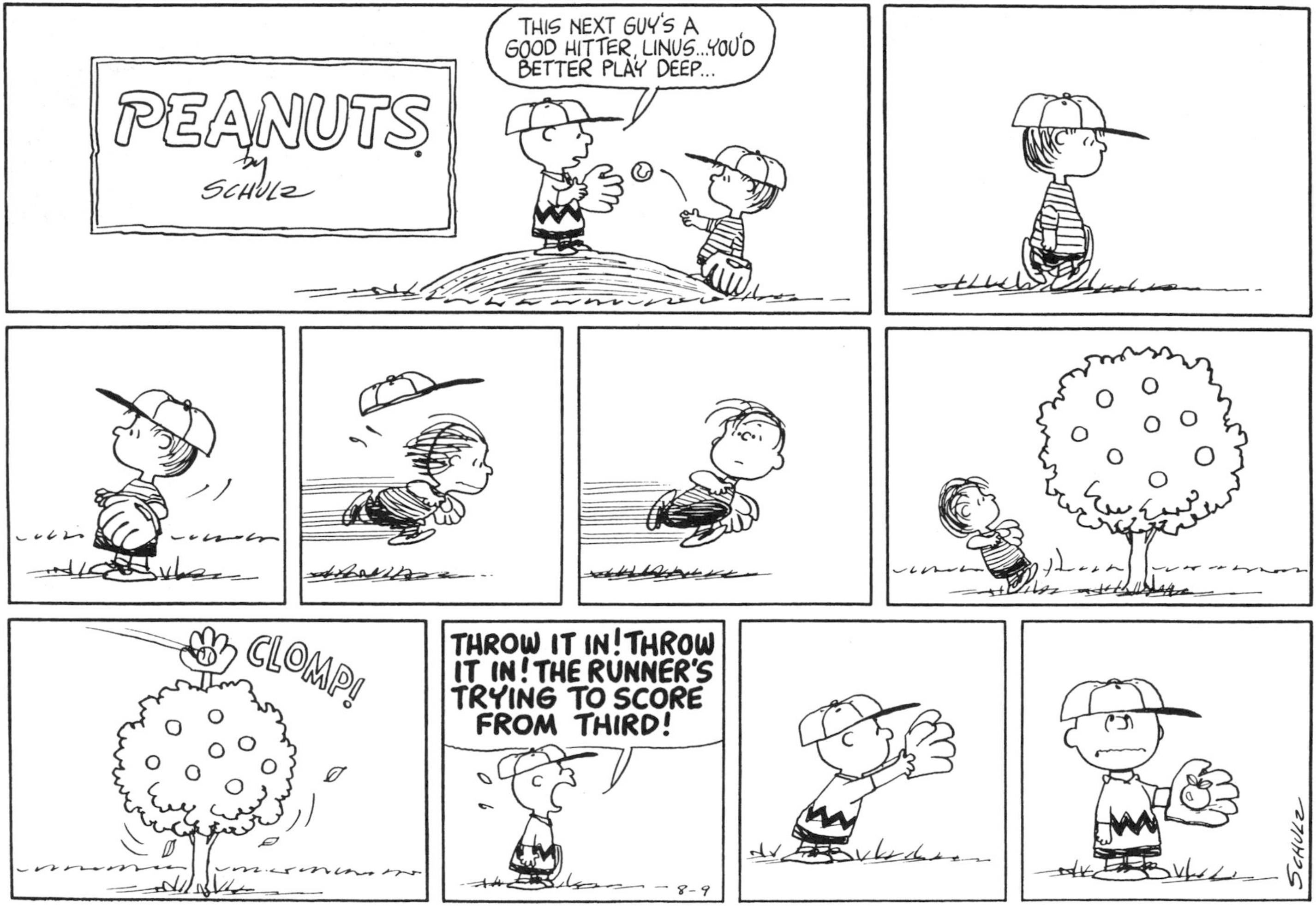
PEANUTS
by SCHULZ
THIS NEXT GUY'S A GOOD HITTER, LINUS...YOU'D BETTER PLAY DEEP...
CLOMP!
THROW IT IN! THROW IT IN! THE RUNNER'S TRYING TO SCORE FROM THIRD!
8-9
SCHULZ

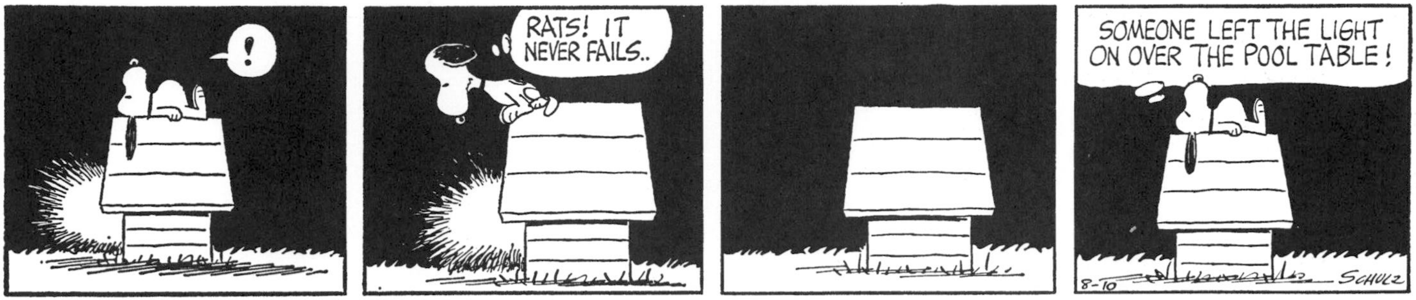
!
RATS! IT NEVER FAILS..
SOMEONE LEFT THE LIGHT ON OVER THE POOL TABLE!
8-10
SCHULZ

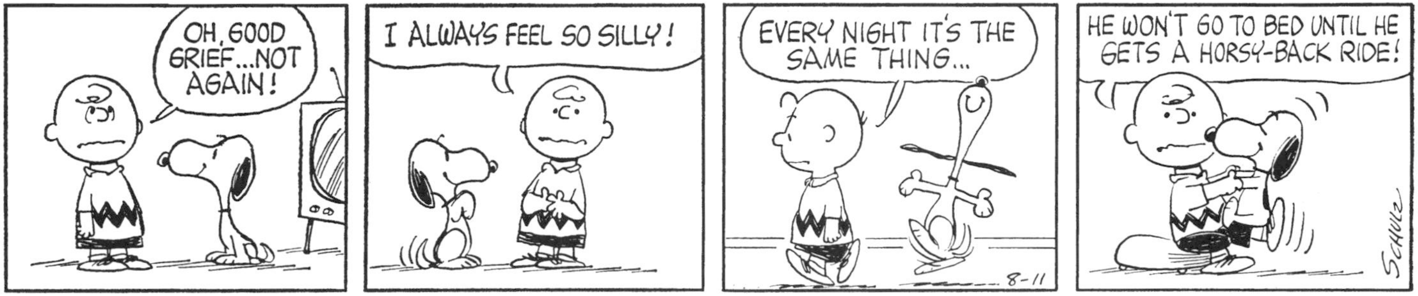
OH, GOOD GRIEF...NOT AGAIN!
I ALWAYS FEEL SO SILLY!
EVERY NIGHT IT'S THE SAME THING...
8-11
HE WON'T GO TO BED UNTIL HE GETS A HORSY-BACK RIDE!
SCHULZ

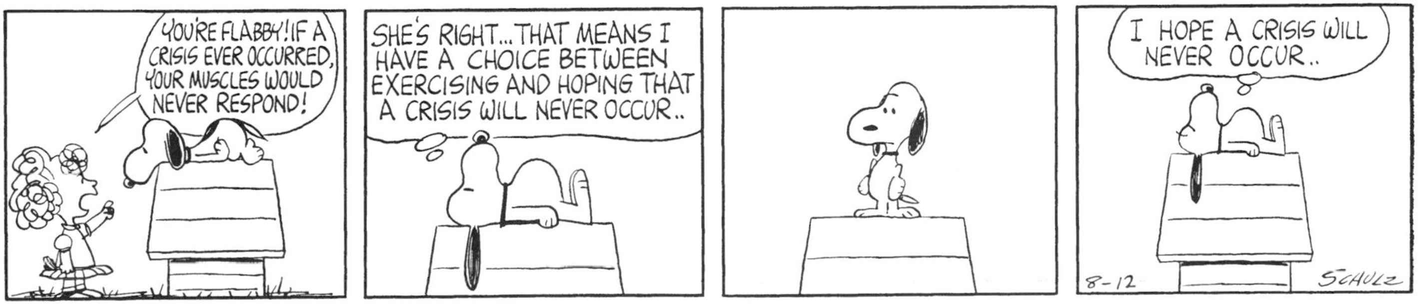
YOU'RE FLABBY! IF A CRISIS EVER OCCURRED, YOUR MUSCLES WOULD NEVER RESPOND!
SHE'S RIGHT...THAT MEANS I HAVE A CHOICE BETWEEN EXERCISING AND HOPING THAT A CRISIS WILL NEVER OCCUR..
I HOPE A CRISIS WILL NEVER OCCUR..
8-12
SCHULZ

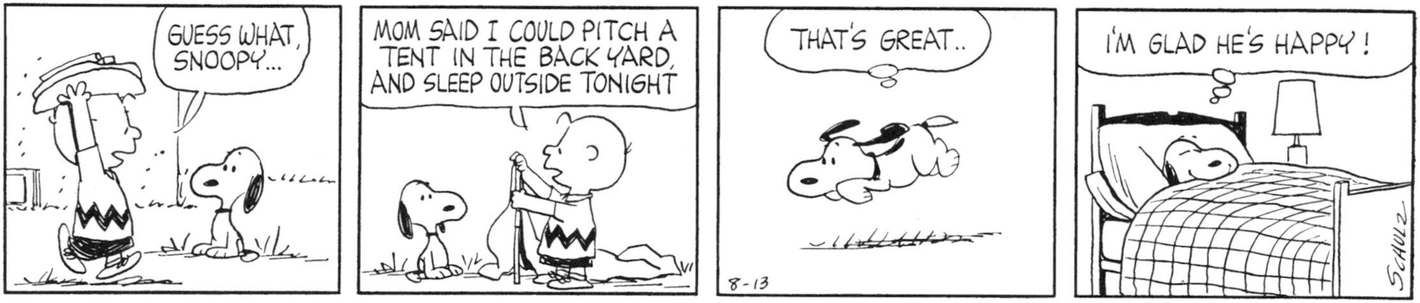
GUESS WHAT, SNOOPY...
MOM SAID I COULD PITCH A TENT IN THE BACK YARD, AND SLEEP OUTSIDE TONIGHT
THAT'S GREAT..
8-13
I'M GLAD HE'S HAPPY!
SCHULZ

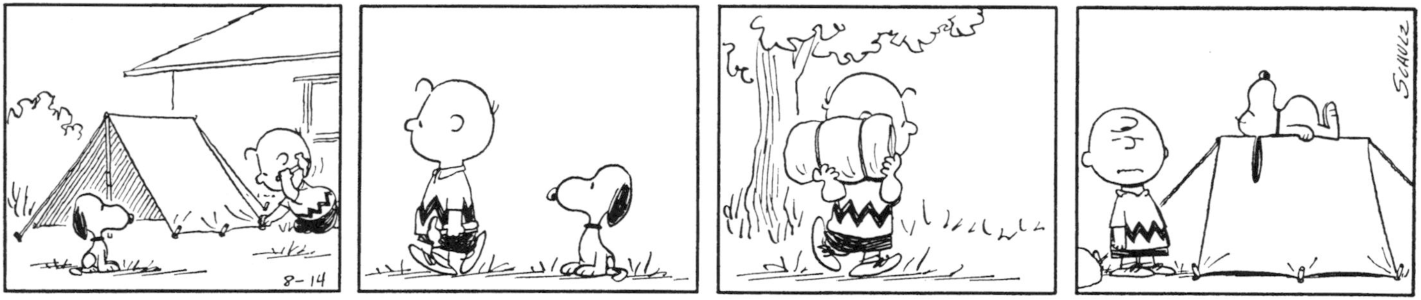
8-14
SCHULZ

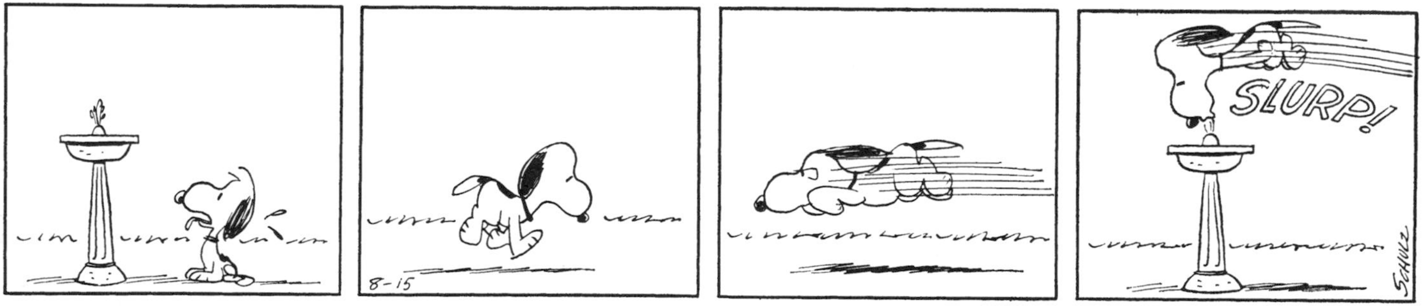
8-15
SLURP!
SCHULZ

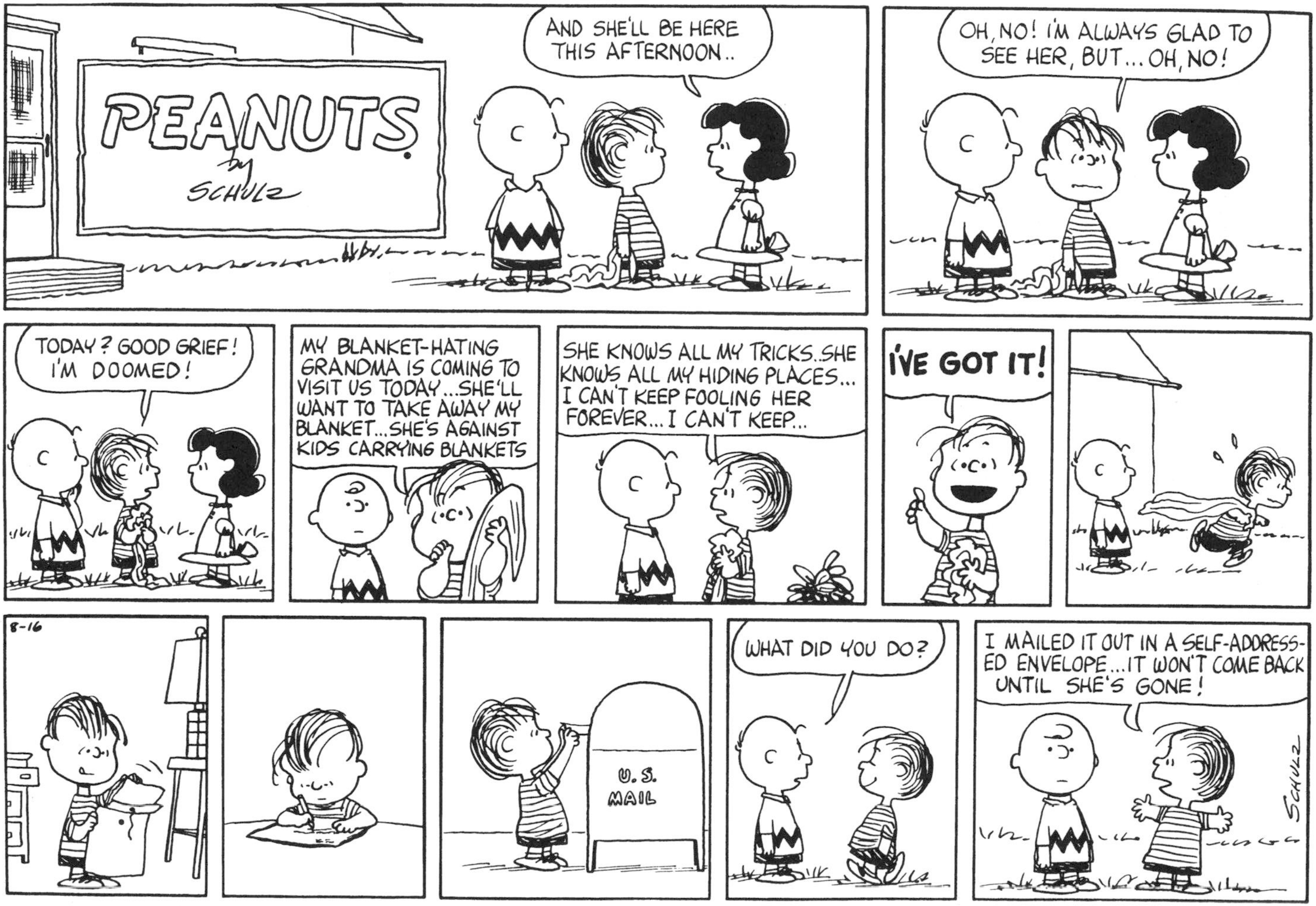
PEANUTS
by SCHULZ
AND SHE'LL BE HERE THIS AFTERNOON..
OH, NO! I'M ALWAYS GLAD TO SEE HER, BUT... OH, NO!
TODAY? GOOD GRIEF! I'M DOOMED!
MY BLANKET-HATING GRANDMA IS COMING TO VISIT US TODAY...SHE'LL WANT TO TAKE AWAY MY BLANKET...SHE'S AGAINST KIDS CARRYING BLANKETS
SHE KNOWS ALL MY TRICKS..SHE KNOWS ALL MY HIDING PLACES... I CAN'T KEEP FOOLING HER FOREVER... I CAN'T KEEP...
I'VE GOT IT!
8-16
U.S. MAIL
WHAT DID YOU DO?
I MAILED IT OUT IN A SELF-ADDRESSED ENVELOPE...IT WON'T COME BACK UNTIL SHE'S GONE!
SCHULZ

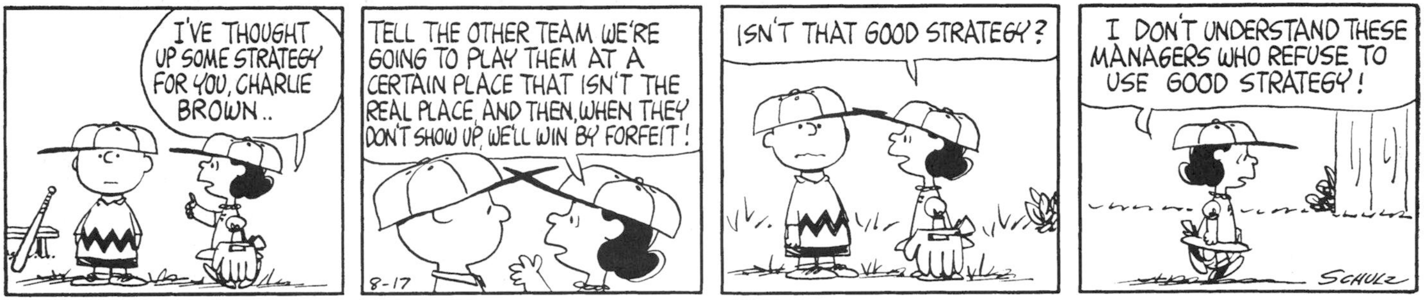
I'VE THOUGHT UP SOME STRATEGY FOR YOU, CHARLIE BROWN..
TELL THE OTHER TEAM WE'RE GOING TO PLAY THEM AT A CERTAIN PLACE THAT ISN'T THE REAL PLACE, AND THEN, WHEN THEY DON'T SHOW UP, WE'LL WIN BY FORFEIT!
8-17
ISN'T THAT GOOD STRATEGY?
I DON'T UNDERSTAND THESE MANAGERS WHO REFUSE TO USE GOOD STRATEGY!
SCHULZ

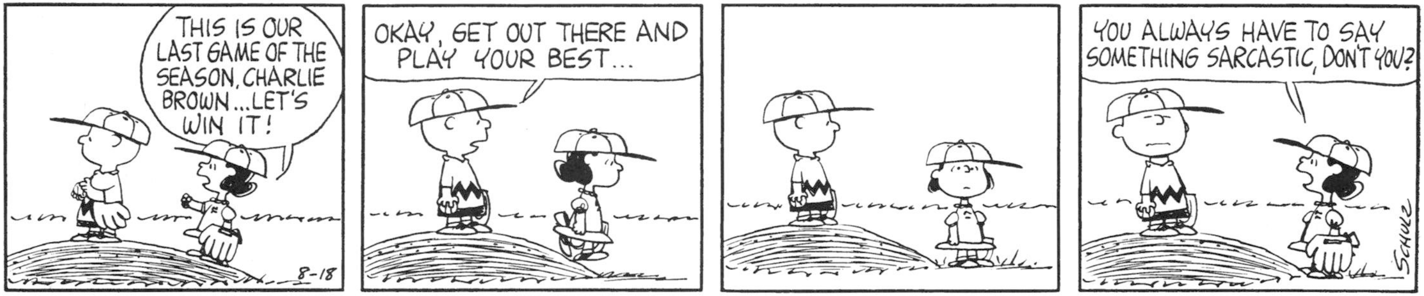
THIS IS OUR LAST GAME OF THE SEASON, CHARLIE BROWN...LET'S WIN IT!
8-18
OKAY, GET OUT THERE AND PLAY YOUR BEST...
YOU ALWAYS HAVE TO SAY SOMETHING SARCASTIC, DON'T YOU?
SCHULZ

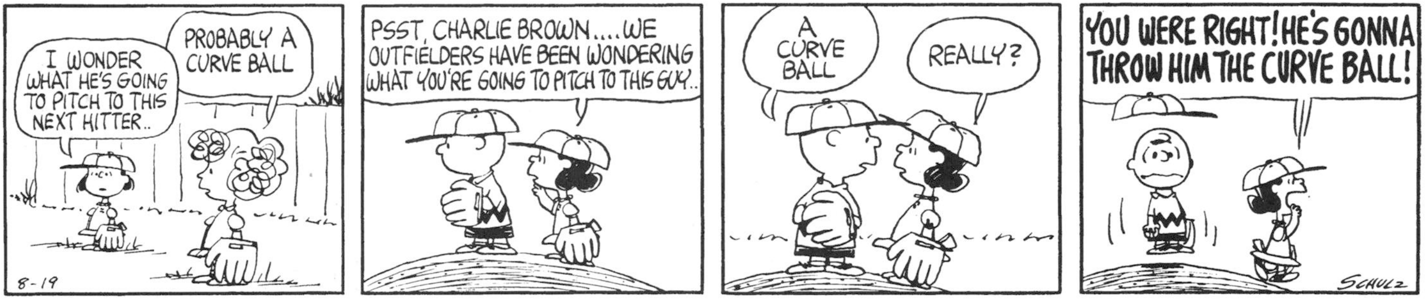
I WONDER WHAT HE'S GOING TO PITCH TO THIS NEXT HITTER..
PROBABLY A CURVE BALL
8-19
PSST, CHARLIE BROWN....WE OUTFIELDERS HAVE BEEN WONDERING WHAT YOU'RE GOING TO PITCH TO THIS GUY..
A CURVE BALL
REALLY?
YOU WERE RIGHT! HE'S GONNA THROW HIM THE CURVE BALL!
SCHULZ

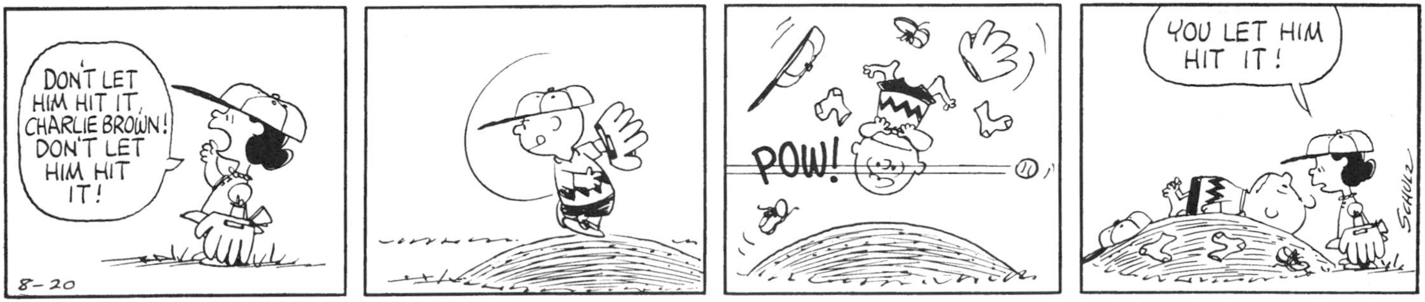

DON'T LET HIM HIT IT, CHARLIE BROWN! DON'T LET HIM HIT IT!
8-20
POW!
YOU LET HIM HIT IT!
SCHULZ

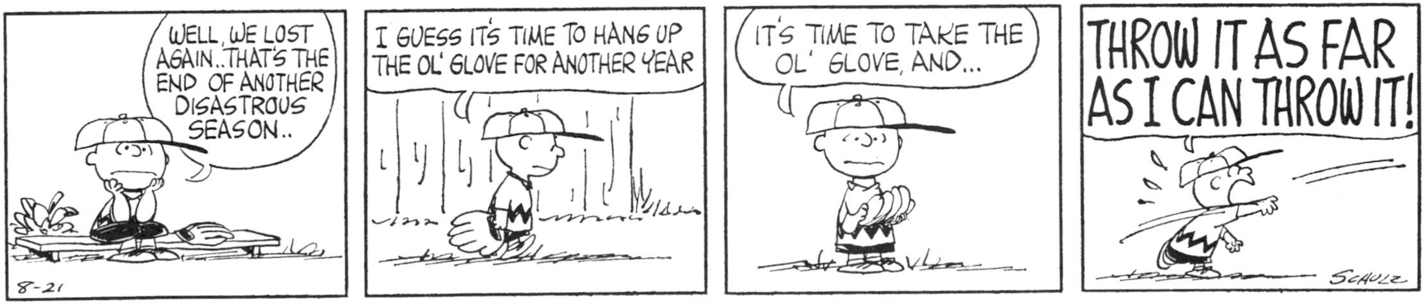

WELL, WE LOST AGAIN..THAT'S THE END OF ANOTHER DISASTROUS SEASON..
8-21
I GUESS IT'S TIME TO HANG UP THE OL' GLOVE FOR ANOTHER YEAR
IT'S TIME TO TAKE THE OL' GLOVE, AND...
THROW IT AS FAR AS I CAN THROW IT!
SCHULZ

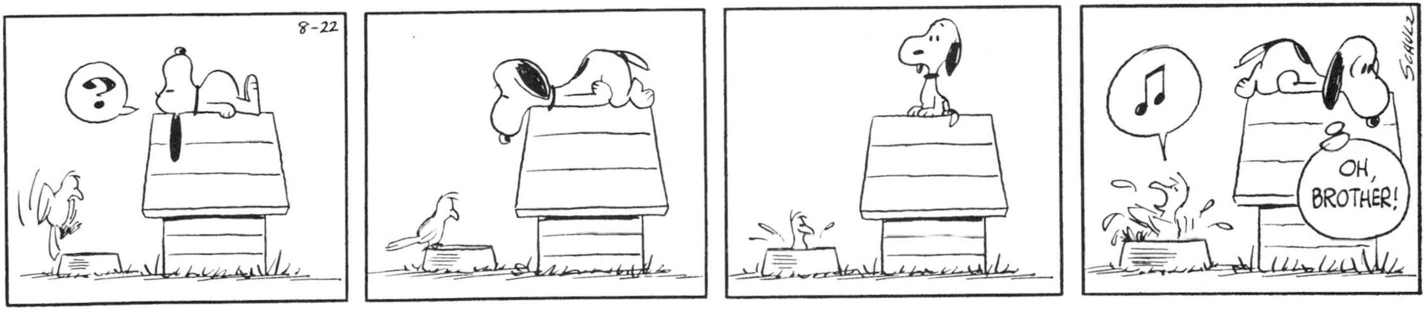

8-22
?
SCHULZ
OH, BROTHER!

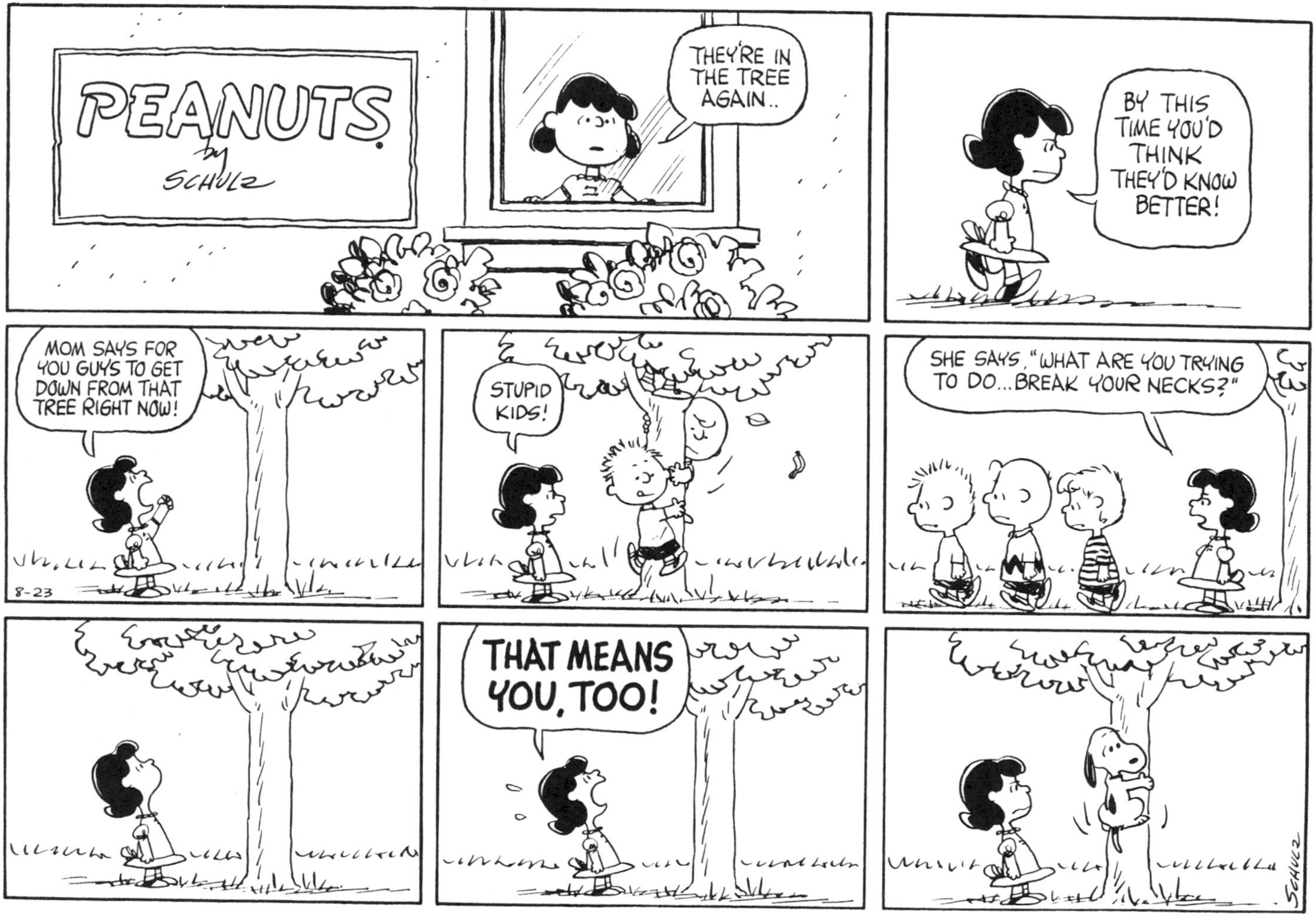
PEANUTS
by SCHULZ
THEY'RE IN THE TREE AGAIN..
BY THIS TIME YOU'D THINK THEY'D KNOW BETTER!
MOM SAYS FOR YOU GUYS TO GET DOWN FROM THAT TREE RIGHT NOW!
8-23
STUPID KIDS!
SHE SAYS, "WHAT ARE YOU TRYING TO DO...BREAK YOUR NECKS?"
THAT MEANS YOU, TOO!
SCHULZ

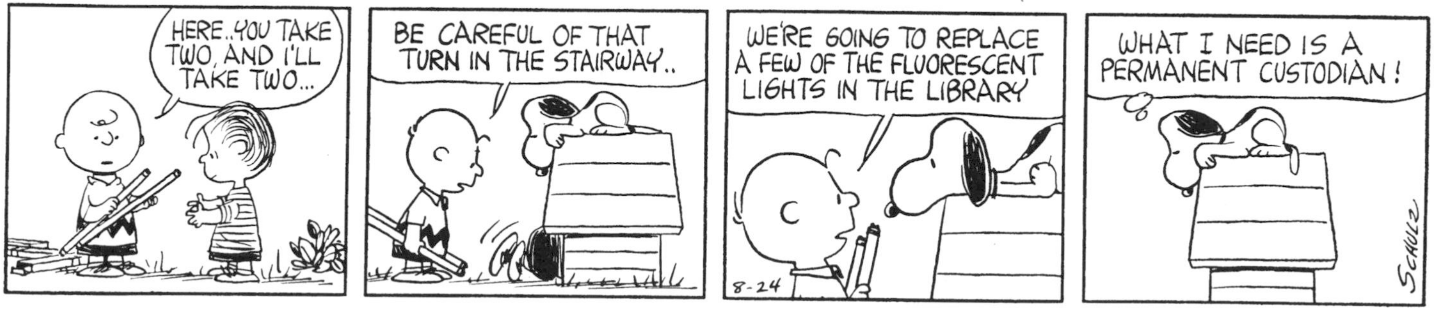
HERE..YOU TAKE TWO, AND I'LL TAKE TWO...
BE CAREFUL OF THAT TURN IN THE STAIRWAY..
WE'RE GOING TO REPLACE A FEW OF THE FLUORESCENT LIGHTS IN THE LIBRARY
8-24
WHAT I NEED IS A PERMANENT CUSTODIAN!
SCHULZ

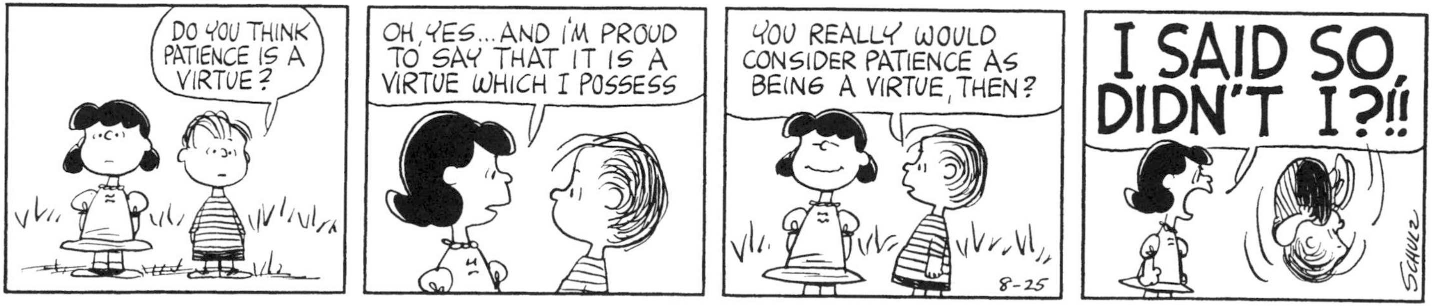
DO YOU THINK PATIENCE IS A VIRTUE?
OH, YES...AND I'M PROUD TO SAY THAT IT IS A VIRTUE WHICH I POSSESS
YOU REALLY WOULD CONSIDER PATIENCE AS BEING A VIRTUE, THEN?
8-25
I SAID SO, DIDN'T I?!!
SCHULZ

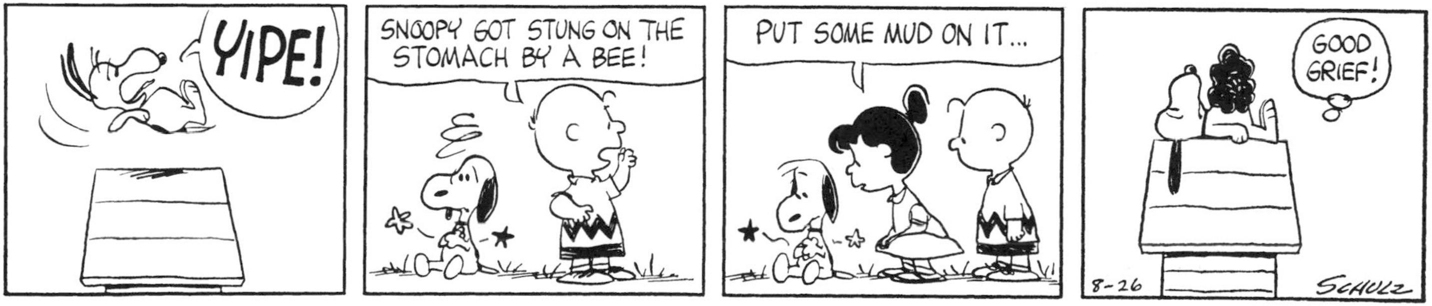
YIPE!
SNOOPY GOT STUNG ON THE STOMACH BY A BEE!
PUT SOME MUD ON IT...
GOOD GRIEF!
8-26
SCHULZ

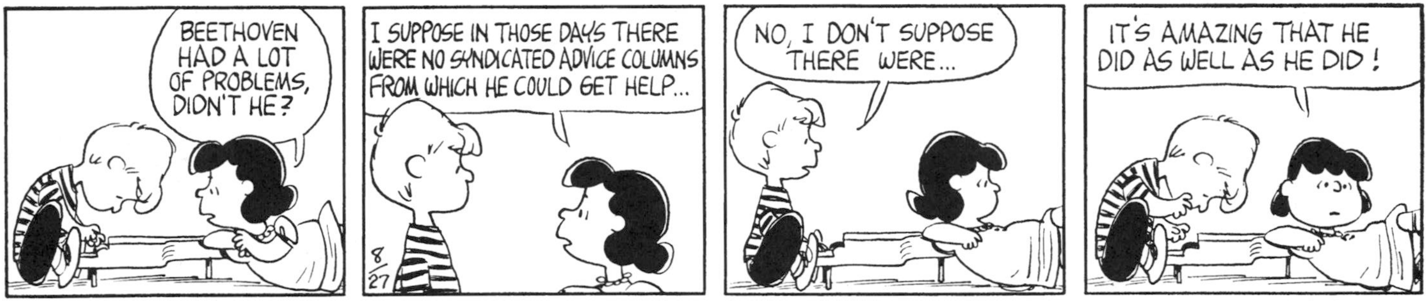
BEETHOVEN HAD A LOT OF PROBLEMS, DIDN'T HE?
I SUPPOSE IN THOSE DAYS THERE WERE NO SYNDICATED ADVICE COLUMNS FROM WHICH HE COULD GET HELP...
8/27
NO, I DON'T SUPPOSE THERE WERE...
IT'S AMAZING THAT HE DID AS WELL AS HE DID!

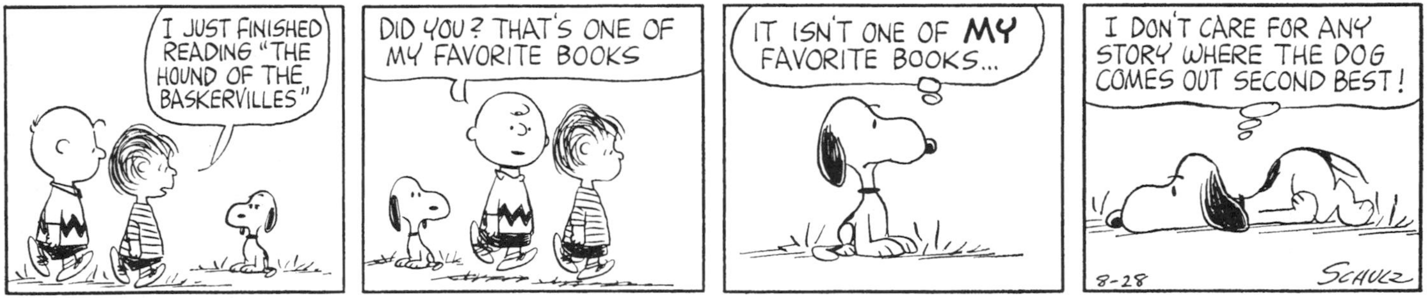
I JUST FINISHED READING "THE HOUND OF THE BASKERVILLES"
DID YOU? THAT'S ONE OF MY FAVORITE BOOKS
IT ISN'T ONE OF **MY** FAVORITE BOOKS...
I DON'T CARE FOR ANY STORY WHERE THE DOG COMES OUT SECOND BEST!
8-28
SCHULZ

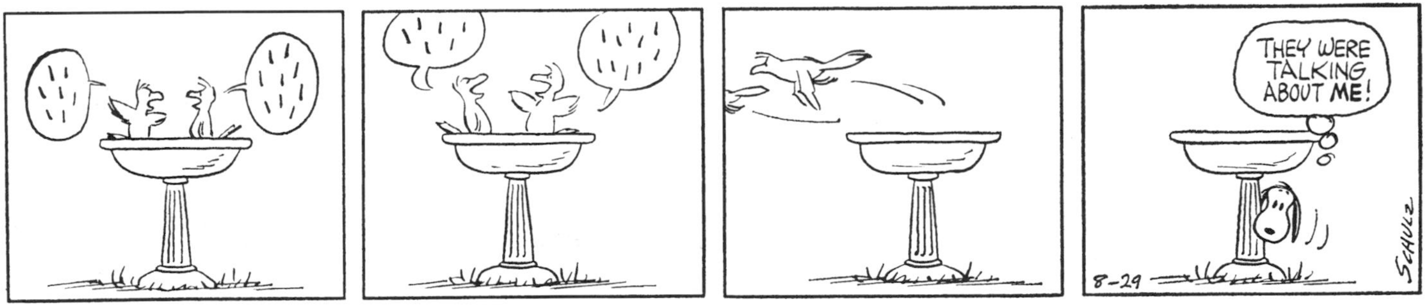
THEY WERE TALKING ABOUT **ME**!
8-29
SCHULZ

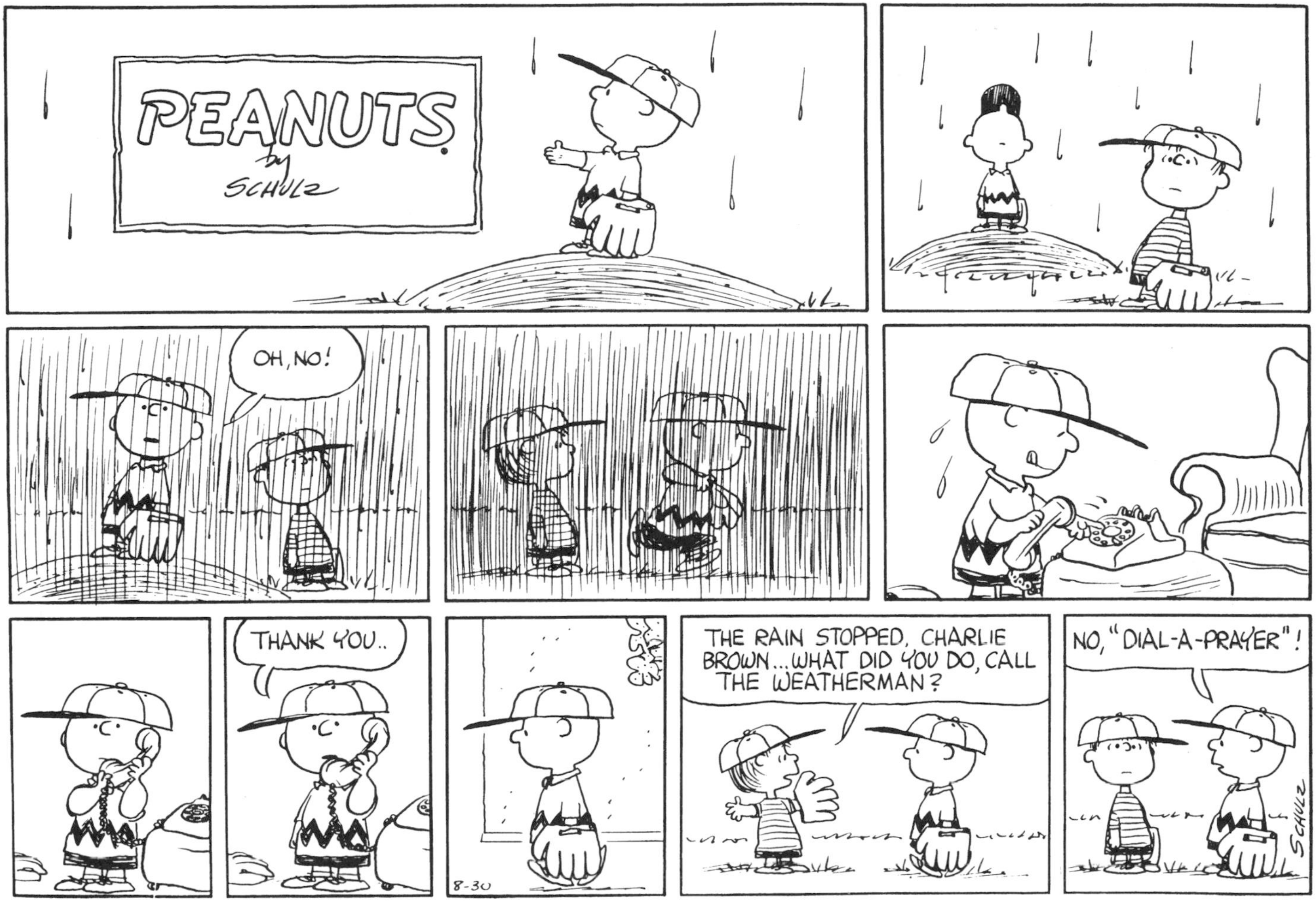
PEANUTS
by SCHULZ
OH, NO!
THANK YOU..
8-30
THE RAIN STOPPED, CHARLIE BROWN...WHAT DID YOU DO, CALL THE WEATHERMAN?
NO, "DIAL-A-PRAYER"!
SCHULZ

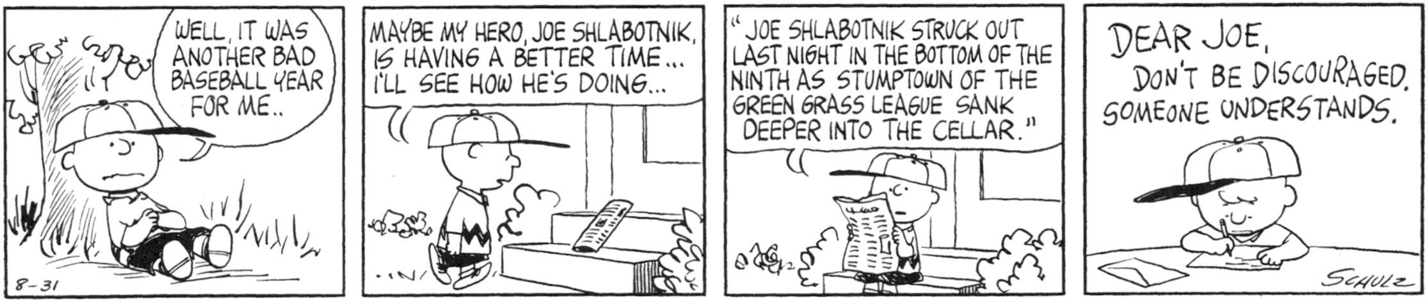
WELL, IT WAS ANOTHER BAD BASEBALL YEAR FOR ME..
8-31
MAYBE MY HERO, JOE SHLABOTNIK, IS HAVING A BETTER TIME... I'LL SEE HOW HE'S DOING...
"JOE SHLABOTNIK STRUCK OUT LAST NIGHT IN THE BOTTOM OF THE NINTH AS STUMPTOWN OF THE GREEN GRASS LEAGUE SANK DEEPER INTO THE CELLAR."
DEAR JOE,
DON'T BE DISCOURAGED.
SOMEONE UNDERSTANDS.
SCHULZ

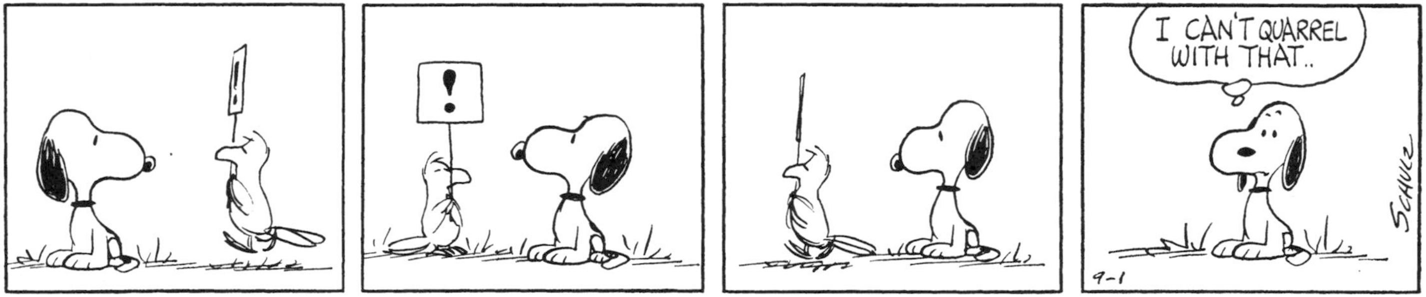
!
!
I CAN'T QUARREL WITH THAT..
SCHULZ
9-1

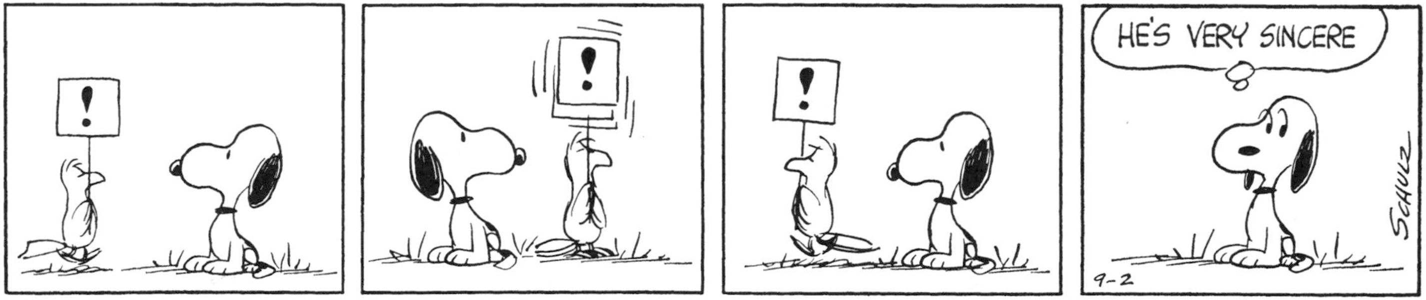
!
!
!
HE'S VERY SINCERE
SCHULZ
9-2

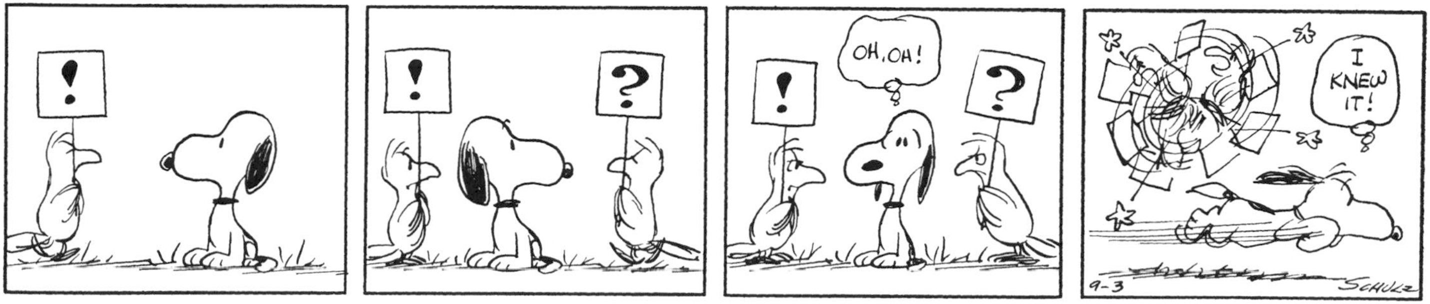
!
!
?
OH, OH!
!
?
I KNEW IT!
9-3
SCHULZ

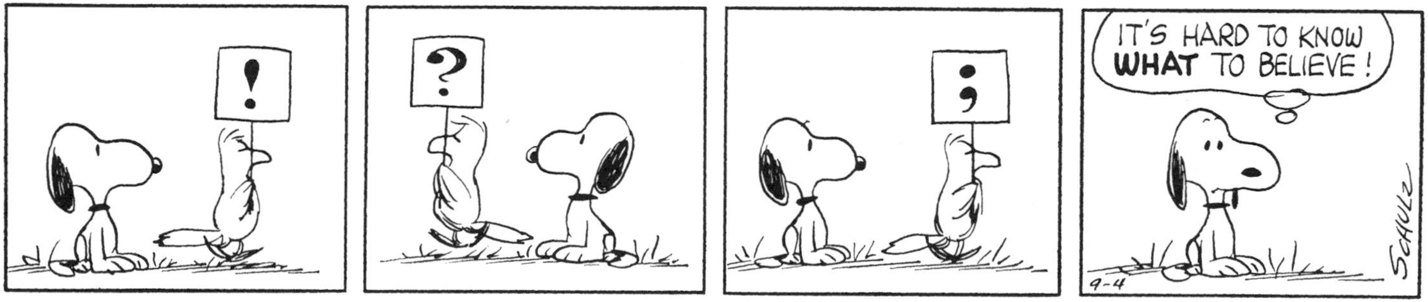
!
?
;
IT'S HARD TO KNOW **WHAT** TO BELIEVE!
9-4
SCHULZ

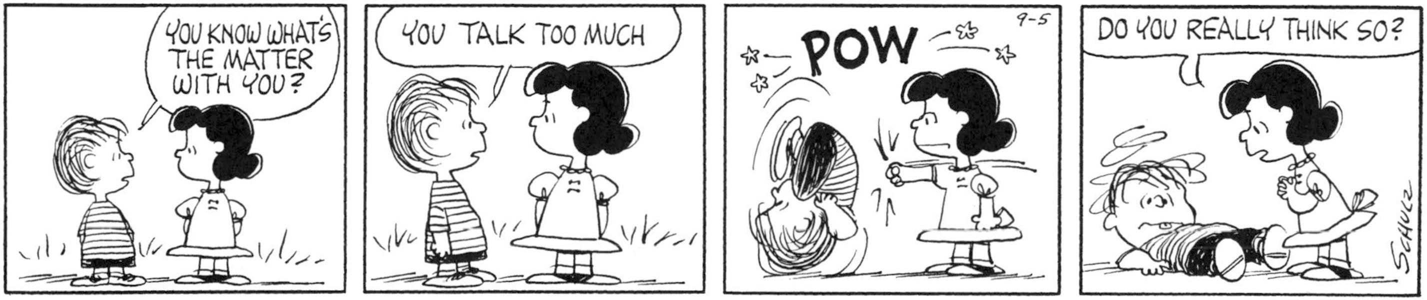
YOU KNOW WHAT'S THE MATTER WITH YOU?
YOU TALK TOO MUCH
POW
9-5
DO YOU REALLY THINK SO?
SCHULZ

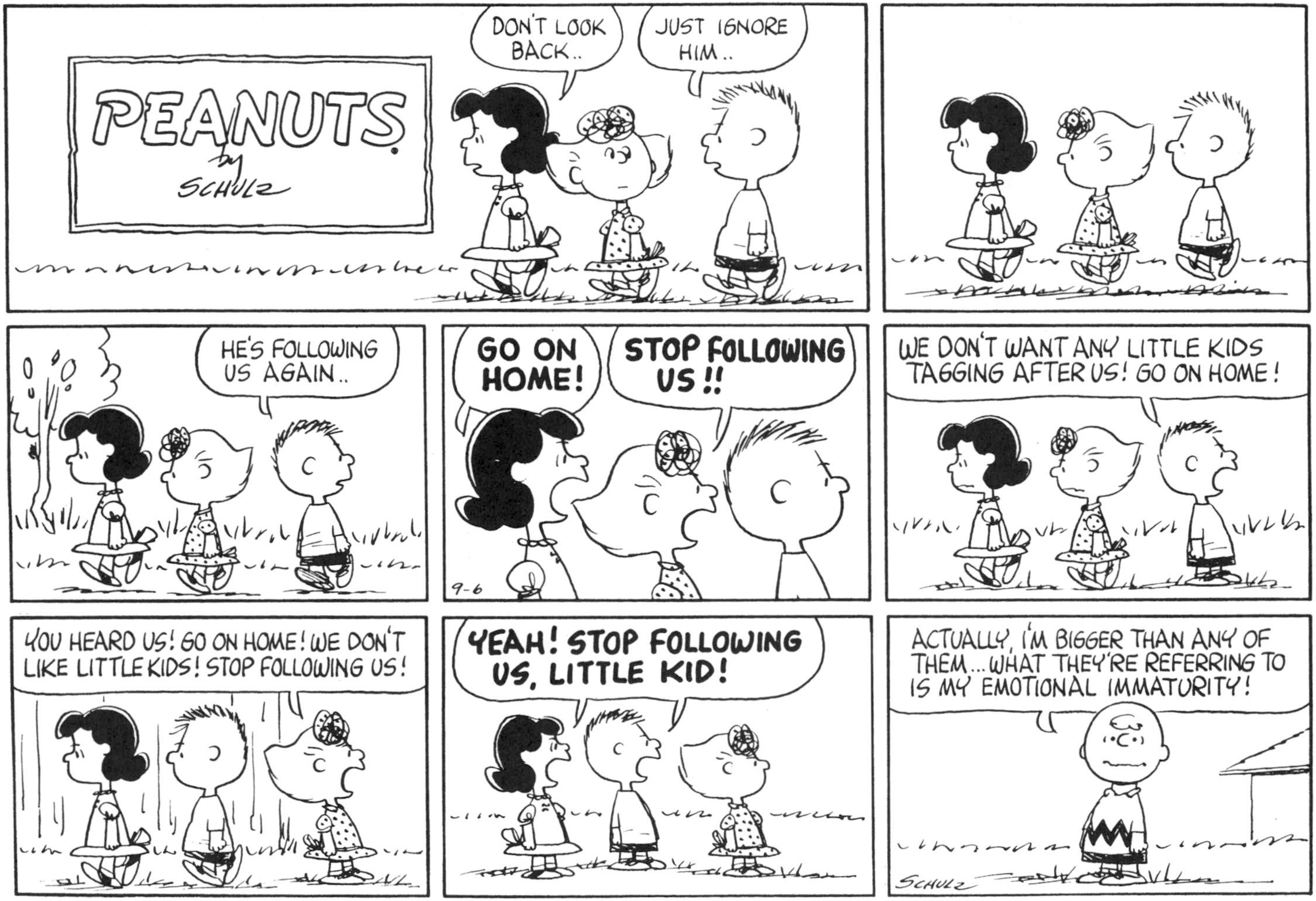
PEANUTS
by SCHULZ
DON'T LOOK BACK..
JUST IGNORE HIM..
HE'S FOLLOWING US AGAIN..
GO ON HOME!
STOP FOLLOWING US!!
9-6
WE DON'T WANT ANY LITTLE KIDS TAGGING AFTER US! GO ON HOME!
YOU HEARD US! GO ON HOME! WE DON'T LIKE LITTLE KIDS! STOP FOLLOWING US!
YEAH! STOP FOLLOWING US, LITTLE KID!
ACTUALLY, I'M BIGGER THAN ANY OF THEM...WHAT THEY'RE REFERRING TO IS MY EMOTIONAL IMMATURITY!
SCHULZ

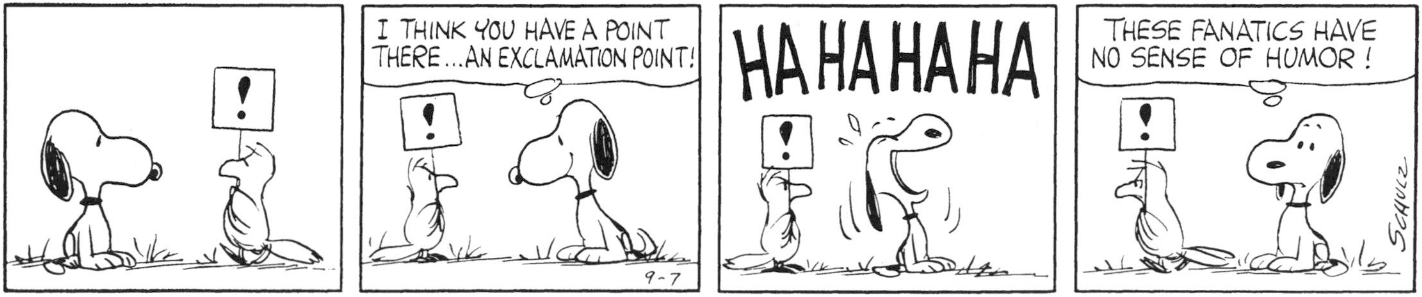
!
I THINK YOU HAVE A POINT THERE...AN EXCLAMATION POINT!
9-7
HA HA HA HA HA
THESE FANATICS HAVE NO SENSE OF HUMOR!
SCHULZ

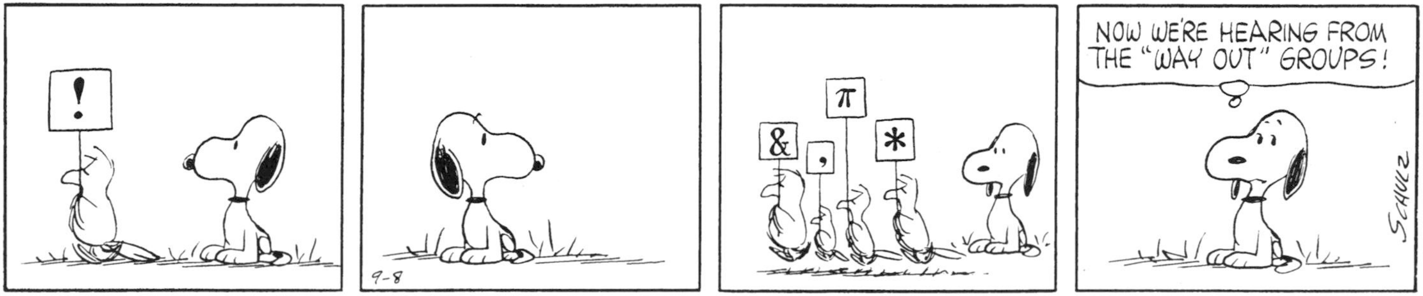
!
9-8
&
,
π
*
NOW WE'RE HEARING FROM THE "WAY OUT" GROUPS!
SCHULZ

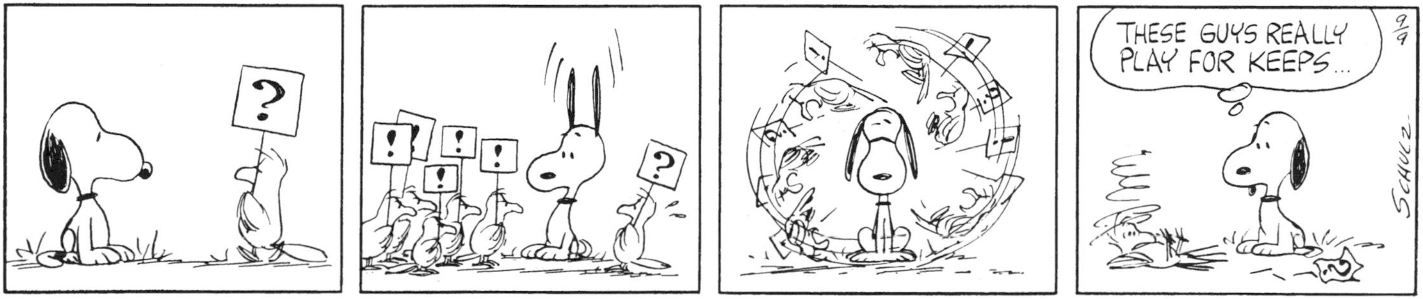
?
THESE GUYS REALLY PLAY FOR KEEPS...
9/9
SCHULZ

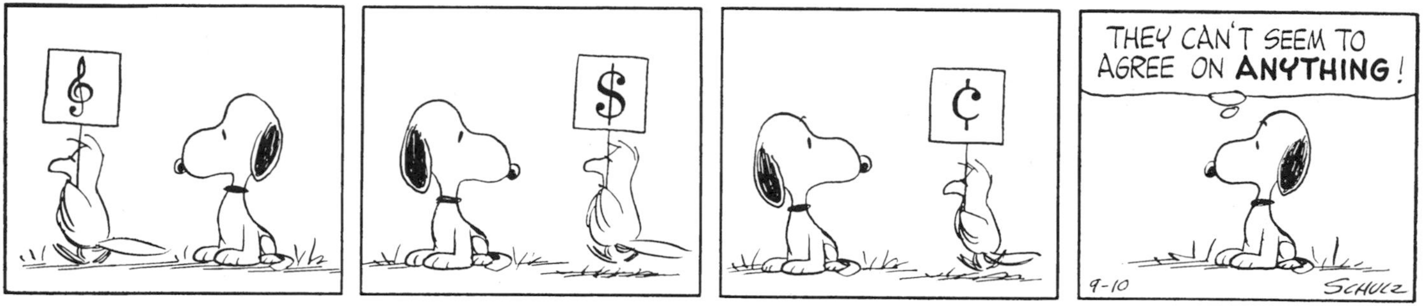
$
¢
THEY CAN'T SEEM TO AGREE ON **ANYTHING**!
9-10
SCHULZ

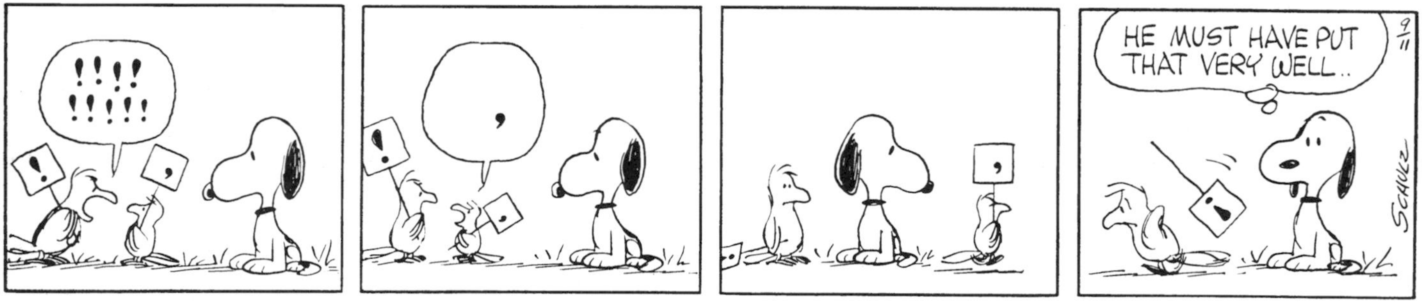
HE MUST HAVE PUT THAT VERY WELL..
9/11
SCHULZ

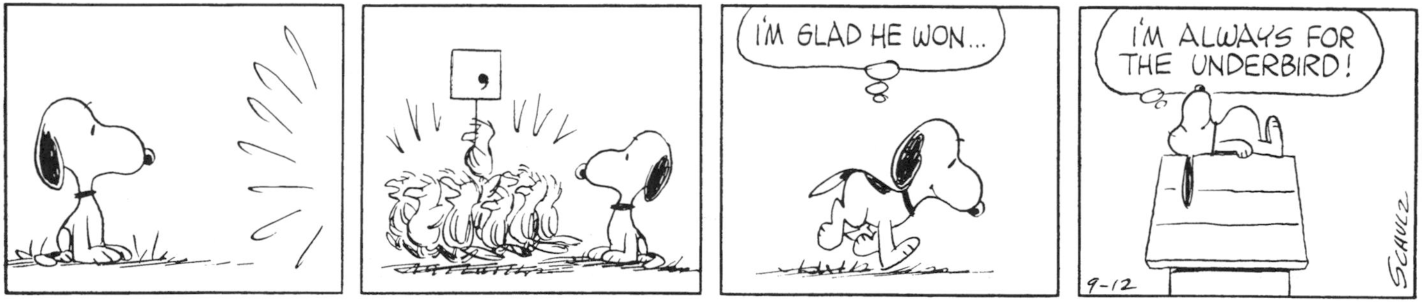
I'M GLAD HE WON...
I'M ALWAYS FOR THE UNDERBIRD!
9-12
SCHULZ

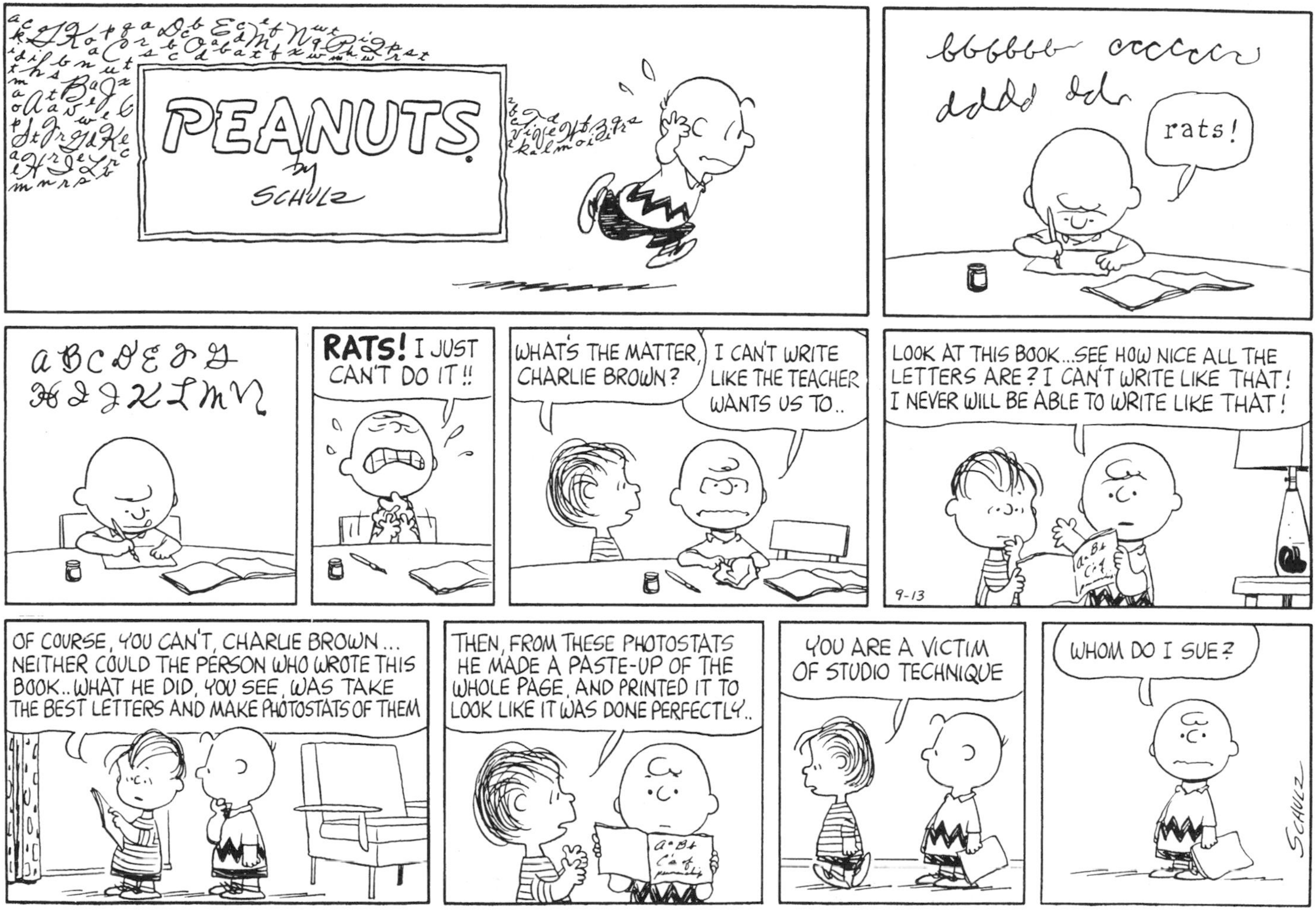

PEANUTS
by
SCHULZ
rats!
RATS! I JUST CAN'T DO IT!!
WHAT'S THE MATTER, CHARLIE BROWN?
I CAN'T WRITE LIKE THE TEACHER WANTS US TO..
LOOK AT THIS BOOK...SEE HOW NICE ALL THE LETTERS ARE? I CAN'T WRITE LIKE THAT! I NEVER WILL BE ABLE TO WRITE LIKE THAT!
9-13
OF COURSE, YOU CAN'T, CHARLIE BROWN... NEITHER COULD THE PERSON WHO WROTE THIS BOOK..WHAT HE DID, YOU SEE, WAS TAKE THE BEST LETTERS AND MAKE PHOTOSTATS OF THEM
THEN, FROM THESE PHOTOSTATS HE MADE A PASTE-UP OF THE WHOLE PAGE, AND PRINTED IT TO LOOK LIKE IT WAS DONE PERFECTLY..
YOU ARE A VICTIM OF STUDIO TECHNIQUE
WHOM DO I SUE?
SCHULZ

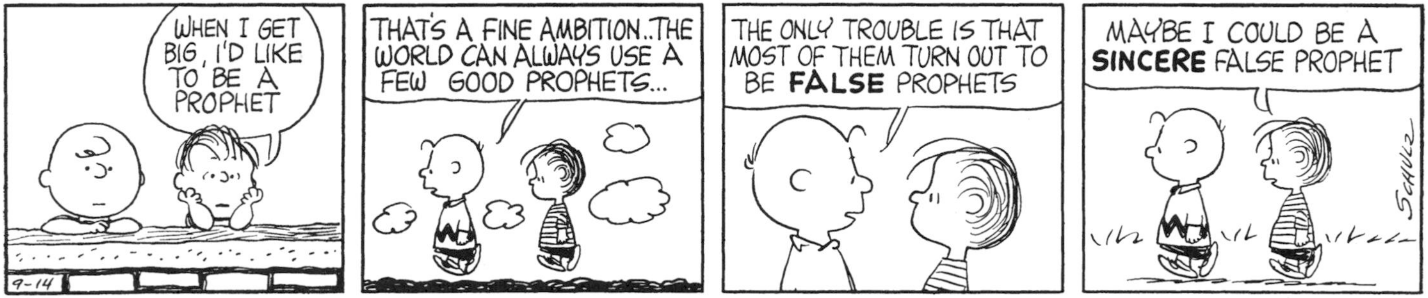
9-14
WHEN I GET BIG, I'D LIKE TO BE A PROPHET
THAT'S A FINE AMBITION..THE WORLD CAN ALWAYS USE A FEW GOOD PROPHETS...
THE ONLY TROUBLE IS THAT MOST OF THEM TURN OUT TO BE **FALSE** PROPHETS
MAYBE I COULD BE A **SINCERE** FALSE PROPHET
SCHULZ

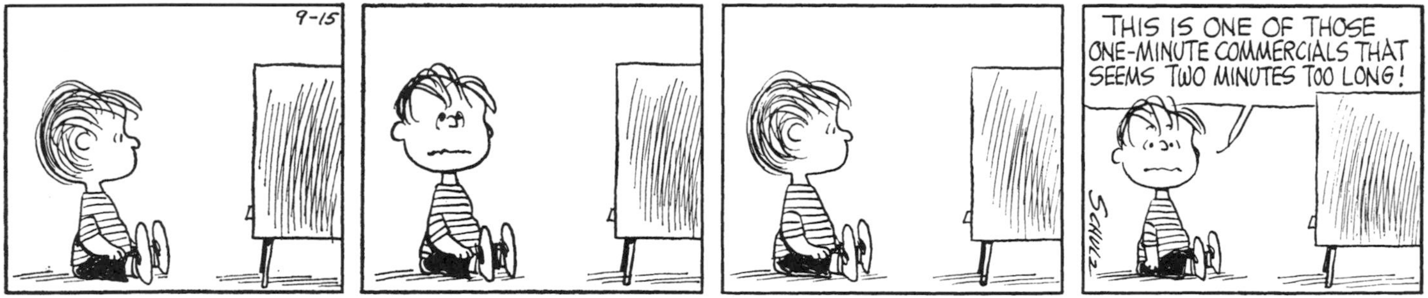
9-15
THIS IS ONE OF THOSE ONE-MINUTE COMMERCIALS THAT SEEMS TWO MINUTES TOO LONG!
SCHULZ

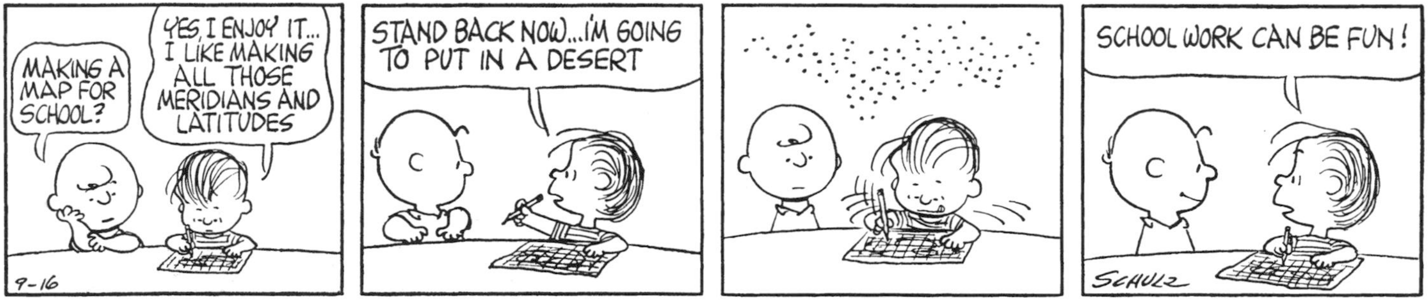
9-16
MAKING A MAP FOR SCHOOL?
YES, I ENJOY IT... I LIKE MAKING ALL THOSE MERIDIANS AND LATITUDES
STAND BACK NOW...I'M GOING TO PUT IN A DESERT
SCHOOL WORK CAN BE FUN!
SCHULZ

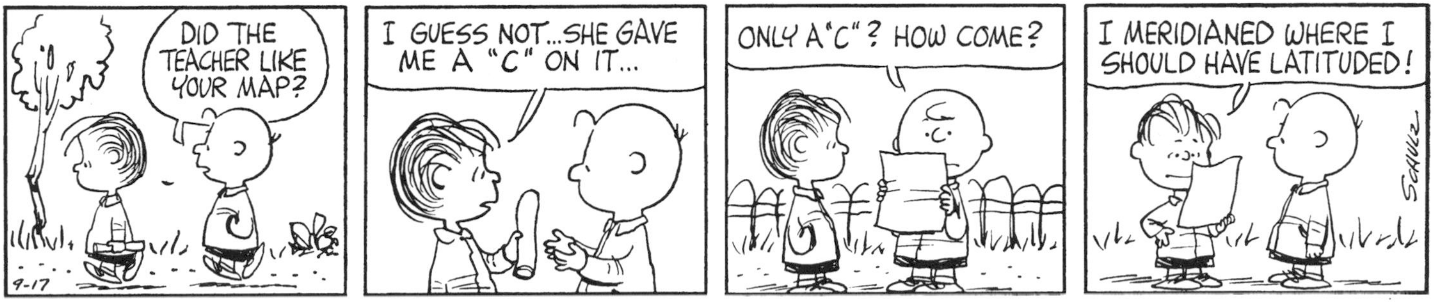
DID THE TEACHER LIKE YOUR MAP?
9-17
I GUESS NOT...SHE GAVE ME A "C" ON IT...
ONLY A "C"? HOW COME?
I MERIDIANED WHERE I SHOULD HAVE LATITUDED!
SCHULZ

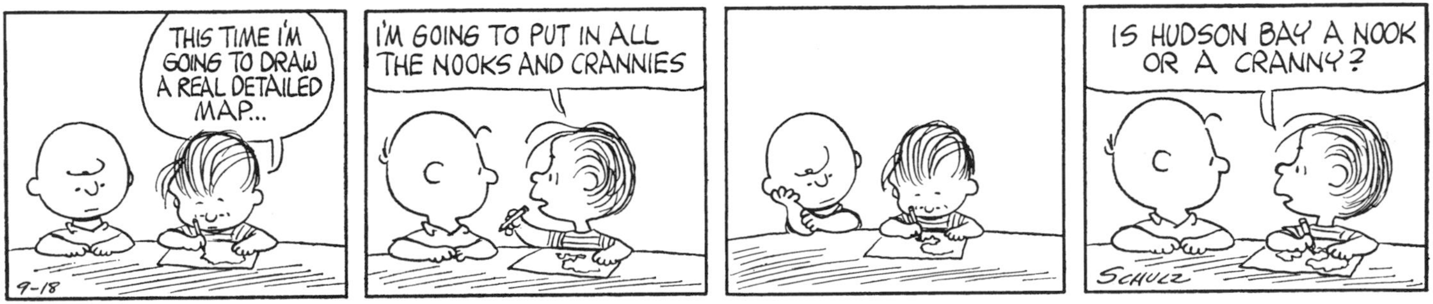
THIS TIME I'M GOING TO DRAW A REAL DETAILED MAP...
9-18
I'M GOING TO PUT IN ALL THE NOOKS AND CRANNIES
IS HUDSON BAY A NOOK OR A CRANNY?
SCHULZ

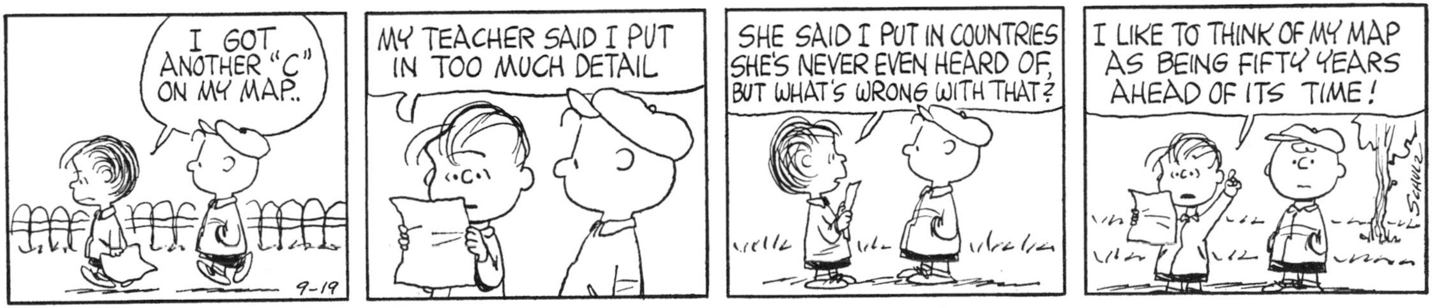
I GOT ANOTHER "C" ON MY MAP..
9-19
MY TEACHER SAID I PUT IN TOO MUCH DETAIL
SHE SAID I PUT IN COUNTRIES SHE'S NEVER EVEN HEARD OF, BUT WHAT'S WRONG WITH THAT?
I LIKE TO THINK OF MY MAP AS BEING FIFTY YEARS AHEAD OF ITS TIME!
SCHULZ

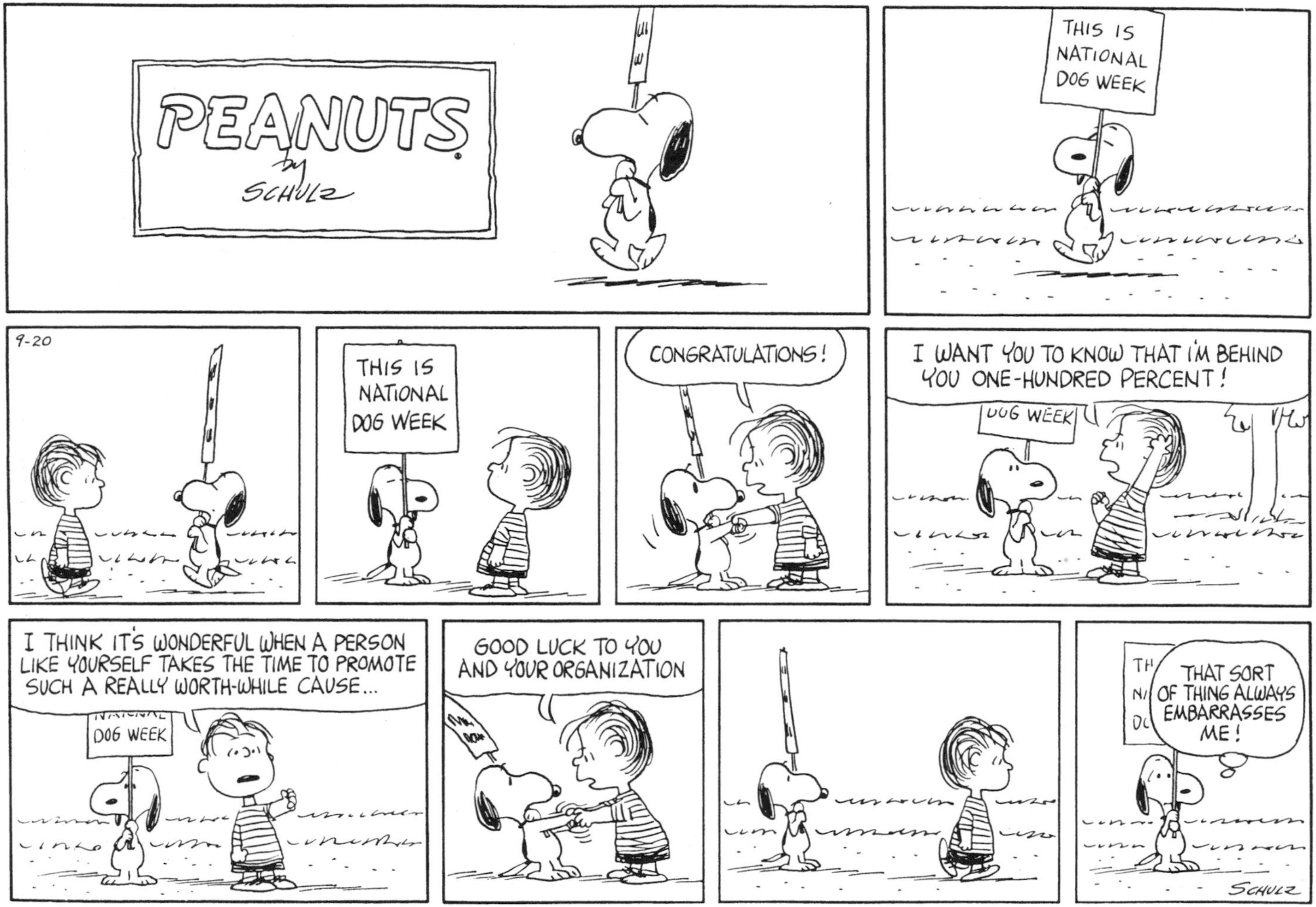
PEANUTS
by SCHULZ
THIS IS NATIONAL DOG WEEK
9-20
THIS IS NATIONAL DOG WEEK
CONGRATULATIONS!
I WANT YOU TO KNOW THAT I'M BEHIND YOU ONE-HUNDRED PERCENT!
DOG WEEK
I THINK IT'S WONDERFUL WHEN A PERSON LIKE YOURSELF TAKES THE TIME TO PROMOTE SUCH A REALLY WORTH-WHILE CAUSE...
DOG WEEK
GOOD LUCK TO YOU AND YOUR ORGANIZATION
THAT SORT OF THING ALWAYS EMBARRASSES ME!
SCHULZ

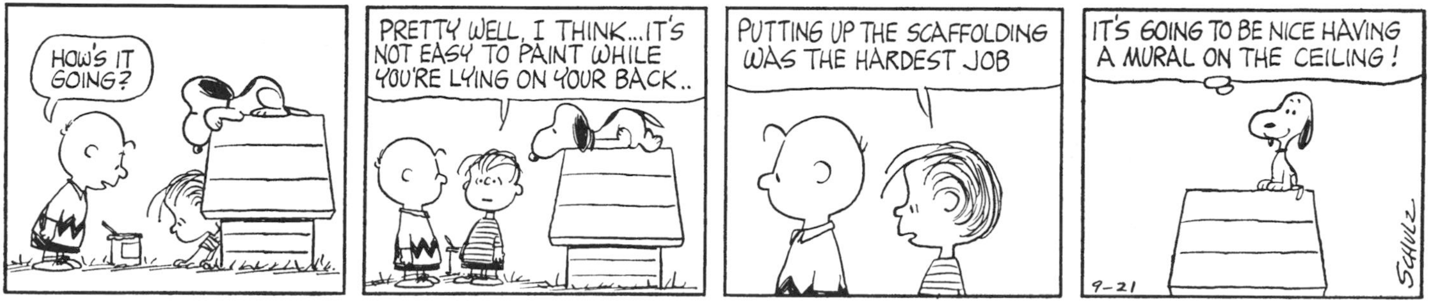
HOW'S IT GOING?
PRETTY WELL, I THINK...IT'S NOT EASY TO PAINT WHILE YOU'RE LYING ON YOUR BACK..
PUTTING UP THE SCAFFOLDING WAS THE HARDEST JOB
IT'S GOING TO BE NICE HAVING A MURAL ON THE CEILING!
9-21
SCHULZ

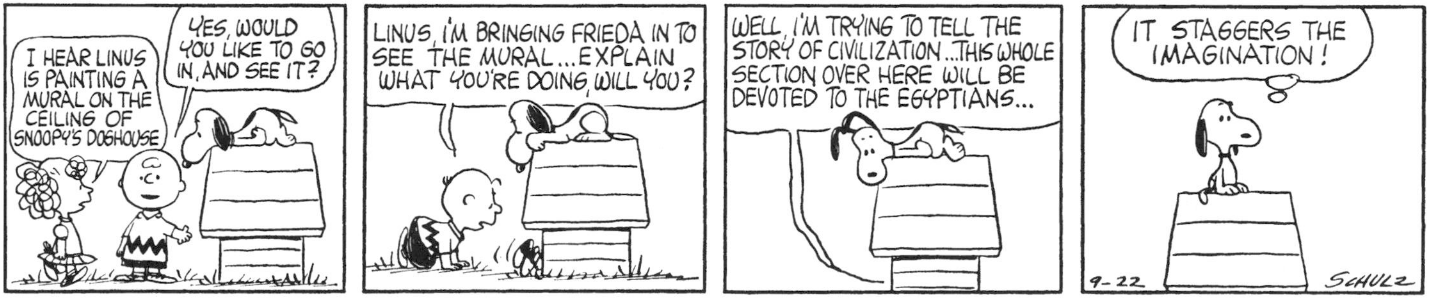
I HEAR LINUS IS PAINTING A MURAL ON THE CEILING OF SNOOPY'S DOGHOUSE
YES, WOULD YOU LIKE TO GO IN, AND SEE IT?
LINUS, I'M BRINGING FRIEDA IN TO SEE THE MURAL...EXPLAIN WHAT YOU'RE DOING, WILL YOU?
WELL, I'M TRYING TO TELL THE STORY OF CIVILIZATION...THIS WHOLE SECTION OVER HERE WILL BE DEVOTED TO THE EGYPTIANS...
IT STAGGERS THE IMAGINATION!
9-22
SCHULZ

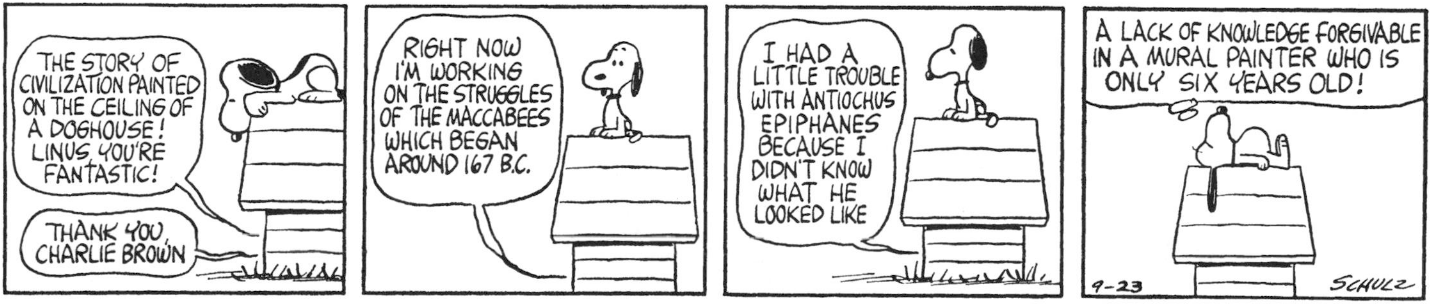
THE STORY OF CIVILIZATION PAINTED ON THE CEILING OF A DOGHOUSE! LINUS, YOU'RE FANTASTIC!
THANK YOU, CHARLIE BROWN
RIGHT NOW I'M WORKING ON THE STRUGGLES OF THE MACCABEES WHICH BEGAN AROUND 167 B.C.
I HAD A LITTLE TROUBLE WITH ANTIOCHUS EPIPHANES BECAUSE I DIDN'T KNOW WHAT HE LOOKED LIKE
A LACK OF KNOWLEDGE FORGIVABLE IN A MURAL PAINTER WHO IS ONLY SIX YEARS OLD!
9-23
SCHULZ

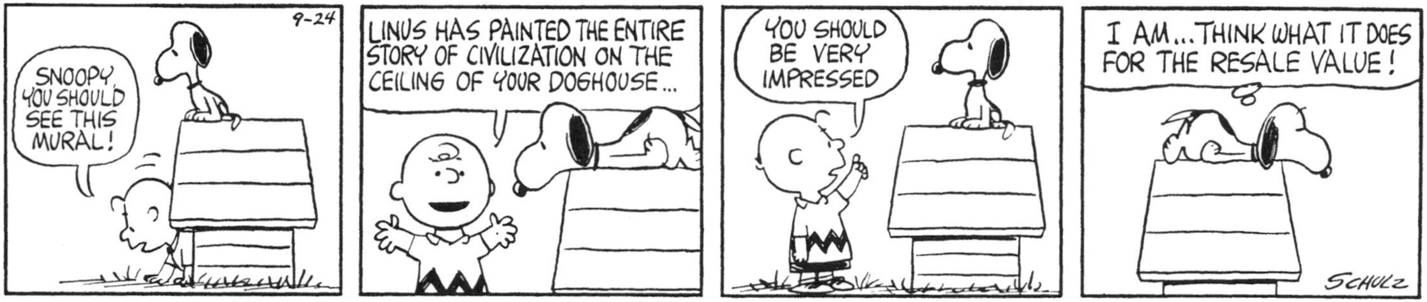
9-24
SNOOPY, YOU SHOULD SEE THIS MURAL!
LINUS HAS PAINTED THE ENTIRE STORY OF CIVILIZATION ON THE CEILING OF YOUR DOGHOUSE...
YOU SHOULD BE VERY IMPRESSED
I AM... THINK WHAT IT DOES FOR THE RESALE VALUE!
SCHULZ

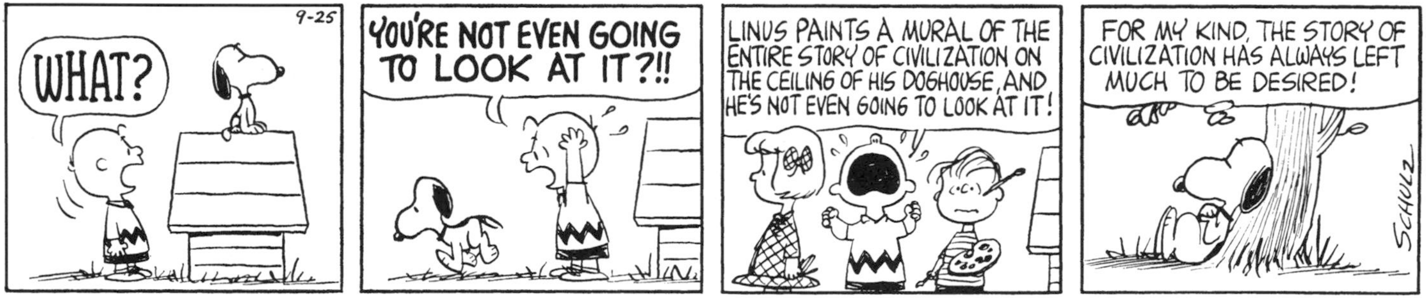
9-25
WHAT?
YOU'RE NOT EVEN GOING TO LOOK AT IT?!!
LINUS PAINTS A MURAL OF THE ENTIRE STORY OF CIVILIZATION ON THE CEILING OF HIS DOGHOUSE, AND HE'S NOT EVEN GOING TO LOOK AT IT!
FOR MY KIND, THE STORY OF CIVILIZATION HAS ALWAYS LEFT MUCH TO BE DESIRED!
SCHULZ

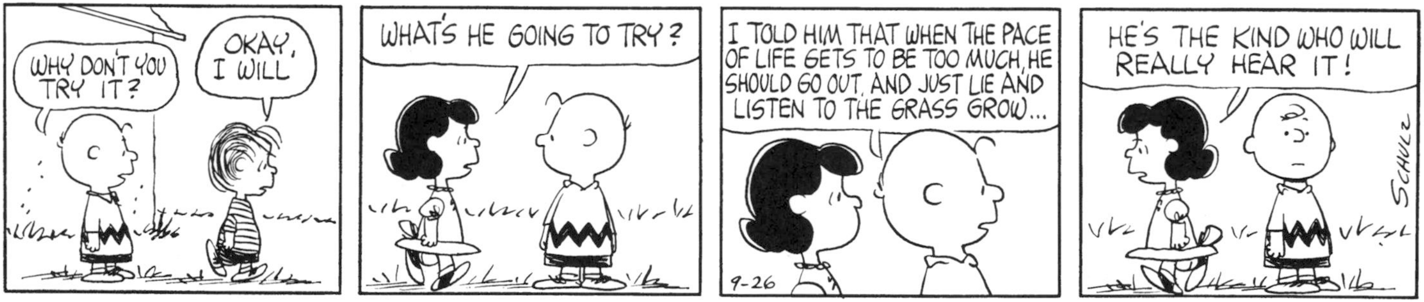
WHY DON'T YOU TRY IT?
OKAY, I WILL
WHAT'S HE GOING TO TRY?
I TOLD HIM THAT WHEN THE PACE OF LIFE GETS TO BE TOO MUCH, HE SHOULD GO OUT, AND JUST LIE AND LISTEN TO THE GRASS GROW...
9-26
HE'S THE KIND WHO WILL REALLY HEAR IT!
SCHULZ

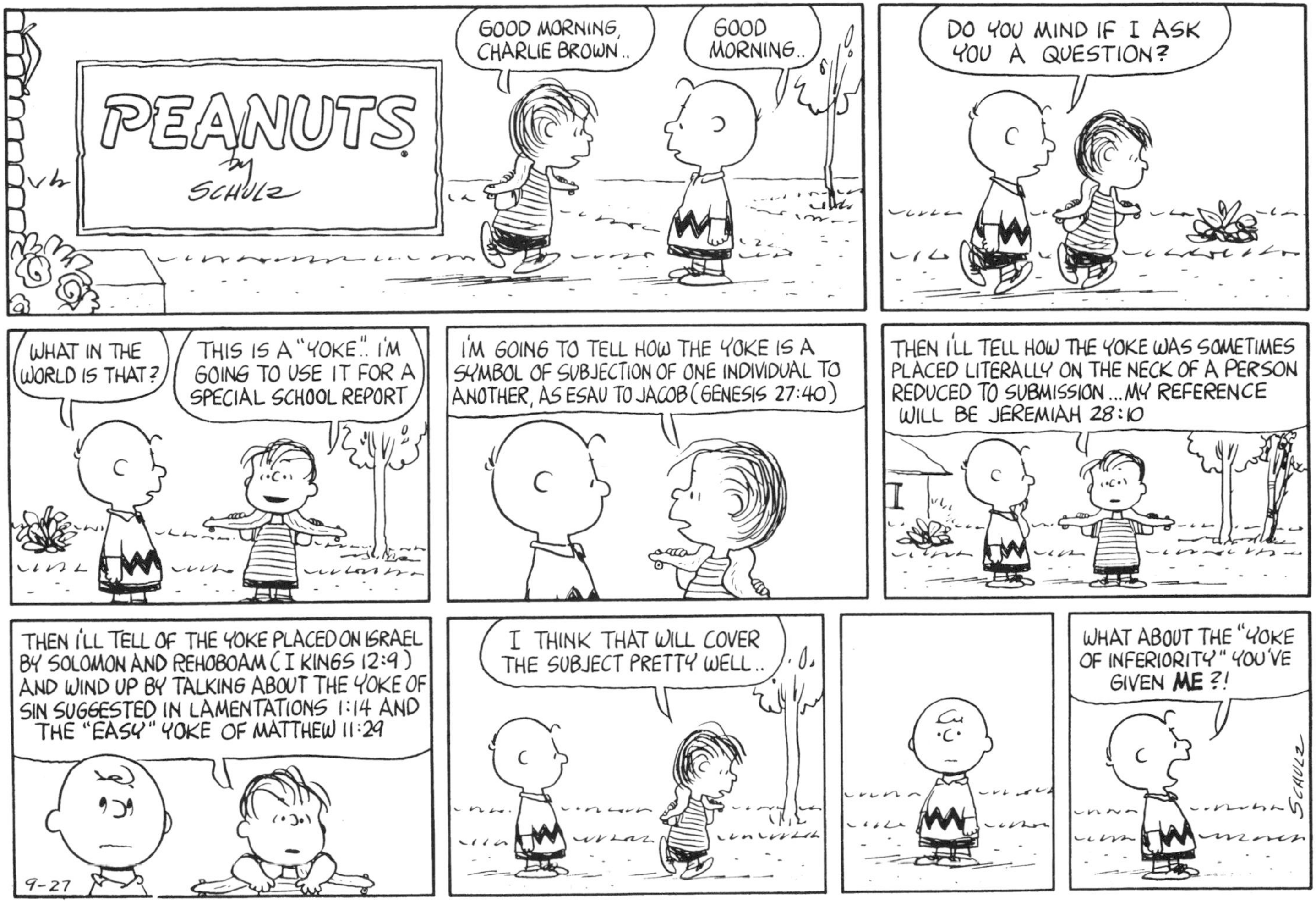
PEANUTS
by SCHULZ
GOOD MORNING, CHARLIE BROWN..
GOOD MORNING..
DO YOU MIND IF I ASK YOU A QUESTION?
WHAT IN THE WORLD IS THAT?
THIS IS A "YOKE".. I'M GOING TO USE IT FOR A SPECIAL SCHOOL REPORT
I'M GOING TO TELL HOW THE YOKE IS A SYMBOL OF SUBJECTION OF ONE INDIVIDUAL TO ANOTHER, AS ESAU TO JACOB (GENESIS 27:40)
THEN I'LL TELL HOW THE YOKE WAS SOMETIMES PLACED LITERALLY ON THE NECK OF A PERSON REDUCED TO SUBMISSION ... MY REFERENCE WILL BE JEREMIAH 28:10
THEN I'LL TELL OF THE YOKE PLACED ON ISRAEL BY SOLOMON AND REHOBOAM (I KINGS 12:9) AND WIND UP BY TALKING ABOUT THE YOKE OF SIN SUGGESTED IN LAMENTATIONS 1:14 AND THE "EASY" YOKE OF MATTHEW 11:29
9-27
I THINK THAT WILL COVER THE SUBJECT PRETTY WELL..
WHAT ABOUT THE "YOKE OF INFERIORITY" YOU'VE GIVEN **ME**?!
SCHULZ

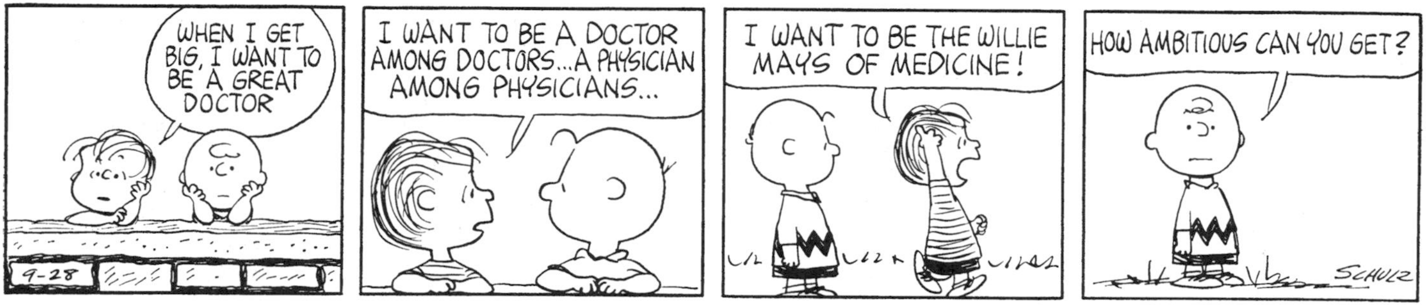
WHEN I GET BIG, I WANT TO BE A GREAT DOCTOR
I WANT TO BE A DOCTOR AMONG DOCTORS...A PHYSICIAN AMONG PHYSICIANS...
I WANT TO BE THE WILLIE MAYS OF MEDICINE!
HOW AMBITIOUS CAN YOU GET?
9-28
SCHULZ

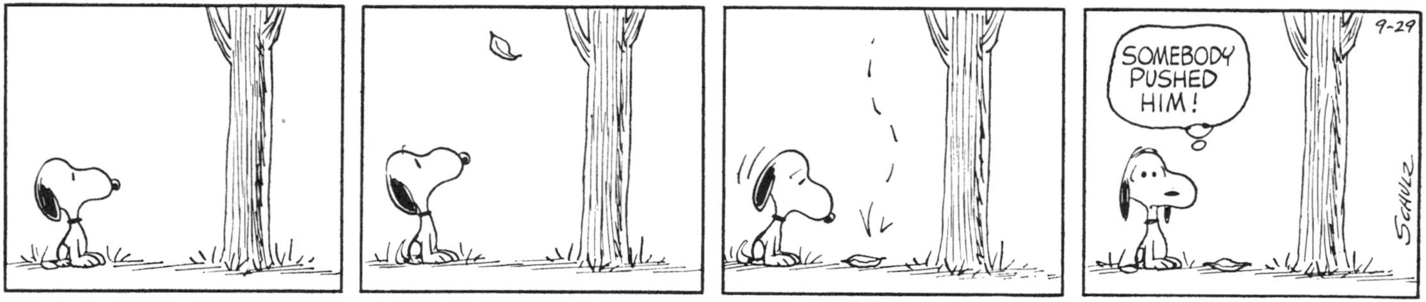
SOMEBODY PUSHED HIM!
9-29
SCHULZ

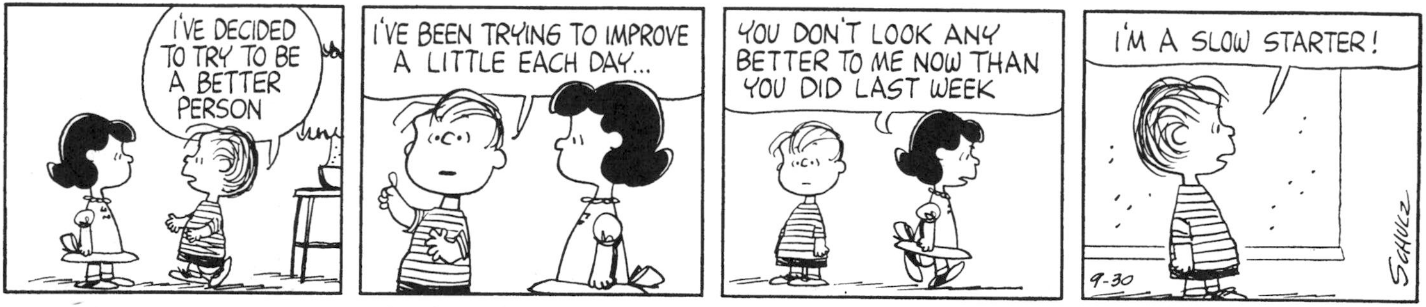
I'VE DECIDED TO TRY TO BE A BETTER PERSON
I'VE BEEN TRYING TO IMPROVE A LITTLE EACH DAY...
YOU DON'T LOOK ANY BETTER TO ME NOW THAN YOU DID LAST WEEK
I'M A SLOW STARTER!
9-30
SCHULZ

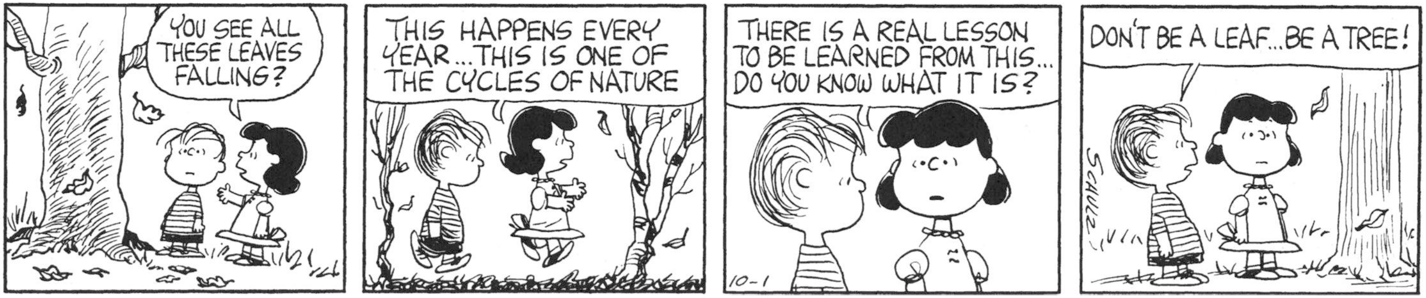
YOU SEE ALL THESE LEAVES FALLING?
THIS HAPPENS EVERY YEAR...THIS IS ONE OF THE CYCLES OF NATURE
THERE IS A REAL LESSON TO BE LEARNED FROM THIS... DO YOU KNOW WHAT IT IS?
10-1
DON'T BE A LEAF...BE A TREE!
SCHULZ

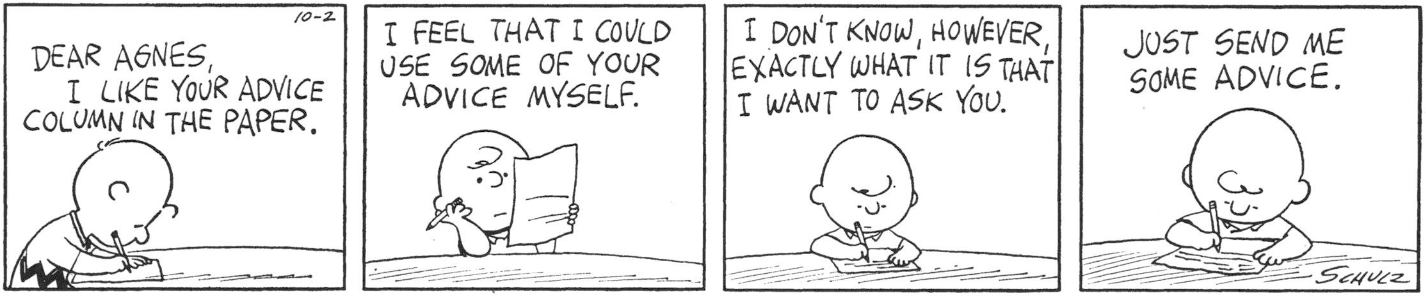
10-2
DEAR AGNES,
I LIKE YOUR ADVICE COLUMN IN THE PAPER.
I FEEL THAT I COULD USE SOME OF YOUR ADVICE MYSELF.
I DON'T KNOW, HOWEVER, EXACTLY WHAT IT IS THAT I WANT TO ASK YOU.
JUST SEND ME SOME ADVICE.
SCHULZ

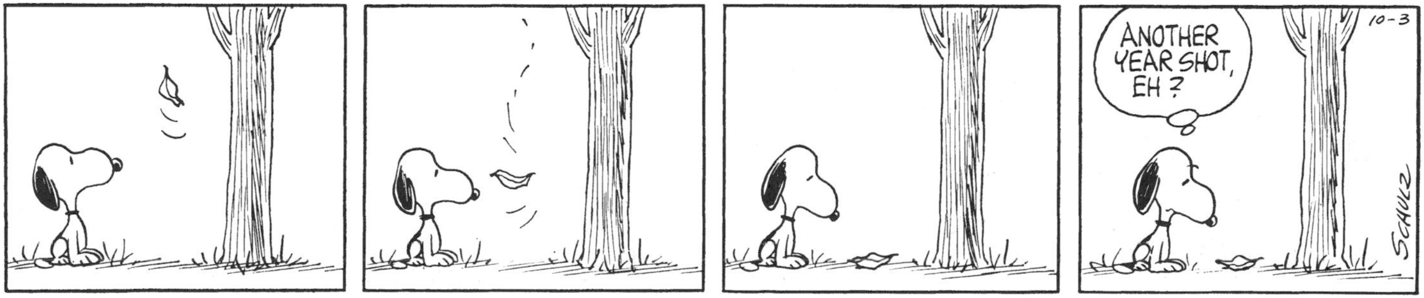
10-3
ANOTHER YEAR SHOT, EH?
SCHULZ

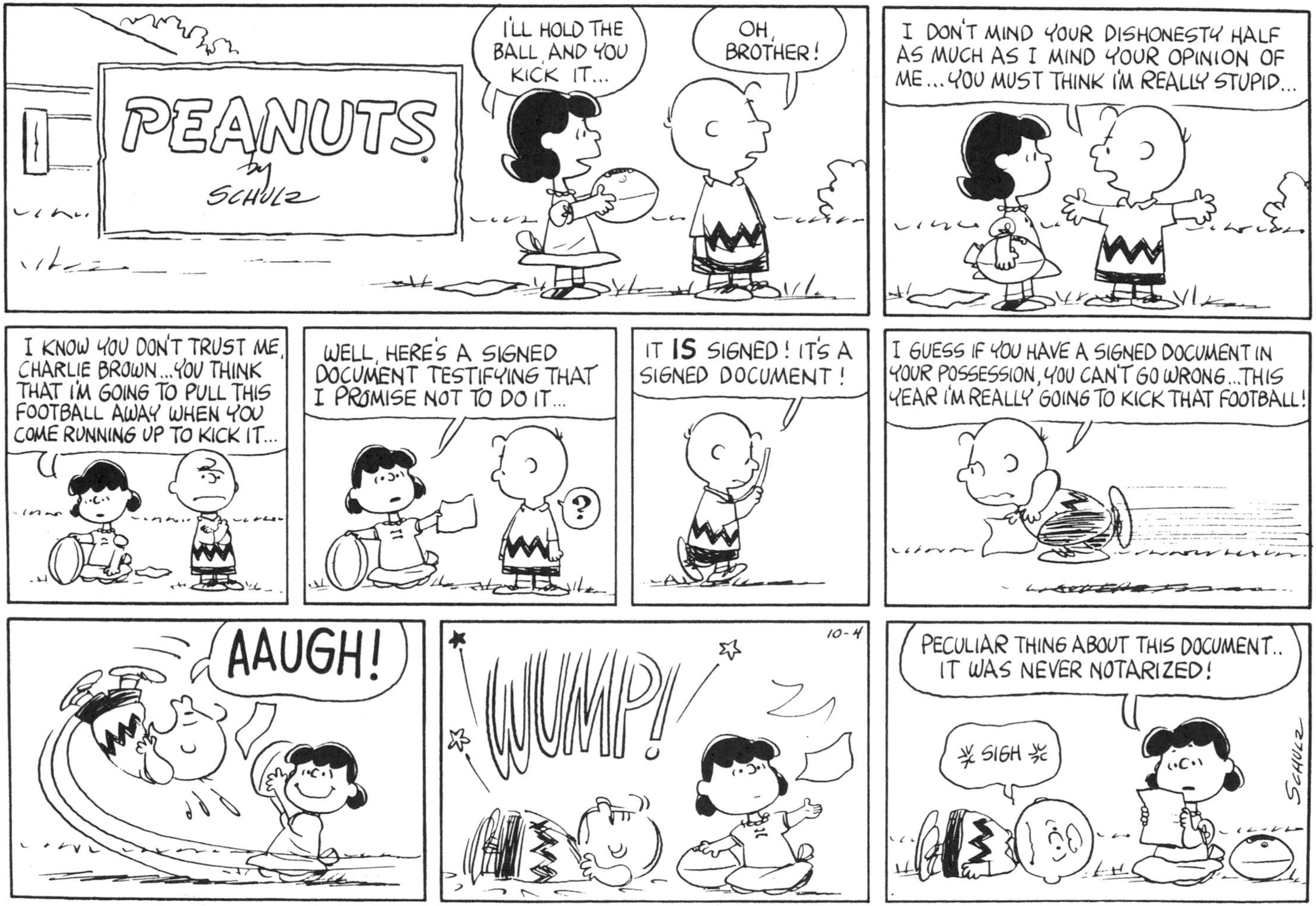
PEANUTS
by SCHULZ
I'LL HOLD THE BALL, AND YOU KICK IT...
OH, BROTHER!
I DON'T MIND YOUR DISHONESTY HALF AS MUCH AS I MIND YOUR OPINION OF ME... YOU MUST THINK I'M REALLY STUPID...
I KNOW YOU DON'T TRUST ME, CHARLIE BROWN... YOU THINK THAT I'M GOING TO PULL THIS FOOTBALL AWAY WHEN YOU COME RUNNING UP TO KICK IT...
WELL, HERE'S A SIGNED DOCUMENT TESTIFYING THAT I PROMISE NOT TO DO IT...
?
IT IS SIGNED! IT'S A SIGNED DOCUMENT!
I GUESS IF YOU HAVE A SIGNED DOCUMENT IN YOUR POSSESSION, YOU CAN'T GO WRONG... THIS YEAR I'M REALLY GOING TO KICK THAT FOOTBALL!
AAUGH!
10-4
WUMP!
PECULIAR THING ABOUT THIS DOCUMENT.. IT WAS NEVER NOTARIZED!
SIGH
SCHULZ

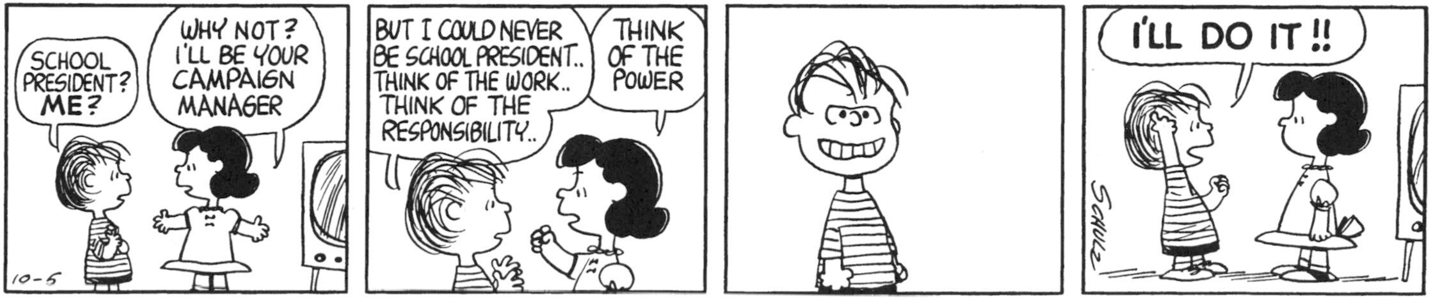
SCHOOL PRESIDENT? ME?
WHY NOT? I'LL BE YOUR CAMPAIGN MANAGER
10-5
BUT I COULD NEVER BE SCHOOL PRESIDENT.. THINK OF THE WORK.. THINK OF THE RESPONSIBILITY..
THINK OF THE POWER
I'LL DO IT!!
SCHULZ

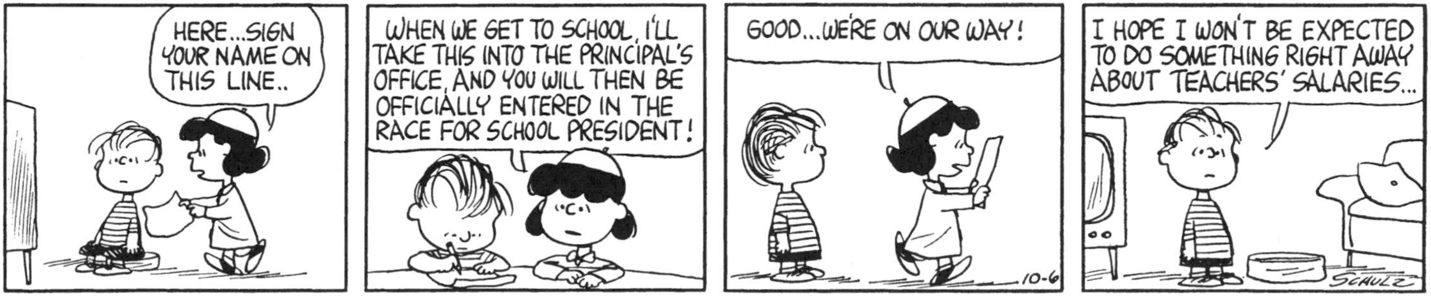
HERE...SIGN YOUR NAME ON THIS LINE..
WHEN WE GET TO SCHOOL, I'LL TAKE THIS INTO THE PRINCIPAL'S OFFICE, AND YOU WILL THEN BE OFFICIALLY ENTERED IN THE RACE FOR SCHOOL PRESIDENT!
GOOD...WE'RE ON OUR WAY!
10-6
I HOPE I WON'T BE EXPECTED TO DO SOMETHING RIGHT AWAY ABOUT TEACHERS' SALARIES...
SCHULZ

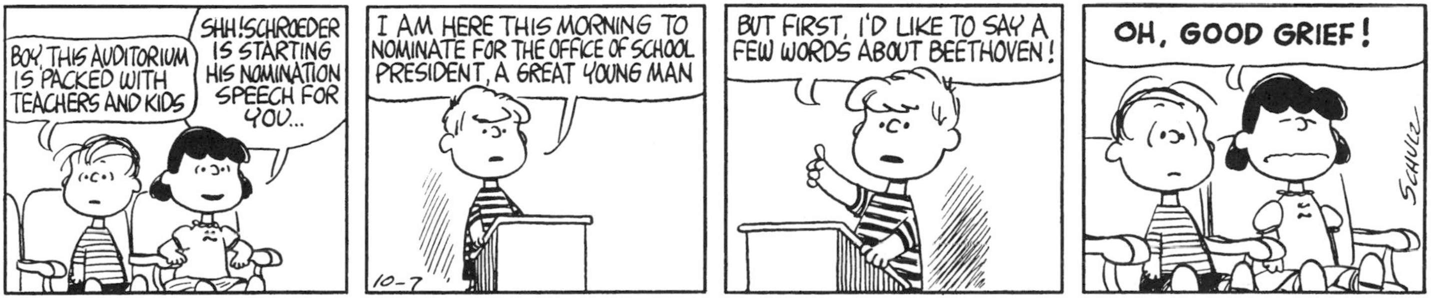
BOY, THIS AUDITORIUM IS PACKED WITH TEACHERS AND KIDS
SHH! SCHROEDER IS STARTING HIS NOMINATION SPEECH FOR YOU...
I AM HERE THIS MORNING TO NOMINATE FOR THE OFFICE OF SCHOOL PRESIDENT, A GREAT YOUNG MAN
10-7
BUT FIRST, I'D LIKE TO SAY A FEW WORDS ABOUT BEETHOVEN!
OH, GOOD GRIEF!
SCHULZ

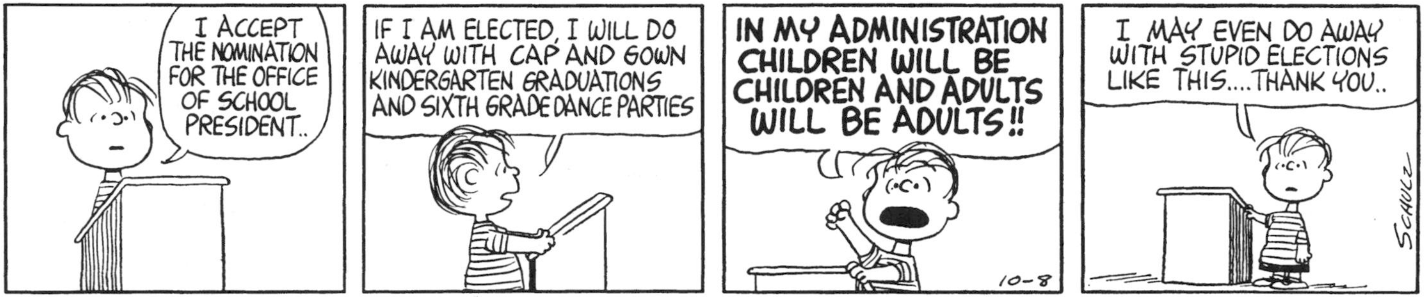
I ACCEPT THE NOMINATION FOR THE OFFICE OF SCHOOL PRESIDENT..
IF I AM ELECTED, I WILL DO AWAY WITH CAP AND GOWN KINDERGARTEN GRADUATIONS AND SIXTH GRADE DANCE PARTIES
IN MY ADMINISTRATION CHILDREN WILL BE CHILDREN AND ADULTS WILL BE ADULTS!!
10-8
I MAY EVEN DO AWAY WITH STUPID ELECTIONS LIKE THIS....THANK YOU..
SCHULZ

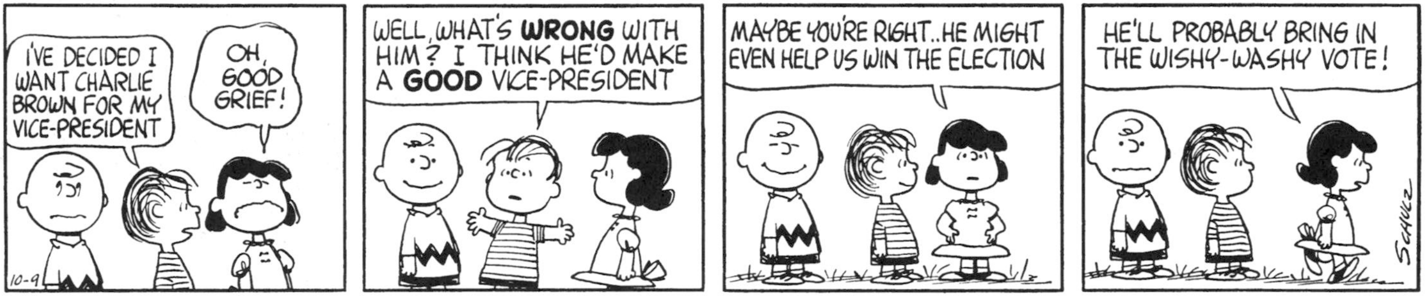
I'VE DECIDED I WANT CHARLIE BROWN FOR MY VICE-PRESIDENT
OH, GOOD GRIEF!
10-9
WELL, WHAT'S WRONG WITH HIM? I THINK HE'D MAKE A GOOD VICE-PRESIDENT
MAYBE YOU'RE RIGHT..HE MIGHT EVEN HELP US WIN THE ELECTION
HE'LL PROBABLY BRING IN THE WISHY-WASHY VOTE!
SCHULZ

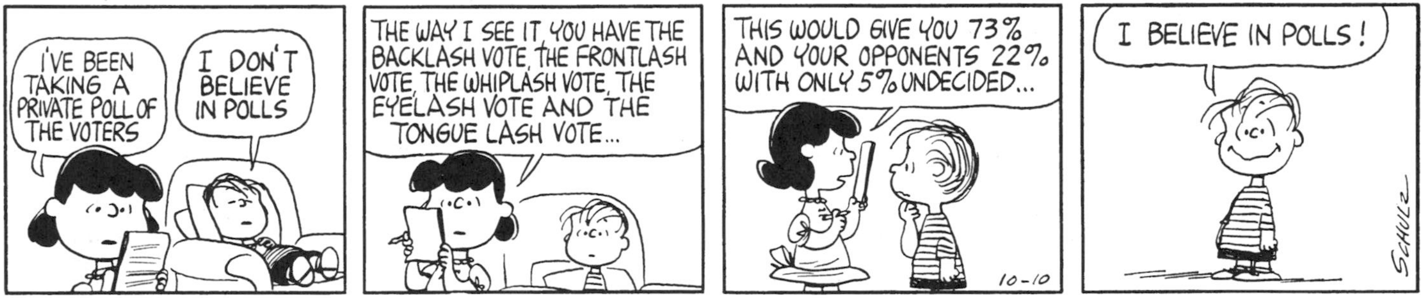
I'VE BEEN TAKING A PRIVATE POLL OF THE VOTERS
I DON'T BELIEVE IN POLLS
THE WAY I SEE IT, YOU HAVE THE BACKLASH VOTE, THE FRONTLASH VOTE, THE WHIPLASH VOTE, THE EYELASH VOTE AND THE TONGUE LASH VOTE...
THIS WOULD GIVE YOU 73% AND YOUR OPPONENTS 22% WITH ONLY 5% UNDECIDED...
10-10
I BELIEVE IN POLLS!
SCHULZ

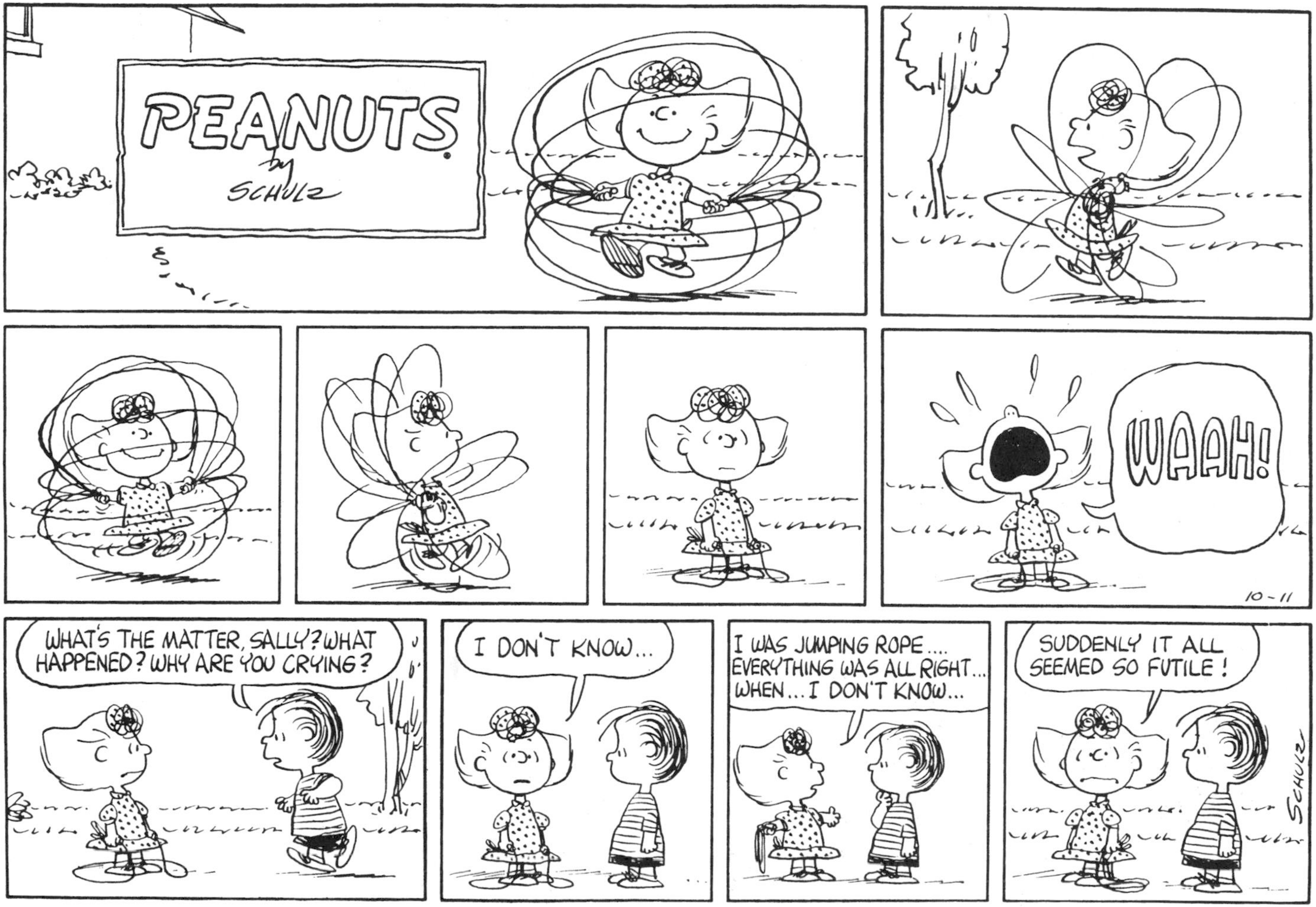
PEANUTS
by SCHULZ
WAAH!
10-11
WHAT'S THE MATTER, SALLY? WHAT HAPPENED? WHY ARE YOU CRYING?
I DON'T KNOW...
I WAS JUMPING ROPE.... EVERYTHING WAS ALL RIGHT... WHEN... I DON'T KNOW...
SUDDENLY IT ALL SEEMED SO FUTILE!
SCHULZ

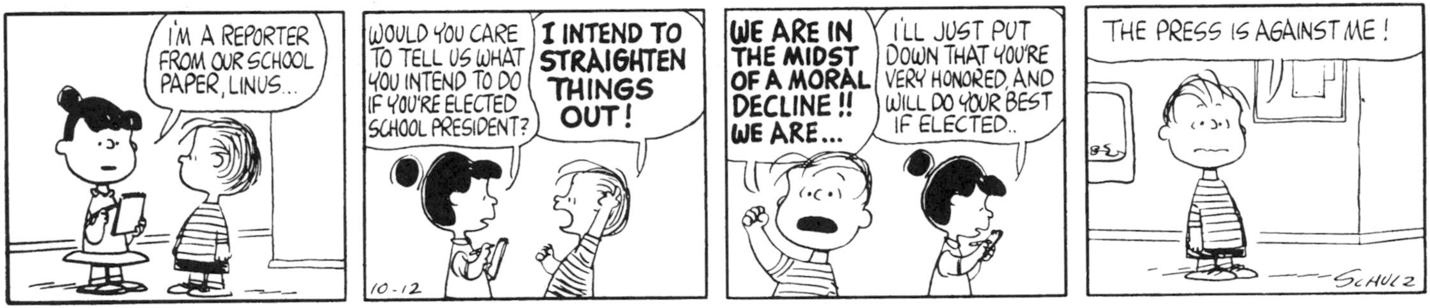
I'M A REPORTER FROM OUR SCHOOL PAPER, LINUS...
WOULD YOU CARE TO TELL US WHAT YOU INTEND TO DO IF YOU'RE ELECTED SCHOOL PRESIDENT?
I INTEND TO STRAIGHTEN THINGS OUT!
10-12
WE ARE IN THE MIDST OF A MORAL DECLINE!! WE ARE...
I'LL JUST PUT DOWN THAT YOU'RE VERY HONORED, AND WILL DO YOUR BEST IF ELECTED..
THE PRESS IS AGAINST ME!
SCHULZ

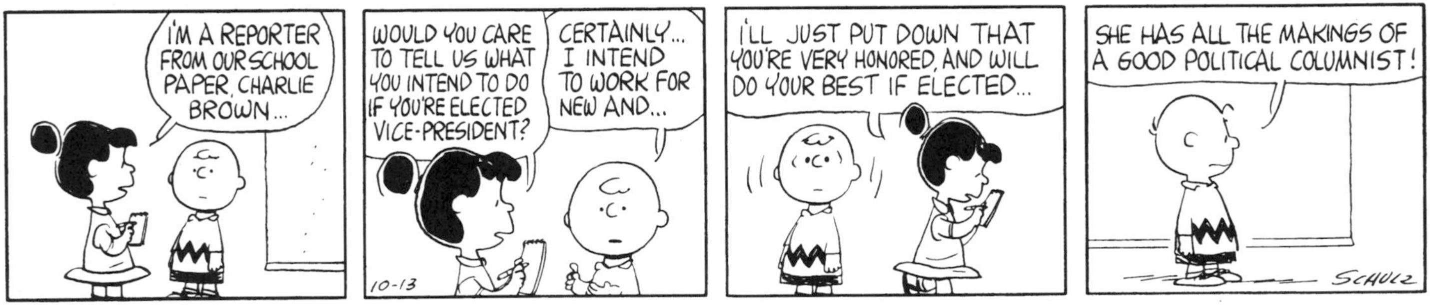
I'M A REPORTER FROM OUR SCHOOL PAPER, CHARLIE BROWN...
WOULD YOU CARE TO TELL US WHAT YOU INTEND TO DO IF YOU'RE ELECTED VICE-PRESIDENT?
CERTAINLY... I INTEND TO WORK FOR NEW AND...
10-13
I'LL JUST PUT DOWN THAT YOU'RE VERY HONORED, AND WILL DO YOUR BEST IF ELECTED...
SHE HAS ALL THE MAKINGS OF A GOOD POLITICAL COLUMNIST!
SCHULZ

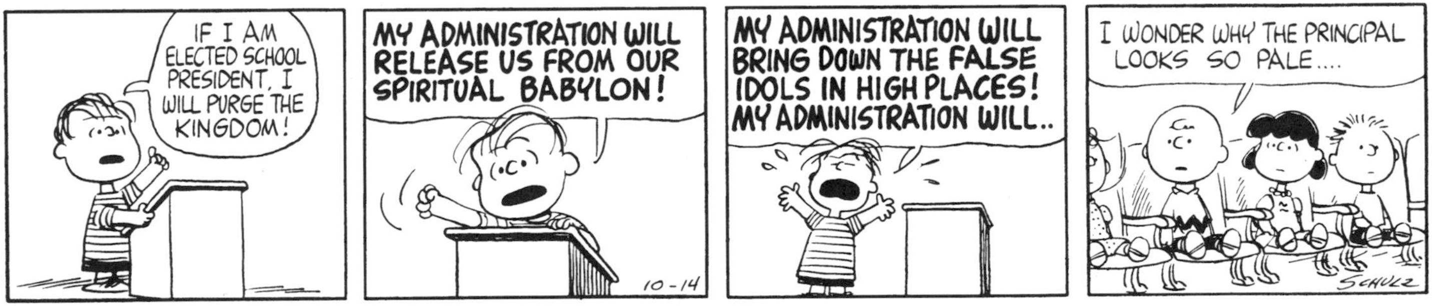
IF I AM ELECTED SCHOOL PRESIDENT, I WILL PURGE THE KINGDOM!
MY ADMINISTRATION WILL RELEASE US FROM OUR SPIRITUAL BABYLON!
10-14
MY ADMINISTRATION WILL BRING DOWN THE FALSE IDOLS IN HIGH PLACES! MY ADMINISTRATION WILL..
I WONDER WHY THE PRINCIPAL LOOKS SO PALE....
SCHULZ

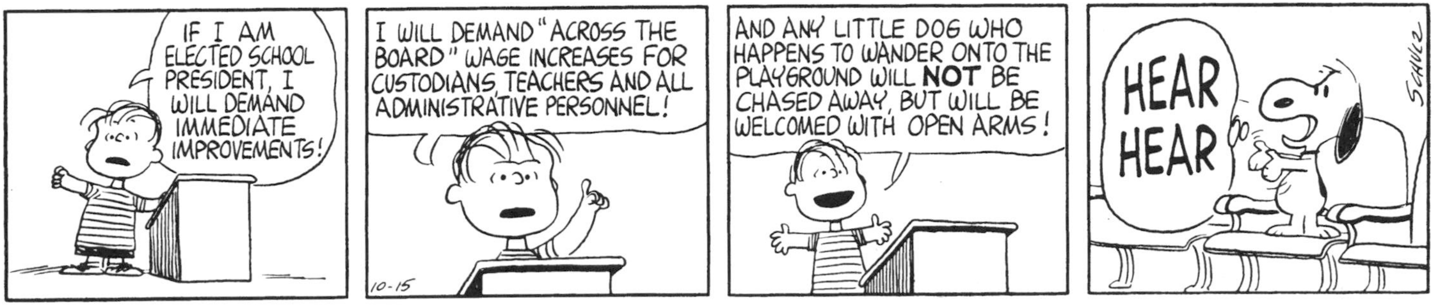
IF I AM ELECTED SCHOOL PRESIDENT, I WILL DEMAND IMMEDIATE IMPROVEMENTS!
I WILL DEMAND "ACROSS THE BOARD" WAGE INCREASES FOR CUSTODIANS, TEACHERS AND ALL ADMINISTRATIVE PERSONNEL!
10-15
AND ANY LITTLE DOG WHO HAPPENS TO WANDER ONTO THE PLAYGROUND WILL **NOT** BE CHASED AWAY, BUT WILL BE WELCOMED WITH OPEN ARMS!
HEAR HEAR
SCHULZ

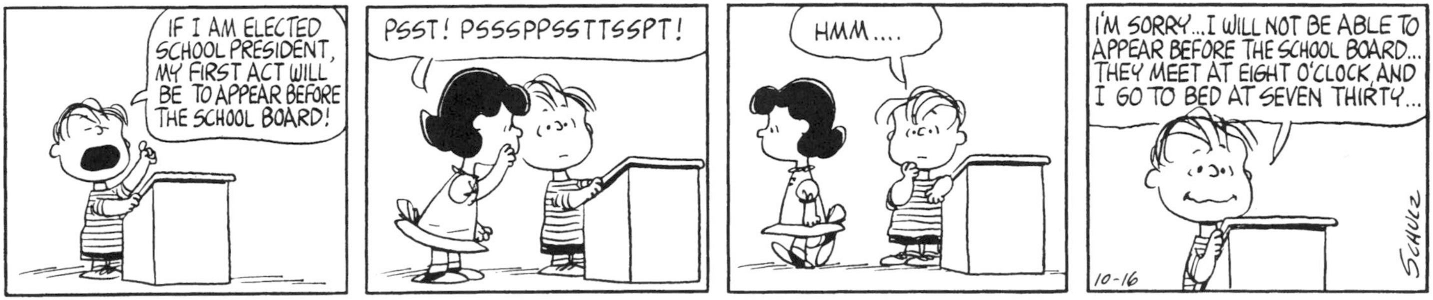
IF I AM ELECTED SCHOOL PRESIDENT, MY FIRST ACT WILL BE TO APPEAR BEFORE THE SCHOOL BOARD!
PSST! PSSSPPSSTTSSPT!
HMM....
I'M SORRY...I WILL NOT BE ABLE TO APPEAR BEFORE THE SCHOOL BOARD... THEY MEET AT EIGHT O'CLOCK, AND I GO TO BED AT SEVEN THIRTY...
SCHULZ
10-16

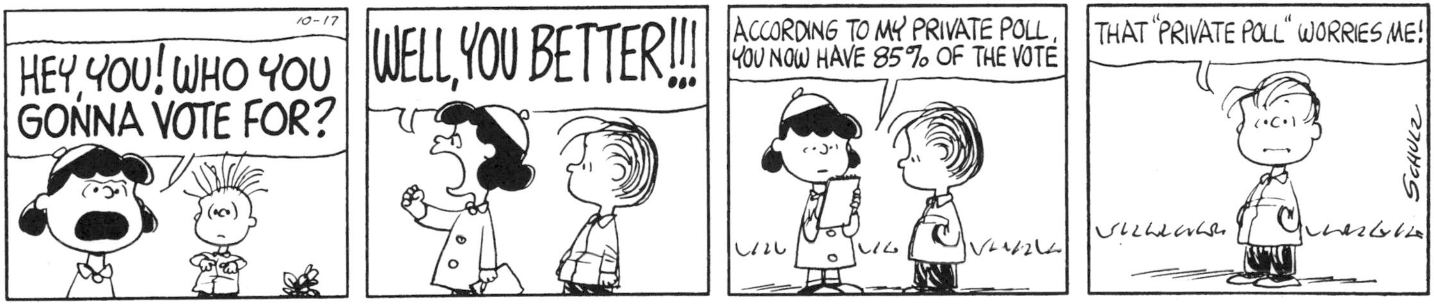
10-17
HEY, YOU! WHO YOU GONNA VOTE FOR?
WELL, YOU BETTER!!!
ACCORDING TO MY PRIVATE POLL, YOU NOW HAVE 85% OF THE VOTE
THAT "PRIVATE POLL" WORRIES ME!
SCHULZ

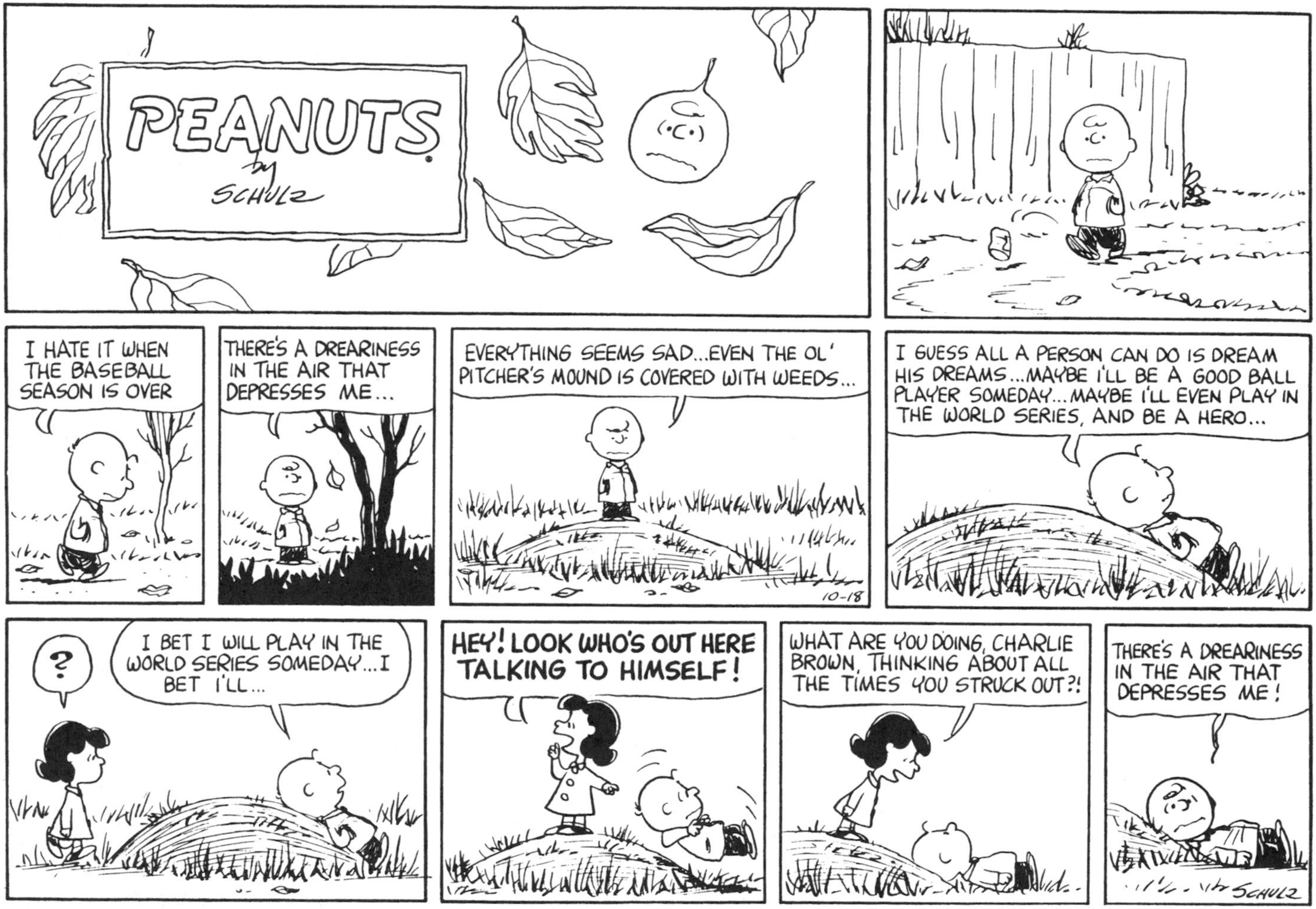
PEANUTS
by SCHULZ
I HATE IT WHEN THE BASEBALL SEASON IS OVER
THERE'S A DREARINESS IN THE AIR THAT DEPRESSES ME...
EVERYTHING SEEMS SAD...EVEN THE OL' PITCHER'S MOUND IS COVERED WITH WEEDS...
10-18
I GUESS ALL A PERSON CAN DO IS DREAM HIS DREAMS...MAYBE I'LL BE A GOOD BALL PLAYER SOMEDAY...MAYBE I'LL EVEN PLAY IN THE WORLD SERIES, AND BE A HERO...
?
I BET I WILL PLAY IN THE WORLD SERIES SOMEDAY...I BET I'LL...
HEY! LOOK WHO'S OUT HERE TALKING TO HIMSELF!
WHAT ARE YOU DOING, CHARLIE BROWN, THINKING ABOUT ALL THE TIMES YOU STRUCK OUT?!
THERE'S A DREARINESS IN THE AIR THAT DEPRESSES ME!
SCHULZ

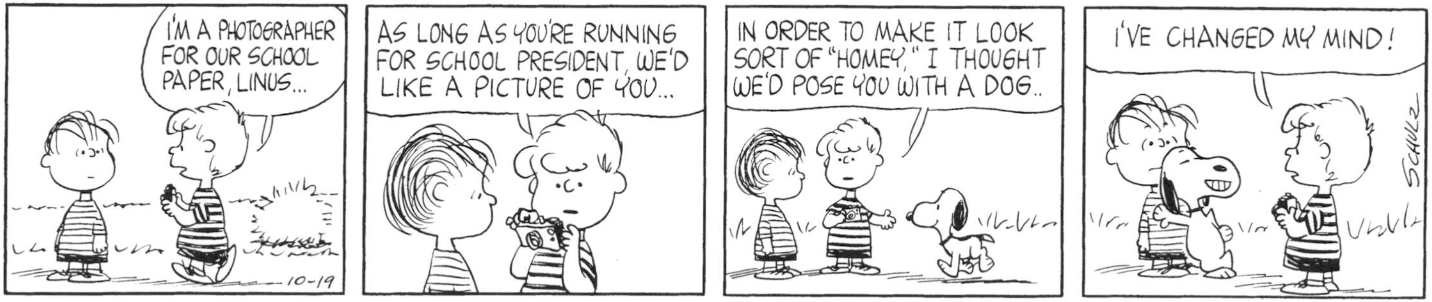
I'M A PHOTOGRAPHER FOR OUR SCHOOL PAPER, LINUS...
10-19
AS LONG AS YOU'RE RUNNING FOR SCHOOL PRESIDENT, WE'D LIKE A PICTURE OF YOU...
IN ORDER TO MAKE IT LOOK SORT OF "HOMEY," I THOUGHT WE'D POSE YOU WITH A DOG..
I'VE CHANGED MY MIND!
SCHULZ

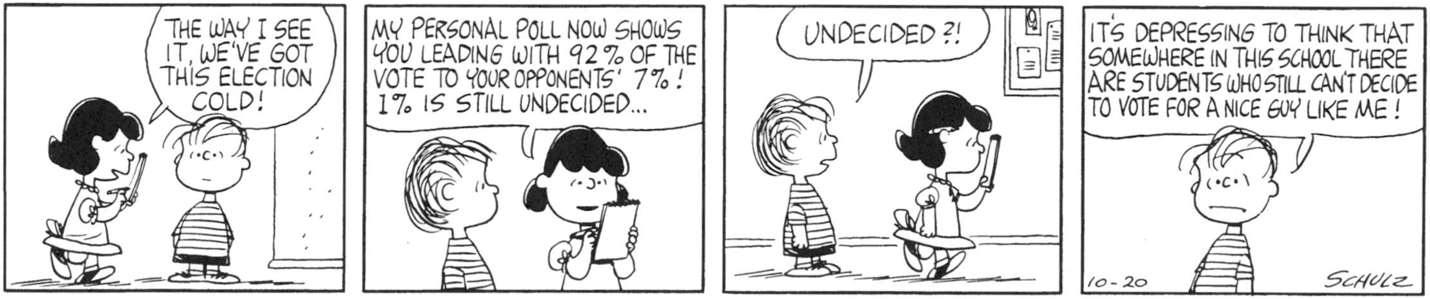
THE WAY I SEE IT, WE'VE GOT THIS ELECTION COLD!
MY PERSONAL POLL NOW SHOWS YOU LEADING WITH 92% OF THE VOTE TO YOUR OPPONENTS' 7%! 1% IS STILL UNDECIDED...
UNDECIDED?!
IT'S DEPRESSING TO THINK THAT SOMEWHERE IN THIS SCHOOL THERE ARE STUDENTS WHO STILL CAN'T DECIDE TO VOTE FOR A NICE GUY LIKE ME!
10-20
SCHULZ

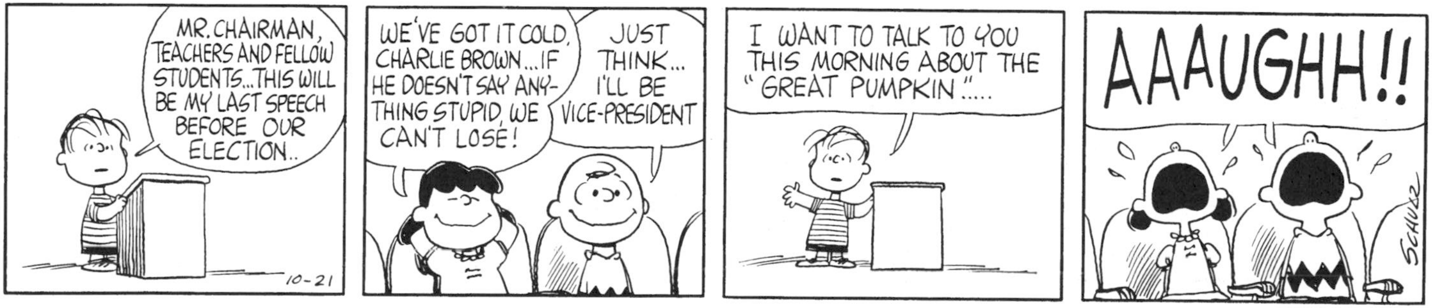
MR. CHAIRMAN, TEACHERS AND FELLOW STUDENTS...THIS WILL BE MY LAST SPEECH BEFORE OUR ELECTION..
10-21
WE'VE GOT IT COLD, CHARLIE BROWN...IF HE DOESN'T SAY ANYTHING STUPID, WE CAN'T LOSE!
JUST THINK... I'LL BE VICE-PRESIDENT
I WANT TO TALK TO YOU THIS MORNING ABOUT THE "GREAT PUMPKIN".....
AAAUGHH!!
SCHULZ

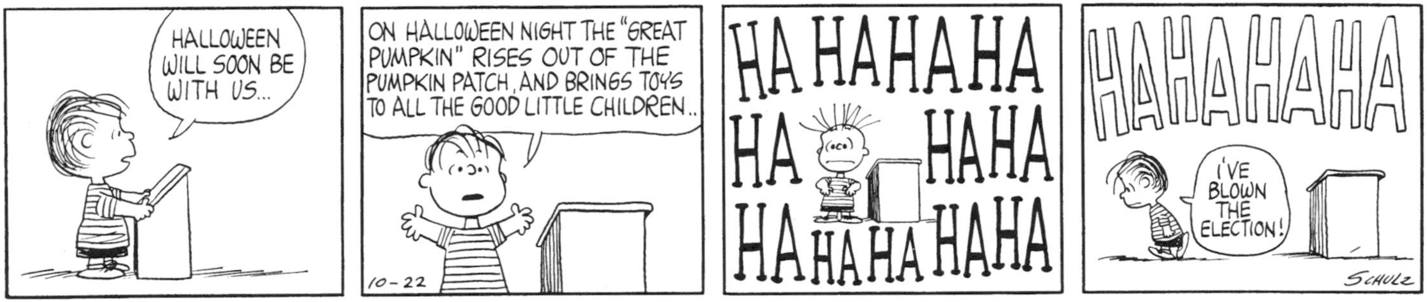
HALLOWEEN WILL SOON BE WITH US...
ON HALLOWEEN NIGHT THE "GREAT PUMPKIN" RISES OUT OF THE PUMPKIN PATCH, AND BRINGS TOYS TO ALL THE GOOD LITTLE CHILDREN..
10-22
HA HAHAHA HA HA HAHA HAHAHAHAHAHA
HAHAHAHAHAHA
I'VE BLOWN THE ELECTION!
SCHULZ

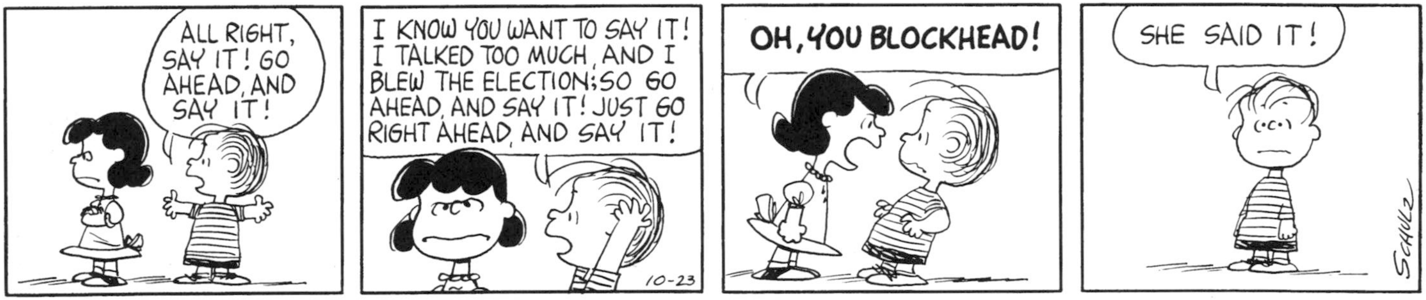
ALL RIGHT, SAY IT! GO AHEAD, AND SAY IT!
I KNOW YOU WANT TO SAY IT! I TALKED TOO MUCH, AND I BLEW THE ELECTION; SO GO AHEAD, AND SAY IT! JUST GO RIGHT AHEAD, AND SAY IT!
10-23
OH, YOU BLOCKHEAD!
SHE SAID IT!
SCHULZ

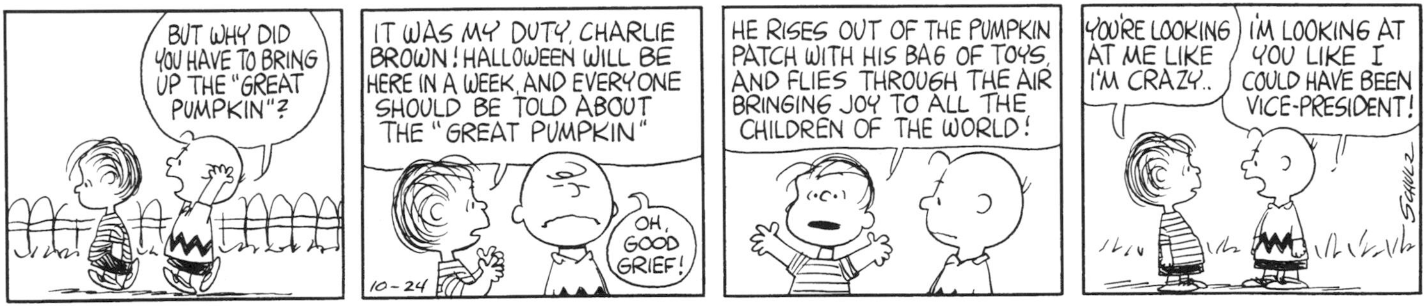
BUT WHY DID YOU HAVE TO BRING UP THE "GREAT PUMPKIN"?
IT WAS MY DUTY, CHARLIE BROWN! HALLOWEEN WILL BE HERE IN A WEEK, AND EVERYONE SHOULD BE TOLD ABOUT THE "GREAT PUMPKIN"
OH, GOOD GRIEF!
10-24
HE RISES OUT OF THE PUMPKIN PATCH WITH HIS BAG OF TOYS, AND FLIES THROUGH THE AIR BRINGING JOY TO ALL THE CHILDREN OF THE WORLD!
YOU'RE LOOKING AT ME LIKE I'M CRAZY..
I'M LOOKING AT YOU LIKE I COULD HAVE BEEN VICE-PRESIDENT!
SCHULZ

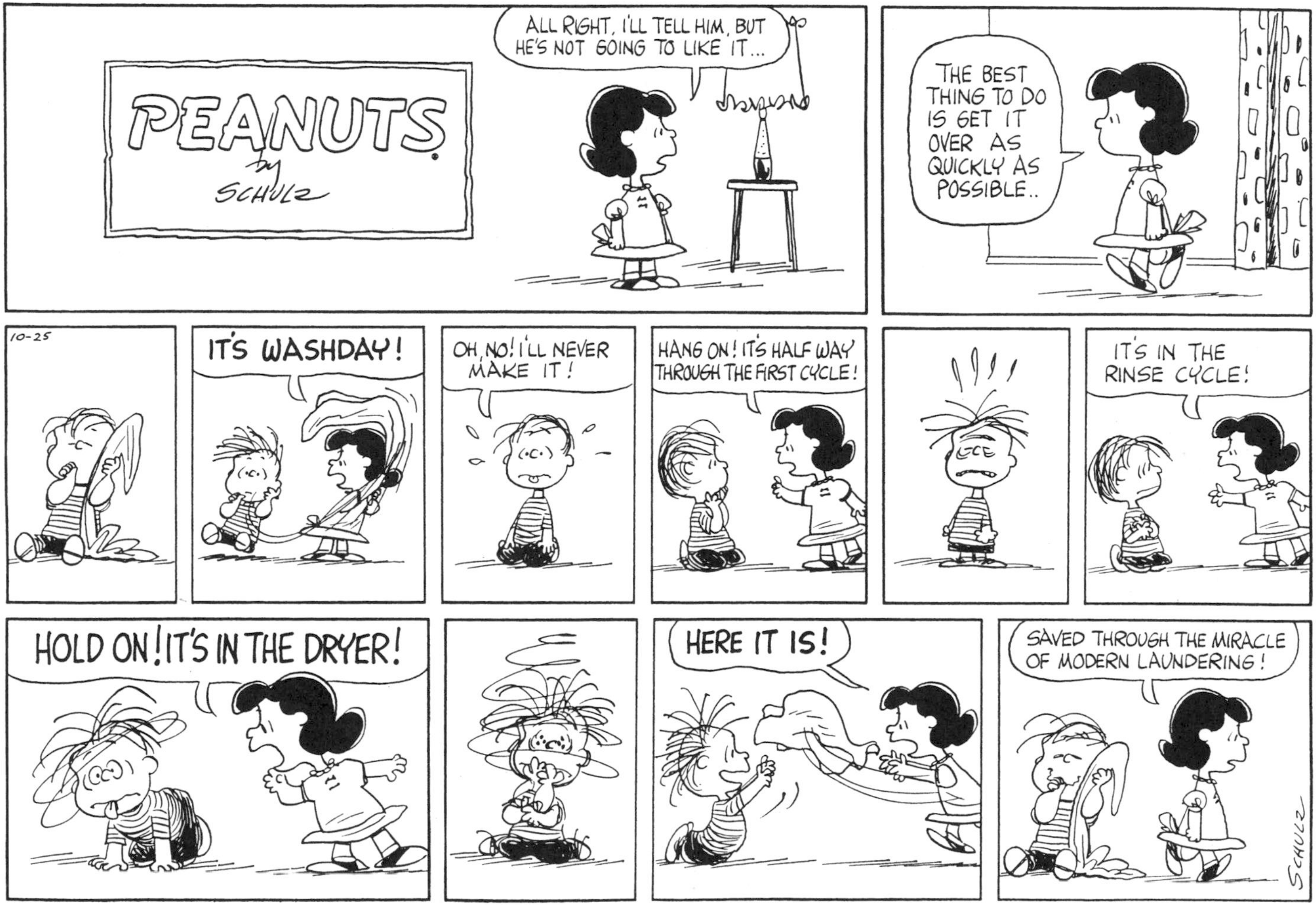
PEANUTS
by SCHULZ
ALL RIGHT, I'LL TELL HIM, BUT HE'S NOT GOING TO LIKE IT...
THE BEST THING TO DO IS GET IT OVER AS QUICKLY AS POSSIBLE..
10-25
IT'S WASHDAY!
OH, NO! I'LL NEVER MAKE IT!
HANG ON! IT'S HALF WAY THROUGH THE FIRST CYCLE!
IT'S IN THE RINSE CYCLE!
HOLD ON! IT'S IN THE DRYER!
HERE IT IS!
SAVED THROUGH THE MIRACLE OF MODERN LAUNDERING!
SCHULZ

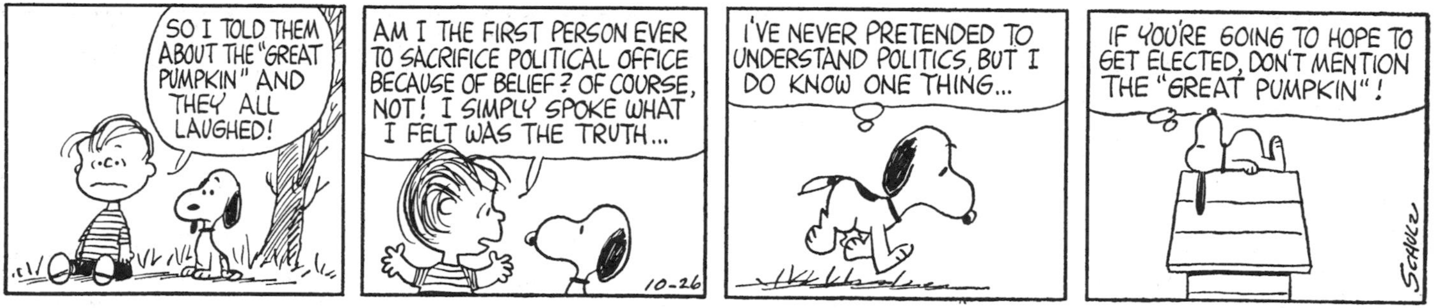
SO I TOLD THEM ABOUT THE "GREAT PUMPKIN" AND THEY ALL LAUGHED!
AM I THE FIRST PERSON EVER TO SACRIFICE POLITICAL OFFICE BECAUSE OF BELIEF? OF COURSE, NOT! I SIMPLY SPOKE WHAT I FELT WAS THE TRUTH...
10-26
I'VE NEVER PRETENDED TO UNDERSTAND POLITICS, BUT I DO KNOW ONE THING...
IF YOU'RE GOING TO HOPE TO GET ELECTED, DON'T MENTION THE "GREAT PUMPKIN"!
SCHULZ

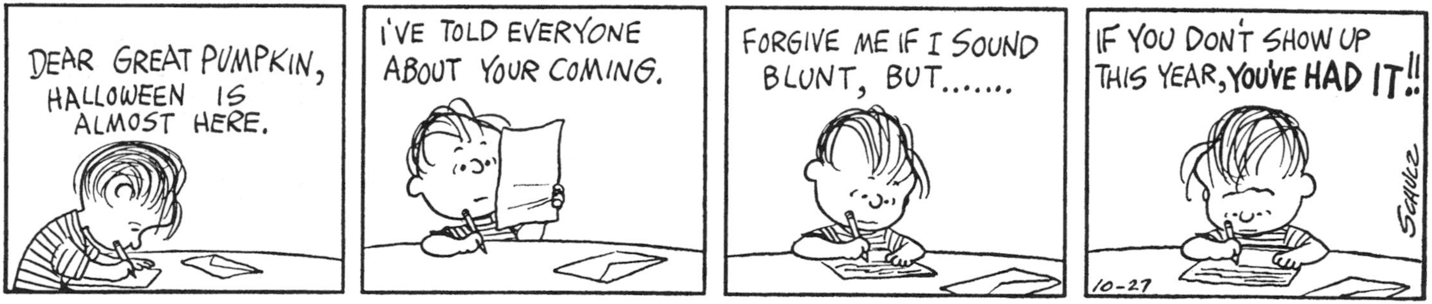
DEAR GREAT PUMPKIN, HALLOWEEN IS ALMOST HERE.
I'VE TOLD EVERYONE ABOUT YOUR COMING.
FORGIVE ME IF I SOUND BLUNT, BUT......
IF YOU DON'T SHOW UP THIS YEAR, **YOU'VE HAD IT!!**
SCHULZ
10-27

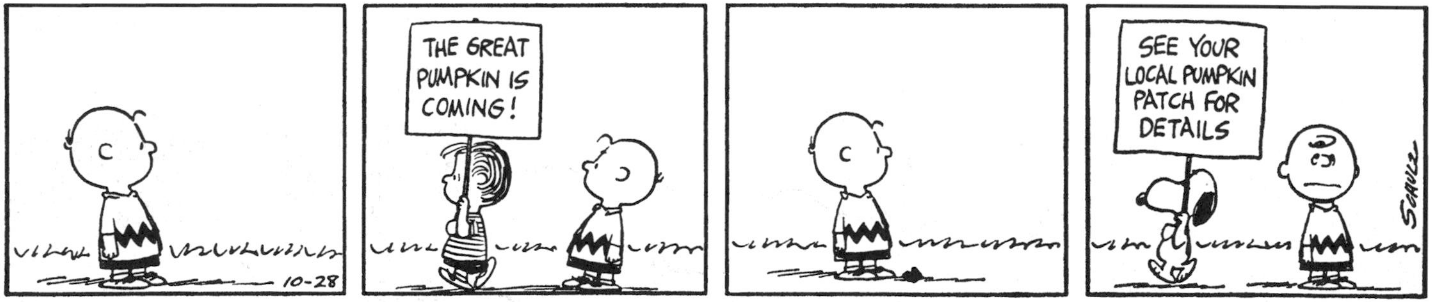
10-28
THE GREAT PUMPKIN IS COMING!
SEE YOUR LOCAL PUMPKIN PATCH FOR DETAILS
SCHULZ

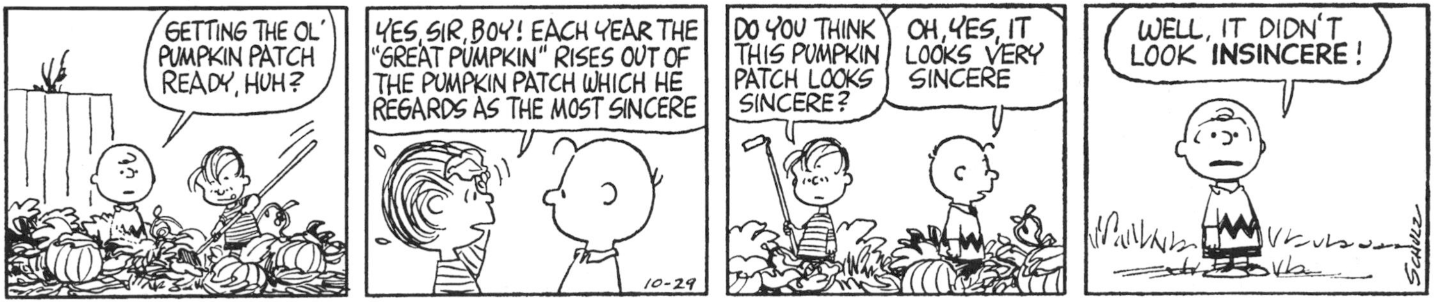
GETTING THE OL' PUMPKIN PATCH READY, HUH?
YES, SIR, BOY! EACH YEAR THE "GREAT PUMPKIN" RISES OUT OF THE PUMPKIN PATCH WHICH HE REGARDS AS THE MOST SINCERE
10-29
DO YOU THINK THIS PUMPKIN PATCH LOOKS SINCERE?
OH, YES, IT LOOKS VERY SINCERE
WELL, IT DIDN'T LOOK **INSINCERE**!
SCHULZ

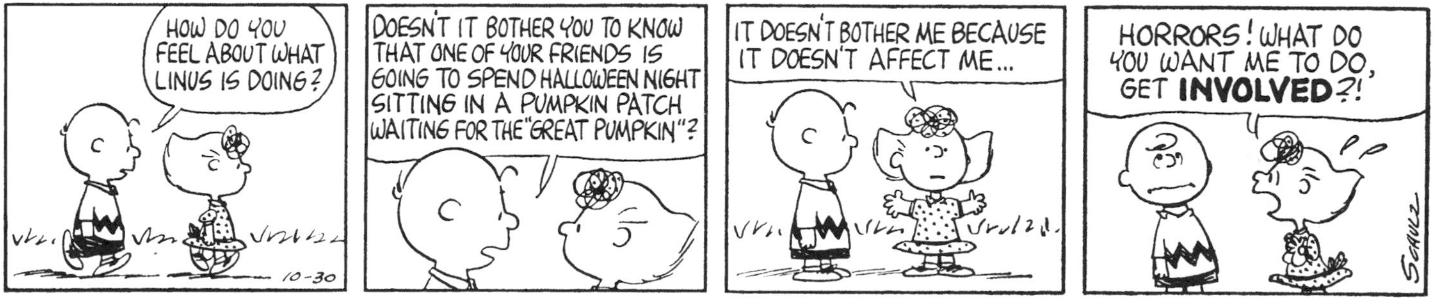
HOW DO YOU FEEL ABOUT WHAT LINUS IS DOING?
10-30
DOESN'T IT BOTHER YOU TO KNOW THAT ONE OF YOUR FRIENDS IS GOING TO SPEND HALLOWEEN NIGHT SITTING IN A PUMPKIN PATCH WAITING FOR THE "GREAT PUMPKIN"?
IT DOESN'T BOTHER ME BECAUSE IT DOESN'T AFFECT ME...
HORRORS! WHAT DO YOU WANT ME TO DO, GET **INVOLVED**?!
SCHULZ

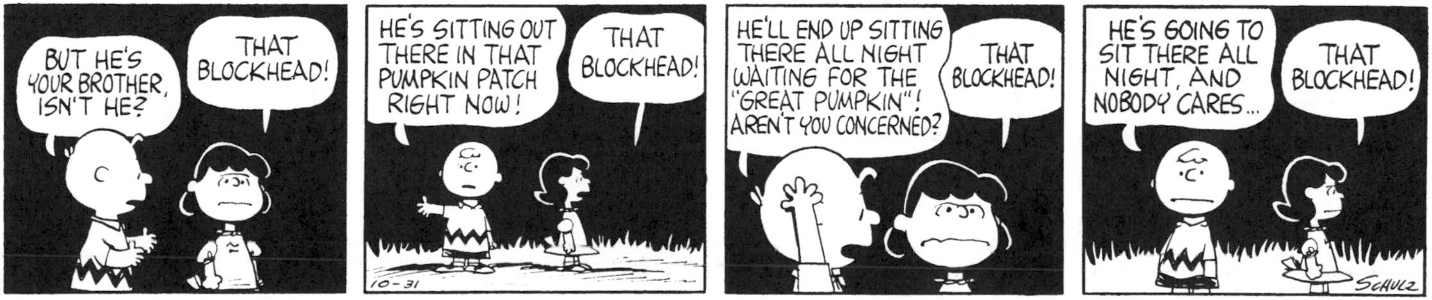
BUT HE'S YOUR BROTHER, ISN'T HE?
THAT BLOCKHEAD!
HE'S SITTING OUT THERE IN THAT PUMPKIN PATCH RIGHT NOW!
THAT BLOCKHEAD!
10-31
HE'LL END UP SITTING THERE ALL NIGHT WAITING FOR THE "GREAT PUMPKIN"! AREN'T YOU CONCERNED?
THAT BLOCKHEAD!
HE'S GOING TO SIT THERE ALL NIGHT, AND NOBODY CARES...
THAT BLOCKHEAD!
SCHULZ

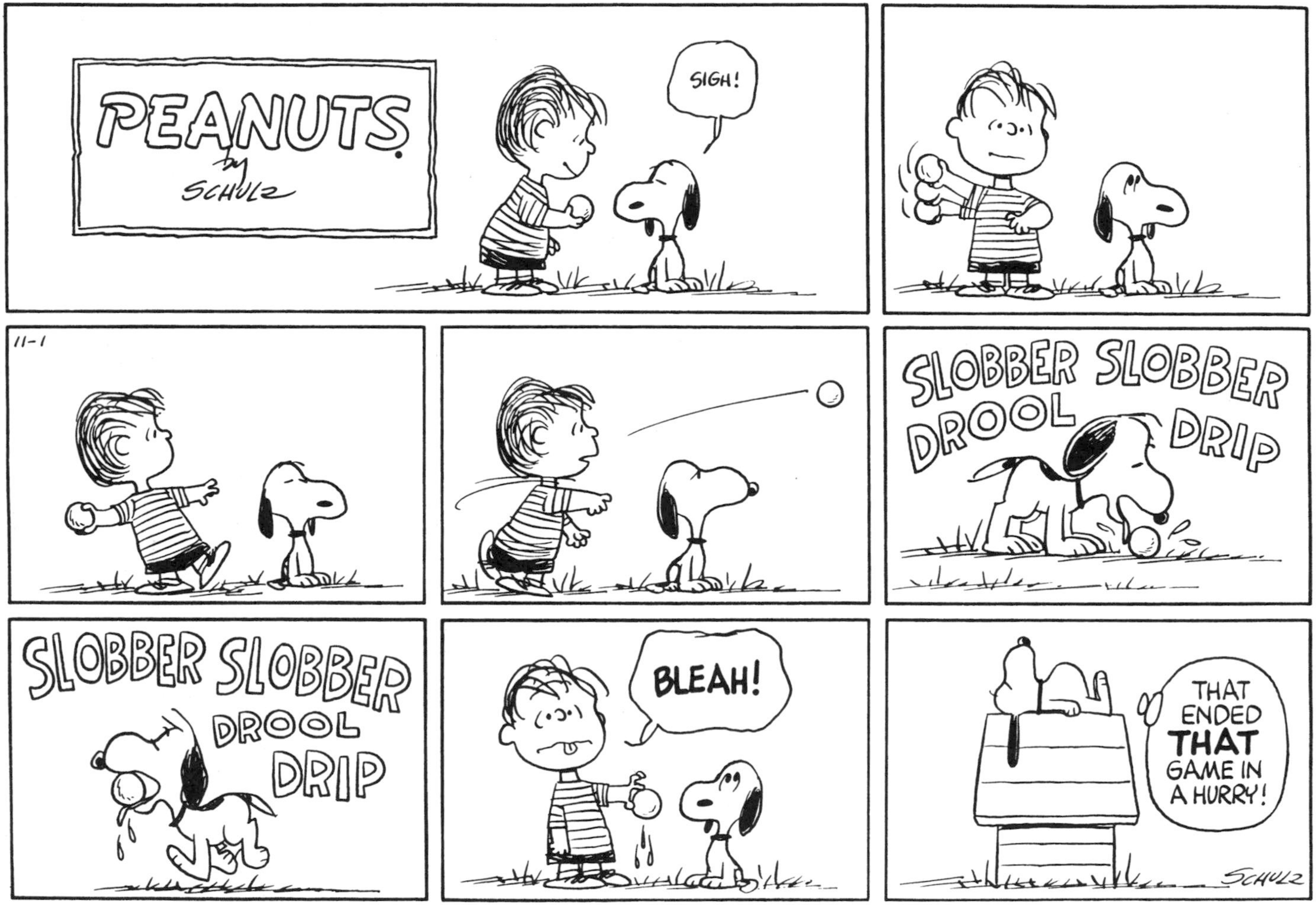
PEANUTS
by
SCHULZ
SIGH!
11-1
SLOBBER SLOBBER
DROOL
DRIP
SLOBBER SLOBBER
DROOL
DRIP
BLEAH!
THAT ENDED THAT GAME IN A HURRY!
SCHULZ

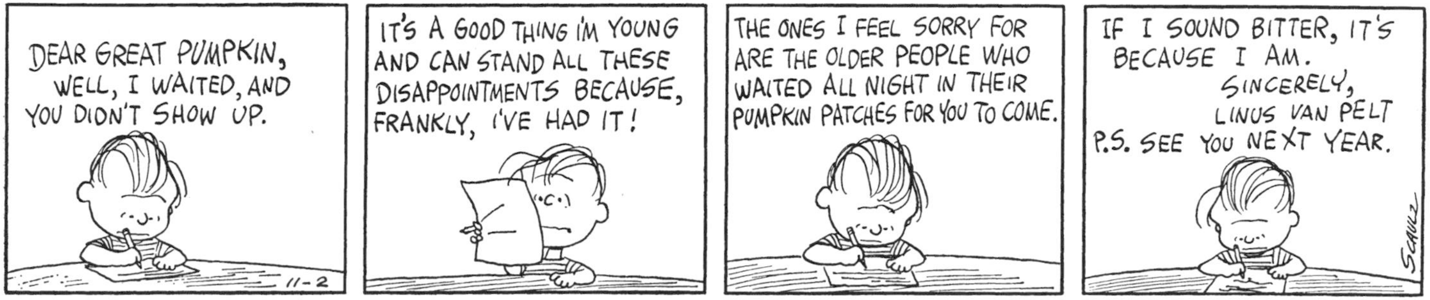
DEAR GREAT PUMPKIN,
WELL, I WAITED, AND YOU DIDN'T SHOW UP.
11-2
IT'S A GOOD THING I'M YOUNG AND CAN STAND ALL THESE DISAPPOINTMENTS BECAUSE, FRANKLY, I'VE HAD IT!
THE ONES I FEEL SORRY FOR ARE THE OLDER PEOPLE WHO WAITED ALL NIGHT IN THEIR PUMPKIN PATCHES FOR YOU TO COME.
IF I SOUND BITTER, IT'S BECAUSE I AM.
SINCERELY,
LINUS VAN PELT
P.S. SEE YOU NEXT YEAR.
SCHULZ

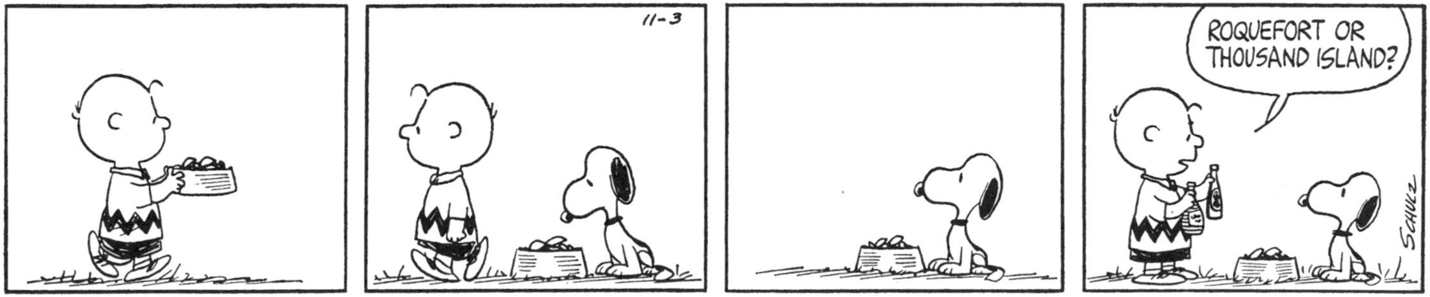
11-3
ROQUEFORT OR THOUSAND ISLAND?
SCHULZ

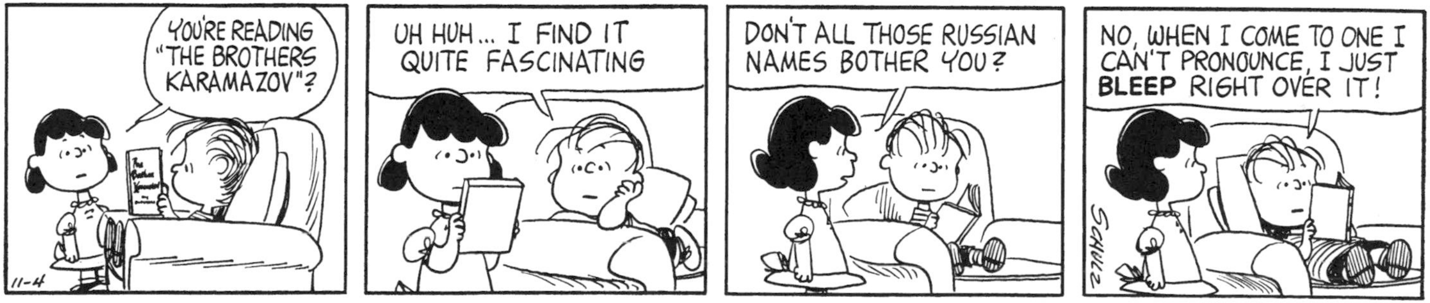
YOU'RE READING "THE BROTHERS KARAMAZOV"?
11-4
UH HUH... I FIND IT QUITE FASCINATING
DON'T ALL THOSE RUSSIAN NAMES BOTHER YOU?
NO, WHEN I COME TO ONE I CAN'T PRONOUNCE, I JUST **BLEEP** RIGHT OVER IT!
SCHULZ

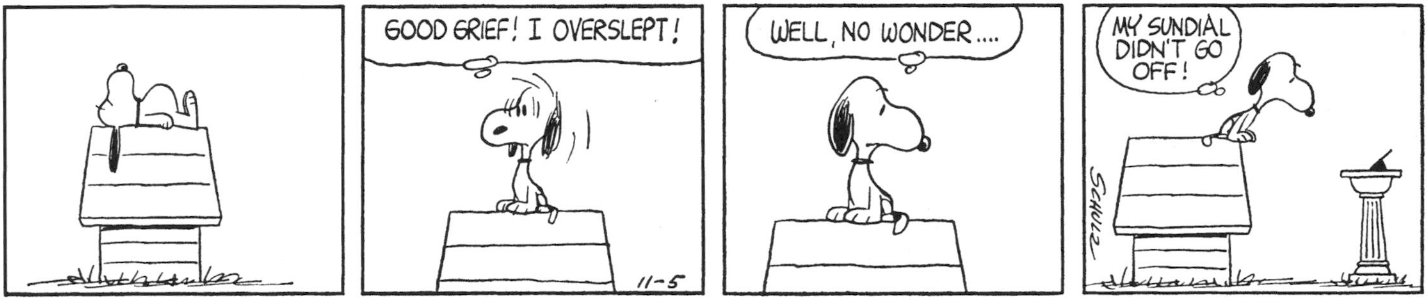
GOOD GRIEF! I OVERSLEPT!
11-5
WELL, NO WONDER....
MY SUNDIAL DIDN'T GO OFF!
SCHULZ

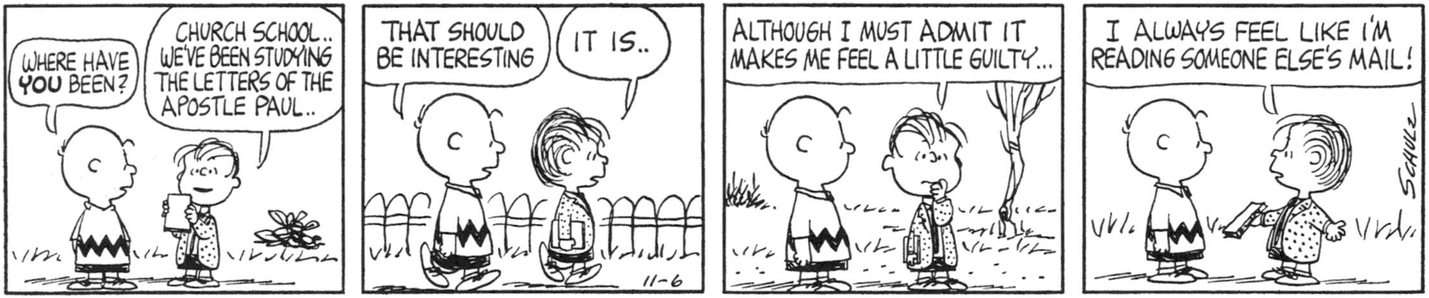
WHERE HAVE **YOU** BEEN?
CHURCH SCHOOL.. WE'VE BEEN STUDYING THE LETTERS OF THE APOSTLE PAUL..
THAT SHOULD BE INTERESTING
IT IS..
11-6
ALTHOUGH I MUST ADMIT IT MAKES ME FEEL A LITTLE GUILTY...
I ALWAYS FEEL LIKE I'M READING SOMEONE ELSE'S MAIL!
SCHULZ

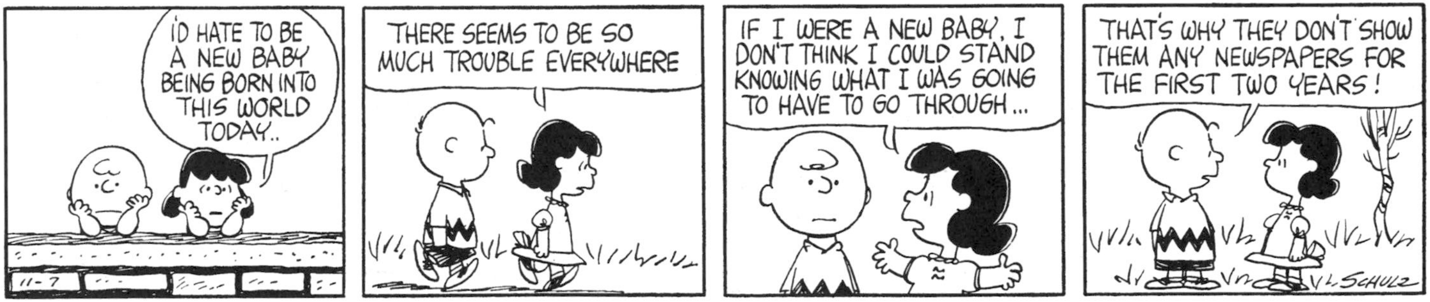
I'D HATE TO BE A NEW BABY BEING BORN INTO THIS WORLD TODAY..
11-7
THERE SEEMS TO BE SO MUCH TROUBLE EVERYWHERE
IF I WERE A NEW BABY, I DON'T THINK I COULD STAND KNOWING WHAT I WAS GOING TO HAVE TO GO THROUGH...
THAT'S WHY THEY DON'T SHOW THEM ANY NEWSPAPERS FOR THE FIRST TWO YEARS!
SCHULZ

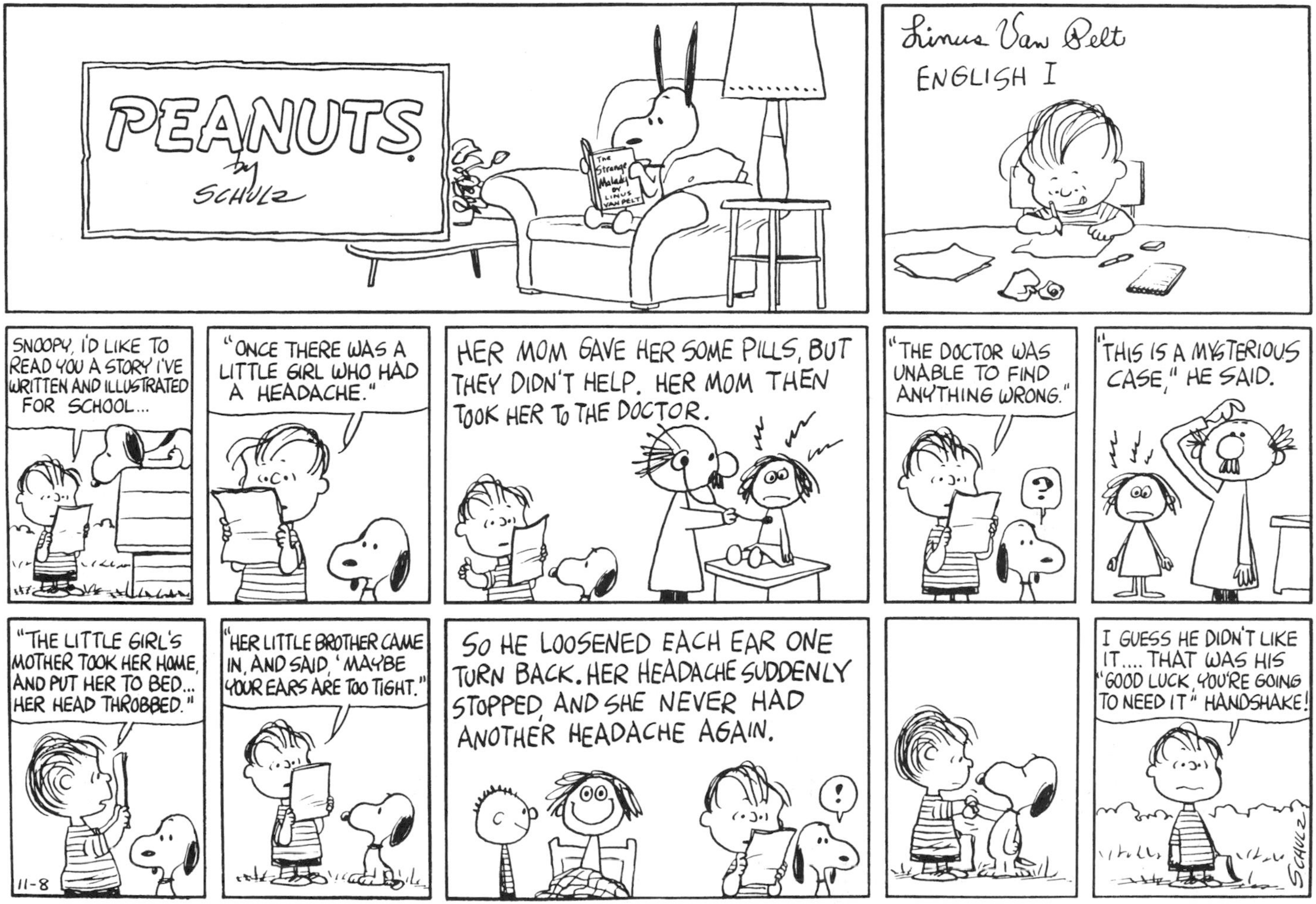
PEANUTS
by SCHULZ
The Strange Malady by Linus Van Pelt
Linus Van Pelt
ENGLISH I
SNOOPY, I'D LIKE TO READ YOU A STORY I'VE WRITTEN AND ILLUSTRATED FOR SCHOOL...
"ONCE THERE WAS A LITTLE GIRL WHO HAD A HEADACHE."
HER MOM GAVE HER SOME PILLS, BUT THEY DIDN'T HELP. HER MOM THEN TOOK HER TO THE DOCTOR.
"THE DOCTOR WAS UNABLE TO FIND ANYTHING WRONG."
?
"THIS IS A MYSTERIOUS CASE," HE SAID.
"THE LITTLE GIRL'S MOTHER TOOK HER HOME, AND PUT HER TO BED... HER HEAD THROBBED."
11-8
"HER LITTLE BROTHER CAME IN, AND SAID, 'MAYBE YOUR EARS ARE TOO TIGHT.'"
SO HE LOOSENED EACH EAR ONE TURN BACK. HER HEADACHE SUDDENLY STOPPED, AND SHE NEVER HAD ANOTHER HEADACHE AGAIN.
!
I GUESS HE DIDN'T LIKE IT.... THAT WAS HIS "GOOD LUCK, YOU'RE GOING TO NEED IT" HANDSHAKE!
SCHULZ

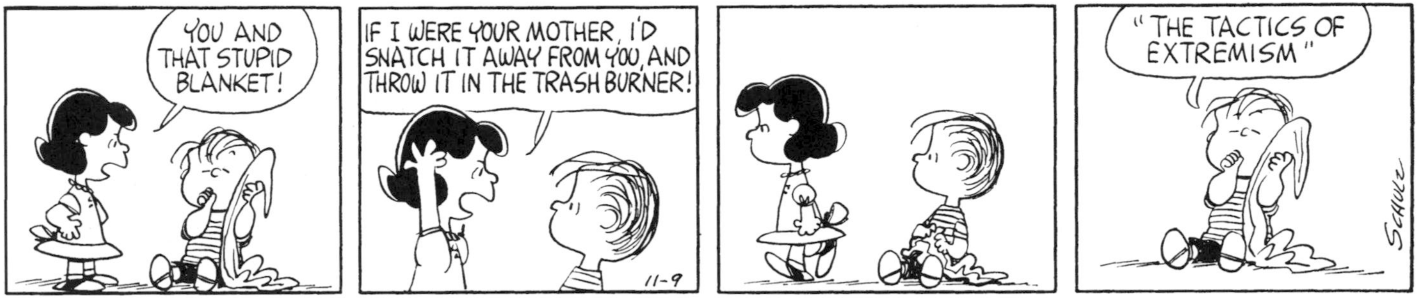
YOU AND THAT STUPID BLANKET!
IF I WERE YOUR MOTHER, I'D SNATCH IT AWAY FROM YOU, AND THROW IT IN THE TRASH BURNER!
"THE TACTICS OF EXTREMISM"
11-9
SCHULZ

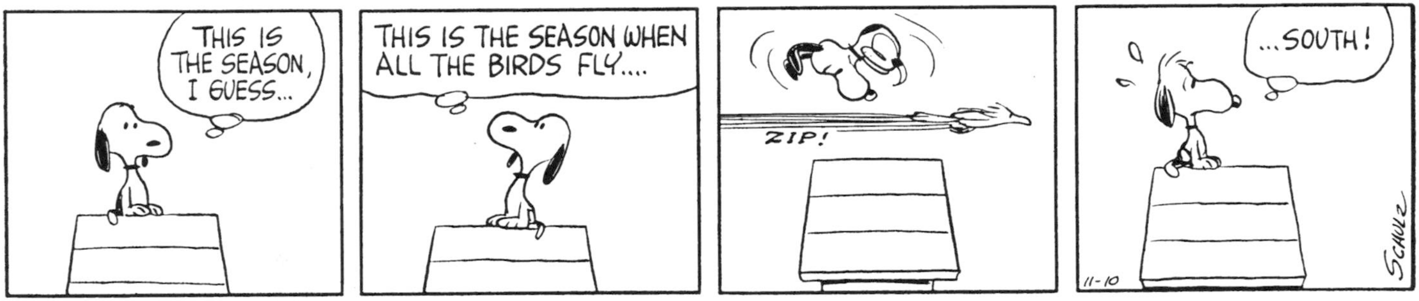
THIS IS THE SEASON, I GUESS...
THIS IS THE SEASON WHEN ALL THE BIRDS FLY....
ZIP!
...SOUTH!
11-10
SCHULZ

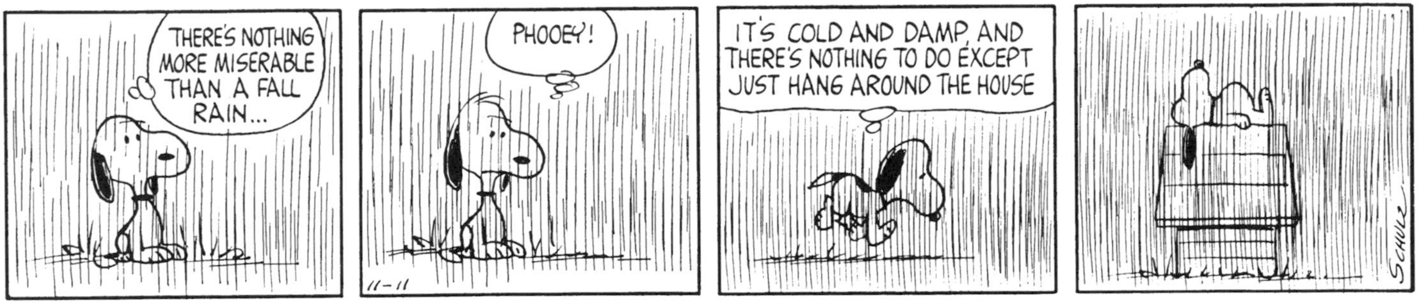
THERE'S NOTHING MORE MISERABLE THAN A FALL RAIN...
PHOOEY!
11-11
IT'S COLD AND DAMP, AND THERE'S NOTHING TO DO EXCEPT JUST HANG AROUND THE HOUSE
SCHULZ

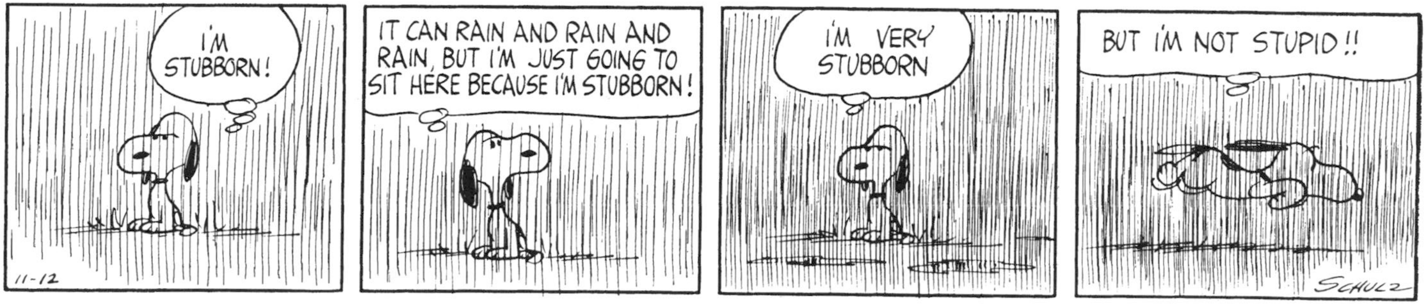
I'M STUBBORN!
IT CAN RAIN AND RAIN AND RAIN, BUT I'M JUST GOING TO SIT HERE BECAUSE I'M STUBBORN!
I'M VERY STUBBORN
BUT I'M NOT STUPID!!
11-12
SCHULZ

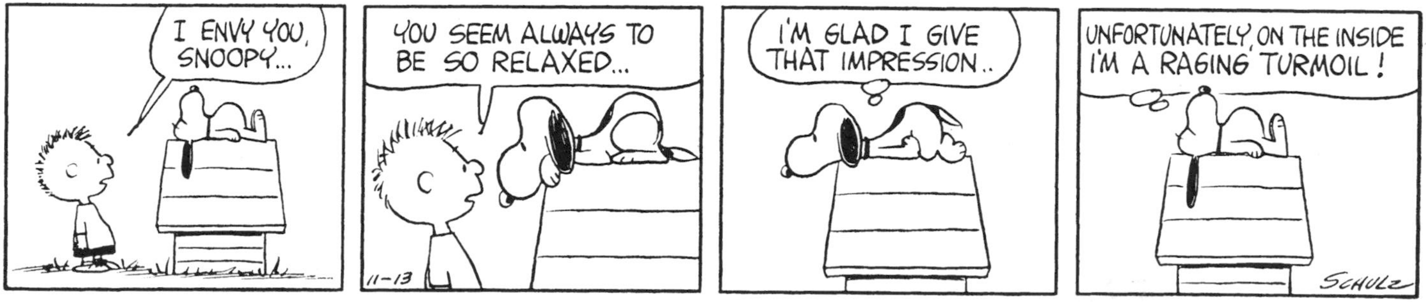
I ENVY YOU, SNOOPY...
YOU SEEM ALWAYS TO BE SO RELAXED...
11-13
I'M GLAD I GIVE THAT IMPRESSION..
UNFORTUNATELY, ON THE INSIDE I'M A RAGING TURMOIL!
SCHULZ

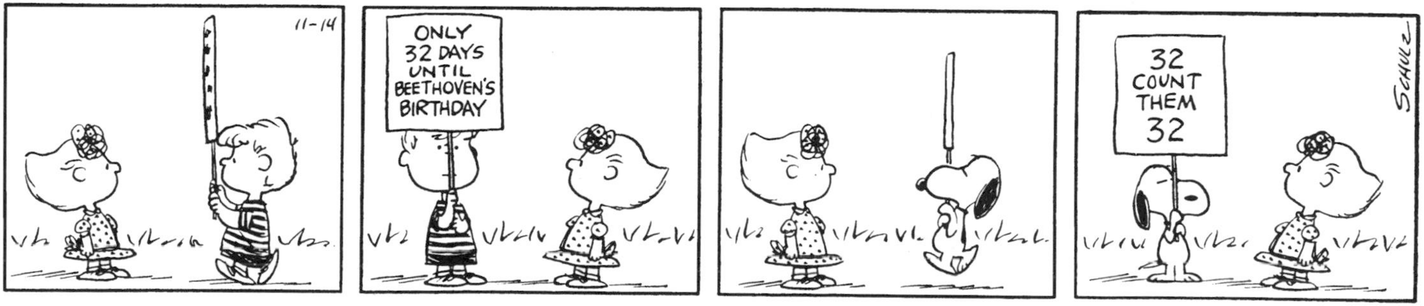
11-14
ONLY 32 DAYS UNTIL BEETHOVEN'S BIRTHDAY
32 COUNT THEM 32
SCHULZ

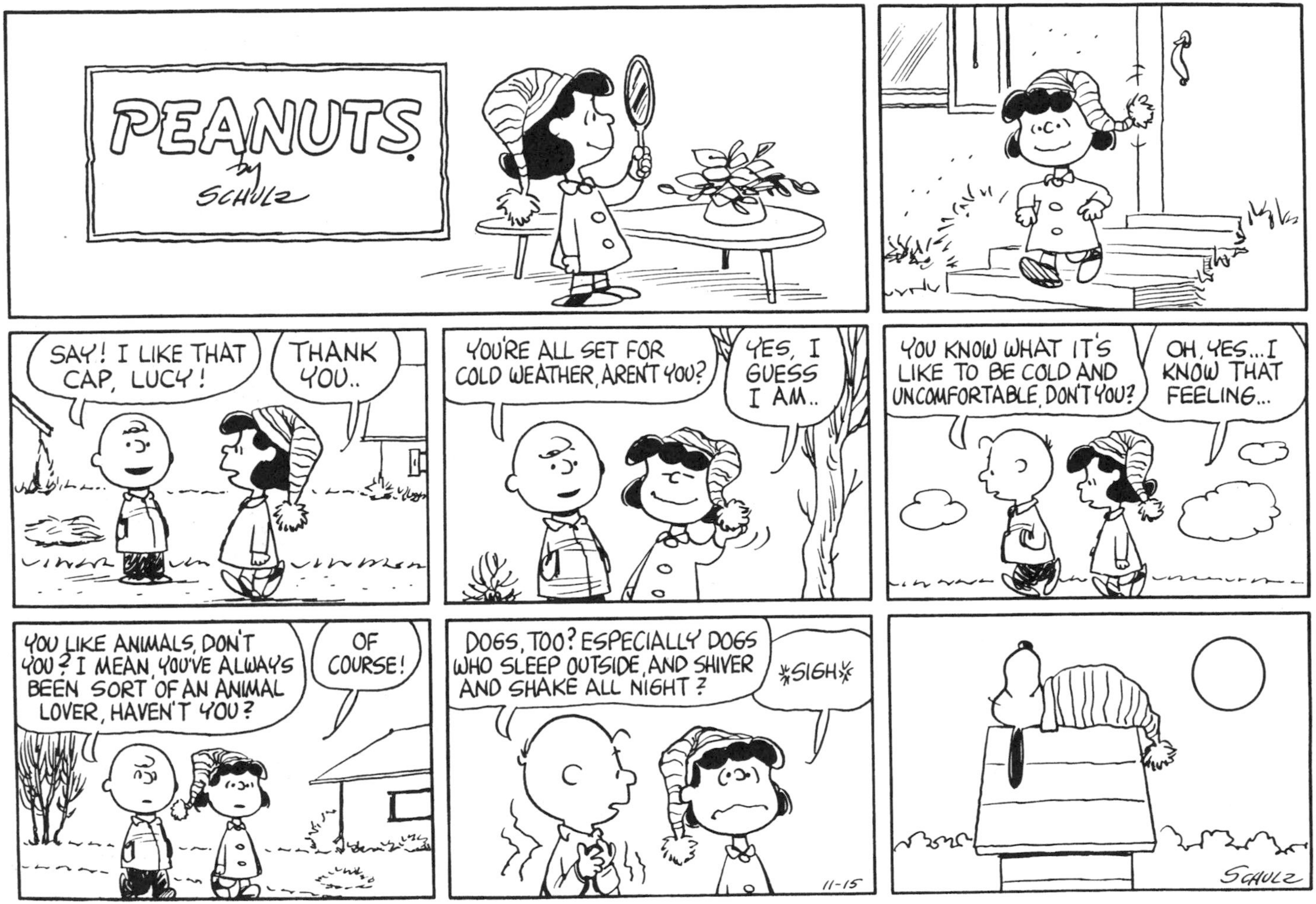
PEANUTS
by SCHULZ
SAY! I LIKE THAT CAP, LUCY!
THANK YOU..
YOU'RE ALL SET FOR COLD WEATHER, AREN'T YOU?
YES, I GUESS I AM..
YOU KNOW WHAT IT'S LIKE TO BE COLD AND UNCOMFORTABLE, DON'T YOU?
OH, YES...I KNOW THAT FEELING...
YOU LIKE ANIMALS, DON'T YOU? I MEAN, YOU'VE ALWAYS BEEN SORT OF AN ANIMAL LOVER, HAVEN'T YOU?
OF COURSE!
DOGS, TOO? ESPECIALLY DOGS WHO SLEEP OUTSIDE, AND SHIVER AND SHAKE ALL NIGHT?
SIGH
11-15
SCHULZ

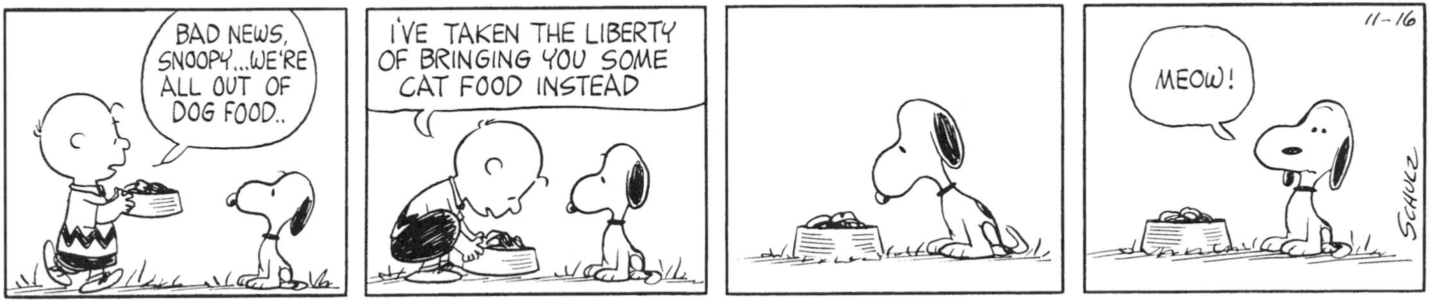
BAD NEWS, SNOOPY...WE'RE ALL OUT OF DOG FOOD..
I'VE TAKEN THE LIBERTY OF BRINGING YOU SOME CAT FOOD INSTEAD
11-16
MEOW!
SCHULZ

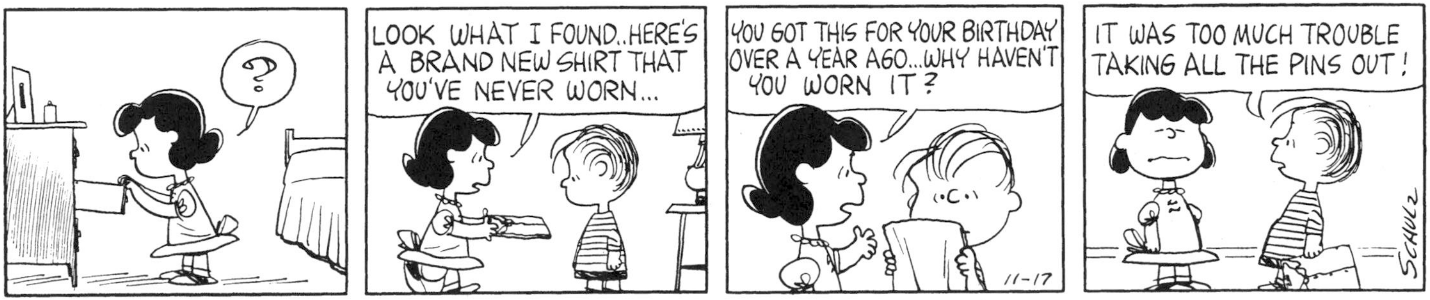
?
LOOK WHAT I FOUND..HERE'S A BRAND NEW SHIRT THAT YOU'VE NEVER WORN...
YOU GOT THIS FOR YOUR BIRTHDAY OVER A YEAR AGO...WHY HAVEN'T YOU WORN IT?
11-17
IT WAS TOO MUCH TROUBLE TAKING ALL THE PINS OUT!
SCHULZ

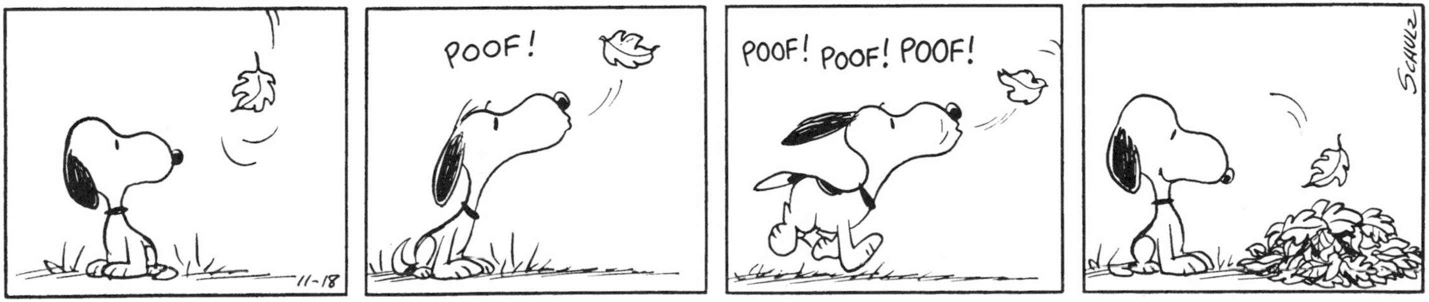
11-18
POOF!
POOF! POOF! POOF!
SCHULZ

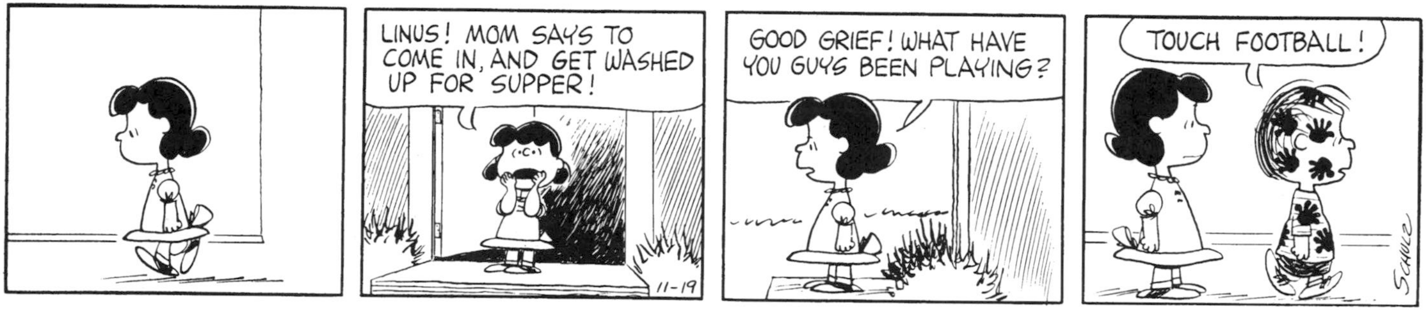
LINUS! MOM SAYS TO COME IN, AND GET WASHED UP FOR SUPPER!
11-19
GOOD GRIEF! WHAT HAVE YOU GUYS BEEN PLAYING?
TOUCH FOOTBALL!
SCHULZ

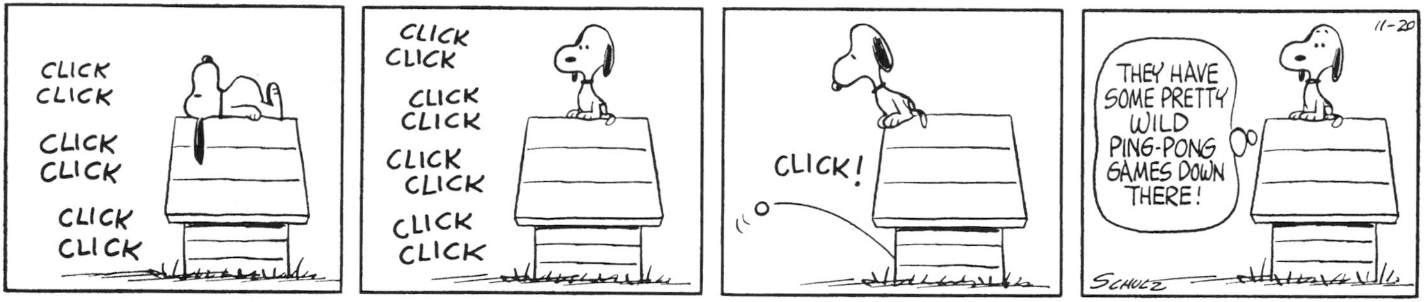
CLICK CLICK
CLICK CLICK
CLICK CLICK
CLICK CLICK
CLICK CLICK
CLICK CLICK
CLICK!
11-20
THEY HAVE SOME PRETTY WILD PING-PONG GAMES DOWN THERE!
SCHULZ

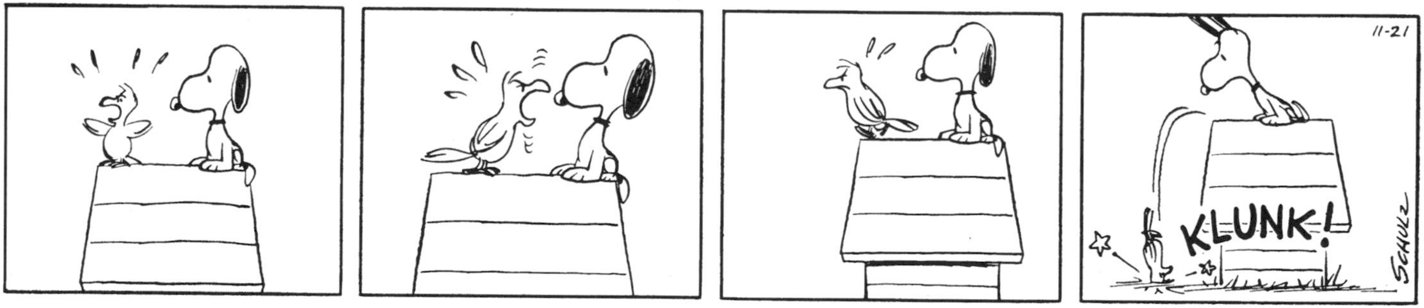
11-21
KLUNK!
SCHULZ

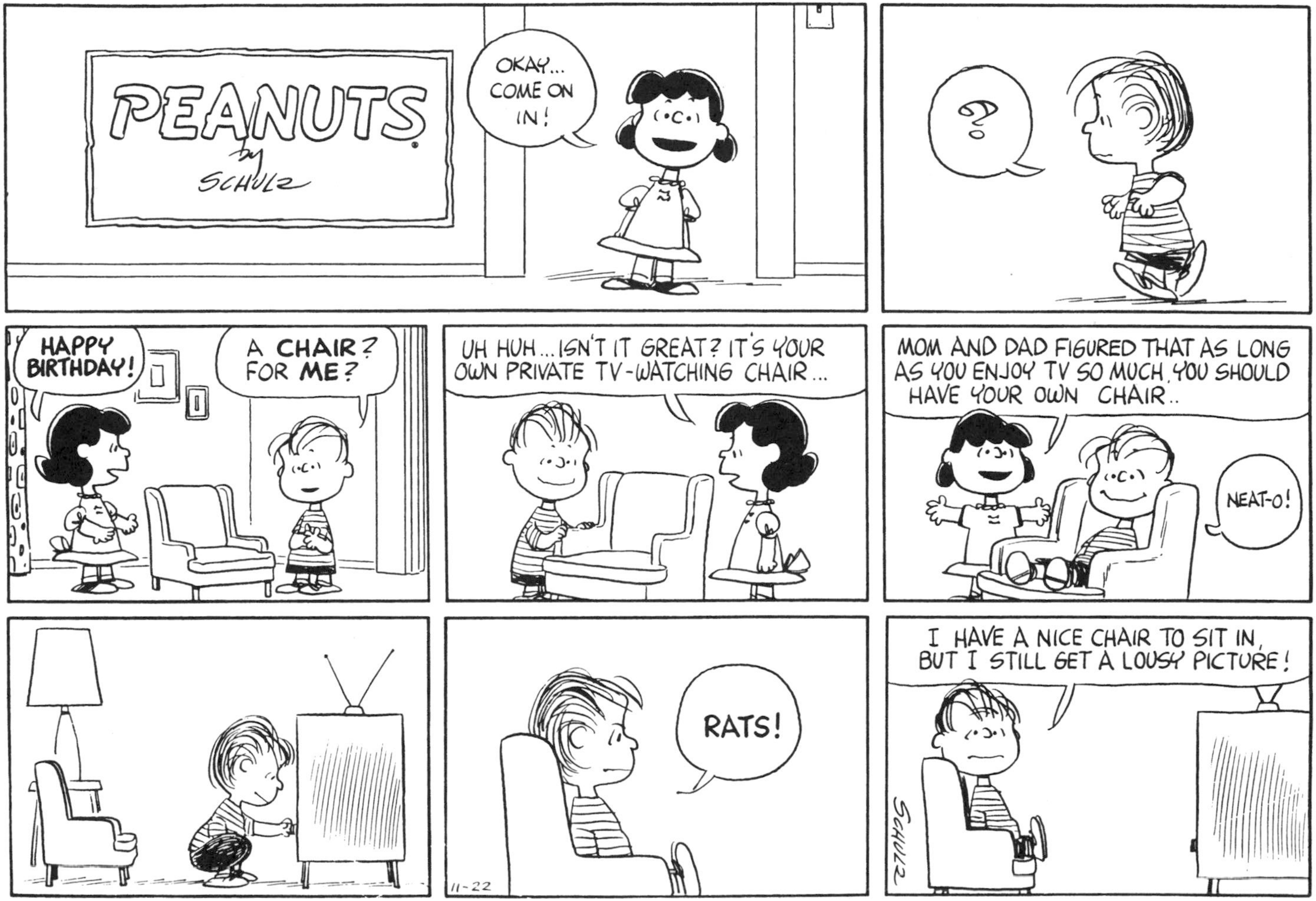
PEANUTS
by
SCHULZ
OKAY... COME ON IN!
?
HAPPY BIRTHDAY!
A CHAIR? FOR ME?
UH HUH... ISN'T IT GREAT? IT'S YOUR OWN PRIVATE TV-WATCHING CHAIR...
MOM AND DAD FIGURED THAT AS LONG AS YOU ENJOY TV SO MUCH, YOU SHOULD HAVE YOUR OWN CHAIR..
NEAT-O!
11-22
RATS!
I HAVE A NICE CHAIR TO SIT IN, BUT I STILL GET A LOUSY PICTURE!
SCHULZ

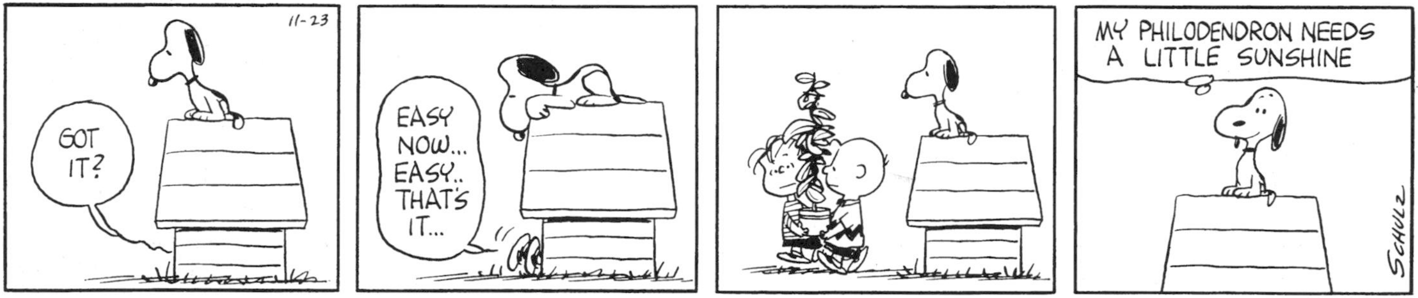
11-23
GOT IT?
EASY NOW... EASY.. THAT'S IT...
MY PHILODENDRON NEEDS A LITTLE SUNSHINE
SCHULZ

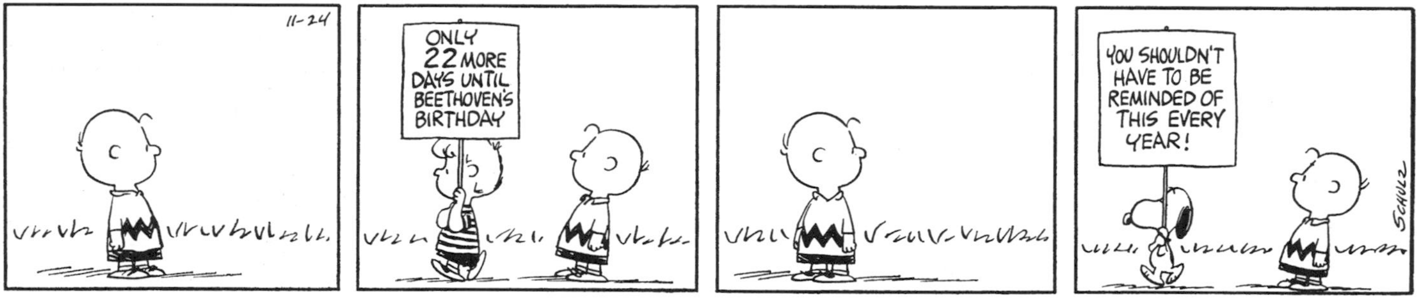
11-24
ONLY 22 MORE DAYS UNTIL BEETHOVEN'S BIRTHDAY
YOU SHOULDN'T HAVE TO BE REMINDED OF THIS EVERY YEAR!
SCHULZ

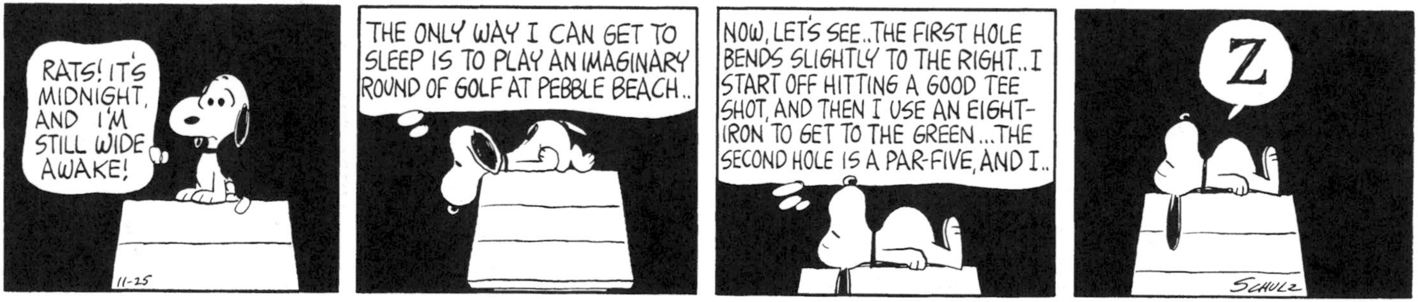
RATS! IT'S MIDNIGHT, AND I'M STILL WIDE AWAKE!
11-25
THE ONLY WAY I CAN GET TO SLEEP IS TO PLAY AN IMAGINARY ROUND OF GOLF AT PEBBLE BEACH..
NOW, LET'S SEE..THE FIRST HOLE BENDS SLIGHTLY TO THE RIGHT..I START OFF HITTING A GOOD TEE SHOT, AND THEN I USE AN EIGHT-IRON TO GET TO THE GREEN ...THE SECOND HOLE IS A PAR-FIVE, AND I..
Z
SCHULZ

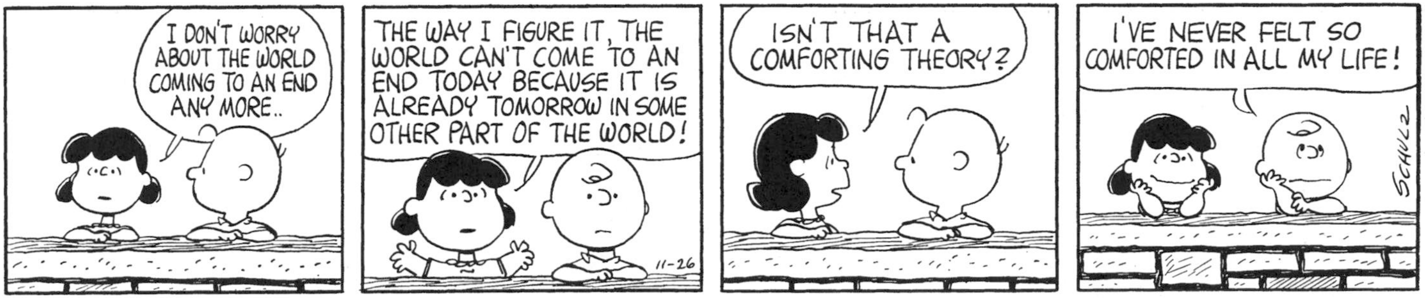
I DON'T WORRY ABOUT THE WORLD COMING TO AN END ANY MORE..
THE WAY I FIGURE IT, THE WORLD CAN'T COME TO AN END TODAY BECAUSE IT IS ALREADY TOMORROW IN SOME OTHER PART OF THE WORLD!
11-26
ISN'T THAT A COMFORTING THEORY?
I'VE NEVER FELT SO COMFORTED IN ALL MY LIFE!
SCHULZ

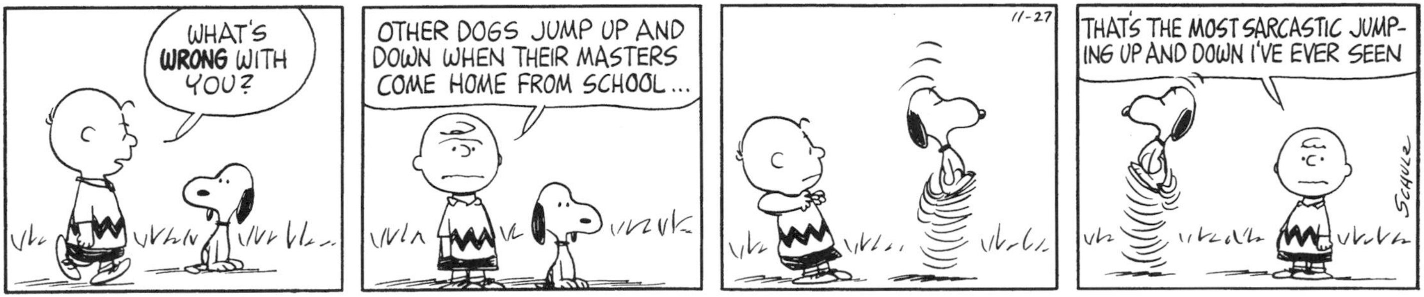
WHAT'S **WRONG** WITH YOU?
OTHER DOGS JUMP UP AND DOWN WHEN THEIR MASTERS COME HOME FROM SCHOOL...
11-27
THAT'S THE MOST SARCASTIC JUMPING UP AND DOWN I'VE EVER SEEN
SCHULZ

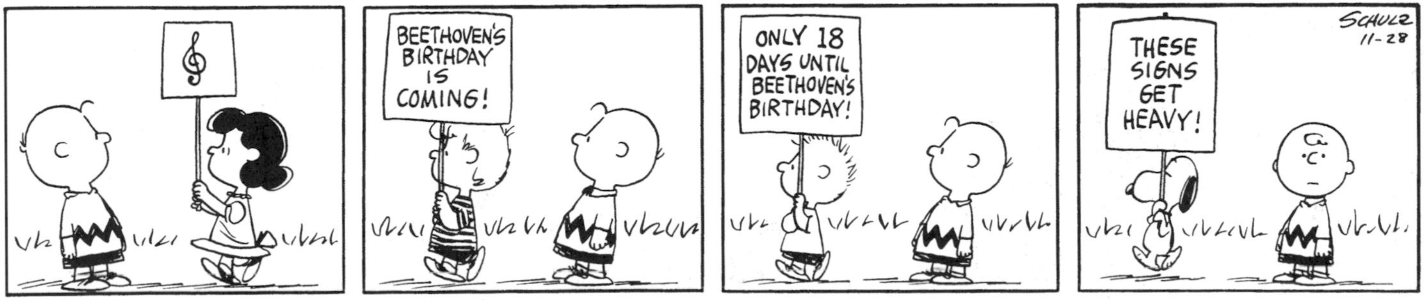
BEETHOVEN'S BIRTHDAY IS COMING!
ONLY 18 DAYS UNTIL BEETHOVEN'S BIRTHDAY!
SCHULZ
11-28
THESE SIGNS GET HEAVY!

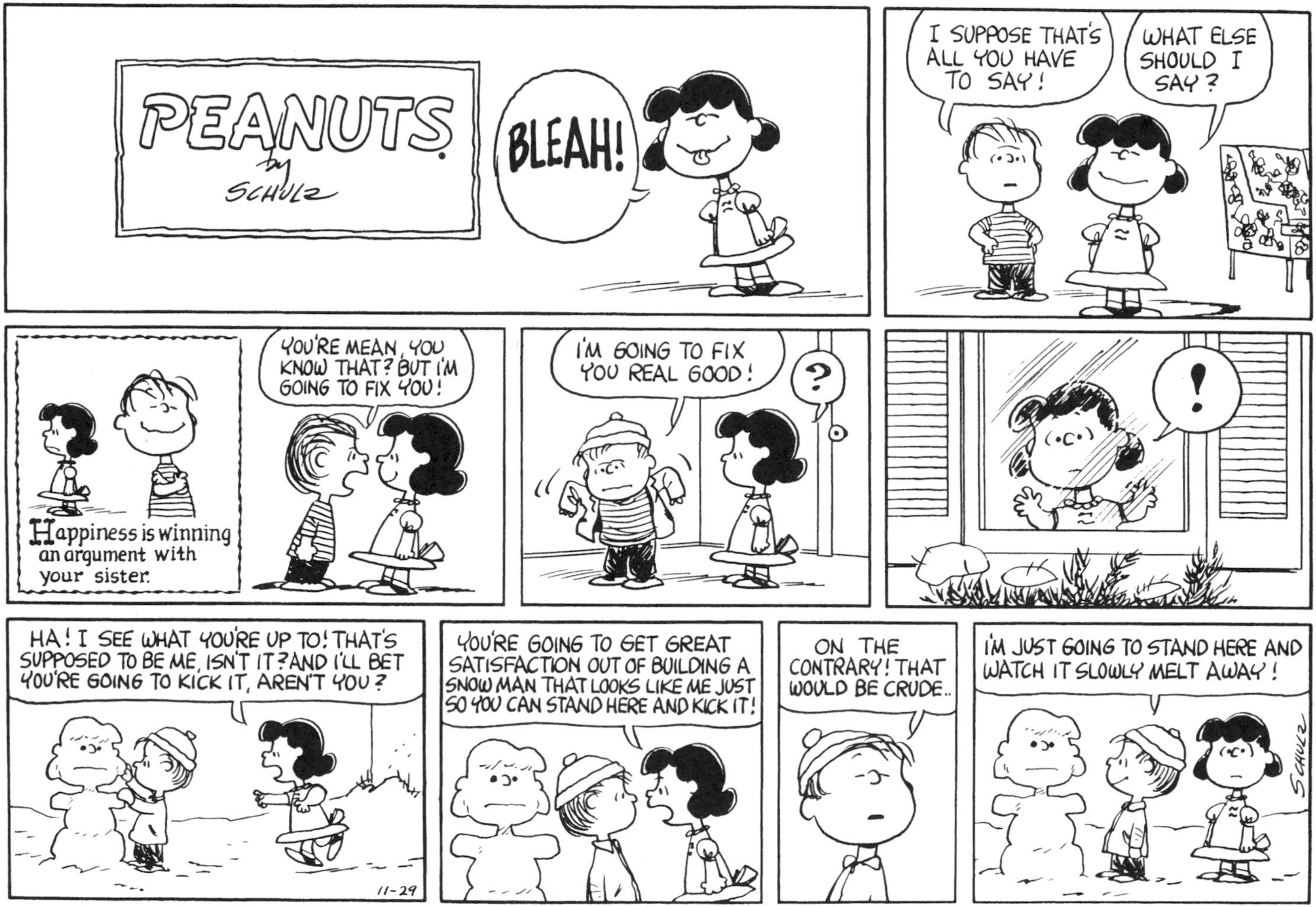
PEANUTS
by SCHULZ
BLEAH!
I SUPPOSE THAT'S ALL YOU HAVE TO SAY!
WHAT ELSE SHOULD I SAY?
Happiness is winning an argument with your sister.
YOU'RE MEAN, YOU KNOW THAT? BUT I'M GOING TO FIX YOU!
I'M GOING TO FIX YOU REAL GOOD!
?
!
HA! I SEE WHAT YOU'RE UP TO! THAT'S SUPPOSED TO BE ME, ISN'T IT? AND I'LL BET YOU'RE GOING TO KICK IT, AREN'T YOU?
11-29
YOU'RE GOING TO GET GREAT SATISFACTION OUT OF BUILDING A SNOW MAN THAT LOOKS LIKE ME JUST SO YOU CAN STAND HERE AND KICK IT!
ON THE CONTRARY! THAT WOULD BE CRUDE..
I'M JUST GOING TO STAND HERE AND WATCH IT SLOWLY MELT AWAY!
SCHULZ

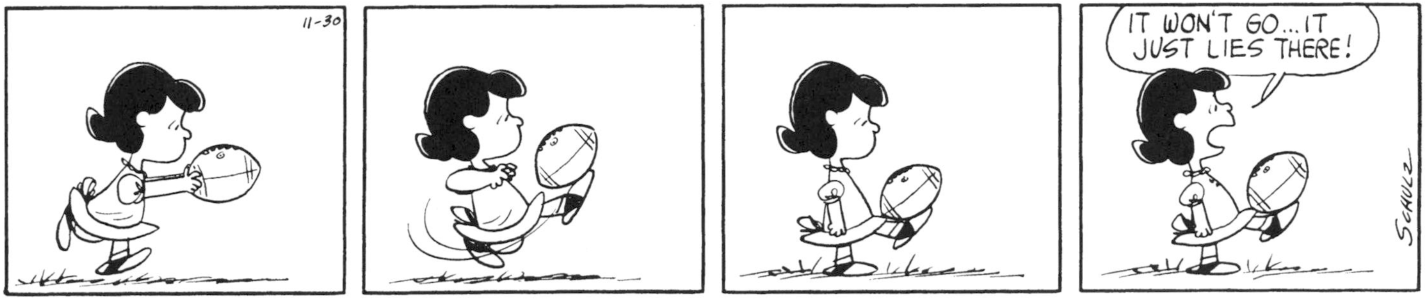
11-30
IT WON'T GO...IT JUST LIES THERE!
SCHULZ

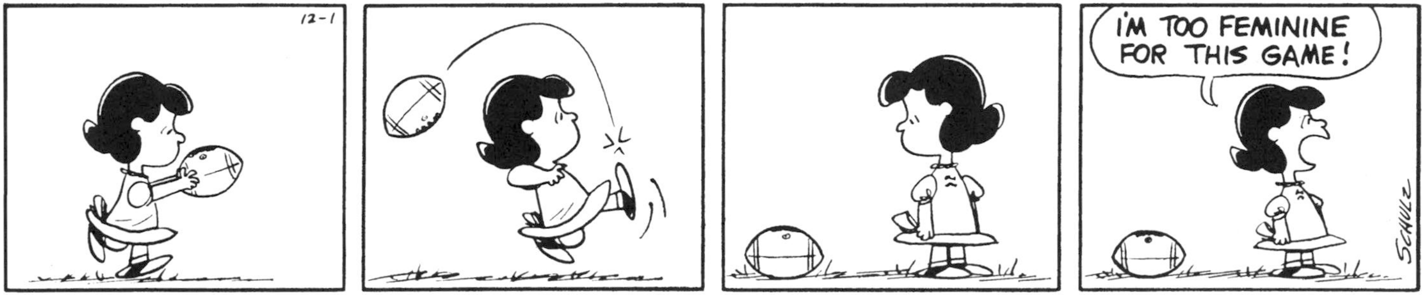
12-1
I'M TOO FEMININE FOR THIS GAME!
SCHULZ

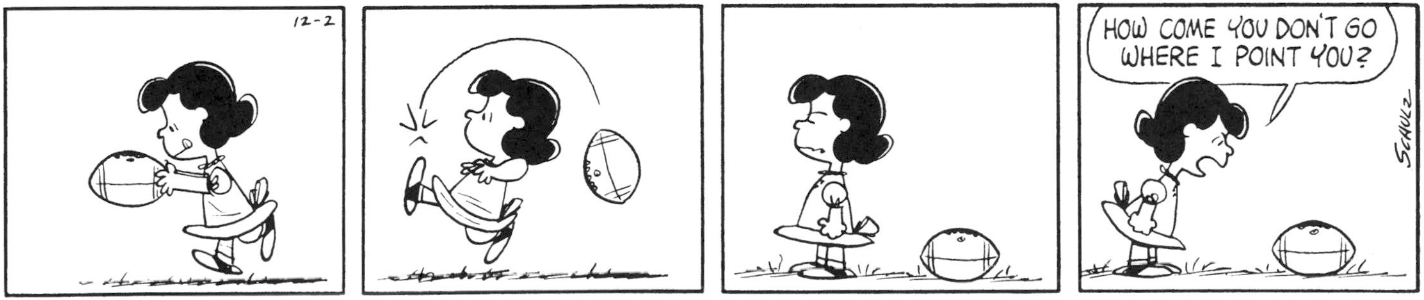
12-2
HOW COME YOU DON'T GO WHERE I POINT YOU?
SCHULZ

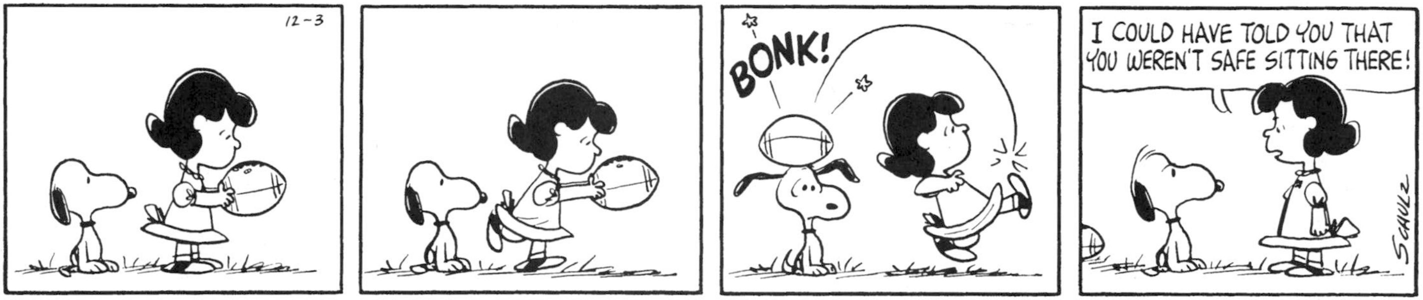
12-3
BONK!
I COULD HAVE TOLD YOU THAT YOU WEREN'T SAFE SITTING THERE!
SCHULZ

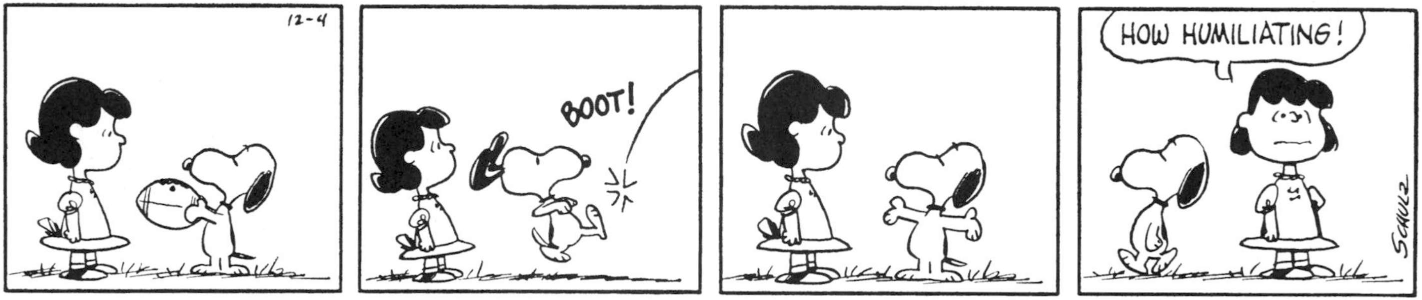
12-4
BOOT!
HOW HUMILIATING!
SCHULZ

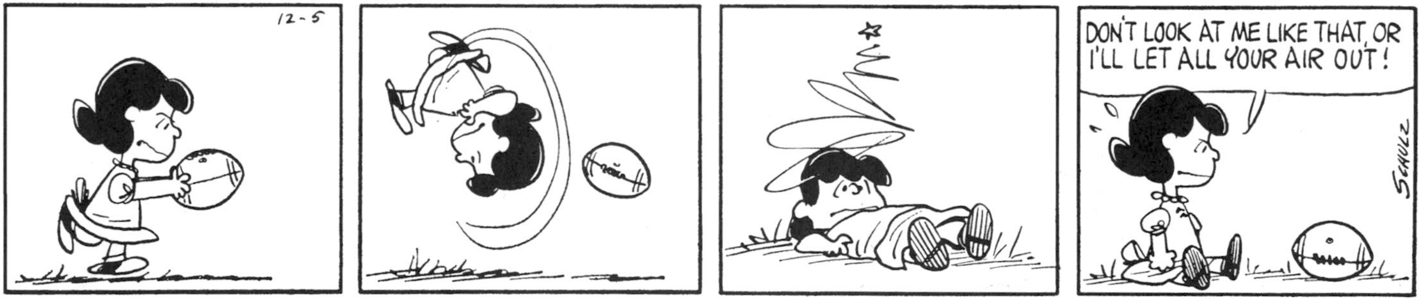
12-5
DON'T LOOK AT ME LIKE THAT, OR I'LL LET ALL YOUR AIR OUT!
SCHULZ

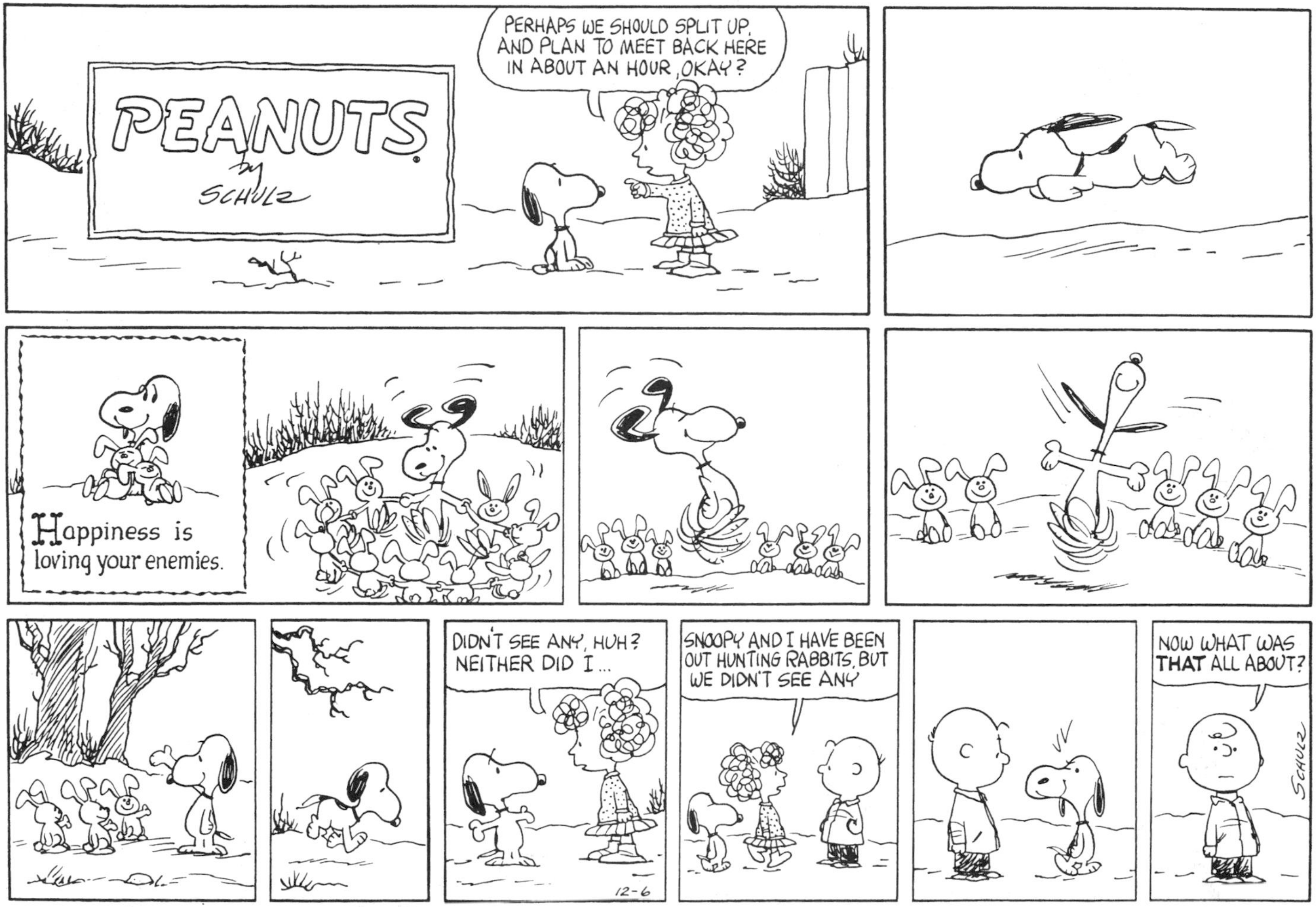
PEANUTS
by SCHULZ
PERHAPS WE SHOULD SPLIT UP, AND PLAN TO MEET BACK HERE IN ABOUT AN HOUR, OKAY?
Happiness is loving your enemies.
DIDN'T SEE ANY, HUH? NEITHER DID I...
12-6
SNOOPY AND I HAVE BEEN OUT HUNTING RABBITS, BUT WE DIDN'T SEE ANY
NOW WHAT WAS THAT ALL ABOUT?
SCHULZ

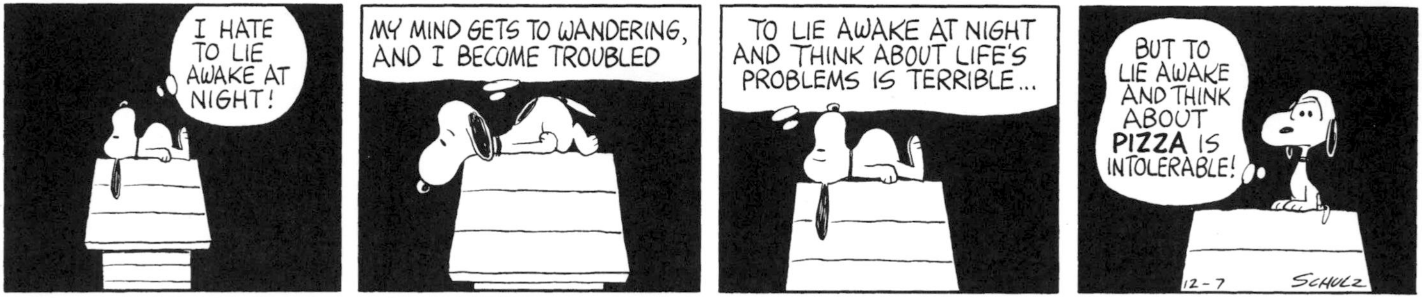
I HATE TO LIE AWAKE AT NIGHT!
MY MIND GETS TO WANDERING, AND I BECOME TROUBLED
TO LIE AWAKE AT NIGHT AND THINK ABOUT LIFE'S PROBLEMS IS TERRIBLE...
BUT TO LIE AWAKE AND THINK ABOUT **PIZZA** IS INTOLERABLE!
12-7
SCHULZ

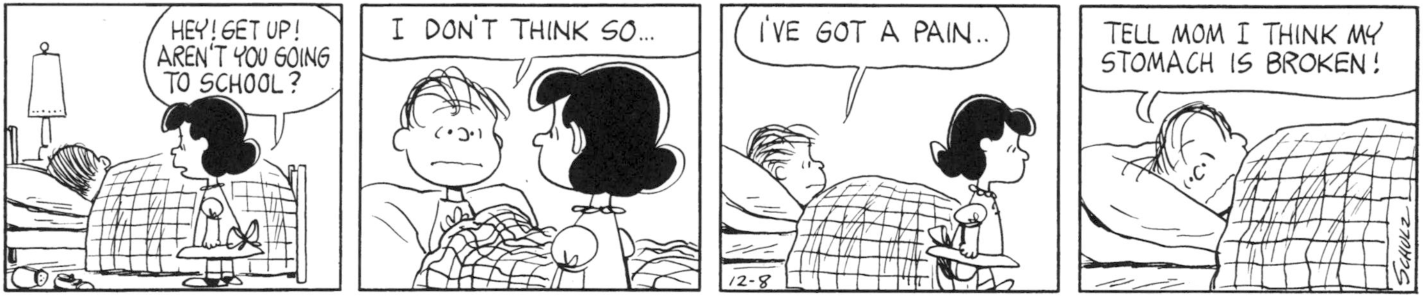
HEY! GET UP! AREN'T YOU GOING TO SCHOOL?
I DON'T THINK SO...
I'VE GOT A PAIN..
12-8
TELL MOM I THINK MY STOMACH IS BROKEN!
SCHULZ

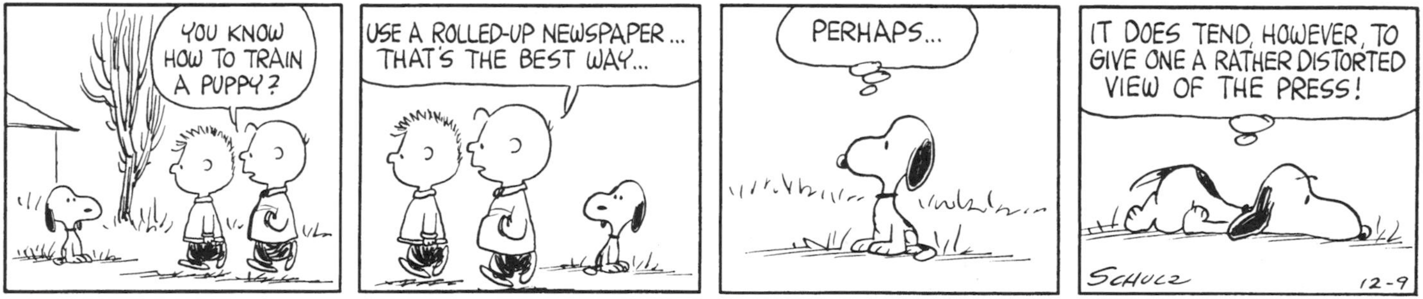
YOU KNOW HOW TO TRAIN A PUPPY?
USE A ROLLED-UP NEWSPAPER... THAT'S THE BEST WAY...
PERHAPS...
IT DOES TEND, HOWEVER, TO GIVE ONE A RATHER DISTORTED VIEW OF THE PRESS!
SCHULZ
12-9

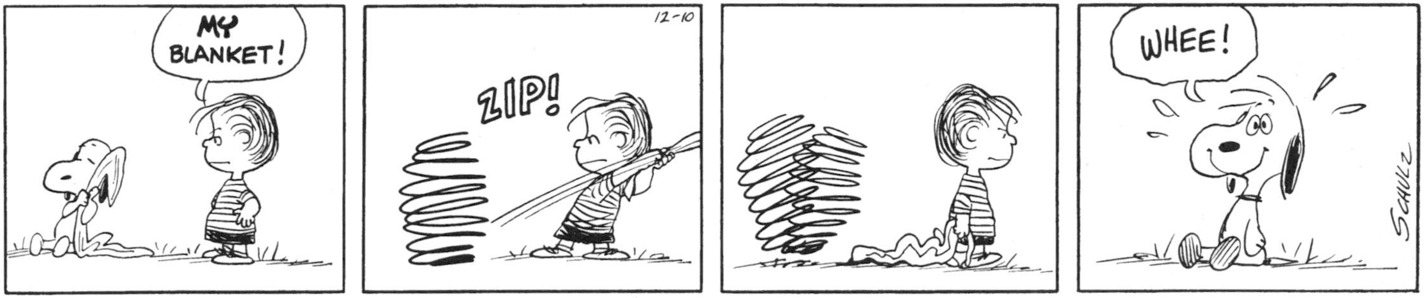
MY BLANKET!
12-10
ZIP!
WHEE!
SCHULZ

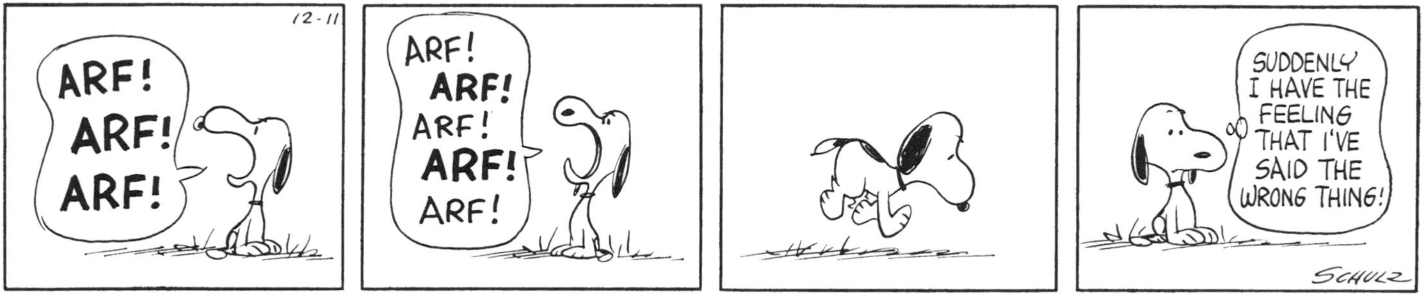
12-11
ARF! ARF! ARF!
ARF! ARF! ARF! ARF! ARF!
SUDDENLY I HAVE THE FEELING THAT I'VE SAID THE WRONG THING!
SCHULZ

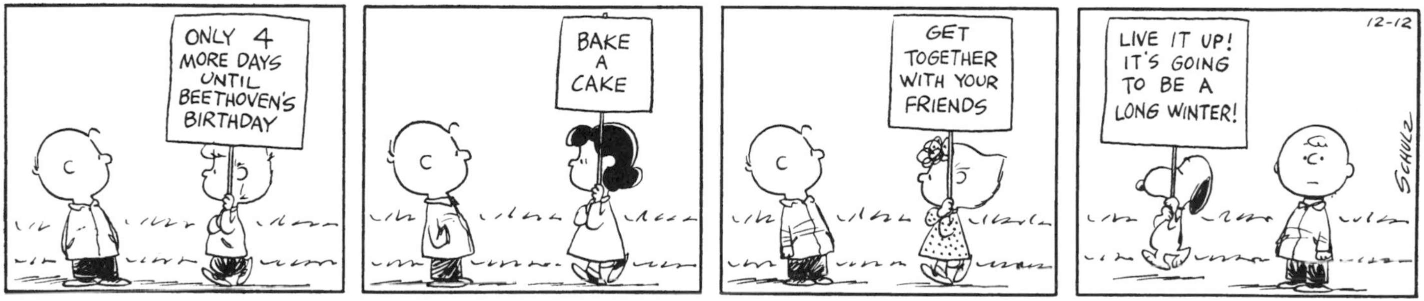
ONLY 4 MORE DAYS UNTIL BEETHOVEN'S BIRTHDAY
BAKE A CAKE
GET TOGETHER WITH YOUR FRIENDS
12-12
LIVE IT UP! IT'S GOING TO BE A LONG WINTER!
SCHULZ

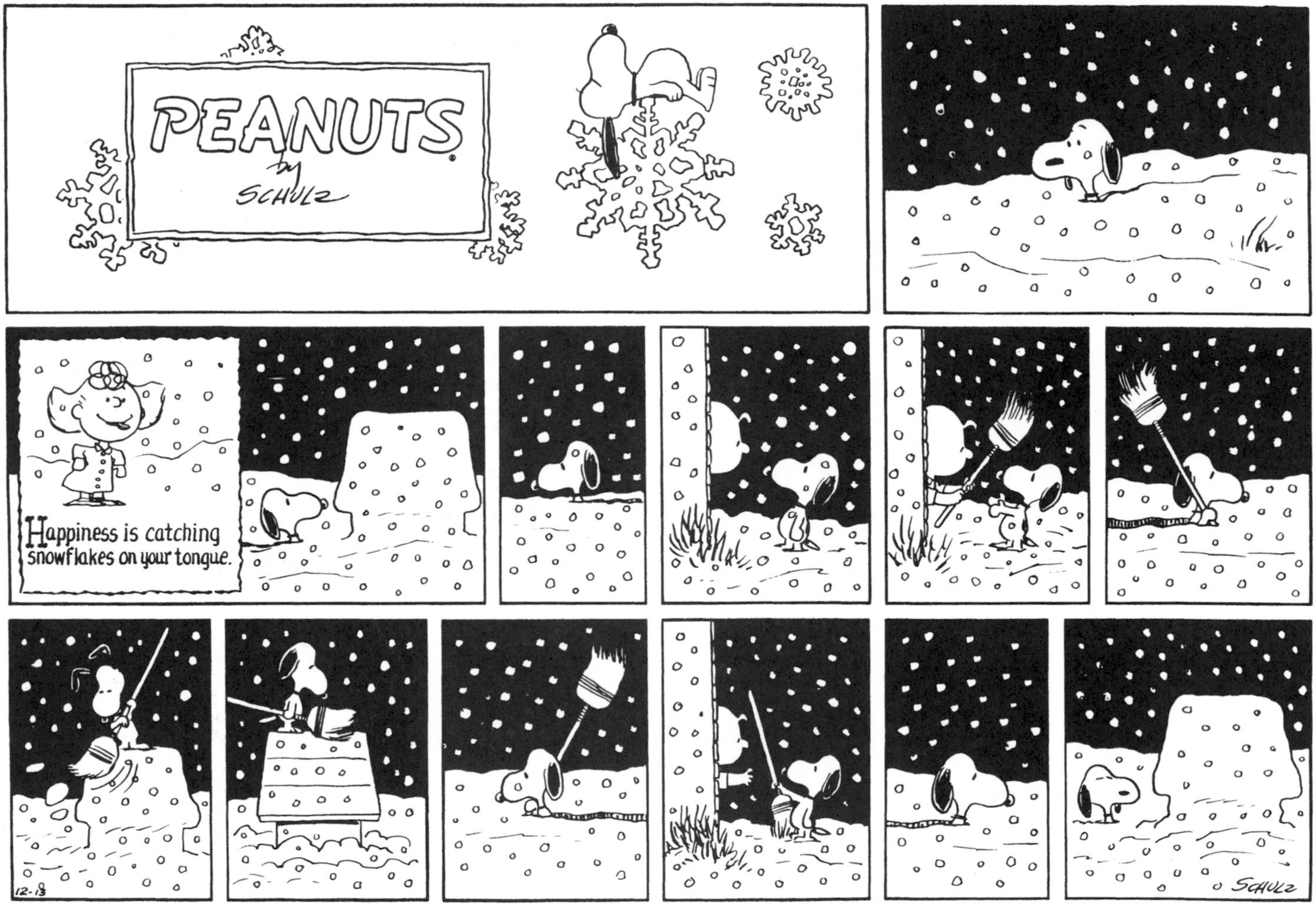
PEANUTS
by SCHULZ
Happiness is catching snowflakes on your tongue.
12-13
SCHULZ

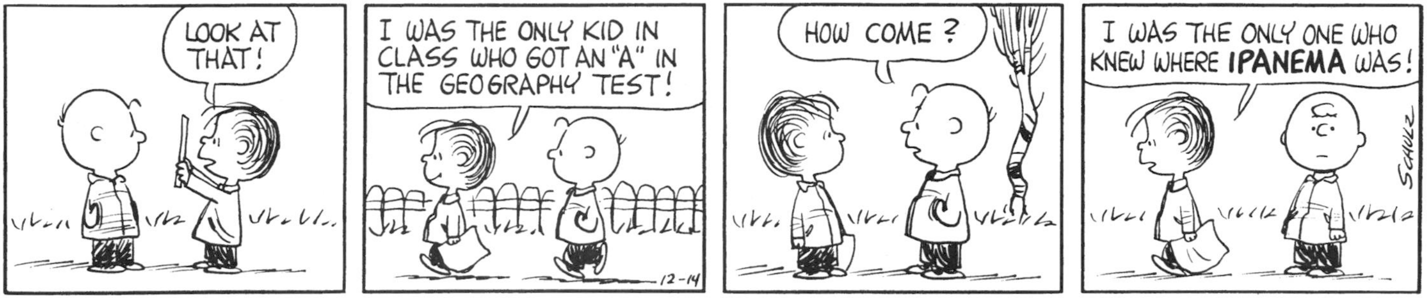
LOOK AT THAT!
I WAS THE ONLY KID IN CLASS WHO GOT AN "A" IN THE GEOGRAPHY TEST!
12-14
HOW COME?
I WAS THE ONLY ONE WHO KNEW WHERE IPANEMA WAS!
SCHULZ

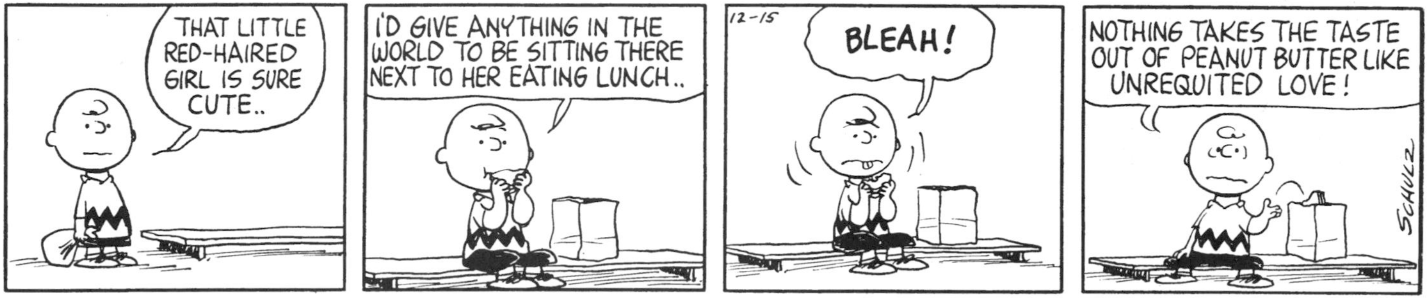
THAT LITTLE RED-HAIRED GIRL IS SURE CUTE..
I'D GIVE ANYTHING IN THE WORLD TO BE SITTING THERE NEXT TO HER EATING LUNCH..
12-15
BLEAH!
NOTHING TAKES THE TASTE OUT OF PEANUT BUTTER LIKE UNREQUITED LOVE!
SCHULZ

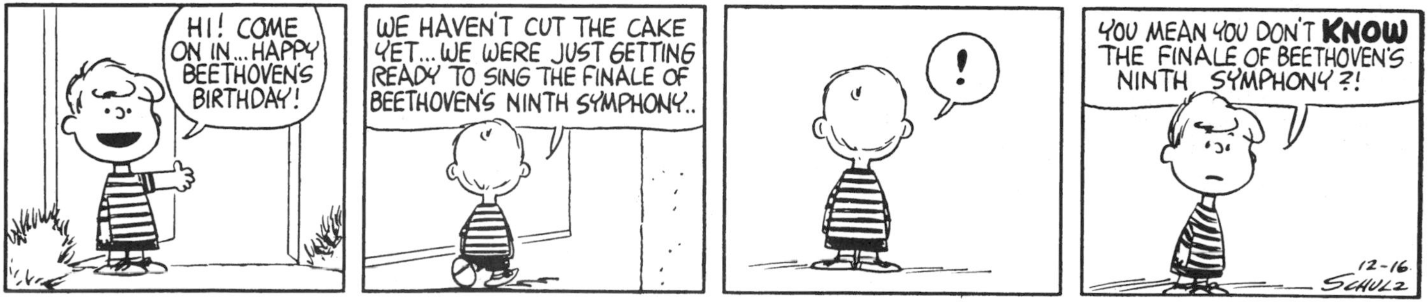
HI! COME ON IN... HAPPY BEETHOVEN'S BIRTHDAY!
WE HAVEN'T CUT THE CAKE YET... WE WERE JUST GETTING READY TO SING THE FINALE OF BEETHOVEN'S NINTH SYMPHONY..
!
YOU MEAN YOU DON'T KNOW THE FINALE OF BEETHOVEN'S NINTH SYMPHONY?!
12-16
SCHULZ

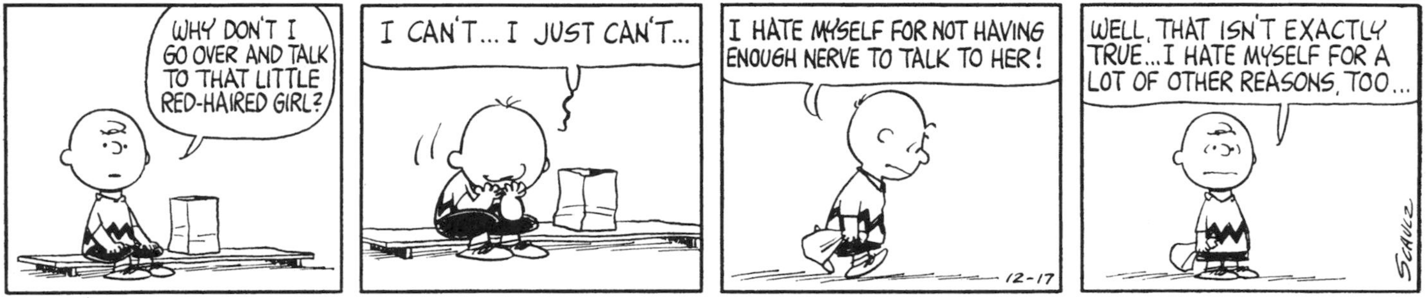
WHY DON'T I GO OVER AND TALK TO THAT LITTLE RED-HAIRED GIRL?
I CAN'T... I JUST CAN'T...
I HATE MYSELF FOR NOT HAVING ENOUGH NERVE TO TALK TO HER!
12-17
WELL, THAT ISN'T EXACTLY TRUE... I HATE MYSELF FOR A LOT OF OTHER REASONS, TOO...
SCHULZ

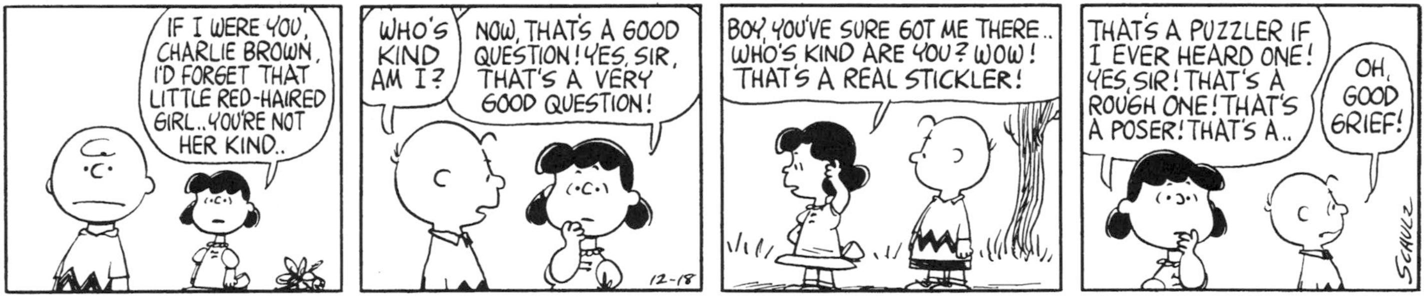
IF I WERE YOU, CHARLIE BROWN, I'D FORGET THAT LITTLE RED-HAIRED GIRL.. YOU'RE NOT HER KIND..
WHO'S KIND AM I?
NOW, THAT'S A GOOD QUESTION! YES, SIR, THAT'S A VERY GOOD QUESTION!
12-18
BOY, YOU'VE SURE GOT ME THERE.. WHO'S KIND ARE YOU? WOW! THAT'S A REAL STICKLER!
THAT'S A PUZZLER IF I EVER HEARD ONE! YES, SIR! THAT'S A ROUGH ONE! THAT'S A POSER! THAT'S A..
OH, GOOD GRIEF!
SCHULZ

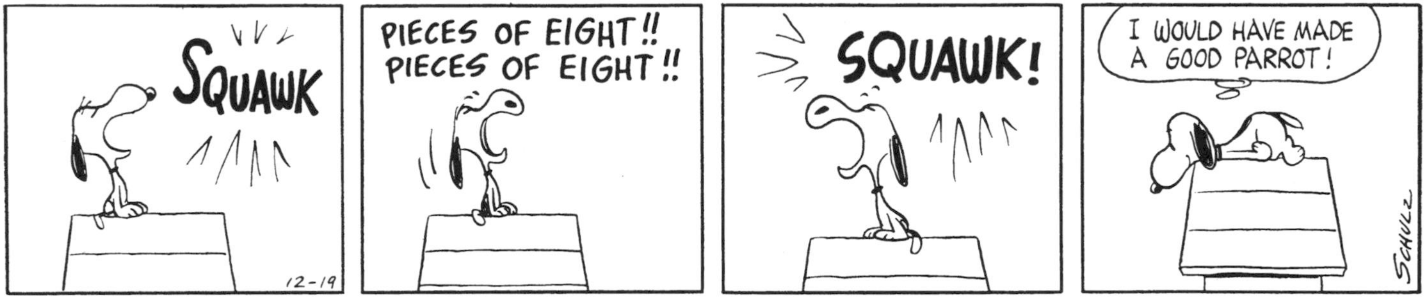
SQUAWK
12-19
PIECES OF EIGHT!! PIECES OF EIGHT!!
SQUAWK!
I WOULD HAVE MADE A GOOD PARROT!
SCHULZ

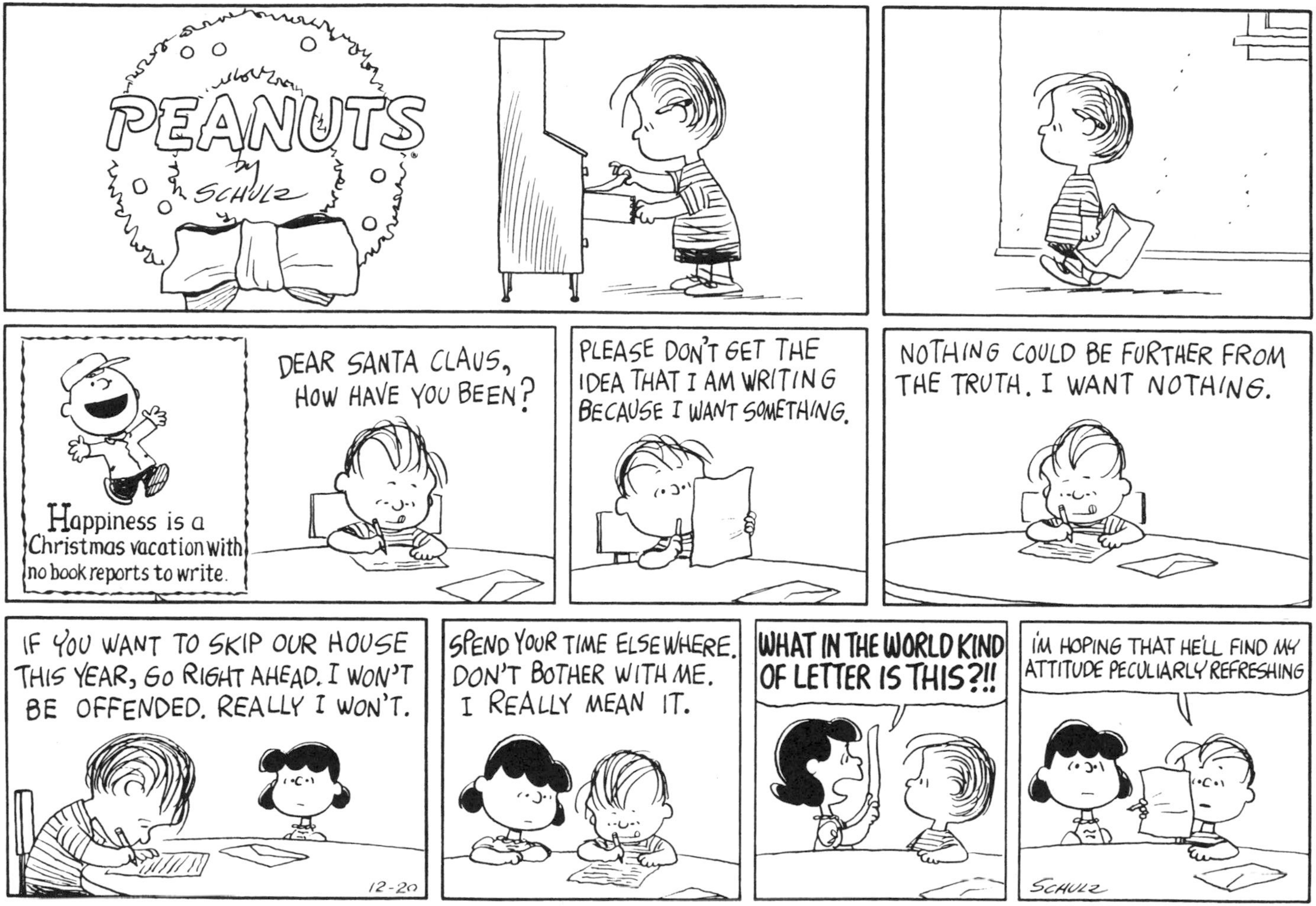
PEANUTS
by SCHULZ
Happiness is a Christmas vacation with no book reports to write.
DEAR SANTA CLAUS, HOW HAVE YOU BEEN?
PLEASE DON'T GET THE IDEA THAT I AM WRITING BECAUSE I WANT SOMETHING.
NOTHING COULD BE FURTHER FROM THE TRUTH. I WANT NOTHING.
IF YOU WANT TO SKIP OUR HOUSE THIS YEAR, GO RIGHT AHEAD. I WON'T BE OFFENDED. REALLY I WON'T.
12-20
SPEND YOUR TIME ELSEWHERE. DON'T BOTHER WITH ME. I REALLY MEAN IT.
WHAT IN THE WORLD KIND OF LETTER IS THIS?!!
I'M HOPING THAT HE'LL FIND MY ATTITUDE PECULIARLY REFRESHING
SCHULZ

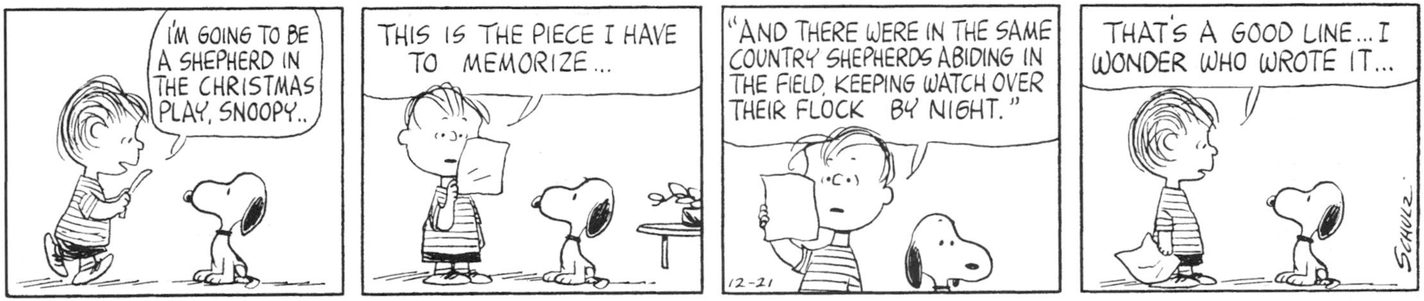
I'M GOING TO BE A SHEPHERD IN THE CHRISTMAS PLAY, SNOOPY..
THIS IS THE PIECE I HAVE TO MEMORIZE...
"AND THERE WERE IN THE SAME COUNTRY SHEPHERDS ABIDING IN THE FIELD, KEEPING WATCH OVER THEIR FLOCK BY NIGHT."
12-21
THAT'S A GOOD LINE...I WONDER WHO WROTE IT...
SCHULZ

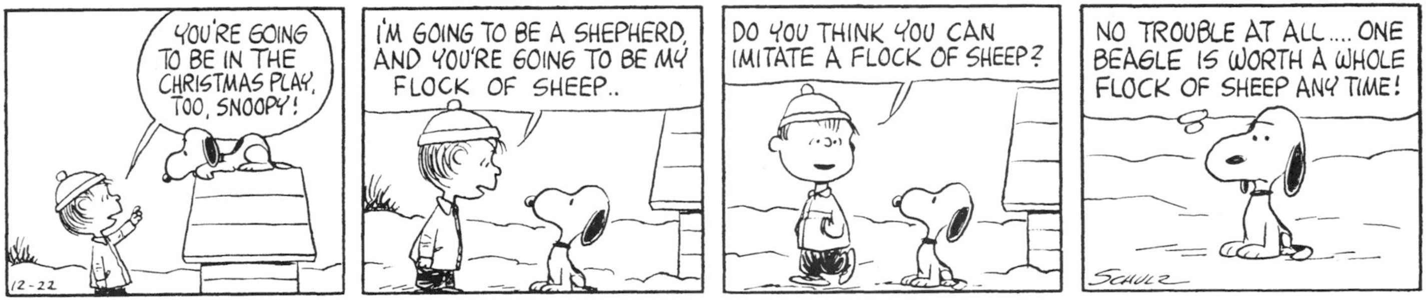
YOU'RE GOING TO BE IN THE CHRISTMAS PLAY, TOO, SNOOPY!
12-22
I'M GOING TO BE A SHEPHERD, AND YOU'RE GOING TO BE MY FLOCK OF SHEEP..
DO YOU THINK YOU CAN IMITATE A FLOCK OF SHEEP?
NO TROUBLE AT ALL.... ONE BEAGLE IS WORTH A WHOLE FLOCK OF SHEEP ANY TIME!
SCHULZ

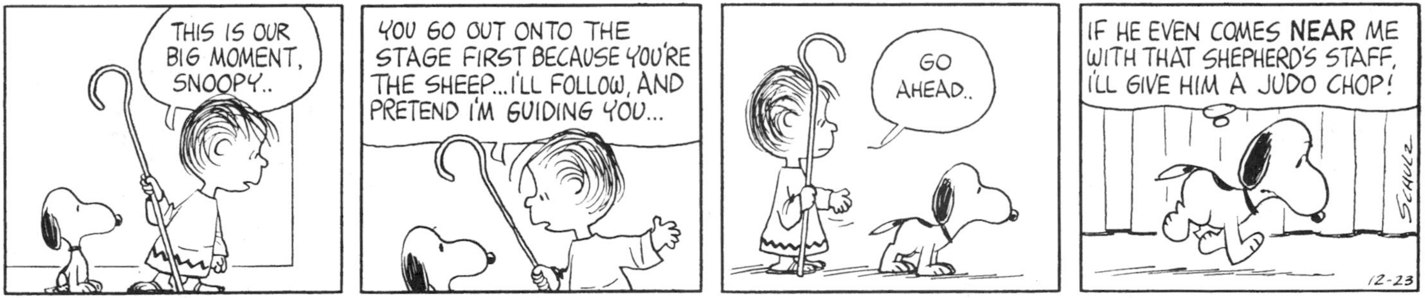
THIS IS OUR BIG MOMENT, SNOOPY..
YOU GO OUT ONTO THE STAGE FIRST BECAUSE YOU'RE THE SHEEP...I'LL FOLLOW, AND PRETEND I'M GUIDING YOU...
GO AHEAD..
IF HE EVEN COMES **NEAR** ME WITH THAT SHEPHERD'S STAFF, I'LL GIVE HIM A JUDO CHOP!
SCHULZ
12-23

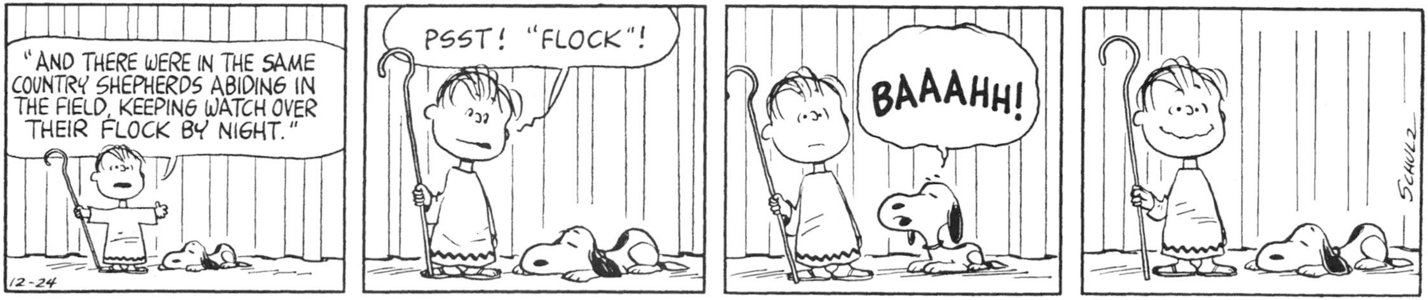
"AND THERE WERE IN THE SAME COUNTRY SHEPHERDS ABIDING IN THE FIELD, KEEPING WATCH OVER THEIR FLOCK BY NIGHT."
12-24
PSST! "FLOCK"!
BAAAHH!
SCHULZ

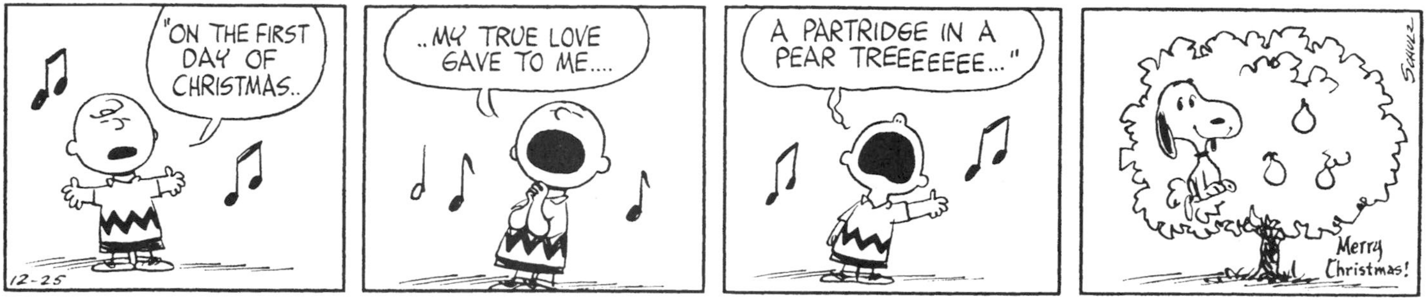
"ON THE FIRST DAY OF CHRISTMAS..
12-25
..MY TRUE LOVE GAVE TO ME....
A PARTRIDGE IN A PEAR TREEEEEEE..."
SCHULZ
Merry Christmas!

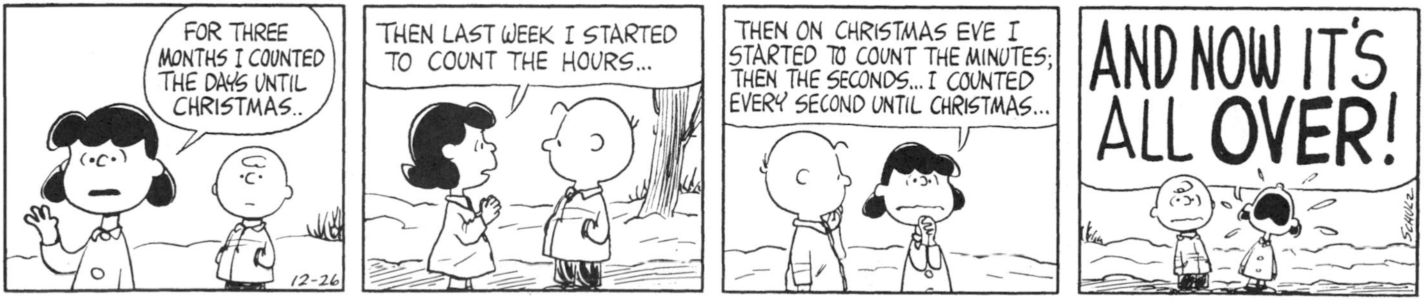
FOR THREE MONTHS I COUNTED THE DAYS UNTIL CHRISTMAS..
12-26
THEN LAST WEEK I STARTED TO COUNT THE HOURS...
THEN ON CHRISTMAS EVE I STARTED TO COUNT THE MINUTES; THEN THE SECONDS... I COUNTED EVERY SECOND UNTIL CHRISTMAS...
AND NOW IT'S ALL OVER!
SCHULZ

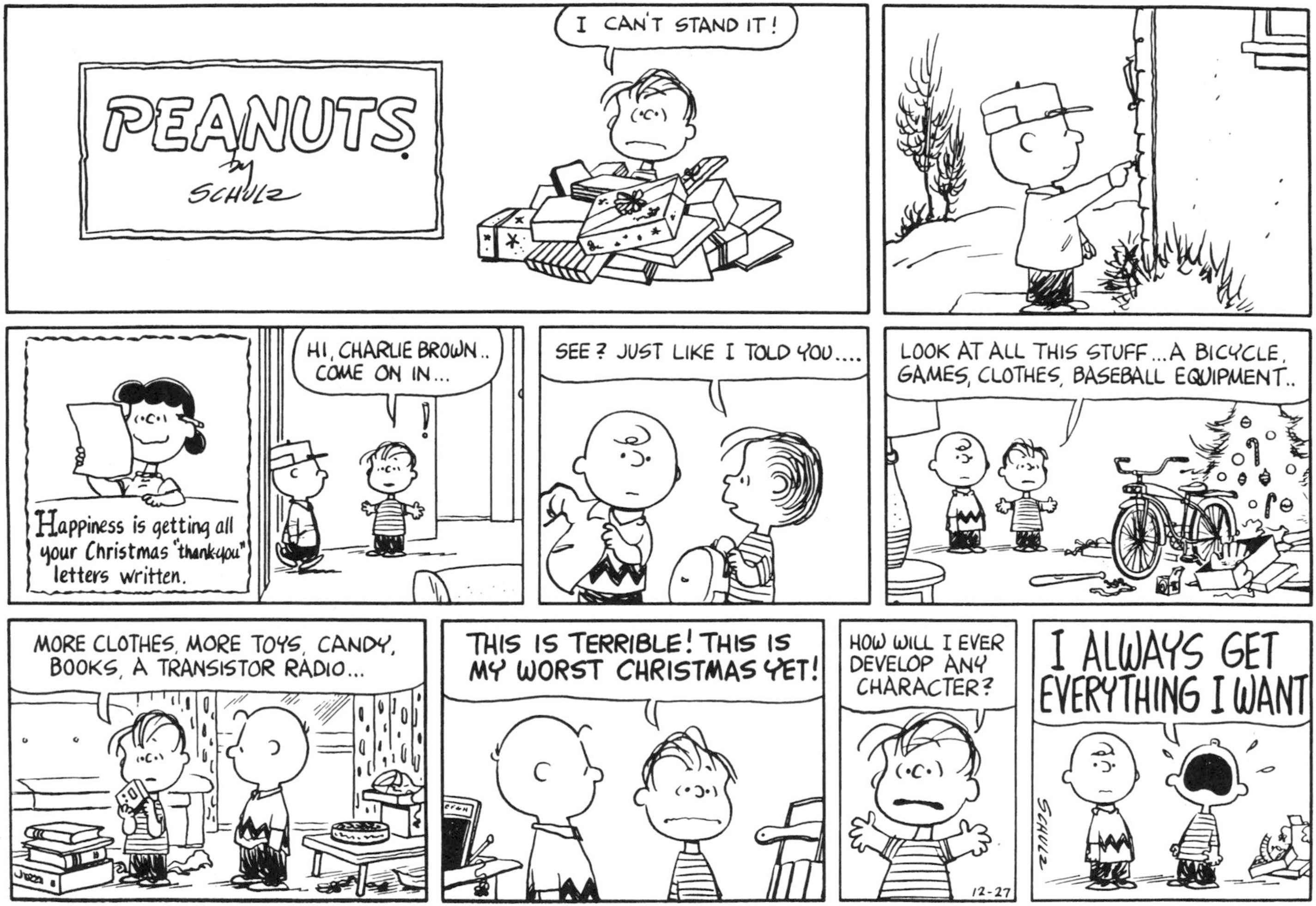
PEANUTS
by SCHULZ
I CAN'T STAND IT!
Happiness is getting all your Christmas "thank-you" letters written.
HI, CHARLIE BROWN.. COME ON IN...
!
SEE? JUST LIKE I TOLD YOU....
LOOK AT ALL THIS STUFF...A BICYCLE, GAMES, CLOTHES, BASEBALL EQUIPMENT..
MORE CLOTHES, MORE TOYS, CANDY, BOOKS, A TRANSISTOR RADIO...
THIS IS TERRIBLE! THIS IS MY WORST CHRISTMAS YET!
HOW WILL I EVER DEVELOP ANY CHARACTER?
12-27
SCHULZ
I ALWAYS GET EVERYTHING I WANT

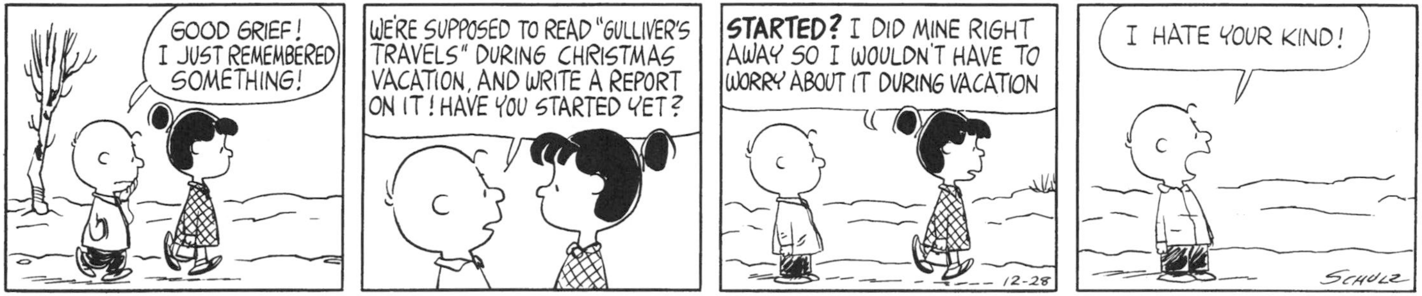
GOOD GRIEF! I JUST REMEMBERED SOMETHING!
WE'RE SUPPOSED TO READ "GULLIVER'S TRAVELS" DURING CHRISTMAS VACATION, AND WRITE A REPORT ON IT! HAVE YOU STARTED YET?
STARTED? I DID MINE RIGHT AWAY SO I WOULDN'T HAVE TO WORRY ABOUT IT DURING VACATION
12-28
I HATE YOUR KIND!
SCHULZ

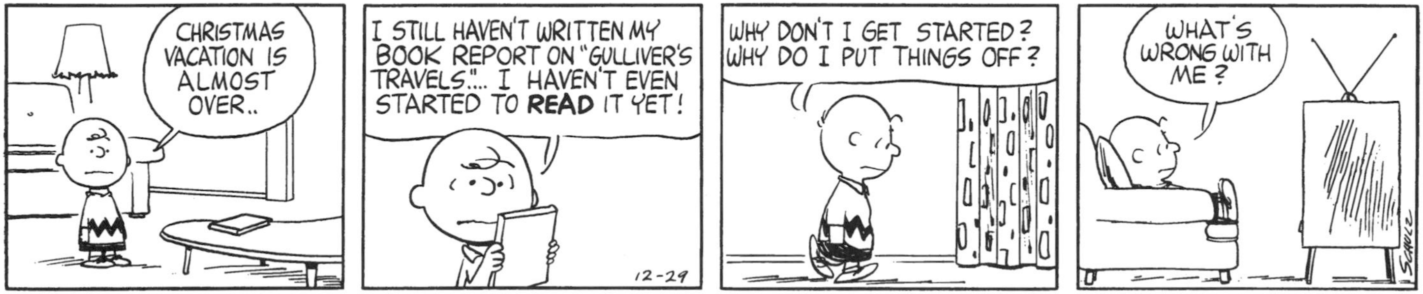
CHRISTMAS VACATION IS ALMOST OVER..
I STILL HAVEN'T WRITTEN MY BOOK REPORT ON "GULLIVER'S TRAVELS"... I HAVEN'T EVEN STARTED TO **READ** IT YET!
12-29
WHY DON'T I GET STARTED? WHY DO I PUT THINGS OFF?
WHAT'S WRONG WITH ME?
SCHULZ

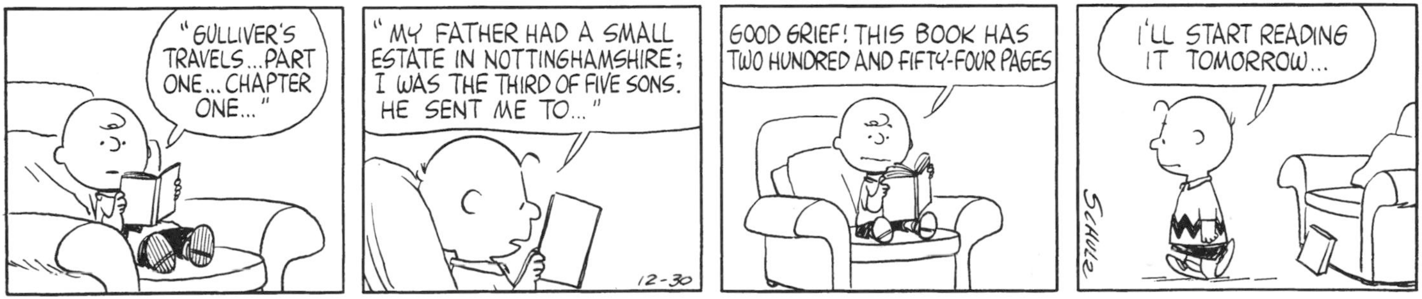
"GULLIVER'S TRAVELS...PART ONE...CHAPTER ONE..."
"MY FATHER HAD A SMALL ESTATE IN NOTTINGHAMSHIRE; I WAS THE THIRD OF FIVE SONS. HE SENT ME TO..."
12-30
GOOD GRIEF! THIS BOOK HAS TWO HUNDRED AND FIFTY-FOUR PAGES
SCHULZ
I'LL START READING IT TOMORROW...

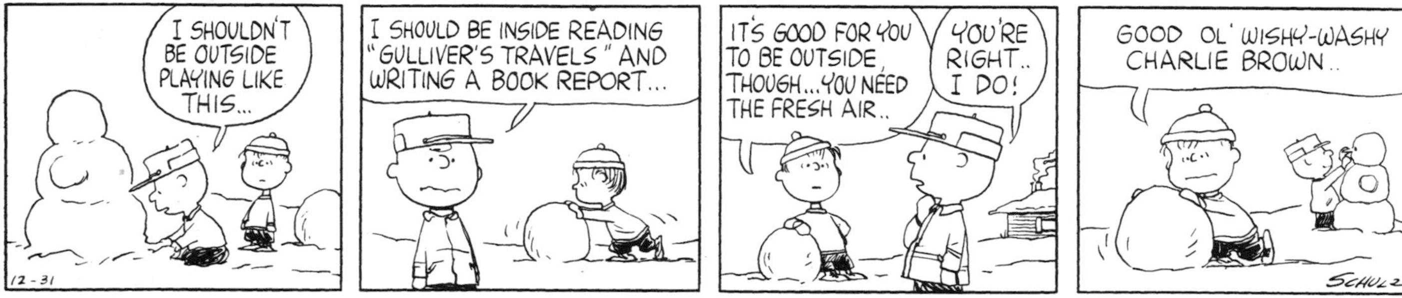
I SHOULDN'T BE OUTSIDE PLAYING LIKE THIS...
I SHOULD BE INSIDE READING "GULLIVER'S TRAVELS" AND WRITING A BOOK REPORT...
IT'S GOOD FOR YOU TO BE OUTSIDE, THOUGH...YOU NEED THE FRESH AIR..
YOU'RE RIGHT.. I DO!
GOOD OL' WISHY-WASHY CHARLIE BROWN..
12-31
SCHULZ

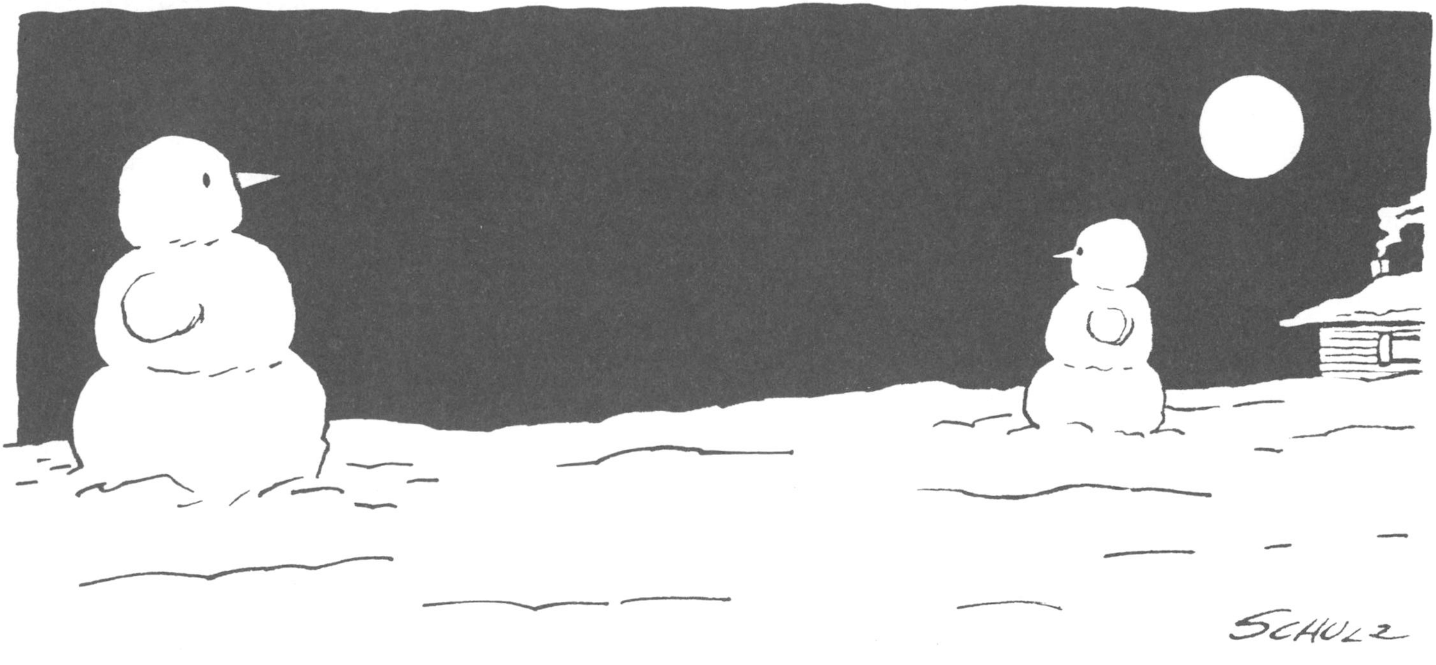
SCHULZ

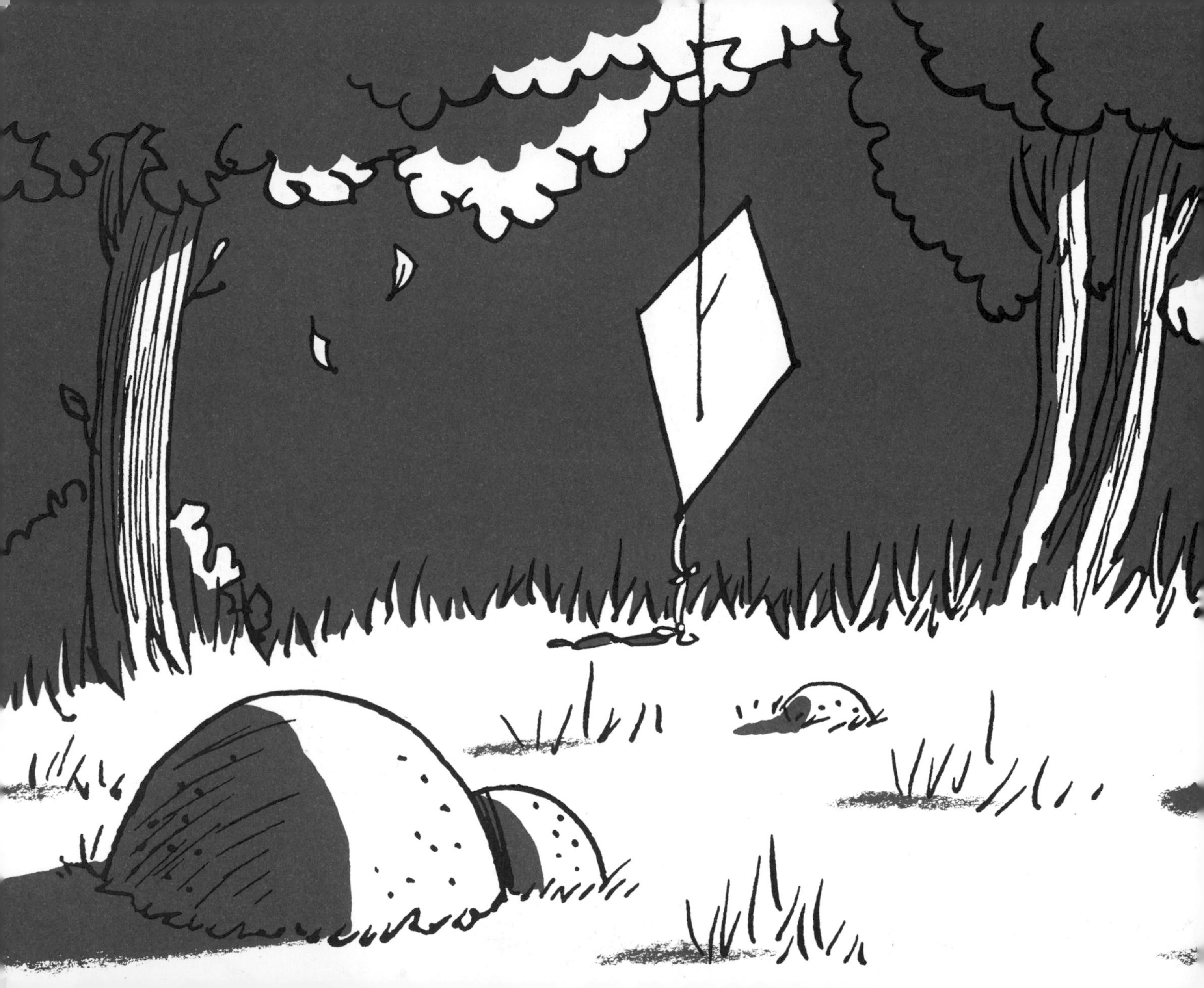

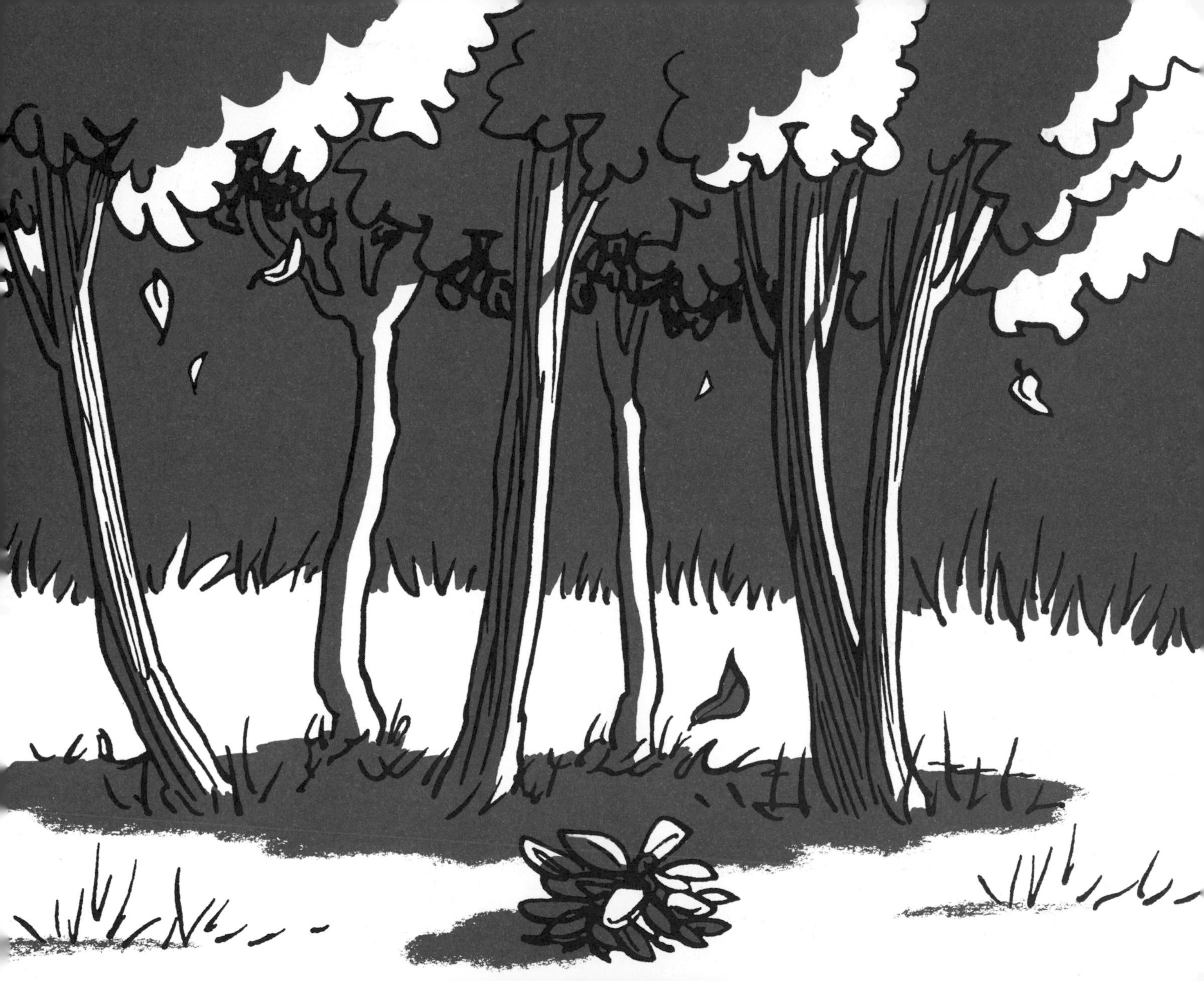

INDEX

DEAR MR. PRODUCER, I WATCHED YOUR ANIMATED CARTOON SHOW ON TV LAST NIGHT. I MUST PROTEST.

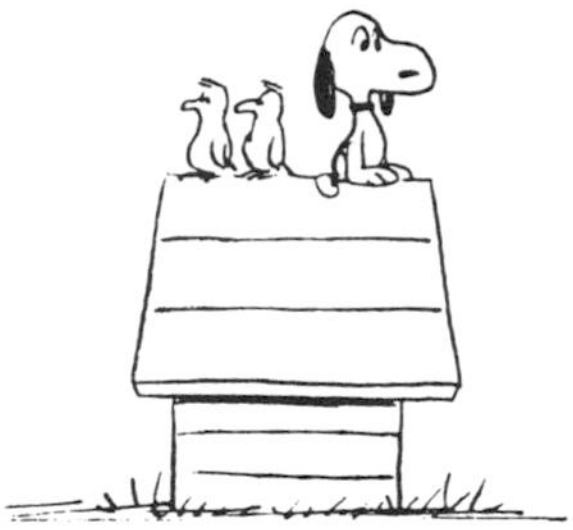

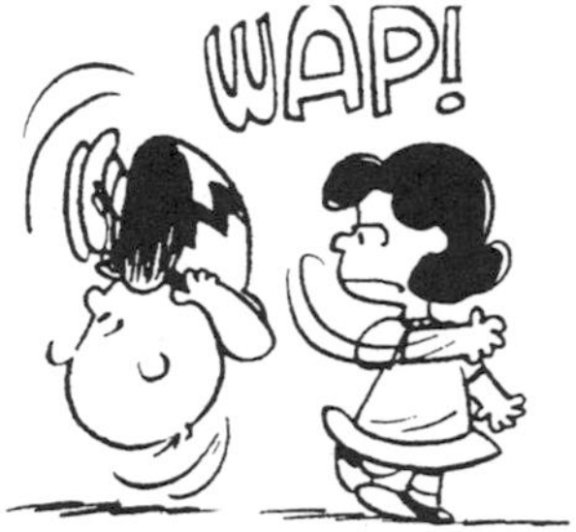
WAP!

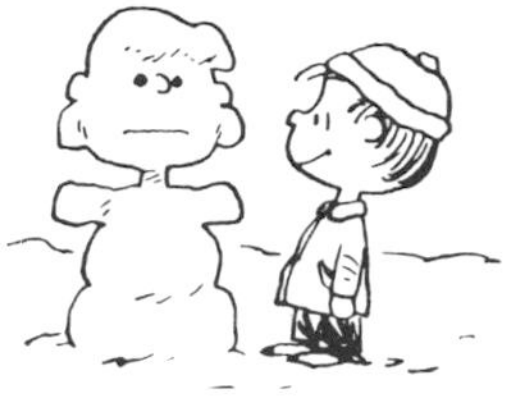

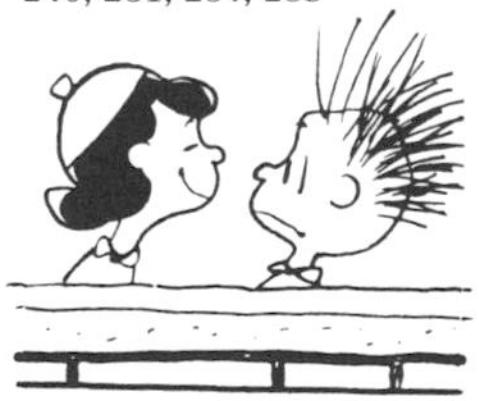

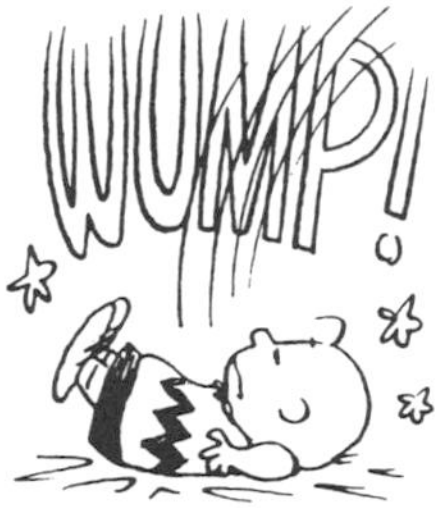

WUMP!

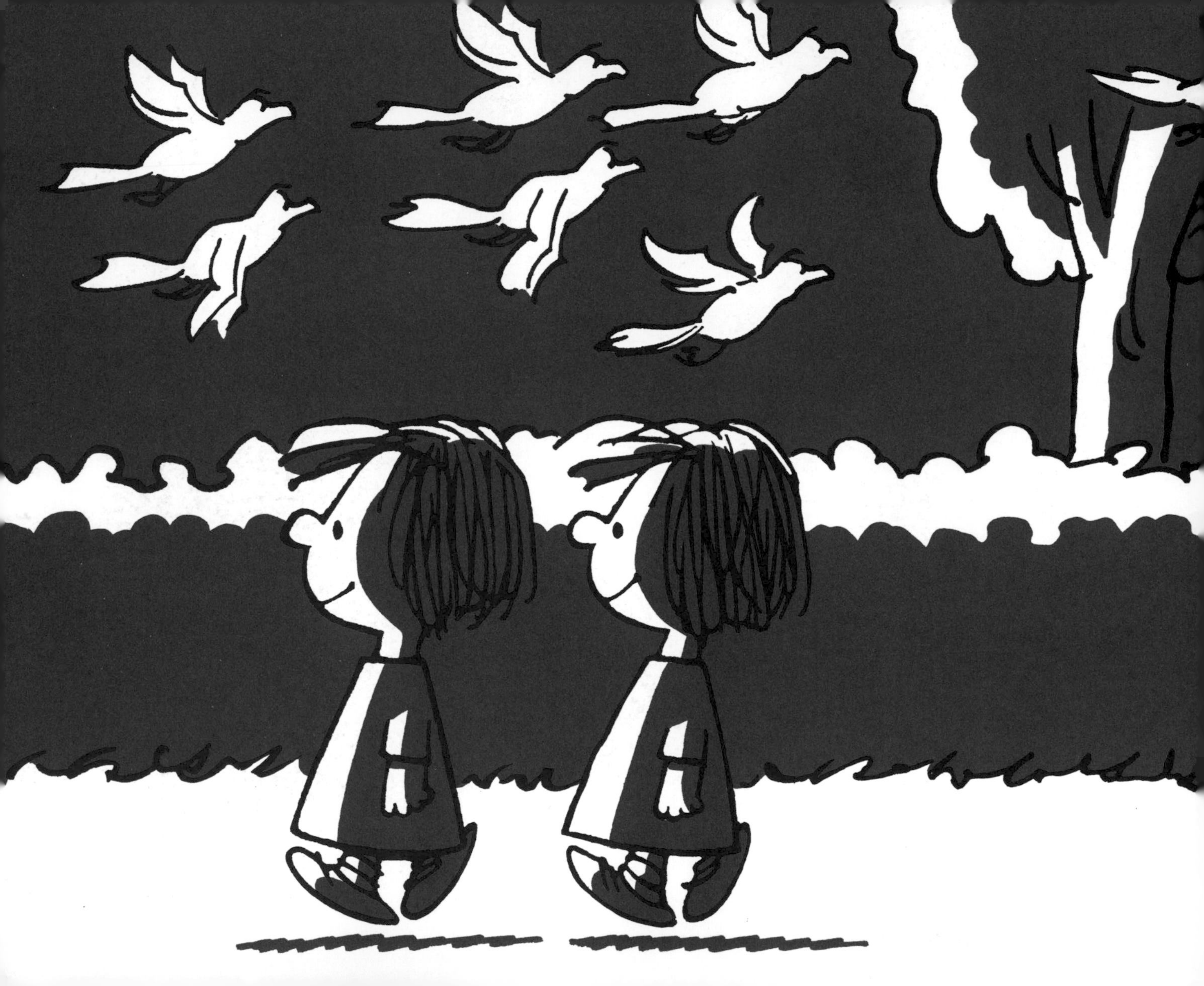

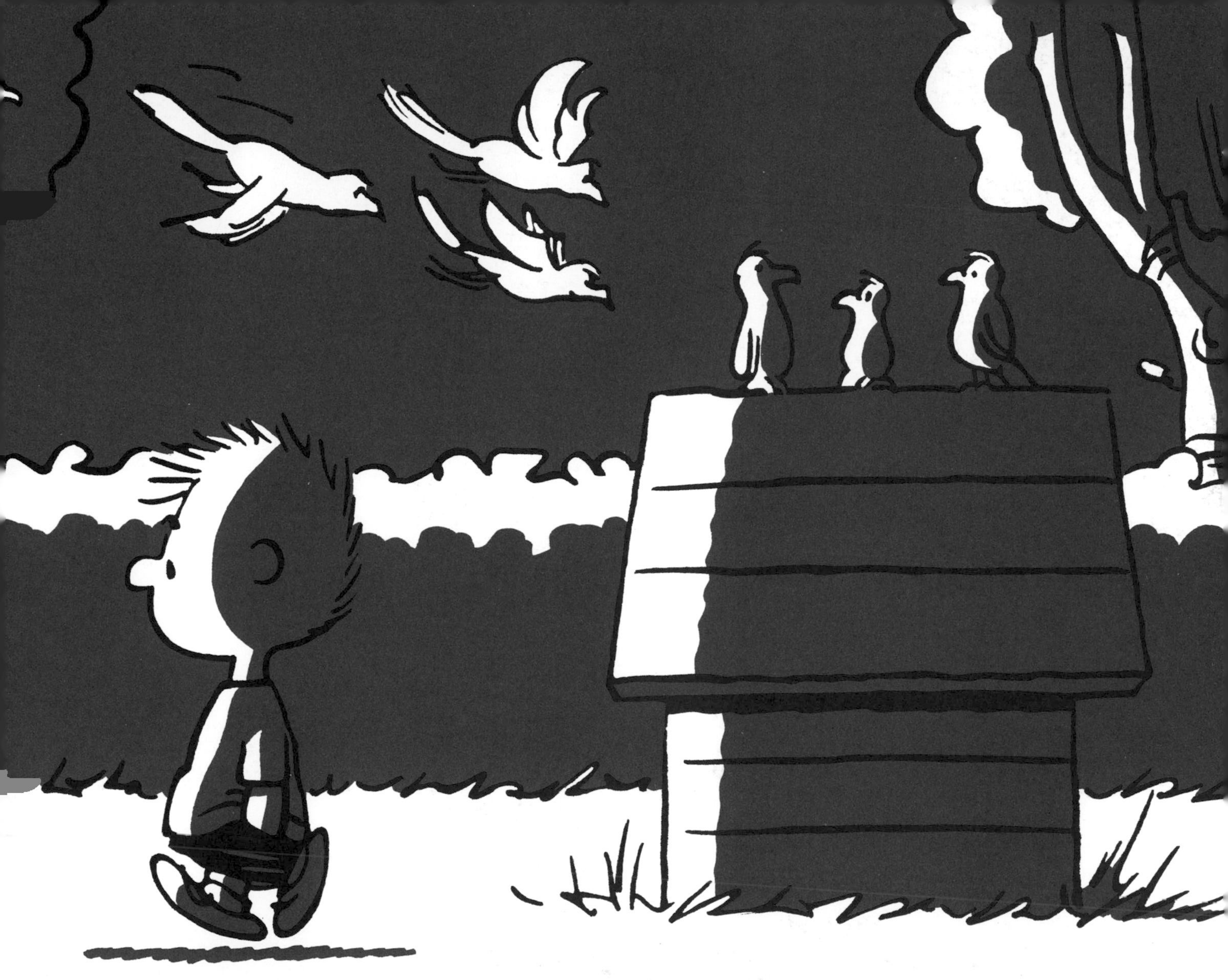

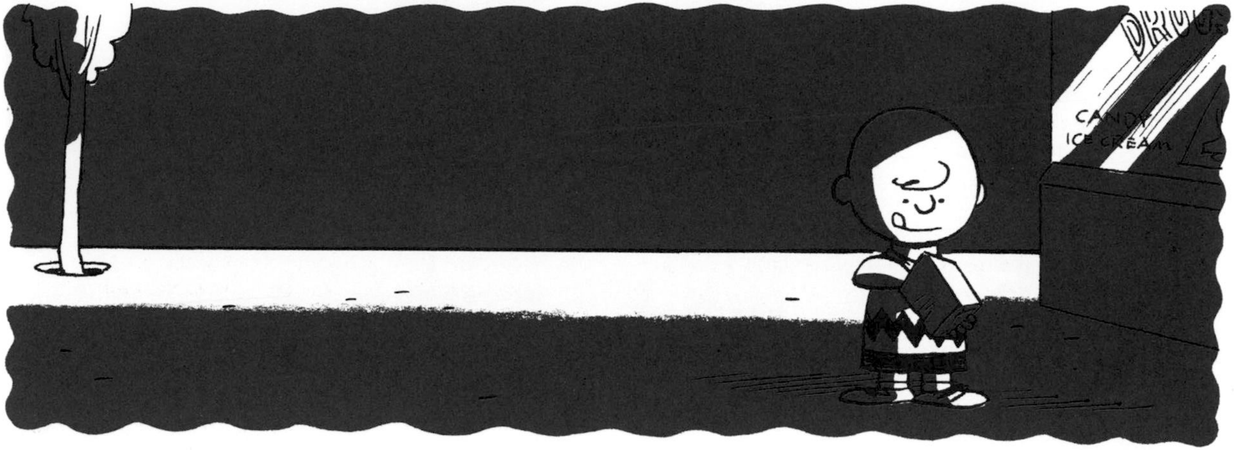

CHARLES M. SCHULZ · 1922 To 2000

Charles M. Schulz was born November 26, 1922 in Minneapolis. His destiny was foreshadowed when an uncle gave him, at the age of two days, the nickname Sparky (after the racehorse Spark Plug in the newspaper strip *Barney Google*).

Schulz grew up in St. Paul. By all accounts, he led an unremarkable, albeit sheltered, childhood. He was an only child, close to both parents, his eventual career path nurtured by his father, who bought four Sunday papers every week — just for the comics.

An outstanding student, he skipped two grades early on, but began to flounder in high school — perhaps not so coincidentally at the same time kids are going through their cruelest, most status-conscious period of socialization. The pain, bitterness, insecurity, and failures chronicled in *Peanuts* appear to have originated from this period of Schulz's life.

Although Schulz enjoyed sports, he also found refuge in solitary activities: reading, drawing, and watching movies. He bought comic books and Big Little Books, pored over the newspaper strips, and copied his favorites — *Buck Rogers*, the Walt Disney characters, *Popeye*, *Tim Tyler's Luck*. He quickly became a connoisseur; his heroes were Milton Caniff, Roy Crane, Hal Foster, and Alex Raymond.

In his senior year in high school, his mother noticed an ad in a local newspaper for a correspondence school, Federal Schools (later called Art

Instruction Schools). Schulz passed the talent test, completed the course and began trying, unsuccessfully, to sell gag cartoons to magazines. (His first published drawing was of his dog, Spike, and appeared in a 1937 Ripley's *Believe It Or Not!* installment.)

After World War II had ended and Schulz was discharged from the army, he started submitting gag cartoons to the various magazines of the time; his first breakthrough, however, came when an editor at Timeless Topix hired him to letter adventure comics. Soon after that, he was hired by his alma mater, Art Instruction, to correct student lessons returned by mail.

Between 1948 and 1950, he succeeded in selling 17 cartoons to the *Saturday Evening Post* — as well as, to the local *St. Paul Pioneer Press*, a weekly comic feature called *Li'l Folks*. It was run in the women's section and paid $10 a week. After writing and drawing the feature for two years, Schulz asked for a better location in the paper or for daily exposure, as well as a raise. When he was turned down on all three counts, he quit.

He started submitting strips to the newspaper syndicates. In the Spring of 1950, he received a letter from the United Feature Syndicate, announcing their interest in his submission, *Li'l Folks*. Schulz boarded a train in June for New York City; more interested in doing a strip than a panel, he also brought along the first installments of what would become *Peanuts* — and that was what sold. (The title, which Schulz loathed to his dying day, was imposed by the syndicate). The first *Peanuts* daily appeared October 2, 1950; the first Sunday, January 6, 1952.

Prior to *Peanuts*, the province of the comics page had been that of gags, social and political observation, domestic comedy, soap opera, and various adventure genres. Although *Peanuts* changed, or evolved, during the 50 years Schulz wrote and drew it, it remained, as it began, an anomaly on the comics page — a comic strip about the interior crises of the cartoonist himself. After a painful divorce in 1973 from which he had not yet recovered, Schulz told a reporter, "Strangely, I've drawn better cartoons in the last six months — or as good as I've ever drawn. I don't know how the human mind works." Surely, it was this kind of humility in the face of profoundly irreducible human question that makes *Peanuts* as universally moving as it is.

Diagnosed with cancer, Schulz retired from *Peanuts* at the end of 1999. He died on February 12th 2000, the day before his last strip was published (and two days before Valentine's Day) — having completed 17,897 daily and Sunday strips, each and every one fully written, drawn, and lettered entirely by his own hand — an unmatched achievement in comics.

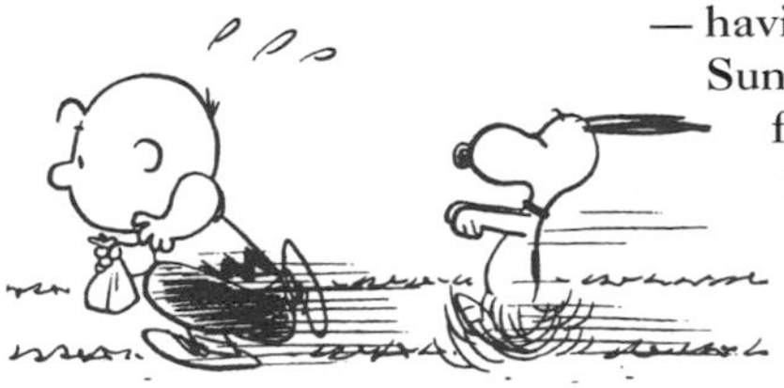

—Gary Groth

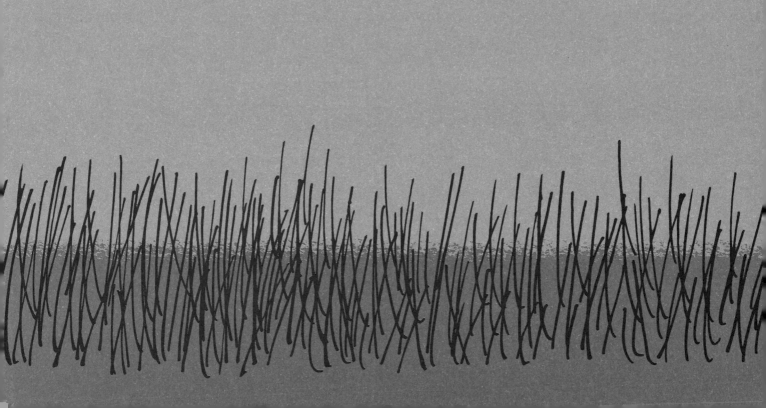

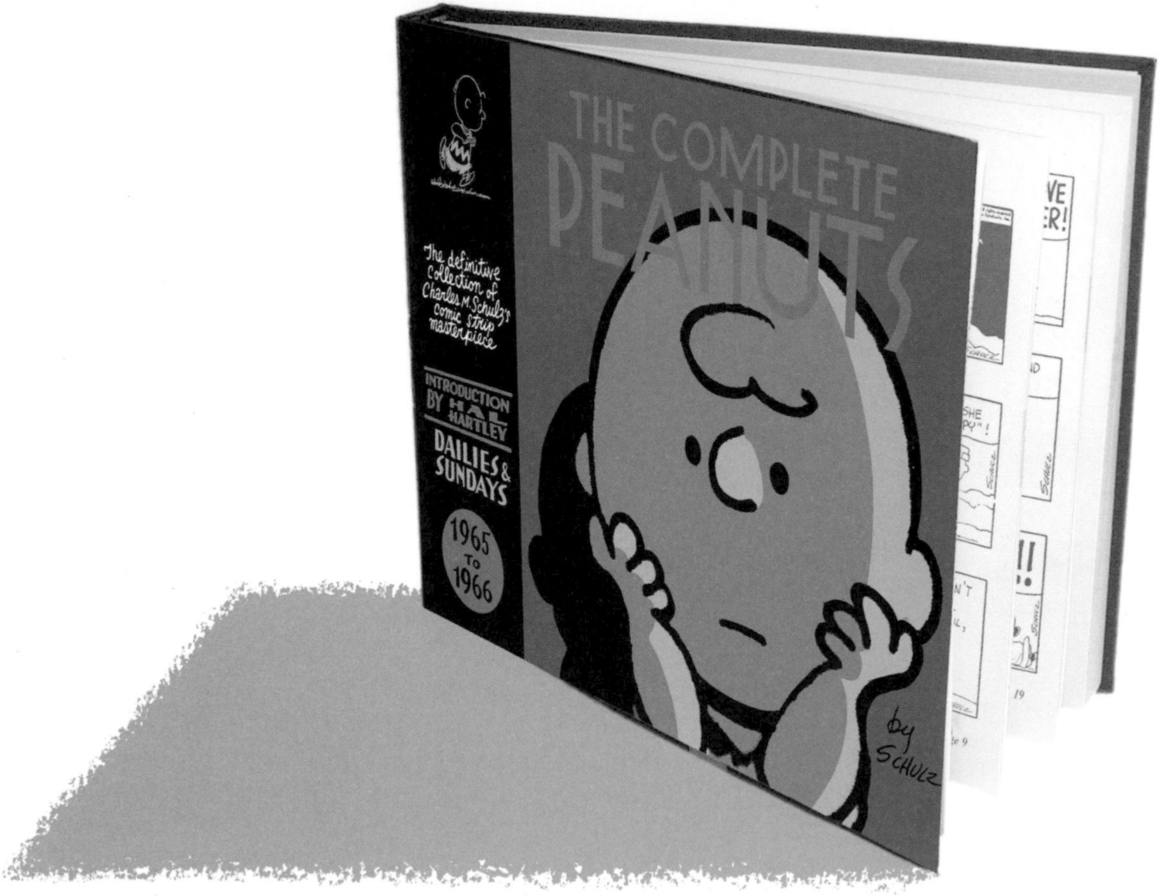
THE COMPLETE PEANUTS
The definitive collection of Charles M. Schulz's comic strip masterpiece
INTRODUCTION BY HAL HARTLEY
DAILIES & SUNDAYS
1965 TO 1966
by SCHULZ

COMING IN THE *COMPLETE PEANUTS: 1965-1966*

The very first World War I Flying Ace sequences... Charlie Brown makes a friend at summer camp... Sally is diagnosed with amblyopia and has to wear an eye patch... Snoopy discovers Thomas Wolfe was right when he revisits the Daisy Hill Puppy Farm... Linus's blanket springs to life and attacks Lucy... Charlie Brown blows a spelling bee... Snoopy's house burns down... and the introduction of Peppermint Patty!